THE POLITICS OF THE PRUSSIAN ARMY

1640–1945

THE POLITICS OF THE PRUSSIAN ARMY 1640–1945

BY

GORDON A. CRAIG

OXFORD UNIVERSITY PRESS
London Oxford New York

OXFORD UNIVERSITY PRESS

London Oxford New York
Glasgow Toronto Melbourne Wellington
Cape Town Ibadan Nairobi Dar es Salaam Lusaka Addis Ababa
Delhi Bombay Calcutta Madras Karachi Lahore Dacca
Kuala Lumpur Singapore Hong Kong Tokyo

Library of Congress Catalogue Card Number: 56-8006
First published by the Clarendon Press, 1955
First issued as an Oxford University Press paperback, with corrections, 1964

This reprint, 1973

Printed in the United States of America

TO THE MEMORY OF

EDWARD MEAD EARLE

TEACHER · CRITIC

FRIEND

PREFATORY NOTE

In this corrected impression, errors of fact made in the original edition have, as far as possible, been eliminated, additions have been made to the footnotes and the bibliography, and in some instances, notably in Chapters XI and XII, a line of argument has been recast in the light of new evidence.

G. A. C.

STANFORD, CALIFORNIA
February, 1964

ACKNOWLEDGEMENTS

I wish to express my gratitude to:

The late Edward Mead Earle, who first encouraged me to undertake the writing of this book;

Felix Gilbert, Hajo Holborn, Theodor Ernst Mommsen, and R. R. Palmer, who read portions of the manuscript and made valuable suggestions for improving it;

The Archivist of the United States, for giving me access to the Groener, Roon, Seeckt, and Stresemann papers; and the staff of the National Archives for their unfailing courtesy and helpfulness;

Colonel C. P. Stacey, Director of the Historical Section, Army Headquarters, Department of National Defence, Ottawa, and the Deputy Director, Lieutenant-Colonel G. W. L. Nicholson, for their kindness in opening the rich resources of the Crerar Military Library to me; and Miss Lola H. Campbell, for her assistance while I was working in that collection;

Fredric Aandahl, Jacob Beam, Elmer A. Beller, Jerome Blum, Moritz J. Bonn, Axel von dem Bussche, Fritz Ernst, Hans Gatzke, B. H. Liddell Hart, Francis Loewenheim, Thuisko von Metzsch, Gerhard Ritter, Herbert Rosinski, R. J. Sontag, Joseph R. Strayer, Gordon B. Turner, and John W. Wheeler-Bennett, for encouragement, suggestions, and material;

The editors of the *Political Science Quarterly*, Columbia University, for permitting me to reprint parts of articles which I wrote originally for that journal;

Harold L. Gordon, Jr., who permitted me to use his unpublished dissertation on the German Reichswehr from 1919 to 1926, and who made available to me some interesting personal correspondence with German soldiers and military administrators;

The Research Committee of Princeton University for generous financial assistance throughout the period of the book's preparation;

Miss Elizabeth d'Arcy, Mrs. Benton Schrader, and Mrs. J. K. Clarke, for typing and re-typing portions of the manuscript; and, last but not least,

My wife and daughters, who have borne with me during the years of research and writing.

For the shortcomings of this book, none of the above-named persons or institutions bears any responsibility. What merits it may have are due in large part to their assistance.

G. A. C.

PRINCETON, N.J.
AND NELSON, N.H.

January, 1955

CONTENTS

INTRODUCTION

THE ROLE OF THE ARMY IN GERMAN HISTORY

We shall wait in vain for the awakening in our country of that public spirit which the English and the French and other peoples possess, if we do not imitate them in setting for our military leaders certain bounds and limitations which they must not disregard. STEIN

Deutschland, ein unendlicher Prolog. CARL ZUCKMAYER

THE experience of fighting two world wars against the Germans has led to much speculation and almost as much writing about 'the German problem', and many facile theories have been advanced to explain the German mind and character. Not the least popular of these has been the theory that the Germans are by nature subservient to authority, militaristic, and aggressive, and that there is very little that any one can do about this except deprive them of the means of making themselves dangerous to their neighbours.

To assign national characteristics to a people is at best a chancy business, and arguments based upon such attribution are apt to fall of their own weight. That authoritarian government, militarism, and aggression have characterized German political life and action in the modern period few would deny. The basic assumption of this book, however, is that these things are not inherent in the German character but are rather—as Franz Neumann has written—'products of a structure which vitiated the attempts to create a viable democracy'.[1]

Inveterate Germanophobes are apt to forget that such attempts were made. Yet it can scarcely be denied that the reforms inaugurated in Prussia after 1807 represented a comprehensive effort to transform the social and political structure of Prussia and to make this state a constitutional kingdom capable of developing in the same direction as the more liberal states of the West. The revolution of 1848, in Prussia and in the other

[1] Franz Neumann, 'Germany and Western Union', *Proceedings of the Academy of Political Science*, xxiii (1949), 262.

German states, was an attempt of the same nature. In the constitutional struggle in Prussia in the 1860's, fought out in the years immediately preceding the unification of Germany under Prussian leadership, organized Prussian liberalism sought to restrict the prerogatives of the Crown and lay the foundations for an effective evolution towards parliamentary democracy. Finally, in the catalogue of earnest attempts to secure reform, the strivings of the Progressive and Socialist parties after 1871 should be mentioned, as should the experiment in republican government which was born of the military collapse of 1918 and was finally defeated by Hitler's rise to power.

It is possible, in short, without doing serious injustice to facts, to regard the history of Germany in the nineteenth and twentieth centuries as one long constitutional struggle, in which the critical battles—those of 1819, 1848, 1866, and 1918—were followed by uneasy truces in which the opposing forces recovered their strength and prepared for new encounters. On the whole, it was the opponents of constitutional reform, liberalism, and democracy who were the more effective fighters. During the nineteenth century, certainly, their defeats were of shorter duration and their powers of recuperation more marked. They could not prevent the promulgation of a constitution in Prussia in 1848, although they tried, and they were forced reluctantly to agree to the unification of Germany in 1871 under a constitution which provided for universal manhood suffrage. But until 1918 they were able successfully to block the introduction into Germany of what were considered in western countries to be the minimal requirements of representative government, namely, the principle of ministerial responsibility and effective parliamentary control over state administration and policy. Indeed, even when the monarchy collapsed in 1918 and Germany acquired a republican constitution, the forces of resistance carried on their fight and were willing in the end, in order to destroy the democratic system, to place the fate of their country in the hands of Adolf Hitler.

In the protracted constitutional struggle, a crucial role was played by the Prussian army. If, as has often been said, the Prussian army made the Prussian state, it is also true that the subsequent political development of Prussia and Germany was dependent, to a far greater extent than is true of any other country, upon the organization of the army, its relationship to the sovereign power, and the will of its leaders. It was the reorganization of the army in the years 1807–13 which made possible Prussia's liberation from French domination and the recovery of her position as a Great Power; and it was the hope of the soldiers who inspired that reorganization—Scharnhorst, Gneisenau, Grolman, and Boyen—that the new army would be the school of a new nation and that the military reforms would be completed by comprehensive political reform. These hopes were defeated, not least by the army's resistance to the liberals in its midst. When Boyen resigned as War Minister in 1819, his action terminated the most hopeful period of reform in Prussian history and, at the same time, indicated that the army had become once more what it had been in the old régime, the strongest supporter of the monarchical state and the most effective and inveterate opponent of political change.

In the years that followed this was adequately demonstrated and was recognized by all those who continued to aspire to liberal or democratic institutions. It is significant that the Prussian liberals in 1848 and in the years 1862–6 sought, first and foremost, to win control over the army, realizing that control over the state would follow naturally if this could be acquired. This challenge the leaders of the army met with determination and with highly effective political tactics. In 1848 they successfully defeated the demand that the army should be bound by an oath to the new constitution, and this dangerous exemption was confirmed in all subsequent constitutional arrangements until 1919. In the so-called *Konfliktszeit* of the 1860's, they effectively defied the right of the Prussian parliament to influence matters of military organization and further demonstrated that the army was responsible to the Crown alone. Finally, after the unification of 1871, when the imperial Reichstag sought to win some measure of influence in military affairs by insisting upon the right to question the War Minister, the army leaders, in a series of adroit administrative adjustments, deprived that official of most of his important functions and relegated authority in all matters of command, organization, and personnel to utterly irresponsible army agencies. The price paid for this was a high degree of administrative confusion and division of authority within the army itself and that had deplorable effects during the First World War; but the immediate objective of these tactics was achieved, and progress towards democracy was blocked by the army's ability to resist parliamentary or popular control.

If the policy of the army was a decisive factor in the domestic history of Germany in the nineteenth century, it was equally important in the field of foreign policy. Alfred Weber has pointed out[1] that one of the most significant developments of the nineteenth century was 'the evolution, inspired by the engineer, of a now fully mechanized militarism which, once drawn into the current of technical revolution, turned the army from a purely subservient instrument of the State into an independent political factor, gradually pursuing its own policies and entering into its own alliances with its own expanding power-drives and more and more monstrous apparatus of destruction'. As early as the 1860's this tendency was noticeable in Prussia and it was precisely in the years in which Prussian arms were forging German unity that the Prussian army chiefs began to meddle in affairs of high policy. In the wars of 1866 and 1870–1 the differences between the military and the civilian leaders with regard to fundamental policy decisions were frequent and sharp, and although Bismarck in most cases successfully maintained the authority of the civilian statesman, it cannot be said that his victory was decisive. Certainly in his twenty years' service as Chancellor he had frequent occasion to complain of the tendency of the military authorities to arrogate to themselves influence in the sphere of foreign policy; during the complicated crisis of 1887, for instance, the success of his diplomacy was seriously jeopardized by their irresponsible activities.

It is perhaps an inevitable concomitant of technical progress that military influence in the direction of foreign affairs should have increased sharply in all countries since 1870. The progressive mechanization of warfare has, for instance, made it essential for policy makers, in time of international tension, to solicit and weigh the advice of army and navy staffs concerning foreign capabilities. In the democratic states it has always been recognized, however, that this broadening of the sphere of military activity is inherently dangerous, and that, unless the right of ultimate decision rests with the civilian authorities, foreign policy will tend to be dictated by military expediency.

In Germany Bismarck at least was conscious of this danger; his successors, however, were less effective than he in keeping

[1] Alfred Weber, *Farewell to European History* (London, 1947), p. 68.

the military within bounds. In consequence the Wilhelmine era was characterized by the progressive usurpation by the military agencies of the authority and functions of the professional diplomats. Operational plans for future wars were adopted, for instance, in a form which seriously limited the diplomatic freedom of the state, although this clearly violated Clausewitz's dictum that strategical ideas should never be considered without due consideration of their political implications. Simultaneously, as international tension mounted, the military advisers of the Crown argued that civilian statesmen had neither the technical knowledge nor the realistic approach which the *Zeitgeist* required and were able to convince the emperor that he should pay less attention to the admonitions of the Foreign Office than to the advice of the General Staff, the *Reichsmarineamt*, and their agents in foreign capitals. 'Wer regiert in Berlin?' cried an exasperated Austrian official in 1914. 'Moltke oder Bethmann?' The German declaration of war and the subsequent course of German policy during the war answered the question in unequivocal terms. The last vestiges of civilian authority in foreign affairs disappeared in the war years, and the professional diplomats were forced either to concur in political decisions which they regarded as mistaken—such as the refusal to promise to evacuate Belgium, the establishment of a kingdom of Poland, the introduction of unrestricted submarine warfare, and the imposition of punitive terms at Brest Litovsk and Bucharest—or to resign their posts.

The policies of the military diplomats led directly to the disaster of 1918 which swept away the monarchical system which the army, by its role in domestic politics, had sought so zealously to maintain. It was natural to expect that the new rulers of Germany would remember the past and profit from it, that they would place effective constitutional limitations upon their military establishment, and would insist henceforth that the army was no more than an instrument of the civilian political authority. The attempt was certainly made, but was hardly successful. From the beginning the republican government was handicapped by its dependence upon the army for protection against revolutionary disturbances. The army chiefs exploited this initial advantage cleverly, and proved as effective in avoiding parliamentary control as their predecessors had been in 1848 and in the *Konfliktszeit*.

All of this was not, of course, immediately clear. In the Weimar Republic the army had to accept, for the first time in its long history, a civilian Minister of War; and the officer corps was forced to do what it had refused to do in 1848—to take an oath of obedience to the constitution of the republic. But these were small things compared to an unhappy truth which emerged more and more clearly as the years passed, namely, that the bulk of the army recognized no real allegiance to the republican régime or to the principles underlying it. The republican government was in fact in the impossible position of relying for protection against dissident groups upon an army which was itself potentially the most dangerous dissident group in Germany. In the Reichswehr of the 1920's, dissatisfaction with the terms of the peace treaty, with the forced reduction of the army in size, and with the consequent slowing down of promotion, made the officer corps contemptuous of the politicians upon whom they blamed these things; and they communicated their own contempt to the troops under their command. The fact that the Allied Powers at Versailles had insisted that the new German army be a small force of long-term professional soldiers merely heightened the effect of this anti-republican indoctrination. In the long run the army became what Gustav Stresemann had warned that it might become, 'a kind of Praetorian guard divorced from and in opposition to the mass of the people'.[1]

In the critical years of the Weimar Republic, as in previous periods of German history, the army played a decisive part in determining the political destiny of the nation. The most dangerous enemies of the republic realized that they could not hope to overthrow it unless they secured at least the sympathetic neutrality of the army; and Hitler for one was guided by that knowledge in all phases of his policy before 1933. Hitler set out deliberately to play upon the dissatisfaction which existed within the army, and while his promises of a restored and expanded military establishment gradually enticed the bulk of the junior officers to his support, his charges that the republican régime lacked national spirit and failed adequately to defend the interests of the state found a sympathetic response in the hearts of the officer corps in general. Thus the fateful political change of 30 January 1933 was supported, at least tacitly, by the army;

[1] Viscount d'Abernon, *An Ambassador of Peace* (London, 1929–30), iii. 56.

and within eighteen months the best-known military journal in Germany was writing:

In the new state of Adolf Hitler, the *Wehrmacht* is no foreign body as it was after the November revolt of 1918. Today it is a part of the organic community and shares in the common distribution of the nation's work; and it follows Adolf Hitler as the Fuehrer of the people with full confidence and with devotion to its great national task.[1]

In the light of what followed the 'revolution' of 1933, these words have a somewhat ironical ring. For the professional officer corps the Hitler period was marked by a long series of humiliations, beginning with the murder of Generals von Schleicher and von Bredow in 1934, made evident to the whole world in the disgraceful dismissal of General von Fritsch in 1938, and ending with the cavalier treatment accorded to professional officers during the campaigns of the Second World War. For more than a century the army had successfully defended its autonomous position in the state, beating off all attempts to impose constitutional restraints upon it and, by these very tactics, frustrating Germany's progress toward democracy. Yet in 1933, when it assented to Hitler's seizure of power, it encompassed its own, as well as Germany's, ruin. Within five years Hitler had accomplished what the liberals of 1848 and 1862 and the republicans and socialists of 1918 had sought to accomplish in vain: he had completely subordinated the army to his own control. And within the space of another two years he had driven it into a war which all responsible German soldiers dreaded—as events were to show, with reason.

Books dealing with the German army are already almost as numerous as the leaves of Vallombrosa. There may be some merit, however, in recounting, in greater detail than has been usual in English and American books on the subject, the history of the political influence and activity of the Prussian-German army. We live in an age in which military influence in both foreign and domestic policy is marked and is growing, and there is little hope that this tendency will be reversed in the foreseeable future. The ideal aim of the healthy state is that its military establishment shall remain merely the executive will of the sovereign power. To fulfil this aim is a task which requires

[1] *Militärwochenblatt*, cxix, Nr. 8 (25 Aug. 1934).

delicacy, patience, and constant vigilance, for military influence manifests itself—as Friedrich Meinecke says[1]—in hidden ways, not always easily detected. Perhaps reflection upon the history of another people, whose political aspirations were defeated in part by their inability to set proper limits to the activities of their military leaders, may help us avoid dangerous mistakes in our own time.

[1] Friedrich Meinecke, *Die deutsche Katastrophe: Betrachtungen und Erinnerungen* (Dritte Auflage, Wiesbaden, 1947), p. 76.

I

THE ARMY AND THE STATE 1640–1807

Le monde ne repose pas plus sûrement sur les épaules d'Atlas que la Prusse sur une telle armée.

FREDERICK II, *after Hohenfriedberg, June* 1745

Der König hat eine Bataille verloren. Ruhe ist die erste Bürgerpflicht.

Government proclamation, after Jena, Oct. 1806.

I

IN his *Deutsche Geschichte* Franz Schnabel has written that the foundation of the Prussian state is the greatest political accomplishment in German history, the more so because the favourable geographical conditions which helped in the formation of other national units were totally lacking in the case of the Hohenzollern domains.[1] The lands which formed the nucleus of modern Prussia were in the seventeenth century scattered in a haphazard fashion across the five parallel streams which flow through northern Germany. Between Ravensberg and Mark and Electoral Brandenburg and East Prussia there was no natural connexion of any kind; and in the confused and fluctuating political conditions of that century there was no reason to suppose that the tenuous ties which bound them to the Hohenzollern dynasty could long be maintained. That they were maintained and that the disparate fragments of territory were forged, not only into a viable political union, but into one which was recognized as a Great European Power, was the result of two things: the political will and sagacity of the Hohenzollern rulers after 1640 and the effectiveness of the army which they created.

When Frederick William, later called the Great Elector, assumed the throne of Brandenburg in 1640, he was confronted with conditions that might well have made him despair. The religious wars that had ravaged the German lands since 1618 had reduced the Elector's authority over his realm to the lowest

[1] Franz Schnabel, *Deutsche Geschichte im 19. Jahrhundert* (Freiburg-im-Breisgau, 1925 ff.), i. 95.

possible point. In an age of war, Frederick William's father had made the fatal mistake of relying for safety upon diplomatic adroitness. His alternation between studied neutrality, half-hearted combinations with the Swedes, and, finally, unwilling support of the Catholic cause were as unedifying as they were ineffective; and in the end his equivocations merely annoyed the Powers he sought to appease. As a result his reign had ended with his Rhineland holdings ringed round by Dutch and Spanish armies, the province of East Prussia in open disaffection, and even Brandenburg itself, with the exception of Berlin and a few fortresses, under foreign occupation.

The new ruler, then, inherited a realm which seemed on the point of dissolution; but, while admitting the gravity of the situation, he refused to be cowed by it. The pitiless realism which was to characterize all of his political thinking did, however, convince him that the time had come to make a clean break with the policy of the past. The Hohenzollerns could not protect their heritage, he felt, by continuing to depend upon diplomatic manœuvre and shifting alliances. 'Alliances', he was to write years later, 'to be sure, are good, but forces of one's own still better. Upon them one can rely with more security, and a lord is of no consideration if he does not have means and troops of his own.'[1] The key to safety lay in military force, and the Elector set out deliberately to create a reliable military establishment.

From the very beginning, the military problem was closely intertwined with the whole question of state administration and local politics. The military weakness of the Elector at the beginning of his reign was largely caused by the desire of the hard-necked notables of his separate provinces to protect the privileges which they had extorted from previous rulers. Chief among these was their control of taxation. The Elector was dependent upon the Estates of Brandenburg, Cleves, Mark, and East Prussia for the funds with which to support his administra-

[1] 'Alliancen seindt zwahr gutt, aber eigene Krefte noch besser, darauff kan man Sich sicherer verlassen, vndt ist ein herr in keiner consideration, wan er selber nicht mittel vndt volck hatt, den das hatt mich, von der zeitt das Ichs also gehalten, Gott sey gedanck(t) considerabell gemacht, vnd beklage allezeitt das Ich im anfange meiner Regirung, zu meinem hochsten nachtheill mich Dauon ableitten lassen, vndt wider meinen willen, anderer Rahdt gefolget.' Political Testament of 1667, in G. Küntzel and M. Hass, *Die politischen Testamente der Hohenzollern* (Leipzig, 1919), i. 56.

tion and pay his troops; and, despite the extraordinary expenses incurred by the war, the Estates had been unwilling to weaken the advantage they held over the ruler by unwise generosity. So niggardly had they been in their grants that, in 1640, the only troops at the disposal of the Elector were a few thousand mercenaries and refugees from other armies—*Landsknechte* of the lowest type, who were incapable of operations against organized forces and who terrorized the provinces they were supposed to defend.[1] To replace these with a reliable army would require the assent of the Estates, and it was doubtful, in view of their past conduct, that this could be obtained.

It was this task, however, which the Elector set himself and which, in the end, he accomplished, with revolutionary political consequences. He started with a gesture which could not help but propitiate the jealous Estates of Brandenburg, by proceeding ruthlessly to eliminate from his existing forces all unruly elements. In the first years of his reign, the undesirable and the unfit were purged; the rebellious colonels who had blackmailed the citizens of the fortress towns were arrested or driven into exile; and the most incompetent of the foreign mercenaries were discharged. What was left was a tiny force of 2,500 men, but this was the nucleus of the standing army of the future. The Estates, grateful for the relief from military anarchy, proved willing to supply the funds necessary to keep this force equipped and even to increase its numbers, and the Elector took advantage of this mood to build up his army rapidly in the last years of the Thirty Years War. In 1648 he had 8,000 men under arms, and the existence of this force was a not inconsiderable factor in securing the concessions made to Brandenburg in the treaties of Westphalia.[2]

Once the war was over, the Estates reverted to the suspicion which had characterized their relations with the ruler in the past, and they made frequent demands in the course of the next thirty years for a substantial reduction of the army. By a mixture of timely concessions, studied evasions, and careful economy, however, the Elector was able to continue his policy of military expansion without serious interference until he was strong enough to defy his critics and destroy their centres of

[1] Gustav Schmoller, 'Die Entstehung des preußischen Heeres von 1640 bis 1740', *Deutsche Rundschau*, xii (1877), 250–7.

[2] Ferdinand Schevill, *The Great Elector* (Chicago, 1947), pp. 124 ff.

resistance. The key to his success in this regard was the famous arrangement which he made with his Brandenburg Estates in 1653. Here, in return for a grant of 530,000 talers, payable in instalments over a period of six years, the Elector made a sweeping grant of power to the great landholders who had been the most intransigent of his antagonists. The estates of these so-called Junkers he transformed from fiefs held in compensation for military and other services into alodial estates held in absolute ownership. Eliminating the legal restrictions which had bound the Junkers in the past, he recognized them as the only class authorized to acquire estates and confirmed and stabilized privileges they had extorted from his predecessors, like exemption from taxation and the right to control the lives of their peasants. Finally, he specifically recognized their authority in local affairs and their right to be regarded as the governing class in all matters that concerned the state as a whole.[1]

To the social and political consequences of this arrangement it will be necessary to return later. The immediately significant result of the compromise of 1653 was that it provided the Elector with the army he desired. It is true that the funds granted in 1653 were sufficient to maintain only a modest force, one which was probably not in excess of 5,000 men; but this was a foundation on which to build, and how quickly and efficiently the Elector could build when given an opportunity, he demonstrated when war broke out between Sweden and Poland in 1655. Pointing to the manifest dangers inherent in this conflict, Frederick William ordered his agents to begin recruiting additional forces in both Brandenburg and the principalities on the lower Rhine and called out the East Prussian militia. The protests of the Brandenburg Estates, who had no inclination to contribute funds for the defence of provinces other than their own, he brushed aside unceremoniously and proceeded to impose a variety of extraordinary taxes to support the new recruits.[2] With this encouragement, his army grew rapidly. Eight thousand men were under arms by September 1655, 22,000 by June 1656, and 27,000 men when the Treaty of Oliva brought the hostilities to an end in 1660.

[1] Hans Rosenberg, 'The Rise of the Junkers', *American Historical Review*, xlix, no. 2 (Jan. 1944), p. 240. Cf. F. L. Carsten, *The Origins of Prussia* (Oxford, 1954), pp. 187–9.

[2] Schevill, *Great Elector*, pp. 195–6; Carsten, *Origins of Prussia*, p. 190.

In Curt Jany's opinion,[1] Prussia's standing army was born during the war of 1655–60. There were reductions in its size after 1660, but they were never as extensive as previous reductions had been;[2] and the Elector and his successors were never again forced to build a military establishment virtually from the ground up when an emergency faced the state. Between 1660 and 1672 the Elector was able to keep between 7,000 and 12,000 men with the colours. To supplement this force he followed a policy of finding state posts for the higher officers who left the service after 1660 and of establishing discharged soldiers as farmers upon his royal domains—thus creating a kind of trained reserve which would be subject to recall in time of war. After 1672, when the expansionist aims of Louis XIV involved the European Powers in a long series of wars, Frederick William's army began to expand again and, thanks to the Elector's ability to exact sizeable subsidies from those who wished his alliance, at a faster rate than before. Nor was the Elector inclined any longer to make concessions to provincial authorities who resisted the rapid increase of his forces. With his Brandenburg Estates he had little trouble after 1653—indeed, there was no further general meeting of the Estates after that year. The Estates of Cleves and Mark and those of East Prussia he now forced into subjection by threatening military execution of his decrees. By 1661 he had compelled his Rhineland provinces to recognize his right to recruit and maintain forces within their borders and, by the middle of the 1670's, his authority was unquestioned in East Prussia as well.[3]

When the Elector died in 1688 he left an army whose strength has been estimated at about 30,000 men.[4] It was a force whose organization had undergone radical change since 1640. The old mercenary system in which the colonels contracted to supply the ruler with regiments of a stipulated size but brooked no interference on his part with the administration and command of their troops, was gradually modified in the course of

[1] Curt Jany, *Geschichte der königlich-preußischen Armee bis zum Jahre 1807* (Berlin, 1928–9), i. 192–3.

[2] Otto Hintze, *Die Hohenzollern und ihr Werk* (7. Auflage, Berlin, 1916), p. 221.

[3] Ludwig Tümpel, *Die Entstehung des brandenburgisch-preußischen Einheitsstaates im Zeitalter des Absolutismus, 1609–1806* (Untersuchungen zur deutschen Staats- und Rechtsgeschichte, ed. by Otto von Gierke, 124. Heft) (Breslau, 1915), especially pp. 49–55, 59–60; Carsten, *Origins of Prussia,* especially pp. 210–17, 219–20, 222–3, 243–52.

[4] Jany, *Preußische Armee,* i. 300–1.

the Great Elector's reign. The first steps were taken toward the modern system of centralized army administration. In 1655 the Elector gave Freiherr von Sparr general command over all troops in the Hohenzollern lands, a step which, theoretically at least, unified the hitherto unco-ordinated provincial forces; and under Sparr's direction a kind of General Staff came into existence which gave some practical meaning, in matters of command, to this concept of unification.[1] Simultaneously the activities of Claus Ernst von Platen, who was appointed as *Generalkriegskommissar* during the Swedish war and was charged with overall supervision of such things as the assembling, remounting, provisioning, and billeting of the army, its payment, stores, and magazines, and the imposition of contributions at home and abroad, also rapidly promoted uniformity within the Elector's army.[2] As a result of these measures the authority of the colonels inevitably declined. Increasingly, the Elector sought to avoid specific contracts (*Kapitulationen*) with individual commanders; progressively he curtailed the colonels' right to commission junior officers and laid the basis for a system in which all officers owed complete allegiance to the ruler as commander-in-chief of the army.[3] Finally, he tried—although

[1] Sparr received the title *Generalfeldmarschalk* in 1658. On the extent of his authority, see Jany, *Preußische Armee*, i. 149 ff. Originally the term *Generalstab* referred to all officers of general grade and all administrative personnel not attached to the regiments or the artillery. The functions of a modern General Staff—the execution of technical studies and the preparation of operational plans—were performed during the Great Elector's reign by the so-called *Generalquartiermeister* and his assistants, under Sparr's general supervision. In time of war the Elector, like Frederick II in a later period, was both commander-in-chief and chief of staff, although Sparr nominally held the latter post in war-time. Ibid., pp. 152–3.

[2] Platen was theoretically responsible to Sparr but, for all practical purposes, worked independently. As early as 1657 Sparr was complaining to the Elector of actions taken by the *Generalkriegskommissar* without his knowledge and orders issued to other officers without his assent. Ibid., p. 153. After Platen's retirement in 1667 the powers of his office did not develop further until the appointment of von Grumbkow in 1679. Under this officer its functions were rapidly expanded, and it developed into the most important authority in the Hohenzollern state, the *Generalkriegskommissar* combining the functions of a minister of war with those of a minister of finance. See Carsten, *Origins of Prussia*, pp. 260–3.

[3] The details of this process are recorded in Schmoller, in *Deutsche Rundschau*, xii (1877), 259. Cf. Jany, *Preußische Armee*, i. 157 ff. It was not until the time of King Frederick William I that the ruler's right of independent creation of officers was unconditionally established, but before his death the Great Elector had made good his right to veto commissions made by the colonels and had also successfully ordered that regimental rank should be determined by seniority. Hans Rosenberg, in *Bureaucracy, Aristocracy and Autocracy: The Prussian Experience, 1660–1815* (Cambridge, Mass., 1958), p. 79, points out that *Kompagniewirtschaft* survived on a limited scale until the army reforms after 1806.

with far less success than one might imagine from reading Kleist's *Prinz Friedrich von Homburg*—to alter the mental outlook of his officers and to persuade them to think of themselves less as speculators and business men than as servants of the state.

Incomplete as they were, these efforts in the direction of centralization were reflected in increased efficiency in the field. During the reign of the Great Elector the army of Brandenburg-Prussia not only demonstrated that it was capable of defending the territories of its ruling house but, by its victories at Warsaw and Fehrbellin, won the consideration and respect of the Great Powers of Europe, a fact adequately demonstrated by the eagerness with which its aid was solicited in the Elector's last years. More tangible benefits were denied him, thanks to the bewildering shifts of the diplomatic alignments of the period; but when his son assumed the title of 'King in Prussia' in January 1701, the failure of any of the Powers to dispute the new title was a belated recognition of the increased stature of the Hohenzollern state and a vindication of the Great Elector's belief that military power alone could make a ruler *considerabell*.

The lesson was not lost upon his successors. The Great Elector's son is generally considered to have been a weak ruler, and certainly his love for ceremonial and display invited the ridicule of his subjects and dismayed the administrators of his revenues. But this first Prussian King nevertheless respected the realities, as well as the trappings, of power; he recognized the army as the bulwark of his authority; and he gradually increased its strength until it stood at a level of 40,000 men. And when his son, the remarkable Frederick William I, came to the throne in 1713, the growth of the army was made the first objective of his policy.

Like the Great Elector, Frederick William I believed that the international position of a prince was determined entirely by the number of troops he could maintain. 'I can but laugh at the scoundrels', he said on one occasion, referring to certain of his father's ministers, 'they say they will obtain land and people for the King with the pen; but I say it can be done only with the sword, otherwise he will get nothing.'[1] Later he took frequent occasion to impress this truth upon his son. 'Fritz, mark my words', he said in 1724, 'always keep up a large efficient army; you cannot have a better friend and without that friend you will not be able to survive. . . . Believe me, you must

[1] Robert Ergang, *The Potsdam Führer: Frederick William I, Father of Prussian Militarism* (New York, 1941), p. 42.

not think about imaginary things; fix your mind on real ones. Have money and a good army; they ensure the glory and safety of a prince.'[1]

Acting upon his own precepts, Frederick William, from the outset of his reign, bent all his energies to the task of increasing the size and efficiency of the army and, at the same time, of freeing it from that dependence upon foreign subsidies which had, in previous reigns, involved the Hohenzollerns in wars which did not always advance their own interests. By a policy of the most rigid economy, in which the Prussian state spent four and five times as much annually on its army as it did on all other obligations, Frederick William increased the size of his military establishment from 40,000 to 83,000 men, a figure which made Prussia's army the fourth largest in Europe, although the state ranked only tenth from the standpoint of territory and thirteenth in population.[2]

This remarkable increase was accompanied by fundamental changes in the composition and personnel of the army and its leaders. The king's greatest source of concern in the early years of his reign was man-power. The fantastic severity which characterized Prussian discipline encouraged desertion. In no single year of this reign did fugitives from the army number fewer than 400, and the total number of desertions between 1713 and 1740 was 30,216. More important sources of attrition were age and sickness which led annually to the discharge of 20 per cent. of the effective force. The king soon found that he could not hope to replace these losses by relying upon volunteers. During his early years, therefore, he resorted increasingly to the impressment of his own subjects and to recruiting—and recruiting which was at times indistinguishable from kidnapping—in neighbouring states. The results of this, however, were scarcely satisfactory. Not only was the king involved continually in disputes with other rulers, who resented the infringement of their rights, but he was confronted in his own lands with mounting public indignation and—and this was probably more troubling to his frugal nature—with an increase in emigration which had deleterious effects upon the economy of the state.[3]

[1] Pierre Gaxotte, *Frederick the Great* (New Haven, 1942), p. 18.

[2] Herbert Rosinski, *The German Army* (rev. ed., Washington, 1944), pp. 12, 16; Ergang, *Potsdam Führer*, p. 63.

[3] Jany, *Preußische Armee*, i. 682, 686; Ergang, *Potsdam Führer*, pp. 72–73. On forced recruiting and impressment of foreigners, see especially Robert Freiherr von

Frederick William I sought to escape these difficulties by making service in the standing army legally binding upon all his subjects. The obligation to defend the country in time of emergency by service in local militias had been assumed ever since the Thirty Years War and had been given legal weight by a regulation of 1701. The militia system had never, however, been systematically applied; the temporary formations were ineffective as reserves for the standing army; and enrolment in the militia had all too often been used as an excuse to escape service in the regular military establishment. Frederick William, then, in the first year of his reign, abolished the existing militia organizations and simultaneously decreed that anyone who left the kingdom in order to escape service in the regular army would be treated as a deserter. By implication this decree established the principle of universal liability to military service.[1]

Over the next twenty years other declarations regularized recruiting procedure, culminating in the decrees of 1732–3 which established the basic features of what came to be called the Prussian canton system. Every regiment in the army was assigned a specific recruiting district; all young males in the district were enrolled upon the regimental recruiting list; and, when the quotas could not be filled by voluntary enlistment, the difference was made up from the eligibles on the rolls.

Although all subsequent canton orders reaffirmed the universal obligation to serve, and although that obligation came to be generally accepted in customary law, neither Frederick William I nor his successors attempted anything approaching universal conscription of Prussian subjects. In practice liberal exemptions were made in the interest of trade, industry, and the public service; the whole upper stratum of society, including the more prosperous artisans and workers in industries which were of interest to the state, were freed of the duty of service; and the burden fell almost exclusively upon the agricultural workers and the less prosperous peasantry.[2] Moreover, even these conscripts were granted very liberal furloughs. In order to safe-

Schrötter, 'Die Ergänzung des preußischen Heeres unter dem ersten Könige', *Forschungen zur brandenburgischen und preußischen Geschichte*, xxiii (1910), 407, 428–9, 455–7, 461; and W. von Schultz, *Die preußischen Werbungen unter Friedrich Wilhelm I und Friedrich dem Großen* (Schwerin, 1887), pp. 8–18.

[1] Max Lehmann, 'Werbung, Wehrpflicht und Beurlaubung im Heere Friedrich Wilhelms I', *Historische Zeitschrift*, lxvii (1891), 265–6.

[2] Jany, *Preußische Armee*, i. 691 ff.; Ergang, *Potsdam Führer*, pp. 75–76.

guard the interests of the large landholders, the peasant conscripts were released from active duty after a two months' drill period every spring and thus, in time of peace, the army was at full strength only in April and May.[1]

Even with this limited application, the canton system was a notable innovation. It assured the army of what was in effect a large trained reserve which could be mobilized quickly in time of emergency. It also wrought an important change in the very character of the military establishment, for, despite the large number of foreign mercenaries in the service, the army would now, at least in time of war, be predominantly national in composition. Finally—and not least important—the accepted convention of a universal obligation to render military service supplied the necessary basis for the thorough-going reorganization of the Prussian army which was to be effected in the Napoleonic period.[2]

Fully as important as the canton system, was the king's successful effort to persuade his nobility to take service in the army. In the proud and truculent barons of his marches he recognized the military virtues of which the state stood in need, and he clearly discerned that these rural lords were the natural leaders of the peasant boys who were now subject to military service. Men cannot be forged into an army by drill and discipline alone. As Hintze has written, the foundation must be prepared by 'fixed ideas and conceptions, inherited and cultivated, and confirmed by tradition'.[3] In order to integrate the rural masses into his military establishment, Frederick William relied upon his Junkers, whose service in the officer corps would effectively introduce into the army a relationship between officer and soldier similar to the traditional relationships of rural society.

The reconciliation of the nobility with the Crown had begun under the Great Elector, the way having been opened by the compromise of 1653. Despite the personal prestige of the Elector, however, and despite the advantages he had been willing to offer the nobles who entered his service, resistance had continued, especially in East Prussia. Frederick William I determined to overcome this as much for political as for military

[1] For the subsequent development of the canton system and a discussion of deferment and furlough policy, see the excellent account in William O. Shanahan, *Prussian Military Reforms, 1786–1813* (New York, 1945), especially pp. 41–60.

[2] Ibid., pp. 41–42.

[3] Otto Hintze, *Historische und politische Aufsätze* (2. Auflage, Berlin, 1908), i. 23.

reasons. 'I will ruin the authority of the Junkers', he said on one occasion, 'and stabilize the sovereignty like a *rocher de bronze*.'[1] At the beginning of his reign he made it illegal for members of the nobility to enter foreign service. At the same time he ordered lists prepared of all young noblemen between the ages of 12 and 18 years and, on the basis of these, personally chose those who were to be admitted to the cadet corps in Berlin, which was the gateway to the officer corps. For a time this practice met with spirited opposition, especially in East Prussia, where some of the hapless candidates attempted to prove that they were not members of the Prussian nobility and hence ineligible for service, while others sought safety in flight. But the king had little patience with such evasions and was not above sending police agents or detachments of troops to round up his prospective officers and to march them to Berlin in gangs.[2]

By 1724 there was scarcely a noble family in the Hohenzollern domains that did not have a son in the officer corps, and by 1740 the king's private battle had been won. This was probably the result, less of his willingness to use force, than of the solid advantages which he held out to his nobility. To the sons of families which often possessed more pride than economic means, he offered an education, a standard of living higher than they could otherwise expect, an opportunity to rise to positions of great military and political authority, and a social position second to none in the state. They were offered also the less tangible, but certainly no less attractive, advantages of association with the king in an honourable calling on terms of complete social equality. In the new officer corps Frederick William wore the same coat as did his captains and lieutenants; with the sole exception of the generals no officer bore any designation of rank, and the ruler and his nobles comprised a closed society governed by the laws of professional competence and feudal honour. It is not surprising that the nobility should find this atmosphere congenial and should come to regard the service, which it entered with initial reluctance, as its natural profession.[3]

[1] Hintze, *Historische und politische Aufsätze*, i. 18. Droysen reports that the king's words were: 'I will reach my goal and stabilize the sovereignty and make the Crown as firm as a *rocher de bronze* and leave to the Junkers the hot air of the *Landtag*.' *Geschichte der preußischen Politik* (Berlin, 1865 ff.), iv, part 2, 198.

[2] Schmoller in *Deutsche Rundschau* (1877), p. 270.

[3] Rosinski, *German Army*, pp. 12–14; Hintze, *Historische und politische Aufsätze*, i.

While the canton system and the mobilization of the nobility for military purposes gave his army a national basis which it had not had before, Frederick William continued along the lines so shrewdly plotted by the Great Elector and advanced the uniformity and centralization of his armed force. Dress and weapons were carefully prescribed by the king and his advisers. In 1714 Frederick William himself wrote the first comprehensive Infantry Regulations ever to be issued to the army, a set of instructions which henceforth governed every phase of the soldier's life in the garrison and the field. The manual exercises and tactical evolutions laid down here, and the endless drilling with which they were impressed upon the troops, gave to Frederick William's infantry a flexibility and precision in manœuvre which had hitherto been unknown in continental armies, while at the same time they produced the rapidity and accuracy of fire which was to make Prussian armies famous throughout all Europe under Frederick William's successor.[1]

For all the importance which he attributed to the possession of an army, Frederick William was very reluctant to use it, and he carefully avoided adventures which might jeopardize the safety of his beloved grenadiers. Not so his son. Even before his accession to the throne the prince, who was to be remembered as Frederick the Great, had chafed at Prussia's inactivity and had been ashamed that, despite her strength, she should be reckoned as a mere pawn on the European chessboard.[2] In his earliest writings he had made it clear that to *corriger la figure de la Prusse* was a necessity if Prussia was 'to stand on her own feet and do credit to the name of her King'.[3] In her present state, Prussia was still a hermaphrodite, more electorate than kingdom;[4] her sprawling provinces offered an open invitation to foreign aggression; consolidation was necessary but could be effected only by new acquisitions; and new acquisitions would necessarily involve resort to force. This being so, Prussia must grasp the first opportunity that presented itself, and Frederick

21–22; Jany, *Preußische Armee*, i. 722, 729; Schmoller in *Deutsche Rundschau* (1877), p. 272.

[1] Ergang, *Potsdam Führer*, p. 66.

[2] G. P. Gooch, *Frederick the Great: The Ruler, the Writer, the Man* (New York, 1947), p. 10.

[3] Heinrich von Treitschke, *German History in the Nineteenth Century* (Eng. trans., New York, 1915–19), i. 59.

[4] Gooch, *Frederick the Great*, p. 12.

found it in the accession of Maria Theresa to the throne of Austria in 1740. As he prepared what can only be called a war of aggression against this ruler, Frederick paid no heed to the legal objections of his ministers or the doubts of his military advisers. Like another great soldier of an earlier era he might well have said:

He either fears his fate too much,
Or his deserts are small,
That dares not put it to the touch,
To gain or lose it all.

When he threw his troops across the frontiers of Silesia in 1740, inaugurating a generation of devastating conflict, Frederick risked nothing less than the utter destruction of his state. But, by winning Silesia, and proving his ability to retain it, he destroyed the old German constitution and raised Prussia to a position of virtual equality with Austria.

The wars of Frederick the Great completed the constructive work of the Great Elector and Frederick William I, at once testing the perfected weapon and achieving the purpose for which it had been forged. 'The twelve campaigns of the Frederician epoch', writes Treitschke, 'have impressed their own stamp forever upon the warlike spirit of the Prussian people and the Prussian army; even today the North German, when war is discussed, involuntarily adopts the expressions of those heroic days and speaks like Frederick of "brilliant campaigns" and "fulminating attacks".'[1] At Mollwitz and Lowositz, at Rossbach and Leuthen, at Zorndorf and Torgau, the army that had been so methodically nurtured by the Great Elector and Frederick William I proved itself, and, at the same time, found the spirit and made the tradition that was to sustain it through all the changes of the coming century.[2] In the fire of the Seven Years War the reconciliation between the king and his nobles was finally completed, and the officer corps became the embodiment of the spirit of devotion to the Crown and the state, while the common foot-soldier gained a consciousness of his own ability which, handed on to his successors, was to make Prussian troops the finest soldiers in Europe. Finally, the achievements of the army crowned with success the process begun in 1640,

[1] Treitschke, *German History*, i. 72–73.
[2] Rosinski, *German Army*, p. 20.

effected a fundamental change in the European balance of power and established beyond question Prussia's title to Great Power status.

II

There was, however, a reverse to the medal. The creation of an army capable of winning international recognition for the Hohenzollern rulers was made possible only by subordinating the total energies of their subjects to the maintenance of that military establishment. The institutional framework, the economic activity, and even the social organization of Prussia were determined in large part by the needs of the army; and if the Prussian state which was thus created was a masterpiece of conscious design, it was, nevertheless, essentially an artificial creation, incapable of natural growth or independent development.

The high degree of centralization which characterized the government of Frederick II was the natural outgrowth of the increasing costs of the military establishment over the last century. The expenses of civil government in the old Electorate of Brandenburg had been extremely modest, and it had been possible, for the most part, to pay them from the income of the royal domains and of those enterprises, like mills and breweries, which were controlled by the Crown. In the Great Elector's time, however, this income proved inadequate to support an army of the size he considered to be necessary, and, during the Thirty Years War and the Swedish war, he was forced to levy new taxes and special contributions—excise taxes on consumers' goods, stamp taxes on legal documents, various poll taxes, a government monopoly on salt, and the like. To collect these monies royal agents were appointed who were called Tax Commissioners (*Steuerkommissare*) or—more significantly in the light of their purpose—War Commissioners (*Kriegskommissare*). Responsible in their activities to provincial *Oberkriegskommissare* and, through them, to the *Generalkriegskommissar* in Berlin, these tax collectors were the standard-bearers of royal authority in every part of the Elector's territories, and inevitably their duties led them to encroach upon the jurisdiction of local magnates and municipal administrations.

As the needs of the army grew, this administration became increasingly elaborate and increasingly centralized. In order to free the army from its dependence upon foreign subsidies, Frederick William I sought to increase revenues by combining the administration of the crown lands with the war commissariats. The General Directory, which he established in 1723, administered the royal domains, collected all taxes, and directed the operations of the mint, the postal system, and the royal monopolies.[1] In addition it assumed the direction of the whole economic life of the state, encouraging foreign immigration, initiating and financing new industries, and, in general, shaping the economic growth of Prussia to the needs of the military establishment. Finally, as developed by Frederick William I and his successor, the General Directory completed the centralization of political authority which had begun when the Great Elector suppressed the provincial Estates. The ministers of the separate departments of the General Directory were invested with political and administrative responsibility; the intermediate boards (*Kriegs- und Domänen-Kammer*) which were established in the provinces were endowed with judicial powers in matters of public law and completely supplanted institutions of local government in the towns and in the western provinces.

Thus, out of the war commissariats of the Great Elector grew the formidable administrative apparatus of Frederick the Great's time—a system which fulfilled the king's requirement that his government should be 'as coherent as a system of philosophy, so that finance, policy and the army are coordinated to the same end: namely, the consolidation of the State and the increase of its power'.[2] The General Directory, the special functional ministries which grew out of it during the reign of Frederick II,[3] and the provincial chambers made possible the organization of the resources of the state for national purposes and provided the machinery for executing the policy which the king determined in his private cabinet.

[1] On the General Directory, see especially Hintze, *Historische und politische Aufsätze*, i. 186–90; Ergang, *Potsdam Führer*, pp. 104–7.

[2] Gooch, *Frederick the Great*, p. 296.

[3] On the progressive specialization of the central branches of Prussian administration and the development of functional ministries, see especially Walter L. Dorn, 'The Prussian Bureaucracy in the Eighteenth Century', *Political Science Quarterly*, xlvii (1932), 75–83. The long-term result of this process, as Dorn points out, was a weakening of the unity of administration which the General Directory originally provided, but this did not become apparent until after the death of Frederick the Great.

The army also had a profound effect upon the social development and class structure of Prussia. To win the landed aristocracy to the army, the Great Elector and his successors had, as we have seen, been prepared to make far-going concessions to them. The partnership which was concluded by the Elector and his Junkers in 1653 was confirmed by his successors. Not only were the Junkers protected economically by being given complete authority over their estates and over the serfs who worked them, but they were permitted, in their own districts, to retain important police, judicial, and administrative functions as well. The centralization which was characteristic of the rest of Prussian administration stopped at the limits of the Junkers' estates. Here the *Landrat*, nominated by his fellow Junkers and appointed by the King, was supreme, and his authority was to remain unaffected by the changes of the revolutionary period.[1]

The right of the nobility to these economic and political privileges was openly championed by Frederick the Great. It was, after all, he pointed out, the sons of the nobility who defended the state; and 'the race is so good that it deserves to be protected in every way'.[2] In Frederick's eyes this protection included a prescriptive right to the highest posts in the civil service and an absolute monopoly of commissions in the officer corps of the army. What Frederick required above all in his officers was a sense of honour—a moral compulsion which forced them, out of respect for themselves and their calling, to bear hardship, danger, and death without flinching and without expectation of reward.[3] This feeling of honour, the king believed, could be found only in the feudal nobility, not in other classes, and certainly not in the *bourgeoisie*, which was driven by material rather than moral considerations and was too rational, in moments of disaster, to regard sacrifice as either necessary or commendable.[4] Although he must have been aware that

[1] Schnabel, *Deutsche Geschichte*, i. 98–99; Rosenberg, *Bureaucracy*, p. 39.

[2] Gerhard Ritter, *Friedrich der Große: ein historisches Profil* (Leipzig, 1936), p. 198.

[3] In a famous description of the officer corps of Frederick II Marwitz speaks of the 'renunciation of all personal advantage, of all gain, of all comfort—yes! of all desire if only honour remains! On the other hand, every sacrifice for this, for their King, for their fatherland, for the honour of Prussian weapons! In their hearts, duty and loyalty; for their own lives no concern! What other class and how many people, above all, in our present age, can pride themselves on such convictions? Model yourselves upon them, posterity, if you would be praised!' *Aus dem Nachlasse Friedrich August Ludwigs von der Marwitz* (Berlin, 1852), i. 307.

[4] Max Lehmann, *Scharnhorst* (Leipzig, 1886–7), ii. 58–59; Jany, *Preußische Armee*, i. 219; Hintze, *Historische und politische Aufsätze*, iii. 20.

some of the great military leaders of the Prussian past—Derfflinger, Lüdcke, and Hennigs, for example—had been of common blood, Frederick wanted only noble officers. He praised the selection policy of his father's time, when:

> On purgea dans chaque régiment le corps des officiers de ces gens dont la conduite ou la naissance ne répondait point au métier de gens d'honneur qu'ils devaient faire, et depuis la délicatesse des officiers ne souffrit parmi leurs compagnons que des gens sans reproche.[1]

He himself improved upon that example, and although he was compelled to permit *bourgeois* officers to serve in his regiments during the Seven Years War, spent the last years of his life cleansing the officer corps of this objectionable material. As a result of his efforts there were in 1806, in an officer corps of over 7,000, only 695 non-nobles, and these for the most part were isolated in the artillery and subsidiary branches of the service.[2]

In comparison with the privileged position of the nobility the lot of the other classes was austere and laborious. In the military state they too had assigned functions. The *bourgeoisie* was expected to produce the weapons and the uniforms for the army and to pay the bulk of the military taxes; the peasantry was to supply both the food and the recruits who would eat it. It would be inaccurate to say that, in return for the required services, these classes received no benefits. The burgher class was, as has already been mentioned, aided by the mercantilist programme of the state and by the planned policy of *Industrialisierung* and, while excluded from ownership of landed estates, was assured of a monopoly of trade and commerce. On the king's domain lands, at least, the peasants were sure of hereditary tenure and were granted a progressive lightening of labour and menial services, while, even on the private estates, the king sought to protect them from expropriation. But it is, nevertheless, impossible to avoid the conclusion that both Frederick William I and his son regarded these classes, in Srbik's telling phrase, as the 'füllende Materie des Staates ohne Selbstexistenz'[3]—as collections of individuals with no private desires or aspirations which required consideration. They were expected to serve the state and its military establishment with complete fidelity; the orders

[1] *Œuvres de Frédéric le Grand* (31 vols., Berlin, 1846–57), i. 192. On Frederick William's policy, see Rosenberg, *Bureaucracy*, 70.

[2] Jany, *Preußische Armee*, iii. 35–37, 418–20; Karl Demeter, *Das deutsche Heer und seine Offiziere* (Berlin, 1930), pp. 8–9.

[3] H. Ritter von Srbik, *Deutsche Einheit* (Munich, 1935–42), i. 106.

which were handed down from above they were to carry out without question; and, for the rest, they were not expected, or permitted, to concern themselves with those matters of high policy which the king decided and his army executed. When the commandant of Berlin, in the first shock of the defeat at Jena, posted a proclamation reading 'The King has lost a battle; calm is the first duty of the citizen!' he was unconsciously writing a commentary on the attitude of enlightened despotism towards the mass of its subjects. They were objects of government rather than participants in it; in the activities of the state their share was the right to obey.

Granted that the middle classes were for the most part narrow in their views, subservient to authority, and interested only in profits, and that the peasantry was, for the most part, a brutish mass with no ambition, the political and social system which had been perfected by the early Hohenzollerns was designed to perpetuate, rather than to correct, these failings. The rigid social stratification and the equally rapidly centralized administration forbade the development of individual initiative; the paternalism of the system stunted and killed energies which might have served the state. Even the much vaunted Prussian bureaucracy was not immune to this stifling atmosphere. Created to serve the army and administer to its needs the civil service was governed in accordance with military principles of rank and discipline.[1] In the time of Frederick William I, as the historian of the Prussian bureaucracy has written,

> ministers of state, like generals and colonels, obeyed unquestioningly and carried out orders with military precision and punctuality . . . Every minister was compelled in his own interest to maintain in his own department the same rigid spirit of order, punctuality and speed which the King enforced on his own ministers. . . . Never before had it been impressed upon the officials so urgently and so unceasingly that they were personally responsible, and never before had personal responsibility been so sternly enforced.[2]

Frederick the Great tightened the discipline of his civil service even farther. Carrying personal government to its furthest extreme he reserved for himself the right of decision in all aspects of state business and was apt to dismiss officials who had ideas

[1] Schnabel, *Deutsche Geschichte*, i. 97.

[2] S. Isaacssohn, *Geschichte des preußischen Beamtentums*, iii (Berlin, 1884), 201–2, quoted in Ergang, *Potsdam Führer*, p. 122.

of their own. As a result he deprived the bureaucracy of that self-reliance which is the mainstay of efficiency, and left it a soulless corporation, politically neutral, and devoid of independent will.[1]

To disperse the cloying atmosphere of paternalism and to open the way for a development of the latent energies of the middle and lower classes would have required fundamental reforms not only in the state administration but also in the social organization of the Prussian people. But, in the last analysis, as long as Prussia was a military state the very prestige of the army made such reform impossible. It was difficult, for instance, to argue that too much discipline was bad for the civil service or, for that matter, for the Prussian people, when the discipline of Prussian troops in the field had won the admiration even of Prussia's antagonists. It was impossible to hope for any real measure of social reform as long as the unity of the officer corps depended upon the protection of the feudal rights of the noble proprietor or as long as hereditary serfdom remained the basis of the canton system.[2] The army moulded the state to its needs; it was now the principal obstacle to political or social change of any kind. While Frederick lived, however, there was little recognition of this basic truth, and virtually no criticism of the preponderant role played by the military in the state. An occasional intellectual might flee the realm, crying—as Winckelmann had done earlier—that Prussia was a gigantic garrison in which arts and literature were impossible and that it was 'better to be a circumcised Turk than a Prussian'.[3] An occasional town councillor might protest to the government against the indignities visited upon civilians by local garrison troops or against the arrogant behaviour of raw lieutenants from the flat lands.[4] But there was no organized movement of protest against the position of the army or, indeed, against any other feature of the authoritarian system. For the most part the inferior classes accepted apathetically the conditions imposed upon them, while the high officials and the educated classes in

[1] Ritter, *Friedrich der Große*, pp. 185, 196; Hintze, *Historische und politische Aufsätze*, i. 190; and especially Dorn in *Political Science Quarterly*, xlvi (1931), 406–7, 414–15, xlvii (1932), 91–94, 267–9. [2] Hintze, *Historische und politische Aufsätze*, iv. 66–67.

[3] Treitschke, *German History*, i. 55.

[4] See, for instance, E. von Conrady, *Leben und Wirken des Generals C. von Grolman* (Berlin, 1894–6), i. 17–20; Jany, *Preußische Armee*, iii. 415 ff.; Hintze, *Historische und politische Aufsätze*, iii. 62.

general remained confident that the existing political and social system was the most efficient and enlightened in Europe.

This was demonstrated all too clearly when the revolution broke out in France in 1789.[1] The initial reaction of Prussian government officials to this event was the patronizing conclusion that the revolution was merely an attempt to apply in France the principles of order and efficiency which were characteristic of Prussian administration. In the early years of the revolution, the *Mittwochgesellschaft*, a literary society of high functionaries, leading members of the clergy and Berlin intelligentsia, held a series of meetings in which the events in France were discussed with interest and with general approval; but its members were not moved to draw any unfavourable comparisons between the new France and the old Prussia. To them, Prussia, far from being a despotic state, was one which assured liberty and well being to its subjects, and hence its government could not be compared with the one that had fallen in Paris. Carl Mangelsdorff, professor of history at the University of Königsberg, wrote in 1790 that the French were justified in revolting against what was patently an insupportable régime, but that civil disobedience of this nature would be odious to Prussians, 'a people happy beyond description'.[2]

The revolution in France remained, then, an interesting drama, but not one that was considered to be instructive. Even such a challenging action as the abolition of the feudal privileges of the French nobility failed to stimulate the desire for similar reform in Prussia, while the spectacle of the French middle classes playing an active role in the politics of their country seems to have stirred up no spirit of emulation.[3] And here it is safe to say that there was no comprehension of one of the most significant results of the upheaval in France—namely, that the French state, by permitting its subjects to share fully in its destinies, had won important new resources of popular energy and national devotion. That Prussia might, and, in her own

[1] For the state of opinion in Prussia during the revolutionary period see O. Tschirsch, *Geschichte der öffentlichen Meinung in Preußen vom Baseler Frieden bis zum Zusammenbruch des Staates* (Weimar, 1933).

[2] Jacques Droz, *L'Allemagne et la Révolution Française* (Paris, 1949), pp. 80–82.

[3] Criticism of the institution of serfdom and discussion of means of freeing Prussian subjects from hereditary burdens and disabilities seems to have been restricted to academic circles, and in particular to the faculty of the University of Königsberg. Ibid., pp. 99–105.

interest, should profit from the French example by instituting political and social reforms, was not even dimly discerned. Among the official and educated classes the prevailing attitude was that the Prussian monarchy had reached the highest degree of perfection and was not susceptible of improvement.[1]

This feeling of invincible superiority lasted throughout the early years of the revolution and was unaffected by Prussia's participation in the campaigns of 1792–5 against France—a war which was never, incidentally, popular in Prussia and which was not characterized by any decisive encounters. It was only in 1806, when a real trial of strength came between Prussia and the new France, that it was demonstrated to be ill-founded. In 1806 all of the basic weaknesses of the absolutist system became manifest. When the victorious armies of Bonaparte entered Berlin after the battles of Jena and Auerstädt, they were greeted at the Brandenburger Tor by representatives of the Berlin magistracy and the local merchants; city officials voluntarily agreed to continue their services for the conqueror; and the burghers of Berlin served without demur in the national guard organized by the French. A similar reception was accorded the French in other Prussian towns; there were few signs of even passive resistance to the foreigner; and the Prussian press treated the shattering events of the recent campaign as indifferently as if they were writing of a war between the Shah of Persia and the Emir of Kabul.[2]

Yet this reaction was not—as some writers have insisted—a result of the spread of revolutionary ideas among the middle classes or of the insidious influence of Freemasonry and French immorality.[3] It was rather a natural consequence of the deficiencies of the political and social principles of the old régime in Prussia. If a people is accustomed blindly to accept authority, it will experience no great difficulty in transferring its allegiance from one authority to another. The institutional framework of the absolute military state did not permit the members of the middle and lower classes to identify themselves in any real sense with the state machine. When that machine collapsed it was only natural that they should accept this fact and adjust their narrow lives to the new circumstances forced upon them.

[1] Ibid., p. 108.

[2] Colmar von der Goltz, 'Roßbach und Jena', *Militärwochenblatt* (Beihefte, 1883), pp. 265–6.

[3] See, for instance, Marwitz, *Nachlaß*, i. 190 ff.

III

In referring thus briefly to the basic weaknesses of the Frederician state, one must add hastily that its collapse, like its rise, was essentially military in nature. German writers who are prone to explain all their military defeats by blaming them on civilian defections have not entirely excluded the defeat of 1806 from this kind of interpretation. 'In 1806', writes one, 'the civil population failed in a higher degree than did the government of the state or the army.'[1] Yet the stab-in-the-back theory is no more valid as an explanation for the failure of Prussian arms against Napoleon than it is for the events of 1918. The Prussian army was soundly beaten in 1806, and the factors which were mainly contributory to its defeat in the field were defects of organization, training, and leadership which had been apparent since 1763.

The decline of the army which had won such signal triumphs in the Seven Years War can be traced back to Frederick the Great himself; and even Treitschke, one of his greatest admirers, is forced to admit that Frederick left the army 'in a worse condition than that in which he had found it on ascending the throne'.[2] There can be little doubt, for instance, that he watered down the canton system to a dangerous degree. Although he was willing to admit on occasion that native soldiers fought Prussia's battles better than foreign mercenaries, Frederick always felt that his subjects served the state better as taxpayers and producers of goods than as soldiers. Whereas in the army of Frederick William I natives had outnumbered foreigners by two to one, Frederick set out deliberately to reverse that ratio. Conscripted cantonists should never, he believed, be in excess of 3 per cent. of the total male population and, even if this meant that some regiments would consist entirely of foreigners, this was preferable to jeopardizing the economic strength of the country. During the last stages of the Seven Years War Frederick resorted to forcible enrolment of prisoners of war and subjects of occupied states rather than increase the size of native contingents; and, in his testament of 1768, he stated flatly that 'useful hardworking people should be guarded as the apple of

[1] C. v. Altrock, *Vom Sterben des deutschen Offizierkorps* (Berlin, 1922), p. 17. See also the same author's 'Jena und Auerstädt. Ein Rückblick und Ausblick', *Militär-wochenblatt* (Beihefte, 1907), 1–25.

[2] Treitschke, *German History*, i. 85.

one's eye, and in wartime recruits should be levied in one's own country only when the bitterest necessity compels'.[1]

From the standpoint of military expediency the first requirement after 1763 was a carefully planned policy to make good the losses suffered by the army in the last seven years. Such a policy might conceivably have been based upon a judicious expansion of the canton system, increasing the number of peasant conscripts or even broadening the system to include wider segments of the population. Frederick's preoccupation with the problem of economic recovery, however, led him to refuse any such solution. The customary exemptions from liability to serve were not only maintained but actually increased in number. In certain areas of the state, the whole population was specifically exempted, this being true, for instance, of Breslau and of other districts of Silesia.[2] In general, conscription in the newly acquired provinces was held at a minimum to prevent the emigration of the population; and freedom from military service was held out as an inducement to prospective immigrants to the Prussian lands. In short, in a period in which Prussian population and territory was growing, the canton system was not adjusted to the changed conditions; and the government sought to make up the inevitable deficiencies in recruitment by filling the quotas with foreign mercenaries.

Despite some professional criticism of the operation of the canton system, Frederick's principles were maintained by his successors. The canton regulations of February 1792 actually expressed pride in the organization of the Prussian state, in which 'beside the mightiest and most formidable army, all the arts of peace bloom, where the compulsion of conscription is moderated as much as possible, and many classes of subjects are hardly disturbed'.[3] The universal obligation to serve in the army remained a fiction throughout the period; the number of mercenaries steadily increased until, in 1804, they comprised almost a half of the army at full strength;[4] and the reliance upon foreign man-power was greater than it had been at any time since the early years of Frederick William I. That the increase of foreigners introduced an element of unreliability

[1] *Werke Friedrichs des Großen* (Berlin, 1913–14), vi. 226–7. See also Erwin Dette, *Friedrich der Große und sein Heer* (Göttingen, 1914), pp. 8–19.

[2] On the operation of canton regulations in Silesia, see Dette, *Friedrich der Große*, p. 12.

[3] Shanahan, *Prussian Military Reforms*, p. 47.

[4] Jany, *Preußische Armee*, iii. 436.

into the army was recognized by a few officers. Between 1802 and 1806 various plans were discussed for supplementing the existing military establishment by organizing a militia which could serve as an active reserve and a home defence force in time of war, and in all of these—and particularly in the plans proposed by Knesebeck and Courbière in 1803 and 1804—some emphasis was placed upon the importance of increasing the native component in the regiments.[1] But these plans were never carried to realization until it was too late, and the principal reason for this was reluctance to eliminate existing exemptions or to broaden the liability to service.

Meanwhile, the practice of furloughing natives for the greater part of the year was continued and extended. In order to reduce the military pay-roll and for reasons of general economy, Frederick the Great had made the annual manœuvre period, during which the army was supposed to be at full strength, shorter than it had been under his predecessor. Frederick William II and Frederick William III went even further, limiting royal manœuvres at times to as little as four weeks, training new conscripts during their first year of service for only ten weeks and granting extensive furloughs not only to the cantonists but to the native professionals as well.[2] That this should have had deleterious effects upon efficiency and discipline is understandable. The bulk of the army was engaged almost perpetually in activities which were remote from the art of war. Meanwhile, the garrisons were filled for the most part with foreign mercenaries, many of them accompanied by their wives and children and forced, in view of their extremely low pay, to undertake menial jobs on a part-time basis in the towns.[3] Descriptions of garrison life in the late eighteenth century make it abundantly clear that under such conditions, no orderly routine or training could be maintained; and the brawling and disorder of the foreign professionals certainly lowered the burghers' respect for the army and contributed to the *Schadenfreude* with which they reacted to the defeat of 1806.

In this general deterioration the much vaunted officer corps was affected fully as much as the rank and file.[4] The flower of

[1] Shanahan, *Prussian Military Reforms*, pp. 73–82.

[2] Ibid., p. 44; Dette, *Friedrich der Große*, p. 14; Conrady, *Grolman*, i. 20.

[3] Jany, *Preußische Armee*, iii. 447.

[4] Some light is thrown upon conditions in the officer corps, and among the garrison troops as well, by an order of Frederick the Great dated 11 May 1763 in

Frederick the Great's officer corps was killed off in the Seven Years War. Frederick's rigid exclusion of *bourgeois* officers from the army after 1763 not only deprived the army of talented and experienced officers but imposed a military burden upon the native nobility which it could not bear alone. The net result of this was that commissions had to be given to foreigners with noble patents, and, although many distinguished officers came to the Prussian service in this way—including Scharnhorst, who was ennobled before his admission to the Prussian army in 1801—many 'adventurers of dubious character', to use Treitschke's phrase, came as well.[1] The officer corps which had, under Frederick William I, become predominantly national in composition, was now less homogeneous and had even less connexion than it had earlier with the population that supported it.

Much more serious than this, however, was the very low state of educational standards throughout the officer corps. This, of course, was not a new development. The educational tone of the Prussian army had been set by Frederick William I and the Old Dessauer, under whose régime, as one observer had written: 'A general was not regarded as uneducated, even though he could barely write his own name. Whoever could do more was styled a pedant, inksplasher and scribbler.'[2] In the subsequent period little improvement was to be noted. Indeed, the problem was aggravated by the tendency of the Junker families to send their sons into the army at an age when they would more profitably have been engaged in acquiring the basic rudiments of mathematics.[3] This practice was encouraged by the critical

which he says: 'Since His Royal Majesty has discovered that most of the officers in the garrisons are so lazy and that they do not even become familiar with the terrain in the vicinity of their garrisons—a knowledge of which is of the highest importance to all officers in case they are sent after deserters—therefore, His Royal Majesty orders that regimental commanders grant leave to the officers, perhaps for one day, so that they can acquire knowledge of the mountainous terrain and acquaint themselves adequately with the *Défilés*, the narrow and hidden paths and the like, and that this must be done in all garrisons when the regiments change their quarters.' *Werke Friedrichs der Großen*, vi. 277. Hans Delbrück, *Geschichte der Kriegskunst im Rahmen der politischen Geschichte*, iv (Berlin, 1920), 289–90.

[1] Treitschke, *German History*, i. 86; Dette, *Friedrich der Große*, p. 61.

[2] Ergang, *Potsdam Führer*, p. 55; Jany, *Preußische Armee*, i. 735; Delbrück, *Kriegskunst*, iv. 298–9.

[3] Frederick the Great once described such officers as 'youth snatched from their mothers' breasts', but he preferred them to *bourgeois* officers. Dette, *Friedrich der Große*, p. 61. Marwitz describes his own military career as beginning in 1791 at the age of 13. *Nachlaß*, i. 44.

need of officer replacements after 1763, but its basic cause was probably a feeling on the part of the native nobility that seniority in grade was more important than cultural achievement.[1] Whatever the cause, the results were deplorable, and the junior grades of the army were filled with callow and boorish youngsters who were not incapable of valour but who lacked the intelligence to make it effective. The reform of the cadet schools by Major von Rüchel in the 1790's and the establishment of four higher military academies between 1763 and 1806 recognized and sought to correct this situation. But the graduates of the latter institutions were few in number, and constituted an inadequate leaven in an officer corps which, in the ranks below major at least, was characterized by abysmal and arrogant ignorance.[2]

If beardless youth was a feature of the lowest grades of the officer corps, age reigned in the positions of high command. In the period after Frederick the Great it seemed literally true that, in Prussia, old soldiers never died. By 1806, of the 142 generals in the Prussian army, four were over 80 years of age, thirteen over 70, and sixty-two over 60; while 25 per cent. of the regimental and battalion commanders had passed the age of 60 also.[3] There is, of course, nothing reprehensible about age in itself, and it has been pointed out that the commanders who won the battles of 1866 and 1870 were in many cases as old as those who lost the battles of 1806.[4] But age that is accompanied by inflexible conservatism may be dangerous, and it is in this sense that years militated against efficiency in the Prussian army. Many of the highest officers in the army of Frederick William II and Frederick William III had been subalterns during the wars of Frederick the Great, and they combined a veneration for Frederician methods with a stubborn reluctance to admit that the practices of warfare may change. They were almost completely blind, therefore, and certainly unresponsive, to innovations which were being introduced abroad.

[1] Jany, *Preußische Armee*, iii. 40, 426 ff.

[2] On military education in this period, see B. Schwertfeger, *Die großen Erzieher des deutschen Heeres: Aus der Geschichte der Kriegsakademie* (Potsdam, 1936), pp. 15 ff.; L. von Scharfenort, *Die königliche preußische Kriegsakademie, 1810–1910* (Berlin, 1910), chap. 1; F. von Rabenau in *Von Scharnhorst zu Schlieffen* (ed. by F. von Cochenhausen, Berlin, 1933), pp. 9–10; Bronsart von Schellendorf, *The Duties of the General Staff* (3rd rev. Eng. ed., London, 1908), pp. 45–46.

[3] Demeter, *Deutsche Heer*, pp. 9 ff.

[4] Jany, *Preußische Armee*, iii. 432–3.

It was in France, which might have been expected to be of special concern to Prussian soldiers, that the most notable military progress was made in the period between the Seven Years War and the beginning of the new century. As early as the 1760's the Marshal de Broglie and the Duke de Choiseul were experimenting with new tactical forms and were laying the basis for the reorganization of the old mass army into independent and self-contained divisions, composed of arms of all kinds and capable of detached manœuvre and action. Simultaneously, artillery operations were being revolutionized by the reforms of Gribeauval, notably the introduction of interchangeable parts, improvement of accuracy of fire, and reduction of the weight of guns. In the years which followed further progress was made along these lines, but even more important changes came as a result of the profound political revolution which began in 1789. The destruction of the old régime and the granting of fundamental rights to all citizens had an immediate effect upon the constitution of the French army. They made possible the creation of a truly national army, and one which, because its rank and file was composed of citizens devoted to the national cause, was freed from the rigid limitations of eighteenth-century warfare. It was no longer necessary for the French to concentrate their forces in close array upon the battlefield, forbidding independent manœuvre lest it lead to mass desertion. The French *tirailleurs* advanced in extended order, fighting, firing, and taking cover as individuals, and the army gained immeasurably in tactical elasticity in consequence. Troops could, moreover, be trusted to forage for themselves, and it was now possible to divorce French units from the cumbersome supply trains and the dependence on magazines which restricted the mobility of the old model armies. This liberation from the tyranny of logistics, combined with the new tactics and the perfected divisional organization, introduced a completely new kind of warfare to Europe—the type of lightning war of which Napoleon showed himself the master in the Italian campaign of 1800.[1]

These changes did not go entirely unnoticed in Prussia.

[1] Delbrück, *Kriegskunst*, iv. 457–84; R. R. Palmer, 'Frederick the Great, Guibert and Bülow; From Dynastic to National War', in *Makers of Modern Strategy: Military Thought from Machiavelli to Hitler*, ed. by Edward Mead Earle, Gordon A. Craig, and Felix Gilbert (Princeton, 1943), pp. 62, 68. See also E. Kessel, 'Die Wandlung der Kriegskunst im Zeitalter der französischen Revolution', *Historische Zeitschrift*, cxlviii (1933).

Shortly after the death of Frederick the Great, the artillerist Tempelhoff and the civilian publicist Georg Heinrich von Behrenhorst warned of the dangers of blind adherence to Frederician principles;[1] and Behrenhorst's pupil, Dietrich Heinrich von Bülow, recognized, although somewhat imperfectly, the importance both of the French *levée en masse* and of the flexibility of Napoleon's operations.[2] The Military Society, a group which was formally established in 1802 and comprised many prominent officers, read papers and held discussions concerning the military innovations in France; and the guiding spirit of this group, Scharnhorst, actively worked for the introduction of divisions of all arms in the Prussian army and for the creation of a popular militia as a reserve force.[3] In 1803 Karl Friedrich Freiherr von dem Knesebeck drew up a far-reaching plan for the reform of the Prussian army, stressing the fact that war had now become a matter of national concern and that attempts must be made to create a more truly national force; and in 1804 General von Courbière urged the creation of a cadre system which would facilitate expansion in time of war.[4]

The existence of these and other reform proposals doubtless proves that the Prussian army was not entirely bereft of intellectual vitality before 1806. The fact remains, however, that none of the suggested reform plans was put into effect in time to do any good. The French experience was not completely convincing to the military advisers closest to the king, and the military theories which commanded the most respect were those of Saldern, Venturini, and Massenbach which portrayed war as a matter of studied manœuvre and mathematical calculation, which stressed the importance of the old parade ground discipline and which continued to praise the line tactics and the oblique attack which Frederick had made famous.[5] Old Field Marshal von Möllendorff, a hero of the Seven Years War, was

[1] See Max Jähns, *Geschichte der Kriegswissenschaften vornehmlich in Deutschland*. 3. Abteilung (Munich, 1891), pp. 2121–33, 2536.

[2] On Bülow, see especially Palmer in *Makers of Modern Strategy*, pp. 69–74, and Jähns, *Kriegswissenschaften*, pp. 2133–45.

[3] Lehmann, *Scharnhorst*, i. 374–85; Gerhard Scholtz, *Hermann von Boyen: ein Lebensbild* (Berlin, 1936), pp. 100–105.

[4] Shanahan, *Prussian Military Reforms*, pp. 75–82. On Knesebeck, see also Max Lehmann, *Knesebeck und Schön* (Leipzig, 1875).

[5] See Jähns, *Kriegswissenschaften*, pp. 1781–2, 1819, 2129, 2529–32. Goltz, who places the onus of responsibility for the defeat of 1806 upon the civilian defection, nevertheless criticizes the 'verkünstelte Auffassung der Kriegführung' which Massenbach preached. 'Roßbach und Jena', p. 290.

apt to greet all suggestions of reform with the words: 'This is altogether above my head.'[1] His influence and that of others like him was instrumental in defeating the suggestions of Knesebeck and Courbière. Against the resistance of this old guard the reformers made very little headway. Some progress was made in lightening the load of baggage which the army was forced to drag with it in its campaigns; there were some minor improvements in ordnance; but the necessity of tactical reforms, or of the political changes which would make them possible, was not recognized. Even the well-proved divisional organization was not introduced until the Prussian army was on the march to Jena, and it consequently merely increased the confusion of that encounter.[2]

Finally, to complete this catalogue of the defects of Prussian military organization, some mention must be made of the administrative complexity and confusion which characterized army administration. A steady process of bureaucratization had taken place since the reign of Frederick William I and, by the end of the eighteenth century, there were five virtually equal and autonomous agencies in the army: the *Militärdepartement* of the General Directory, the Governors of the Garrisons, the General Inspectors, the so-called *Oberkriegskollegium*, and the *Generaladjutantur*.[3] The *Militärdepartement*, through which Frederick William I had exercised his authority in administrative matters, had, in the subsequent period, been deprived of much of its effective power. The governors of the big garrisons were virtually independent of its control, as were the general inspectors who, since 1763, had been allowed to exercise supervision over recruiting. The *Oberkriegskollegium* had been created in 1787, ostensibly to control and co-ordinate the various competing agencies and to bring all military matters once more under central direction. But from the very start matters affecting command and military operations were specifically reserved for the king's decision and the relationship between the new agency and the commanding generals was left conveniently vague.[4] In

[1] Treitschke, *German History*, i. 177.

[2] Shanahan, *Prussian Military Reforms*, pp. 80–87; Lehmann, *Scharnhorst*, i. 412–13; Conrady, *Grolman*, i. 45–46.

[3] *Das königliche preußische Kriegsministerium*, 1809–1909 (Mit allerhöchster Genehmigung S.M. des Kaisers und Königs zum nichtamtlichen Gebrauch herausgegeben u. bearbeitet vom Kriegsministerium) (Berlin, 1909), p. 28.

[4] Günther Wohlers, *Die staatsrechtliche Stellung des Generalstabes in Preußen und*

actuality, the *Oberkriegskollegium* proved incapable of co-ordinating even the purely administrative functions of the army. Its authority was always contested by the *Militärdepartement* and its position was gradually undermined by the *Generaladjutantur.*

This last body, out of which was to grow the all-powerful Military Cabinet of the nineteenth century, had its beginnings in the first years of Frederick William I. Originally it was a small group of officers who served as personal aides of the king and who handled his military correspondence. The army list of 1741, for instance, describes the royal suite as comprising four *Generaladjutanten* with the rank of colonel and five *Flügeladjutanten* with the rank of major,[1] but the numbers and the rank varied from time to time. Because of their access to the sovereign, the adjutants, if they were gifted and energetic men, had an opportunity to exert considerable influence, and, under Frederick William II and Frederick William III, they did so. Indeed, in 1787, when the *Oberkriegskollegium* was established, Frederick William II simultaneously made Colonel von Geusau, his *Generaladjutant von der Infanterie*, the channel through which all military matters were brought to his attention and through which his commands were communicated to other agencies.[2] Armed with this power—the so-called right of *Vortrag*—Geusau, his successor Lieutenant-Colonel von Manstein and the *Generaladjutant der Kavallerie*, Bischoffswerder, played a very active role not only in matters affecting the armed establishment but in politics as well.[3] In the strictly military sphere they gradually weakened the position of the *Oberkriegskollegium*, for that body could present its views to the sovereign only through the adjutants. In addition, they added to the general administrative confusion of the army and the state as a whole, since all of the conflicting agencies, including the civilian ministers, vied for their favour, while the adjutants themselves were not averse to playing one off against the other in order to maintain and increase their own influence.[4]

dem deutschen Reich (Bonn, 1921), p. 10; Ernst R. Huber, *Heer und Staat in der deutschen Geschichte* (1. Auflage, Hamburg, 1938), pp. 113–14; R. Schmidt-Bückeburg, *Das Militärkabinett der preußischen Könige und deutschen Kaiser* (Berlin, 1933), p. 8.

[1] Bronsart von Schellendorf, *Duties of the General Staff*, p. 13.

[2] Jany, *Preußische Armee*, iii. 150–2; Schmidt-Bückeburg, *Militärkabinett*, pp. 2–4.

[3] See, for instance, Marwitz, *Nachlaß*, i. 83.

[4] Schmidt-Bückeburg, *Militärkabinett*, pp. 6–8; H. O. Meisner, *Der Kriegsminister, 1814–1914* (Berlin, 1940), pp. 7 ff.

As a result of this bureaucratic rivalry, the one relatively hopeful administrative development of this period—the attempt to establish an effective General Staff—was far less successful than it could have been. Some of the functions which we associate with general staff work had been performed, ever since the time of the Great Elector, by the *Generalquartiermeisterstab*, but it was not until the very end of the eighteenth century that much thought was devoted to the question. In 1800, however, General Lecoq, of the quartermaster-general's staff, attempted a more systematic description of what a staff's duty should be[1] and, in the following year, Colonel von Massenbach applied his fertile brain to the same task. In two long memoranda Massenbach urged that the quartermaster-general's staff be reorganized into three brigades, each charged with operational studies for a given area, that the staff as a whole prepare war plans against all possible contingencies, that it hold regular staff exercises to familiarize its members with terrain problems, that it accumulate intelligence with regard to foreign conditions and forces, that its members alternate between service with the staff and service with troop units and, finally, that the head of the quartermaster-general's staff have direct access to the king and the right to express his opinions upon military matters.[2]

From the beginning, these plans were contested by the other military agencies. Field Marshal von Möllendorff, the head of the *Oberkriegskollegium*, feared that the preparation of war plans would lead to indiscretions which would help potential enemies; General von Zastrow felt that an agency which set out to develop 'Field-Marshal's talents' in officers would merely promote insubordination; Generalmajor von Köckritz, the head of the *Generaladjutantur*, opposed Massenbach's plans on general principle, probably fearing that the projected organization would reduce his own authority.[3] The general-quartermaster's staff was in fact reorganized, roughly in accordance with Massenbach's ideas, in 1803, but it started its new existence with the other agencies hostile and with certain other deficiencies which weakened its effectiveness. Its new chief, Generalleutnant von Geusau, was simultaneously charged with the direction of the Engineering Corps and the War Department of

[1] Bronsart von Schellendorf, *Duties of the General Staff*, pp. 15–16.

[2] Walter Görlitz, *History of the German General Staff* (New York, 1953), pp. 20–21.

[3] Ibid., pp. 21, 23.

the *Oberkriegskollegium*, a multiplication of function which aggravated the already fantastic complexity of military administration. The chiefs of the three brigades of the staff—Generalmajor von Phull, Massenbach himself, and Scharnhorst—were men whose conceptions of strategy and tactics were at hopeless variance and who were, in addition, temperamentally incompatible.[1] The new organization began now to be called the General Staff, but no one had a clear idea of its functions or its authority.

While the inadequacies and abuses noted above did not entirely escape the attention of military reformers in the years after 1800, the true extent of the decay that had affected the armed establishment since 1763 was never realized. The aura of invincibility which had surrounded the army as a result of Frederick's victories had not been entirely dissipated in the years that had followed. Even the disappointing campaigns of 1792–5 which might, to a discerning critic, have revealed disturbing defects of discipline and leadership,[2] do not seem to have shaken the belief of the average officer that, in any real trial of strength, the Prussian army was unbeatable. Certainly, as the government, increasingly irritated by Napoleon's pretensions and by French violations of Prussian territory, began to move closer to war in 1805, the soldiers had no doubt that they could put the Corsican in his place. It is true that some generals close to the king, and especially Massenbach, were opposed to a war with France, but Massenbach's attitude was determined more by political bias than by military considerations, for he hated the English and the Russians and dreamed of a Franco-Prussian crusade against the latter.[3] With this exception, it should be noted that the Prussian war party of 1805 was predominantly military in character and was, moreover, led by that reforming element which should have been most conscious of Prussia's incapacity for a major campaign. While the junior officers of the Berlin garrisons sharpened their swords on the steps of the French Embassy,[4] men like Scharnhorst, Rüchel, and Blücher brought to bear all the influence

[1] Görlitz, *General Staff*, p. 22; Lehmann, *Scharnhorst*, i. 339 ff.; Bronsart von Schellendorf, *Duties of the General Staff*, pp. 20–21.

[2] See, for instance, Treitschke, *German History*, i. 147–53.

[3] See Lehmann, *Scharnhorst*, i. 417 ff., and the damaging, if biased, portrait in Marwitz, *Nachlaß*, i. 140–6.

[4] J. G. Droysen, *Das Leben des Feldmarschalls Grafen York von Wartenburg* (Berlin, 1854), i. 119.

which they possessed in high places, in order to convince the king that war was necessary.[1] They did not all, perhaps, possess the sublime faith of the unnamed colonel who regretted that his 'Kerls' had to carry sabres and muskets, since cudgels would be sufficient to drive the 'French curs' from the land;[2] but they were, when the king finally decided on war with France in 1806, confident in victory.

This confidence was sadly belied. Boyen was later to write of the events of 1806 that 'there have been few campaigns in which such numerous and, often, such incomprehensible blunders piled up on top of each other'.[3] The diplomatic preparation for the war was ludicrously bad. In 1805, when both the Austrians and the Russians were in the field against Napoleon, the Prussian government had vacillated until the best opportunity for action had passed; in August 1806 it bolted into war with Austria neutral and Russia in no position to supply supporting forces. The mobilization for war was disorderly and incomplete; no attempt was made to call up the forces of East Prussia; and, against a French army of 160,000, the Prussians sent only 128,000 into the field. This force was placed under the command of the aged Duke of Brunswick, whose circumspect hesitation in the campaigns of 1792–5 was no earnest of energetic leadership, who had no clear strategic plan, and who was so incapable of understanding the importance of staff work that he made little use of the talents of Scharnhorst, who was assigned to his headquarters as chief of staff. Effective leadership would have been impossible, however, even under a more gifted *Feldherr* than Brunswick, for the administrative confusion that had plagued the army in peacetime followed it into the field. Any unified direction of the war was made impossible by the arrival of the king at army headquarters in September and, from that time on, the war was conducted by committee meetings in which the field commander's energies were drained away in profitless debates with members of the royal suite, cabinet councillors, and the general adjutants, who now assumed the position of the king's private General Staff.

These protracted discussions left the initiative entirely to Napoleon, and they were still going on when his armies drove through the Thuringian Forest and overwhelmed the Prussian

[1] Lehmann, *Scharnhorst*, i. 397–8.
[2] Görlitz, *General Staff*, p. 26.
[3] Scholtz, *Boyen*, p. 107.

advance guard at Saalfeld on 10 October. This defeat caused consternation in Prussian headquarters, and, with his left flank threatened, Brunswick decided to retreat in order to protect his line of communications. This decision made impossible a concentration of Prussian forces which might still have staved off disaster. As a result, moving with a rapidity which bewildered the Prussian command, Napoleon forced the issue upon an army composed of detached and unco-ordinated fragments. The emperor himself fell upon Hohenlohe's corps at Jena, and operating with a heavy numerical superiority and command of the high ground, swept the field. Simultaneously, Davout threw himself against Brunswick's flank at Auerstädt and, with only 26,000 men at his disposal, decisively defeated a force almost twice as large, thanks largely to the reluctance of General von Kalkreuth to commit his reserve of 12,000 men without explicit orders. Through the early hours of 14 October the Prussian grenadiers stood bravely against the murderous fire of the French *tirailleurs*, winning Napoleon's unstinted admiration; but by noon morale had begun to crack. At Auerstädt, Brunswick, trying to rally a badly shaken division, was shot through both eyes and borne dying from the field; and this loss deepened the growing discouragement. General retreat was begun and, by evening, had degenerated into a rout as fugitives from both battles rushed pell-mell in the direction of the fortress of Magdeburg.[1]

The events that followed form one of the least glorious chapters in Prussian military annals, for the will to continued resistance seems to have died at Jena and Auerstädt, and only a few of the commanders tried to rally their forces for a new stand. Scharnhorst, separated from his post at royal headquarters in the confusion of the fight, joined Blücher's corps and served as chief of staff while the hussar officer stubbornly fought his way, with the artillery which he had saved from the defeat and the support of York's *Jaeger*, over the Harz toward Mecklenburg, deflecting French forces which might otherwise have thrust their way into East Prussia. But Blücher and Scharnhorst were almost alone in carrying on the fight and even they, for

[1] The fullest account of these battles and of subsequent operations will be found in Oscar von Lettow-Vorbeck, *Der Krieg von 1806 und 1807* (4 vols., Berlin, 1892–9). For shorter accounts, see E. Leidolph, *Die Schlacht bei Jena* (2. Auflage, Jena, 1901), F. N. Maude, *1806, the Jena Campaign* (London, 1909), and the standard biographies of such participants as Scharnhorst, Blücher, and York.

lack of food and ammunition, were forced to surrender to the French in the neighbourhood of Lübeck. For the rest, the collapse of the Prussian army was complete and disgraceful. At Magdeburg, General von Kleist and twenty-three other generals, with 24,000 men under their command, capitulated without a fight; and the commanders of the fortresses of Erfurt, Hameln, Spandau, Küstrin, and Stettin did the same. After having won his way with 12,000 men from Jena to Prenzlau, where he was virtually within sight of safety, Hohenlohe lay down his arms on the advice of his chief of staff, Massenbach. Having demonstrated that it was deficient in talent, the officer corps seemed intent upon proving itself bankrupt of valour as well.

His western provinces overrun by French armies, Frederick William III retired to East Prussia and tried, in alliance with the Russians, to retrieve his fortunes. The campaign of 1807 was marked, however, mainly by more debates of the kind that preceded Jena and Auerstädt, and the Prussian and Russian staffs were never able to agree upon a strategic plan. In February Scharnhorst distinguished himself once again when his leadership of the pitifully small remnant of the Prussian army deprived Napoleon's advance guard of victory at Preußisch-Eylau. But the allied force failed to seize the opportunity presented by this temporary disruption of the emperor's plans and stood inactive while Napoleon brought up the bulk of his forces.[1] The French began their big offensive in June and, on the 14th, rolled up the main Russian body at Friedland. After this, Tsar Alexander had no stomach for further resistance and hastened to come to terms with the Corsican with scant regard for the feelings of his desperate ally.

Abandoned to his fate, Frederick William III met Napoleon at Tilsit on 9 July and received his terms. If he expected moderate treatment he did not get it. In brief, the king was asked to submit to the loss of approximately half of his territory and his subjects, to promise to pay heavy contributions to his enemy, and to support a large army of occupation; and, since he no longer had an effective fighting force, he had no choice but to agree. The terms were completely shattering, and they encompassed the destruction of the old Prussian state. This need not, however, be attributed to vindictiveness on the part

[1] Lehmann, *Scharnhorst*, i. 484–522.

of the French Emperor. In reality, the Prussia which had been created and made a major power by the exertions of its army had now been swept away by the failure of that army to adjust itself to changing methods of warfare and by the unwillingness of its rulers to exploit the undeveloped energies of the Prussian people.

II

REFORM AND REACTION

1807–40

Frisch auf, mein Volk! Die Flammenzeichen rauchen,
Hell aus dem Norden bricht der Freiheit Licht! ARNDT.

Though soldiers are the true supports,
The natural allies of Courts,
Woe to the Monarch who depends
Too much on his red-coated friends;
For even soldiers sometimes think—
Nay, Colonels have been known to reason—
And reasoners, whether clad in pink,
Or red, or blue, are on the brink
(Nine cases out of ten) of treason. THOMAS MOORE.

In the months that followed the capitulation of Tilsit, only the most optimistic could place much faith in the continued existence of Prussia as an independent state. Napoleon quickly revealed his intention of transforming the shattered land into a satellite of his empire, and important sections of the Prussian people seemed all too willing to submit to that fate. Among the middle classes and the aristocracy, the military débâcle bred widespread defeatism and a not inconsiderable degree of opportunism; and among the intellectuals voices were soon raised to argue the advantages of adhering to Napoleon's new European order even if this should involve the reduction of Prussian sovereignty. Simultaneously, in the great mass of the population, there was little evidence of resentment over Prussia's humiliation and even less of any popular desire to avenge it.

It is all the more remarkable, therefore, that, within six years, this apathetic acceptance of defeat was overcome and that Prussia was foremost among those states which combined to defeat and expel the Corsican. This recovery was the work primarily of a small group of devoted and patriotic reformers, chief among whom were Stein, Scharnhorst, Gneisenau, Boyen, and Grolman. While admitting the military deficiencies which had led to the rout at Jena, these men clearly recognized the deeper causes of Prussia's collapse—the gulf which existed between the state machine and the Prussian people, which made it impossible for the people to identify themselves with their government and which deprived the state of popular support in time of crisis. To bridge this gulf and to inspire a new sense of devotion to the Prussian state was the end objective of the social, political, and military reforms instituted by Stein and his colleagues in the years after 1807; and the immediate results of their effort were reflected in the successful war against Napoleon in 1813–14 and in the popular enthusiasm with which it was supported by the Prussian people.

Despite their success in liberating Prussia from foreign domination, the reformers, in the long run, failed to attain their goals. It may be, as Herbert Rosinski has written, that they over-estimated the Prussian state's capacity to abandon its fundamental traditions.[1] It is certainly true that they failed to foresee that, once Prussia had been freed from the yoke of the foreigner, the governing class would tend to revert to its ancient ways. When that tendency asserted itself after 1814, the reformers showed little political skill in resisting it; and by 1819 they had been driven from power, their political and social programme had been frustrated and distorted, and their hope that Prussia might become a progressive state with representative institutions had been defeated. The period of reform was succeeded, after 1819, by a period of reaction, during which the old frustrations of the Prussian people appeared in new forms and during which the army, which Scharnhorst and Boyen had sought to transform into an object of popular pride, became once more the target of popular resentment.

I

The period of the reforms may be said to have begun in July 1807 when King Frederick William III appointed a Military Reorganization Commission and instructed it to investigate the recent campaign, to cashier and punish those officers whose conduct had been improper, and to propose changes in army organization, supply, service regulations, selection of officers, and education and training. The establishment of such commissions was not new, and, after a major defeat like Jena, some sort

[1] Rosinski, *German Army*, p. 42.

of investigation was to be expected. There was less immediate expectation that the commission would propose any startling changes in the existing system. In the eyes of many senior officers—including Count Lottum, one of the original members of the commission, and generals York and Knesebeck—the defeat of 1806 had been caused by no fundamental defects in the military or political system but rather by a combination of incompetent leadership and bad luck. Consequently, although they believed that the more patent abuses should be corrected, they saw no necessity for anything in the nature of basic reorganization and reform.[1]

From this kind of superficial patchwork, the Prussian state was saved by two circumstances. The first was the fact that the Military Reorganization Commission, after some initial internal disharmony, came to be dominated by Scharnhorst and his disciples Gneisenau, Boyen, and Grolman.[2] The second was Napoleon's insistence in July 1807 on the dismissal of Hardenberg, the king's chief minister, an event which led Frederick William to recall the Baron vom Stein to his service and to intrust him with the direction of all internal and external affairs.[3] The ascendancy of Scharnhorst and Stein gave the post-war reorganization its distinctive character and made the years 1807–15 one of the most promising periods of reform in German history.[4]

Temperamentally, Stein and Scharnhorst were poles apart. The minister was violent, emotional, and so passionate in advocating his views that he had, after a previous term of office, been dismissed by the king as a 'refractory, insolent,

[1] Huber, *Heer und Staat*, p. 122; Jany, *Preußische Armee*, iv. pp. 2–3.

[2] For a balanced account of the changes in the membership of the commission, see Shanahan, *Military Reforms*, pp. 100–2. Max Lehmann's interpretation (*Scharnhorst*, ii, esp. 8–37), which stresses the struggle between the reformers and the conservatives on the commission, has been disputed most recently by Rudolf Stadelmann, 'Das Duell zwischen Scharnhorst und Borstell in Dezember 1807', *Historische Zeitschrift*, clxi (1940), pp. 263–76.

[3] Max Lehmann, *Freiherr vom Stein* (3 vols., Leipzig, 1902–5), ii. 109 ff.

[4] The commanding role of Scharnhorst in the reform period was admitted, although somewhat grudgingly, by his most inveterate opponents. Thus Marwitz wrote: 'The ideologues and the philosophes have praised [Scharnhorst] much too much, as if he were the greatest of heroes and as if he had saved the Prussian State single handed. This is going too far! But it was nevertheless truly fortunate for the country that he came to the side of the King and held the rudder in military affairs, for everything permanent and essential which was established between 1807 and 1813 originated with him.' *Nachlaß*, i. 300–1.

obstinate and disobedient official';[1] the soldier was silent and withdrawn, a man who looked more like a school-teacher than an officer of the king, and one whose calm tenacity in adversity was in sharp contrast to Stein's furious rages.[2] In their political and social philosophy, however, and in their attitude toward the recent defeat, their attitudes were remarkably similar. Both realized that Jena and Auerstädt represented more than a military misfortune, that they were, in fact, a terrible judgement against the political and military system of the past. Both felt, moreover, that the most shameful aspect of the recent débâcle was the fact that the Prussian people had so openly disassociated themselves from the fate of their government and their army. This deplorable absence of a popular sense of duty and sacrifice in extremity was clear proof, they believed, that the mass of the population regarded the state as a mere instrument of oppression and the army as an alien establishment serving the king rather than the land.[3] If Prussia was to survive, the interest of the masses in their state must be awakened and they must be persuaded to serve it willingly. As Stein wrote, after his first audience with the king in August 1807: 'The chief idea was to arouse a moral, religious and patriotic spirit in the nation, to instil into it again courage, confidence, readiness for every sacrifice in behalf of independence from foreigners and for the national honour, and to seize the first favourable opportunity to begin the bloody and hazardous struggle.'[4]

The reformers were unanimous in their belief, however, that this regeneration was unlikely, if not impossible, under existing conditions. How could a peasant in the Mark be expected to act like a responsible citizen as long as he continued to be held in hereditary bondage to the local landholder? How could the

[1] Freiherr vom Stein, *Briefwechsel, Denkschriften und Aufzeichnungen* (Berlin, 1931) ii. 1963; G. Ritter, *Stein, eine politische Biographie* (Stuttgart, 1931), i. 269–79.

[2] See, for instance, Rudolf Stadelmann, *Scharnhorst, Schicksal und geistige Welt* (Wiesbaden, 1952), p. 91.

[3] Oberpräsident von Schön, who played a prominent part in the reforms and the subsequent liberation of Prussia, testified to this popular antipathy to the army when, writing to Droysen late in his life, he said, 'the army had tyrannized the people too long before 1806'. J. G. Droysen, *Briefwechsel*, ed. by R. Hübner (Stuttgart, 1929), i. 656.

[4] Stein, *Briefwechsel*, vi. 167.

middle classes of the towns be expected to recognize their duties to the state as long as they were barred from any participation in local government? And how, above all, could Prussian subjects who were called to the colours be expected to fight loyally and bravely in an army which showed no respect for their individual moral worth, which allowed them no opportunity for advancement during their service, and which regarded them as cannon fodder rather than as citizens?[1] Certainly an amelioration of the burdens of the past and a grant of basic social and political privileges to all Prussian subjects were the prerequisites of the revival needed to free Prussia from French domination. And because they believed this to be true, the reformers could not be satisfied with the kind of superficial reform which the more conservative members of the ruling class considered adequate. Stein embarked on the programme which was to bring the abolition of hereditary serfdom in October 1807 and the institution of local government in the cities in November 1808, and which he hoped would be crowned by a thorough-going reform of the central government and the establishment of some form of national representation which would bring 'harmony between the spirit of the Nation and that of the agencies of the State'.[2] Scharnhorst and his colleagues on the Military Reorganization Commission set out not only to correct the deficiencies which had been revealed at Jena but also, in Scharnhorst's words, 'to raise and inspire the spirit of the army, to bring the army and the nation into a more intimate union and to guide it to its characteristic and exalted destiny'.[3]

[1] Hintze, *Die Hohenzollern*, p. 445.

[2] The words quoted are from Stein's Nassau Memorandum of June 1807. See Freiherr vom Stein, *Briefwechsel*, ii, 210 ff.

[3] Huber, *Heer und Staat*, pp. 126–7. Gerhard Ritter, writing with special reference to Gneisenau's views, sums up the programme of the reformers by saying: 'The annulment of bondage, the awakening of a feeling for the worth of the individual in every subject, the abolition of the old brutal discipline in the army, the encouragement of the military spirit in the people by means of all the resources of national education—these were the prerequisites for the creation of a people's army, the excellence of which would be based on a sense of honour and a love of country rather than on slavish obedience.' *Staatskunst und Kriegshandwerk*: *Das Problem des 'Militarismus' in Deutschland*, i (Munich, 1954), 99. In 1807, Gneisenau wrote: 'From time immemorial every effort has been made to make men useful to the State machine . . . but far less has been done to make them free and noble and independent so that they believe that they are a part of the whole and that they possess a value in themselves.' G. H. Pertz and Hans Delbrück, *Das Leben des Grafen Neithardt von Gneisenau* (Berlin, 1864 ff.), i. 319–20.

Before these more ambitious plans could be considered, however, the commission had to devote its energies to that subject which was of closest interest to the king, namely, the punishment of those officers who had violated the Prussian code of honour in the recent campaign by capitulating to the enemy without cause or without adequate show of resistance. This promised to be a painful and complicated business, and the commission, in view of the other tasks confronting it, sought to avoid becoming involved in it. In this it was successful. After its members had gone on record in favour of stringent punishment for all officers found guilty of dishonourable conduct, the king referred the post mortem on the Jena campaign to a separate investigating commission. The labours of this body were protracted until 1814, in part because of the difficulty of locating witnesses, in part because of the loss of the army's plans and papers during the retreat. In the end only 208 officers were found guilty, including all of those who had surrendered fortresses, except Blücher who had capitulated at Lübeck only after his supply of food and ammunition was exhausted. Aside from this, the purge of incompetent and superannuated officers, which was hotly discussed in the press immediately after the defeat, was much less extensive than is often supposed, and many of those who were accused of defection in 1806 and 1807 were allowed to retrieve their reputations in the war of 1813.[1]

The reformers on the commission were well pleased to be free of this aspect of the military reorganization, for their chief interest lay less in sitting in judgement on the officer corps of the past than improving the quality of the officers of the future. The reform party in general were of the opinion that the best way of accomplishing this was to put an end to the aristocratic monopoly of the officer corps. Scharnhorst pointed out that the Prussian nobility had not in the past been notable for educational zeal or interest in improving their military proficiency and he attacked the theory, held so tenaciously by officers like York and Marwitz,[2] that the middle classes were temperamentally

[1] On this subject, cf. Lehmann, *Scharnhorst*, ii. 41–55 and Shanahan, *Prussian Military Reforms*, pp. 105–9. See also Marwitz, *Nachlaß*, i. 189.

[2] Marwitz until the end of his life argued that he would put more faith in wartime 'in the son of a poor landholder or officer, who suffers in want in his manor or his garrison, than in the son of a rich man who owes his wealth to speculation or, indeed, to bankrupts'. *Nachlaß*, i. 305 ff. See also Walther Kayser, *Marwitz*

unsuited for the art of war.[1] Grolman was even more outspoken than his chief: 'In order to fight', he wrote, 'it is not necessary to belong to a special class. The melancholy belief that one must belong to a special class in order to defend the fatherland has done much to plunge it into the present abyss, and only the opposite principle can pull it out again.'[2] With these views Stein was in complete accord. Certainly it was not the Junker class who would rescue Prussia from her present extremity. 'What can we expect', the minister wrote, 'from the inhabitants of these sandy steppes—these artful, heartless, wooden, half-educated men—who are really capable only of becoming corporals or book-keepers?'[3] The time had come, he and the other reformers argued, to open the officer corps to talented members of the middle class and to make educational qualification the decisive fact in securing a commission.

Despite his natural antipathy to daring innovations, the king placed no immediate obstacles in the way of the reformers in this matter. It is probably true that his bitterness at the conduct of the aristocracy, and the officer corps in particular, led him to regard the middle classes with more affection than might have been expected.[4] Grolman was encouraged to work out the details of a new system of officer selection, and his efforts resulted in the order of 6 August 1808 which declared that:

> A claim to the position of officer shall from now on be warranted, in peace-time by knowledge and education, in time of war by exceptional bravery and quickness of perception. From the whole nation, therefore, all individuals who possess these qualities can lay title to the highest positions of honour in the military establishment. All social preference which has hitherto existed is herewith terminated in the military establishment, and everyone, without regard for his background, has the same duties and the same rights.[5]

(Hamburg, 1936), pp. 184, 187, and Friedrich Meusel, ed. 'Marwitz' Schilderung der altpreussischen Armee', *Preußische Jahrbücher*, cxxxi (1908), 460–84.

[1] Lehmann, *Scharnhorst*, ii. 60. This marked an advance over Scharnhorst's early thinking on the subject. See Eleftherios Sossidi, *Die staatsrechtliche Stellung des Offiziers im absoluten Staat* (Berlin, 1939), pp. 41 ff.

[2] Conrady, *Grolman*, i. 151. On Grolman's career, see Oberst von Hoepfner in *Militärwochenblatt* (Beiheft, Oct. 1843), pp. 2–23.

[3] Friedrich Meinecke, *Das Leben des Generalfeldmarschalls Hermann von Boyen* (Stuttgart, 1895–9), i. 169.

[4] This is the opinion of Eugene N. Anderson in his perceptive chapter on the king in his *Nationalism and the Cultural Crisis in Prussia, 1806–1815* (New York, 1939), esp. pp. 278–9.

[5] Demeter, *Deutsche Heer*, p. 15; Conrady, *Grolman*, i. 159–62.

To implement this sweeping statement, regulations were issued putting an end to the system whereby Junkers of 12 and 13 years were permitted to serve as corporals until they could be commissioned. From now on, any young man who had reached the age of 17 years and had served three months in the ranks could take regimental examinations for admission to the rank of cornet (*Portepéefähnrich*), fourteen of whom were authorized for each infantry regiment and eight for each cavalry regiment. The new examination system was applied also to promotions to the higher grades. Before the cornets were admitted to the grade of lieutenant, they were forced to undergo a second examination before a board in Berlin; and it was intended—at least originally—that all officers should pass examinations before promotion to a higher grade.[1]

These innovations were regarded with horror by the officers of the old school. The admission of the *bourgeoisie* to the officer corps they regarded as an attack upon their own class and an unjust deprivation of prerogatives which belonged to them. When Prince William sought to defend the new regulations, the fiery and melodramatic General York is reported to have said: 'If your royal highness deprives me and my children of our rights, what foundation is left for your own?'[2] The conservatives—including such members, or former members, of the commission as Lottum and Borstell[3]—felt that the emphasis on book-learning was ill-advised, since 'too much learning kills character',[4] and they did not hesitate to intimate to the king that the elaborate system of examining boards would destroy the intimate relationship which had always existed between the sovereign and his officers. These arguments were not without effect and, even at the very inception of the new system, important reservations were made. In the instructions to the examining commissions it was pointed out that 'knowledge and scholarship are not the only qualifications which mark a useful officer; presence of mind, ready perception, precision, correctness in his duty and propriety in his deportment are essential qualities which every officer must possess'.[5] This was doubtless a

[1] Lehmann, *Scharnhorst*, ii. 55–67; Shanahan, *Prussian Military Reforms*, pp. 131–3.

[2] Demeter, *Deutsche Heer*, p. 16. See also Droysen, *York*, pp. 183–4.

[3] On Borstell, see especially Stadelmann in *Historische Zeitschrift*, clxi (1940), 263–76. See also Demeter, *Deutsche Heer*, pp. 13–15.

[4] So Marwitz, *Nachlaß*, i. 306.

[5] Demeter, *Deutsche Heer*, p. 80.

reasonable safeguard against excessive emphasis upon book-knowledge, but it was certainly open to abuse by prejudiced examiners. In addition, a royal order of March 1809 reaffirmed the king's right to appoint commanding officers at his own discretion—a reminder to the reformers that he did not intend to allow his royal rights to disappear.[1]

These reservations could not alter the fact, however, that the reformers had effected a serious breach in the old system. The opening of the officer corps to the middle classes and the new emphasis upon educational qualifications, supplemented the reforms inaugurated by Stein to lower class barriers and to remove social inequalities. The conservatives were at this time powerless to introduce more than minor modifications in the new regulations, since the memory of Jena was still sharp and the need for intelligent officers apparent. Thus Scharnhorst was able to go on his way and to supplement the order of August 1808 with a thorough-going reorganization of the military schools. By the middle of 1810 all of the old basic schools, except the *Kadettenhaüser* in Berlin and Potsdam, had been dissolved. In their place new schools of war were established in Berlin, Königsberg, and Breslau, offering nine-month courses to give candidates for commissions 'whatever is required by those who desire to be officers'. For the 'spiritual advancement' of officers in general a superior military academy—the germ of the later *Kriegsakademie*—was founded in Berlin, where small groups of selected officers were given a three-years' course in military specialties, including mathematics, tactics, strategy, artillery, military geography, French and German, physics, chemistry, horse care, and mess administration.[2] The upper class of this academy, the so-called *Selekta*, became the chief recruiting ground for the General Staff, and it was in the training of future staff officers that Scharnhorst's disciples, Clausewitz and Tiedemann, first won renown throughout the army.[3] The effect of these changes was not immediate, but it was important. The proper relationship between book-learning and soldierly qualities was to be a matter of heated controversy until late in the century; but there can be no doubt that the number

[1] Rosenberg, *Bureaucracy*, p. 217; Shanahan, *Prussian Military Reforms*, p. 132, n.

[2] Schwertfeger, *Die großen Erzieher*, p. 15. See also Bronsart von Schellendorf, *Duties of the General Staff*, pp. 47 ff.

[3] F. von Rabenau in *Von Scharnhorst zu Schlieffen*, pp. 36–37.

of well educated and cultivated officers was greatly increased by Scharnhorst's reforms, and it became now less fashionable to model one's conduct on that of the Old Dessauer.

The reform of the officer corps was perhaps the most successful aspect of the work of the Military Reorganization Commission. Their progress in reorganizing the army as a whole into an effective fighting force was slower, and their achievements less spectacular. There was, of course, good reason for this. The structure of the army and the machinery for conscription had to be overhauled completely in view of Napoleon's virtual control of the Continent, which made foreign recruiting impossible and forced Prussia, with greatly reduced territory, to rely entirely on native forces. It was, moreover, difficult to set a limit to the size of the standing army without knowing what Napoleon would permit and what the shattered finances of the state would stand. Throughout 1807 and 1808 the commission was forced to think in terms of reduction rather than of expansion; it operated on the assumption that the country could support an army of six divisions of all arms; and a series of cabinet orders set the new limits for infantry, cavalry, and artillery units. But these plans were changed almost as quickly as they were drawn up; and the new tables of organization had to be completely recast in September 1808 when Napoleon, by the Treaty of Paris, imposed an overall limit of 42,000 men on the Prussian army. As a result of this the projected six division army had to be discarded in favour of one composed of six combined brigades—each consisting of seven to eight battalions of infantry and twelve squadrons of cavalry—and three brigades of artillery.[1]

The Treaty of Paris not only imposed restrictions upon the size of the standing army but forbade extraordinary measures for national defence or the formation of a civil guard.[2] The latter condition was an even more serious blow to the reformers than the former, and Scharnhorst, Gneisenau, and Grolman tried in vain to induce the king to refuse to accept it, since it threatened to make impossible the fulfilment of their plans for complete reform of the conscription system and the establishment of a truly national army. Gneisenau in particular feared that the

[1] The details will be found in Shanahan, *Prussian Military Reforms*, pp. 109–14, 128–9, and Jany, *Preußische Armee*, iv. 20 ff.

[2] Shanahan, *Prussian Military Reforms*, p. 152.

treaty would encourage the natural timidity of the king and persuade him to be content with a mere reorganization of the old style standing army, the kind of army which, he wrote scornfully, 'had contributed more than anything else to the enervation and degeneration of peoples, which destroyed the warlike spirit of the nation and its sense of community by relieving the other sections of society from the duty of directly defending the State'.[1] Although some members of the commission had, during the early months of its labours, talked in terms of perpetuating the old canton system with all of its exemptions, the reform party—both those on the commission and those, like Stein and Oberpräsident Schön, who were active in civil affairs—were determined that the principle of universal liability must be firmly applied and that all young men who were not called into the standing army must be made liable for service in some kind of national militia. In a memorandum to the king on 15 March 1808 the commission unanimously recommended the application of the principle of universal service; and in December of the same year they elaborated this demand by recommending universal conscription for all men between 20 and 35. They recommended further that no exemptions of any kind should be allowed; that the selection for the regular army should be by lot; and that plans for a reserve militia, working in conjunction with the regular army, should be made.[2]

It is impossible to over-estimate the importance which the reformers attributed to this aspect of their work. In a letter written after his second dismissal from office, Stein insisted that only the union of standing army and national militia would give actuality to 'universality of responsibility for service in war, binding upon every class of civil society', and added: 'Through this it will be possible to inculcate a proud warlike national character, to wage wearying distant wars of conquest and to withstand an overwhelming enemy attack with a national war.'[3] Hermann von Boyen, who as a cornet had heard Kant lecture at Königsberg and had subsequently made a serious study of his philosophy, shared Stein's views.[4] To Boyen, indeed, a truly

[1] R. Vaupel, *Stimmen aus der Zeit der Erniedrigung* (Berlin, 1923), p. 67.

[2] Huber, *Heer und Staat*, p. 130.

[3] Freiherr vom Stein, *Staatsschriften und politische Briefe*, ed. by Friedrich Thimme (Leipzig, 1921), p. 57.

[4] Boyen's memoirs were edited by Friedrich Nippold and published under the

national army appeared as 'the school of the nation' of the future, teaching the citizens who served in it the meaning of duty and preparing them for intelligent participation in public life.[1] In order that it might do this successfully Boyen had long argued the necessity of abolishing the brutal discipline of the old army, and it was primarily due to his influence and that of Gneisenau, that the new Articles of War, which were issued on 3 August 1808, abolished corporeal punishments for minor breaches of discipline and set up a system of military justice which protected the individual soldier from arbitrary verdicts of local commanders.[2] The new articles were obviously designed to reduce the repugnance to military life felt by those classes which in the past had been exempt from military service but who now—if the reformers had their way—would serve either in the standing army or in the national militia. It is significant that the articles specifically declared that 'in the future every subject of the state, without regard for birth, will be obliged to do military service under conditions of time and circumstance still to be determined'.[3]

It was easier, however, to persuade the king to sign such declarations of principle than it was to induce him to give them actuality. In December 1808, when the commission, as has already been mentioned, recommended the establishment of universal conscription, the king took no action. Frederick William had no desire to see the professional army replaced by a more popular one, and he was encouraged in his resistance by his financial advisers, who told him it would ruin the state, by men like Niebuhr who opposed it out of religious conviction, and by provincial authorities who regarded it as a dangerous

title *Erinnerungen aus dem Leben des Generalfeldmarschalls Hermann von Boyen* (3 vols., Stuttgart, 1889–90). They cover only the period before 1813. For Boyen's career as a whole see especially Friedrich Meinecke, *Das Leben des Generalfeldmarschalls Hermann von Boyen* (2 vols., Stuttgart, 1895–9); his comments on this work in *Erlebtes 1862–1901* (Leipzig, 1941), p. 221; his essay 'Boyen und Roon' in *Historische Zeitschrift*, lxxvii (1896), most recently reprinted in *Preußich-Deutsche Gestalten und Probleme* (Leipzig, 1940); and his brief comments on Boyen in *Die deutsche Katastrophe* (Dritte Auflage, Wiesbaden, 1947), pp. 154–5. Like Scharnhorst, Boyen was taken up by Nationalist Socialist historians, some of whom tried to make him a spiritual precursor of Adolf Hitler. See, for instance, Scholtz, *Boyen*, esp. pp. 98–99.

[1] Meinecke, *Boyen*, i. 101–2, 192 ff.

[2] Ibid., 106 ff.; Boyen, *Erinnerungen*, i. 132, 210, 316–18, 411–21, 476–80; Lehmann, *Scharnhorst*, ii. 24, 99 ff., 124–5. Huber, *Heer und Staat*, p. 136; Shanahan, *Prussian Military Reforms*, pp. 136–9; Lehmann, *Freiherr vom Stein* (Leipzig, 1902–5), ii. 546–7.

[3] Shanahan, *Prussian Military Reforms*, p. 137.

French idea.[1] As for the plans for a national militia, the king regarded them with disfavour from the very first. What he knew of the history of England and France convinced him that militias were inimical to royal authority, and he feared, moreover, that the creation of a second force would lower the prestige, and eventually the efficiency, of the standing army.[2] The Treaty of Paris was a blow to the reformers because it gave the king an additional reason for refusing to follow their programme; and their cause was even more seriously injured in November 1808 when Napoleon once more asserted his influence in Prussian affairs and forced the dismissal of Stein from office. The fall of this indomitable fighter for basic reform rejoiced the hearts of conservatives like York, who wrote: 'One mad head is already severed; the remaining rabble of serpents (*Natterngeschmeiß*) will die in its own poison.'[3] This prophecy was premature, but it nevertheless seemed true that the influence of the reformers was on the wane. Certainly they made no immediate progress with their plans for universal conscription or for a national militia. Until 1813 the old canton system, with all the customary exemptions, remained in force, and no steps were taken to erect supplementary popular formations.

Retention of the canton system not only blocked the basic objectives of the reformers but made impossible any appreciable increase in the size of the army. Attempts were made after 1807, and especially after 1809, to build up the strength of the forces, primarily by means of the so-called *Krümper* system, whereby each company or squadron annually gave leave to a prescribed number of trained men and replaced them with raw recruits. The belief that this originated as a plan for evading the terms of the treaty with France and that it succeeded in training a secret army of 150,000 men has long since been exposed as a patriotic legend.[4] The *Krümper* system, first suggested by Scharnhorst in July 1807, was designed merely to train replacements for war; it was not applied to the whole army until 1809 and was interrupted in 1811; and it was far less

[1] Max Lehmann, 'Zur Geschichte der preußischen Heeresreform von 1808', *Historische Zeitschrift*, cxxvi (1922).

[2] Lehmann, *Scharnhorst*, ii. 97–99.

[3] Droysen, *York*, pp. 190–1. On the reliance which Scharnhorst placed in Stein, see Lehmann, *Stein*, ii. 541.

[4] See Shanahan, *Prussian Military Reforms*, pp. 159–78; Jany, *Preußische Armee*, iii. 468; iv. 41. Cf. Lehmann, *Scharnhorst*, ii. 157–9.

effective than has been imagined. At the outbreak of war in 1813 the Prussian army and its trained reserves numbered only 65,675 officers and men.[1]

It need not be concluded from all this, however, that the accomplishments of the reformers were trifling. While it is true that they had been checked in their desire to form a truly national military establishment, they had at least laid the foundations upon which such a force could be established at some later date. Moreover, such reforms as the opening of the officer corps to the middle classes and the revision of military justice, which were animated by the same philosophy as Stein's reforms of the civil government, were received with favour by the general public and helped to reduce the popular bitterness against state and army which had been so strong after Jena. The reformers were realistic enough to understand that they must now wait upon events, in the hope that the growing arrogance of Napoleon and the increasing popular irritation at French exactions would compel the king to abandon his cautious course and take up arms again. When he did this, they were determined to persuade him to complete the work begun so well in 1807 and 1808 and to create the citizen army from which they expected so much.

Quite apart from this Scharnhorst and his colleagues had good reason for satisfaction, for, in the field of technical efficiency, they had effected decided improvements in the existing armed force. The basic equipment of the army, from uniforms to ordnance, was studied with a critical eye. Diligent attempts were made to improve the supply and efficiency of small arms and artillery, and new foundries were established for the manufacture of arms, although the rate of output was always severely limited by the shaky finances of the state. In the field of tactics, serious efforts were made to benefit from French practice, and new training manuals were written which emphasized the use of light troops, the columnar battle formation, and the co-operation of all arms in the field. With respect to the last of these, the brigade organization which was introduced after the French treaty of 1808 enabled infantry and cavalry units to train together and to become accustomed to the kind of collaboration in the field that had been so conspicuously absent in 1806. It made possible also a complete overhauling of the

[1] Shanahan, *Prussian Military Reforms*, p. 178.

supply services, and distribution and accounting of supplies were now centralized under the authority of a newly established War Commissariat with representatives in each of the six brigades.[1]

By all odds the most important of these technical innovations was the establishment of the new Ministry of War in March 1809. In this, as in many of the military reforms, Stein's influence is to be noted, and the new agency grew in a sense out of that minister's campaign against irresponsible government and multiplication of function in the state administration. In a memorandum of 23 November 1807 Stein recommended the unification of the whole administration of the state under the direction of five ministries, the responsible heads of which should form a *Staatsministerium* and report directly to the king. One of these ministries, he urged, should be a Ministry of War, capable of unifying all military matters under its control.[2] The king, always more responsive to plans of reform which affected the civil administration than to projects which touched on his military prerogatives, waited for eight months before giving tentative approval to this idea, and it was not until December 1808 that definite orders were issued creating a Ministry of War.

These orders declared that the new ministry would have authority 'over everything which pertained to the military and to its constitution, its establishment and its maintenance and . . . everything which hitherto lay within the jurisdiction of the *Oberkriegskollegium*, the *Militärdepartement* of the General Directory, the Provincial Magazine Departments of Silesia and Prussia as well as the *Generalintendantur*. . . .'[3] The new ministry was divided into two departments, a General Department of War (*Allgemeine Kriegsdepartement*) and a Military Economy Department (*Militär Ökonomiedepartement*). The first of these, which was to deal with all matters of administration and command, comprised three divisions, the first handling questions of personnel, including promotions, pay, decorations, justice, and dismissal, the second dealing with training, education, war plans, and mobilization, and the third having supervision over artillery, engineering, fortifications, ordnance, and the testing of inven-

[1] See Lehmann, *Scharnhorst*, ii. 136 ff., 153 ff., 222 ff.; Shanahan, *Prussian Military Reforms*, pp. 141–3, 179–85.

[2] Lehmann, *Stein*, ii. 369 ff., 376–8; *Scharnhorst*, ii. 134.

[3] *Das Königliche Preußische Kriegsministerium*, pp. 6–8; Schmidt-Bückeburg, *Militärkabinett*, pp. 15 ff.

tions. The Military Economy Department, with four divisions, was to concern itself with all matters of finance and supply.[1]

Having granted this much the king, characteristically, baulked at the final step needed to complete the reform. Doubtless fearing to give too much power in military affairs to any single individual[2] he refused to appoint a Minister of War. Instead, Scharnhorst was made head of the General Department of War, with the additional title Chief of the General Staff, while Graf Lottum, a conservative, was made Chief of the Military Economy Department. Both officers were granted the right of conferring directly with the king and communicating, when necessary, with other ministries and department heads.

Although the Ministry of War was not united under a single minister until 1814, the king's caution was not productive of very great harm. After the ministry began to function, in March 1809, it was dominated by the personality of Scharnhorst, and the two departments seem to have worked together amicably. It was natural that the commanding generals, who were placed, in peace-time, under the authority of the ministry, should have resented the new creation;[3] and, indeed, throughout its long existence until 1918, the Ministry of War was forced, not always with success, to fight for its powers and its very existence. But in the period under review its position was not seriously challenged, and it was permitted to give a degree of unity to the military establishment which had been unknown during the old régime. The competing agencies whose strife had contributed so directly to the confusion at Jena now disappeared or were subordinated to the new ministry. Thus the functions of all-powerful *Generaladjutantur* were absorbed by the first division of the General Department of War, under Grolman; the old *Generalquartiermeisterstab* surrendered its duties to the second division of that department, where Boyen was the first division chief; and the *Oberkriegskollegium* and the *Militärdepartement* disappeared completely.[4] This centralization was in itself a hopeful

[1] Lehmann, *Scharnhorst*, ii. 208–11.

[2] Ibid. The king may also, however, have been influenced by the fact that Scharnhorst, the obvious candidate for minister, was junior in grade to many other officers in the service.

[3] Ibid., 211–12.

[4] Schmidt-Bückeburg, *Militärkabinett*, pp. 16–20. Grolman served as head of the first division for only two months. He was succeeded by Colonel Hake and, in

augury for the future. Even more so was the fact that, by the terms of its creation, the new ministry was to work in constant collaboration with the other four ministries, and its minister was to be a member of the central ministry of state. If applied in the proper spirit, this meant that military affairs would no longer constitute a province all their own, isolated from other aspects of the state administration. This, the reformers believed, would also hasten the day when the gulf between the army and civil society would be bridged.

II

In April 1809 long gathering difficulties between Austria and France came to a head; Austrian troops burst into Bavaria; and their commander, the Archduke Charles, called upon all Germans to raise the standard of freedom and to drive the French Emperor back over the Rhine.[1] The response in Prussia was immediate and passionate; and if one seeks the first tangible result of the reform programme of 1807–9, he will find it perhaps in the desire for war which now manifested itself. There was little trace now of the spiritless passivity which had marked the aftermath of Jena. Within the army itself, both the reformers and the extreme conservatives believed that Prussia, despite the deficiencies which still existed in her forces, must seize this opportunity. Such past opponents of the reforms as Kalkreuth and Borstell called openly for intervention, while Marwitz and Knesebeck offered their services to Austria.[2] Nor was the desire for war confined to military circles. Those patriots who, like Arndt and Fichte,[3] addressed their appeals to the general public were greeted with enthusiasm; and when Major von Schill, on his own initiative, led a force of about one hundred hussars from the drill-ground in Berlin to attack the kingdom of Westphalia,[4] his ill-fated expedition aroused such a storm of emotion that Borstell warned the king that disciplinary

February 1810 when Hake became head of the Military Economy Department, by Boyen. See Boyen, *Erinnerungen*, ii. 12.

[1] On the origins and significance of the Austrian war, see the general accounts in Srbik, *Deutsche Einheit*, i. 168 ff., and Schnabel, *Deutsche Geschichte*, i. 398.

[2] Lehmann, *Scharnhorst*, ii. 263–7.

[3] For a perceptive treatment of the nationalism of these much abused figures, see Hans Kohn, 'Arndt and the Character of German Nationalism', *American Historical Review*, liv (1949), 787–803; 'The Paradox of Fichte's Nationalism', *Journal of the History of Ideas*, x (1949), 319–43.

[4] See Treitschke, *German History*, i. 402–3.

action against the insubordinate officer might very well cause a revolution in Berlin.[1]

The leaders of the reform party tried to persuade the king to take advantage of the state of public opinion. Scharnhorst not only urged an immediate alliance with Austria, but offered a new plan for giving actuality to the principle of universal service—a plan whereby immediate steps would be taken to supplement the standing army with a trained reserve, composed of former soldiers, with a number of volunteer *Jaeger* battalions, to be formed by members of the propertied classes who could equip and mount themselves.[2] Frederick William, however, had no desire for heroic deeds. There is more than a little truth in Lehmann's verdict that, in this crisis in his country's fortunes, the king acted like a man who was 'completely convinced of the superiority of his opponent, the depravity of his people and the incompetence of his advisers and his commanders'.[3] He did enter into relations with the Austrian government, and he seems to have made promises of support, but these were always conditional upon assurances which no one could give in 1809. The king wanted to be convinced that Russia would not object to Prussian intervention, that Britain would effectively support the enterprise, and that Austria and Prussia could in fact defeat Napoleon. In his heart he believed none of these things and, because of this, he would neither commit himself to war nor implement any of Scharnhorst's plans. Not even Napoleon's set-back at Aspern could move him from his fearful torpor; and, when Wagram put an end to all the high hopes of 1809, Frederick William's reaction was closer to self-satisfaction than to discomfiture. The patriots, however, were left shaken and discouraged by the issue of the war. Old Blücher, the defender of Lübeck, who had promised the king that with 30,000 men he would drive the French out of Germany, retired in anger to his headquarters at Stargaard, and alarming reports were soon being circulated to the effect that the old warrior was in a state of mental collapse and believed himself pregnant of an elephant.[4] Gneisenau resigned from the army, although he

[1] Lehmann, *Scharnhorst*, ii. 268–70.

[2] Ibid., p. 288.

[3] Ibid., p. 295.

[4] Boyen, *Erinnerungen*, ii. 106–8; E. F. Henderson, *Blücher and the Uprising of Prussia against Napoleon, 1806–1815* (London, 1911), pp. 47–48. Blücher was also reported to believe that he was being persecuted by the French, who were hiring agents to keep the floor of his quarters so hot that it could not be walked upon. It

continued to serve the state as a secret agent and undertook missions to London and St. Petersburg; and Grolman, who had served as a staff officer in the Austrian army during the brief campaign, departed for England and, in the spring of 1810, entered a newly formed foreign legion in Spain where he was to serve with distinction until 1812.[1]

This discouragement deepened in 1810 and 1811 as Napoleon, pressed in other quarters, began to increase his exactions in Prussia. In January 1810 the emperor peremptorily demanded the payment of the indemnity called for under the treaty of 8 September 1808. When the Dohna–Altenstein ministry pleaded for a new extension, Napoleon showed that he had not been insensible to the efforts made by Scharnhorst to restore Prussia's military might. He suggested that, unless the Prussian government wished to surrender the province of Silesia in lieu of the indemnity, they had better be prepared to raise the money by reducing the Prussian army to a royal guard of 6,000 men. The ensuing crisis brought the fall of the ministry which —thanks to a spirited fight by Scharnhorst—had suggested that the cession of at least part of Silesia was preferable to the complete destruction of the army; and in the end Silesia was saved also when Hardenberg became *Staatskanzler* in June and succeeded in convincing the emperor's representative that the required moneys would be raised without delay.[2] Even so, the crisis was almost disastrous for the hopes of the patriots. Hardenberg's financial measures seriously reduced the funds available for the army, while his administrative reforms aroused a degree of internal dissension and bickering that dissipated the unity and optimism of the previous year.[3] Moreover, although Napoleon relented, he demanded a sacrifice before doing so, and Scharnhorst was forced to retire from his position at the head of the *Allgemeine Kriegsdepartement*, an event which weakened the unity and will of that body, although Scharnhorst was permitted to continue his supervision of staff and engineering functions.

is possible that these fancies were not unconnected with injudicious tippling. In any event, they passed.

[1] Hoepfner in *Militärwochenblatt* (Beihefte, 1843), pp. 7–8.

[2] Treitschke, *German History*, i. 412–13; Hintze, *Die Hohenzollern*, p. 461; Lehmann, *Scharnhorst*, ii. 308 ff.

[3] On Hardenberg's reforms, cf. Hintze, *Die Hohenzollern*, pp. 462–6 and Treitschke, *German History*, i. 428–48. Some impression of the hatred they inspired among the landholders of Brandenburg and East Prussia, and conservative circles in general, may be gained from Marwitz, *Nachlaß*, i. 322 ff.

Finally, the emotional storms which filled the year 1810, together with the sudden death of his wife, plunged the king into a mood of fatalistic submission to the blows of fate. The queen herself, shortly before her death, had written:

> It becomes ever clearer to me that everything had to come as it has come. Divine providence ushers in a new age, and there will be a different order of things, for the old has outlived itself. . . . We went to sleep on the laurels of Frederick the Great who, master of his century, created a new age. We have not progressed with it and it has passed us by. . . . It is abundantly clear that everything that has happened and is happening . . . is only the beginning of the road to a better goal. But this goal seems to lie in the remote distance; we shall apparently not live to reach it. As God wills! Everything as He wills![1]

Grief-stricken by his loss, Frederick William adopted this philosophy as his own and, turning to religion for consolation, seemed indifferent to the fate of his country.[2]

During the course of 1811 this attitude of the king reduced the reformers to despair. It was in this year that the first clear signs of an eventual break between France and Russia became apparent, and the reform party reacted to this as they had to the Austrian war of 1809. Once more they urged the king to sanction plans for mobilizing the full strength of Prussian manpower. Their principal spokesman on this occasion was Gneisenau, the hero of the siege of Kolberg in 1806 and a man who had come to the conclusion that Prussia would be saved only by a mass rising of her people, who, once they had saved the state, would be entitled to a constitution and all the other privileges of representative government. In the summer of 1811 Gneisenau drew up an eloquent and detailed memorandum to the king, urging him, upon the first sign of war between France and Russia, to summon his people to the colours. In the margins of this document the king scribbled two comments: 'Nobody would come!' and 'Good—as poetry!' Stung by the latter of these, Gneisenau wrote: 'Religion, prayer, love of one's ruler, love of the fatherland—these things are nothing else than poetry. There is no lifting of the heart that is not atune to poetry. The man that acts only in accordance with cold calculation becomes an inveterate egoist. Upon poetry is founded the

[1] Hintze, *Die Hohenzollern*, pp. 461–2.

[2] Anderson, *Nationalism*, p. 289.

security of the throne.'[1] Frederick William does not seem to have replied.

But it was not the king alone who stood in the way of the reformers. Hardenberg was also still unconvinced of the advisability of their projects. Although, in reactionary circles, the new Chancellor was supposed to be of the same stripe as Stein, Scharnhorst, and Gneisenau, his position was, in reality, quite distinct from theirs. He possessed far less faith in the masses than did Gneisenau, for instance, and the idea of the nation in arms was in consequence less attractive to him. His main interest, moreover, lay in the field of foreign affairs, in which his talent was comparable with that of Metternich and Talleyrand; and his vision was keener and his sense of realities more accurate than that of the reform party. His desire to free Prussia from the French yoke was tempered by a disinclination to substitute a Russian preponderance in central Europe for that of France; and he was unwilling to merge Prussia's fortunes with those of Russia until he was sure of the ultimate intentions of the Tsar. Throughout the latter half of 1811, then, Hardenberg moved cautiously and, while Scharnhorst was authorized to hold conversations with the Russians, the Chancellor investigated the advantages of a military alliance with Napoleon, meanwhile throwing his influence against any schemes of mobilization.[2]

By late fall, Franco-Russian relations reached their ultimate point of deterioration, and both countries began to exert pressure on the Prussian government. Napoleon now insisted that Prussia either enter the Rhine Confederation or conclude an unconditional offensive-defensive alliance with France; the Tsar, on his side, promised to protect Prussia from the consequences of refusing the French terms. Forced to choose between alternatives, Hardenberg threw in his lot with the reform party and advised alliance with Russia. The king, unfortunately,

[1] Pertz, *Gneisenau*, ii. 191 ff. Ritter believes that Gneisenau's plans for a mass rising were so impractical as to cast doubt on his political judgement. See *Staatskunst und Kriegshandwerk*, i. 103.

[2] On Hardenberg, see the judgement of his contemporaries Marwitz (*Nachlaß*, i. 332 ff.) and Schön (Droysen, *Briefwechsel*, i. 713). See also Hintze, *Historische und politische Aufsätze*, iii. 66–67; P. Rohden, 'Die klassische Diplomatie im Kampf um das europäische Gleichgewicht', *Europäische Revue*, xv (1939), 259; and Paul Haake, 'König Friedrich Wilhelm III., Hardenberg, und die preußische Verfassungsfrage', *Forschungen zur brandenburgischen und preußischen Geschichte*, vols. xxvi (1913) to xxxii (1919) and esp. xxx (1918), 348. On his diplomacy in 1811, see Lehmann, *Scharnhorst*, ii. 359 and Meinecke, *Boyen*, i. 211–21.

was not convinced by this late conversion and—to the horror of the reformers and of the bulk of the army—he decided, in November 1811, to submit to Napoleon and to conclude the alliance desired by the emperor.

The Franco-Prussian treaty, which was ratified in March 1812, seemed to render meaningless everything that had been done to strengthen the army since 1807. Its most important provision was that which stipulated that Prussia, in the event of a Franco-Russian war, would supply the emperor with an auxiliary army of 20,000 men; but there were other clauses which seemed equally shameful. No mobilization orders or troop movements were to be permissible in Prussia without Napoleon's assent; two of Prussia's fortresses were to be occupied by French units immediately; and all the rigours of French occupation were to be restored. The effects of the pact were completely demoralizing. Three hundred Prussian officers—almost a fourth of the officer corps—submitted their resignations in disgust; and among those who now left the king's service were numbered Boyen and Clausewitz. The latter officer wrote of the treaty: 'I believe, I must confess, that the shameful blot of a cowardly capitulation is never wiped away; that this drop of poison in the blood of a people is transmitted to posterity and will cripple and undermine the energy of later generations.'[1] Scharnhorst also requested retirement, and, although this was denied on the advice of Hardenberg, the leader of the military reformers surrendered his post as Chief of the General Staff to Colonel von Rauch and withdrew to Breslau where he found many of his disgruntled disciples and where Blücher also was living in impatient exile.[2]

The gloom of the Breslau circle was not, however, of long duration. Supported by an unwilling corps of Prussian troops under York's command, Napoleon advanced into Russia in July. By December his disorganized forces were reeling back across East Prussia; and Prussia's great opportunity had arrived.

It was not to be expected that the king would realize this immediately. His palace in Berlin was remote from the scene of

[1] Hintze, *Die Hohenzollern*, p. 467.

[2] Lehmann, *Scharnhorst*, ii. 402–25, 428 ff., 446; Droysen, *York*, i. 296–8. Blücher had been banned on Napoleon's request because of his encouragement of secret arming in Pomerania. See Boyen, *Erinnerungen*, ii. 138, 187–91.

the French disaster, and it is clear that he did not believe the excited reports that poured in upon him. Frederick William, indeed, seemed to place trust only in the genius of Napoleon, and, since he could not forget that Wagram had followed Aspern, he prevented any ministerial action designed to take advantage of the French reverses. But the power to control events was now snatched from the sovereign's hands. On 30 December General York—acting completely on his own responsibility—concluded the convention of Tauroggen with the commander of the advancing Russian forces, withdrew his auxiliary corps from the fighting, and announced their neutrality.[1]

And before the startled king had an opportunity to repudiate this action, Stein arrived in East Prussia as an agent of the Russian court, arranged with York for the summoning of an East Prussian *Landtag*, and persuaded that body to mobilize a *Landwehr* of all able-bodied men between 18 and 45 years, to defend the province from French reprisals.[2]

After this there was no turning back. The king transferred his headquarters from Berlin to Breslau, where the reform party was in the ascendancy, and almost immediately appointed a committee, of which Scharnhorst was the dominant member, to increase Prussia's armed strength as quickly as possible. The first orders issued by this body merely mobilized the standing army to full strength, increased the number of regiments, and distributed the trained men throughout the new formations. On 3 February, however, the first of the steps long desired by the

[1] Gallons of ink have been expended on analyses of York's action, and the question of insubordination has been hotly debated. See, for instance, Walter von Elze, *Der Streit um Tauroggen* (Breslau, 1926). In a book written during the national socialist period, E. R. Huber argued that the convention was an act of defiance, a violation of the officers' oath, and an appeal to the ancient *Widerstandsrecht*, the right of the *Volk* to protect itself against a monarch who threatened it. 'The oath to the colours binds the army no longer', Huber wrote, 'when it is ordered to fight on the side of the hereditary enemy. . . . The convention of Tauroggen was an act of the greatest constitutional importance; it demonstrated that the King also had an office which made him responsible to the *Volk* and that at that moment when the King failed them, the army and the *Volk* must make decisions by themselves and on their own responsibility.' (*Heer und Staat*, pp. 163 ff.) For other views, see Droysen, *Briefwechsel*, ii. 66 and *York*, i. 419 ff.; Lehmann, *Knesebeck und Schön*, pp. 75–76; and Treitschke, *German History*, i. 491–2. Hintze argues that York recognized the risks involved but acted in the belief that he was doing what the king secretly desired. *Die Hohenzollern*, pp. 468–9. Yet it is worth noting that the king always harboured a silent distrust of York after this and that, even after the liberation, the convention was never officially recognized as an act of state.

[2] Lehmann, *Stein*, iii. 218 ff.; Shanahan, *Prussian Military Reforms*, pp. 193–6.

reformers was realized when authorization was given for the formation of volunteer *Jaeger* detachments and the first appeal was made to the propertied classes who had in the past been exempt from conscription. On 9 February, at long last, universal conscription became a reality, when all existing exemptions were terminated for the duration of the war. When, on 17 March, a royal order announced the creation of a *Landwehr* on the East Prussian model, to comprise all men aged 17–40 who were not serving in the regular army or the *Jaeger*, and when, a month later, the *Landsturm* edict made all men hitherto unaffected responsible for home defence and guerrilla operations in case of need, the reformers' dream of the nation in arms had finally been clothed in actuality.[1]

In January and February, when the first of these orders were being issued, the purpose of the hasty mobilization had not been made clear. Prussia had repudiated her obligations to Napoleon without a formal agreement of any kind with Russia, and her legal position approximated that of neutrality. In the minds of the thousands of volunteers pouring into Prussian cantonments, there was, however, no doubt; they knew that their purpose was to fight France and their unanimity swept the king along with them. Frederick William did, momentarily, play with the idea of an armed mediation between France and Russia and actually sent a special mission to the Russian headquarters which Stein had some difficulty in side-tracking.[2] This, however, was the last hesitation before the plunge. On 27 February a military alliance was concluded with Russia; on 16 March Frederick William declared war on Napoleon; and on the following day he issued the famous address 'An mein Volk', in which, for the first time in Prussian history, a monarch explained to his people the compelling reasons for the sacrifices he was now to demand of them.[3]

The so-called war of liberation was the testing ground of the work of the reformers and, during its course, that work was pronounced good. In 1813 Prussia sent approximately 280,000 men into the field—some 6 per cent. of her total population—a burden which would have been insupportable without the kind

[1] Shanahan, *Prussian Military Reforms*, pp. 197–213. On the democratic implication of the *Landsturm*, see Schnabel, *Deutsche Geschichte*, i. 503–6.

[2] Lehmann, *Stein*, iii. 248 ff.; Boyen, *Erinnerungen*, ii. 337–9.

[3] Hintze, *Die Hohenzollern*, p. 471.

of total mobilization upon which Scharnhorst and his colleagues had insisted. The percentage of this total that represented trained manpower was relatively small; in March 1813 first-line troops numbered only about 68,000 officers and men; and these fully trained units were badly depleted in the first battles at Groß-Görschen and Bautzen.[1] The voluntary *Jaeger* detachments, however, soon demonstrated their value as reservoirs of officer replacements; while the *Landwehr*, after some initial confusion and some popular resistance to conscription on the part of the people of Silesia who had always been exempt from service, not only made good the losses in the line but provided the means for rapid expansion of total strength.[2] This was accomplished, moreover, without sacrificing the original character of the *Landwehr* as a separate militia. During the reorganization of the armed forces during the armistice of June 1813, suggestions that the *Landwehr* recruits be added to line units in small numbers were firmly rejected, partly because of the king's jealous desire to preserve the professional spirit of his line army but also because reformers like Boyen sought successfully to maintain the uniqueness of the *Landwehr* as a citizen army with its own leadership and its own developing tradition. The *Landwehr*, then, was organized into regiments with separate designation and distinct uniforms and fought side by side with the regiments of the line. By mid-1813 it comprised thirty-eight infantry regiments and thirty cavalry regiments and had reached a strength of approximately 120,000 men. Without this supplement to the standing forces Prussia could not have played such a prominent part in the subsequent campaigns.[3]

It is more difficult to establish the extent to which the work of the reformers influenced the psychological mood in which the war was fought by the Prussian people. Much has been written about the popular enthusiasm of 1813 and doubtless much of it is exaggerated; but that there was a sharp contrast with the mood of 1806 there can be no doubt.[4] The king

[1] Some figures are given in Shanahan, *Prussian Military Reforms*, pp. 206–7, 218–24.

[2] On the problems involved in raising the *Landwehr*, ibid., pp. 207–11. See also Boyen, *Erinnerungen*, iii. 93–95.

[3] Shanahan, *Prussian Military Reforms*, pp. 219–21; Schnabel, *Deutsche Geschichte*, i. 503.

[4] See, above all, Treitschke, *German History*, i. 506 ff. A fictional treatment of the popular temper in the winter of 1812–13 will be found in Fontane's *Vor dem Sturm.*

himself was clearly surprised by the response to his message and by the floods of volunteers who applied at recruiting stations. Hatred of France was doubtless a primary motive in this upsurge of patriotism; but it is worth noting that enthusiasm for war was most exalted in the educated middle class, the class which had been most noted for its apathy in 1806. In view of this it is reasonable to conclude that the reforms which had been primarily designed to appease the *bourgeoisie* and to reconcile it to the army had achieved their purpose.

There is no question that the efficiency of the armies which now marched against Napoleon benefited from Scharnhorst's work. If they were weak in artillery and short of small arms and ammunition in the first months of the fighting, they made up for these deficiencies by the excellence of their leadership. Their commanding generals—Blücher, York, Kleist, and Bülow—were unaffected by the doubts and the failure of nerve which had crippled the High Command in 1806 and which were not absent in some of their allies in 1813; while the subordinate officers, thanks to the reorganization of the officer corps, proved, in general, that they were willing to take the initiative and were not afraid of responsibility. Perhaps the most notable feature of the new army was the excellence of the staff work throughout the campaigns. For the first time in the history of the army responsible staff officers were assigned to all commanding generals and corps commanders—Gneisenau to Blücher, Boyen to General von Bülow, Grolman to Kleist, Rauch to York, Clausewitz to Thielmann, Reiche to Zieten, and Rothenburg to the Korps Tauentzien—and for the most part they were received well and consulted constantly. York, it is true, greeted his chief of staff, Colonel von Rauch, with the words: 'I need no chief of staff, although if I've got to have one, you are the one I would always prefer'; and Zieten's *chef* complained bitterly that he was given nothing to do.[1] But these cases were overshadowed by the success of Grolman's and Boyen's work with their commanders, and by the inspired collaboration of Blücher and Gneisenau. Blücher, who recognized both his own shortcomings and the genius of his chief of staff, relied implicitly on Gneisenau's judgement; and he was not wholly joking when—while receiving an honorary degree at Oxford after the war—he remarked: '*Nu*, if I am to become a doctor, you must at least

[1] F. von Cochenhausen in *Von Scharnhorst zu Schlieffen*, pp. 105–7.

make Gneisenau an apothecary, for we two belong always together.'[1]

It was Gneisenau who took over Scharnhorst's duties as Chief of the General Staff when the leader of the military reform party met his tragic death as a result of a wound received at Groß-Görschen. The choice was a fortunate one, for Gneisenau, alone of the reformers, possessed the military talent of his great chief, and his strategical sense has, indeed, been compared favourably with that of Napoleon.[2] Like Scharnhorst he never wavered in his belief that intelligence made as great a contribution to victory as bravery; and he insisted that staff officers must share the responsibility for operational decisions made by their commanding officers. This insistence, and Gneisenau's readiness to support his staff officers in disputes with the commanding generals, strengthened the position of the General Staff and gave it an *esprit* which it was not to lose until the days of Hitler. Gneisenau's other achievements in the French war are equally notable. To him is owed the development of the Prussian technique of command, characterized by clear and comprehensive formulation of objective but always leaving room for individual initiative and freedom of action. Finally, it was his spirit which impressed upon the army in these campaigns of 1813 and 1814 that preference for *Vernichtungsstrategie*—the eschewal of the war of manœuvre and the constant search for the opportunity to destroy the enemy's forces—which, as formulated by Clausewitz, was to dominate Prussian military thinking throughout the nineteenth century.[3]

[1] Varnhagen von Ense, *Blücher* (new ed., Berlin, 1933), p. 270. Blücher is certainly one of the most attractive figures in this period. Described by Schön as 'complete bravery, but in heroic human form' (Droysen, *Briefwechsel*, ii. 43), the commander of the Silesian army was unassuming and modest to the point of exaggeration. Once during the campaign of 1813 he amused and perplexed his *chef* by saying: 'Gneisenau, if I had only learned something, what might not have been made of me! But I put off everything that I should have learned. . . . Instead of studying, I have given myself to gambling, drink, and women; I have hunted and perpetrated all sorts of foolish pranks. And that's why I don't know anything now. Yes, the other way I would have become a different kind of fellow, believe me; something could have been made out of me.' Varnhagen von Ense, p. 342. On Blücher, the soldier, see Henderson, *Blücher*, and W. von Unger, *Blücher* (2 vols., Berlin, 1908).

[2] Schnabel, *Deutsche Geschichte*, i. 555.

[3] On Clausewitz's writing, which will not be treated at any length here, there is a voluminous literature. See, above all, H. Rothfels, 'Clausewitz' in *Makers of Modern Strategy*, pp. 93–113, with the appended bibliography; Herbert Rosinski, 'Die Entwicklung von Clausewitz' Werk "Vom Kriege" im Licht seiner "Vorreden"

Once hostilities had begun, the reform party found themselves confronted with new problems and with new antagonists. Napoleon's recovery from his Russian disaster was rapid and formidable, and in the first of their clashes with him, at Groß-Görschen and Bautzen, the Russian and Prussian allies had reason to believe that they would not defeat him definitively without additional support. Attempts to win Austrian aid were consequently redoubled and, while they were successful in the end, the Austrian adhesion to the cause introduced military and political complications of the gravest importance. For Austria, under Metternich's leadership, fought the war with none of the nationalistic fervour of 1809 but in a spirit of cold calculation reminiscent of the *Kabinettskriege* of the eighteenth century.[1] The stormy ebullience of the Prussian patriots and their impatient desire to advance to the gates of Paris found no echo in Vienna. Metternich was bent on restoring the eighteenth-century balance of power; he was apprehensive of the results of too complete a French defeat; he had visions of exorbitant post-war demands by Russia and, perhaps, an attempt by Alexander to place a Swedish satellite upon the throne of France; and he was irritated by the upsurge of nationalism in Prussia.[2] His caution and circumspection was reflected in the strategy of Prince Karl zu Schwarzenberg, the Austrian *Feldmarschall* who became commander-in-chief of the allied armies after Austria became a member of the coalition. Thus, while the autumn campaign of 1813 brought such heartening triumphs as Gneisenau's fight on the Katzbach, Kleist's victory at Nollendorf, and Blücher's advance over the Elbe, it was marked also by continual bickering between the allies and by a fatal lack of co-ordination in decisive moments.

Thus also, when the allies had inflicted their crushing defeat upon Napoleon at Leipzig in October 1813, the opportunity for a speedy pursuit of his disorganized army was not exploited to the full; and in the months that followed the union of the allies deteriorated swiftly.[3] In February 1814, when they were poised on the borders of France, Schwarzenberg was insisting that the time had come to retreat and negotiate a peace, and Metternich

und "Nachrichten", *Historische Zeitschrift*, cli (1935), 278–93; and Ritter, *Staatskunst und Kriegshandwerk*, i. 67–96.

[1] Srbik, *Deutsche Einheit*, i. 194–205.

[2] See, for instance, Ritter, *Staatskunst und Kriegshandwerk*, i. 105 ff.

[3] Schnabel, *Deutsche Geschichte*, i. 528 ff.; Treitschke, *German History*, i. 615 ff.

was arguing the advantages of leaving France her natural boundaries and Bonaparte his throne. At this critical stage, Blücher's headquarters—already suspect in Austrian eyes as a 'nest of Jacobins'—fought desperately for a continuation of the war; and Grolman deserves credit for having persuaded the Tsar and Frederick William to authorize the union of Blücher's and Bülow's forces and to permit them to open an offensive of their own.[1] This decision, in the end, forced the resumption of the general advance but did not eliminate the political differences within the coalition. It was not until Napoleon's intransigence at Chatillon had demonstrated the futility of negotiation with him, that the Austrians yielded to the persuasive arguments of Lord Castlereagh, concluded the agreement of Chaumont, and accepted Gneisenau's war plan.[2] After that the end desired by the Prussian reformers was attained quickly. In March the allied armies entered Paris; Napoleon was taken into custody; and Stein, with a sigh of dour satisfaction, could say: 'The fellow is overthrown.'[3]

The remark was essentially true, despite the fact that the Corsican still had one throw to make. The desperate adventure of the Hundred Days called the allied armies back into the field in 1815; and the collaboration between Blücher and Gneisenau and the will of the Prussian levies were once more put to the test. But Ligny and Waterloo merely confirmed the earlier result, while proving once more the merit of the work begun in 1807 by Scharnhorst.

III

The reformers had served their country well and, when Napoleon was safe on St. Helena and hostilities had finally come to an end, this was recognized by the Crown. In addition to the popular adulation which greeted them wherever they went, Blücher, Gneisenau, Boyen, Grolman, and others received formal honours, pecuniary emoluments, appropriate raises in rank, and positions of honour and responsibility in the state.

[1] On this crisis, see Pertz and Delbrück, *Gneisenau*, iv. 71–88; Conrady, *Grolman*, ii. 193 ff.; and F. von Cochenhausen, 'Vor 125 Jahren. Politische und militärische Führung im Feldzug 1814', *Wissen und Wehr*, xx (1939), 81–100.

[2] Rohden in *Europäische Revue*, xv (1939), 162. On the decisive role of Castlereagh, see C. K. Webster, *The Foreign Policy of Castlereagh, 1812–1815* (London, 1931), pp. 226–9.

[3] Treitschke, *German History*, i. 649.

The bestowal of these dignities, however, could not hide the fact that their relationship with the king was somewhat strained. This fact did not promise well for the permanence of the changes they had effected in the past or for the completion of their programme by basic constitutional reform.

The fact of the matter was that, even when they were winning battles for him, the reformers had done little to ingratiate themselves with their sovereign and that, in 1814 and 1815, their conduct often irritated and frightened him. Blücher and Gneisenau's insistence upon their own war plan, during the inter-allied crisis of February 1814, had turned out well in the end; but the violent manner in which they had argued their case, and their blunt refusal on several occasions to execute orders from general headquarters, had been alarming. It smacked vaguely of insubordination, and it recalled to the king's mind the revolt of Schill in 1809, a thing of which he did not wish to be reminded.[1]

Their attitude during the peace negotiations at Vienna had been even worse. They had been bitterly critical of the procedure of negotiation and of the tactics of the Prussian representatives—Boyen, indeed, over a very trifling matter, had fought a rather foolish duel in Vienna with Wilhelm von Humboldt[2]—and they had been patently disgusted with the territorial arrangements concluded. Filled with a nationalistic fervour, they had championed schemes of German unity in which the king had no interest or pushed plans for a Prussian hegemony in northern Germany which he felt were impractical.[3] They had not only insisted that Prussia must be allowed to annex all of Saxony, but they had been willing to fight a new war against Austria in order to secure this accretion of territory. In late 1814, indeed, Gneisenau, Boyen, and Grolman had prepared plans for such a war and had argued that Britain would stand idly by, and Russia and Württemberg give active aid, while the Prussian army destroyed Austria and remodelled Germany.[4]

[1] Pertz and Delbrück, *Gneisenau*, v. 20 ff.

[2] See especially *Wilhelm und Caroline von Humboldt in ihren Briefen*, ed. by Anna von Sydow (Berlin, 1906–16), iv. 542–6.

[3] Even Blücher, whose political views were less radical than those of the other reformers, had written to Scharnhorst in 1813 that 'not only Prussia but the whole German fatherland must be aroused and the nation must be created'. Erich Brandenburg, *Die Reichsgründung* (2 vols., Leipzig, 1914), i. 68. See also Meinecke, *Boyen*, ii. 40 ff.

[4] Meinecke, *Boyen*, ii. 13–22.

These fancies were rudely shattered when Austria concluded a secret alliance with France and Britain in January 1815, and two months later the belligerence of the Prussian soldiers had been diverted by Napoleon's attempt to recapture power. But even after the campaign of 1815 and after the peace conference had finished its work, the reform party had continued to raise difficulties. In November, for instance, Blücher flatly refused to obey orders to evacuate France because he felt that certain fortresses should first be surrendered to Prussia as pledges; and he had given way only after Hardenberg had formally complained to the king of his recalcitrance.[1]

In any circumstances, the king would have objected to these actions; he had additional reason for annoyance, however, in the fact that they aroused unfavourable comment abroad. The Austrians in particular were beginning to view Prussian policy with grave suspicion; and Friedrich von Gentz was advising Metternich that Prussia was clearly bent on destroying Austrian influence in Germany.[2] But Austria was not alone in this. The Tsar was reported to be disturbed by the unwholesome influence of the Prussian military reformers and was supposed to have said to his generals: 'It is possible that some time we shall have to come to the aid of the King of Prussia against his army.'[3] Britain's attitude towards Prussia had also become one of chilly reserve; and, in December 1815, Castlereagh was writing to his envoy in Berlin:[4]

> With all that partiality and a grateful admiration of the conduct of that nation [i.e. Prussia] and its armies in the war, I fairly own that I look with considerable anxiety to the tendency of their politics. There certainly at this moment exists a great fermentation in all orders of the State, very free notions of Government, if not principles actually revolutionary, are prevalent, and the army is by no means subordinate to the civil authorities.

The king could not avoid sensing this growing coolness in other capitals; Hardenberg was warning him that the attitude of the soldiers was not helping Prussia's position; and since Frederick William wished to retain the respect and the friendship of his fellow rulers, he became increasingly critical of

[1] Haake in *Forschungen*, xxviii (1915), 213–14.

[2] Meinecke, *Boyen*, ii. 5.

[3] Ibid., p. 73.

[4] H. G. Schenk, *The Aftermath of the Napoleonic Wars* (New York, 1947), pp. 116–17. Schenk also quotes the lines from Moore which are reproduced at the head of this chapter.

Gneisenau and those who shared his views. Even before the end of the military campaigns he confided to an English military observer that Gneisenau was too clever for his own good; and his *Generaladjutant*, von dem Knesebeck, wrote to Pozzo di Borgo in October 1815 that the king was worried about the influence of Gneisenau and his associates on the cabinet and was resolved to get rid of them.[1]

This change in the king's feelings played into the hands of all those who felt that Stein and Scharnhorst had 'brought revolution into the country' and who believed that the civil and military reforms would lead to a destruction of the monarchy and to a war of the propertyless against the propertied.[2] This opposition had long been in existence—the so-called Perponcher Club, where men like Kalkreuth, Jagow, and York met and grumbled about Scharnhorst's ideas, had been founded in the winter of 1807–8,[3] while the *Christlich-deutsche Tischgesellschaft*, an association of officers, landholders, professional men, and *literati*, had been agitating against all reforms since 1811[4]—but it had never been very effective. Now, under the leadership of the Minister of Police, Prince Wittgenstein, and Duke Karl von Mecklenburg, it began to get the upper hand.

The triumph of the reaction was, however, a gradual process. In 1814 and 1815 the position of the reformers still seemed secure, and the permanence of the reforms certain. In June 1814, for instance, the king not only perpetuated the administrative reform of 1809 but completed the unification of the *Kriegsministerium*. The dual organization of that body was terminated; the old General Department of War and the Military Economy Department were dissolved; and a single unified ministry, with authority over all aspects of military administration, was created.[5] Moreover, after Gneisenau had indicated

[1] Ritter, *Staatskunst und Kriegshandwerk*, i. 140–1. In the subsequent period the king's suspicions of Gneisenau increased. In a letter of January 1818 Clausewitz wrote: 'The confidence which the King placed in him [Gneisenau] . . . seems to have been weakened by insinuations'; and he noted that, although Gneisenau had recently returned to Berlin, three weeks had passed without the king inviting him to dine. Eberhard Kessel, 'Zu Boyens Entlassung', *Historische Zeitschrift*, clxxv (1953), 48.

[2] See, for instance, Marwitz, *Nachlaß*, i. 291–2.

[3] Droysen, *Briefwechsel*, ii. 20.

[4] Schnabel, *Deutsche Geschichte*, i. 472–3.

[5] For details of the reorganization see Meisner, *Der Kriegsminister*, p. 11; Schmidt-Bückeburg, *Militärkabinett*, p. 28.

his preference for a field command, the king had appointed, as Minister of War, Hermann von Boyen, of all the reformers the one who had been closest to Scharnhorst.

Boyen's principal objective was to make permanent the work of his former chief. He realized that, in conservative circles, there was a desire to put an end to universal military service, now that the war was over, and to return to the canton system which had reflected and buttressed the traditional social structure. Prince Wittgenstein, who was not above using his police agents to spy on the new War Minister, was arguing openly that 'to arm a nation means merely to organize and facilitate opposition and disaffection',[1] and was advocating both the termination of universal conscription and the abolition of the *Landwehr*. Boyen worked swiftly to counteract this campaign and, with the aid of Grolman, now Chief of the General Staff and head of the second division of the War Ministry, he succeeded.

In the summer of 1814 Boyen and Grolman drafted, and persuaded the king to accept, the law which regulated military service in Prussia until the 1860's. Promulgated in September, this new *Wehrgesetz* announced that all male Prussians, upon reaching their twentieth birthday, would be liable to military service. They would be enrolled, successively, for three years in the standing army, for two years in the active reserve, for seven years in the first levy of the *Landwehr*, which in time of war would serve with the field army, and for seven years with the second levy of the *Landwehr*, which in time of war would occupy fortresses and perform duties of home defence. Only during the first three years would they serve continuously; but until they reached the age of 39 they would have a clearly defined military status and would be called for brief periodic training; and even after that, in time of national emergency, they would be liable for service in the *Landsturm*. The reformers calculated that by combining the principle of universality with a relatively short term of service in the standing army, Prussia would have an army of 500,000 men, but would have to support, at any one time, only the 130,000 who were on active duty.[2]

With the publication of this law, the last possibility of a

[1] Meinecke, *Boyen*, ii. 310.

[2] On the law of 3 September 1814, see Meinecke, *Boyen*, i. 398 ff.; Schnabel, *Deutsche Geschichte*, ii. 310 ff.; Huber, *Heer und Staat*, pp. 148 ff.; F. von Rabenau, 'Zur 90. Wiederkehr des Todestags des Generalfeldmarschalls v. Boyen', *Militärwissenschaftliche Rundschau*, iii (1938), 32 ff.

return to the canton system, with its liberal exemptions, disappeared. The only modification of liability which was allowed was made in the interests of higher education. Hardenberg and other ministers argued that, to interrupt the education of young men destined for the professions, the sciences, or the state service, would do irreparable harm to the nation, and, very reluctantly, Boyen introduced a provision whereby young people 'of the educated classes' who could outfit and arm themselves could be admitted in *Jaeger* battalions as one-year volunteers (*Einjährig-Freiwillige*) and released at the end of twelve months' service. This aspect of the law was much criticized, and justifiably so in its original form, when commanding officers were permitted to decide who belonged to 'the educated classes'. In 1822, however, a new order stipulated that volunteers would be accepted only after passing an examination at the end of the *Tertia* in the Gymnasia; and, in this form, the institution of *Einjährige* was to last until 1918.[1]

Boyen's law also assured the continuation of the *Landwehr*, an institution of which he had the greatest expectations. In August 1814, at a banquet following his investment with an honorary degree at the University of Berlin, Blücher had toasted 'the happy union of the warrior and civilian society by means of the *Landwehr*'.[2] Boyen agreed with the sentiment. If the standing army was designed to awaken the martial spirit in the people as a whole, the *Landwehr*, in his mind, was designed to provide a bond of intimacy between military and civilian society, preventing mutual antipathy and assuring the continuation of the concept of a civilian army.[3] In drafting the law for the reorganization of the *Landwehr*, which was promulgated in November 1815, Boyen, therefore, stipulated that, although in war-time it would unite with the standing army on the brigade level, in time of peace it would retain its original character as a national militia, that its units would have an intimate relationship with the district in which they were stationed, that their officers would be men of property and demonstrated leadership nominated by the district (*Kreis*) government and elected by the other officers of the unit, and that they would be inspected by

[1] Schnabel (*Deutsche Geschichte*, ii. 315–16) points out that university pressure was not without influence in securing this provision of the law. On Boyen's attitude, see Meinecke, *Boyen*, ii. 136–41.

[2] Varnhagen von Ense, *Blücher*, p. 274.

[3] Meinecke, *Boyen*, ii. 164–77; Schnabel, *Deutsche Geschichte*, ii. 313.

special *Landwehrinspekteure* who were responsible to the Ministry of War.[1]

Boyen's success in carrying this programme, and his effective defence of it in 1817, when a financial crisis brought it under sharp attack,[2] delighted those who had participated in the reforms of 1807–8—Stein, now in retirement, Oberpräsident Schön, Gneisenau, and Blücher, both on inactive service,[3] and Clausewitz who was now engaged on the strategical works which were to make him famous. It was only natural that they should redouble their efforts now to secure that reform which they desired to crown their work—a basic constitutional reform which, as a minimum, would bring a written constitution and some form of national representation. This had been implicit in the military reforms from the beginning. The reform party had always taken the position that the duty of military service should be balanced by the right to some share in the politics of the state; and Boyen particularly had always thought of the reformed army as a school for teaching the people how to bear civic responsibility. But, in trying now to secure the political reforms which might have inaugurated an era of gradual progress toward representative institutions, the reform party met forces which proved too strong for them; and their efforts precipitated a full-scale constitutional crisis which put an end to their influence in the state and delivered Prussia into the arms of reaction.

It was perhaps unfortunate that the man who led the fight for constitutional reform was Wilhelm von Humboldt. Now that Stein had left the public arena, Humboldt was generally recognized as Prussia's most distinguished public servant and most enlightened mind. As Minister of Culture in the period of reform he had been chiefly responsible for the founding of the University of Berlin; at the Congress of Vienna, despite the distinguished company in which he had found himself, he had demonstrated a gift for organization and a thorough grasp of

[1] Schnabel, *Deutsche Geschichte*, ii. 313–14; Meinecke, *Boyen*, ii. 178–9; Sossidi, *Offizierkorps*, pp. 71–72.

[2] On this crisis, and Boyen's brilliant 'Exposition of the Principles of the Former and the Present Prussian Military Organization', see Treitschke, *German History*, ii. 473–4; Meinecke, *Boyen*, ii. 299–309.

[3] Gneisenau retired from the General Kommando am Rhein at the end of 1816, while remaining an active general. His headquarters at Koblenz had always been an object of suspicion to the reactionaries and had been referred to as 'Wallensteins Lager in Koblenz'. Pertz and Delbrück, *Gneisenau*, v. 4–37.

diplomatic technique. As a political philosopher he was known for his markedly liberal views and for his unwavering advocacy of a written constitution which would embody representative institutions and the principle of ministerial responsibility.[1] In February 1819, when Humboldt was brought into the *Staatsministerium* and given jurisdiction over matters concerning the provincial estates and local government, it was widely believed that progress towards constitutional reform would be forthcoming. This was certainly the belief of Boyen who—despite their differences at Vienna—had become one of Humboldt's most fervent admirers and who welcomed his admission to the ministry.[2]

These hopes were not to be realized. Whatever his qualities as a thinker, Humboldt did not possess the talents which would have been required to master the tangled political situation in which he found himself. He proved maladroit both in his assessment of political realities and in his judgement of people. He over-estimated the extent of his own authority and failed completely to fathom the shrewd tactics of the reactionary party at the court. And, worst of all, he threw away the opportunity to exert the influence he undoubtedly possessed in order to engage in a bitter personal battle with the Chancellor Hardenberg.

Hardenberg's attitude was, to be sure, ambiguous.[3] He was not opposed to the granting of a constitution or to the establishment of a national representative body. He had, indeed, championed these things on more than one occasion. But his principal interest lay in the perfection of the state administration and he was not willing to jeopardize his chances of completing this by taking a doctrinaire stand on the constitutional question. He realized, moreover, that any basic constitutional change would have wide-spread repercussions in the other German states and would certainly affect Prussia's relations with Austria. This argued the necessity of caution and very careful consideration of diplomatic consequences.

Humboldt showed no appreciation of this point of view.

[1] The best treatment of the public aspects of Humboldt's life is S. A. Kaehler, *Wilhelm von Humboldt und der Staat* (Munich, 1927). See also the older work by Bruno Gebhardt, *Wilhelm von Humboldt als Staatsmann* (2 vols.; Stuttgart, 1899).

[2] Kaehler, *Humboldt*, p. 398.

[3] See the diverse views in Treitschke, *German History*, ii. 451–2; Kaehler, *Humboldt*, p. 418; Meinecke, *Boyen*, ii. 369–70; and Haake in *Forschungen*, xxxii (1919), 112 ff.

Morally offended by Hardenberg's rather irregular private life, he seems to have regarded the Chancellor as one whose only serious purpose in politics was remaining in power. He made no attempt to reach an understanding with Hardenberg and, after becoming an active member of the ministry of state in August 1819, bitterly criticized the constitutional draft which Hardenberg had prepared in the same month, and sought to organize the rest of the ministry against him. This delighted the reactionary members of the ministry, particularly Wittgenstein, who flattered and encouraged Humboldt in the knowledge that they would be the beneficiaries of the consequent confusion.[1]

This confusion was brought to a head in September when, after a series of conversations between Hardenberg and Metternich at Teplitz and Carlsbad, the king announced Prussia's adherence to the so-called Carlsbad Decrees, which were designed to put an end to revolutionary agitation in all German states. There can be little doubt that Hardenberg's role in this was a minor one, and that the king—terrified by the excesses of the *Burschenschaft* and the murder of the dramatist Kotzebue by a deranged student in March—would, in any circumstances, have insisted upon the agreement.[2] Humboldt, however, refused to recognize this and opened a full-scale attack upon Hardenberg as the author of a Prussian capitulation. He was supported by Beyme, the Minister of Finance, and Boyen. The War Minister, indeed, in a pointed memorandum, argued that the Carlsbad Decrees represented an unwarranted intrusion into Prussian affairs and that the implied Austro-Prussian alliance was unrealistic in view of the natural antipathy of the two Powers and their irreconcilable interests in Germany.[3]

The reactionary party now had the opportunity for which they had long been waiting. Humboldt they could leave to the tender mercies of Hardenberg, for the Chancellor was now thoroughly aroused and had determined to make Humboldt's dismissal the condition of his own retention of office. Wittgenstein and his followers concentrated their fire on Boyen. They knew that the king had always been uncertain about the War Minister, for, as Clausewitz was to write in December 1819,

[1] Kaehler, *Humboldt*, pp. 422 ff.; Haake in *Forschungen*, xxxii (1919), 129–36.

[2] Kaehler, *Humboldt*, p. 426.

[3] Treitschke, *German History*, iii. 265; Meinecke, *Boyen*, ii. 373 ff.

Boyen was 'too much a plant from Scharnhorst's bed not to be always somewhat more uncongenial to him than another man would have been in his position'.[1] They realized shrewdly that Boyen's attack on the Carlsbad Decrees would further weaken the king's confidence in him; and, therefore, they redoubled their attacks upon the new military constitution and, in particular, upon the *Landwehr*, with the obvious intention of goading Boyen into some new indiscretion.

By 1819 the *Landwehr* was very vulnerable to criticism, for its efficiency had deteriorated sharply in the four years of peace. It had been assumed originally that a large part of the force would be composed of trained soldiers who had served in the line army. The continued financial weakness of the state, however, imposed serious limitations on the size of the line army, and the military authorities had drifted into the practice of assigning recruits who could not be accommodated in line regiments to the reserve or the *Landwehr* after a very sketchy training period. Moreover, again for financial reasons, the exercises of the first levy of the *Landwehr* had been reduced from two fourteen-day periods annually to one, while those of the second levy had been discontinued completely. Simultaneously, as an increasing number of officers were recruited from the *Einjährig-Freiwillige*, whose training had been limited to one year, the quality of leadership deteriorated also. It was only natural that these deficiencies of training should be revealed with distressing clarity in the annual manœuvres, as they were, for instance, in the autumn of 1818.[2]

All of this gave the Wittgenstein party an additional argument to use with the king, who was always sensitive to criticism of the efficiency of his army. They had long insisted that the *Landwehr* was unreliable politically, that it was a refuge for dissidents and conspirators, and that its leaders harboured nationalist aspirations which might well involve Prussia in war with the other German states;[3] and Boyen's Carlsbad memorandum seemed to give credence to at least the last of these points. But the military inadequacy of the *Landwehr* enabled them to argue that,

[1] Kessel in *Historische Zeitschrift*, clxxv (1953), 53.

[2] Meinecke, *Boyen*, ii. 203 ff. and *Preußisch-deutsche Gestalten und Probleme*, pp. 105–8; Conrady, *Grolman*, iii. 68 ff.; Treitschke, *German History*, ii. 500 ff.; Schnabel, *Deutsche Geschichte*, ii. 319–24.

[3] See, for instance, the account of Wittgenstein's and Mecklenburg's agitations in June and July 1819. Haake in *Forschungen*, xxxii (1919), 135.

if Prussia should find herself at war, she would be unable to defend herself and that, consequently, the time had come for the king to submit the *Landwehr* to closer supervision. Perhaps because he was irritated over Boyen's alliance with Humboldt, the king agreed.[1] In December 1819, at the same time that Hardenberg's conflict with Humboldt came to a head, the king peremptorily demanded a closer fusion between the *Landwehr* and the line, and a fundamental reorganization which included the disbanding of thirty-four *Landwehr* battalions, the elimination of the separate system of inspection hitherto enjoyed by the *Landwehr*, the assignment of regular line officers to all field commands, and the incorporation of the sixteen *Landwehr* brigades into divisions of the line even in peace-time.[2]

Boyen's reaction to this was, as the reactionary party had hoped, immediate and uncompromising. The king's order, he felt, marked the beginning of the end for the *Landwehr* as conceived in 1814. Once it had lost its equality of status with the line, it would gradually be subjected to the narrow discipline and the unenlightened political views which had always characterized the standing army and its officer corps; and inevitably the progress made towards a reconciliation between the army and civilian society would be reversed. Rather than be a party to that, Boyen submitted his resignation and, although the king rather half-heartedly urged him to stay, persisted in taking his departure.[3] His closest associate, Grolman, did the same, in a terse note to the king which said: 'In view of existing circumstances and of the distressing years I have lived through since 1815, I am compelled to resign.'[4] Simultaneously, because of Hardenberg's insistence, Humboldt and Beyme were dismissed from the *Staatsministerium*. The party of reaction had swept the board, and the last of the reformers had been driven from positions of power and responsibility.[5]

[1] It should be noted, however, that the king had been meditating a reorganization of the *Landwehr* since March. See Conrady, *Grolman*, iii. 74.

[2] Ibid.; Treitschke, *German History*, iii. 271; Schnabel, *Deutsche Geschichte*, ii. 320. Henceforth, the division was to consist of one brigade of the line, one *Landwehr* brigade, one cavalry brigade, plus artillery and technical troops.

[3] Meinecke, *Boyen*, ii. 381.

[4] Treitschke, *German History*, iii. 270.

[5] In a letter of December 1819 Clausewitz was critical of Boyen's resignation for precisely this reason, saying, 'I do not think it right to yield the battlefield so completely to the men of 1806'. See Kessel in *Historische Zeitschrift*, clxxv (1953), 53.

IV

Friedrich Meinecke has called the year 1819 the 'year of misfortune in the nineteenth century' and has always maintained that the ministerial crisis which brought it to an end was one of the most important turning points in German history.[1] At the risk of indulging in speculation, one can agree with this point of view. If Humboldt had been less doctrinaire in 1819, and if there had been a higher degree of tactical collaboration between Hardenberg, Boyen, Beyme, and himself, some measure of constitutional reform, providing for a national representative assembly and a degree of ministerial responsibility, might have been achieved. However limited such a grant might have been, it could have supplied a basis for future progress toward a more liberal form of government; it might have reduced the harsh antipathy which existed after 1819 between Prussia and the more liberal states of southern Germany; it might even have made possible a solution of the German question without resort to the kind of war that had to be waged in 1866, with southern Germany ranged in the enemy camp;[2] and, finally, it might, by providing a means of alleviating social tensions, have freed Prussia, and the Germany she came to dominate, from that complex of fears, frustrations, and belligerence which was to cause so much trouble to the rest of the world in the nineteenth and twentieth centuries.

It was impossible to hope for any of these things after 1819. The fall of Boyen and Humboldt effectively killed the plan for a national representative body. Hardenberg, it is true, persisted in his efforts to secure a constitutional grant, but he was now in a position of isolation, and his efforts finally came to nothing in 1821 when Wittgenstein and the crown prince, who was enamoured of highly romantic feudal concepts of government, persuaded the king to revive the old provincial estates instead of promulgating a general constitution.[3] In 1823 the king followed this advice and established eight provincial *Landtage*, which were designed, however, to meet only at three-year intervals and to possess only advisory powers. The additional fact that these bodies were dominated by the landed aristocracy made it unlikely that they would advocate any progressive ideas. Their

[1] Meinecke, *Erlebtes, 1862–1901*, p. 208; *1848: eine Säkularbetrachtung* (Bonn, 1948), p. 9.

[2] On this, see Hintze, *Staat und Verfassung*, ed. by Fritz Hartung (Leipzig, 1941), p. 439.

[3] Haake, in *Forschungen*, xxxii (1919), 165–7; Treitschke, *German History*, iii. 568 ff.

creation suggested rather a renewal of the old alliance between the Crown and the nobility against the social and political aspirations of the rest of the people; and this suggestion was further underlined by the progressive watering down of Stein's peasant reform and local government ordinances and by the continued retention of the patrimonial rights of justice by the *Rittergutsbesitzer* of the eastern districts.[1]

In the period of political reaction which now opened, however, Wittgenstein and his associates did not secure the fundamental changes in the constitution of the army which they desired. No thought was given to the revival of the canton system, and the principle of universal service was firmly maintained. Attempts were made, indeed, to make it more effective. In 1833, when it was recognized that Prussia's population was increasing at a faster rate than the ability to support the line army, and that consequently large numbers of Prussian youth were being exempted from service, the term of service was lowered provisionally from three years to two. It was hoped that this would make the application of the law of 1814 more equitable, that it would increase the number of recruits who passed through the line army, and that, in time, it would also improve the quality of the *Landwehr*, in which they were enrolled after their line service. The change of 1833 did not accomplish everything that was expected of it, but it brought some improvement and it maintained the fundamental principle of the law of 1814.[2]

With regard to the general efficiency of the army, the period after 1819 was marked by slow and steady progress. In the line army at least, important improvements were made in training programmes, basic equipment, artillery, and small arms; the Prussian army was the first in Europe, for instance, to be completely equipped with the new percussion small arms and, as early as the 30's, Dreyse was conducting the experiments which were to produce the famous needle-gun (*Zündnadelgewehr*) which was to help win the battle of Königgrätz.[3] There is little doubt,

[1] Schnabel, *Deutsche Geschichte*, ii. 287–98.

[2] Treitschke, *German History*, vi. 62–63; Meinecke, *Boyen*, ii. 459–62, 540 ff.

[3] Treitschke, *German History*, vi. 63. It was this breech-loading rifle which inspired an English versifier to write in 1866:

> The needle gun, the needle gun,
> The death-defying needle gun;
> It does knock over men like fun—
> What a formidable weapon is the needle-gun! *Punch*, li (1866), 31.

moreover, that in staff work the Prussian army was superior to any in Europe at this time.[1] The work which had been begun by Scharnhorst and Grolman was continued after 1819 by Müffling and Krauseneck. The duties of the General Staff were systematized, a Topographical Bureau and a Historical Section were established, annual reconnaissance tours (*Generalstabsreisen*) were introduced as a regular feature of staff training, and increasing care was taken in planning and criticizing the elaborate autumn manœuvres of the army. In the 30's a commission of the General Staff was making the first study of the importance of rail transport in troop mobilization, and this too was to have a decided effect upon Prussian superiority in the field in the 1860's. Finally, by the regular alternation of staff officers between the Great General Staff in Berlin and troop units, some of the lingering suspicion of these intellectuals began to die away.[2]

The administrative unity of the army which had been accomplished between 1809 and 1814 was also for the most part maintained, although there were intimations that this would not always be so. Even before Boyen's fall, the king had shown signs of a desire to revive the old *Generaladjutantur*. In 1816 he had made Colonel Job von Witzleben, the chief of the personnel section of the War Ministry, the head of his private correspondence bureau or Military Cabinet, and in 1818 he had increased the ambiguity of Witzleben's position by raising him to the rank of *Generalmajor* and appointing him *Generaladjutant*. Despite his great personal influence, however, Witzleben continued to regard the War Minister as his superior and, in his time, the Military Cabinet did not become the irresponsible agency which it became in the latter half of the century.[3] In the same way the reorganization of the General Staff as a department separate from the War Ministry in 1821 did not have the effect

[1] See especially Dallas D. Irvine, 'The Origin of Capital Staffs', *Journal of Modern History*, x (1938), 161–79; and 'The French and Prussian Staff Systems before 1870', *Journal of the American History Foundation*, ii (1938), 192–203.

[2] Müffling was Chief of the General Staff from 1821 to 1829; Krauseneck from 1829 to 1848. For their work, see Bronsart von Schellendorf, *Duties of the General Staff*, pp. 26 ff.; and Bockmann in *Von Scharnhorst zu Schlieffen*, pp. 121 ff. Some interesting details on the work of the Topographical Bureau and the Historical Section will be found in W. Bigge, *Moltke* (Munich, 1901), i. 31–34; Max Jähns, *Feldmarschall Moltke* (Berlin, 1894), pp. 32 ff.; Major Ollech, 'Reyher', *Militärwochenblatt* (Beihefte, 1879, nrs. 5–6), especially pp. 42–44; Albrecht Graf von Roon, *Denkwürdigkeiten* (Berlin, 1905), i. 92. On railroads see especially E. A. Pratt, *The Rise of Rail-Power in War and Conquest, 1833–1914* (New York, 1915).

[3] On this see especially Schmidt-Bückeburg, *Militärkabinett*, pp. 28–32.

of creating a competing agency, for the Chief of the General Staff had no access to the king except through the War Minister and he was specifically instructed to remain in an intimate relationship with the minister who was, in effect, his chief.[1] As in the case of the Military Cabinet, the separate and very fateful role of the General Staff was a thing of the future.

The fall of the reformers did, however, have other and less beneficial results. There is no doubt, for instance, that the social and educational reforms effected in the officer corps by Scharnhorst were weakened after 1819. General Hake, who was War Minister from 1819 to 1833, had none of the reformers' faith in education, and privately believed that an officer was competent if he could read, write, and figure. 'Just show me', he said on one occasion, 'anyone who later on had needed much more.'[2] While the general level of education remained much higher than it had been in the old régime, and while standards in the *Allgemeine Kriegsschule* were raised progressively by the efforts of men like Rühle von Lilienstern and Clausewitz,[3] educational deficiencies among the general run of officers were sufficiently glaring to require special regulations in 1836 and 1844, which ordered officers to improve their intellectual attainments so that the dignity of their calling could be preserved.[4] Moreover, in order to maintain the aristocratic preponderance in the officer corps, there was some deliberate evasion of the educational requirements for a commission. Between 1818 and 1839 the number of *Kadettenanstalten*, designed to give an education to the sons of the impoverished nobility, was doubled; officer candidates were admitted at the age of 11 on the recommendation of the commanding officers of the schools and with the approval of the king; and they were admitted to the army at the age of 17 regardless of the grade they had attained.[5]

Even more serious in its long-range results was the growth of professionalism in the army. After Boyen's fall, the younger officers ceased to be 'Boyensche' in their ideals and interests, and

[1] Huber, *Heer und Staat*, pp. 337–8; Meisner, *Der Kriegsminister*, p. 48; Wohlers, *Generalstab*, pp. 24–28.

[2] Reinhard Höhn, *Verfassungskampf und Heereseid: Der Kampf des Bürgertums um das Heer, 1815–1850* (Leipzig, 1938), p. 265.

[3] On Rühle, see the biographical sketch in *Militärwochenblatt* (Beihefte, Oct.–Dec. 1847).

[4] Demeter, *Deutsche Heer*, pp. 84–85.

[5] Sossidi, *Offizierkorps*, p. 69; Alfred Vagts, *A History of Militarism* (New York, 1937), pp. 180–1.

his conception of the enlightened citizen soldier who played a full and active role in the life of the society to which he belonged died away.[1] In its place there grew the concept of the army as a special calling, followed by technicians who were essentially separate from civilian society. The growth of this tendency can be found in the heated debates concerning the curriculum of the *Allgemeine Kriegsschule*, and the forced, although gradual, retreat of Rühle von Lilienstern from his insistence that his programme should include instruction in cultural, as well as purely military, subjects.[2] It can be found also in the military literature of the period, notably in Blesson's *Betrachtungen über die Befugnis des Militairs, an politischen Angelegenheiten des Vaterlands Theil zu nehmen*, published in 1821. Here the author argued that 'the soldier belongs to a special class', that as a professional he had no right to share in the politics of the day, and that to participate in—or even think about—matters which were not within the military sphere was dangerous, since 'the deliberating soldier is really no longer a soldier but a mutineer'.[3] In this attitude, one sees opening out once more that gulf between the military and civilian society which had had such ruinous effects before 1806.

There were, indeed, many other signs that the old antipathy between the army and the people was reasserting itself. The importance of the crisis of 1819 had not been lost upon the middle and lower classes. In the period of reaction that followed, came the first stirrings of an organized liberal movement in Prussia, a movement animated by desires for constitutional reform and for a foreign policy which would solve the nationalist aspirations of the German people by creating a united nation. Baulked of progress in either direction, the liberals became increasingly critical of the government and, simultaneously, of the army. It was in this period that the deification of the *Landwehr* began and that its achievements in the war of liberation began to be praised at the expense of the line army. It was in this period that the works of the south German writer Karl von Rotteck began to enjoy a wide popularity; and Prussian liberals faithfully repeated his arguments against the standing army, claiming that it was a tool of despotism, that its recruits were deliberately alienated from civilian society and indoctrinated

[1] Erich Marcks, *Männer und Zeiten* (Leipzig, 1912), i. 303–6.
[2] Schwertfeger, *Große Erzieher*, pp. 43 ff.
[3] Höhn, *Verfassungskampf*, pp. 222–3.

with scorn of humanitarian values and disrespect of law, that it was inimical to the development of industry and the arts and the sciences, and that it should be abolished and replaced by an expanded national militia.[1]

These high-flown arguments would have meant little if the government and the army itself had not acted in a way designed to give them validity. But the close—and to liberals unpopular—alliance with Austria after 1819 seemed to indicate that the king and his closest advisers were more interested in repressing liberal agitation than they were in fulfilling Prussia's national aspirations, and that they regarded the army less as a means of defence against the foreigner than as a weapon against their own people. This was, indeed, almost explicitly admitted in Rudloff's *Handbuch des preußischen Militärrechts*, which appeared with royal approval in 1826, and in the works of other professional military publicists, where the role of the army as 'a factor of order' in society was given great emphasis.[2] In addition, the brutality with which troops conducted themselves on occasions when they were, in fact, called out to preserve order—as in the case of disturbances among the journeymen tailors in Berlin in 1830[3] and during the so-called Fireworks Revolution of August 1835 in the same city[4]—seemed to indicate that the army was animated by a genuine contempt for civilians, as did numerous cases of caste arrogance on the part of individual officers.[5]

These abuses could not help but make the army an object of popular suspicion and dislike. In the years between 1819 and 1840 everything that Scharnhorst and his disciples had done to reconcile the military establishment with civilian society had been destroyed; the army was once more widely regarded as the main barrier to social progress; and it was clear that, in the event of a major domestic upheaval, its existence would be in jeopardy.

[1] On Rotteck, ibid., pp. 19 ff.

[2] Ibid., pp. 227–36, 252 ff.

[3] Treitschke, *German History*, v. 216.

[4] Veit Valentin, *Geschichte der deutschen Revolution, 1848–49* (Berlin, 1930), i. 55.

[5] See, for instance, the case of Blücher's grandson who, in 1823, cut down an actor named Stich in the course of a nocturnal love affair. Treitschke, *German History*, iv. 209. For other instances, see M. Boehn, *Biedermeier. Deutschland von 1815–1847* (Berlin, n.d.), pp. 285–7.

III

FREDERICK WILLIAM IV, THE ARMY AND THE CONSTITUTION 1840–58

'Damals lagen wir alle auf dem Bauche.'
FREDERICK WILLIAM IV, *recollecting the events of 18–19 March 1848.*

'Nur dadurch, daß das alte Verhältnis von König und Heer unangetastet bleibt, daß an dem ohne Beispiel dastehenden Verwachsensein beider nicht gerüttelt wird, kann das Heer bleiben was es ist, die feste Säule, auf der die Monarchie ruht.'
FREDERICK WILLIAM IV *to his ministers, 1 July 1849.*

IN the fourth decade of the nineteenth century the Prussian monarchy was once more shaken to its very foundations, although this time the upheaval was domestic rather than foreign in origin. The advent of a new ruler to the throne in 1840 heightened desires which had been frustrated in 1819 and encouraged the middle and lower classes to believe that an era of political and social reform was opening. The unwillingness of the new monarch to fulfil the expectations which he had aroused, however, and the simultaneous deepening of distress among the journeymen of the towns and the agricultural proletariat resulted in popular disorders of a kind unknown in previous Prussian history; and the ineptitude of the government in dealing with these led finally to the revolution in Berlin on 18 March 1848, during which the king was virtually taken prisoner by the populace of his capital and was forced temporarily to submit to its desires.

In the tumultuous political activity of 1848, the Prussian army played a decisive, if not *the* decisive, role. It was the conduct of the troops in the city and the attitude of their leaders, which precipitated the rising of 18 March; it was the confused, and not entirely intentional, withdrawal of the troops from the city on 19 March which placed the party of constitutional reform in effective control of events. Yet it was clearly realized by the leaders of that party that their position was insecure as long as they had not subordinated the military establishment to their control. Thus, when Prussia's first elected National Assembly convened in April 1848, the liberal groups which dominated it worked feverishly to introduce basic military reforms, to restrict the royal power of command over the armed forces, and to transform the army into a body whose first allegiance would be to the constitution which they had undertaken to create.

These efforts came to nothing. The inability of the liberal and democratic groups to concert on a constructive military programme prolonged the Assembly's work until the end of the year and gave the king and his closest advisers time in which to recover from the panic which had paralysed their will in March. In November 1848, after long and painful hesitation, the king ordered army detachments to re-enter Berlin; and, as Wrangel's hussars rode through the Brandenburger Tor, the liberal revolution came to an abrupt and sorry conclusion. A month later, it is true, Prussia received a constitution from the hands of her king, but it was a document which included few of the features desired by the liberals and one which, moreover, left untouched the military prerogatives of the Crown.

The events of 1848 could not help but widen the gulf which already existed between military and civilian society. The forced withdrawal from Berlin on 19 March in circumstances which resembled a military defeat was a humiliation which affected the officer corps as a whole and, in the ensuing period, this found natural expression in the heightened arrogance and contempt which marked their dealings with civilians. Of greater significance, perhaps, was the fact that in the highest ranks of the officer corps, and especially among those officers closest to the king, the memory of the March days was accompanied by a confirmed belief that a renewal of revolutionary agitation was certain in the near future. This conviction was so firmly held that, for ten years after 1848, these men tended to regard the army primarily as a domestic police force and to oppose any foreign policy which might lead to military commitments outside the borders of the state, even when Prussia's natural interests were involved. This attitude contributed to Prussia's capitulation to Austrian demands at Olmütz in 1850 and to the vacillations of her policy during the Crimean War, while simultaneously it increased the numbers of those who believed that the Prussian army had lost the spirit of 1740 and 1813 and had degenerated into a mere tool of domestic oppression.

I

Frederick William IV, the monarch who presided over these events, was a man whose character and talents have received more widely divergent historical judgements than any other Prussian ruler with the possible exception of William II, whom —it must be added—he resembled in marked particulars.[1] This difference of historical opinion is understandable if it is remembered that the king's contemporaries, and even his closest associates, experienced difficulty in making up their minds concerning their sovereign, and that their attitude alternated, as his reign progressed, between admiration, exasperation, and despair. 'The master's head', one of his ministers said in a tone of bafflement, 'is organized differently than that of other men';[2] and this sentiment, and the mood in which it was uttered, came to be widely shared.

Despite the amazing range of his interests, which led many people to regard him as a mere dilettante, Frederick William IV had genuine political ability. So stern a critic as Bismarck was to write that, in statesmanlike insight, the king often surpassed his ministers;[3] and it is certainly true that, in assessing a political situation and seeing the various factors involved, he was unequalled by any of his advisors. But this gift of analysis was not accompanied by the more substantial gifts of practicality and determination. Hintze has written that the king's character was more that of the artist than that of the practising politician.[4] Frederick William's penchant for abstruse theory, involved manœuvre, and complicated political combinations would seem to bear this out. He appeared, indeed, deliberately

[1] Judgements of the king range from the angry criticism of Treitschke (*German History*, vi. 304 ff.) to the measured defence of Max Lenz ('1848', *Preußische Jahrbücher*, xci (1898), 533–44) and, more recently, from the severe critique of Veit Valentin (*Deutsche Revolution*, i. 31–37) to the qualified admiration of Kurt Borries (*Preußen im Krimkrieg* (Stuttgart, 1930), *passim*). A good résumé of the literature on Frederick William IV will be found in Elisabeth Schmitz, *Edwin von Manteuffel als Quelle zur Geschichte Friedrich Wilhelms IV* (Berlin, 1921), pp. 3–15. There is no biography of the king which utilizes the abundant materials on his reign, although that of H. von Petersdorff, *König Friedrich Wilhelm der Vierte* (Stuttgart, 1900), is still useful if used with caution.

[2] Marcks, *Männer und Zeiten*, i. 266.

[3] See, however, Bismarck's considered opinion in his memoirs. Bismarck, *Die gesammelten Werke* (1st ed., Berlin, 1924 ff.) [hereafter cited as Bismarck, *G.W.*], xv. 190–1, 546–7.

[4] Hintze, *Die Hohenzollern*, pp. 516–17.

to avoid the direct and simple solutions to the problems of politics, as if they were beneath his dignity.[1] Combined with this, he possessed a dangerous tendency to irresolution when matters of importance were pressing for solution. This was not attributable to lack of will, for at frequent intervals in his reign, especially when his own principles were under attack, Frederick William showed that he had no lack of courage or steadfastness. But when the occasion demanded initiative and determination he was apt to be overcome by the complications which his foresight revealed to him and to sacrifice action to debate or speculation.

But even more dangerous than these qualities, especially in the first years of his reign, was the king's unfortunate, and unfailing, ability to arouse in others mistaken ideas concerning his intentions and objectives. A man of great personal charm and endowed with superb oratorical gifts,[2] Frederick William was able to move assemblies of his subjects to transports of enthusiasm which in the end were generally proved to be misplaced. It was this above all which made the early years of his reign 'a long concatenation of misunderstandings'.[3] In his first appearances before his subjects—in that dramatic moment in the coronation in Berlin, for instance, in which he spoke directly to the throng of the intimate ties between a monarch and his people and asked them for an open manifestation of their allegiance—Frederick William appeared in the mantle of the liberal ruler who was determined to sweep away the reactionary prohibitions of the past and to inaugurate a period of progress and reform; and this impression was strengthened by such early actions as the lightening of restrictions on the press and the recalling of Hermann von Boyen to the direction of the Ministry of War.[4] In view of these things it was perhaps natural for those sections of society which were suffering economic distress to look upon the new ruler as one who would solve their problems, and for all those who had absorbed the doctrines of western liberalism to regard him as a potential supporter of their demands. These assumptions were, none the less, ill-founded.

[1] Leopold von Gerlach, *Denkwürdigkeiten* (2 vols., Berlin, 1892), i. 510, 514.

[2] Erich Kaeber, *Berlin 1848* (Berlin, 1948), p. 27.

[3] Treitschke, *German History*, vi. 308.

[4] On Boyen's appointment, see the letters of the king reprinted in Boyen, *Erinnerungen*, vol. iii, pp. ix–x.

The king's oratorical flights were not without significance, but they marked his remoteness from the interests and desires of his subjects rather than his identification with them. He could call upon his people to give oral expression to their allegiance because this gesture appealed to his sense of the dramatic and because it recalled to his romantic imagination a time when German warriors beat upon their shields while their new chief was crowned. But at the same time, Frederick William never for a moment doubted that allegiance was owed to a king as a matter of right. He had a much more exalted conception of his office than any of his predecessors; and, in a world which was becoming increasingly dominated by industrialism, he was one of the few remaining rulers who sincerely believed in the divine right of kings.[1] In view of this, there could scarcely be any fundamental agreement between him and the growing party which advocated liberal reform. To Frederick William all of the doctrines of liberalism were pernicious outgrowths of the French Revolution, that apocalyptic horror which had disturbed the divine order.[2]

The appointment of Boyen, the granting of an amnesty to political prisoners, the cessation of that censorship and thought-control which had been associated with the Carlsbad Decrees and the other liberal actions with which the king inaugurated his reign, were dictated primarily by a romantic desire to appear as a wise and magnanimous father of his people;[3] they had no deeper significance, and the king himself was doubtless surprised by the reaction they aroused. In any event, he discovered very quickly that his first acts of state had created a difficult, and potentially dangerous, situation. The general impression in the country was that the reforming activity of the period of liberation was now to be resumed and that, specifically, the constitution and the national representative assembly which Frederick William III had promised, but never granted, would quickly be established. The newspaper press, which—thanks to the king's orders—was permitted to print political material for the first time in a generation, eagerly discussed the constitutional question; dozens of pamphlets and fly-sheets appeared, citing abuses which should be corrected by the supposedly pending

[1] Petersdorff, *Friedrich Wilhelm*, pp. 1–3.

[2] Valentin, *Deutsche Revolution*, i. 31.

[3] Hintze, *Die Hohenzollern*, p. 519.

legislation;[1] the king was the recipient of numerous petitions, including one from Oberpräsident von Schön, who argued that a constitutional grant would be the logical conclusion of the work of 1807–13;[2] and Boyen—who, to his great embarrassment, was surrounded by enthusiastic crowds singing *Landwehr* songs whenever he appeared in public[3]—was so impressed by the general air of expectation that he warned the king that something must be done to satisfy it.[4]

All of this was highly irritating to Frederick William and seemed, indeed, to verge upon treasonable presumption. He made it quite clear to Schön and Boyen that he had not the slightest intention of issuing a written constitution. Simultaneously, he rejected any suggestion of a truly national legislative assembly elected by the people, and devised a highly complicated substitute, which took more than five years to elaborate and which pleased no one when it was finally revealed to the public in February 1847. The king did make a grudging concession to the desire for an assembly. The February patent of 1847 stipulated that the existing provincial *Landtage* should, at the king's pleasure, be summoned to meet as a united diet and should, on those occasions, be privileged to approve state loans and new or increased taxes, to give advice concerning pending government action, and to address petitions to the monarch, with the understanding that no petition should be re-submitted once it had been rejected by the Crown. But Frederick William's obvious intention of convoking this body as infrequently as possible was made clear in the simultaneous creation of two additional bodies: a standing committee on the state debt which was to be elected by the united diet and which was authorized to report to it when it re-convened; and a larger committee, comprising delegates elected by the provincial diets, which would meet every four years and which would have precisely the same functions as the united diet itself. Why there should be three overlapping agencies instead of the one assembly which was generally desired, the February patent did not make clear. The glaring duplication of function, and the extreme vagueness in the definition of the powers assigned to the three new bodies, bewildered and disgusted those who had expected

[1] On the newspaper agitation see Boehn, *Biedermeier*, pp. 111 ff.

[2] See Hintze, *Die Hohenzollern*, p. 521.

[3] Treitschke, *German History*, vii. 400–1.

[4] Meinecke, *Boyen*, ii. 570 ff.

something which would be comparable to the legislative assemblies of England and France.[1]

Their disappointment deepened when the first united diet was assembled in Berlin on 11 April 1847. In his opening address to this body Frederick William flatly avowed his repugnance for the doctrines of the constitutional reformers. 'No power on earth', he said, 'will ever force me to transform the natural relationship . . . between prince and people into a conventional, constitutional one; neither now nor ever will I permit a written piece of paper to force itself, like some second providence, between our Lord God in heaven and this land, to rule us with its paragraphs and, through them, to replace the ancient sacred loyalty.' He called upon the delegates to abjure the radical theories of liberalism which would undermine the state and the church; he reminded them that they represented the estates of the realm—the aristocracy, the *bourgeoisie*, and the peasantry—and not the people as a whole; he added that an assembly which tried to be responsive to public opinion was 'un-German' and would inevitably come into conflict with the Crown; and he concluded this homily by asserting that a Prussian king must rule in obedience to the laws of God and the country and in accordance with his own free will; he neither could, nor should, rule in accordance with the will of the majority.[2]

No assembly thus admonished could be expected to go about its business in a happy frame of mind. In the sessions of the united diet, the long accumulating exasperation over the king's handling of the constitutional issue was given full expression. Frederick William was not, of course, without defenders, including one young and very *farouche* deputy named Bismarck-Schönhausen who in his maiden speech not only attacked the basic conceptions of the constitutional reformers but found occasion also to challenge the liberal theory that the rising of 1813 had been successful because the people had been fighting for political freedom as well as for liberation from French domination.[3] On the other hand, many delegates who were normally conservative in their political views joined with the advocates of liberal reform in attacking the inadequacies of the

[1] On the February patent of 1847, see Fritz Hartung, *Deutsche Verfassungsgeschichte vom 15. Jahrhundert bis zur Gegenwart* (2. Aufl., Leipzig, 1922), p. 151.

[2] Hintze, *Die Hohenzollern*, p. 525.

[3] Bismarck, *G.W.*, x. 3–4; Erich Eyck, *Bismarck: Leben und Werk* (3 vols., Zürich, 1941–4), i. 64–66.

February patent and in petitioning the king for an extension of the powers of the united diet, for the recognition of its right to meet at two-year intervals, and for the abolition of the separate committee of delegates from the provincial diets. When the king held firmly to his declared policy, these delegates became as stubborn and as unco-operative as their sovereign. Thus, the elections of the delegations for the supplementary committees were accompanied by bitter protests and numerous abstentions; and later, when the king requested approval of two important state loans, he was met by an uncompromising refusal. After this, it was hopeless to expect that any useful work would be accomplished; and the diet was dissolved in a general atmosphere of recrimination and disillusionment.

The first united diet was not, however, without historical significance. If they had done nothing else, the debates had clarified the great issue of the day. They had convinced many of the delegates—and many of those who read the exhaustive press accounts of the diet's sessions—that the king, despite all his rhetorical flourishes, was a convinced absolutist at heart and that political and social progress would not be achieved with his help. Once the king was seen for what he was, there came, throughout the country, a definite hardening of opposition to the Crown and to those weapons with which it maintained its absolute authority.

Chief among those weapons was the regular army, and it is significant that, in the last stages of the session of the united diet, representatives of the *bourgeoisie* had seen fit to attack the social privileges of the officer corps, the inequities of military justice, and the dangerous antipathy which existed between the army and civil society.[1] These attacks came to nothing at this time, but they revealed at least an additional reason for the growing unpopularity of the king among the middle and lower classes. At the outset of his reign it had been expected that he would check the growing arrogance of the officer corps and the misconduct of troops toward civilians; and his appointment of Boyen as War Minister had seemed an earnest of his intention to return to the military ideals of the reform period. These expectations had been betrayed, and the abuses of the army had not only continued but were by now a dangerous threat to social peace.

[1] Valentin, *Deutsche Revolution*, i. 74.

Boyen's second term as War Minister was characterized by constructive work which further increased the technical proficiency of the army. Under his direction the rations and pay of officers and men were improved, a revised code of military punishments and a perfected manual on marksmanship were issued, some improvements were made in the curriculum of the superior military schools, and—most important—the whole army was equipped with the Dreyse needle-gun.[1] On the other hand, his return to the War Ministry had no effect upon the prevailing tendencies within the army—the trend to professionalism, the increasing political conservatism of the officer corps, and the steady alienation of the military establishment from civilian society. His personal authority was by no means as great as it had been in 1814; he had serious differences of opinion with such subordinates in the ministry as General Reyher and his aide Griesheim; and his orders were challenged frequently by the commanding generals—notably by the Prince of Prussia, commanding the *Gardekorps*, by Prince Charles, and by Count Friedrich Dohna, the commandant at Königsberg, all men of inflexibly conservative, if not reactionary, views who regarded Boyen with grave suspicion. Of even graver import was the fact that the king himself, despite the honours with which he loaded Boyen at the outset of his reign, made little attempt to support his War Minister in disputes. As a result Boyen was gradually reduced to the position of a liberal figure-head who was retained because of his popular appeal but who had no real authority.[2]

Certainly it was ironical that during this last term of a man who had striven throughout his life to reconcile the soldier and the civilian, there were more frequent and more bloody clashes between the military and civilians than at any time in previous Prussian history. In 1844, for instance, the whole city of Königsberg was aroused when a young lieutenant named Leithold accused a local barrister of *lèse majesté*, called him out, and killed him in a duel. In face of a widespread agitation in the officer corps for Leithold's complete exoneration, Boyen insisted upon appropriate punishment. He had only partial success, however,

[1] Meinecke, *Boyen*, ii. 536–7; Rabenau in *Militärwissenschaftliche Rundschau*, iii (1938), 37.

[2] See, for instance, Meinecke, *Boyen*, ii. 570 ff., although the author elsewhere tends to minimize the whittling away of Boyen's authority.

and his attempt to assuage the inflamed public temper in Königsberg was in any case counteracted by the king's insistence upon intervening personally in the affair. When the burghers of the city criticized the conduct of the local garrison in general, Frederick William charged them with disloyalty and warned them haughtily that persistence in this attitude would lead him to withdraw his favour from them.[1]

The Königsberg affair was not without an element of humour, for it threatened at times to degenerate into a debate concerning the right of officers of the king to walk in public parks. In subsequent years, however, there were much uglier affairs. In August 1846, during the annual *Martinskirmeß* in Köln, serious disorders broke out when the police tried to stop the jokes and demonstrations which, as usual, marked this popular festival. Troops had to be called in to quell the disturbances, and these acted with an enthusiastic brutality which caused widespread indignation.[2] The number of incidents of this kind was increased by the sharpening of economic distress in the mid-forties. In the towns this period was marked by a steady advance of industrialism with all the social dislocations which this implied, while the rural areas experienced a series of poor harvests, a steady depression of agricultural wages, and a high incidence of typhus and cholera. In view of the apparent inability, or unwillingness, of the government to do anything to alleviate this situation, unemployed artisans and the agricultural proletariat indulged in sporadic but belligerent demonstrations. The municipal and rural police were usually inadequate to control these, and there was an increasing tendency for local bureaucrats to call for troops at the first sign of trouble. Before 1847 there had—in addition to the Köln affair—been pitched battles between troops and workers in most of the garrison towns and in the weaving districts of Silesia;[3] and the opening of the united diet in 1847 coincided with the outbreak of the so-called 'Potato Rebellion' in Berlin, during which mobs, incensed by the high price of potatoes, rioted and plundered for three days until order was restored by the Alexander Regiment, the Gardekürassiere, and a battalion of Franconian troops which were rushed to

[1] Ibid., p. 577; Treitschke, *German History*, vii. 408–9. Valentin (*Deutsche Revolution*, i. 43) has the lawyer killing the lieutenant, in addition to other inaccuracies.

[2] Valentin, *Deutsche Revolution*, i. 60–61.

[3] Ibid., 57–60.

Berlin.[1] This repeated employment of troops for police purposes made the uniform an object of hatred to the working classes; and the army authorities fed this popular antipathy by deliberately discouraging any fraternization between troops and civilians and by changing garrisons at regular intervals so that the soldiers should acquire no deep affection for the garrison town or its inhabitants and should thus have no sentimental qualms when asked to use musket butt or bayonet against them.[2]

As the year 1848 opened, the atmosphere of optimism and hope which had surrounded the accession of Frederick William IV had been completely dissipated. The reform-conscious middle classes had lost all confidence in their ruler, in his chosen ministers, and in the army whose abuses he condoned. The city and rural working classes had long ago concluded that the government's only answer to economic distress was the employment of force to prevent its being called to their attention. Although very few in the governing class seemed aware of the impending danger, the situation had deteriorated so far that continued obtuseness on the part of the government would inevitably produce a domestic upheaval of drastic proportions. Obtuseness, however, was a commodity with which the king, his ministers, and his army chiefs were well supplied, as the events of March were to prove.

II

On 23 February 1848 the government of Louis Philippe of France was overthrown by revolution, an event which aroused feverish excitement throughout Germany and which was in the end succeeded by similar risings in all the major capitals, including Berlin. In view of the wide incidence of revolution in 1848, some Prussian historians, especially those who are sympathetic to Frederick William IV, have argued that nothing could have prevented what happened in Berlin in March.[3] This thesis has the great advantage of being incapable of disproof, yet it is not very satisfactory. A close review of the actions of the Prussian government in the three weeks which intervened between the Paris rising and that in Berlin makes it difficult to avoid the conclusion that, whether revolution was inevitable or not, the men

[1] Kaeber, *Berlin 1848*, pp. 12–13.

[2] Valentin, *Deutsche Revolution*, i. 60.

[3] See, for instance, Max Lenz in *Preußische Jahrbücher*, xci (1898), 535.

who were governing Prussia at this critical hour did everything in their power to make it so. And this was especially true of the most highly placed officers of the army, who betrayed an appalling degree of political short-sightedness and military incompetence.

Perhaps the most significant characteristic of military thinking, once the news from Paris had been received, was a stubborn insistence that the remorseless employment of military force was the only means of preventing a repetition of the Paris experience in Berlin. Although several of the king's civilian advisers were convinced that it was not too late for the king to retrieve his position and that immediate concessions to the widespread demands for constitutional and social reform would end the disorders which were now breaking out, none of the officers in contact with the King—with the possible exception of General von Pfuehl, the military governor of Berlin—had any sympathy with this point of view.[1]

They argued that the disorders were being fomented by hordes of alien revolutionaries and agents of foreign powers—a suggestion that was demonstrably false[2]—and that concessions of any kind would be so evident a sign of weakness that they would jeopardize the security of the throne. It is possible to detect in these arguments a desire to force the issue. Some of the most influential military leaders seem to have awaited the beginning of the shooting with actual eagerness and to have feared only that something might intervene to prevent the *battue*. This was certainly the attitude of the king's *Generaladjutant*, Leopold von Gerlach, who insisted that 'the only way to combat the revolution was to avoid concessions of any kind and, instead of calling *Landtage*, to assemble an army'.[3] It seems also to have represented the views of the Prince of Prussia, who wanted to have it understood that, once troops were committed to the streets, they would be authorized to use their weapons

[1] See the testimony of the state councillor Nobiling who was in close contact with all the military leaders in Berlin at this time. Felix Rachfahl, 'König Friedrich Wilhelm IV und die Berliner Märzrevolution im Lichte neuer Quellen', *Preußische Jahrbücher*, cx (1902), 277–9.

[2] The story of the foreign agitators is repeated faithfully in Meyerinck, 'Die Tätigkeit der Truppen während der Berliner Märztage des Jahres 1848', *Militär-wochenblatt* (Beihefte, 1891), pp. 99 ff. For convincing evidence concerning its falsity, see Rachfahl, pp. 291–2 and Rudolf Stadelmann, *Soziale und politische Geschichte der Revolution von 1848* (Munich, 1948), p. 46.

[3] Gerlach, *Denkwürdigkeiten*, i. 130–1.

since 'the masses must see that they can accomplish nothing against the military'.[1]

The chief fear of the soldiers was that the king might fail them. Frederick William's unsoldierly bearing, his awkwardness in the saddle, and his propensity for making jokes about his own mistakes at military reviews had long irritated them and made them suspect that he lacked the virtues of his forebears;[2] while his February patent of 1847—which had seemed so inadequate to liberals—had appeared to them as a revolutionary gesture which proved the king's political unreliability. Generalleutnant von Prittwitz—who had commanded the troops during the Berlin disorders of 1847 and who now, early in March, was made assistant to the easy-going military governor of Berlin—was particularly fearful lest the king should be persuaded to make political concessions. In his conversations with the king, Prittwitz urged first, that the Berlin garrisons be reinforced as quickly as possible and, second, that the king and his family should withdraw from the city. Meanwhile, the general privately ordered his officers to keep complete written records of their duty assignments and to collect any written material 'which some day will give chapter and verse concerning events which are still hidden in the bosom of the future'.[3] This curious order was plainly designed to protect the army from responsibility for any quixotic gesture on the part of their royal commander; and it is an interesting indication of the army's gnawing fear that the king might be less determined to defend the absolutist system of the past than the army itself.

For these military fears there was some excuse, for the king's conduct was ambiguous in the extreme. He was obviously impressed by the sharp increase in political agitation in his capital city—an increase which was due not only to the news from Paris but also to such things as the partial shut-down of the Borsig works and other firms in consequence of the prevailing trade depression.[4] But in face of the growing popular turbulence he

[1] Karl Haenchen, 'Neue Briefe und Berichte aus den Berliner Märztagen des Jahres 1848', *Forschungen zur brandenburgischen und preußischen Geschichte*, xlix (1937), 262.

[2] See, for instance, Prinz Kraft zu Hohenlohe-Ingelfingen, *Aus meinem Leben* (4 vols., Berlin, 1897–1907), i. 4; Rachfahl in *Preußische Jahrbücher*, cx (1902), 461–2.

[3] Karl Haenchen, 'Aus dem Nachlaß des Generals von Prittwitz', *Forschungen zur brandenburgischen und preußischen Geschichte*, xlv (1933), 101–2.

[4] Valentin, *Deutsche Revolution*, i. 416–18.

followed no clear line of policy, but tacked erratically between the line proposed by his ministers and that championed by his military advisers. When the former urged that a liberal gesture was necessary to allay public opinion, the king showed his customary talent for procrastination and when, finally, on 6 March, he appeared to give in, it was only to announce that he had decided to approve the right of the united diet to meet periodically—a concession which satisfied no one. On the other hand, Frederich William refused to commit himself to the policy of complete intransigence desired by the soldiers. He did authorize the summoning of reinforcements from garrisons in Potsdam, Frankfurt an der Oder, Halle, and Stettin, but he could not be prevailed upon to discuss seriously the possibility of fighting in the city, to issue clear orders to his commanders against the eruption of such fighting, or to clarify the muddled relationship between the military governor of Berlin, the *Stadtkommandant* (General von Ditfurth), the commander of the *Gardekorps* and General von Prittwitz.[1] Nor would he make up his mind to leave Berlin.[2]

This studied avoidance of a policy was an invitation to trouble. On the one hand, the city filled up with troops—for the most part raw recruits from rural areas under the command of ambitious young officers who were burning with a desire to teach the city *canaille* a lesson; on the other, political meetings and demonstrations in favour of far-reaching constitutional and social changes now became daily occurrences. Given this juxtaposition of forces, clashes were likely, and they were now made certain by the action of the president of police, Minutoli, an official whose gifts of persuasion were superior to his judgement. Minutoli's police force comprised only 40 sergeants and 120 gendarmes and although he was empowered to organize a voluntary force of auxiliaries—the so-called *Bürgerschutzkommission*—he had no confidence in his ability to control the situation; and he convinced the king that army troops should be authorized to support the police and, by their presence, to overawe the lower classes whose insolence, he argued, was

[1] On the confusion of military command in Berlin, see Haenchen in *Forschungen*, xlix (1937), 256–7; and Rachfahl in *Preußische Jahrbücher*, cx (1902), 271–4.

[2] The king later said that, as early as 14 March, he had wanted to leave Berlin but had been persuaded to stay. Rachfahl, p. 288. See also Gerlach, *Denkwürdigkeiten*, i. 133, and E. L. von Gerlach, *Aufzeichnungen aus seinem Leben und Wirken* (2 vols., Schwerin, 1903), ii. 8.

becoming insupportable.[1] The king's assent touched off the series of bloody incidents which began on 13 March and culminated in the pitched battles of the 18th and 19th.

The mere appearance of troop detachments in the streets reawakened memories of the *Feuerwerkskrawall* of 1835 and the Potato Rebellion of 1847, and served to inflame the public temper. Whereas most of the public meetings attended by Berliners since the rising in Paris had been conducted in a temperate and even jocular atmosphere, those held under the surveillance of troops took on a spirit of open hostility to the government. Marching columns were jeered at by the crowds, and individual soldiers were insulted and, in some cases, attacked. The troops in their turn, made nervous by this universal hostility, began to lash back brutally at their tormentors whenever an occasion presented itself. On 13 March a detachment of cavalry broke up a meeting on Unter den Linden and there was some hacking at the crowd which resulted in minor casualties;[2] on the 14th a squadron of *Gardekürassiere* launched a pointless attack upon ten civilians in the Brüderstraße;[3] and on the 15th a gathering outside the *Schloß* was dispersed by infantry which fired into the crowd.[4] The 16th of March was marked by even more serious clashes. Another demonstration near the *Schloß* was dispersed by cavalry, and serious bloodshed was prevented only when General von Pfuehl intervened personally and countermanded the Prince of Prussia's orders which had authorized the officers to commence firing if the crowd hesitated to disband.[5] On the same day, in the vicinity of the Opera House, some members of the *Bürgerschutzkommission*—perhaps over impressed by their new authority and the beauty of their white brassards and truncheons—manhandled a peaceful crowd and were attacked in turn by it. While they were retreating in

[1] On Minutoli's role, see Kaeber, *Berlin 1848*, pp. 38 ff.

[2] Valentin, *Deutsche Revolution*, i. 421.

[3] A. Wolff, *Berliner Revolutions-Chronik* (Berlin, 1852), i. 73 ff.

[4] See the eyewitness accounts assembled by Haenchen in *Forschungen*, xlv (1933), 110 ff., and the semi-official account by Meyerinck in *Militärwochenblatt* (Beihefte, 1891), pp. 104–6.

[5] Pfuehl stepped between the troops and the crowd, saying to the company commanders: 'I am old enough and will gladly risk my life if I can spare the blood of citizens.' Kaeber, *Berlin 1848*, p. 47. The Prince of Prussia protested against his action, saying that it 'compromised' the army, and Pfuehl tendered his resignation—although it was not accepted. Valentin, *Deutsche Revolution*, i. 424. See also Gerlach, *Denkwürdigkeiten*, i. 131.

disorder, a detachment of troops commanded by a Captain von Cosel appeared on the scene and directed a fusillade of shots which caused several deaths.[1] News of this last incident spread with amazing rapidity; hatred of the military now became general; and it is perhaps significant that the first attempts at building barricades took place on the same day.

The seriousness of all this could not escape the king. Even before the first bloodshed in Berlin, he had been receiving anxious messages from the provincial *Oberpräsidenten* saying that they could not be held responsible for the security of their provinces if the government did not take some ameliorative action and suggesting that at least the united diet should be convoked as quickly as possible. On 14 March the king had made up his mind to follow this advice and to have that body meet at the end of April.[2] The sharp deterioration of the situation in Berlin, however, and the staggering news which was received on the 16th, to the effect that Vienna had risen in revolt and that Metternich had fled the city, persuaded the monarch to go even further. In a remarkable change of heart—and one which affected the Prince of Prussia and Leopold von Gerlach with indignation and despair—he authorized his minister Bodelschwingh[3] to prepare a patent which was designed to satisfy the political desires of his subjects. This document, which Frederick William signed late in the night of 17 March, announced that the united diet would assemble on 2 April, that the demands for an extension of its powers, made at the previous session, would be granted, and that the king was prepared now to grant a constitution to the nation. Frederick William took note also of the intense interest of his subjects in the German question by promising to initiate action calling for a thorough reform of the Germanic Confederation,[4] and, in a supplementary statement, he announced the lifting of all restrictions upon the press.[5]

So comprehensive were these declarations that they touched on virtually all of the demands which were raised most

[1] Rachfahl in *Preußische Jahrbücher*, cx (1902), 277; Haenchen in *Forschungen*, xlv (1933), 114 ff.

[2] Petersdorff, *Friedrich Wilhelm*, pp. 74 ff.

[3] On Bodelschwingh, see Treitschke, *German History*, vii. 430.

[4] On the king's position concerning the question of German unity, see below, pp. 128 ff.

[5] Gerlach told Bodelschwingh that he would rather have cut off his own hand than sign these edicts. Gerlach, *Denkwürdigkeiten*, i. 133–4.

frequently at political meetings and demonstrations, with one significant exception. Nothing was said about the withdrawal of the troops from Berlin, something which, in view of the incidents of 16 March, was desired generally throughout the city. At least one of the king's aides, General von Pfuehl, the governor of Berlin, recognized the gravity of this omission and recommended that the troops brought in from the provinces be returned to their normal garrisons, while the local contingents should be temporarily confined to their *Kaserne*.[1] The king not only paid no attention to this but, on the morning of the 18th, yielded to the desires of some of his more reactionary confidantes, like Generals von Alvensleben and Rauch, and transferred the command of all troops in Berlin from Pfuehl to General von Prittwitz.[2] Because of this action, Frederick William must bear much of the responsibility for what happened on the afternoon of 18 March.

Certainly it seems clear that, but for the presence of the military, the 18th would have been a day of civic rejoicing and general relaxation of tension. During the morning the king received delegations from the city magistracy and from the municipal governments of other towns. He explained the forthcoming concessions to them and graciously received their expressions of relief and gratitude. At about two o'clock in the afternoon, the patents signed on the previous evening were promulgated and were received with immediate and general enthusiasm. A huge throng, comprising both working-class people and members of the wealthier and more substantial strata of society, converged upon the palace and forced their way into the *Schloßplatz* with the evident intention of paying tribute to their sovereign. After the unhappy troubles of the past week, Berlin seemed about to fall into a carnival mood.

As the throng entered the palace square, however, General von Prittwitz was oppressed with fears concerning the king's personal safety and, placing himself at the head of a detachment of cavalry, rode slowly toward the crowd, ordering it to disperse. At the sight of the uniforms, the happy mood of the demonstrators disappeared at once. Menacing shouts of '*Militär zurück*!'

[1] Valentin, *Deutsche Revolution*, i. 426 ff.

[2] The transfer was effected very suddenly while Pfuehl was absent from the castle on a brief visit to his family. See Rachfahl in *Preußische Jahrbücher*, cx (1902), 290–1.

were raised and there was a general surge toward the horses. It was at this point that Major von Falkenstein, seeing Prittwitz hemmed in by angry civilians, undertook on his own responsibility to lead two companies of the Kaiser Franz Infantry Regiment into the square. As these became involved in the confused mêlée, the rifles of two men in the foremost rank of the first company were discharged, either because of the nervousness of the soldiers or of the jostling of the crowd. There was a moment of transfixed silence, and then a howl of 'Treachery!' from the throng, followed by a scattered volley from the troops. Horrified, several of the king's civilian aides and some members of the municipal government, who had been watching from the palace windows, rushed to the square and sought to restore order. They were listened to neither by the enraged citizenry nor the now thoroughly aroused troops. Grimly and methodically, the infantry cleared the square, but the crowd withdrew only to carry word of the incident to the rest of the city and, before the soldiers' work was done, barricades were being erected across all the principal approaches to the castle and the city was in a state of revolt.[1]

The first reaction of the army, both officers and men, to these events seems to have been one of relief. Prittwitz wrote later: 'Extremely beneficial to the soldiers was the feeling of having finally shaken off the burden of the mass of the people, of having a definite enemy in front of them and of having reached the end of the hitherto existing trial of their patience.'[2] The majority of the high-ranking officers in the royal castle were relieved because the outbreak of fighting seemed to simplify the issues. It was simply a matter now of persuading the king to leave the city until the army completed the job of restoring order. At a meeting in the castle shortly after the incident in the *Schloßplatz*, it was suggested that the king retire to Potsdam at once. An officer who was, within a matter of months, to enjoy the full confidence of the king, Rittmeister Edwin von Manteuffel, adjutant to Prince Albrecht, objected to this, saying that the

[1] This famous incident has been described many times. Some interesting eye-witness accounts will be found in Karl Haenchen, *Revolutionsbriefe 1848* (Leipzig, 1930), pp. 49 ff., and in the same author's article in *Forschungen*, vol. xlv (1933) which includes Major von Falkenstein's explanation of the shots which began the engagement. The official military version of the incident will be found in Meyerinck, *Militärwochenblatt* (Beihefte, 1891), esp. pp. 112 ff.

[2] Kaeber, *Berlin 1848*, p. 71.

king was, after all, a descendant of Frederick the Great, who would never have considered such a retreat. At this point, General von Thile, a close military adviser of the king since 1840, turned upon Manteuffel and said sharply:

> You stay out of this with your emotional speechifying. In the first place, no man knows what Frederick the Great would have done in such a case; in the second place, the king can very well be a descendant without being Frederick the Great himself. The situation is very serious, and it is necessary to take measures against Berlin which it would be not at all seemly to carry out under the eye of the king and which his heart would not permit to be carried out in his presence. The way things stand, and in view of the king's character (*Individualität*), he must leave, and he must give orders to the commanding general, authorizing him, independently and on his own responsibility, to bring Berlin unconditionally to order.[1]

The military, however, soon made two unpleasant discoveries. In the first place, the king would neither leave the city nor relinquish complete control to the army chiefs. Throughout the 18th and the 19th he remained in the castle, sunk for the most part in a bewildered torpor but sporadically summoning up his energy and issuing orders which contravened the military designs. In the second place, the army leaders learned to their surprise that the restoration of order was not going to be an easy matter.

Immediately after the incident in the *Schloßplatz*, the troops had sallied forth from the castle and from the other garrisons in the city and set about the job of reducing the barricades and dispersing those who defended them. Theoretically, this should have been no difficult task. The barricade fighters were manual workers, led for the most part by students whose enthusiasm was greater than their military skill. They were poorly armed, often with nothing but clubs and paving stones, and, with the exception of two small and erratic guns, had no artillery. The barricades had been hastily built and were often placed at unstrategic points; while communication between the various strong-points held by the burghers was never effectively maintained.[2] But the military, too, suffered from grave disadvantages. As has already been pointed out, the majority of the troops were new recruits, and, while they were led by experienced

[1] Rachfahl in *Preußische Jahrbücher*, cx (1902), 302–3.

[2] Valentin, *Deutsche Revolution*, i. 430.

officers, their leaders knew little about the kind of fighting they were now expected to do. The army manuals had nothing to say about street fighting. It was not, indeed, until Cavaignac had subdued Paris and Windischgrätz had retaken Vienna that theories concerning the proper way to take corner houses began to be formulated and the relative advantages of frontal and oblique assaults on barricades were discussed scientifically.[1] Bewildered by the complexity of the city streets, continually frustrated by the re-building of obstacles in districts which they had fancied they had cleared, and disconcerted by unorthodox missiles like chimney pots and boiling water which dropped on their heads from the roofs above, the troops found their task hazardous and wearying.[2] Apart from some isolated engagements near the various garrisons and at the Friedrichsbrücke and the Cölnisches Rathaus,[3] Prittwitz's main effort was directed from the *Schloßplatz* northward along Königsstraße in the direction of the *Alexanderplatz*. It took his troops four hours to reach the edge of this last objective, and when a lull in the fighting intervened at 7.30 in the evening, the progress made was not very encouraging.

On the evening of the 18th, Georg von Vincke, a moderate conservative who had led the opposition party in the first united diet, went to the castle to urge the king to do everything in his power to end the fighting. He argued that the troops would have to be withdrawn, since they were weary, badly supplied, and very close to complete discouragement. 'What should I do?', asked the king. 'What if the people win?' Vincke answered.[4] It was a troubling question, and the king doubtless thought of it at midnight when he had a long interview with Prittwitz. The general now seemed prey to many new doubts and fears. He explained that his plan was to take a section of the city and to await the effect of this upon the populace. He added, however, that if the rising continued for more than a couple of days, his troops would be at a decided disadvantage. They were not

[1] See the interesting remarks on street fighting by the noted civilian writer on military affairs, Bernhardi, in *Aus dem Leben Theodor von Bernhardis* (9 vols., Leipzig, 1893–1906), iii. 260.

[2] The general nature of the fighting is described in Haenchen in *Forschungen*, xlix (1937), 258 ff.; by Meyerinck in *Militärwochenblatt* (Beihefte, 1891), 115 ff.; and in Generalkommando des Gardekorps, 'Zum 18. März 1848', *Preußische Jahrbücher*, cxii (1903), 327 ff.

[3] Gerlach, *Denkwürdigkeiten*, i. 136–7.

[4] Schmitz, *Manteuffel als Geschichtsquelle*, p. 36.

in sufficient number to take the city street by street, and new reinforcements from outside the city could not be authorized without jeopardizing the security of other centres. The barricade fighters already had the great advantage of complete familiarity with the terrain; and a prolongation of the fighting would accustom them to action under fire. Prittwitz cited a French theory, from Maison's critique of Marshal Marmont's conduct of the street fighting in Paris in 1830, to the effect that failure to put down a rising within the first days should be followed by a withdrawal of troops from the city and the institution of a blockade and siege. He suggested that the government might have to act upon this prescription.[1]

This quite clearly startled the king. Shaken by the events of the day, he had been trying to convince himself that they were all a horrible mistake and that somehow they would go away. At the same time he awaited with fear and trembling news of similar risings in his other cities, news which would certainly come if the fighting was prolonged. Aside from that, the thought of continued bloodshed was entirely repugnant to his humane nature, and he could not be expected to relish a plan which involved the military investment of his capital city and the systematic reduction of large areas of it to rubble. When he had heard Prittwitz out, Frederick William pulled himself together and firmly ordered the general to attempt no new advances. Then, retiring to his study, the king sat down to compose an address 'To my dear Berliners', a document which, however much it bore witness to its author's desire for social peace, was to become a source of acrimonious controversy and almost indescribable confusion.

If the king wished to allay the heightened passions of his subjects, the tone of his address was ill-adapted for that purpose. There was no admission of guilt here and no excuses for the conduct of his troops. Frederick William chided his subjects for rising against their 'King and loyalest friend'. He expressed the belief that 'the rebellious and insolent demands' and the defiance of order had been the work of a few disturbers of the peace, 'a rabble of rascals, for the most from abroad'. He spoke of 'the victorious progress of his troops'—a reference which, in view of the facts, was dangerously capable of arousing derision. On the positive side, however, the address contained a proposal de-

[1] Rachfahl in *Preußische Jahrbücher*, cx (1902), 305 ff.

signed to win over moderate opinion. If the citizens would level their barricades and send 'men of the real old Berlin spirit' to him, the king promised to withdraw his troops from the city with the exception of forces which would be adequate to protect the palace, the armoury, the national bank, and a few other points.[1]

Early in the morning of the 19th, representatives of various civic groups appeared at the castle and held discussions with the king's ministers. In these talks there was a certain amount of mutual recrimination; but in the end the delegations accepted the spirit of the king's proposal and promised to try to secure the reduction of the barricades. They were at least partially successful, for in mid-morning word came to the castle that some of the street barriers were already removed. It was at this point that the ambiguity of the royal address became painfully evident. Exactly how was the retreat to be effected? Was it—now that the burghers had demonstrated their good faith—to be immediate and general? Was it to be piecemeal, the troops co-ordinating their withdrawal with the progressive reduction of the street barriers? Or was any movement of retreat to await the final and complete removal of the barricades? The king had once more secluded himself and would give no clarifying order. In default of this, the generals in the palace and the king's ministers, notably Bodelschwingh, became involved in a prolonged and bitter wrangle which made clear decisions impossible.[2]

In the circumstances the clarification of the royal order had to be made by Prittwitz. The general was more keenly aware of the harsh realities of the military situation than the contentious groups in the castle, and it seems clear that he regarded the debate over the various methods of retreat as academic. On the morning of the 19th, Prittwitz's most pressing consideration was the morale of his troops. In the course of the night he had already had to order his cavalry units, who had proven them-

[1] The complete text of the address is in Wolff, *Berliner Revolutions-Chronik*, i. 201–2.

[2] Bodelschwingh insisted that the king desired a complete withdrawal of the troops to the *Schloß* and the *Zeughaus* as soon as the first barricades were levelled, and he has been accused of falsifying the king's intentions and causing the deterioration of the military situation by issuing orders in this sense to the field commanders. See Gerlach, *Denkwürdigkeiten*, i. 140 ff., and Petersdorff, *Friedrich Wilhelm*, pp. 85 ff.

selves ill-adapted to attacks on barricades, to withdraw to Potsdam; and he had also been forced to withdraw a battalion of the *Leibregiment* and one of the Guards from the fight because of poor discipline under fire.[1] Prittwitz was sure that any retreat would deepen the general sense of discouragement and that, as long as any strong concentrations of troops remained in the city, there would be a danger of a general collapse of morale. Certainly armed forces could not be expected to stand in the *Schloßplatz*, exposed to the insults of the crowds, without either retaliating against their tormentors, which the king apparently did not desire, or fraternizing with the crowds, which would be disastrous.[2] Prittwitz never wavered in his original belief that, if retreat of any kind was necessary, it should be a general retreat from the city itself. Consequently, as the confusion deepened and communication between the various isolated units became increasingly faulty, the general cut through the welter of contradictory instructions emanating from the castle and ordered the detachments under his command to return to their normal quarters. The provincial troops were instructed to evacuate the city immediately, the local troops to withdraw to their *Kaserne*. The commanders of these latter contingents were, however, authorized to withdraw from the city also, if they could not hold their garrisons without resort to weapons or if the discipline of their troops began to waver; and, in the next two days, these officers took advantage of this authorization and marched their troops out of the capital.[3]

It is perhaps too much to accuse Prittwitz of 'oppositional defiance'[4] and of attempting to force the king to agree to his plan for a blockade and siege. It is evident, however, that in his orders he had greater consideration for the security and the honour of his troops than for the desires of his sovereign, which he considered unrealistic.[5] And it is perfectly clear that his

[1] Valentin, *Deutsche Revolution*, i. 439.

[2] Some contemporaries, including officers under Prittwitz's command, believed that his concern over morale was exaggerated. See Haenchen in *Forschungen*, xlix (1937), 271. This is the view also of Meyerinck in *Militärwochenblatt* (Beihefte, 1891), p. 161.

[3] Ibid., pp. 162 ff.; Rachfahl in *Preußische Jahrbücher*, cx (1902), 421 ff., 449 ff.

[4] The phrase is Rachfahl's in 'Zur Berliner Märzrevolution', *Forschungen*, xvii (1904), 214. Gerlach also speaks of Prittwitz's 'innere und auch äussere Opposition gegen die Person des Königs'. *Denkwürdigkeiten*, i. 729–30.

[5] This is the conclusion of Friedrich Thimme, although he absolves Prittwitz from the charge of deliberate disobedience of orders. 'König Friedrich Wilhelm IV,

orders brought the play of events in Berlin to an abrupt and dramatic *dénouement*. At about noon on the 19th the king was informed not only that troops were leaving the city and that the armoury and other strong points were completely unprotected, but that the castle itself was defended by only two battalions, a force insufficient even to keep the *Schloßplatz* cleared. 'But that is not possible!', the king cried, gazing with consternation at the military members of his staff. There was a hurried consultation in which signs of panic were evident. Then Edwin von Manteuffel, reversing the opinion which he had expressed the night before, urged the king to place himself in the midst of the remaining troops and to leave the city with them. The way to the Brandenburger Tor was still open, he said; the mob would be surprised and without leadership; and the king would escape to come and fight another day. 'Manteuffel', someone growled, 'what responsibility are you taking on yourself?' 'Full responsibility before God and men', the *Rittmeister* answered, 'when nobody has any advice and it is a matter of the king's safety.'[1]

Manteuffel's advice was hotly contested by Count Arnim von Boytzenburg, whom the king had chosen to head a new ministry appointed on this day. It would be better now to put his trust in the people, Arnim argued. No king who had abandoned his capital had ever been allowed to return to it. Manteuffel denied this, citing the case of Henri IV, and the debate went on. It was clear that the king was impressed by Manteuffel's counsel.[2] As usual, however, he was incapable of acting swiftly and, when he had finally persuaded himself that withdrawal was advisable, it was too late. For now came the shattering news that the *Schloßplatz* was filled with people, that all retreat was cut off, and that the crowd was calling for the king to come and view the bodies of those slain on the previous day.

There was no way now of avoiding this painful ceremony. At almost the precise moment at which, twenty-four hours earlier, the fighting had begun, the King of Prussia was standing bareheaded and submissive before his jubilant subjects. Before the

General von Prittwitz und die Berliner Märzrevolution', *Forschungen*, xvi (1903), especially 580–2. It is worth noting that the king never forgave Prittwitz for these orders which he interpreted as defiance of instructions. Gerlach, *Denkwürdigkeiten*, ii. 21, 49.

[1] Rachfahl in *Preußische Jahrbücher*, cx (1902), 441–3.

[2] In 1853 the king presented Manteuffel with a plate showing Henri IV's triumphant return to Paris. E. L. von Gerlach, *Aufzeichnungen*, ii. 240.

afternoon was over, he had authorized the creation of a civilian defence force (*Bürgerwehr*) and transferred to it all responsibility for the maintenance of order in the capital. Two days later Frederick William rode around the city, accompanied by his newly appointed liberal ministers and wearing a red, white, and gold cockade. Deprived of the support of his army, the very substance of Hohenzollern authority, the king seemed to have lost all will to resistance, and to have become, as the Tsar commented savagely, 'a king of the streets' (*Pflasterkönig*)[1] if not indeed—in the words of a modern historian—a king of shadows.[2]

III

The officer corps of the army watched all this with growing bitterness. The establishment of the *Bürgerwehr* was clearly a blow to the position of the army in the state, and the surrender of the sentry posts at the *Schloß* to this body of pseudo-soldiers seemed an almost unbearable humiliation.[3] The king's statement to a group of deputies from Liegnitz and Breslau on 22 March, which promised that, once a constitution was drawn up, he would require the army to take an oath to it,[4] was received with anger and incredulity by men who had always prided themselves on the fact that they owed allegiance only to the king himself. But even worse was to follow. On 25 March Frederick William rode to Potsdam and addressed the officers of the units concentrated there. Although he thanked them for their services in the recent fighting, his further remarks left a feeling of profound disillusionment. Bismarck has described the angry rattle of sabres which greeted the monarch's expressions of faith in his loyal Berliners and his praise of the services of the *Bürgerwehr*;[5] and Prittwitz wrote later that, after the king had discussed the promised concessions in a manner which seemed to indicate that they had his full approval and that the old monarchical Prussia was a thing of the past, 'the officers went down the ramp from the marble gallery to the *Lustgarten* feeling the way a drenched poodle might'.[6]

[1] Srbik, *Deutsche Einheit*, i. 331.

[2] Stadelmann, *Soziale und politische Geschichte*, pp. 55–56.

[3] See the account of the lieutenant commanding the *Königswache* at the time of the transfer. Haenchen in *Forschungen*, xlv (1933), 121 ff.

[4] Höhn, *Verfassungskampf*, p. 142.

[5] Bismarck, *G.W.*, xv. 22.

[6] Rachfahl in *Preußische Jahrbücher*, cx (1902), 459–60. See also Hohenlohe-Ingelfingen, *Aus meinem Leben*, i. 68 ff.

It was after this meeting that Albrecht von Roon, whose loyalty to the monarchy was unquestioned, expressed sentiments which might almost be regarded as mutinous. In a letter to his wife, Roon wrote: 'The army is now our fatherland, for there alone have the unclean and violent elements who put everything into turmoil failed to penetrate.' The just prerogatives of the army, he continued, were being forgotten, 'as if the Prussian National Army was nothing but a homeless rabble of bought mercenaries which must remain without rights and subordinate to the sovereign will of philistines and proletarians. But the army shall and must play a role in the evolutionary process in which we are involved; it has a right to that.'[1] There were many officers who felt, with Roon, that the king was, by his concessions to the revolution, abandoning his army. To a countess whose son had been killed in the Berlin fighting, one officer said: 'Fortunate Frau von Zastrow, your son is at least dead, but what is to become of our sons?'[2] And on 28 March the king's old adviser, General von Thile, wrote to Frederick William expressing his concern over the sense of despair which hung over the officer corps and urging his sovereign not to forget that the army was the 'only pillar' upon which he could 'still securely lean'.[3]

The pessimism of Roon was as premature as the advice of Thile was unnecessary. It was true that the Prussian monarchy had suffered a humiliating defeat on 18–19 March and that, in consequence of this, the king had been forced to make concessions to popular demands. What the soldiers failed to realize was that those concessions were largely verbal in character; none had yet been translated into legal and binding terms. Moreover, the events of 18–19 March had not altered fundamentally any of the king's basic political convictions. He was still a complete absolutist at heart and had every intention of resisting the diminution of any of his royal prerogatives. Chief among these was his uncontested right of command over the army concerning the importance of which he, as a Hohenzollern, did not need to be reminded.

The first intimation that the king intended to be less submissive than his public utterances might indicate came before

[1] Roon, *Denkwürdigkeiten*, i. 152 ff.
[2] Valentin, *Deutsche Revolution*, i. 453.
[3] Haenchen, *Revolutionsbriefe*, p. 57.

the month of March was over. On the 29th the king appointed a new ministry headed by Ludolph Camphausen, with David Hansemann as Minister of Finance and Freiherr von Arnim-Suckow as Minister for Foreign Affairs. These three men were ardent constitutional reformers and admirers of the British political system; and their elevation to office seemed an additional indication that fundamental changes were in the offing. It is possible that Camphausen and his colleagues believed this themselves, and conceived of themselves as forming a cabinet which would determine Prussian policy and be responsible to the new National Assembly which was soon to be elected. If this was the case, the king soon disabused them of the notion. He made it clear that his ministers were responsible only to him and that, far from determining policy, their duty was merely to consult with him as individuals and, after he had decided the policy which was to be followed, to defend it before the Assembly and the people as a whole. It was clear that Frederick William would not tolerate the English version of cabinet solidarity which Prussian liberals admired so heartily. His ministers were to be his servants and nothing else.[1] It was evident also that he had no intention of giving his ministers his full confidence or relying solely on them for advice. Although it was supposed that the events of 18–19 March had put an end to the secret cabinet government of the past and had separated the king effectively from reactionary counsellors, a so-called '*ministère occulte*'[2] was in formation before the end of March. This camarilla, which included such pronounced conservatives as Leopold von Gerlach, General von Rauch, Count Dohna, Count von der Groeben, the cabinet counsellor Niebuhr, and Edwin von Manteuffel, had its headquarters at Potsdam and, especially after the king took up his residence there in April, was as frequently consulted by the sovereign as were his ministers and often had more influence than they.[3]

[1] It took a little time for the Camphausen ministry to realize all the implications of the king's position, but there should have been no doubts in their mind after the king's letter of 20 May to Camphausen. See Erich Brandenburg, ed., *König Friedrich Wilhelms IV Briefwechsel mit Ludolf Camphausen* (Berlin, 1906), pp. 104 ff.

[2] The phrase is Gerlach's. *Denkwürdigkeiten*, i. 150.

[3] On the camarilla, see Fritz Hartung, 'Verantwortliche Regierung, Kabinette und Nebenregierungen im konstitutionellen Preußen 1848–1918', *Forschungen*, xliv (1932), especially 5–7; Schmidt-Bückeburg, *Militärkabinett*, pp. 51–53. A literary description of the camarilla's power will be found in Gutzkow's *Ritter vom Geiste*, especially in the chapter 'Die Gesellschaft und die "Kleinen Cirkel".' See also

From the very beginning Frederick William was on guard against attempts on the part of the Camphausen ministry to place limitations on his authority in military affairs. During the troubles which broke out in the Polish districts of Posen in April, he issued orders to the commanding general there without consulting the ministry at all and, in doing so, helped to confuse, and defeat, the delicate policy they were seeking to execute.[1] On 13 May the ministers as a body sent an indignant note to the king, asking him in the future 'in all military matters to stop communicating directly with individual commanders and to permit such communication to take place only through the agency of the responsible War Minister'.[2] On the following day, in a letter to Camphausen, Frederick William answered blandly: 'I tell you that no one could be more in accord with the principles . . . of all constitutional governments than I. I must, however, explain at the same time that the extension of these principles to the army is justified by no constitution.'[3] When the ministry continued to express its dissatisfaction with this reasoning, the king stated his position more tartly. On 4 June he wrote that the principle of complete royal authority in military affairs must be maintained in Prussia 'which cannot be conceived of without the absolute unity of the King with his army, because any infringement of that absolute unity would be the death sentence of Prussia at home and abroad . . .'.[4]

While the king was thus demonstrating his determination to avoid ministerial dictation, the scene was being set for a more public discussion of the constitutional and military questions. In April the second united diet convened in Berlin in accordance with the king's declaration of 14 March. Its members clearly recognized, however, that the events of the 18th and 19th had irretrievably destroyed the authority of a body which had always, after all, been a poor excuse for a national parliament. Therefore they confined themselves to passing a few exceptional laws establishing complete freedom of the press and of assembly and to making the necessary arrangements for the election of a national constituent assembly which would,

E. Kohn-Bramstedt, *Aristocracy and the Middle Classes in Germany* (London, 1937), pp. 81–83.

[1] On the situation in Posen, see Valentin, *Deutsche Revolution*, i. 539 ff.

[2] Haenchen, *Revolutionsbriefe*, pp. 97–98.

[3] Brandenburg, *Briefwechsel mit Camphausen*, p. 83.

[4] Ibid., p. 145.

presumably, translate the work of March into legislative terms.[1]

The first Prussian National Assembly was elected by universal and equal manhood suffrage and secret ballot and was convoked on 22 May 1848. It was a unicameral body of about 400 members, drawn predominantly from the middle sections of society. Both the great landed proprietors and the manual workers were very lightly represented. *Bourgeois* proprietors, prosperous peasants, manufacturers and merchants, schoolteachers, and ministers and artisans from the larger towns were in greater number, while almost half of the members were drawn from the state and city bureaucracy and from the legal profession.[2] Despite the general social homogeneity of the body, there were deep political divisions in the Assembly. In general, there were three main groupings. The Right, led by Baumstark and Reichensperger, was the party of resistance, opposing all attacks on the pre-March system and dubious concerning constitutional projects which threatened to change the monarchical régime. The Centre, which was divided into a right wing whose most conspicuous member was Hans Victor von Unruh and a left wing headed by Rodbertus, Gierke, and Schultze-Delitzsch, advocated a moderate constitutional régime and the consolidation of the gains which they felt had been achieved by the March rising. The Left, under the leadership of Waldeck, Jacoby, Stein, and d'Ester, expressed more extremely democratic sentiments and favoured a sharper reduction of royal authority if not the actual establishment of a republican régime.[3]

While natural, these divisions were of extreme importance for the political future of Prussia. The Assembly had been elected for the purpose of drawing up a constitution. Had they confined themselves to this duty and worked with dispatch, Prussia's constitutional system could probably have been firmly established by the end of the summer of 1848, and the position of the king and the army could have been regulated in accordance with liberal principles. In actuality, however, the Assembly's deliberations were marked neither by concentration nor speed. The work of drafting the constitution was relegated to committees on which the various factions wrangled interminably, with

[1] Hartung, *Verfassungsgeschichte*, p. 152.

[2] Figures are given in Valentin, *Deutsche Revolution*, ii. 42–43.

[3] Ibid., pp. 44 ff.

the result that a finished draft did not reach the plenum until October. The plenary sessions were given over to long debates on subjects which often had little connexion with the Assembly's mandate and which were seldom resolved. Inevitably, this procedure led to a gradual deterioration of the Assembly's public stature and, by doing so, strengthened the hand of the king and gave the forces of reaction an opportunity to recover.

With regard to military affairs, the Assembly would have been well advised to concentrate upon the constitutional issues involved, to define with precision the powers of the king and the War Minister and to make provision for a clear and unequivocal military oath of allegiance to the constitution of the state. The members of the Left, however, were less interested in these matters than they were in elaborate and essentially impractical plans for a complete reorganization of the army. At the very outset of the Assembly's sessions, on 30 May, this was made clear in a speech by the Left deputy Jung who called for a return to the ideals of the period 1807–13, asserting that Scharnhorst had wanted to create 'das volkstümliche Heer' but that this had degenerated with the passage of time into 'das unvolkstümliche Militär'.[1] In subsequent days a good deal of the deputies' time was devoted to listening to long attacks upon the *Kadettenhäuser*, the system of military justice and the privileges of the officer corps.[2] Eventually—but very slowly—a pattern emerged in this welter of argument. The Left took the position that the time had come to abolish the regular army, which had been the source of so many of the country's ills, and to replace it by a genuine *Volkswehr* or popular militia which would be 'the surest, the only guarantee of civil freedom'.[3]

Had such a proposition been debated on 20 March 1848 it might very well have been accepted. At that time, hatred of the army was general and the transfer of police powers in Berlin from the regular military establishment to the *Bürgerwehr* had been acclaimed as the first step toward the abolition of the old military system. Unfortunately, it was soon all too evident that the *Bürgerwehr* was no model of military efficiency.[4] The original enthusiasm with which the citizen-soldiers had taken

[1] *Verhandlungen der constituirenden Versammlung für Preußen 1848* (Berlin, 1848), i. 197.

[2] Höhn, *Verfassungskampf*, p. 145.

[3] Valentin, *Deutsche Revolution*, ii. 289–90.

[4] On the organization, composition, and leadership of the *Bürgerwehr*, see Kaeber, *Berlin 1848*, pp. 115ff.

up the task of local defence had rapidly been replaced by boredom and laxity; and as early as 21 March, municipal authorities had had to request the return of a few battalions of regular troops to Berlin to help relieve the *Bürgerwehr* of the burden they had assumed.[1] And now came an event which not only irretrievably destroyed confidence in that organization, but made respectable people suspicious of all arguments in favour of popular militias. On 14 June an excited mob, carried away by a sudden flare-up of the spirit of 18 March, attacked the Berlin armoury, overpowered the guard, rifled the stores of arms and ammunition, and began to prowl about the streets in a definitely menacing way. In the resultant disorders the organization, leadership, and morale of the *Bürgerwehr* were demonstrated to be hopelessly inadequate, and, after the restoration of peace, its commander, Major von Blesson, was dismissed and the structure of the force was completely overhauled.[2]

The troubles in Berlin represented a significant turning point in the history of the Prussian revolution of 1848. They effected a subtle shifting of political opinion to the right as the middle groups of society began to lose their revolutionary ardour and to long for the security of the pre-March period.[3] Simultaneously, they led to a sensible diminution of criticism of the old military system and a definite waning of support for radical projects of reform. In the Assembly the left factions persisted for a while in their efforts to replace the line army with a new popular force of some kind; but by the beginning of August the idea of a *Volksbewaffnung* had ceased to be a practical political proposition.[4]

The shift in public temper was encouraging to the army, and the first signs of a recovery from the disillusionment and moral collapse of March became evident. In July a group of officers, in an obvious attempt to counter assaults upon the military, founded a journal called the *Deutsche-Wehrzeitung*. The editors announced bluntly that their purpose was to fight against 'the

[1] Kaeber, *Berlin 1848*, pp. 97–99; Haenchen, *Revolutionsbriefe*, pp. 59, 64–65.

[2] Valentin, *Deutsche Revolution*, ii. 69 ff.; Kaeber, *Berlin 1848*, pp. 168 ff.

[3] The effect of the *Zeughaussturm* upon moderate opinion was so damaging to the party of extreme democratic reform that some of its members believed that the attack on the armoury had been deliberately provoked by reactionaries to discredit the revolutionary cause. See, for instance, Stephan Born, *Erinnerungen eines Achtundvierziger* (Leipzig, 1898), pp. 141–2. See also Stadelmann, *Soziale und politische Geschichte*, p. 87.

[4] See Höhn, *Verfassungskampf*, pp. 145–8; and, for the fruitless project for an enlarged civil guard, *Verhandlungen der constituierenden Versammlung*, iii. 2096–2111.

demon of revolution' and to combat 'the modern artifice which seeks to separate the Prince and the people by making the latter believe that the interest of Princes is quite different from that of their peoples'.[1] Simultaneously, from the inner sanctum of the War Ministry itself came a stream of pamphlets, penned by the gifted Lieutenant-Colonel von Griesheim. Some of these gave technical answers to the Assembly's criticism of military institutions; others—like the provocative 'Only Soldiers Help against Democrats'—were obviously designed as counter-revolutionary propaganda.[2] Nor were these writings without effect on public opinion. There has been little occasion in these pages to comment on events which were taking place elsewhere in Germany, but it should be remembered that in Frankfurt at this time another assembly composed of delegates from all German states, was seeking to create a united Germany on a constitutional basis and had already organized a provisional imperial government with an Austrian archduke as imperial vicar (*Reichsverweser*) pending the election of an emperor. On 16 July the War Minister of this Frankfurt government, in a circular note to all German governments, ordered them to parade their troops on 6 August and to have read to them a declaration announcing the assumption by the *Reichsverweser* of supreme command over all German troops.[3] The news of this stimulated Prussian military publicists to feverish activity. The *Deutsche-Wehrzeitung* launched a spirited campaign against compliance with the Frankfurt circular; and Griesheim, in a widely read pamphlet entitled 'The German Central Power and the Prussian Army', poured scorn on the idea that Prussian soldiers would allow themselves to be submerged in a German army. So violent were his appeals for popular resistance to the pretensions of Frankfurt, that one member of the Prussian Assembly demanded that he be arrested for high treason and incitation to riot;[4] but his arguments were nevertheless greeted with enthusiasm by all classes of society and were repeated by journals of widely differing political convictions, and there can be little doubt that Griesheim and his colleagues were largely responsible for the approval which

[1] Höhn, *Verfassungskampf*, pp. 282 ff.

[2] On Griesheim, see especially 'Zur Erinnerung an General von Griesheim', *Militärwochenblatt* (Beihefte, 1854). This article is unsigned but appears to have been written by Albrecht von Roon. See Roon, *Denkwürdigkeiten*, i. 291.

[3] On this affair, see Haenchen, *Revolutionsbriefe*, pp. 131 ff., 142 ff., 151; Gerlach, *Denkwürdigkeiten*, i. 178.

[4] Höhn, *Verfassungskampf*, p. 292, n.

greeted the government's decision to evade full compliance with Frankfurt note.[1]

This literary activity indicated a return of confidence on the part of the army which boded ill for the Prussian National Assembly's hope of consolidating the gains of 18–19 March. It is from this point on that the military leaders who stood closest to the king began eagerly to discuss the possibility of a restoration of the pre-March system by *coup d'état*. Thus, as early as July, Ludwig von Gerlach suggested to his brother Leopold that the time was ripe for the establishment of a military dictatorship, and the *Generaladjutant* admitted the desirability of this, although he added, with an oblique reference to the suppression of the Parisian workers by General Cavaignac in June, that 'a military [reactionary] ministry . . . can come only when we have "cavaignac-ed" the sovereign people'.[2]

These first stirrings of counter-revolutionary activity, and the simultaneous founding of numerous reactionary political clubs and associations—like the *Verein für König und Vaterland* in Brandenburg[3]—alarmed the Left and Centre of the Assembly and induced the deputies not only to apply themselves more diligently to the job of drafting a constitution but also to concentrate their attention upon the political attitude and activity of members of the officer corps. Provisions were now written into the constitutional draft for a formal oath of allegiance to the constitution to be taken by all officers. Simultaneously, the Assembly undertook to purge the officer corps of all reactionary officers.

The immediate occasion for this latter move was a serious brush between a battalion of troops stationed at Schweidnitz and the local citizens in the course of which the soldiers had fired upon a demonstration, killing fourteen people. This was altogether too reminiscent of army actions under the old régime to pass unnoticed; and it led to a long debate in the National Assembly at the conclusion of which, on 9 August, the deputies passed two resolutions. The first of these—proposed by a deputy from Breslau named Stein—read:

The War Minister, in an order to the army, shall express his

[1] Höhn, *Verfassungskampf*, pp. 293–4; Valentin, *Deutsche Revolution*, ii. 61, 228.

[2] E. L. von Gerlach, *Aufzeichnungen*, i. 538.

[3] Kohn-Bramstedt, *Aristocracy and Middle Classes*, pp. 88–89; Eyck, *Bismarck*, i. 102–5; Stadelmann, *Soziale und politische Geschichte*, p. 94; Kaeber, *Berlin 1848*, pp. 183 ff.

desire that the officers shall abstain from reactionary agitations, that they shall not only avoid conflicts of any kind with civilians but also, by advances to the burghers and union with them, shall give evidence of their desire to co-operate, with honesty and devotion, in the realization of a constitutional legal system.[1]

At the same time the Assembly accepted the so-called Schulz-Wanzleben resolution which stipulated that officers who found the above resolution incompatible with their political conviction should, as a matter of honour and duty, resign from the army.[2]

These resolutions infuriated the king. Up to this time he had studiously avoided any conflict with the Assembly; but he made it clear now to his ministers that he would not permit any attempts on the part of that body to interfere with his command of the army. Since the resolutions were an obvious infringement of his royal *Kommandogewalt*, they must, he insisted, be defied. Thoroughly aroused, Frederick William actually drafted a haughty message to the Assembly, instructing that body to confine itself to the tasks for which it had been elected and warning that further attempts to meddle with 'the inviolable rights of Our Crown' would be opposed 'with strength and vigour and all the power which We have received from God'.[3]

The Hansemann-Auerswald ministry, which had succeeded Camphausen and his colleagues after the June rising in Berlin, was placed in an insupportable position by the intransigence of the sovereign. They were better informed concerning the temper of the Assembly than Frederick William, and they feared that disclosure of the king's views might lead to an ascendancy of the Left in that body and to a new wave of radical resolutions. On the other hand, Frederick William made it very clear that he could no longer work in confidence with them unless they sabotaged the Assembly's campaign against the army.[4] Hansemann and his colleagues tried to follow a middle course. They decided to suppress the king's message and, instead, sought to convince the Assembly that—while every effort would be made to correct the political attitude of the officer corps—the general order demanded by the Stein resolution would make such correction more difficult, rather than easier, and hence should not

[1] *Verhandlungen*, iii. 1730–1.

[2] Ibid., p. 1741.

[3] Haenchen, *Revolutionsbriefe*, p. 167.

[4] Brandenburg, *Reichsgründung*, i. 241–2.

be insisted upon.[1] As was perhaps natural, these lame explanations and promises enraged the deputies, and, on 7 September, they re-passed the Stein and Schulz resolutions and demanded that they be carried out to the letter.[2] The Hansemann ministry immediately tendered its resignation, and the king accepted it on 10 September.

In military circles these events were greeted with a sharp increase in the desire for a military *coup d'état* which would put an end, once and for all, to the Assembly and all its works. The force for such an action was, indeed, available, for, on 26 August, the confused and fruitless war between Denmark and the German confederation had come to an end, and the Prussian troops which had been involved in this had been withdrawn to their own country. Immediately after their arrival the king appointed their leader, General von Wrangel, commanding general of all troops between the Elbe and the Oder.[3] Wrangel's military talents were extremely limited—as he had just demonstrated in Holstein and as he would make abundantly clear in the same theatre in 1864[4]—but he possessed great energy and had a decided flair for the dramatic gesture.[5] He demonstrated this now by celebrating the assumption of his new command with a speech which was heard from one end of Prussia to another.

> My task [he announced] is to restore public peace in these lands, wherever it is disturbed and whenever the strength of the good citizens is not adequate for the purpose. I indulge myself with the definite hope that I shall have no occasion to intervene with military power, for my confidence in the citizens . . . stands fast. . . . There are in the country, however, elements which want to seduce people nto illegalities. They are, it is true, few in number, but they push themselves forward all the more strongly, while the good elements hold back. To these last I will from now on be a powerful support, in order to make easier for them the maintenance of public order, without which no legal freedom is possible.[4]

[1] Höhn, *Verfassungskampf*, pp. 150–1.

[2] For the debate preceding this action, see *Verhandlungen*, iv. 2678 ff., 2777 ff.

[3] Gerlach, *Denkwürdigkeiten*, i. 198.

[4] See, for instance, Hohenlohe-Ingelfingen, *Aus meinem Leben*, iii. 8–15.

[5] It was said of him that he deliberately copied the idiosyncrasies of Blücher to the extent of learning to speak with a Berlin dialect. Valentin, *Deutsche Revolution*, ii. 246–7. For more respectful appraisals of Wrangel, see Kurt von Priesdorff, *Soldatisches Führertum* (7 vols., Hamburg, 1936), and F. von Meerheimb, 'Graf v. Wrangel, Kgl. Pr. Generalfeldmarschall', *Militärwochenblatt* (Beihefte, 1877), pp. 355–418.

[6] Meerheimb, p. 388.

This menacing oration, with its intimation that the army would soon reclaim its position as the *Ordnungsfaktor* in the state, and its additional injunctions to the troops to ignore false promises made by 'unknown persons' and to obey the orders of their officers implicitly, was greeted with jubilation in army circles. Helmuth von Moltke, still a relatively junior officer in the General Staff, reflected what must have been a general attitude in the army. On 21 September he wrote to his brother Adolf:

> We now have 40,000 men in and around Berlin; the critical point of the whole German question lies there. Order in Berlin, and we shall have order in the country. . . . They [presumably the King and his advisers] now have the power in their hands and a perfect right to use it. If they don't do it this time, then I am ready to emigrate with you to Adelaide. The next few days must bring great things.[1]

These hopes were, for the time being, to remain unrealized. The king did seriously consider the possibility of annulling the Assembly vote of 7 September by royal declaration, of dissolving the National Assembly, and of using troops to overawe his capital.[2] But his old habit of indecision at critical moments reasserted itself. There were rumours of approaching disorders in Berlin and, before the end of the month, there were, indeed, some attempts to build barricades in a few thoroughfares.[3] The king, to his credit, shrank away from the thought of renewed bloodshed and decided in favour of the prudent course. He authorized General von Pfuehl to form a ministry and to seek a *modus vivendi* with the Assembly; and Pfuehl, on 23 September, issued to the commanding generals the kind of order which the Stein resolution had demanded.[4]

This apparent capitulation to the Assembly exasperated the officer corps to an almost uncontrollable degree. The *Deutsche-Wehrzeitung*, while counselling obedience to the royal decision, made no attempt to disguise the bitterness which that decision aroused.[5] Individual officers were outspoken in their criticism of the king. At Charlottenburg, Wrangel grumbled about the drift toward 'republicanism'; and, at the end of the month, he

[1] Jähns, *Moltke*, p. 171.

[2] See, for instance, Haenchen, *Revolutionsbriefe*, pp. 175 ff.

[3] Valentin, *Deutsche Revolution*, ii. 247.

[4] Haenchen, *Revolutionsbriefe*, pp. 178–9, 183–7; Höhn, *Verfassungskampf*, pp. 155–6.

[5] Ibid., pp. 301–6; Roon, *Denkwürdigkeiten*, i. 208.

paid an unauthorized visit to Berlin and made a highly provocative, if somewhat confused, speech in which he made uncomfortable references to his desire not to have to shoot citizens, complained fretfully about conditions in Berlin, and added: 'This must change, and it will change; I will bring you good with order; this anarchy must stop! I promise you this and a Wrangel has never broken his word.'[1]

It is impossible to say to what extent this army reaction influenced the king in the policy which he followed in subsequent weeks. It seems clear that, since the very beginning of the controversy over the Stein resolution, Frederick William had become increasingly sensitive to army criticism of his actions, and there were times when he appeared to admit that there were limits to his ability to refuse to satisfy military desires. Thus, in September, in the course of a conversation with Leopold von Gerlach, he had suddenly remarked: 'For the sake of the army speed is needed, for I wouldn't blame it if, in the belief that I was abandoning it, it should place William on the throne.'[2] Again, in early October, while discussing the Assembly's constitutional draft with Gerlach, the king bitterly criticized its inclusion of an oath for the army, saying: 'This oath would cost me all my officers and is therefore impossible.'[3] In view of these random comments, it may be true that the army's sharp criticism of Pfuehl's action was responsible for Frederick William's decision to repudiate the policy of his new ministry. It is equally possible, however—and, in view of the king's character and political convictions, not at all unlikely—that the appointment of the Pfuehl ministry was simply a manœuvre to gain time and that the king never intended to implement the promises which it made to the Assembly.

Whatever the truth of the matter, during the month of October, while Pfuehl sought to convince the Assembly of the king's good intentions, in which he himself honestly believed, Frederick William was gradually drifting toward *coup d'état*. He obliquely gave his blessing to Wrangel's conduct by dispatching his portrait to the general's headquarters;[4] and, through the agency of the camarilla, he opened negotiations with the man he desired as Pfuehl's successor—Count Brandenburg, the com-

[1] Meerheimb in *Militärwochenblatt* (Beihefte, 1877), pp. 389–91.

[2] Gerlach, *Denkwürdigkeiten*, i. 193.

[3] Ibid., 215.

[4] Meerheimb in *Militärwochenblatt* (Beihefte, 1877), p. 393.

mander of the VI Armeekorps in Breslau, a man of determination and energy and one who had publicly stated his belief in the necessity of putting down the 'seditious activity' in Berlin.[1] He still hesitated to make an open avowal of his stand—as late as 23 October he was anxiously asking his friend Count Stolberg whether he should 'continue the constitutional comedy . . . or suddenly march in with Wrangel and then, as conqueror, fulfil the letter of my promises?'[2]—but events now forced his hand.

On 28 October Windischgrätz began the bombardment that was, three days later, to restore imperial authority in Vienna and to mark the turning of the tide of revolutionary fortunes in Germany. The significance of this was not lost in Berlin. The city was immediately thrown into an uproar of excitement, and the democratic movement, which had become increasingly active in the past three months, had won many converts among the factory workers and had even penetrated the ranks of the *Bürgerwehr*, sought, in a series of noisy demonstrations, to re-awaken the revolutionary zeal of 18 March. In the Assembly itself the Left factions demanded that the government give immediate aid to the beleaguered citizens of Vienna. This demand was rejected by the majority on 31 October, but only after a stormy debate which concluded with the deputies being manhandled by a mob as they left the Chamber. Pfuehl himself had to take refuge in the home of the Left deputy Jung where he took tea with that politician's wife, an incident which completed the discrediting of the unfortunate minister.[3]

Under the influence of these events the king finally took the plunge over which he had hesitated so long. On 2 November the Assembly was informed that Brandenburg was forming a ministry. That minister waited precisely one week, while tension in the city mounted. Then, on 9 November, he announced that the meetings of the Assembly would be suspended until 27 November at which time it would re-convene at Brandenburg. On the following day, Wrangel, who had been urging action

[1] Gerlach, *Denkwürdigkeiten*, i. 220 ff.; Haenchen, *Revolutionsbriefe*, pp. 211 ff.; Stadelmann, *Soziale und politische Geschichte*, pp. 148–9.

[2] Stolberg-Wernigerode, *Anton Graf zu Stolberg* (Munich, 1926), p. 121.

[3] On the debate, see *Verhandlungen*, viii. 506 ff. The camarilla used the Pfuehl incident to persuade the king that it would be disgraceful to retain him any longer in office. The reactionary *Kreuzzeitung*, playing on the fact that Pfuehl was the leading spirit in a Berlin swimming club, wrote: 'The swimming master was drowned in Madame Jung's teacup.' E. L. von Gerlach, *Aufzeichnungen*, ii. 21.

for the past week, received the orders he had been waiting for and entered Berlin with 13,000 men and 60 guns.

Momentarily it appeared as if these actions would meet resistance. Some of the members of the Assembly refused to disband and barricaded themselves within the Chamber; the Democratic Central Committee sought to mobilize street-fighters; and some detachments of the *Bürgerwehr* seemed willing to defend the rights they had won on 19 March. In the end, however, all this came to nothing. The story is told of Wrangel's being informed that his wife had been seized by democrats, who threatened to kill her if he did not stop his advance on the city. The general went on his way imperturbably and was heard, some time later, murmuring: 'I wonder whether they have really hanged her? I hardly believe so.'[1] The anecdote is probably apocryphal but it might as well have been true. The fact of the matter was that the reconquest of Berlin by royal forces was accompanied by neither organized resistance nor by individual acts of terrorism. Wrangel's forces were hailed by the solid mass of the middle class, long weary of the insecurity and discomforts of a people's revolution. The *Bürgerwehr*, as Griesheim jeered, 'held still as lambs and let themselves be disarmed';[2] the deputies evacuated the Chamber within the fifteen-minute period allowed them by Wrangel, who sat meanwhile in a chair in the street glancing at his watch; a detachment of workers from the Borsig plant who were assembled before the *Schloß* disbanded with no more than a formal protest; and, with that, all opposition came to an end. On 12 November Wrangel ordered the immediate closing of all political clubs, the prohibition of assemblies of more than twenty persons, the imposition of police censorship of all publications, and the formal dissolution of the *Bürgerwehr*. He then concentrated his troops at all important points and waited for his king to exploit the bloodless victory he had won.[3]

IV

If Wrangel and the reactionary camarilla expected now that the clock would be turned back with a vengeance, they were

[1] Hohenlohe-Ingelfingen, *Aus meinem Leben*, i. 100 ff.

[2] Höhn, *Verfassungskampf*, p. 343.

[3] A detailed description of Wrangel's entry into Berlin is given by Meerheimb in *Militärwochenblatt* (Beihefte, 1877), pp. 394–6.

bitterly disappointed. The king, it is true, was, in the first days after the entry of the troops, in an exultant and arrogant mood and seemed prepared to repudiate all of the concessions and promises which he had made since 18 March. He found, however, that his new Minister President would have none of these tactics. Count Brandenburg argued that provocative gestures would merely reanimate the revolutionary zeal of the Prussian people and would cause new domestic disorders at a time when Prussian unity was desirable. Brandenburg realized that, with the victory of the Austrian government over the revolution, a duel would begin between Austria and Prussia for the domination of the rest of Germany; and he was anxious to avoid problems which could only weaken Prussia's foreign policy.[1] The Minister President argued that, with his throne secure once more and protected by his loyal troops, the king could afford to be magnanimous. And surely the most striking show of magnanimity would be to grant a constitution to his subjects, provided, of course, that such grant was made independently by the monarch and of his own free will.

The king was surprised and indignant at these proposals, but in the end he gave way, partly because he himself was becoming engrossed in foreign affairs, partly because Brandenburg threatened to resign unless his advice was followed, and partly, perhaps, because it was his nature to be inconsistent.[2] On 5 December 1848, then, the hapless National Assembly, still bickering and protesting, was declared dissolved by royal decree; and, on the same day, Prussia became, at long last, a constitutional state with the promulgation of the royal *charte*.[3]

Although modelled after the Belgian constitution, there was no essential similarity between this new document and any of the constitutions of the liberal west. At the very outset, the Prussian constitution repudiated all doctrines of popular sovereignty and reaffirmed the principles of divine-right monarchy. Provision was made for a bicameral legislature, with an upper house composed of members who were elected by the provincial

[1] Stadelmann, *Soziale und politische Geschichte*, pp. 149–50; Eyck, *Bismarck*, i. 113.

[2] To Gerlach the king professed to be infuriated by Brandenburg's proposals. *Denkwürdigkeiten*, i. 242, 244–8. That the idea of a constitution freely granted by the Crown was not new to him, however, is shown by his letter of 23 October to Stolberg, cited above, p. 119.

[3] See Edwin von Manteuffel's draft of the promulgation message in Haenchen, *Revolutionsbriefe*, pp. 247–8.

and district governments, and a lower house which was elected by universal suffrage. But, while the powers of the legislature were rather loosely defined, its limitations were sharply delineated. The Crown was given a right of absolute veto over all legislation; it had extensive rights to declare a state of siege and to suspend civil liberties; and its privilege of promulgating emergency decrees was virtually unlimited.[1]

Moreover, despite the specious liberality of the original document, which—as Count Brandenburg predicted—had a favourable public reaction, the government clearly intended from the beginning to revise the constitution in a conservative direction as soon as it was expedient to do so. As early as May 1849 the use of universal suffrage in elections to the lower house was replaced by an elaborate system which divided electors according to the amount of taxes they paid and made certain that the preponderance of seats in the chamber would be filled by representatives of the wealthier classes. In subsequent months the king's revisions justified Karl Francke's later complaint that 'in Berlin they are picking away at the constitution like an artichoke'.[2] By February 1850, when the so-called 'revised constitution' was put in force, the provision for unrestricted freedom of the press had been modified, the *Bürgerwehr*—one of the chief gains of the March revolution—had been abolished, and the upper house of the legislature had been transformed into a kind of house of peers, in which princes and *Standesherren* held seats by prescription and a large percentage of the members were appointed directly by the king.

The critical question of the role of the army in the state had been passed over in silence in the constitution promulgated on 5 December 1848, although the king had once more intimated publicly that the army would take an oath to the constitution.[3]

[1] For the constitution and its revision see above all G. Anschütz, *Die Verfassungsurkunde des preußischen Staates* (Leipzig, 1912). Useful short discussions will be found in Hartung, *Verfassungsgeschichte*, pp. 151–5, and 'Die Entwicklung der konstitutionellen Monarchie in Preußen', in *Volk und Staat in der deutschen Geschichte* (Leipzig, 1940), pp. 208–12; Huber, *Heer und Staat*, pp. 179 ff; and Kurt Kaminski, *Verfassung und Verfassungskonflikt in Preußen, 1862–66* (Berlin, 1938), pp. 19–22.

[2] Max Duncker, *Politischer Briefwechsel aus seinem Nachlaß* (*Deutsche Geschichtsquellen des 19. Jahrhunderts*, xii) (Stuttgart, 1923), p. 51.

[3] The constitutional draft adopted by the Brandenburg ministry made provision for an army oath. It seems to have been deleted at the last moment on the initiative of Edwin von Manteuffel. See Schmitz, *Manteuffel als Geschichtsquelle*, p. 61.

This led to wide-spread indignation in military circles, and the *Deutsche-Wehrzeitung* conducted a spirited campaign in which it argued that, once it had taken the oath, the army's 'strength for the fatherland would be broken', that 'it would not save the State a second time as it has saved it now', and that the Crown would be left 'helpless in the face of future attacks by democracy'. The king was the recipient of a flood of petitions from pensioned and active officers, *Offiziervereine* and patriotic societies urging him to protect the army from a step which could only be destructive of discipline, efficiency, and loyalty to the Crown.[1] The extent to which this campaign influenced the king's thinking is not known, but it is significant that article 108 of the revised constitution of 1850 stated flatly that 'an oath by the army to the constitution will not take place', while articles 44–47 reaffirmed the king's powers of command and appointment in the army.[2] Thus, to all intents and purposes, the army was left outside the constitution, subject only to the king's control and serving to protect his authority against legislative encroachment.

All of this seemed adequately to preserve the traditional prerogatives of the Crown. Yet, even after the revisions had been made, Frederick William suffered from grave doubts concerning the advisability of pursuing the policy which his Minister President had insisted upon; and it was only after Count Brandenburg had emphatically pressed all of his previous arguments that the king capitulated and, on 6 February 1850, took an oath to observe and defend the new constitution.[3] In this instance, if not in others, the king's indecision was a tribute to his political intelligence. He sensed that his oath was in a very real sense an admission that the constitutional struggle which had begun in March 1848 was ending, not with a definitive victory of the Crown, but with a very uneasy compromise.

[1] Höhn, *Verfassungskampf*, pp. 343–56.

[2] Ibid., p. 358; Huber, *Heer und Staat*, p. 192; Schmidt-Bückeburg, *Militärkabinett*, p. 39.

[3] Brandenburg, on more than one occasion, was reduced to despair by the king's vacillations, and was reported to have said that he was reminded of the fate of the Stuarts. Gerlach, *Denkwürdigkeiten*, i. 391; Duncker, *Briefwechsel*, p. 20. On the attempts of the Gerlach circle to prevent the king's oath, see Gerlach, *Denkwürdigkeiten*, i. 400 ff. The influence of Joseph Maria von Radowitz seems to have swung the tide in Brandenburg's favour. Ibid., i. 797–8, 827–8; Petersdorff, *Friedrich Wilhelm*, pp. 165 ff. On the oath-taking ceremony, see, *inter alia*, *Aus dem Leben Bernhardis*, vi. 174.

Despite the safeguards provided for royal authority, the growing liberal opposition in Prussia had won a *point d'appui* which they had not had before 1848. They now had a parliament in which to air their grievances, and the lower house of that body had, by the recognition of the principle of ministerial responsibility and of parliamentary control over the budget, been given important powers. It was true that these powers were ill defined,[1] but what was to prevent a future parliament from seeking to clarify or expand them? And even if the king's emergency powers provided a means of governing in defiance of parliament, would not the continued employment of those powers involve the government in new crises, which would place public security and royal authority in jeopardy? In the last analysis the new constitution was an attempt to base a political system upon a marriage between an imperfect constitutionalism and an ill-disguised absolutism.[2] The king was intelligent enough to doubt the workability of such an experiment, even while he assented to it.[3]

The king's fears were shared by the more perceptive of his military advisers, who, once they had recovered from their jubilation over the issue of the oath controversy, became aware that the new constitutional régime would, in two vital respects, endanger the army.

In the first place there was the problem of the Minister of War. As a minister of the king, he—alone of all the officers in the army—was required to take an oath to defend the constitution. Presumably this meant that he would be honour-bound to observe article 44 of the revised constitution, which stipulated that all acts of government must be countersigned by the

[1] Frederick William IV never abandoned his belief that the ministers were responsible to him rather than to the Chamber. The difficulties caused by this are analysed in Hartung, 'Nebenregierungen', in *Forschungen*, xliv (1932), 8–17. The budget right was qualified by a stipulation that refusal to approve a budget could not prevent continued collection of existing taxes. See Schmitz, *Manteuffel als Geschichtsquelle*, p. 61.

[2] 'Verhüllter Absolutismus und Scheinkonstitutionalismus sind das innere Wesen dieser Verfassung.' Kaminski, *Verfassung*, p. 31. See also pp. 35 ff. where the author talks of a '*Kompromißverfassung* incapable of reconciling the opposites from which it stemmed'. A similar interpretation will be found in Carl Schmitt, *Staatsgefüge und Zusammenbruch des zweiten Reiches: Der Sieg des Bürgers über den Soldaten* (Hamburg, 1934), pp. 9, 11. Huber, in *Heer und Staat*, esp. pp. 187 ff., argues that the constitution represented a complete victory of the king over the revolution, but his case is neither convincing nor consistent.

[3] See Gerlach, *Denkwürdigkeiten*, i. 708.

minister within whose jurisdiction they fell and must be defended by him in the parliament. Did this, however, imply that ordinances affecting the army had to be countersigned and thus exposed to discussion in the *Landtag*, and, if so, how was this to be reconciled with article 46 of the constitution, which reserved the right of the supreme command over the army to the king, to whom the Minister of War, by another oath, owed complete fidelity? The king's view was that the Minister of War need countersign, and assume responsibility before parliament for, only those military decrees which were purely administrative in character, whereas, in the case of all military decisions made by the king in his capacity as supreme commander of the army, the Minister of War was responsible only to the king and to his own conscience and need neither sign nor allow them to be discussed in parliament. This theory was difficult to understand, let alone implement. It became increasingly evident, as the years passed, that the Minister of War was placed in an almost impossible position. If he tried sincerely to observe the principle of ministerial responsibility he became involved in serious difficulties with the king and lost the confidence of the officer corps who regarded themselves as beyond the constitutional pale and who resented any discussion of military matters in parliament. If he gave his oath to the king precedence over his constitutional oath, he invited parliamentary attacks upon himself and upon the military establishment. Between 1850 and 1857, two ministers of war—Generals von Strotha and von Bonin—lost their posts because they found it impossible to balance their conflicting loyalties and because they ended by becoming 'too constitutional' for the king and for the army, while a third—General von Waldersee—went so far in the other direction that he alienated the lower house of the parliament completely. Thus, in the post-revolutionary period, the Minister of War became the living embodiment of the fateful dualism which characterized the new governmental system, and his required appearances before parliament tended increasingly to provoke criticism of the army and the political ideals for which it stood.[1]

[1] The major work on this complicated subject is F. Freiherr Marschall von Bieberstein, *Verantwortlichkeit und Gegenzeichnung bei Anordnungen des Obersten Kriegsherrn. Studie zum deutschen Staatsrecht* (Berlin, 1911). For shorter treatments, see Schmidt-Bückeburg, *Militärkabinett*, pp. 39–45 and Meisner, *Der Kriegsminister*,

In the second place the army was now in the position of having to have its budget approved by the lower house of the parliament, and the military leaders soon discovered that this arrangement placed very awkward restrictions upon their freedom of action in military affairs. In the years following 1848 the army chiefs, for instance, desired to effect a thorough-going expansion of the military establishment, and it was considered desirable also to reward the army for its loyalty in 1848 by introducing a general increase in pay and allowances. The Ministry of War noted that such an increase had been granted in the Austrian army, and it expressed the fear that failure to imitate this would cause deterioration of morale and discipline.[1] When this question was raised in 1851, however, the War Ministry's proposals were rejected by the civilian ministers of the king on the grounds that the lower house of the parliament would certainly vote down any budget which included them.[2]

In taking this attitude the civilian ministers were being completely realistic. A Chamber in which the liberal opposition was becoming steadily stronger could not be expected to favour any rewards to the army for its services in 1848. Once the constitutional régime had been introduced it was difficult enough to secure approval for normal military budgets; requests for increased appropriations were subjected to very critical scrutiny and often led to noisy debates in which liberal antipathy to the army was given open expression and ancient, as well as recent, incidents of military arrogance toward civilian society were cited to prove that the army deserved no consideration.[3]

For perhaps the first time in its existence the Prussian army was, in short, placed in a position in which it was forced, for

pp. 16ff. An interesting, though highly prejudiced, discussion of the difficulties of the War Minister in these years will be found in a letter of 8 July 1864 from Edwin von Manteuffel to Albrecht von Roon in the Roon Nachlaß currently housed in the Militärgeschichtliches Forschungsamt in Freiburg im Breisgau.

[1] In 1851 Stockhausen said that officers and men were already repeating bitterly: 'The Moor has done his duty; the Moor can go.' Stolberg-Wernigerode, *Stolberg*, p. 97.

[2] Gerlach, *Denkwürdigkeiten*, i. 675–9, 693–8.

[3] The incidents which aroused most indignation in liberal circles in the 1850's were the duel in March 1855 between Freiherr von Patow, a member of the Hansemann ministry in 1848, and a young officer, Graf Schlieffen (see Duncker, *Politischer Briefwechsel*, p. 66), and the death of Police President von Hinckeldey in a duel caused by his attempts to break up a gambling club frequented by officers in 1856 (see *Aus dem Leben Bernhardis*, ii. 284ff.).

material reasons, to worry about its public reputation and popularity. Although it is difficult to cite specific evidence, there are strong indications that the army administration recognized this fact and indulged in a deliberate attempt to glorify the army in the eyes of the people by encouraging the production of works which praised the valour and the achievements of Prussian arms. The historical period which was most suitable for this purpose was that of the war against Napoleon; and it is perhaps no mere coincidence that the 1850's saw the publication of Varnhagen von Ense's *Bülow*, of Pertz's volumes on Gneisenau —which lauded their subject's military talents but played down his political views—and of the memoirs of General von Müffling, of General von dem Knesebeck, and of Ludwig von der Marwitz, all of which discussed the campaigns of 1813–15 in a manner designed to exalt the reputation of the line and the officer corps, while passing over or depreciating those aspects of the liberation which might serve as a source of inspiration to contemporary liberalism.[1] It would be unjust to accuse the army authorities of being responsible in any way for the works of Willibald Alexis, whose highly romanticized patriotic novels concerning the liberation period—notably *Isegrimm* and *Ruhe ist die erste Bürgerpflicht*—were appearing in this same decade;[2] but at least they put no obstacles in the writer's way. This was not true in the case of other authors who threatened to write books which were critical of the army or which discussed incidents which the army desired to have forgotten. While Droysen was writing his adulatory work on York, which appeared in 1851–2, he was given permission to use the papers of the General Staff and was subjected to no censorship. When it was suggested that he might write a similar work on Scharnhorst, and when he indicated that, in doing so, he might be critical—as Scharnhorst would certainly have been critical—of prevailing tendencies in the army and the state, the General Staff firmly vetoed the project.[3] In the same way, when General von Prittwitz wrote a frank account of the events in Berlin on 18–19 March 1848, in an attempt to avoid being made the scapegoat for the military débâcle, he could find no printer who dared publish his book,

[1] On the Marwitz memoirs, see Droysen, *Briefwechsel*, ii. 45–49; on Müffling's, ibid., i. 746; and on Knesebeck's, Max Lehmann, *Knesebeck und Schön*, p. 8.

[2] See Treitschke, *German History*, vii. 139–40.

[3] Droysen, *Briefwechsel*, ii. 458 ff., 466–7, 508–9, 697–8, 700–1; Hintze, *Zur Theorie der Geschichte*, ed. by Fritz Hartung (Leipzig, 1942), p. 207.

and in the end his manuscript was held in a secret file in the General Staff archives until the end of the century.[1]

In the political circumstances of the 1850's, however, it is doubtful whether any propaganda campaign, however skilfully devised and executed, could have lessened parliamentary criticism of the army or made it easier for the military establishment to secure appropriations. In any parliament, requests for military funds are expected to be accompanied by a convincing explanation of the purpose for which they are needed. If the Prussian military chiefs had been able to justify their requests by arguing that a strong army was needed to assure the successful execution of Prussia's foreign policy, they would have experienced little difficulty, even at the hands of the liberal opposition. This, however, they could not do, for they were never able, in the years 1850–7, to convince the liberals that the government or the army had a foreign policy, unless it was the kind of policy defined by Bernhardi in 1857, one 'whose only content was fear of revolution'.[2]

The liberals themselves had very definite ideas about the kind of foreign policy which Prussia should be pursuing. In German affairs they wanted a policy which would seek to solve the German question along the general lines laid down at the Frankfurt Assembly in 1848–9—namely, the union of all German states except Austria into a federative empire with the Prussian King as its ruler. In European affairs in general they advocated collaboration between the new constitutional Prussia and the liberal powers of the West against the country which they considered to be the source and inspiration of international reaction, namely, Russia. Prussia's course in international affairs in the 1850's seemed, however, to be in contradiction to both of these desires.

With regard to the German question, Frederick William IV had flatly repudiated the work of the Frankfurt Assembly when, in April 1849, after completing their plan for a unification of Germany, the members of that Assembly had offered the imperial crown to him. Almost immediately, however, as if to prove that his previous action was not purely negative in character, the king had advanced a substitute plan which, in its main outlines, had emanated from the teeming brain of his close

[1] Haenchen in *Forschungen*, xlv (1933), 102–8.

[2] *Aus dem Leben Bernhardis*, ii. 336.

friend and adviser, Joseph Maria von Radowitz.[1] The Radowitz plan was based upon what he called the 'narrower and the wider union'. It proposed the formation of a German federation from which Austria was to be excluded but which would be bound in perpetual alliance with Austria and would co-operate in all matters of foreign and commercial policy with her. 'To the foreigner', Radowitz said, 'Germany can and must show herself to be a unit';[2] and the Austria-German alliance would make this possible. The narrower union, from which Austria was to be excluded, would be organized in general along the lines laid down at Frankfurt but would be freed from most of the liberal-constitutional ideas introduced into the Frankfurt plan. The executive power would be composed of a college of princes under the Presidency of the King of Prussia and would have an absolute veto right in all legislative matters. The legislature would comprise a House of States, formed of envoys from the various German governments, and a National Assembly whose members were elected by indirect franchise based on status and property qualifications; and financial power would be divided between these two bodies. The fundamental rights of the citizen, which had formed such a conspicuous feature of the Frankfurt constitution, were to be curtailed and left to be adopted at the discretion of the separate member states.[3]

Despite its illiberal features, which Frederick William took pleasure in emphasizing, this project had some attractive features. It did provide for national unity in matters of foreign policy, and Lord Palmerston spoke of it later as 'a very good European arrangement'.[4] It did, moreover, provide for a German National Assembly, something that had long been desired by German liberals.[5] But whatever its advantages, the plan was impractical, for it incurred the inflexible antagonism of the Austrian government. Throughout the latter half of 1849 Austrian diplomacy, under the skilful guidance of Prince Felix

[1] On Radowitz, see especially Friedrich Meinecke, *Radowitz und die deutsche Revolution* (Berlin, 1913).

[2] Friedrich Meinecke, ed. *Joseph von Radowitz: Ausgewählte Schriften und Reden* (*Der deutsche Staatsgedanke*, erste Reihe, xvi), pp. 141 ff.

[3] William Harbutt Dawson, *The German Empire* (New York, 1919), i. 76.

[4] Ibid.

[5] It should be noted that, in June 1849, seventy-five members of the Frankfurt Assembly met at Gotha and declared their support for the Radowitz plan of union, asserting that the aims of Frankfurt were more important than the form in which they were achieved. Srbik, *Deutsche Einheit*, ii. 25–26.

zu Schwarzenberg, sabotaged Prussian efforts to secure the approval of other German governments for the Radowitz plan; and in 1850 the Austrian minister, whose *Gewaltnatur*—as Friedjung has written—'drove him to decisions by force',[1] bluntly confronted Prussia with a choice between abandonment of the project or war.[2]

For Prussia to capitulate before this threat would, Radowitz insisted, be tantamount to abandoning her position of leadership in Germany and casting doubt upon her right to be considered as a Great Power.[3] Yet, as the crisis came to a head in the late summer of 1850, the author of the union project found himself virtually isolated at the Prussian court. The king was plainly horrified at the thought of serious conflict with Austria for, despite his apparent enthusiasm for Radowitz's project, he still held to the romantic notions of his youth, according to which the Austrian Emperor was the natural ruler of the Germanies with the Prussian King standing at his side as his loyal retainer and *Reichserzfeldherr*.[4] Shaken by the apparent imminence of war, Frederick William was readily susceptible to the arguments of his more reactionary advisers—Otto von Manteuffel within the ministry, Leopold von Gerlach, Edwin von Manteuffel, and the other members of the secret camarilla, and virtually all of the soldiers in high administrative posts including General von Stockhausen, the Minister of War. These men, motivated by their fear of liberalism and their belief that the strength of the army should be reserved as a safeguard against a renewal of revolutionary agitation on the home front, showed

[1] Heinrich Friedjung, *Oesterreich von 1848 bis 1860* (2. Aufl., 2 vols., Stuttgart, 1912), ii. 30–31.

[2] This is, of course, a very simplified summary of a complicated situation. The diplomatic manœuvres of 1849 and the early months of 1850 are exhaustively treated in Srbik, *Deutsche Einheit*, ii. 21 ff., 41 ff., and Meinecke, *Radowitz*, pp. 342, 351–6, 374, 387, 393 ff. The most thoughtful analyses of Schwarzenberg's talents and policy will be found in the former of these, in Friedjung's *Oesterreich*, in Louis Eisenmann, *Le Compromis austro-hongrois de 1867* (Paris, 1904), especially p. 156, and in Josef Redlich, *Emperor Francis Joseph* (New York, 1929), pp. 34–39, 65–73. Adolph Schwarzenberg, *Prince Felix zu Schwarzenberg, Prime Minister of Austria, 1848–52* (New York, 1946) is superficial.

[3] Meinecke, *Radowitz*, pp. 442–3. In July Radowitz told Leopold von Gerlach that, if Prussia gave up the union plan, she would be 'degraded and destroyed thereby'. *Denkwürdigkeiten*, i. 504–5.

[4] Meinecke, *Radowitz*, pp. 88–89. The idea of any definite separation between Austria and the rest of Germany was repugnant to the king. It would, he said, leave Germany without Trieste and the Tyrol, which would be 'worse than a face without a nose'. Petersdorff, *Friedrich Wilhelm*, pp. 68–69.

a high degree of skill in devising reasons for a Prussian surrender to Austrian demands. While Stockhausen stressed the inadequacy of the regular forces, the financial weakness of the state, and the political inadvisability of attempting to mobilize the *Landwehr*,[1] the Gerlachs and the Manteuffels insinuated that war would benefit only the liberals and the democrats and that, by releasing the force of revolution once more, it would destroy the institution of monarchy in Prussia, if not in Europe as a whole.[2] They were able to argue, also, that if persistence in the Radowitz policy led to war with Austria, Russia would intervene on the side of the enemy—a thesis which derived some plausibility from the Tsar's known dislike for Prussia's new constitutional order and his obvious concern over the Austro-Prussian conflict.[3]

It is impossible to say what might have happened if the king had rejected these views and supported Radowitz to the end. It is highly likely, in view of Schwarzenberg's character, that war with Austria would have resulted; it is considerably less probable that Russia would, in fact, have intervened.[4] In the event that she had not, Prussia's hopes of success were by no means as uncertain as Stockhausen and others indicated. In the decisive crown council of 2 November, the Prince of Prussia insisted vehemently that the Prussian army was prepared to fight and win, and he is reported to have withdrawn from the council room in tears when the Manteuffel party triumphed.[5] Four years later, when Prince Kraft zu Hohenlohe-Ingelfingen went to Vienna as military attaché, he was shocked by the

[1] On Stockhausen's position, see Srbik, *Deutsche Einheit*, ii. 44, 55; Meinecke, *Radowitz*, p. 443; Droysen, *Briefwechsel*, i. 662; Gerlach, *Denkwürdigkeiten*, i. 468, 503, 513 ff. On other aspects of his career, and his eventual dismissal because of financial differences with the Chamber and with his fellow ministers, see ibid., pp. 603, 632, 637, 639, 645, 668, 675, 678, 680, 693, 702, 706, 714.

[2] See the significant admission by Gerlach. Ibid., p. 561.

[3] According to Gerlach, the Tsar warned Frederick William in a letter in June that changes in European treaties that were made without the approval of the co-signatories must be considered as aggression. Ibid., p. 491. Despite his warm personal feelings for the Prussian King, Nicholas viewed the course of Prussian domestic policy with grave suspicion. As early as December 1849 he had said to the Prussian minister: 'Parliaments in Germany and also in Prussia are prejudicial to all thrones!' Friedjung, *Oesterreich*, ii. 19. Later he was reported to have offered Frederick William 300,000 men to enable him to abrogate the constitution. Meinecke, *Radowitz*, p. 431. He clearly regarded Radowitz as the king's evil genius. Ibid., p. 452; Srbik, *Deutsche Einheit*, ii. 63–64.

[4] See especially Srbik's discussion of this question. Ibid., pp. 73–75.

[5] Roon, *Denkwürdigkeiten*, i. 261–2.

disorganization, the lack of leadership, and the faulty training of the Austrian imperial forces, and concluded that 'it would have been child's play for us in 1850 to throw the whole Austrian army, in the deplorable state in which it was at that time, neck over crop'.[1]

Whatever the military chances they were not taken. In November 1850 Frederick William IV withdrew his support from Radowitz and authorized his ministers to make a settlement with Austria on Schwarzenberg's own terms. On 29 November, at Olmütz, Otto von Manteuffel formally abandoned Prussia's plans for the reorganization of Germany and agreed to the re-establishment of the old Germanic confederation, the inadequacy of which had been generally recognized for two generations. To Prussian liberals, who had rallied behind the Radowitz plan, the Olmütz convention—soon known as 'the shame' or 'the humiliation' of Olmütz—was completely disillusioning; and it coloured their attitude toward the government's foreign and military policy for the next fifteen years. It seemed perfectly clear, especially if one listened to the jubilant chorus raised in court and military circles after Olmütz,[2] that the government had deliberately subordinated its foreign interests to ideological considerations, that its alliance with the forces of European reaction had been confirmed, and that its armed force would be employed in the future only to combat revolution, especially on the home front. It was inevitable, in these circumstances, that the parliamentary representatives of liberalism would grasp every possible opportunity to hamper the expansion of the army and deny its financial requests.

Parliamentary opposition was increased by the course followed by the government during the Crimean War. In that

[1] Hohenlohe-Ingelfingen, *Aus meinem Leben*, i. 296.

[2] Srbik, *Deutsche Einheit*, ii. 85; W. von Schweinitz, ed., *Denkwürdigkeiten des Botschafters H. L. von Schweinitz* (2 vols., Berlin, 1927), i. 40. In military circles, especially among those officers who were to rise to high command in the next generation, there were dissenting voices. See Freiherr von Loë, *Erinnerungen aus meinem Berufsleben* (2. Aufl., Stuttgart, 1906), p. 13. Commenting on the general withdrawal in foreign affairs that followed Olmütz, Helmuth von Moltke said: 'If victory over democracy bears such fruits, one would almost prefer to summon it up again!' Rudolf Stadelmann, *Moltke und der Staat* (Krefeld, 1950), p. 112. On the divided opinions in conservative and even reactionary circles and their political consequences, see Gerhard Ritter, *Die preußischen Konservativen und Bismarcks deutsche Politik* (Heidelberg, 1913), pp. 10–11.

conflict, liberal and popular opinion was strongly in favour of collaboration with the Western Powers, as were, indeed, influential conservative groups. Once again, however, the camarilla showed its talent for seeing policy in purely ideological terms, and while they were never strong enough to secure the alliance with Russia which they seemed to desire, they had sufficient influence to block all attempts at union with Britain and France and to make Prussian neutrality seem, to Prussian citizens as well as to foreigners, a pro-Russian policy.[1] The full extent of their activities—their secret liaison with the Russian court through the office of the Prussian military plenipotentiary in St. Petersburg[2] and their disclosure to the Russians of official correspondence with foreign powers and confidential information concerning Prussian mobilization plans[3]—was not publicly known; but enough was suspected to cause grave parliamentary troubles for the government and for the army, the majority of whose officers were popularly suspected of being 'Russians'.[4] In March 1854, when the government asked the *Landtag* for a credit of 30 million marks, the Chamber referred the request to the *Budgetkommission* which demanded a clear exposition of the government's intentions and accused it and the army of working for an alliance with Russia. The Minister for War, General von Bonin, tried to dispel these suspicions by saying that 'the Government has as little consideration for such an [alliance] as Solon had for parricide in his code of laws'.[5] The effect of this brave announcement was considerably weakened, however, by Bonin's abrupt dismissal from office after he had been accused by other high ranking officers of seeking, by anti-Russian

[1] The most satisfactory account of Prussia's policy during the Crimean War is Kurt Borries, *Preußen im Krimkrieg* (Stuttgart, 1930). For the incredible confusion caused by the king's practice of giving encouragement to factions with widely diverse views on policy, see also Hartung, 'Nebenregierungen', in *Forschungen*, xliv (1932), 14–17.

[2] The reports of this officer, Lieutenant-Colonel H. zu Münster, were not communicated to the Prussian Ministry, and the minister president was ignorant of their contents until he arranged to have some of them stolen by a spy. See H. von Poschinger, ed., *Unter Friedrich Wilhelm IV: Denkwürdigkeiten des Ministerpräsidenten Otto von Manteuffel* (3 vols., Berlin, 1901), iii. 49 ff., 83 ff. See also 'Politische Briefe des Grafen Hugo zu Münster an Edwin von Manteuffel', *Deutsche Revue*, 38. Jg., especially pp. 183–97, 326–37. On the origins and importance of the post of military plenipotentiary in St. Petersburg, see below, pp. 261–66.

[3] *Aus dem Leben Bernhardis*, ii. 184, 199.

[4] Ibid., pp. 230, 243; Hohenlohe-Ingelfingen, *Aus meinem Leben*, i. 228–9.

[5] Borries, *Preußen im Krimkrieg*, pp. 131–2, 156 ff.

remarks, 'to create a schism in the Prussian army' and 'to throw a firebrand between the army and the people'.[1]

In retrospect it must be admitted that the policy of neutrality pursued by Frederick William IV in subsequent months was the course best designed to protect Prussian interests and to preserve her independence as a Power.[2] The benefits accruing from the king's course were not, however, immediately discernible; liberal opinion identified him with the reactionary group which had most intimate contact with him; and the determination with which the king avoided subordinating his policy to that of Austria was less widely remarked than the actions of some of his officials—the appearance, for instance, of Field Marshall von Wrangel and his staff at a *te deum* to celebrate the Russian capture of Kars in December 1854,[3] and the public symbols of mourning worn by Guard officers after the death of Tsar Nicholas in March of the following year.[4] The net effect of the war was, therefore, to confirm the belief of the liberals in the Chamber that their government, and the army that supported it, were completely reactionary and that whatever powers were vested in the Chamber by the constitution must be used to oppose announced policy.

It was only natural that the army, in its turn, should resent the restrictions it encountered. Officers who had fought the revolution in 1848, and who had believed their fight won when the oath controversy was settled in their favour, became convinced that now their victory had been nullified by the privileges granted to the parliamentarians. Military journals became increasingly critical of the '*Montesquieu'schen Kinkerlitzchen*' of the Chamber and increasingly outspoken in their demands that military matters should be reserved to professionals and not decided in debates on the military budget.[5] Technicians who recognized the necessity of reforming and expanding the army as a precaution against the troubled situation left by the Crimean War found it easy to believe that the obstacles placed in their way by parliament were animated by lack of patriotism

[1] R. Koser, 'Zur Geschichte der preußischen Politik während des Krimkriegs', *Forschungen*, ii (1889), 235 n. See also Borries, 139 ff., and Gerlach, *Denkwürdigkeiten*, ii. 142, 145, 147.

[2] This is Borries's view. For a brief summary of the positive gains achieved by Prussian policy, see Srbik, *Deutsche Einheit*, ii. 265.

[3] Gerlach, *Denkwürdigkeiten*, ii. 370.

[4] *Aus dem Leben Bernhardis*, ii. 224–6.

[5] Höhn, *Verfassungskampf*, pp. 364 ff.

or by darker motives. As early as 1851 Griesheim had written pessimistically that the army was an island in society, ringed round by hostile forces.[1] As the reign of Frederick William IV came to an end, it was generally believed in the army that the military was going to be forced soon to fight again for its existence; and Gustav Freytag was writing with alarm:

> The Junkers, the Guard and the Berlin court nobility live in an atmosphere which is reminiscent of the French restoration under Louis XVIII. . . . In all circles of German government, they are predicting a second 1848, and dire and urgent warnings are coursing through Berlin.[2]

In these circumstances it was not difficult to prophesy the coming of a major crisis in which the constitutional position of the army would be the question at issue.

[1] Ibid., pp. 369–70.

[2] Duncker, *Politischer Briefwechsel*, p. 80.

IV

THE ARMY REFORM AND THE CONSTITUTIONAL CONFLICT 1859–1866

'How can the three-year service be given up during his reign without bringing shame upon the personal position of the All-Highest? . . . The army will not understand it; its confidence in the King will be shaken.' EDWIN VON MANTEUFFEL *to Albrecht von Roon, 3 April 1862.*

'The military are panting after riots like the hart after the water-brooks.' MAX DUNCKER *in 1862.*

IN October 1857, worn out by the emotional storms that had filled the last decade, Frederick William IV suffered a physical and mental collapse and was forced to entrust the cares of his office to his brother, Prince William of Prussia. In the course of the year that followed it became apparent that there was no hope of the king's recovery. A formal regency was, therefore, established in October 1858, and Prince William began the reign which he was to continue, as king and emperor, for thirty years, and during which his state was destined to fight three victorious wars, to assert its dominance over the whole of Germany, and to assume a commanding position in the European constellation of Powers.

In the early years of William's reign it would have required remarkable powers of divination to foresee these future glories. Within fifteen months of his accession to power, the prince regent ordered his ministers to submit to parliament a bill calling for the reform and expansion of the Prussian army. The Chamber, unconvinced of the necessity and offended by the form of the project, insisted upon amendments which the Crown was disinclined to grant; and the mutual intransigence of the sovereign and the parliament led inevitably to a constitutional conflict which, on more than one occasion, brought William to the verge of abdication and which, through the bitterness of the passions it aroused, threatened to destroy the very fabric of the state.

The constitutional conflict has justifiably been called 'the central event in the domestic history of Germany in the last hundred years'.[1] During its course the forces of organized Prussian liberalism made their last determined attempt to win a decisive influence over the military establishment of the state. This effort failed, in part because of the skilled tactics of Otto von Bismarck, who at the height of the struggle assumed direction of the royal cause, but in part also because of the divided aims of the liberals themselves and their tendency to subordinate their domestic objectives to their desire for national greatness. The so-called Indemnity Act of September 1866, by which the Chamber gave retroactive approval to the military reforms which had been enacted without its consent, was an act of capitulation from which middle class liberalism never recovered, and its effects have been felt in German history down to our own day.

This, however, is not the whole story. Had the military chiefs had their way, the defeat of the liberals would have been accompanied by the termination of the constitutional experiment and a retreat to a system of complete absolutism. For reasons that will be discussed below, Bismarck prevented the realization of these ambitions. The end of the *Konfliktszeit* was celebrated neither by the abrogation nor by the modification of the Prussian constitution; and, however definitive the defeat of the liberals may have been, it did not free the military establishment from the restrictions of the constitutional régime.

For the army this result was a disappointment and a source of future danger; and the concern of the military leaders grew steadily as Bismarck elaborated his plans for the reorganization of Germany after 1866. They discovered to their dismay that the parliamentary prerogatives to which they had objected most strenuously in Prussia were perpetuated in the constitutional arrangements for the North German Confederation of 1867 and for the new German Reich of 1871, and were vested, moreover, in legislative bodies which, unlike the Prussian Chamber, were elected by direct universal manhood suffrage. The army chiefs had every reason to fear that this widening of the constitutional system to fit the new imperial framework would facilitate the growth of new and more radical opposition parties which, sooner or later, would again contest the absolute supremacy of the Crown in military matters; and the later

[1] Schmitt, *Staatsgefüge und Zusammenbruch*, p. 10.

history of the century was to prove them justified in this apprehension.

I

Historians have long speculated whether the conflict of the 1860's could not have been avoided. Certainly the prince regent had no desire to become involved in political troubles like those which had filled the previous reign. The years had tempered the reactionary views which he had expressed so openly in 1848; and the willingness with which he took the oath to defend the constitution—although his brother had explicitly advised him not to do so[1]—indicated that he wanted no new embroilments with the representatives of the people. Nor were there any immediate signs in the Prussian parliament of a desire to engage in a new struggle with the Crown. Although the *Landtag* elections of November 1858 resulted in a surprising defeat for Prussian conservatism and gave control of the new Chamber to a liberal coalition, the leaders of the new majority were extremely moderate in their views and seemed to be more interested in questions of tax reform than in the troublesome problems of royal and parliamentary prerogatives. In general, moreover, the liberals had greeted the accession of the new ruler with surprising cordiality, and this had turned to open enthusiasm after his first ministerial appointments.[2] Many of their leaders, including men who had been prominent in the parliamentary opposition during the March days, now preferred, if possible, to co-operate with the regent and his ministers rather than to follow the negative tactics of criticism and obstruction.[3] Even in military matters, in which the Prussian Chamber was traditionally sensitive, such co-operation was not absolutely impossible. Like William himself, the liberals had been highly critical of the weakness of Prussia's foreign policy in the last decade, and, in principle, they had no objection to reforms which were designed to make that policy more effective.

[1] In a political testament written before his collapse, Frederick William IV had advised his successor to withdraw the constitution of 1850 and to replace it with a royal *Freibrief*. Hintze, *Die Hohenzollern*, p. 564.

[2] The ministry of Otto von Manteuffel was dismissed on 6 November 1858 and was replaced by one which was composed of liberal conservatives who had opposed the reactionary tendencies of the last eight years and which included, as Minister of War, the popular General von Bonin.

[3] See, for instance, Duncker, *Politischer Briefwechsel*, p. 79.

The political atmosphere of Prussia was still, however, poisoned by the memory of 1848, and the Chamber could not be expected to be completely objective about military matters. If the liberals, in principle, believed that Prussia should have a stronger army, they nevertheless suffered from a gnawing fear that such an army might be used to suppress constitutional liberties in the country. And this fear was now reinforced by the manner in which the regent's reform plan was formulated and by its specific proposals concerning the length of military service and the position of the *Landwehr*.

The story of the evolution of the army reform bill of 1860 is a very tangled one, not only because of the technical issues which had necessarily to be considered but also because the discussion of those issues inspired a remarkable amount of dissension and intrigue within the higher levels of the army itself. Serious consideration of reform plans began as early as October 1857, when Prince William—not yet formally installed as regent—requested the ministry to draw up a list of changes which might improve the efficiency of the armed establishment. In February 1858 the ministry forwarded its suggestions, which were based on an earlier study by Lieutenant-Colonel von Clausewitz. These were aimed primarily at correcting the system of conscription which had, over the course of the years, failed to keep pace with the growth of national population. The ministry pointed out that since 1820 Prussia's population had increased from 10 to 18 millions, whereas the number of recruits taken annually into the army had remained at about 40,000. This meant that an increasing number of those young men who were physically best prepared to serve were escaping military duty entirely, while much older men, who were the heads of families, were required to continue their *Landwehr* duty and would presumably be expected to perform front-line service in time of war. To correct this obviously inequitable system and to make possible an expansion and rejuvenation of line and *Landwehr*, the ministry suggested that the term of service be legally set at two years instead of three and that the annual levies be increased in size.[1]

While he was considering these proposals the prince, in July 1858, received a long memorandum on the state of the armed

[1] Erich Marcks, *Kaiser Wilhelm I* (4. Aufl., Leipzig, 1900), p. 170; F. Löwenthal, *Der preußische Verfassungsstreit, 1862–1866* (Altenburg, 1914), pp. 26–27.

forces from General Albrecht von Roon, a man with whom he had been on terms of intimacy since 1854, when they were both stationed at Koblenz. In words which could not help but strike a responsive chord in William's breast, Roon described the dangerous state of international relations and the perils in which Prussia might become involved unless she built up her armed forces rapidly. He agreed with the experts of the Ministry of War that the annual cadres must be increased in size, although he insisted that, for proper training of recruits, the three-year term of service must be retained. He urged also that every effort must be made to increase the number of trained officers and non-commissioned officers, and suggested that new military schools be established to serve that purpose. But the most emphatic passages of Roon's memorandum concerned the *Landwehr*, and he made no attempt to hide his conviction that that body represented the main drag upon the efficiency of the Prussian army. The *Landwehr*, he argued, was a 'politically false' institution because it no longer impressed the foreigner, while, in view of the fact that 'every *Landwehrmann* has become an elector, thanks to our present parliamentary form of government', the government could not employ it like any normal military force but had to consider the wishes of its members. The *Landwehr* was also a 'militarily false' institution because it lacked proper discipline and was devoid of the quality which Roon described as the 'eigentlichen richtigen festen Soldatengeist'. Roon proposed what amounted to the destruction of the *Landwehr* as a separate arm in the military establishment—the complete absorption of the first levy of that force by the line army by means of the formation of mixed batallions in which the *Landwehr* recruits would be trained and led, in peace-time and in war, by professional officers, and the relegation of the second *Landwehr* levy to nominal defensive functions to which little prestige was attached.[1]

It is perhaps difficult to reconcile this memorandum with Roon's later statement that, at the time of the introduction of the army reform, he had no political designs and was 'guided solely by technical motives'.[2] Yet it is probably true that Roon's

[1] Roon, *Denkwürdigkeiten*, i. 346 ff. The memorandum is printed in its entirety in the same work, ii. 521 ff.

[2] See R. Hübner, *Albrecht von Roon: Preußens Heer im Kampf um das Reich* (Hamburg, 1933), p. 84.

proposals were dictated primarily by the military deficiencies of the *Landwehr*, which had been widely recognized since the 1840's.[1] For the idealism which had inspired Hermann von Boyen when he drew up the *Landwehrordnung* of 1815, Roon had neither sympathy nor understanding. He had made his way to the top of the army in a time when—as Erich Marcks has written—'the philosopher was retreating and the expert was coming forward'.[2] As a man who had worked for forty years to make himself a competent professional soldier and who was devoted to his calling, Roon found it incongruous that the state should be forced to rely so heavily upon a force which was composed of, and led by, men whose principal interests and activities were civilian in nature. An uncompromising realist, Roon saw history as 'the fight for power and increase of power'.[3] If Prussia was to maintain and improve her European position, she would do so only with sword in hand. The basic prerequisite of success was a large, well-trained and well-disciplined army, and one led by professional officers rather than by barristers and merchants whose interest in the trade of arms was only incidental.

As a professional soldier, however, Roon had no comprehension of the political implications of his proposals. His weakness in this respect was immediately recognized by the regent's new Minister of War, Eduard von Bonin.[4] Bonin, who himself admired the work of his great predecessor Boyen, realized the popular veneration in which the *Landwehr* was held; and his immediate comment upon Roon's memorandum was that, if implemented, it would 'separate the army from the country' and create a situation in which Prussia would 'lose the essential condition of her existence', namely, the confidence of the people in the army.[5] Had Bonin made a clear-cut issue of this, much subsequent trouble might have been avoided. Instead of doing so, however, he seems to have attempted to dispose of Roon's awkward proposals by a mixture of procrastination and

[1] See, for instance, *Aus dem Leben Bernhardis*, ii. 336–42, iii. 243–4. Ranke, commenting on its weaknesses in a conversation with Moltke, had gone so far as to say: 'Olmütz war eine Rettung!' Meinecke, *Boyen*, ii. 567.

[2] Marcks, *Männer und Zeiten*, i. 303–4.

[3] Friedrich Meinecke, 'Boyen und Roon', *Historische Zeitschrift*, lxxvii (1896).

[4] On Bonin's earlier term as Minister of War, see above, pp. 125, 133–4. His military talents are touched on in Thilo Krieg, *Constantin von Alvensleben* (Berlin, 1903), p. 14.

[5] Marcks, *Wilhelm I*, pp. 178–9.

constitutional objection and to have been confident that, in the long run, his own influence over the regent would be stronger than Roon's. At the outset he reminded William that the co-operation of the *Landtag* was necessary if any military re-organization was to be effected and suggested that, apart from the *Landwehr* issue, Roon's proposals would involve such a heavy drain upon the resources of the state that the Chamber would not assent to them. In subsequent months, as the regent pressed for action, Bonin reiterated this and similar arguments. Meanwhile, in an appearance before the Chamber during the session of 1859, he assured certain deputies who asked for information about the government's intentions concerning the *Landwehr* that the projected reorganization would not depart from the principles underlying the legislation of 1814 and 1815.[1] This statement also seems to have been an expression of Bonin's confidence in his own ability to guide the regent's thinking.

In reality the War Minister's objections and delays irritated William profoundly, especially as the situation caused by the outbreak of the Italian war made the expansion of Prussian forces more urgent; and this fact played into the hands of Bonin's enemies at court. Chief among these was Edwin von Manteuffel, the Chief of the Military Cabinet, who had reasons for opposing Bonin which were only remotely connected with the question of military reform. Manteuffel objected bitterly to Bonin's interpretation of the prerogatives of his office, and notably to the War Minister's insistence that he be consulted on all military matters, that he be allowed to counter-sign all important military orders and that all royal communications to the commanding generals pass through his hands.[2] He argued that Bonin's penchant for the 'so-called constitutional method of doing business' would destroy the intimate relationship between the Crown and the army. Even before the reform question came to a head, the cabinet chief's constant complaints to the regent had succeeded in making William suspicious of Bonin;[3] and the War Minister's attitude on the reform question

[1] Löwenthal, *Verfassungsstreit*, p. 29; Ritter, *Staatskunst und Kriegshandwerk*, i. 162.

[2] Manteuffel's objections to Bonin's conduct of his office are most clearly stated in a letter from Manteuffel to Roon dated 8 July 1864. The original of this is in the Roon Nachlaß currently housed in the Militärgeschichtliches Forschungsamt in Freiburg im Breisgau.

[3] See Schmidt-Bückeburg, *Militärkabinett*, pp. 66–68, and Meisner, *Kriegsminister*, pp. 23–24. By July 1859 William was weary of these controversies and had pen-

provided Manteuffel with another excuse for urging his elimination. With the help of his friend, the *Generaladjutant*, Gustav von Alvensleben, Manteuffel now intimated to William that Bonin's objections to the proposed reforms were irrelevant and quixotic, if not influenced by ulterior motives.

Under this influence the regent finally decided in September 1859 to by-pass the Ministry of War and to assign the duty of drafting a reform bill to a special military commission under the chairmanship of General von Roon. In appointing this body William specifically ordered its members, as they went about their work, to be guided solely by military expediency and to exclude all other considerations. This outraged Bonin and—even when the commission had made some concessions to his point of view on the *Landwehr* question—he stubbornly insisted that its work was unrealistic, since its proposals would involve an insupportable increase in the military budget.[1] Losing all patience with his Minister of War, the regent sent him a tart note in November in which he said flatly: 'In a monarchy like ours, the military point of view must not be subordinated to the financial and economic, for the European position of the State . . . depends upon it.'[2] Recognizing at long last that his fight was lost, Bonin immediately submitted his resignation. After a month's delay—a rather clumsy attempt on the regent's part to hide the differences among his military advisers from the public eye[3]—his place at the Ministry of War was filled by Albrecht von Roon.

Roon's appointment brought reassurance to those who feared that the constitutional powers of the Minister of War might be used to weaken the royal power of command and to impose restrictions upon the army. In the new minister's scale of

cilled on one of Bonin's letters the querulous complaint: 'Der Kriegsherr kommandiert die Armee und nicht der Kriegsminister.'

[1] Bonin's associates in the Ministry of War blamed the regent's military entourage, and Manteuffel in particular, for encouraging William to write new and expensive provisions into the reform bill, and said that these additions were so numerous that Bonin gave up in despair. *Aus dem Leben Bernhardis*, iii. 295, 309–10.

[2] Marcks, *Wilhelm I*, pp. 178–9. There is a striking similarity between the regent's argument here and that advanced in an earlier letter from Manteuffel to Roon in which the Chief of Military Cabinet had written: 'Der preußische Staat ist in einer Lage, wo er *le tout pour le tout* spielen muß; nur durch die Tüchtigkeit der Armee kann er Chancen haben; darf man diese gefährden durch Unterordnung militärischer Lebensbedürfnisse unter finanzielle Nebenrücksichten?' Roon Papers: Manteuffel to Roon, 30 September 1859.

[3] See Hübner, *Roon*, p. 69.

values, loyalty to the sovereign superseded all others.[1] He liked to think of himself as 'a sergeant in the great company of which the King was the captain';[2] and he found it inconceivable that others should seek to contest royal commands or impose their will upon the Crown. 'My Prussian soldier's heart', he was to write William on a later occasion, 'cannot bear the thought of my King and master subordinating his will to that of another.'[3] Although he had played no part in the intrigue against Bonin, he did not regret his going and was puzzled only that the regent had not dismissed him earlier. After all, Bonin too was a soldier and should have known how to obey. His persistent refusal to execute royal orders showed that he believed that William was 'a Childerich to master and to hold in tutelage and that his designated Pipin was the constitutional Minister of War! Thank God that that is *not* so! Otherwise we should have come a great step closer to sovereignty of the people and a republic.'[4] Before Roon accepted his new office he told William bluntly that he did not hold by 'all of this constitutional business', that he could only serve as an 'expert adviser' (*Fachminister*), and that, if the regent wanted a minister of the 'right constitutional perfume', he had better look elsewhere.[5] In view of this kind of frankness it is understandable that reactionaries of the Gerlach stripe should have hailed Roon's appointment with enthusiasm and seen in it the beginning of an assault upon the settlement of 1850.[6]

In justice to Roon it must be pointed out that he was far less reactionary than those who cheered him. His greatest ambition was to wipe out the shame of Olmütz and to assert Prussia's dominance in Germany—a programme which was far from representing the wishes of the Gerlach circle. The settlement of 1850 he regarded as an accomplished fact and, provided no attempt was made to interfere with the army, he had no desire to subvert it. These views were, however, inadequately appreciated, and if the extreme conservatives were misled in their judgement of the new War Minister, so were the liberals in the Chamber. To the latter, Roon seemed a mere tool of the Junker class, and the knowledge that his appointment had come as a

[1] See especially Meinecke in *Historische Zeitschrift*, lxxvii (1896).
[2] Roon, *Denkwürdigkeiten*, ii. 151.
[3] Eyck, *Bismarck*, i. 362.
[4] Roon, *Denkwürdigkeiten*, i. 399.
[5] Ibid., pp. 398, 406.
[6] See, for instance, Gerlach, *Denkwürdigkeiten*, ii. 709.

result of a dispute over the nature of the army reform bill made it inevitable that the bill would be given a critical reception in parliament.

If the circumstances of the bill's preparation awakened suspicions in the *Landtag*, the specific clauses of the proposed reform confirmed them. The recommendations made by the regent's special commission were not essentially different from those in Roon's original memorandum. The reorganization bill called for so decided an increase in the number of Guard and line infantry and cavalry regiments that the size of the standing army would be practically doubled. The *Landwehr*, simultaneously, was to be sharply reduced, its second levy disappearing completely, its younger recruits henceforth assigned to the army reserve, and the 116 batallions that were left being designated for fortress duty and deprived of all offensive weapons. As both Roon and the War Ministry experts had advised from the beginning, the annual levy of recruits was to be increased to 63,000. The term of service would henceforth be three years with the line, five years in the reserve, and eleven years in the *Landwehr*.[1] Funds were asked to make these changes possible and also to provide for the necessary expansion of the officer corps and the construction of barracks, schools, and training grounds.[2]

The first feature of the bill to excite comment when it was introduced in the Chamber in February 1860 was the estimated cost of the changes it envisaged. Although Bonin, a year before, had promised the deputies that the reorganization would not be extensive, the government was now asking for an increase in the military budget of some $9\frac{1}{2}$ millions of thaler and was stating frankly that even this might not be adequate. It was not only the liberal groups in the Chamber who were worried by this. Prussia was still suffering from the repercussions of the economic depression of 1857. To vote the necessary funds would, it was believed, either burden Prussia with a deficit like that of Austria or necessitate a sharp expansion of the tax load. Neither alternative was very attractive.[3]

[1] There were differences according to the branch of service in which a man was enrolled. Cavalry recruits were to serve four years in the line; infantrymen, pioneers, and naval recruits, three.

[2] For details, see Löwenthal, *Verfassungsstreit*, pp. 34–36.

[3] Egmont Zechlin, *Bismarck und die Grundlegung der deutschen Großmacht* (Stuttgart, 1930), pp. 173 ff.

Apart from the financial aspects, caustic criticism was directed against the provisions for the reduction of the *Landwehr* and the increase in the length of service, the conjunction of which seemed a baleful portent to all liberals. As Bonin had predicted, the attack on the *Landwehr* evoked memories of 1813 and awakened a stubborn determination to protect one of the last remaining fruits of the reform period. 'We cleave to the *Landwehr*', wrote one aroused deputy, 'with religious fanaticism, with the whole weight of our youthful memories.'[1] The liberals were convinced that the *Landwehr* had proven its military worth beyond any reasonable doubt, and they suspected therefore that the government, in reducing its power, was seeking to destroy the bulwark of the people's liberty. The same suspicion influenced their attitude to the proposed lengthening of the term of service. The Prussian army had operated on the basis of the two-year term since 1834; and many famous soldiers from Grolman and Witzleben to Prittwitz and Peucker had declared that adequate for thorough training. It was known that the regent and Roon considered a third year necessary to imbue recruits with an *esprit de corps*, a sense of military honour, a proper devotion to the state and the monarch, and a professional attitude.[2] But was not this merely an attempt to alienate the recruits from the ways of civilian society and to convert them into degraded and unreflecting supporters of absolutism? The liberals wanted no army that was animated only by the principles of *Kadavergehorsam*; and the reorganization bill, with its apparent repudiation of the ideals of Scharnhorst and Boyen, seemed to threaten them with that.

After some preliminary skirmishing, then, the Chamber sent the bill, on 15 February, to its committee on military affairs. Even among the liberals who dominated this body, there was no disposition to reject the government's proposals outright; and the so-called old liberals in particular were anxious to arrange a compromise which would permit the army to be expanded.[3]

[1] Eyck, *Bismarck*, i. 344. [2] Zechlin, *Grundlegung*, pp. 176–7, 179 ff.

[3] *Aus dem Leben Bernhardis*, iii. 272–3. Heinrich von Sybel, for instance, believed that since the liberals were in the majority in the Chamber they should act as the governmental, rather than the opposition, party, and should accept the bill so as to be in a position later to claim credit for its passage. Ibid., pp. 313–14. See also Ritter's remarks on the tendency of the old liberals to regard the *Landwehr* as an outmoded institution, while opposing extension of the term of service. *Staatskunst und Kriegshandwerk*, i. 166–7.

It was soon realized, however, that an effective compromise was unlikely. The questions at issue were by this time being debated far beyond the walls of the legislative chambers; and during the committee deliberations the members received unmistakable indications of strong public opposition to the proposed reduction of the *Landwehr* and to the three-year service term. Even those who feared that their opposition might drive the regent into the arms of the reaction, therefore, felt obliged to withhold their approval from these features of the bill.[1] On the other hand, the representatives of the government and of the army who testified before the committee were completely unco-operative. Not only did they insist flatly upon the *Landwehr* and service provisions, but they also refused to give any detailed information concerning the planned expenditure of the moneys requested. The regent himself took the position that the committee was incompetent to review individual items of the proposed budget;[2] and Roon defended his sovereign's decision in this matter with a scornful arrogance which led to several acrimonious passages between him and the committee chairman.[3]

In the end, therefore, the committee followed the lead of its chairman, Georg von Vincke-Hagen, and its *rapporteur*, the retired General von Stavenhagen. In principle they approved the expansion of the armed establishment. They drew up, however, a long list of specific amendments designed to cut some 6,789,000 thaler from the budget, including a request for a reduction in the proposed number of new regiments, especially Guard regiments which were highly unpopular in liberal circles. They demanded that the two-year service be retained except in the case of cavalry units; and, finally, they insisted that the traditional form of the *Landwehr* be preserved.[4]

There was not the slightest doubt that the Chamber would approve the recommendations of its military committee. Fully aware of this the government, on 5 May, indulged in a surprising manœuvre. The much-criticized army reform bill was

[1] Bernhardi, who believed the bill should be accepted, wrote on 15 April: 'These people believe they have to vote against the government bill . . . simply because they are afraid of the voters, of public opinion so-called—from lack of moral courage.' *Aus dem Leben Bernhardis*, iii. 318.

[2] Schmidt-Bückeburg, *Militärkabinett*, pp. 68 ff.

[3] See Roon Papers: Manteuffel to Roon, 15 May 1860.

[4] Löwenthal, *Verfassungsstreit*, pp. 39 ff.

withdrawn from consideration, and in its place the government asked for a grant of 9 million thaler in excess of the normal budget, to strengthen the army during the next fourteen months. In making this request Finance Minister von Patow stressed the fact that this would be a provisional grant of funds, that granting it would not prejudice later decisions which would have to be made concerning army organization, and that the moneys would be used only to strengthen units which were already authorized by existing laws—specifically, the service law of 1814 and the *Landwehrordnung* of 1815.[1]

For all of those liberals who wished to perpetuate the atmosphere of the 'New Era', these assurances seemed to offer a means of avoiding an action which, they felt, might antagonize their ruler irretrievably. No one seems to have asked how far Patow could claim to be speaking for the regent. The moderate majority in the Chamber took his promises at their face value and, on 15 May 1860, voted the required sums.

This action proved to be a tactical mistake of the highest order.

II

The Chamber's opposition to the reform bill had, meanwhile, caused indignation and alarm among the soldiers who were closest to the regent. They resented the parliamentarians' refusal to accept their professional advice concerning the changes which should be effected in the army; and they found it easy to believe that some secret design lurked behind that refusal. In March the publicist Theodor von Bernhardi talked with former War Minister von Stockhausen and was appalled to discover that the general apparently believed that revolution was imminent. This, said Stockhausen, was what came of the regent's flirting with liberalism. It was all too apparent that the liberals wished to get rid of the professional army so that they could attempt once more to take over the state.[2] Nor was Stockhausen alone in these fears. In the royal entourage even men who were far from reactionary in their views began now to be oppressed by memories of 1848 and to indulge in the most fantastic fears. In this atmosphere it was not difficult for the inveterate opponents of the constitutional system to come forward.

Among this last group the strongest personality, and certainly

[1] Löwenthal, *Verfassungsstreit*, pp. 41–42; Brandenburg, *Reichsgründung*, i. 423.
[2] *Aus dem Leben Bernhardis*, iii. 279.

the most influential, was the man who had engineered Bonin's fall, Edwin von Manteuffel. Among all the political generals who appear in the German history of the nineteenth century Manteuffel stands out as the most interesting and the most controversial. A gifted military administrator, a diplomatist of more than ordinary competence, and a field commander who was to prove himself in the campaigns of 1866 and 1870, Manteuffel was never far from the centre of the political stage during his lifetime, and it is probable that he failed to rise to that position of eminence later attained by Bismarck only because of the distrust caused by his intense personal vanity and his burning ambition. Even his admirers were at times repelled, or amused, by Manteuffel's conscious attempt to model himself after such giants of the past as Epaminondas, Hannibal, and Wallenstein;[1] and Bismarck, who was often irritated by his airs, once dismissed him as 'a fantastic corporal'.[2] Yet even with his defects there was nothing ignoble in Manteuffel's character. If, throughout his life, he yearned for greatness, he did so only that his greatness might give him an opportunity to serve his king and his country. All things considered, the judgement passed on him by General Schweinitz is probably more just than those of his contemporary critics or those of most liberal historians. 'A burning love for his country', Schweinitz wrote, 'true piety, enthusiasm for the noble and the sublime filled this true Prussian heart; Christian humility and classical greatness of soul united in this man and made him, to whom nature had given the bent to fanaticism, a model of those virtues upon which Prussia's greatness is founded.'[3]

Politically, Manteuffel was an unwavering absolutist and, in his mind, the greatest mistake ever made by the Prussian monarchy had been its decision to grant a constitution to the Prussian people. This action, he believed, had prevented the definitive crushing of the revolution in 1848 and had exposed the monarchy to the danger, indeed the certainty, of new attacks. Since 1850 Manteuffel had awaited with gloomy anticipation

[1] As a tribute to Epaminondas, Manteuffel at one time considered naming his first-born sons Leuctra and Mantinea. He was so fascinated by the character of Wallenstein that he was reputed to have memorized all of Schiller's drama on that hero. See especially Ludwig Dehio, 'Manteuffels politische Ideen', *Historische Zeitschrift*, cxxxi (1925), 63-64.

[2] Eyck, *Bismarck*, i. 281-2.

[3] Schweinitz, *Denkwürdigkeiten*, i. 242-3.

the hour when the forces of liberalism and democracy would make their new bid for power. When the Chamber forced the withdrawal of the army reform bill in 1860, he was sure that that hour had come.[1]

Finding his darkest prognostications confirmed, however, Manteuffel threw himself into the fight with vigour and with a kind of solemn joy. His romantic imagination and his love for historical models led him to think of the regent as being in the position of Charles Stuart, menaced by the rebellious Commons; and he fancied himself as another Strafford, standing beside the sovereign in this crisis and, if necessary, giving his life that the royal position might be maintained.[2]

Like Strafford also, Manteuffel called for the policy of Thorough; and it is this that makes his role in the constitutional struggle important. From 1860 to 1866 he was the leader of that party in the state that rejected all idea of compromise with the opposition and called for the imposition of the royal will even at the cost of civil war. As early as 11 March, he made his position perfectly clear in a letter to Roon:[3]

> I have always found in my twelve years of experience in revolutionary life [he wrote] that when a question of principle rises, all the world counsels concession and compromise and advises against bringing matters to a head; and that when this or that minister has acted upon these rules of prudence and the momentary mood has passed, then everyone says: 'How could he have given in like that?'

He was determined that, as long as he had any influence, there would be no compromise with the Chamber. On the contrary, the policies which he advocated seemed at times designed to force things to an issue, even to provoke revolution, on the assumption that the subsequent suppression of the rebels would enable the Crown to dispense with the constitution and re-establish the pre-1848 political system.

It is perhaps an indication of Manteuffel's compelling person-

[1] These passages, and subsequent ones on Manteuffel, are based on an earlier study by the author, and the earlier text has sometimes been closely followed. See Gordon A. Craig, 'Portrait of a Political General: Edwin von Manteuffel and the Constitutional Conflict in Prussia', *Political Science Quarterly*, lxvi (1951), 1–36.

[2] '. . . [Manteuffel's] ideal was Lord Strafford in prison, who, when he was condemned to die for his royalism, wrote to his King pleading that he confirm this death sentence, since his execution was at this moment the only possible salvation for the monarchy.' Hohenlohe-Ingelfingen, *Aus meinem Leben*, iii. 172.

[3] Roon Papers: Manteuffel to Roon, 11 March 1860.

ality that both the regent and Roon should have followed his lead almost blindly in the early stages of the dispute with the Chamber and that it was not until mid-1862 that they became fearful of the extreme measures he advocated. Certainly Manteuffel's influence was at work in the determination of the tactics followed by the Crown after the withdrawal of the army reform bill in May 1860 and in the regent's authorization of measures which were clearly at variance with the spirit of Finance Minister von Patow's declaration to the Chamber.

At the beginning of the year, even before the bill had been sent to the Chamber, the prince regent had taken the first steps toward realizing his desired reform of the army by authorizing the creation of certain new 'combined regiments', designed to replace existing *Landwehr* units.[1] When the Chamber refused to approve the bill, however, the legality of the new formations was dubious; and it remained so even after the deputies had made their provisional grant of funds for military purposes. If Patow's assurances meant anything, these funds could not be employed to effect fundamental changes in the structure of the army; and it would seem to follow, therefore, that they could not be used to support 'combined regiments' the purpose of which was to facilitate the reduction of the *Landwehr*. Strictly speaking the new units should have been disbanded. The regent hesitated, however, to give them up; and he was encouraged in this by his Chief of Military Cabinet. Manteuffel, indeed, urged that, despite the Chamber's action, the units should be organized definitively, commissioned, and entered into the line of battle. Either to disband them or to consider them provisional formations would be an admission that the Chamber had the right to determine the strength and organization of the army. 'I consider the state of army morale and its inner energy imperilled and the position of the prince regent compromised', he wrote to Roon, 'if these regiments are not established definitively at once.'[2] 'Your Excellency said recently that to make the army really strong is the best and most influential measure against the attacks of the opposition—and I am also convinced of that. Reasoning helps little; facts convince.'[3]

[1] Löwenthal, *Verfassungsstreit*, p. 44.

[2] Roon Papers: Manteuffel to Roon, 29 May 1860. In another letter of the same date Manteuffel intimated that he would not feel bound by Patow's declarations. The question, he said, was 'whether the King or Minister Patow was war-lord'.

[3] Ibid., 26 June 1860.

Manteuffel was using similar arguments in his talks with the regent[1] and was apparently pleading his cause well, for, in the last months of 1860, William proceeded to issue the desired orders to the new regiments. Moreover, after the death of his brother and his own succession to the royal title, William went a step further. He announced that on 18 January 1861 he would dedicate the standards of the new regiments at the tomb of Frederick the Great. A gesture so provocative was sure to cause a sharp deterioration of relations between Crown and parliament, a prospect which did not please William's civilian ministers. Accordingly they sent one of their number, Rudolf von Auerswald, to Manteuffel, urging him to dissuade the king from proceeding with the ceremony. Auerswald found Manteuffel delighted with the royal announcement and in his most arrogant mood. Coldly he said:

> I do not understand what Your Excellency desires. His Majesty has ordered me to arrange a military ceremony. Am I to renounce this because there are a number of people sitting in a house in the *Dönhoffplatz*, who call themselves a *Landtag* and who may be displeased with this ceremony? I fail to see how these people concern me. As a general, I have never yet been ordered to take my instructions from these people.[2]

The dedication, then, took place as scheduled; and it has justly been considered the decisive event in securing the success of the military reforms.[3] The future organization of the army and the fate of the *Landwehr* had, in effect, been decided by a royal *fait accompli*. The action enraged liberal opinion; and, throughout the parliamentary session of 1861, there were heated attacks against the military caste and considerable talk about cutting the military budget.[4] But the moderate liberals still hesitated to take up the gage thrown down by the Crown, and they ended the rhetorical exercises by making another provisional grant of funds to the government, insisting, however, that in the next session a comprehensive military service law be placed before the Chamber for consideration.[5]

This timid action should have been enough to convince the king that Manteuffel's talk of a liberal conspiracy against the

[1] Roon Papers: Manteuffel to Roon, 17 July 1860.

[2] Hohenlohe-Ingelfingen, *Aus meinem Leben*, ii. 255–6.

[3] See, for instance, Zechlin, *Grundlegung*, p. 183.

[4] Löwenthal, *Verfassungsstreit*, pp. 49–50.

[5] Ibid., pp. 54–57.

Crown was, at the very least, exaggerated. But William was so irritated by attacks on his beloved army that his mind was closed to cooler calculations and, in any event, his attention was now diverted by another theatrical gesture on the part of his Chief of Military Cabinet. In the spring of 1861 an obscure city councillor named Carl Twesten wrote a brochure in favour of retention of the two-year service law in the course of which he accused the Military Cabinet, and Manteuffel personally, of seeking to divorce the army completely from the Prussian people, and warned that this could easily 'produce an atmosphere of distrust and hostility between the military and civil society such as existed in its fullest flower before 1806'.[1] Manteuffel immediately placed before Twesten the alternatives of withdrawing his views[2] or fighting a duel, and, when Twesten chose the latter, shot him through the arm.

Before proceeding with this *opera bouffe* affair—which gave wide publicity to a pamphlet which would otherwise have dropped into obscurity—Manteuffel informed all of his associates that his action was necessitated by the fact that Twesten was a tool of the secret revolutionary party which was plotting to overthrow the state. He doubtless believed this himself[3] and he certainly convinced the king that it was true; for William, far from being outraged by the presumption of his cabinet chief, wrung his hands in despair at the thought that he might be expected to punish Manteuffel for his courage. He wrote to his War Minister:

> At this moment, to be deprived of Manteuffel's services, to have him hunted out of my presence by the triumph of democracy—the bother that this event will cause in my intimate circle—these are things which can rob me of my senses because they impress yet another unhappy stamp upon my reign. *Wo will der Himmel mit mir hin*![4]

Manteuffel, characteristically, insisted upon being punished and spent some weeks in fortress detention at Magdeburg, playing the role of Strafford with great enjoyment. 'The more severe

[1] *Was uns noch retten kann*, especially pp. 61, 77–82.

[2] Manteuffel did not restrict his demand to a withdrawal by Twesten of personal remarks about him but demanded, in effect, that he renounce the entire contents of his pamphlet. This Theodor von Bernhardi, among others, found completely unjustifiable. *Aus dem Leben Bernhardis*, iv. 131–2.

[3] Schmitz, *Manteuffel als Geschichtsquelle*, pp. 42–43.

[4] Roon, *Denkwürdigkeiten*, ii. 21.

the king seems to be to me here, the better position he and Your Excellency will be in to be severe to the other side . . . Liberalism and Jacobinism and Parliamentarianism.' He urged Roon to stiffen the king's resistance and to remind him of the words of Maria Stuart, in Schiller's drama: 'Bleibt bei der Sache, Lord, und weicht nicht aus.'[1]

Such warnings, however, were now scarcely necessary. Events in the latter half of 1861 caused a virtual panic in royal circles and created precisely the emotional atmosphere which was most favourable to Manteuffel's plans. The principal cause of this was a marked shift to the left on the part of parliamentary liberalism, the foundation of the *Deutsche Fortschrittspartei*, and the decisive victory of this party in the *Landtag* elections of 6 December. Now the strongest single party in the Chamber, the D.F.P. called for a much more aggressive programme than the moderate liberal groups which had dominated the Chamber since 1859; it was pledged to the progressive development of the constitutional system, the reform of the upper house, and a more complete realization of the principle of ministerial responsibility; and, with respect to the army, it was insistent upon retention of the two-year service, maintenance of the *Landwehr*, and close supervision of the military budget.[2]

The programme and the electoral victory of the D.F.P. caused consternation among the king's military advisers. Roon, whose letters in the course of 1861 were filled with dark references to encroaching chaos and yawning abysses at the foot of the throne,[3] began now to talk ominously of eliminating the Chamber completely.[4] Prince Frederick Charles, the Hotspur of the court, wanted to purge the ministry of unsound elements and place a soldier, preferably Roon, at its head.[5] In a conversation with Max Duncker in January 1862, Colonel von Seidlitz said: 'In high military circles, they are afraid of everything. They are talking of a *coup d'état*; they suspect a great revolution'; and he went on to say that telegraph lines were being laid

[1] Roon Papers: Manteuffel to Roon, 6 July 1861. How little Roon needed this advice is shown in Ritter, *Staatskunst und Kriegshandwerk*, i. 180–1, 184–5.

[2] Kaminski, *Verfassung*, pp. 60–1; Eyck, *Bismarck*, i. 370–1; Zechlin, *Grundlegung*, pp. 201–2.

[3] Roon, *Denkwürdigkeiten*, ii. 38 ff.

[4] *Aus dem Leben Bernhardis*, iv. 172 ff.

[5] Roon, *Denkwürdigkeiten*, ii. 58–59, 62. On the prince's views, see also *Prinz Friedrich Karl von Preußen, Denkwürdigkeiten aus seinem Leben*, ed. by Wolfgang Foerster (2 vols., Stuttgart, 1910), i. 268.

between the castle and the various garrisons in Berlin, and that Field Marshal Wrangel had advised the queen to have iron gratings put in her windows.[1] Manteuffel, meanwhile, was urging the king to make even more elaborate preparations against the time of trouble. In the course of 1861 his friend General Hiller von Gärtringen, who had carried the challenge to Twesten, had prepared an operations plan for the expected campaign in Berlin. This involved the immediate strengthening of the Berlin garrisons; the placing of artillery in prepared trenches at Windmühlenberg and of light mortars on the roof of the *Schloß*; the withdrawal of the royal family from Berlin at the first sign of disorder—obviously a reflection of Manteuffel's memories of March 1848; and a systematic and remorseless conquest of the city by the army.[2]

In the months preceding the elections this plan was discussed thoroughly in the Military Cabinet and in the presence of the king; and in January 1862 the king adopted a modification of the Hiller–Manteuffel plan. In the event of a rising in Berlin this envisaged the employment against the rebels of 34,500 infantry and engineers, 16,000 horse, and 100 field pieces, the local units operating outward from the area of the *Schloß* and the provincial regiments enveloping and assaulting the city from without. Sealed orders were sent to the units which would be used in this campaign, with instructions that they were to be opened only upon telegraphic advice. These orders included explicit instructions that negotiations with the rebels would be considered a violation of military honour and that officers surrendering their posts to the rebels would be tried by military tribunal.[3]

This was, ostensibly, a defensive plan, a necessary precaution against the threat of revolution; but there is every reason to believe that the leading spirit behind it, Edwin von Manteuffel, was eager to have it put into effect even if he had to provoke the Chamber into revolution. And Manteuffel's influence seemed never greater than it was during the first months of 1862; both the king and Manteuffel's nominal superior, War Minister Roon, were apparently completely under his spell. In

[1] Duncker, *Politischer Briefwechsel*, 305.

[2] Ludwig Dehio, 'Die Pläne der Militärpartei und der Konflikt', *Deutsche Rundschau*, ccxiii (1927), 93–94.

[3] Ibid., pp. 94 ff. These orders were not called back until after the end of the Danish war in 1864.

March 1862—after the Chamber had refused the three-year service law, rejected the government's request for funds, and demanded a complete itemization of the budget[1]—Manteuffel not only urged dissolution of the Chamber but insisted that, because of its inability to control the Chamber, the ministry should be purged of its more liberal members and reformed in a conservative direction.[2] When both these measures were taken, Bernhardi recognized them as a sign that Manteuffel had reached the goal toward which he had been working 'with shrewd calculation'.[3] There were, indeed, indications that strong action was not far off. On 23 March Bernhardi spent the evening with Roon, and the War Minister expressed the opinion that, if the forthcoming elections were unfavourable to the government, it could hardly be expected 'to sheathe its sword and retreat'. Bernhardi said: 'Then we may be in position in June in which a *coup d'état* is unavoidable'; and Roon answered: 'On that I am determined.'[4] Bernhardi was inclined to dismiss this as scare talk, but three days later General Peucker told him that the new ministry expected a rising before the May elections, and was confident that it would be suppressed and would be followed by a thorough-going political reaction. Peucker added that troops in Berlin were restricted to their quarters and that live ammunition had already been distributed. Bernhardi wrote in his diary: 'I am convinced that these things emanate not from Roon and the ministers but from a quite different source'[5]—presumably from Manteuffel.

In these weeks following the dissolution of the *Landtag* the constitutional conflict came to full crisis, and had there been even a minor outbreak of disorder in Berlin it seems probable that the secret orders would have been put into effect. In that case Manteuffel might very well have realized his dream of entering the pages of history as the great soldier-statesman in Prussia's critical hour. For the kind of warfare that would have ensued in Berlin he had a stronger will than Roon and more

[1] On this, see Löwenthal, *Verfassungsstreit*, pp. 69 ff.; Kaminski, *Verfassung*, pp. 61 ff.; A. Wahl, *Beiträge zur Geschichte der Konfliktszeit* (Tübingen, 1914), pp. 13–14.

[2] Roon Papers: Manteuffel to Roon, 7 March 1862. Roon also had long been critical of some of his colleagues, suspecting them of a desire to compromise with the Chamber. See *Denkwürdigkeiten*, ii. 23–24. On 19 March the liberal conservatives Auerswald, Schwerin, and Patow were dismissed. Ibid., p. 70.

[3] *Aus dem Leben Bernhardis*, iv. 238.

[4] Ibid., pp. 255–6.

[5] Ibid., p. 260.

military ability than Wrangel;[1] and, once his plans had led to the complete suppression of the rebels, he would have earned the right to direct the backward revision of the constitution. Indeed, throughout the spring and summer of 1862, there was talk, at least in the reactionary group headed by the Gerlachs and Kleist-Retzow, of elevating Manteuffel to the position of Minister President.[2]

Manteuffel's great hour, however, never arrived. At this crucial moment in Prussian affairs both the king and Roon began to entertain doubts concerning the advisability of bringing matters to a head. At the beginning of April the king—in despair over the opposition of the Chamber—intimated that he was confronted with a choice between concessions to the opposition or abdication. This horrified Manteuffel, and he pleaded with the king to stand firm. As he wrote later:

> I told the King that I had advised him four years ago that we were living in a revolution; but the question was whether he would act like Charles I and Louis XVI and allow power to be wrested from his hands before it came to an open fight. Today he still had power and had the army; if, however, he gave way at the expense of the army, in order to secure favourable election results, he would still not secure that objective but would only shake the army's confidence in his firmness.[3]

To Roon, who was also beginning to wonder whether it would not be wise to seek a compromise with the Chamber, even at the expense of the three-year service, Manteuffel made the same arguments. In a letter of 3 April he pointed out that the king had identified himself so definitely with the lengthened service term that a compromise would now be regarded by the army as a surrender. The fight must go on, he insisted, and, if the elections were not favourable to the royal cause, then 'we shall see bloody heads, and *then* good elections results will come. . . . The views of the king must be maintained; nothing must happen to compromise him.'[3] Five days later Manteuffel sent

[1] In the event of fighting in Berlin, Wrangel was to be over-all commander of the troops. See Dehio in *Deutsche Rundschau*, ccxiii. 96.

[2] Ritter, *Die preußischen Konservativen*, p. 69.

[3] Dehio in *Deutsche Rundschau*, ccxiii. 99. Wrangel told the king that abdication would be desertion in the face of the enemy and threatened him with the mutiny of the whole army.

[4] Roon Papers: Manteuffel to Roon, 3 April 1862.

another urgent reminder to his colleague. 'In 1848', he wrote, 'purely political considerations induced the late King to break off the fight; he gave them priority over the purely military; he thought that the soldiers would understand that he would be able to return to the military principle—he desired to do so twelve hours later—he could no longer do so; their faith in his firmness was gone.'[1]

There can be no doubt that these arguments were effective, at least as far as the king's attitude was concerned. Indeed, it seems likely that, if it had not been for Manteuffel's influence, the differences between the Chamber and the Crown could have been adjusted before the end of 1862. The fact that the D.F.P. increased its parliamentary strength in the *Landtag* elections of May 1862, had a depressing effect upon the king's ministers; and the strongest personality among them, the new Finance Minister von der Heydt,[2] undertook to investigate once more the possibility of an arrangement with the opposition. Negotiations with the Chamber revealed a desire to temporize there also. Accordingly, Heydt persuaded his ministerial colleagues, including Roon, to recommend the retention of the two-year service term if the Chamber would vote the funds necessary to support the military reforms. The War Minister, indeed, actually announced his support of this bargain to an enthusiastic Chamber on 17 September. On the same day, however, in two dramatic meetings with his ministers, the king refused absolutely to give way on the service issue, declaring that, unless he could rule in accordance with the dictates of his conscience, he would abdicate.[3] Horrified by this announcement, Roon reversed his position completely and abandoned the compromise which had been so painfully arrived at. Infuriated by the unreliability of their colleague, Heydt and the ministers Holzbrinck and Bernstorff handed in their resignations, while the Chamber, with a justifiable sense of having been betrayed, rejected the military budget out of hand.[4] Manteuffel's indoctrination of his sovereign had, in short, suc-

[1] Roon Papers: Manteuffel to Roon, 8 April 1862.

[2] On Heydt see Alexander Bergengrün, *Staatsminister August Freiherr von der Heydt* (Leipzig, 1908), especially pp. 298–308.

[3] Löwenthal, *Verfassungskonflikt*, pp. 99–104; Zechlin, *Grundlegung*, pp. 291–8.

[4] Roon's behaviour is favourably analysed in Harbou, *Dienst und Glaube in der Staatsanschauung Albrecht von Roons* (Berlin, 1936), pp. 68, 73 ff., 122–3, and Marcks, *Männer und Zeiten*, i. 317–18.

ceeded in cutting off even the provisional funds which the Chamber had granted heretofore.[1]

If, on the other hand, Manteuffel's hope was to create a situation in which a *coup d'état* was made inevitable he was disappointed. However much the Chief of the Military Cabinet might yearn for bloody heads and the kind of open conflict which would justify a return to absolutism, the king had no stomach for such a trial by arms. The frequency with which he reverted to the idea of abdication made this abundantly clear. And that meant, of course, that the elaborate plans for a campaign in Berlin, which had been approved in January 1862, would never be put into effect unless the Chamber itself took the initiative and precipitated a revolution. There was no likelihood of this. Despite its aggressive programme, the D.F.P. did not want to fight a revolution to secure it. Predominantly drawn from the middle economic groups, its members remembered the disorders of 1848 with something less than pleasure; and in any case—as Johannes Ziekursch has written—barristers and business men do not man barricades.[2] The deputies placed their reliance, not in revolt, but in the expected results of their financial boycott of the government.

With both sides refusing then to make the final resort to force, the conflict became perforce a struggle of attrition, the main campaigns of which would have to be fought in parliament. In such a contest Manteuffel could not hope to play a dominant role; decisions on questions of principles and tactics would be made, in the last analysis, by the king's ministers who had to face the opposition in parliament. The Chief of the Military Cabinet had, moreover, by encouraging the king's stubbornness, unwittingly prepared the way for the minister who was to win an even higher degree of the king's confidence than he himself possessed and who was gradually, although not without some difficulty, to push him from the centre of the political stage. For, in September 1862, in a desperate attempt to escape from the ministerial crisis which his own intransigence had precipitated, the king called to office Otto von Bismarck-Schönhausen.

[1] The influence of Manteuffel and the other soldiers was not lost on contemporaries. Duncker wrote on 21 September: 'The military party does not become weary of telling the king that the army will leave him if he concedes the two year service.' *Politischer Briefwechsel*, p. 335.

[2] Johannes Ziekursch, *Politische Geschichte des neuen deutschen Kaiserreiches* (3 vols., Frankfurt, 1925-32), i. 64-65.

III

The Bismarck who came to power in 1862 was a different man from the young backwoodsman who had preached a philosophy of primitive absolutism in the united diet of 1847. The Junker politician of that earlier period had been transformed by twelve years of diplomatic experience into a statesman whose views were no longer in accordance with those of his reactionary patrons. As early as 1850 he had indicated the profound difference which existed between his own thinking and that of men whose fear of revolution led them to subordinate foreign to domestic policy and to allow Prussia's external interests to be guided by ideological considerations. 'The only sound basis for a great State', he had written at that time, 'is stately egoism and not romanticism, and it is not worthy for a great State to fight for a cause which has nothing to do with its own interest.'[1] Six years later, in the so-called *Prachtbericht* from Frankfurt, he had more explicitly stated what he considered Prussia's interest to be and where he believed stately egoism must lead her. Prussia's mission, he said, was to extend her power and territory in Germany, and this could be accomplished only at the expense of Austria.

> Because of the policy of Vienna, Germany is clearly too small for us both; as long as an honourable arrangement concerning the influence of each cannot be concluded and carried out, we will both plough the same disputed acre, and Austria will remain the only state to whom we can permanently lose or from whom we can permanently gain. . . . For a thousand years intermittently—and, since Charles V, every century—the German dualism has regularly adjusted the reciprocal relations [of the two Powers] by a thorough internal war; and in this century also no other means than this can set the clock of evolution at the right hour. . . . In the not too distant future, we shall have to fight for our existence against Austria and . . . it is not within our power to avoid that, since the course of events in Germany has no other solution.[2]

During the years that followed the Crimean War Bismarck had held fast to these views. He was bitterly scornful of the sentimentalists who wished to come to Austria's aid during the Italian war of 1859; and he had protested to General von Alvensleben that it would be more in accord with the true interest of

[1] Bismarck, *G.W.*, x. 103. [2] Ibid., ii. 142.

the state for Prussian troops to take advantage of Austria's troubles and to 'move south with boundary posts in their knapsacks'.[1] Now, in 1862, as he assumed the Minister Presidentship, there was no doubt that he was desirous of moulding Prussian policy to the requirements of his own realistic opportunism.

Bismarck's foreign plans necessarily influenced his attitude toward the tangled controversy between Crown and Chamber. Determined to put an end to the policy of drift that had characterized Prussia's foreign relations since 1850 and to inaugurate a policy which would almost inevitably lead to a struggle with Austria, the new Minister President wished to remove the constitutional issues which were presently preventing national unity and strength.[2] In the trials that lay ahead Prussia would require all her energies and resources, the intelligence and industry of the middle classes, as much as the courage and professional skill of the officer corps. Bismarck was fully in accord with the technical considerations which had motivated the army reform; and he completely agreed that the king's power of military command and military affairs in general must not be subjected to parliamentary control. In assuming office he had promised the king that he would fight for these things; but he was determined that in doing so he would not deliver himself into the hands of the reactionary party, which had no sympathy for his foreign objectives. This consideration excluded the possibility of resorting to a domestic *Putsch* and of seeking to destroy parliament and revoke the constitution of 1850. On the contrary, Bismarck was intent upon reaching some kind of reconciliation with the parliamentary opposition, and he described his objective as being 'an understanding with the majority of the deputies which will not at the same time prejudice the future authority and governmental powers of the Crown or endanger the proficiency of the army'.[3]

Despite the general belief that his advent to power heralded extreme reactionary measures[4] and despite his first forthright

[1] Eyck, *Bismarck*, i. 321.

[2] Bismarck himself said that a prolongation of the crisis would be 'an essential and grave obstacle to our prestige and our action abroad'. Zechlin, *Grundlegung*, pp. 324–5.

[3] Kaiser Friedrich III, *Tagebücher von 1848–1866*, ed. by H. O. Meisner (Leipzig, 1929), p. 505. Thus Bismarck defined his objective in a letter to the crown prince dated 13 October 1862.

[4] See O. Nirrnheim, *Das erste Jahr des Ministeriums Bismarcks* (Heidelberg, 1908), pp. 58 ff.

utterances to the Chamber, which seemed to support this belief,[1] Bismarck's principal efforts during his first month of office were devoted to a search for an arrangement which might remove the current stalemate. These, however, failed to achieve tangible results, partly because of liberal suspicions of the new minister,[2] but in large part also because Bismarck's freedom of negotiation with the deputies was severely restricted by the fixed prejudices of his king. William's stubbornness was encouraged, as usual, by his military advisers, some of whom were fully as suspicious of Bismarck as were the liberals;[3] and the Minister President soon learned that his nicest calculations could be disrupted by this kind of backstairs influence.

This discovery was made when, in collaboration with his friend Roon, Bismarck, in October 1862, conceived an entirely new approach to the army dispute.[4] The two ministers drafted for submission to the Chamber an army service bill which provided first, that the size of the army would henceforth be fixed at a given percentage of the population—probably 1 per cent. This army would consist of two elements: long-term volunteers (*Capitulanten*) comprising one-third of the total force; and conscripts who would serve for only two years. To support the volunteer formations—the existence of which would presumably reduce the number of conscripts called annually—all eligible males who were placed in the *Ersatzreserve* instead of being called up, and all actual conscripts who wished to be sure that their term of service would not exceed two years, would pay a special tax (*Einstandsgeld*). Finally, instead of having to pore over the complicated details of a military budget, the Chamber would henceforth automatically grant a fixed annual sum (*Pauschquantum*) per soldier in the army.

This plan could not help but be attractive to elements of the opposition, and therein lay its shrewdness. The provision for two-year service for conscripts would satisfy one of the liberals'

[1] Löwenthal, *Verfassungsstreit*, pp. 116–21.

[2] See the accounts of Bismarck's conversations with Twesten and Simson in ibid., p. 116, and Zechlin, *Grundlegung*, pp. 324–5.

[3] Manteuffel was especially so. See Roon Papers: Manteuffel to Roon, 4 October 1862.

[4] Ludwig Dehio, 'Bismarck und die Heeresvorlagen der Konfliktszeit', *Historische Zeitschrift*, cxliv (1931), 31 ff. The plan was drafted by Roon, but Dehio's argument that Bismarck was the moving spirit behind it is convincing. Cf. Ritter, *Staatskunst und Kriegshandwerk*, i. 192–3, 364.

most important demands, while the introduction of volunteer contingents and the elaborate scheme of taxes for their support seemed to promise that well-to-do young men might be exempted from active service in peace-time. Behind these concessions to the opposition, however, lay very tangible advantages for the Crown. The *Pauschquantum* scheme was a clever blow at the budgetary rights of the Chamber; and the royal *Kommandogewalt* would certainly be strengthened by the proposed removal of the questions of army strength and finance from the area of parliamentary discussion.

It is impossible to say what effect this plan would have had if submitted to the Chamber. It seems likely that if it had not won the opposition it might have split it. It never had a chance to do either, for it was effectively sabotaged by Edwin von Manteuffel. Doubtless moved in part by growing jealousy of Bismarck but certainly more by his hatred of concession in any form, he argued that the prospective advantages to the Crown were outweighed by the moral victory which the admission of the two-year service would give to the opposition. Moreover, to allow the peace-time strength of the army to be fixed by a law, however permanent, was to weaken the whole constitutional position of the Crown. The king had always insisted that, in military affairs, the Chamber had only a budgetary right; decisions on size, organization, and command of the army were made by the king alone.[1] These arguments were perhaps not convincing to Bismarck, but they were to the king. Overborne by the eloquence of his Chief of Military Cabinet, he refused to countenance the plan.[2]

Bismarck must have been aware after this experience that further attempts at this time to seek a compromise with the Chamber would be inadvisable, if not dangerous. In the minds of the king and his military entourage they would only arouse doubts concerning his reliability and firmness of purpose, and he might find himself going the way of Patow and Heydt and other ministers who had been too lenient in their dealings with the deputies. From now on he was forced to be more royalist than the king, and, as he said, with a regretful reference to the *Pauschquantum* scheme: 'Two-year service with *Capitulanten* would be adequate for the infantry; but if the King takes his

[1] Roon Papers: Manteuffel to Roon, 5 December 1862.

[2] Dehio in *Historische Zeitschrift*, cxliv. 37–41.

stand on ten-year service I will not withhold my obedience from him in the matter.'[1]

In his dealings with the Chamber during the next two years, the Minister President's behaviour was designed to satisfy the most exacting enemy of parliamentary government. Roon's '*Gardeleutnantsmanier*' had always exasperated the deputies;[2] but in the contemptuous and arrogant manner in which he conducted his parliamentary duties, Bismarck proved far more offensive than his colleague. Refusing to be discountenanced by the Chamber's refusal to approve the government's budget for 1863, he blandly informed the enraged deputies, at the end of the session of 1862 and again at the opening of the new session in January 1863, that the Crown had no intention of allowing the whims of parliament to disrupt the processes of government. If the Chamber, because of doctrinaire ambition, failed to do its duty, then that agency which held the monopoly of power in the state—namely, the Crown—must go its own way, for it was unthinkable that the normal life and activities of the state should be brought to a standstill.[3] If the Chamber persisted in its refusal to vote funds, he said on another occasion, 'we will take the money where we find it'; and he proceeded to demonstrate that this could be done without difficulty. While the deputies made long, and often learned, speeches about the government's violation of the constitution, the Minister President ordered the bureaucracy to disregard the constitutional issue and to perform their normal duties with promptitude and loyalty. Lest there be any mistake about his meaning in this respect he inaugurated a campaign against 'oppositional civil servants'—punishing or dismissing national, provincial, and

[1] Bismarck, *G.W.*, xiv. 628.

[2] Duncker, *Politischer Briefwechsel*, p. 311.

[3] Nirrnheim, *Das erste Jahr*, pp. 144 ff.; Löwenthal, *Verfassungsstreit*, pp. 133, 146. There had, even before Bismarck's elevation to power, been considerable discussion in royal circles concerning possible legal justification for a budgetless régime. The most popular theory, which was called the *Lückentheorie*, held that, since the constitution provided no procedure which could be followed when the Chamber refused to pass a budget, the king must resort to his antecedent residuary power in order to carry on the government. Justifications were based also on the fact that the constitution had originated in a free action of the Crown; and it was argued also that the Chamber's action was illegal without the concurrence of the *Herrenhaus* (which, in 1862, passed the budget that had been rejected by the Chamber). In general, Bismarck avoided legalistic explanations and based his case purely on grounds of expediency and national security. See Huber, *Heer und Staat*, pp. 220 ff.; Löwenthal, *Verfassungsstreit*, p. 133; Zechlin, *Grundlegung*, pp. 353–4; and especially Kaminski, *Verfassung*, p. 94.

city officials who publicly supported opposition policies or were associated in any way with the D.F.P., and appointing and promoting only bureaucrats known to be faithful to the Crown.[1] It did not take much of this to obviate the possibility of the Chamber's receiving encouragement or aid from the civil service. Properly intimidated, the Prussian bureaucracy went about its business—recruiting the troops considered necessary for national security and collecting the taxes with which to pay for their sustenance and for the other functions of the government.[2]

While thus demonstrating the impotence of the opposition, Bismarck showed a high degree of skill in manœuvring the deputies into false positions. The session of 1863—which was otherwise unproductive—was rich in examples of this. During the meetings of the Military Commission, for instance, War Minister von Roon went out of his way to catechize the deputies on the meaning of patriotism, with some unkind references to the Chamber's lack of that quality. This drew from Heinrich von Sybel a spirited rejoinder in which he challenged Roon's right to speak of patriotism, describing the War Minister as 'a man who has contributed more than any other to the disruption of legal relationships in the fatherland' and urging him to demonstrate his own public spirit by ceasing to be 'an obstacle to peace between the King and the people'. Roon declared this an unjustified attack and, when his remarks were interrupted by the presiding officer, objected to this also as an illegal attempt to discipline one of the king's ministers. Bismarck seized upon this incident and insisted that no ministers would appear before the Chamber until that body had specifically disclaimed any desire to impose its own rules upon the ministers; and this action led to a flurry of charges and counter-charges, an extraordinary address from the Chamber to the king, and a refusal on William's part to receive it, and, finally, the dissolution of the Chamber in circumstances that hardly redounded to its dignity.[3]

[1] The necessity of such a campaign was emphasized by Bismarck as early as 13 October 1862 in a letter to the crown prince. Friedrich III, *Tagebücher*, pp. 505–6. For details, see Löwenthal, *Verfassungsstreit*, pp. 135–6, 190 ff.; Kaminski, *Verfassung*, pp. 77–78; Eugene N. Anderson, *The Social and Political Conflict in Prussia, 1858–1864* (Lincoln, Nebraska, 1954), pp. 386 ff.

[2] Hartung in *Volk und Staat*, p. 215.

[3] Nirrnheim, *Das erste Jahr*, pp. 165–7; Löwenthal, *Verfassungsstreit*, pp. 175–6; Eyck, *Bismarck*, i. 489–91. See also *Aus dem Leben Bernhardis*, v. 109.

The skill and brutality of Bismarck's tactics in the Chamber, the inflexibility with which he propounded the royal point of view on the military question, and his simultaneous ability to provide the funds which were essential for government operations brought the Minister President at least one tangible advantage. They removed whatever lingering doubts the sovereign may have had concerning the reliability of his Minister President. William had called Bismarck to office with some trepidation, fearing the 'eruptive and eccentric' strains in his character;[1] and he had not been wholly reassured by the famous interview with Bismarck on 22 September 1862. In the storms of the session of 1863, however, he acquired confidence in his Minister President's domestic policy, and before long he was leaning on him more heavily than he had on any of his former civilian ministers. Even in such a delicate situation as that caused by the crown prince's public attack upon governmental policy in June 1863, the king solicited Bismarck's advice concerning the punishment which was to be administered to his son.[2] For Bismarck personally this was encouraging; and, as the king's confidence deepened, his minister's authority became less susceptible to interference from irresponsible influences and '*Nebenregierungen*' at the court.[3]

Aside from this Bismarck's position was still a difficult one at the end of 1863. Throughout the year there had been little indication of weakness or discouragement on the part of the embattled opposition; and in the elections of October the D.F.P. increased its strength once more, while only thirty-eight deputies who could be considered completely in accord with

[1] Zechlin, *Grundlegung*, pp. 309 ff.

[2] In a speech at Danzig on 5 June, the crown prince had spoken out against Bismarck's new restrictions upon the press. His remarks aroused wide enthusiasm in liberal circles. Since the prince was an army officer, he was theoretically liable to trial for breach of discipline, and there was some talk of his being sentenced to at least a brief term of fortress detention. Bismarck was opposed to any step that might make a martyr of the heir apparent and was reported to have said to the king: 'Deal gently with the young Absalom! Your Majesty should avoid any decision *ab irato*; reason of state alone should be your standard.' Lenz, *Geschichte Bismarcks*, p. 191. The king followed this advice and contented himself with a stern letter to the crown prince in which, while forgiving him for his conduct, he reproached him for seeking to lead an opposition movement and for asking the people to choose between father and son. Duncker, *Politischer Briefwechsel*, pp. 348 ff. After this, the prince withdrew almost completely from politics. On the affair in general, see *Letters of the Empress Frederick*, ed. by Sir Frederick Ponsonby (London, 1929), pp. 40–48.

[3] See Hartung, 'Nebenregierungen', in *Forschungen*, xliv (1932), 30.

government policy were elected to seats in the Chamber. These results were so shattering that the king was, at least momentarily, plunged into gloom, and, looking moodily out of the castle window, was heard to grumble: 'Down there in the *Schloßplatz* they'll put the guillotine up for me.'[1]

If Bismarck was more sanguine, it was because he was looking far beyond the hubbub of the electoral campaign and was beginning to see, in the foreign field, possibilities of confounding and, eventually, reconciling, the parliamentary opposition. Bismarck had always realized that a large part of the opposition to the army reform was based on a fixed liberal belief that the government had no intention of using the augmented forces for any but domestic purposes.[2] He had told the king in 1862 that, if he would promise to use his army to support the programme of the German National Union, an organization which advocated the exclusion of Austria from Germany and the fusion of the German states into an empire with the Prussian King at its head, all objection to his military plans would disappear forthwith.[3] William's response convinced Bismarck that he could not expect the king to support a deliberately anti-Austrian policy. Unlike his Minister President, William thought of foreign policy, not in terms of *Staatsräson*, but in terms of family and traditional relationships; and, in common with soldiers like Manteuffel and Moltke,[4] he regarded Austria as Prussia's natural ally in the not unlikely contingency of a future war with France.

Bismarck was, then, debarred from following openly any policy which might be interpreted as anti-Austrian and had to pursue his own foreign objectives by indirection. It was only natural that the D.F.P., which called for Prussian support of

[1] *Aus dem Leben Bernhardis*, v. 124.

[2] For contemporary expressions of this belief, see Nirrnheim, *Das erste Jahr*, pp. 18–21.

[3] Ziekursch, *Politische Geschichte*, i. 210. See also Bismarck's letter to Roon of 2 July 1861. Roon, *Denkwürdigkeiten*, ii. 30–31. One of the most thoughtful contemporary observers, Konstantin Rössler, wrote in November 1862 that, if Bismarck would make a daring and progressive effort to solve the German problem, 'then everything that he has said, done and permitted today and yesterday will be forgotten in a few days. Then it will be all over with the Reaction and also with the Opposition. After some initial resistance, the summons of a nation, which is now being driven to despair by speeches, will be transmitted through the German provinces with the speed of an avalanche. . . . The German nation will shout with jubilation: "A dictatorship for a man!"' Nirrnheim, *Das erste Jahr*, pp. 122 ff.

[4] On Moltke's views on foreign policy, see Chapter V below.

the unitary programme of the *Nationalverein*,[1] should have viewed his direction of the country's external relations with extreme suspicion. Bismarck's one successful stroke in foreign policy in 1863, indeed, aroused the D.F.P. to a pitch of fury and aggravated, rather than alleviated, the situation in the Chamber. The action in question was Bismarck's conclusion in February 1863 of a secret convention with the government of the Tsar, providing for common action in suppressing a revolt which had recently broken out in Russia's Polish provinces. The Prussian Minister President had lent himself to this arrangement for reasons not generally understood at the time and often misinterpreted since. He had acted out of fear that the Tsar might defer to the wishes of Napoleon III, the Emperor of the French, and might give the Poles their freedom. If he did so, Prussia would have a new and troublesome neighbour on her eastern flank, at the very least a centre from which disaffection could be encouraged in Prussia's Polish districts, at the worst a French camp on the Vistula.[2] In addition, such a creation would further cement the friendship between Russia and France, which might then be formalized into an alliance which Austria might find it to her interest to join. With such a combination dominating Europe, the outlook for Prussia would be dark, especially in view of Napoleon's interest in a general *remaniement de la carte* which would give France the left bank of the Rhine. In concluding his convention with the Russians, then, Bismarck was seeking to avoid future troubles by checking the pro-French tendency of Russian policy. In this he was successful, but only at the expense of a hardening of the Prussian Chamber's opposition to his policies.[3]

The convention with Russia, however, had results which even Bismarck's fertile imagination could not have foreseen and which, in the end, gave him the opportunity both to ease his domestic difficulties and advance his foreign plans. The support of Prussia encouraged the Tsar to resist the pressure of Britain and France and to put down the Polish revolt by force of arms. The diplomatic crisis caused by this Russian decision left a heritage of bitterness not only between Russia and the Western

[1] Brandenburg, *Reichsgründung*, i. 426; Eyck, *Bismarck*, i. 370–1.

[2] See C. Friese, *Russland und Preussen vom Krimkrieg bis zum polnischen Aufstand* (Berlin, 1931), pp. 295 ff.

[3] On the reaction of the Chamber, see Löwenthal, *Verfassungsstreit*, pp. 156 ff., Nirrnheim, *Das erste Jahr*, pp. 308 ff., and *Aus dem Leben Bernhardis*, v. 32 ff.

Powers but also—thanks to the deplorable vacillations of British policy—between Britain and France.[1] In consequence the power relationships of Europe were in a state of some confusion by the end of 1863; and the tensions among the Powers prevented speedy and effective collaboration on their part to liquidate the dangerous situation which now came to a head in the duchies of Schleswig and Holstein.

This is not the place to discuss the complications of the dispute between Denmark and her semi-autonomous duchies, their agitation for freedom, and the decision of the Germanic Confederation to support them in acquiring it. Nor is there, in a chapter concerned with the Prussian constitutional conflict, any necessity for giving an exhaustive account of Bismarck's diplomacy during the involved affair.[2] In brief, Bismarck, taking advantage of the divided counsels of the other Great Powers, led his country to war against Denmark in January 1864. This action was taken in collaboration with Austria, and its ostensible purpose was not to detach the duchies from Denmark, as the Germanic Confederation wished, but rather to force the Danish government to recognize the validity of the Treaty of 1852 which had governed Denmark's relations with Schleswig and Holstein in the past. Privately, Bismarck believed from the beginning that a return to the legal basis of 1852 would prove impossible, and that the fate of the duchies would, in the end, be determined by Austria and Prussia. It was his hope, furthermore, that he would be able to persuade his king to demand the title to the duchies by right of conquest and, in the event that Austria refused to agree to this, to carry his point by force of arms.[3]

[1] See R. W. Seton-Watson, *Britain in Europe, 1789–1914* (Cambridge, 1937), pp. 432–8.

[2] For detailed accounts see Lawrence Steefel, *The Schleswig-Holstein Question* (Cambridge, Mass., 1932); Rudolf Stadelmann, *Das Jahr 1865 und das Problem von Bismarcks deutscher Politik* (Munich, 1933); Chester W. Clark, *Franz Joseph and Bismarck: The Diplomacy of Austria before the War of 1866* (Cambridge, Mass., 1934); and, more recently, the fourth volume of Srbik's *Deutsche Einheit*.

[3] In December 1862 Bismarck wrote to the Prussian minister in Karlsruhe: 'I haven't the slightest doubt that the whole Danish business can be settled in a manner desired by us only by war', but he added that Prussia was not prepared to fight a war 'in order to set up a new Archduke in Schleswig-Holstein who will vote against us in the Confederation'. Eyck, *Bismarck*, i. 553 ff. The crown council of 3 February 1864 seems to have been the first occasion on which Bismarck suggested to the king that Prussia should annex the duchies after the war. Steefel, *Schleswig-Holstein*, pp. 107–8.

All of these calculations were accurate, and all of these hopes were fulfilled. The divisions of the Powers and the stubbornness of the Danes combined to make impossible a return to the *status quo ante bellum* in the duchies; and, when Danish resistance was finally beaten down, Schleswig and Holstein passed into Austro-Prussian control. Almost immediately differences arose between the two partners concerning the ultimate disposal of the conquered territory, a fact that was not surprising in view of Bismarck's skilful technique of blocking all proposals which threatened to make impossible the eventual acquisition of the duchies by Prussia. While Austrian irritation mounted the Prussian minister was able to convince his sovereign—although the process took some time—that his confidence in Austria had been misplaced and that his ally was, in reality, seeking to defeat Prussia's legitimate aspirations. Once this idea had been firmly implanted, the clock of evolution had been set at the right hour, and the miserable dispute over the duchies was resolved in the shock of arms between the two great German Powers.

Long before that eventuality had arrived, the evolution of Bismarck's foreign policy had begun to have perceptible effects upon the attitude of the Chamber in the domestic conflict. The first reaction to the declaration of war against Denmark was outright opposition, inspired principally by the government's avowed intention of restoring the arrangement of 1852 in the duchies. Insistent upon the liberation of the duchies from Denmark and their establishment as an independent state under the rule of the Duke of Augustenburg, the D.F.P. and the deputies of the left centre joined in attacks on the government's policy and, in January 1864, refused its request for permission to float a loan to support the military operations.[1] Once the fighting had begun, however, the unity and the fervour of this opposition began to diminish. Bismarck had long held that, if they were given a foreign success sufficiently striking to inflate their self-esteem, the Prussian people would forget their internal grievances; and this now proved true. As Prussian troops won their first victories against a foreign foe, enthusiasm was widespread in the country, and, especially after the daring assault on Düppel on 18 April, the Chamber too became susceptible to the prevailing emotion.[2] There was, to be sure, nothing ap-

[1] Löwenthal, *Verfassungsstreit*, pp. 211–20.

[2] Droysen described the Düppel operation as 'one of those events which mark an

proaching a full-scale surrender. Indeed, when the Chamber reconvened in January 1865 there was the usual spate of speeches accusing the government of violation of the constitution; and Roon's new draft of the military reorganization bill was, like his previous drafts, voted down by the Military Commission. But it was clear that many of the deputies had been moved by the passage in the speech from the throne in which the king had argued that the successes in Denmark justified the government's military demands; the tone of the debates was far less bitter than in previous sessions, and more than one observer felt that even the inveterate followers of the D.F.P. programme would be willing to compromise if a golden bridge were built for them by the government.[1]

Bismarck, on his part, was willing to be reasonable also. He had never wavered in his desire to reconcile the Chamber, if possible, before the nation became involved in a war with Austria, and, during the first months of 1865—especially after Bismarck had sent the so-called February terms to Vienna demanding what amounted to complete control over the duchies[2]—relations between the two Powers deteriorated so rapidly that war seemed probable before summer. In May, therefore, when a member of the old liberal section in the Chamber named Bonin came forward with a new compromise plan, which made some trifling concessions to the D.F.P. position on the military question while retaining all the essential features of the original reorganization plan,[3] the Minister President seized upon it, convinced Roon of its workability, and submitted it to the king with the approval of the whole ministry.

Once again, however, the possibility of a bargain with the Chamber was defeated. Among the extreme conservatives the recent military victories had revived the hope that the Crown

epoch in a nation's history'. *Aus dem Leben Bernhardis*, vi. 110–11. Perthes wrote to Roon: 'Now the army knows what it is and what it can do, and Prussia, Germany and Europe know it also.' Roon, *Denkwürdigkeiten*, ii. 236.

[1] See *Aus dem Leben Bernhardis*, vi. 152–3.

[2] See, *inter alia*, Srbik, *Deutsche Einheit*, iv. 237 ff., and Stadelmann, *Das Jahr 1865*, pp. 25 ff. In Prussia the early enthusiasm for the Duke of Augustenburg was long since dead, and annexationist sentiment was strong in all parties. Mommsen, Sybel, Duncker, Treitschke, the *Preußische Jahrbücher*, the *Grenzboten*, and the majority of army officers favoured annexation. Srbik, iv. 228.

[3] The plan provided for a reduction of the size of the annual contingents, an increase in the proportion of *Capitulanten* to conscripts and the shortening of the three-year term by a few months. Stadelmann, *Das Jahr 1865*, pp. 31–32.

might yet be persuaded to return to the ways of reaction; and there had been much talk, after the Danish campaign, of the possibility of an 'inner Düppel'.[1] In February 1865 Bernhardi talked with General von Alvensleben and found him so outspoken in his criticism of the Chamber that the publicist concluded that 'the coterie Prince Charles, Manteuffel, Alvensleben, Pückler etc. believe now that they are strong enough to work openly for their ultimate objective—the abrogation of the Constitution'.[2] Bernhardi's suspicions were well grounded. By May Manteuffel at least was making no secret of his belief that the time for revoking the constitution was approaching. In a letter to the king dated 28 May the Chief of the Military Cabinet argued that if—as seemed likely—Prussia had to fight a war, and if, as a result of it, she acquired new territory, this enlargement of the national domain would make the old constitution unworkable. Meanwhile, the king's moral authority would be so great that the country would accept any legal changes which he might recommend. This, he implied, would be a God-given opportunity to dispose of constitutionalism once and for all; and it would be the king's duty to take advantage of it.[3]

Even before he had written this letter, Manteuffel had killed Bismarck's latest attempt to reach an understanding with the Chamber. Although the Minister President himself, in a two-hour conversation, sought to win over the cabinet chief, Manteuffel remained inflexibly opposed to anything that might be interpreted as a concession on the part of the Crown. Like his friend Alvensleben, he maintained that every revolution in history had started because the reigning monarch had been willing to compromise.[4] On 2 May, he wrote to the king:[5]

Who rules and decides in Prussia, the King or the ministers? . . . Your Majesty's ministers are loyal and devoted, but they live now only in the atmosphere of the Chamber. If I may express my opinion, it is this: Your Majesty should hold no council but should write to Minister Bismarck saying: 'Now that I have read the proposal, I have decided that the government will not agree to it.'

[1] Ritter, *Die preußischen Konservativen*, p. 116.

[2] *Aus dem Leben Bernhardis*, vi. 171. When Bernhardi expressed the opinion that an attempt to do away with the constitution would be a misfortune for the country, Alvensleben said that 'the people could perfectly well adjust themselves to the old conditions'.

[3] Stadelmann, *Das Jahr 1865*, pp. 79 ff.

[4] *Aus dem Leben Bernhardis*, vi. 200.

[5] Stadelmann, *Das Jahr 1865*, pp. 31 ff.

The king followed this advice.[1]

After this blow Bismarck was determined to secure Manteuffel's removal from Berlin, and he was strongly seconded in this by his friend the War Minister. Roon had long since lost sympathy for the domestic views of Manteuffel and Alvensleben. He could still on occasion become so irritated with the Chamber that he would yearn for 'a skilful and powerful attack to clear the beasts out of the arena', but in his reflective moments he could see no advantages in a return to stark reaction.[2] Like Bismarck his main interest lay now in the development of the critical Austrian question, and he shared the Minister President's anger over Manteuffel's meddling in a scheme which had been designed, after all, to unite the energies of the nation for the war that lay ahead. Roon's personal relations with Manteuffel had also deteriorated sharply since 1862 largely because of the cabinet chief's unwillingness to recognize that he was Roon's subordinate and his habit of acting in the king's name in military matters without consulting the War Minister.[3] Roon agreed with Bismarck, then, that Manteuffel would be less dangerous if he were detached from the king's immediate circle. An opportunity for effecting this was finally found when it became necessary to appoint a man of personal stature and diplomatic skill to the difficult and important post of Governor of Schleswig; and, although it was not easy, Bismarck and the War Minister succeeded in persuading the king that Manteuffel was the indispensable man for that assignment.[4] Thus, the powerful cabinet chief moved on to a new phase in his crowded career, and, although his penchant for interfering with Bismarck's designs was to be indulged on many other occasions, he had no further influence on the evolution and termination of the domestic conflict.

Moreover, Manteuffel's hope that a successful war would

[1] On the day following Manteuffel's letter the king wrote to Roon that he could not impose a humiliation on the army 'after it had come out of a war with glory'. Roon, *Denkwürdigkeiten*, ii. 331.

[2] See, for instance, ibid., pp. 348 ff.

[3] See Roon Papers: Manteuffel to Roon, 19 February, 5 March, 8 December 1862. During the Danish campaign Roon had a stormy scene with Manteuffel at Karlsbad and accused him of withholding from him action reports sent from the commanding generals to the king. Ibid., Manteuffel to Roon, 8 July 1864.

[4] Roon Papers: Note by Roon, 13 May 1865; Manteuffel to Roon, 29 June 1865. *Aus dem Leben Bernhardis*, vi. 211; *Auswärtige Politik Preußens* (1858–71), ed. by Reichsinstitut für Geschichte (Oldenburg, 1932 ff.), vi. 140.

prepare the way for a destruction of the constitutional régime was doomed to disappointment. As he went ahead with his plans for the struggle against Austria, Bismarck realized that victory over that antagonist would open a new era in German history. The specific Prussianism of Manteuffel and his kind would be a thing of the past. For good or ill, Prussia would have to assume the responsible leadership of the German states and would have to find solutions for a host of entirely new problems. After the war, then, there would be even greater need for an end to domestic disaffection and the union of all classes behind the Crown. The prerequisite for this, he was sure, was a settlement with the Chamber which, while sacrificing none of the essential rights of the Crown, would be sufficiently conciliatory to assure the co-operation of the liberals in the promotion of future national aims.

IV

The Chamber's ardour for a continuation of the fight against the government had been waning ever since 1864; in 1866 it disappeared completely. The deputies could derive little satisfaction from a contemplation of the results of their refusal to vote any funds for the government since 1862. Bismarck had been able to find means of defraying not only the normal costs of government but the extraordinary expenditures necessitated by his foreign policy as well. In Roon's memoirs there is an intriguing note dated 1 August 1865 in which the War Minister writes:[1]

> We have enough money to give us a free hand in foreign policy, if necessary to mobilize the whole army and to pay for a whole campaign. This lends to our conduct toward Austria the necessary *aplomb*. . . . Where does the money come from? [We get it] without any breach of the law, principally through an arrangement with the Cologne-Minden Railway, which I and even Bodelschwingh [the Minister of Finance] regard as *very profitable*.

This sort of thing provided the necessary *aplomb* for the fight against the Chamber also; and the government's patent ability to disregard that body tended to remove whatever zest the conflict may have had for the liberals in the now distant days of 1862.

Aside from this the liberal deputies found themselves being

[1] Roon, *Denkwürdigkeiten*, ii. 354.

forced into a position which threatened to deprive them of the support, not only of the masses, but also of the middle classes who elected them. This was especially true after Bismarck, in April 1866, re-opened the German question by declaring that Prussia desired the calling of a German parliament elected by direct and universal suffrage to reform the Germanic Confederation.[1] This declaration was designed to embarrass the Austrian government, in which it succeeded, but also to arouse the enthusiasm of all those who had hoped one day to see Germany a united nation. It was in effect a promise that, under Prussian leadership, that goal would be attained. It made the position of the opposition in the Prussian Chamber, many of whose members had fought for unity in 1848 and had, more recently, agitated for the objectives of the *Nationalverein*, appear both inconsistent and unpatriotic.

It is significant that as war came closer the liberal press, long openly critical of all phases of Bismarck's policy, began to swing to his support; and once hostilities had started the conversion of publications like the *Kölnische Zeitung*, the *Preußische Jahrbücher*, and *Grenzboten* became complete.[2] This in itself was a sign that the Prussian middle classes were giving up the fight, and this was confirmed decisively even before it was certain that the war effort would be successful. The elections for the new Chamber of Deputies were held on the day of the battle of Königgrätz and were over before the news of the overwhelming Prussian victory had been received. Nevertheless, while the conservatives increased their seats from 38 to 142, the D.F.P. received the smallest number of mandates in its history and, even combined with the left centre, would henceforth constitute a minority in the Chamber.[3]

It was a minority which was, nevertheless, important to Bismarck, for he knew that he could expect from its members more understanding of, and support for, his future German policy than he could from many of the triumphant conservatives.[4] He therefore proceeded with the plan which he had first outlined in a series of conversations with liberal leaders in the spring of 1866—that of saving the collective face of the Chamber

[1] Srbik, *Deutsche Einheit*, iv. 347 ff.

[2] Ibid., p. 429.

[3] The figures were: conservatives 142 seats; old liberals 26; clericals 15; Poles 21; left centre 65; D.F.P. 83. Löwenthal, *Verfassungsstreit*, p. 290.

[4] Ritter, *Die preußischen Konservativen*, p. 173.

by a public admission that the budgetless régime had been in violation of the constitution and by a request that the Chamber legitimize past expenditures by an act of indemnity.[1] He had no doubt now that the Chamber would be co-operative; his real difficulty was rather that of persuading the king to admit that the conduct of his government had not been entirely legitimate. This proved no easy task, but there was no Manteuffel at the king's elbow on this occasion and Bismarck had—not for the last time in his career—allowed it to be rumoured that he would resign if the king did not give way.[2] Despite a flurry of alarmist messages from Kleist-Retzow and other Junker notables[3] and a good deal of haggling over matters of form, William surrendered to the determination of his Minister President.

Thus, at the opening of the new *Landtag* on 5 August the king, in his address from the throne, recognized that the government's long rule without budget was contrary to the law of the state, adding, however, that the government had acted in accordance with the dictates of duty and conscience, and that its measures were all vital to the security of the state and hence necessary. He gave no assurances concerning the government's conduct in the future. Later, indeed, in an informal comment made after the Chamber's reply to the *Thronrede*, he was to mutter that he had had to act as he had done and would always do so again if similar circumstances arose—a remark which the ministers hastily described as off the record and having no legal significance.[4] After listening obediently to their ruler, the Chamber, in a general atmosphere of resignation, debated the proposed act of indemnity, and, on 3 September, it was passed by a vote of 230 to 75.[5]

The passage of this law has been called the Caudine yoke of Prussian liberalism;[6] and there can be little doubt that this is an apt description. It was all too clear, in the course of the debate, that many members of the former opposition were intent now only on proving their patriotism. Watching the eagerness with which they grasped the olive branch which

[1] On the background of the indemnity, see Löwenthal, *Verfassungsstreit*, pp. 292 ff.; Kaminski, *Verfassung*, pp. 102 ff.

[2] Löwenthal, *Verfassungsstreit*, p. 293.

[3] Ibid., p. 294; Ritter, *Die preußischen Konservativen*, pp. 174 ff.

[4] Kaminski, *Verfassung*, p. 110.

[5] Ibid., pp. 106 ff.

[6] Ziekursch, *Politische Geschichte*, i. 197 ff.

Bismarck held out to them, Wilhelm Liebknecht commented caustically:[1]

> The oppressors of yesterday are the saviours of today; right has become wrong and wrong right. Blood appears, indeed, to be a special elixir, for the angel of darkness has become the angel of light, before whom the people lie in the dust and adore. The stigma of violation of the constitution has been washed from his brow, and in its place the halo of glory rings his laurelled head.

The indemnity debate broke what was left of the D.F.P. in two. In October 1866 twenty-four members of its parliamentary section, led by Twesten, Lasker, Forckenbeck, and Bennigsen, announced their complete acceptance of the aims of Bismarck's foreign policy, adding that, in domestic affairs, they would observe 'the duties of a vigilant and loyal opposition'. This marked the birth of the National Liberal party which was to be the chief spokesman of the middle classes in the next generation; but the gulf that was to separate its principles from those of the opposition of the *Konfliktszeit* may be judged by the words of one of its members, who said: 'The time of ideals is past. . . . Politicians must today ask themselves less what is desirable than what is attainable.'[2] This was burying the past with a vengeance; and it may well be taken as the epitaph of middle class liberalism in Prussia.

There is, however, another aspect of the indemnity legislation that demands consideration. Perhaps the most distinctive feature of the September settlement was the silence which both parties to it observed with regard to the issue which had caused the original dispute—the army reform. Approval for the departures made from the service law of 1814 was neither sought by the government nor granted by the Chamber. The exultant conservatives claimed at the time—and the point has been made often since[3]—that this avoidance of the military issue implied that the Chamber had tacitly accepted, not only the reforms, but also the theory that the military rights of the Crown were absolute and not susceptible to parliamentary interference of any kind. This is a debatable point[4] and, in any case, an academic one. After 1866 the attitude of the Prussian

[1] Quoted in Rudolf Olden, *History of Liberty in Germany* (London, 1946), p. 106.

[2] Eyck, *Bismarck*, ii. 322 ff.

[3] See, for instance, Huber, *Heer und Staat*, pp. 240 ff.

[4] See the views of Carl Schmitt, *Staatsgefüge und Zusammenbruch*, p. 11.

Chamber toward the royal prerogative was not of decisive importance. The principal arena in which the relationship of the army to the state was to be discussed henceforth was, from 1867 to 1871, the parliament of the newly created North German Confederation and, after 1871, the Reichstag of the German Empire.

It is true that, in its first consideration of military affairs, the parliament of the North German Confederation did not hesitate to accept the substance of a reorganization bill drafted by the Prussian military commission of 1859. It passed a service law which required conscripts to serve for three years with the line, four years in the active reserve, and five additional years in the reformed *Landwehr*; it imposed this on the territories acquired by Prussia as a result of the recent war, and it provided the funds to maintain an army equal to 1 per cent. of the national population until 1871. But there was no assurance that this ready compliance would last. Bismarck had hoped that the deputies would accept a *Pauschquantum* scheme similar to that of 1862, which would make the army budget inflexible and permanent and obviate the necessity of budget debates. This proved impossible; and the vehemence with which the parliamentarians insisted upon retaining at least a periodic right to debate the size and budget of the army showed that even the cowed liberals were not prepared to admit that military affairs were a private preserve of the Crown.

Moreover, new political forces were now emerging whose conduct could not be expected to be determined by the experience and the precedents, real or imaginary, of the *Konfliktszeit*. Partly because of the requirements of his foreign policy, partly because he had desired a counterweight to middle-class liberalism, Bismarck had become the champion of universal suffrage, and this principle became the basis of the constitutional arrangements of 1867 and 1871. This opened the way for the development of new political parties appealing to, and claiming to represent, the working classes; and, considering the traditional attitude of the German working classes toward the military caste, these new parties could hardly be expected to agree with the conservative theory that the military issue had been settled once and for all in September 1866.

In the constitutional conflict of the 60's the army had been saved from a determined effort on the part of the middle-class liberals to subject it to civilian control. Thanks to the surrender of its antagonists to the wave of patriotism engendered by its victories in the field, it had been saved also from the serious possibility of a renewal of the fight by the liberals. But its successes had not been accompanied—as some of its leaders had hoped—by a destruction of the constitutional régime. It would still have to worry about budgets, and it would still have to expect that those who were empowered to vote budgets would insist upon prying into matters of military organization and personnel. The fight to make the army completely autonomous within the state was not yet won; and the fact that this was fully realized by the leaders of the army themselves was to be shown by the defensive character of their parliamentary tactics and their administrative reforms in the period after 1871.

V

WAR AND DIPLOMACY IN THE PERIOD OF UNIFICATION

Our diplomats plunge us forever into misfortune; our generals always save us. MOLTKE *in the 1850's.*

Lieber Moltke, gehst so stumm
Immer um den Brei herum?
Bester Moltke, nimm's nicht krumm:
Mach' doch endlich Bumm, Bumm, Bumm!
Popular jingle sung during the bombardment dispute.

DURING the tangled course of the constitutional dispute, Bismarck had been almost constantly at odds with military politicians, and it was only with the greatest of difficulty that he had been able to make good his right to be considered as the king's principal adviser in matters of state policy. But it was not only in the domestic field that he found himself embroiled with the soldiers. Before the fight over the reorganization of the army was terminated, wars had been fought and won against Denmark and Austria. In each of those conflicts, and in the struggle against France which began in 1870, the Prussian Minister President discovered that the army leaders had a tendency to regard war as a province in which they alone had competence, that they were reluctant to admit that the civilian ministers had any authority to influence the course of operations and that they were dangerously willing, in the name of military expediency, to disregard important considerations of international diplomacy.

The relationship between civilian and military leadership in war-time is always delicate, and it is understandable that soldiers should resent what appears to them to be the unwarranted intrusion of politicians into their own professional sphere. Germany's greatest military philosopher, however, had warned his colleagues against claims of self-sufficiency in time of war. War, Clausewitz had written, is merely the continuation of diplomacy intermingled with other means; and the political leaders of the state must determine its scope and objectives and exercise the overall direction of its course.

> It is wholly [their] business, and can only be [theirs], to determine what events and what shifts in the course of negotiations properly express the purpose of the war. . . . It is a senseless proceeding to consult the soldiers concerning plans of war in such a way as to permit them to pass purely military judgements on what the ministers have to do; and even more senseless is the demand of theoreticians that the accumulated war material should simply be handed over to the field commander so that he can draw up a pure military plan for the war or for a campaign.[1]

During the wars of unification Bismarck seemed to understand Clausewitz better than the soldiers who so frequently paid lip-service to his doctrines. Bismarck's attempts to establish the principle of civilian responsibility for the direction of the war effort were bitterly opposed; and, although he had his way in the main, the soldiers—as experience in later years was to demonstrate—remained unconvinced of the validity of his views.

I

Bismarck's differences with the soldiers began with the war against Denmark in 1864, and they were rooted in the very nature of that conflict. Some reference has been made above[2] to Bismarck's motives in 1864; and here it need only be emphasized that, while his ultimate objective was the acquisition of the duchies of Schleswig and Holstein, he found it expedient to disguise this and to begin the campaign against the Danes in collaboration with Austria. An Austrian alliance was the best assurance, he believed, against the intervention of the other Great Powers—Great Britain and Russia, who had always been sensitive concerning the position of Denmark, and France, who could be expected to intervene in any dispute which promised to bring her advantage. 'We learned in the year 1849', Bismarck is reported to have said, 'that it is bad to stand one against four. Two against three is a better relationship.'[3]

[1] General Carl von Clausewitz, *Hinterlassene Werke über Krieg und Kriegführung* (Berlin, 1857), iii. 124.

[2] See above, Chapter IV, pp. 169–70.

[3] Heinrich Friedjung, *Der Kampf um die Vorherrschaft in Deutschland* (10th ed., Stuttgart and Berlin, 1916), i. 76.

The Austrian government agreed to the alliance, partly because they feared isolation and partly because they were convinced that Prussia would act in any event and they preferred to be in a position to exercise some control over her.[1] But, even more apprehensive of international complications than Bismarck, they went ahead very hesitantly and with an obvious desire to avoid committing anything that might be interpreted as an act of violence. In the treaty of 16 January 1864 with Prussia they stipulated only that, if the Danes refused an ultimatum to withdraw those measures which were in violation of the international settlement of 1852, Austrian and Prussian forces would occupy the duchy of Schleswig and the two governments would subsequently decide in common the nature of the settlement with Denmark.[2] The Austrians were apparently hoping that the Danes would cave in at the first show of force and that no extensive military operations would be necessary.

This Austrian reluctance to think in terms of a real military commitment was the source of Bismarck's first disputes with his generals. In December 1862 the Chief of the General Staff, Helmuth von Moltke, had written two memoranda on the possible course of a war with Denmark.[3] He pointed out that without an effective fleet in Danish waters it would be impossible to strike directly at the heart of Danish power, Copenhagen. This left two possibilities. If the bulk of the Danish army elected to make a stand in the defensive works on the Schleswig border, they might be encircled and destroyed. If they decided, however, to fall back to the much more heavily fortified positions at Düppel and Fredericia, which could be taken only by very costly frontal assault, the best means of forcing them to capitulate would be by by-passing these and occupying all of Jutland.

The substance of Moltke's memoranda was incorporated in the draft instruction which was prepared for the guidance of Field Marshal von Wrangel, the commander of the allied force. The meeting called by the king on 20 January to discuss this draft degenerated into a stormy altercation between Bismarck

[1] Friedjung, op. cit., pp. 79–80; Srbik, *Deutsche Einheit*, iv. 109–11.

[2] Clark, *Franz Joseph and Bismarck*, pp. 59 ff.

[3] Helmuth von Moltke, *Militärische Korrespondenz*, 1864, nos. 1, 2 [Moltke's *Militärische Werke* (Berlin, 1892–1912)].

and the soldiers. The Minister President insisted that any intimation of a possible campaign in Jutland would frighten the Austrians and give them an excuse for backing out of the alliance which they had signed only four days before. War Minister von Roon, on the other hand, argued that a war limited to the duchy of Schleswig had no meaning and could have no possibility of success and added that, if there were doubts about the Austrians' zeal in the common cause, it would be advisable to discover as quickly as possible how much reliance could be placed upon them. He was supported in these views by the king.

Bismarck, however, was determined that the doubts and hesitations of Vienna must not be reinforced by Prussian mistakes and—as on a number of other occasions—showed himself perfectly willing to lay down his office if his advice was not followed. The thought that the statesman he admired so deeply might resign shocked Roon, and he anxiously sought, and in the end succeeded in finding, a compromise. Since the question of occupying Jutland was not yet vital, no mention was made of it in the instructions to Wrangel. They stated only that the field marshal's objective would be to engage and destroy the Danish army before it succeeded in withdrawing to Düppel and other fortified debarkation points, that every victory should be followed by an energetic pursuit of the beaten foe, and that once Schleswig was occupied measures should be taken to prevent the re-entry of the Danes.[1]

This formula avoided trouble only momentarily. The Danes having rejected the ultimatum, the Austro-Prussian forces crossed the border of Schleswig on 1 February. They were unable, however, to force a battle on the Danes, who abandoned their forward positions and withdrew to the security of Düppel. The thought of assaulting this formidable strong-point did not arouse any enthusiasm in Wrangel's headquarters. Instead, the staff reverted to Moltke's original plan of battle, and, on 14 February, Wrangel informed Berlin that, unless he received orders to the contrary, he intended to advance into Jutland on the 17th.

By this time the king had seen the merit of Bismarck's original objections to this idea, for he had been informed by his envoy

[1] For this and much that follows in this chapter, see the excellent account in Anneliese Klein-Wuttig, *Politik und Kriegführung in den deutschen Einigungskriegen* (Abhandlungen zur mittleren und neueren Geschichte, lxxv) (Berlin, 1934), 7–9.

in Vienna that the emperor desired no extension of the fighting beyond Schleswig—a warning reinforced by the Austrian ambassador, who told Bismarck that an advance farther north would necessitate the negotiation of a new agreement between the allies. William resolved to send his Chief of Military Cabinet, Edwin von Manteuffel, to Vienna to persuade the emperor of the necessity of a campaign in Jutland. Meanwhile, however, he instructed Wrangel to hold his position on the northern borders of Schleswig.[1]

To give that ancient warrior instructions of any kind was at best a chancy business. Wrangel had received the command of the joint force principally because the Austrians had insisted that, if their troops were to serve under a Prussian commander, he must be a senior general with war experience—qualifications which Wrangel alone in the Prussian officer corps possessed.[2] But age had strengthened the eccentric strain in his character, and visitors to the Prussian headquarters came away with grave doubts concerning his mental stability. On 9 February the crown prince wrote in his diary: 'At certain moments Wrangel is really half foolish, and the energy and vigour with which he was once filled shows itself now only in stubbornness and vanity.'[3] He drove his staff to distraction with senseless orders and with personal abuse; he made life as miserable as possible for the diplomatic representatives attached to his headquarters;[4] and he made no secret of the fact that he detested Bismarck and believed that the Minister President was deliberately placing obstacles in his way.[5]

It cannot be said with certainty that Wrangel deliberately

[1] Klein-Wuttig, *Politik und Kriegführung*, p. 10.

[2] Hohenlohe-Ingelfingen, *Aus meinem Leben*, iii. 15, n.

[3] Friedrich III, *Tagebücher von 1848–1866*, pp. 252–3. On a later occasion the crown prince wrote that whenever he gave advice to Wrangel which was later proved to be correct, the field marshal 'wants always to kiss me. Then he weeps, promises all sorts of things, &c. In short, he is a completely amazing old owl, who at certain times, especially when he hasn't slept well, is unbelievably confused or pig-headed.' Ibid., p. 266.

[4] See the remarks of the Austrian commissioner in Graf Revertera, 'Rechberg und Bismarck', *Deutsche Revue*, xxviii (4) (1903), 9. In March, Friedrich von Holstein, the grey eminence of the Foreign Office in the post-Bismarckian period, was sent to Wrangel's headquarters as a diplomatic attaché. He wanted to see the front lines, and a safe tour was arranged for him. Wrangel, however, suggested that he be taken to a position where the Danes could shoot at him. Hohenlohe-Ingelfingen, *Aus meinem Leben*, iii. 108. See also Friedrich von Holstein, *Lebensbekenntnis*, ed. by W. Rogge (Berlin, 1932), pp. 41 ff.

[5] Friedrich III, *Tagebücher*, pp. 242, 246.

disobeyed the order to hold his troops behind the Schleswig border; but he certainly did not take the trouble to see that it was communicated swiftly and accurately to his unit commanders. As a result, despite the prohibition laid down in Berlin, a detachment under General von Mülbe advanced into Jutland on 18 February and invested the town of Kolding.

This was a step which was certain to cause trouble in Vienna. It could not, however, be corrected, for the withdrawal of Mülbe's troops would reveal to the other Great Powers that differences existed between the German allies, and this might encourage them to intervene. All Bismarck could do, then, was to redouble his efforts to convince the Austrians that the occupation of Jutland was necessary. Once he had accomplished that, he could—as he said in a later conversation with Roon concerning Wrangel—give 'the old baby new boots to paddle in the water with'.[1] Immediately, however, he insisted that a peremptory order be sent to the field marshal forbidding any further advance.

This new order, which was received on 19 February, completely infuriated Wrangel. Without consulting his staff he dispatched a long and querulous telegram to the king in which he said: 'To recall the Prussians from their career of victory is quite impossible for me, for the curse of the fatherland would strike even my grandchildren [if I should do so]. The diplomats may counsel such a thing, but they may be sure that their name will be affixed to the gallows.' He awaited with 'reverent expectation', he added, a royal command to leave Kolding and strike to the north.[2]

He received no such order. Attention in Berlin was now riveted on the negotiations which Edwin von Manteuffel was conducting with the Austrians. That these should succeed appeared now to be absolutely essential, for the Kolding incident had elicited a note from the French government, and the tone of the press in both Paris and London was becoming menacing.[3]

The choice of Edwin von Manteuffel as special envoy to Vienna at this juncture had been dictated by the fact that his well-known sympathies for Austria would make him *persona gratissima* to the emperor and his advisers. This very qualification,

[1] Roon, *Denkwürdigkeiten*, ii. 210. [2] Bismarck, *G.W.*, iv. 328.
[3] Klein-Wuttig, *Politik und Kriegführung*, p. 16.

however, involved some degree of risk. Manteuffel was an impulsive man who had difficulty in disguising his personal views on any subject, and he had a private solution for Austro-Prussian differences. It was his belief that Austria would not only co-operate in the necessary extension of the hostilities but would also give Prussia a free hand in the disposal of the duchies after the fighting was over if the Prussian government would promise to help Austria reconquer Lombardy, which she had lost in 1859, in 'the next war'.[1] This, incidentally, was not original with Manteuffel. The great majority of Prussian officers regarded France as the real enemy and believed that a close alliance with Austria would be necessary when the inevitable war on the Rhine broke out. Many of them, in addition, felt that it had been a mistake not to fight on Austria's side in 1859 and were willing to make reparation for that mistake by assuming obligations in Italy, especially if concessions in this form might remove the tension which had existed between Austria and Prussia since 1850. In 1861, during the fruitless negotiations with Austria on the reform of the army of the German confederation, Moltke and Gustav von Alvensleben, the Prussian representatives, had urged that a Prussian guarantee of Venetia would provide the basis for a comprehensive agreement with the Austrians, and they had made no attempt to hide their displeasure when the Foreign Minister, Schleinitz, had persuaded the regent that such a commitment would be inadvisable.[2]

Bismarck, who was less inclined than the soldiers to think in terms of traditional friendships and enmities, was not prepared to make promises to the Austrians which might be a source of embarrassment at a later date. He saw to it that Manteuffel was not authorized to extend the discussions in Vienna beyond the scope of the Danish issue. Perhaps to his surprise, Manteuffel raised no objections, but bent himself to his task with complete obedience to his instructions. Moreover, against the military,

[1] Srbik, *Deutsche Einheit*, iv. 126–33.

[2] On this see especially Rudolf Stadelmann, 'Moltke und die deutsche Frage', in Kurt von Raumer and Theodor Schieder, eds. *Stufen und Wandlungen der deutschen Einheit* (Stuttgart, 1943), and the documents on the military talks of 1861 in the first volume of H. Ritter von Srbik, ed. *Quellen zur deutschen Politik Oesterreichs* (Oldenburg, 1934–8) and the second volume, first part, of *Auswärtige Politik Preußens*. After the failure of these talks Moltke said: 'If people would only leave military-political matters to regulation by a few clever and reliable officers, without diplomats, they would get together to everyone's satisfaction.' Stadelmann, *Moltke und der Staat*, p. 138.

political, and financial arguments which the Austrians raised against any extension of the fighting in the north, he brought to bear a diplomatic skill and a personal charm which won the complete admiration of his hosts.[1] Gradually he succeeded in allaying the Austrian fears and, by the first week in March, he had persuaded the Vienna government to give up its opposition to the advance into Jutland. The Austrians insisted that the principal objective of future fighting must be the capture of Düppel and of the island of Alsen, both parts of Schleswig, but agreed that Wrangel should be authorized to advance as far into Jutland as was necessary to prevent enemy operations from the direction of Fredericia.[2]

At the last moment this painfully negotiated settlement was jeopardized by another of the aged field marshal's irresponsible gestures. News reached Berlin that, in violation of the explicit orders sent to him on 19 February, Wrangel had allowed a patrol to make a sally to the north. Raging over this new instance of military disregard of diplomatic considerations, Bismarck persuaded the War Minister to send the culprit a stinging reprimand for having acted 'contrary to the very concise royal orders, on the exact observation of which the Ministry of Foreign Affairs bases its statements to foreign cabinets. . . . Under the given circumstances and in order to direct our foreign affairs safely and without the appearance of ambiguity, I must consider it absolutely imperative that the renewal of such steps be prevented by resolute measures.'[3]

The incident, happily, had no effect upon the agreement with Austria, which was signed on 6 March, and it was Bismarck's last serious brush with Wrangel, for the field marshal, after a month of uneventful campaigning in Jutland, was—to the satisfaction of diplomats and soldiers alike—relieved of his command in mid-May. Long before that happened, however, the Minister President had become involved in other differences with the military.

Even before the end of the Vienna talks the British government had proposed to the belligerents that a conference meet in London to discuss the restoration of peace; and on 7 March

[1] At the end of the mission the Austrian minister Rechberg said: 'If ever again a disagreement should arise between Berlin and Vienna, may the King send back General Manteuffel at once.' Clark, *Franz Joseph and Bismarck*, p. 99, n.

[2] Klein-Wuttig, *Politik und Kriegführung*, pp. 17–18.

[3] Bismarck, *G.W.*, iv. 328–9, 352–3.

the Austrian and Prussian governments had announced that they would be prepared to discuss the question of an armistice and participation in a conference. This ready compliance was activated by the desire to propitiate the other Great Powers; in actuality the British request was highly embarrassing to Bismarck. Prussian arms had as yet won no impressive success against the Danes, and the Minister President was resolved not to appear before an international conference until they had done so. The meeting of the conference could, of course, be postponed by haggling over armistice terms and by raising technical points concerning representation, and throughout the months of March and April Bismarck showed great skill in devising delaying tactics.[1] But simultaneously he was forced to persuade the soldiers to win a victory, and he realized that the exploit best calculated to win the respect of Europe for Prussian arms would be the taking of Düppel.

While Wrangel had advanced into Jutland, the siege of Düppel had been entrusted to Prince Frederick Charles. This commander was impressed by the strength of the Danish position and less so with the arguments which came from Berlin. 'Is it supposed to be a political necessity to take the bulwarks?' he wrote to the king. 'It will cost a lot of men and money. I don't see the military necessity.'[2] The prince was supported by his own chief of staff, Blumenthal, and by the Chief of the General Staff as well. 'Any reasonable soldier must see', wrote Moltke, 'that a quick decision at Düppel is not to be expected and that time is needed. . . . One cannot express sanguine hopes, and a good rider doesn't encourage his best horse to make a jump which will break its neck. Our troops will certainly show what they can accomplish, but the assault must be prepared.'[3] Moltke, at least, envisaged an eventual attack on Düppel. Frederick Charles, on the other hand, seemed to prefer almost any operation except the one desired. He argued that an amphibious assault on Alsen would yield greater results; he weighed other substitute plans; and he constantly inveighed against the '*Hofkriegsrat*' in Berlin who was attempting to dictate to him.[4]

[1] Steefel, *Schleswig-Holstein Question*, pp. 203 ff.; Klein-Wuttig, *Politik und Kriegführung*, p. 22.

[2] Friedrich Karl, *Denkwürdigkeiten*, i. 307 ff.

[3] Moltke, *Militärische Korrespondenz*, 1864, no. 48.

[4] Friedrich Karl, *Denkwürdigkeiten*, i. 328.

The Düppel dispute was, in a sense, a forerunner of the much more acrimonious controversy over the bombardment of Paris in 1871, when Bismarck again, for political reasons, insisted on an operation which aroused misgivings in the minds of the field commanders. In the earlier case, however, in contrast to the latter, he had important allies among the soldiers themselves. The supreme war lord, King William, was uncomfortably aware that, in the fighting so far, the Austrian troops had shown themselves to better advantage than the Prussians, and he was anxious to show the Prussian people that the hotly contested reorganization of the army had in fact brought an increase in efficiency. He had no sympathy with Frederick Charles's complaints and procrastinations. He was tired, he told one visitor, of campaigns that went around strong-points like a cat around hot broth. He needed Düppel so that people would learn to respect Prussian arms.[1]

In the military hierarchy proper, the War Minister loyally supported Bismarck's views, while Edwin von Manteuffel once more proved that, when the occasion moved him, he could be a very effective supporter. The Chief of the Military Cabinet took it upon himself to break down Frederick Charles's hesitation, bombarding him with inspirational messages and visiting him at his headquarters to go over the assault plans in detail. As early as 10 March, he had written to the reluctant commander:

> If your royal highness goes on demanding more weapons, if you go on postponing the attack, then doubts will arise in people's minds concerning your royal highness's determination; and I should not desire, for the sake of the army and of the person of your royal highness and of the hope which I place in it, that an armistice should be concluded while our troops were still standing *in front of* Düppel. This is a matter not of the importance of the position, not of the question whether it can be held without Alsen, whether Alsen should be captured, whether without Alsen's capture the taking of Düppel is not worthless—this is a matter of the renown of the Prussian army and the position of the King in the councils of Europe. The prize is worth streams of blood, and for its sake that blood will be spilled with joy by everyone from the highest officer down to the drummer boy.[2]

In a letter to Roon at the same time, Manteuffel scoffed at the

[1] Hohenlohe-Ingelfingen, *Aus meinem Leben*, iii. 145.

[2] Friedrich Karl, *Denkwürdigkeiten*, i. 317.

Alsen plan, which he said would be at the mercy of the wind and the Danish fleet; and he urged the War Minister to see that the king did not waver, since his own pen, employed in this purpose, might be too weak alone.[1]

It took another full month before Frederick Charles's resistance was finally overcome.[2] Even at the end he insisted that militarily he had every reason to oppose the operation and that he was yielding for political reasons alone.[3] But yield he did. The storm of Düppel took place on 18 April, and the Prussian troops, showing a gallantry under fire that fulfilled their king's fondest expectations, overran the Danish positions. The news of the victory had an electrifying effect in Prussia, and—as has been noted above—the wave of patriotism which it inspired began the undermining of liberal resistance to absolutism on the home front. Many former opponents of the government felt with Droysen that Düppel was 'one of those events that mark an epoch in a nation's history',[4] and allowed their new found pride in Prussian military prowess to overcome their constitutional principles.

The immediate effect of Düppel, however, was that it made it possible for Prussia to participate in the London conference as a Power that had proved itself in the field. Düppel was, indeed, the key to Prussian success at London; after the taking of the *Schanzen* there was little likelihood that the other Powers would threaten Prussia with war if she did not yield to their demands, and this was proved during the crucial discussions on a partition line for Schleswig, when the French refused to entertain a British proposal for joint pressure on Prussia.[5]

On the other hand, the victory at Düppel not only increased the self-esteem of the soldiers but aroused in them a suspicion that what they had won in the field might be lost at the conference table. Even those officers closest to the court did not always understand the tactics which Bismarck employed before and during the conference which opened in London on 25 April.[6]

[1] Roon Papers (National Archives): Manteuffel to Roon, 12 March.

[2] Ibid., 22 March, 29 March, 17 April.

[3] Friedrich Karl, *Denkwürdigkeiten*, i. 339.

[4] *Aus dem Leben Bernhardis*, vi. 110–11.

[5] *Origines diplomatiques de la guerre de 1870–1871*, iii. 190–1, 201 ff.; Eyck, *Bismarck*, i. 627 ff.

[6] On the conference see Steefel, *Schleswig-Holstein Question*, pp. 227 ff.; Eyck, *Bismarck*, i. 618–25.

They failed to see that the Minister President—in order to keep the Austrians happy, to outmanœuvre the other Powers and to discredit the Danes who were insanely intransigent—was willing on occasion to accept compromises and make concessions, the more so because—suspecting from the beginning that the conference would not succeed in effecting a settlement[1]—he knew that his promises would not have to be fulfilled. The soldiers took a shorter view of things and regarded the concessions as signs of weakness and as a betrayal of those who had fallen at the *Dannewerk* and before Düppel.

Thus, there was a good deal of grumbling about the terms of the armistice, which left Prussian troops in possession of the greater part of Jutland but forbade them to levy contributions on the population, who remained under the authority of the local Danish government. Moltke felt that this destroyed the whole purpose of the recent campaign which had been to deny the resources of the province to the Danish government,[2] while Roon wrote uneasily about the disadvantages of an arrangement which left the conquered foe master in his own house while the victor was a scarcely tolerated guest. There was a good deal of perturbation over Bismarck's apparent willingness to demand less territory from the Danes than the soldiers thought they were justified in asking. And there was great indignation at the end of May when, in view of the fact that the conference was just barely getting down to the essential issues, Bismarck agreed to the extension of the armistice for another month.

In this last case, protests from the military led Bismarck to say plainly that it was not the business of the army to express opinions on political questions. This elicited an interesting comment from the War Minister. Writing on 29 May Roon said: 'There has been, and is now, hardly any army that regarded itself and understood itself to be *purely* a political instrument, a lancet for the diplomatic surgeon.' All armies have opinions, and to neglect these is to run the danger of blunting their effectiveness. 'And the more developed the professional sense of an army the more sensitive and touchy [*kitzlicher*] it is to anything which hurts, or seems to hurt, its interests and prerogatives.' In the present situation, the army is justified in being

[1] Friedrich III, *Tagebücher*, p. 328.

[2] Moltke, *Militärische Korrespondenz*, 1864, no. 81.

opposed to a long armistice which places it in an exposed position in a foreign land; and it has a right to have its opinion considered. After all, Roon reminded the Minister President, 'when a government depends—and this is our situation—particularly upon the armed part of the population . . . the army's views on what the government does and does not do is surely not a matter of indifference'.[1] Even coming from a friend of years' standing, these words had a somewhat menacing ring.

On the whole, however, none of these post-Düppel differences amounted to anything. Bismarck had his way and was permitted to direct Prussian strategy in London as he saw fit. In late June the conference, as he had predicted, came to an unsuccessful conclusion. The German allies returned to the attack, the Danes were beaten to their knees and sued for peace on 12 July, and, in the peace that followed, Schleswig and Holstein were handed over to the joint supervision of Austria and Prussia. With these results the soldiers had no real reason to be dissatisfied.

Seen in retrospect, Bismarck's disputes with the military during the Danish war were minor in nature. The most irritating ones—the troubles with Wrangel—were caused more by violent personal antipathies than by differences in principle. In other instances, when Bismarck's diplomatic strategy upset the operational calculations of the professionals, the Minister President was fortunate in being able to count on the political sense of high-ranking officers like Manteuffel and Roon. The War Minister especially was close enough to Bismarck to appreciate his difficulties and, although he could and did protest vehemently on occasion, he always in the end subordinated his professional scruples to the demands of politics. This was all the more important because, during the Danish war, Roon was still, in the eyes of the king, the uncontested head of the military hierarchy.

In the next six years, however, the situation was to change radically. The rise of the General Staff and its virtual supersession of the War Ministry as the chief military agency in time of war created new problems for the Prussian Minister President. Bismarck's conflict with the General Staff reached its point of highest emotional intensity during the war against France in 1870–1, but its roots are to be discovered in the Austrian war of 1866.

[1] Roon, *Denkwürdigkeiten*, ii. 244–6.

II

The origins and early development of the General Staff have already been touched upon.[1] By the 1860's it had won the respect of the Prussian officer corps but, since it had had few opportunities in the long period of peace to demonstrate its effectiveness, was accorded none of the veneration which came to be associated with it later in the century. Moreover, within the overall organization of the army it remained a subordinate agency. It is true that in 1821, when Rühle von Lilienstern became Chief of the Second (or General Staff) Department of the War Ministry, it was discovered that he was junior in grade to General von Müffling, who was serving in that department; and Müffling was consequently detached from the War Ministry and given the title of Chief of the General Staff of the Army. While this represented a breach in the unified organization of the army which Scharnhorst had effected, the new arrangement did not alter the essential subordination of the General Staff to the War Ministry. Its chief was not given the right to report directly to the king or, for that matter, even to the War Minister, but had to act through the General War Department of the War Ministry.[2] When matters of war and peace were discussed in royal council, he was rarely present, nor was his advice often solicited. His relationship with the commanding generals of the army was, moreover, ill defined, and it was by no means clear whether he would be permitted to give them directives in time of war or whether he would even be expected to appear at field headquarters.

The transformation of the General Staff into the agency charged with jurisdiction over all questions of command and the recognition of its chief as the highest adviser of the king in matters of warfare was the achievement of Helmuth von Moltke. It was not, however, an overnight accomplishment. Moltke was made Chief of the General Staff when William I first became regent of Prussia in 1857. He received a significant increase in authority two years later when War Minister von Bonin gave him the right to report directly to him rather than through the *Allgemeine Kriegsdepartement*.[3] Nevertheless, in the subsequent

[1] See above, Chapter I, pp. 6, 31; Chapter II, pp. 45, 63, 78.

[2] See Schmidt-Bückeburg, *Militärkabinett*, pp. 30–31; Bockmann in *Von Scharnhorst zu Schlieffen*, p. 121; Huber, *Heer und Staat*, pp. 337–8; Meisner, *Kriegsminister*, p. 48.

[3] Schmidt-Bückeburg, *Militärkabinett*, p. 70.

period, as the reorganization of the army stood in the foreground, Moltke was completely overshadowed by Bonin's successor Roon.

At the beginning of the Danish campaign, Moltke's influence was almost negligible. Operational directives were sent directly to the field command from the War Ministry; and Moltke seems to have had no authority over, or contact with, either Wrangel or that commander's chief of staff, Vogel von Falckenstein.[1] If it had not, indeed, been for his private correspondence with Colonel von Blumenthal, who was serving as Prince Frederick Charles's *chef*, he would have been completely in the dark concerning events in Schleswig.[2]

At the end of April 1864, however, Edwin von Manteuffel became convinced that Falckenstein was contributing to the confusion that had come to characterize Wrangel's headquarters and urged Roon to send Moltke to replace him.[3] Roon followed this advice, and Moltke finished the war as chief of staff to Wrangel and, when the field marshal was replaced by Frederick Charles, to the prince.[4] It was generally recognized that he was largely responsible for the planning and direction of the successful operation against Alsen, which brought the war to a close.[5] As a result of this his position in the army, and especially with the king, was enormously strengthened. In the period that followed the campaigns in Schleswig and Jutland, William's respect for the Chief of the General Staff apparently deepened. To the crucial crown councils which debated the policy to be adopted *vis-à-vis* Austria, Moltke was usually invited and his views were always listened to with respect.[6] It is probably true that William was impressed also by the technical excellence of the mobilization and *Aufmarsch* plans which the Chief of Staff worked out for the coming campaign in Bohemia.

When, precisely, William became an admirer of Moltke is a matter of speculation. What is known is that, at the very outset

[1] Schickfus in *Von Scharnhorst zu Schlieffen*, pp. 163–4.

[2] Jähns, *Moltke*, pp. 345, 351.

[3] Roon Papers (National Archives): Manteuffel to Roon, 30 April 1864.

[4] On the excellent relations between Moltke and Frederick Charles, see Friedrich Karl, *Denkwürdigkeiten*, i. 350–7.

[5] Schickfus in *Von Scharnhorst zu Schlieffen*, p. 168.

[6] See, for instance, on his participation in the *Kronrat* of 29 May 1865, A. O. Meyer in *Festgabe für Srbik* (Berlin, 1938); *Auswärtige Politik Preußens*, vi. 174; Srbik, *Deutsche Einheit*. iv. 251 ff. On the *Kronrat* of 28 February 1866, see *Auswärtige Politik Preußens*, vi. 611.

of hostilities against Austria, on 2 June 1866, a royal cabinet order stated that from now on the commands of the General Staff would be communicated directly to the troops and no longer through the mediation of the War Ministry.[1] For the duration of the war at least, the General Staff had been released from its subordination to the ministry.

On the basis of this elevation of the chief of staff, the official historians of the General Staff have erected a theory intended to explain the controversies between the civilian and military leadership of the Prussian state in the years that followed. 'When Moltke on 2 June finally stepped into Roon's place as the first military adviser of the King', they have written, 'he must have appeared to Bismarck to a certain extent as an intruder. It is from this standpoint that the later friction between Bismarck and the General Staff is to be understood.'[2] The implication here is that Bismarck took the initiative in quarrelling with the General Staff and its chief because he resented the apparent demotion of his old friend and collaborator.

In view of the fact that there is no evidence to show that the Minister President did actually object to the royal order of 2 June, this is not a very satisfactory theory. Nevertheless—although not for the reason cited in the General Staff history—the replacement of Roon by Moltke was an important cause of the troubles that followed. Roon, who had a highly developed political sense, recognized the paramountcy of politics even in time of war and understood the diplomatic necessities which on occasion led Bismarck to intervene in the sphere of military operations. Moltke, on the other hand, who possessed a much more intense *Fachnatur* than the War Minister, was never able completely to reconcile himself to these elementary laws of statesmanship.

He did, it was true, acknowledge both civilian supremacy and the primacy of politics. But, accustomed to thinking in terms of pure strategy and to drawing up plans of almost mathematical exactitude, he was irritated by the disruption of his calculations by unpleasant political realities. His irritation led him, indeed, to attempt the impossible task of delineating the exact boundaries

[1] O. von Lettow-Vorbeck, *Geschichte des Krieges von 1866*, i (Berlin, 1896), 104.

[2] *Moltke in der Vorbereitung und Durchführung der Operationen. Kriegsgeschichtliche Einzelschriften hrsg. vom Großen Generalstab.* Heft xxxvi (1905), 54–55.

between politics and strategy, apparently in the hope that he would be able to keep them separate. Once the political goal of the war had been determined and the decision to open hostilities had been taken, he seems to have believed, considerations of strategy became paramount. In the first operational plan which he drew up for the campaign against Denmark, he went so far as to say that, from the time that mobilization began, 'neither diplomatic negotiations nor political considerations should interrupt the further military progress',[1] and this principle found expression in his later war plans also. Politics, in short, was to be decisive before the beginning and after the end of hostilities, but not in between. 'In his linear logical way Moltke thought that he had solved the problem in the form of a simple division of function [*Arbeitsteilung*]' between the politician and the strategist.[2]

The impracticability of this division was demonstrated during the Danish war, and the demonstration was repeated in 1866. Even during the mobilization phase of the Austrian conflict, Bismarck had caused a temporary disruption of Moltke's plans. Worried by the uncertain attitude of Napoleon III, the Minister President, without informing Moltke, persuaded the king to revoke orders which would have withdrawn the Eighth (Rhenish) Army Corps from the Rhine provinces so that they could join the main force which was making the drive into Bohemia. Moltke, when he learned of the change, was able to have the original orders restored by arguing the necessity of having a numerical superiority when contact was made with Benedek's army, but the incident must have been irritating and was certainly not forgotten.[3]

Once the hostilities had begun, a more serious example of the Minister President's readiness to intervene in the operational sphere occurred. In the west, Prussia's first objective was to knock Austria's German allies out of the war before their

[1] Moltke, *Militärische Korrespondenz*, 1864, p. 16.

[2] Stadelmann, *Moltke und der Staat*, p. 41. See also Gerhard Ritter, 'Politik und Kriegführung im bismarckischen Reich', in *Deutschland und Europa: Festschrift für Hans Rothfels*, ed. by W. Conze (Düsseldorf, 1951), p. 79, and *Staatskunst und Kriegshandwerk*, i. 247 ff.

[3] Lettow-Vorbeck, *Geschichte des Krieges von 1866*, i. 99. Klein-Wuttig (*Politik und Kriegführung*, pp. 37–38) tends to minimize this incident, but it is significant that it is stressed in most of the military literature. See *Moltke in Vorbereitung*, pp. 54–55; Frh. von Freytag-Loringhoven, *Politik und Kriegführung* (Berlin, 1918), p. 154; Haeften, 'Bismarck und Moltke', *Preußische Jahrbücher*, clxxvii (1919).

troops could effect a junction with the main Austrian army; and General von Falckenstein had been ordered by Moltke to direct his operations against the Hanoverians and then, after defeating and disarming them, to turn his forces against the Bavarian army. On 19 June, however, Bismarck dispatched to Falckenstein's headquarters a telegram which he had received from his representative in Karlsruhe, which read in part: 'The German confederative army is still fully disorganized. A speedy advance by Prussia against Frankfurt-am-Main would make any organization impossible and would easily lead to a second Rossbach.'[1] Apparently under the influence of this communication, Falckenstein, when he lost contact with the Hanoverian army on 22 June, broke off the pursuit and began an advance over Kassel toward Frankfurt. This might have proved to be a costly decision, but Moltke was able, by employing other troops, to intercept the Hanoverians and force them to capitulate; and, that done, he peremptorily ordered Falckenstein to stop his advance on the capital of the *Bund* and to turn his forces against the Bavarians.[2]

While Falckenstein was doubtless chiefly to blame in this affair, Bismarck would have been better advised to communicate the information which he had received from Karlsruhe to Moltke, rather than sending it directly to the western field headquarters. The excuse that can be given for his action is that the new administrative system which the royal order of 2 June had created had not yet taken hold, and it was not, indeed, until after Königgrätz, that Moltke's authority was clearly recognized, even by the soldiers themselves.[3] Information came to the king, to Bismarck, and to Roon from every conceivable source; no system had been worked out yet for handling it and seeing that it was communicated to the Chief of the General Staff; and Bismarck was not alone in sending news to interested field commanders without consulting Moltke.[4] Even so, the incident was unfortunate. It must have reinforced the suspicion of Bismarck which was beginning to develop among General

[1] Lettow-Vorbeck, *Geschichte des Krieges von 1866*, iii (Berlin, 1902), 52.

[2] Blume, 'Politik und Strategie: Bismarck und Moltke 1866 und 1870/71', *Preußische Jahrbücher*, cxi (1903), 235.

[3] A division commander, receiving orders from Moltke at Königgrätz, is reported to have said, 'This is all very well, but who is General Moltke?' Holborn in *Makers of Modern Strategy*, p. 176.

[4] Klein-Wuttig, *Politik und Kriegführung*, p. 43.

Staff officers,[1] while making it difficult for them to appreciate the Minister President's more justifiable incursions into the operational sphere in the last weeks of the war.

On 3 July the Prussian armies smashed the forces of Benedek at Königgrätz. Moltke had conceived of the battle as one of encirclement, but his hopes were not in this respect fulfilled. Thanks to faulty communication between the First and Second Prussian armies, the Austrians, while losing a fourth of their strength, were able to withdraw and to fall back across the Danube towards Vienna.[2] The Prussian military were eager for a prompt and vigorous pursuit. Moltke, who had no way of knowing the confusion which reigned in Austrian military councils at this time, believed that the enemy was capable of further offensive action and might even be able to withdraw fresh troops from the Italian theatre unless he was forestalled.[3] At the same time the king and his military entourage were anxious to crown the recent victory by a triumphal entry into Vienna. All of William's previous hesitations about taking up arms against his former ally had disappeared with the firing of the first shots, and he was intent now only on crushing the Austrians and imposing a punitive peace upon them.[4]

Two days after Königgrätz, however, the Emperor of the French intervened between the belligerents, proposing an armistice and the beginning of peace talks; and Bismarck recognized that, once he had taken this step, Napoleon could not, without serious loss of face, permit it to be disregarded. Bismarck had no objection to allowing the emperor the satisfaction of having arranged a peace, provided that peace brought to Prussia the territorial gains which he had already privately defined. He was determined that Austria should be expelled from Germany and that both Schleswig and Holstein should be handed over to Prussia. In addition, he desired either the reformation of the *Bund* in such a manner as to give Prussia unquestioned domination over north Germany or the actual acquisition, from Kurhesse, Hanover, and Saxony, of territory which would bring Prussia three to four million new subjects.[5] Despite the attitude

[1] Here again it is significant that Blume, who was attached to the General Staff in 1870–1, makes much of the incident. *Preußische Jahrbücher*, cxi.

[2] Holborn in *Makers of Modern Strategy*, p. 184.

[3] Klein-Wuttig, *Politik und Kriegführung*, pp. 46, 60–62.

[4] On the king's attitude, see A. O. Meyer, *Bismarck: Der Mensch und der Staatsmann* (Stuttgart, 1949), pp. 321–2.

[5] Bismarck, *G.W.*, vi. 44.

of the French Foreign Minister, Drouyn de Lhuys, and the envoy he had sent to Prussian headquarters—both of whom made no secret of the fact that they were opposed to annexations in any form—Bismarck believed that it might be possible to persuade the emperor to agree to his north German demands; but he sensed that Napoleon's jealous regard for his own prestige would make him unalterably opposed to additional annexations of Austrian territory or to a victor's triumph in Vienna. At the same time there was no assurance that the emperor would agree to the north German claims; there was always the possibility that Napoleon, through ambition or mortified pride, might decide to launch an attack against the Rhine provinces. In such case a Prussian army, the bulk of which was on its way to Vienna, would be at a serious disadvantage.

The task of winning Napoleon's support for his programme of annexations Bismarck entrusted to the Prussian ambassador in Paris, Count Robert von der Goltz, and the ensuing negotiations proved to be difficult and time-consuming.[1] Simultaneously, as an additional safeguard against France, Bismarck had to explore the possibility of direct negotiations with Austria, and he thought it prudent to watch his Italian ally closely lest the Austrians should attempt to conclude a separate peace with the idea of detaching the armies operating in the south. These parallel negotiations were so delicate that the Minister President felt it necessary to guard against any indiscretion from the military side, either in the form of declarations concerning territorial expectations or of military operations which would jeopardize the chances of an advantageous peace.

The victory at Königgrätz had not unnaturally inspired widespread speculation about Prussia's coming territorial gains, and the soldiers were as prone to this intellectual exercise as public opinion in general. Prussian headquarters was filled with talk concerning the necessity of acquiring Saxony and parts of Bavaria, the advantages of taking the Bohemian districts of Reichenberg, Karlsbad, and the Egertal as a protective *glacis* and of making other attractive annexations. On 9 July Bismarck wrote to his wife:

Everything goes well with us, despite Napoleon. If we are not

[1] See Hermann Oncken, *Die Rheinpolitik Kaiser Napoleons III. von 1863 bis 1870* (Stuttgart, 1926), i. 320 ff., and Herbert Rothfritz, *Die Politik des preußischen Botschafters Grafen Robert von der Goltz in Paris, 1863–69* (Abhandlungen zur mittleren und neueren Geschichte, lxxiv) (Berlin, 1934), pp. 85–97.

excessive in our demands and do not believe that we have conquered the world, we will attain a peace which is worth our effort. But we are just as quickly intoxicated as we are plunged into dejection, and I have the thankless task of pouring water into the bubbling wine and making it clear that we don't live alone in Europe but with three other Powers who hate and envy us.[1]

The available evidence does not reliably indicate which members of the king's military entourage expressed ambitious territorial designs or what tactics Bismarck used to counter their arguments.[2] All that can be said with certainty is that no public declaration concerning war aims was issued by Prussian headquarters, and that the Minister President succeeded even in avoiding a specific discussion of the subject with his king, lest it tie his hands in his negotiations with Napoleon.[3]

If this was difficult, it could have been no more so than the task of restraining the soldiers from driving against Vienna. In one of the many military councils held in the weeks after Königgrätz, Bismarck interrupted a discussion of the necessity of dictating peace in Vienna by asking why it was necessary for the army to stop there. Why not pursue the Austrians into Hungary and, since it would be difficult to maintain communications with the rear, go on to Constantinople, found a new Byzantium, and leave Prussia to her fate?[4] Beneath the sarcasm lay a real fear, not only of the political disadvantages of a campaign against Vienna, but of the disaster which might befall Prussia if the French attacked while her troops were committed deep within the Austrian empire. This fear led Bismarck to use every argument and delaying tactic at his command to postpone further operations, and, in using them, he had no hesitation about invading the soldiers' professional sphere and raising technical military objections to their views. Thus, at Czernahora on 12 July, he boldly intervened in a debate concerning the advisability of storming the fortifications at Floridsdorf—possession of which Prince Frederick Charles considered necessary as the first step toward the crossing of the Danube and the beginning

[1] Bismarck, *Briefe an seine Braut und Gattin*, ed. by Fürst Herbert Bismarck (Stuttgart, 1900), p. 572.

[2] The evidence is discussed in Klein-Wuttig, *Politik und Kriegführung*, pp. 47–51.

[3] Ibid., pp. 49–50.

[4] R. von Keudell, *Fürst und Fürstin Bismarck: Erinnerungen aus den Jahren 1846–72* (Berlin, 1901), p. 297.

of the march toward the Austrian capital;[1] and on other occasions also he showed that he was unwilling to regard military matters as the sole property of the generals. That the soldiers should have resented this is understandable.

The decisive brush with the soldiers came on 19 July. Six days earlier Goltz had persuaded the Emperor of the French to agree to a programme of terms which included the exclusion of Austria from Germany, the formation of a north German federation under Prussian leadership, and the continued independence of the south German states.[2] No mention whatsoever was made in this bill of particulars of Prussian annexations of any kind, and Bismarck angrily commanded his ambassador to press this point, which he now regarded as essential. Before any progress could be made in this regard, the French persuaded the Austrian government to accept these terms as a basis for negotiations for peace, and, on 19 July, the French envoy at Prussian headquarters made it clear to Bismarck that the emperor expected the Prussian government likewise to accept and to conclude an immediate armistice of five days' duration.

Acceptance of the French demand involved the risk that Napoleon would subsequently refuse to countenance any Prussian accretions of territory. Refusal, on the other hand, might precipitate a two-front war, and Bismarck was unwilling to accept this as long as there was a chance of winning French assent to his proposed annexations. He seems to have believed also that the significant omission in the French programme was due to Goltz's failure to make the importance of Prussian territorial gains sufficiently clear to the emperor, and that it could still be corrected. He urged, therefore, that the French request be granted.

The army chiefs, on the other hand, realized that this was a political gamble, and they felt that the chances of success were not great enough to justify accepting an arrangement which would bring with it pronounced military disadvantages. In their eyes a five-day truce at this juncture would enable the Austrians to bring up new supplies and regroup their still disorganized forces, while it would completely destroy the momentum

[1] On Czernahora, see Bismarck's own account in *G.W.*, xv. 271–3; and Hermann Gackenholz, 'Der Kriegsrat von Czernahora', *Historische Vierteljahrschrift*, xxvi (1931).

[2] Rothfritz, *Goltz*, p. 89; and Oncken, *Rheinpolitik*, i. 351 ff.

of the Prussian advance.[1] The plans for a crossing of the Danube had now been perfected,[2] and the majority of the commanders probably shared the views of *Generaladjutant* von Boyen, who noted on 19 July that the advance guard was only four miles from the river and added: 'Its bank can be reached tomorrow; the crossing will be easy or difficult, depending on what luck we have; I count with complete confidence on the former. In eight days it will be all over, if the diplomats, who attach themselves to every honourable war like bugs to a bed, don't destroy the sport for us.'[3]

As far as Moltke is concerned, the Chief of the General Staff does not seem—in contrast to some of his colleagues—to have placed much importance upon the conquest of Vienna as such. But he still believed that the Austrians were capable of renewed action unless their gathering forces were subjected to new hammer blows. From a memorandum which Roon wrote to him on the evening of 19 July it is clear that Moltke was in favour of an immediate crossing of the Danube, and it is reasonable to suppose that he argued in favour of this in the crucial discussions which took place in the presence of the king earlier in the day.[4] Moltke was probably less concerned about offending the French than Bismarck, for he was confident that, if it was necessary, Prussia could carry on a successful war against both France and Austria.[5] In 1868, indeed, in a conversation with the British Foreign Secretary, Lord Clarendon, he expressed regret that the opportunity had not been seized immediately after Königgrätz to complete the unification of Germany by smashing France.[6]

The discussions of 19 July in the Prussian headquarters were protracted and stormy, and Bismarck's views were contested both by the king and by the generals.[7] The Minister President's political arguments were reinforced, however, by Roon's grave doubts concerning the advisability of attempting a Danube crossing before recent losses in man-power had been made good,

[1] See Lettow-Vorbeck, *Geschichte des Krieges von 1866*, ii. 644.

[2] Moltke, *Militärische Korrespondenz*, 1866, no. 186.

[3] *Erinnerungen aus dem Leben des General-Adjutanten Kaisers William I. Hermann von Boyen*, ed. by W. von Tümpling (Berlin, 1898), p. 179.

[4] Klein-Wuttig, *Politik und Kriegführung*, pp. 74–76.

[5] Moltke, *Militärische Korrespondenz*, 1866, no. 329; Jähns, *Moltke*, pp. 437 ff.

[6] Newton, *Lord Lyons, A Record of British Diplomacy* (London, 1913), i. 202; Stadelmann, *Moltke und der Staat*, pp. 168–9.

[7] Keudell, *Fürst und Fürstin Bismarck*, pp. 296–7.

supplies and ammunition replenished, and communications to the rear strengthened; and, in the end, it was decided that Bismarck should be authorized to accept the French programme and grant the five-day truce. His calculation that the French emperor would be reasonable in the matter of annexations, which had aroused misgivings in headquarters, was quickly justified, for, on 22 July, Goltz wired from Paris that Napoleon would not object to Prussia's acquiring as many as four million new subjects in northern Germany, although he was anxious that the kingdom of Saxony should not disappear completely from the map. Personally, Bismarck had been willing to take less than the emperor was now prepared to tolerate. As it was, he was able to lay before his king an impressive list of territories which were his for the asking: the *Kurfürstentum* of Hesse, the duchy of Nassau, the free city of Frankfurt, all of the kingdom of Hannover and the duchies of Schleswig and Holstein.

Even these rich offerings did not seem, however, sufficient to appease the king's hunger for territory. He was indignant at the thought that Saxony should be spared; he still believed that Austria should not be permitted to go scot-free, and, significantly, he feared that the army would reproach him for what he regarded as inadequate compensation for the victory won. It was only after many emotional scenes—which are described, not without some exaggeration, in Bismarck's memoirs[1]—that his resistance was worn down by the Minister President's argument that it would be foolish to run the risk of a new war after having gained so much. With bad grace the sovereign gave way, scribbling angrily in the margin of Bismarck's final memorandum on the subject: 'If what the army and the country are justified in expecting—that is, a heavy war indemnity from Austria or an acquisition of land sufficient to impress the eye—cannot be obtained from the vanquished without endangering our principal objective, then the victor at the gates of Vienna must bite into this sour apple and leave to posterity the judgement of his behaviour.'[2] The king's capitulation made possible the conclusion of preliminaries of peace, which were signed on 26 July.

In Bismarck's struggle with the king the military seem to have played no significant role, and the soldiers were, in general,

[1] See Bismarck, *G.W.* xv. 277–9. Also Friedrich III, *Tagebücher*, pp. 470–5.

[2] Bismarck, *G.W.*, vi. 81.

satisfied with the peace that was concluded.[1] It would be a mistake to assume, however, that their satisfaction was sufficient to overcome their accumulated resentment against the Minister President. Moltke and the admiring circle of 'demi-gods' who surrounded him in the General Staff remembered Bismarck's meddling with the mobilization orders and his communication with Falckenstein; and they had watched his active participation in the military councils after Königgrätz with mounting irritation. Bismarck is certainly correct in stating that his behaviour during the Czernahora talks of 12 July outraged the General Staff and made its members resolve that, in future wars, politicians would not be given the right to meddle in professional matters.[2] The extent to which they were willing to go in pursuit of this objective is shown in the attitude they adopted toward Bismarck during the Franco-Prussian war.

III

From the very beginning of this new conflict there was evidence that the General Staff intended, as far as possible, to prevent the Chancellor[3] and—because of his past support of Bismarck—the War Minister as well, from having any real contact with the operational aspects of the war. To exclude Roon from the military conferences which were held as the fighting progressed proved to be impossible. Although officers like Verdy, one of the three division chiefs on the General Staff,[4] and Waldersee, one of the king's aides-de-camp (*Flügeladjutanten*), made no secret of the fact that they thought that the War Minister's proper place was in Berlin, supervising the supply system and dealing with problems of replacements,[5] Roon remained at field headquarters and, together with Moltke, the Quartermaster-General Podbielski, the Chief of Military Cabinet Tresckow, and the crown prince, participated in the conferences which were held each morning at ten o'clock in the

[1] See Klein-Wuttig, *Politik und Kriegführung*, pp. 78–79.

[2] Bismarck, *G.W.*, xv. 271–2.

[3] Bismarck's official title was now Chancellor of the North German Confederation.

[4] The others were Bronsart von Schellendorf and Brandenstein, like Verdy, lieutenant-colonels.

[5] I. von Verdy du Vernois, *With Royal Headquarters, 1870–1871* (London, 1897), p. 39; *Denkwürdigkeiten des Generalfeldmarschalls Alfred Grafen von Waldersee*, ed. by H. O. Meisner (Stuttgart, 1925), i. 37, 85. Moltke agreed with this view. *Gesammelte Schriften und Denkwürdigkeiten* (Berlin, 1891–3), iii. 423–4.

presence of the king.[1] Bismarck, however, was no longer invited to these meetings as he had frequently been in 1866;[2] and, what is more important, no arrangement was made at the beginning of the fighting to keep him informed concerning the progress of operations or the intentions of the high command.

Bismarck does not seem initially to have objected to this arrangement and, in the first stage of the war, there was no very good reason why he should. There was no secret about the direction and objective of Prussian operations, which were designed to seek out and destroy the French army. It was only after the battle of Sedan, when Bismarck began to investigate the possibilities of peace and when military movements could conceivably disrupt negotiations in progress, that the Chancellor began to feel that vital information was being withheld from him deliberately. He was informed neither of the plans for the advance into France after Sedan nor of the design to encircle Paris; and, despite his repeated requests for improved communication between the General Staff and his own office, it was not until 15 October—six weeks after Sedan—that an arrangement was made to provide him with copies of telegrams sent from field headquarters to the German press.[3] Even this concession was made grudgingly and administered in a slipshod manner, and Bismarck was soon writing stiffly to Moltke to request that 'I receive continuous information concerning military proceedings and, if this does not seem possible in any other way, [that I receive it] by means of the simultaneous communication of the telegrams which are designed for the Berlin press, the content of which is still in most cases new to me when I read it five days later in the newspapers.'[4]

Long before he wrote this letter, however, Bismarck had acquired other reasons for complaint against the General Staff. In the first days after Sedan, when the headquarters was established at Rheims, he had become involved in a bitter controversy with the 'demi-gods' and with the quartermaster-general as a result of certain instructions which he had given to Stieber, the chief of the *Feldpolizei*. Stieber had been placed under the

[1] Moltke, *Gesammelte Schriften*, iii. 428.

[2] How this change was effected is not clear. Bismarck claims that, on the way to the front, he heard General Podbielski boasting that a military boycott would be imposed on him, but the veracity of this story has been doubted. See Bismarck, *G.W.*, xv. 312.

[3] Ibid., vi b, 659.

[4] Ibid., 558.

orders of the General Staff for the duration of the war, although his duties led him to deal with questions which were of interest and importance to Bismarck.[1] When the Chancellor instructed the police chief to reprimand the *maire* of Rheims for having announced his allegiance to the new government in Paris, officers of the staff protested that he was interfering in matters of military administration—a charge which led to an explosion of indignation on Bismarck's part and an acrimonious exchange between him and Moltke.[2]

The Stieber affair was trifling in itself and had no further consequences. It did reveal, however, that the officers of the General Staff were attempting to draw a rigid line of demarcation between military affairs and political affairs and that they were determined that the line should not be crossed even by the king's first minister. Their ideas, moreover, concerning what lay within the military sphere proper were remarkably ambitious, as Bismarck discovered as he turned his mind, in September and October, to the question of arranging peace.

In the French war, as in all his wars, the Chancellor was concerned over the international situation and was apprehensive lest other Powers intervene before his political objectives had been attained. As early as August there had been indications that the Russian government was considering the possibility of calling a conference to end the conflict,[3] and this in itself was enough to make Bismarck anxious to end hostilities at the first favourable opportunity. In the confused political situation which followed the French emperor's capitulation at Sedan and the republican revolution in Paris, the chief obstacle to peace lay in the difficulty of finding a government which was capable of conducting negotiations and willing to make the territorial cessions which Bismarck considered indispensable. On the whole, the Chancellor felt that he had more to gain from a continuation of the imperial régime in France than from the the new government in Paris. He was aware, however, that Napoleon III or his son could not hope to regain and consolidate power unless provided with sufficient military strength to put

[1] See Klein-Wuttig, *Politik and Kriegführung*, p. 93, where Stieber's own memoirs are cited on this point.

[2] *Denkwürdigkeiten des Generals und Admirals Albrecht von Stosch*, ed. by Ulrich von Stosch (Stuttgart, 1904), p. 196; Haeften, in *Preußische Jahrbücher*, clxxvii. 89.

[3] Kurt Rheindorf, *Die Schwarze Meer- (Pontus-) Frage vom Pariser Frieden von 1856 bis zum Abschluß der Londoner Konferenz von 1871* (Berlin, 1925), pp. 78 ff.

down domestic dissidence. After Sedan there was only one organized French force which might become available for this purpose, and that was the army of Bazaine which was beleaguered in the fortress of Metz. Bismark, then—in a series of very complicated negotiations[1]—set about investigating the possibility of combining the capitulation of Metz with a definitive peace which would give Prussia what she desired but would free Bazaine's army to place the emperor or his heir firmly on the throne of France.

In the long run these negotiations came to nothing, primarily because neither Napoleon nor the empress, who had removed to London, would make the territorial promises which Bismarck required; and late in October this diplomatic episode was terminated by the capitulation of Bazaine. The significant point here, however, is that while there was still a chance that an arrangement might be made with the Bonapartes, the soldiers placed every possible obstacle in the way of Bismarck's efforts to effect this result. The most glaring example of military obstructionism came when Bismarck persuaded the king to authorize a safe-conduct for General Bourbaki, permitting the French officer to leave Metz, travel to London to consult the empress, and then return to his post within the fortress. Prince Frederick Charles, who commanded the Prussian forces investing Metz, had objected from the start to Bismarck's dealings with Bazaine and his agents, apparently fearing that the Chancellor intended to deprive him of the honour of receiving Metz's capitulation. When Bourbaki returned from London, the prince delayed giving him permission to re-enter the fortress for so long that, in disgust, Bourbaki travelled to Tours and offered his services to the newly organized army of the Government of National Defence.

When Bismarck received word of this, he wrote a long letter to Frederick Charles's chief of staff.[2]

> I appeal to your Excellency's clear judgement [he wrote] and to your own perception, so that you will understand how discouraging it must be for me when, through this kind of failure to execute explicit royal orders, the danger arises that in the whole constellation of political calculations one single cog, which is necessary in its place, will refuse to do its work. How can I have the courage to

[1] These are discussed in detail in Klein-Wuttig, *Politik und Kriegführung*, pp. 94–127.

[2] Bismarck, *G.W.*, vi b, 552–3.

proceed with my work if I cannot count on royal orders . . . being faithfully executed? . . . Your Excellency knows that my whole energy has been devoted, and with success, to providing for the victorious progress of our arms a free field, undisturbed by foreign influence. I must then demand that the army show the same confidence in me that His Majesty the King has shown in his approval of my plans. . . .

The behaviour of Prince Frederick Charles was not, unfortunately, unique. Bismarck's designs were opposed by other high-ranking officers, chief among whom was Moltke. Like his subordinates, the Chief of the General Staff tried to insist on an artificial separation of politics and strategy, and he regarded all matters touching on the prospective capitulation of Metz as belonging exclusively to his own sphere of competence. But Moltke's attitude was complicated by other factors. For one thing, he clearly regarded Bismarck's fears of foreign intervention as being unrealistic and, consequently, saw no reason why his military plans should be disrupted by diplomatic considerations.[1] Aside from this, his deep hatred of France[2] made him unwilling to countenance any peace terms until the last organized forces in the country had been utterly smashed; and this and his personal contempt for the imperial régime made him inflexibly opposed to the idea of a Bonapartist restoration.

Moltke did not hesitate to express his opposition in words, both at the time of the Bourbaki affair and later, and his sentiments were faithfully echoed by the other high-ranking officers at headquarters. Bismarck was justly indignant at this incursion into his professional field by men who were so jealous of their own. 'It is exactly as if I gave a lecture about the placing of a battery in this or that place', he said on one occasion;[3] and he complained to his wife that 'the military gentlemen make my work terrifically difficult for me! They lay their hands on it and ruin it and I have to bear the responsibility!'[4] The Chancellor was powerless to prevent this sort of thing, however; and, in the opinion of the Grand Duke of Baden, it was Moltke's arguments which turned the king definitely against the idea of restoring

[1] See Stadelmann, *Moltke und der Staat*, pp. 210–11.

[2] On Moltke's attitude towards France, see ibid., pp. 179–96.

[3] Moritz Busch, *Tagebuchblätter* (Leipzig, 1899), i. 298.

[4] Bismarck, *Briefe an seine Gattin aus dem Kriege 1870/71* (Stuttgart, 1903), p. 54.

Napoleon III.[1] Had Bismarck's negotiations not failed for other reasons, this act of persuasion might have been enough to cause their breakdown.

At the end of October, when Metz finally fell, Bismarck's relations with the military were already on the worst possible footing. He had come, moreover, to realize that Moltke was his most formidable antagonist in royal headquarters, an opponent whose influence on the king was all the more to be feared because he was—in Bismarck's words—'a *verknöcherter Generalstabsmensch* who doesn't understand anything about politics'.[2] It was the danger implicit in this apparent blindness to political factors that led the Chancellor to go on the offensive against the General Staff in November and December when the question of the fate of Paris became the subject of debate.

Paris had been encircled by Prussian armies ever since the middle of September, but no preparations had been made for the assault or even the bombardment of the city. The bulk of military opinion, indeed, was opposed to any form of attack on the capital. Moltke, as a student of Clausewitz, was temperamentally averse to siege warfare, preferring operations in the open field. As early as 1844, in his history of the Russo-Turkish campaign, he had stated that 'cities of a half million population will certainly not be taken by force of arms but must fall by themselves'.[3] His opinion had been strengthened by his study of the Crimean War. His admirer Verdy was certainly expressing Moltke's views when, in December 1870, he wrote a memorandum in which he compared a siege of Paris with that of Sevastopol, and argued that the Prussian army could not afford the losses suffered by the forces which had taken the Russian city, and that 'a thorough bombardment is, under the prevailing circumstances, an impossibility.'[4]

Bismarck was not convinced by this reasoning, especially in view of the time that the military had had to make preparations,

[1] Hermann Oncken, *Großherzog Friedrich I. von Baden und die deutsche Politik* (Berlin, 1927), ii. 167.

[2] *Bismarcks großes Spiel. Die geheimen Tagebücher Ludwig Bambergers*, ed. by Ernst Feder (Frankfurt-am-Main, 1932), p. 207.

[3] Jähns, *Moltke*, p. 534.

[4] Verdy, *With Royal Headquarters*, pp. 159–60. There were moments—in October, for instance—when Moltke seemed to desire bombardment, but in general he sided with the technicians who opposed it, and he always resented Bismarck's intervention in the matter. See Paul Bronsart von Schellendorf, *Geheimes Kriegstagebuch, 1870–1*, ed. by Peter Rassow (Bonn, 1954), pp. 18–19, 156, 204.

and he was assured by Roon that the necessary guns and ammunition could be provided for the bombardment. This being so, the Chancellor insisted that an active attempt be made to force the surrender of Paris. He was motivated here by events in the sphere of international politics and, primarily, by the sudden declaration by the Russian government that they would no longer observe the Black Sea clauses of the Treaty of 1856. Bismarck had no fundamental objection to this Russian stroke, but it had produced a sharp reaction in other capitals and, in order to prevent the situation deteriorating into a general European war with unforeseen consequences, the Chancellor had proposed an international conference to validate the Russian action. The disadvantage of this lay in the fact that, once the neutrals were assembled at the council table, they might feel called upon to attempt to end the Franco-Prussian war as well.[1] Bismarck preferred to end his wars in his own way and he was, therefore, anxiously desirous of a military victory so impressive that the French might be induced to seek terms. The surrender of Paris might, he thought, produce this result, and he demanded, therefore, that the bombardment begin.

Despite these pressing diplomatic considerations, it was not until late in December that Bismarck's arguments prevailed. In his struggle to persuade the king, he was opposed at every turn by the soldiers, all of whom—with the exception of Roon—fought against the bombardment. The crown prince's influential chief of staff, General Blumenthal, who would be responsible for the operation once it had begun, was especially outspoken. The French, he fumed, would die of hunger like mad dogs; the bombardment would not hasten this result and was pointless.[2] Obviously thinking of the ill effects of a bombardment which might prove in the end to be ineffective, Blumenthal wrote in his diary that Bismarck's 'politics should have nothing to do with this question; it is a purely military one; and the honour of the army is at stake'. He would rather give up his command, he added, than yield to the 'infantile counsels' which came from the Chancellor.[3]

[1] Rheindorf, *Pontusfrage*, pp. 99 ff.; Horst Michael, *Bismarck, England und Europa, vorwiegend von 1866–1870* (Munich, 1930), pp. 307 ff.; Klein-Wuttig, *Politik und Kriegführung*, pp. 132–3.

[2] *Bismarcks großes Spiel*, pp. 27–28.

[3] Albert Count Blumenthal, *War Journals, 1866 and 1870–71* (London, 1903), p. 197. See also Stosch, *Denkwürdigkeiten*, p. 217; Bronsart von Schellendorf, *Kriegstagebuch*, pp. 188, 192, 200, 204, 220–1, 226; Kessel, *Moltke*, pp. 577 ff.

Against this obstructionism Bismarck mobilized the resources of public opinion, and soon German newspapers were demanding an attack on Paris and popular songs were being composed to encourage Moltke to begin the shelling of the city.[1] This further infuriated the soldiers, and Blumenthal expressed what must have been the opinion of most of his colleagues, when he wrote: 'If we allow ourselves to be driven by the so-called "Voice of the People", as the newspapers call it, to adopt measures in opposition to reason and to all military science, it will be an end to generalship. The people will have to try us by court-martial, turn us out and appoint in our places lawyers and newspaper correspondents.'[2]

Bismarck, nevertheless, had his way; but, by the time the bombardment was started, on 27 December,[3] the Chancellor's relations with the soldiers and, above all, with Moltke were so strained that the crown prince became seriously worried about the disunity among the king's advisers. In a conversation with the prince on 8 January, Moltke said that he had the impression 'that the *Bundeskanzler*, in military matters just as much as in politics, wants to decide everything by himself, without paying the slightest attention to the responsible experts'. The chief of staff added that Bismarck was always sending queries to the General Staff about matters touching on secret strategical plans, and that he had on several occasions had to reject these without ceremony.[4] Moltke was so bitter that the crown prince decided that an attempt must be made to effect a reconciliation between the two antagonists. He accordingly invited them to dine with him on 13 January, but succeeded only in embroiling them further, since Bismarck took advantage of the occasion to vent his long-accumulated wrath against Moltke's subordinates in the General Staff.[5]

If the crown prince's attempt at mediation accomplished anything, it revealed that the differences between the Chancellor and the chief of staff went far beyond the merely technical aspects of the bombardment issue. On 8 January Moltke admitted that, as far as he was concerned, the real importance of

[1] See chapter heading. [2] Blumenthal, *War Journals*, pp. 229–30.

[3] On the start of the bombardment, see Hohenlohe-Ingelfingen, *Aus meinem Leben*, iv. 343 ff.

[4] Kaiser Friedrich III, *Das Kriegstagebuch von 1870–71*, ed. by H. O. Meisner (Berlin, 1926), p. 319.

[5] Ibid., pp. 325–6.

the fall of Paris would be that it would release troops for a decisive campaign against the French levies which had been raised in the south.[1] In short, as the crown prince noted a few days later, Bismarck wanted peace, but Moltke desired a war of extermination.[2] Since the chief of staff was already intent on future operations, he regarded the approaching fall of the capital not as an opportunity to end the conflict but as an event which would have no more significance than the capitulation of Metz. Indeed, in a memorandum addressed to the king on 14 January, he revealed that he thought Paris should be treated no differently than Metz. Not only the forts, but the city itself, must be surrendered, he insisted. The capital must be occupied by German troops and placed under martial law, which would be administered by a German governor through the Paris police and the National Guard. The line troops and the Mobile Guards must be disarmed and sent as prisoners to Germany; and all eagles and flags must be given up to the victors.[3]

In discussing this memorandum with one of the crown prince's aides, Moltke said, rather naïvely, that he had confined himself to purely military issues, leaving politics to Count Bismarck.[4] It is difficult to conceive, however, of a plan which was likely to have more far-reaching and more unpleasant political repercussions than this. If the king had accepted the memorandum and if Moltke had been placed in charge of the negotiations for the surrender of Paris—as he had been at Sedan and as he seemed to expect to be now—it is reasonable to suppose that the negotiations would have broken down hopelessly and the war been indefinitely extended or, conversely—if the Paris government had the temerity to consider the terms—that the chaos of the Commune would have come sooner than it did come and would have been blamed on the Germans. In either case, the possibility of neutral intervention would have been enormously enhanced.[5]

Bismarck's plans were so directly threatened by the implications of Moltke's memorandum that he resolved, at all costs, to see that the chief of staff was excluded from the negotiations

[1] Oncken, *Friedrich von Baden*, ii. 300–1.

[2] Friedrich III, *Kriegstagebuch*, p. 325.

[3] A. O. Meyer, 'Bismarck und Moltke', in *Stufen und Wandlungen der deutschen Einheit*, pp. 338–40.

[4] Friedrich III, *Kriegstagebuch*, pp. 483–4.

[5] See A. O. Meyer in *Stufen und Wandlungen*, pp. 332–3.

for the surrender of Paris. On 14 January he too sent a memodum to the king in which he stressed the imminent danger of intervention by the other Great Powers, and insisted that the question of Paris must be coupled with that of peace—a peace, moreover, which, while bringing Germany a sizeable indemnity and the cession of territory on the eastern frontier, would spare the capital any unnecessary humiliation.[1] Then, in a second memorandum four days later, he raised a more fundamental issue. Seizing upon certain correspondence which Moltke had been conducting with the Governor of Paris without consulting him in advance, the Chancellor intimated strongly that Moltke was exceeding his duties and requested that no negotiations of any kind with authorities in the city should be permitted unless he was privy to them.[2]

What went on inside the king's mind as relations between Bismarck and Moltke reached their final crisis is not known. In the long series of disputes since the beginning of the war, the sovereign had seemed, on the whole, to be more sympathetic to the soldiers than to his Chancellor.[3] Now, however, he reversed his position completely. On 20 January, when the French expressed a desire to discuss terms, he authorized Bismarck to begin armistice talks—an action which foreshadowed the end of Moltke's ideas of an extension of the war. And five days later he at last took action to end the bitter struggle over spheres of competence and to satisfy Bismarck's frequent complaints concerning the boycott imposed on him by the General Staff.[4] Two royal orders of 25 January stipulated, first, that Moltke was to engage in no correspondence with French authorities in either Paris or Bordeaux without first learning from the king whether Bismarck should be consulted, and, second, that the Chancellor was to be kept fully informed about the course of future military operations and was to be given an opportunity to present his views concerning them.[5]

The Chief of the General Staff seems to have been stunned by the receipt of these orders. His first impulse was to resign his office and, on the evening of 25 January, he drafted a letter to the

[1] Bismarck, *G.W.*, vi b, 665 ff. [2] Ibid., p. 673; Kessel, *Moltke*, pp. 585 ff.

[3] See, for instance, Bronsart von Schellendorf, *Kriegstagebuch*, pp. 233–7.

[4] The most recent of these had been on 9 January. See Bismarck, *G.W.*, vi b, 658 and, on Bismarck's determination to force this issue, Waldersee, *Denkwürdigkeiten*, i. 116–17.

[5] Klein-Wuttig, *Politik und Kriegführung*, pp. 152–3.

king in which he defended himself against charges of having indulged in political activity and of having failed to keep Bismarck informed of operations and suggested, rather sarcastically, that it might be best, in the interest of unity, to allow Bismarck to advise the king in military matters and to bear the responsibility for future operations.[1] After a night's reflection Moltke composed a second memorandum[2] which was somewhat calmer in tone but which still contained a strong defence of his own actions and placed the responsibility for past disputes on Bismarck's shoulders. In addition, the chief of staff drew a distinction between military operations which had been executed and those which were still in prospect. Information concerning the former he was willing to transmit to the Chancellor, he said, and had in fact done so. 'On the other hand, to give information concerning operations planned or still in the course of being carried out to anyone except the generals charged with their execution, I would consider as a breach of duty.'

But the most interesting passage in this revised memorandum, which was sent to the king on 29 January,[3] dealt with Moltke's conception of his own office.

> I believe [he wrote] that it would be a good thing to settle my relationship with the Federal Chancellor definitively. Up till now I have considered that the Chief of the General Staff (especially in war) and the Federal Chancellor are two equally warranted [*berechtigte*] and mutually independent agencies under the direct command of Your Royal Majesty, which have the duty of keeping each other reciprocally informed.

Coming from the chief of staff who, until 1859, had not been permitted to report directly even to the War Minister, this was

[1] This first memorandum was drafted by Bronsart von Schellendorf. Bronsart, *Kriegstagebuch*, pp. 309–11. The idea of forcing the issue in this way seems to have been much on Moltke's mind. In a letter which Verdy wrote to the Austrian Chief of General Staff Beck in 1896 he recalled the struggle with Bismarck and said that, a few days before the capitulation of Paris, Moltke said, 'There will be nothing left for me but to request His Majesty to hand over to this high dignitary [Bismarck] the duties of a Chief of the General Staff of the Army as well.' Edmund von Glaise-Horstenau, *Franz Josephs Weggefährte* (Zürich, Leipzig, and Vienna, 1930), p. 472.

[2] Copies of both memoranda are reproduced in Stadelmann, *Moltke und der Staat*, pp. 434–8.

[3] It was earlier believed that Moltke decided against sending the memorandum to the king and buried it, and the earlier draft, in his files. See Haeften in *Preußische Jahrbücher*, clxxvii. 99 ff., and Klein-Wuttig, *Politik und Kriegführung*, p. 154. The records of the Military Cabinet, however, prove that the second memorandum was, in fact, sent to the king. Stadelmann, *Moltke und der Staat*, p. 505.

a remarkable claim; and its importance is not diminished by the fact that the king apparently decided to disregard it.[1]

The sovereign, indeed, after he had made up his mind to support his Chancellor, never wavered again. There was an atmosphere of general mortification in the General Staff as Bismarck conducted the armistice talks with Jules Favre on 26 January and made decisions on such matters as which of the Paris forts would have to be surrendered and who was to have the honour of the last shot.[2] Albrecht von Stosch, who was serving on the staff of the crown prince, wrote at this time that he had never seen such bitterness directed against one man as was shown toward Bismarck in field headquarters.[3] But this did not alter the fact that the Chancellor had won his private campaign. The terms arranged for the surrender of Paris were in accordance with his, rather than Moltke's, ideas;[4] during the armistice he was always invited to attend discussions of operations which might yet have to be attempted;[5] and the final peace terms were arranged under his direction and without significant interference by the military. It has sometimes been argued that, in the question of the territorial annexations demanded of France, Bismarck surrendered, against his better judgement, to the pressure of the military, especially in the question of Metz.[6] But the Chancellor's opinions concerning the advisability of taking Metz had varied widely during the war,[7] and even at the end he seems to have been undecided. On 21 February he said: 'The soldiers . . . will not want to do without Metz, and perhaps they are right.'[8] His final decision to include the fortress in the German demands cannot, therefore, be fairly described as a capitulation to military opinion.

IV

In the three wars of the unification period, Bismarck had successfully maintained the principle of the predominance of politics in war-time. It had, however, become progressively

[1] The draft answer in the files of the Military Cabinet does not touch on any of the real issues raised by Moltke. See Stadelmann, *Moltke und der Staat*, p. 505.

[2] Ibid., p. 250.

[3] Stosch, *Denkwürdigkeiten*, p. 227.

[4] A. O. Meyer in *Stufen und Wandlungen*, pp. 334–5.

[5] See, for instance, Stadelmann, *Moltke und der Staat*, p. 251.

[6] See A. O. Meyer in *Stufen und Wandlungen*, p. 336.

[7] Klein-Wuttig, *Politik und Kriegführung*, pp. 158–62.

[8] Busch, *Tagebuchblätter*, ii. 168–9.

more difficult for him to do so; and, what is more significant, his victory had not convinced the soldiers that he was right. Shortly after the Franco-Prussian war had ended Moltke wrote in a famous essay on strategy:

Politics uses war for the attainment of its ends; it operates decisively at the beginning and the end [of the conflict], of course in such manner that it refrains from increasing its demands during the war's duration or from being satisfied with an inadequate success. . . . Strategy can only direct its efforts towards the highest goal which the means available make attainable. In this way, it aids politics best, working only for its objectives, but in its operations independent of it.[1]

Here again, unaffected by the events of the recent war, was the demand for a line of demarcation between politics and strategy which would free the strategist from civilian interference. Generations of officers, trained in the General Staff by Moltke, were to accept this as doctrine and were to attempt, with disastrous results, to apply it in the First World War.

[1] Moltke, 'Über Strategie', *Militärische Werke*, ii. 291.

VI

THE STATE WITHIN THE STATE
1871–1914

Versailles is the birthplace of a military absolutism like that brought to bloom by Louis XIV. LUDWIG WINDTHORST *in 1871.*

Naja, in Uniform, da gehts ja, da macht man Figur, das gibt n kolossalen Halt, da is man n ganz anderer Kerl. Wissense — in Staatsbürjerkluft — da komm ick mir immer vor wie ne halbe Portion ohne Mostrich. SCHLETTOW *in* ZUCKMAYER'S *Der Hauptmann von Köpenick.*

IN May 1870 the Bavarian statesman Hohenlohe and the historian Sybel watched a military parade on the Kreuzberg. Hohenlohe wrote later:

> The whole garrison of Berlin had turned out. A great show of princes, generals and so forth. I mingled with the crowd and was struck by the interest manifested by the lowest of the people in things military. No trace of the former animosity against the military which used to be noticeable among the lower classes. The commonest working man looked on the troops with the feeling that he belonged or had belonged to them. Everywhere stories of Königgrätz, Düppel, &c., by old service men who were among the spectators.[1]

Had Hohenlohe attended a similar ceremony a year later, after the war against France had been won, he would doubtless have remarked that popular enthusiasm for the army was even more pronounced. There can be no doubt that the three victorious wars inspired a deep and abiding pride in German arms, not only among the Prussian people, but also among the subjects of the other German states which were now absorbed in the new empire. They had the further happy result of alleviating the bitterness that had been the legacy of the constitutional struggle and of converting many of the army's most inveterate opponents into admirers and supporters.

It would have been well for the German empire if its leaders

[1] *Memoirs of Prince Chlodwig zu Hohenlohe-Schillingsfürst* (London, 1906), ii. 11.

had properly appreciated this fund of goodwill and had striven to build upon it a permanent reconciliation between army and people. The military hierarchy, however, made arrogant by its successes, seemed intent only on winning what it had not been able to win during the *Konfliktszeit*, complete freedom from the budgetary powers of parliament, and this, not unnaturally, led, first, to parliamentary resistance and, later, with the growth of the Progressive and Social Democratic parties, to a renewed attempt to impose democratic controls on the military establishment. Within three years of the ceremony at Versailles, which crowned the unification of Germany, the old conflict had been renewed; and it continued with mounting intensity until the outbreak of war in 1914.

To the political generals of the period after 1871 the thought of using a military *coup d'état* to escape from their constitutional difficulties occurred as frequently as it had to their predecessors in the 1860's. No serious attempt was made, however, to try this extreme and hazardous experiment. Instead, to defend themselves against what they considered to be the forces of revolution, the army chiefs relied on two principal lines of policy. In the first place, they progressively reorganized military administration in such a way as to withdraw the most vital military matters from the jurisdiction of the only person whom parliament could hold accountable for them—the War Minister—and to entrust them to constitutionally irresponsible agencies like the Military Cabinet and the General Staff. Secondly, they adopted a policy of officer selection which was deliberately designed to withhold commissions from persons with unorthodox social and political ideas and to maintain the officer corps as a bulwark of royal absolutism.

These military policies were encouraged by Bismarck who, especially after 1879, began to lose faith in the constitutional arrangements of which he himself had been the author; and they were accepted by Bismarck's successors. In the short run they were successful policies, for the army defeated all parliamentary attempts to control its activities, while the officer corps preserved its cohesiveness and its feudal relationship to the Crown. But this success was achieved only by destroying the organizational unity of the army, which had in consequence to suffer, in the pre-war years and during the war also, from administrative confusion, duplication of function, and interdepartmental rivalry. Meanwhile, the social attitudes and policies of the army and the political activities of some of its leaders convinced the parliamentary opposition that the officer corps had become a praetorian guard which had no essential connexion with the society which supported it, and led them inevitably to the conclusion that, if democracy were ever to make progress in Germany, the old army system must be overthrown completely.

I

As a result of the extension of Prussian hegemony over all of Germany, the military powers of the Prussian ruler had been greatly expanded. When the constitution of the North German Confederation was adopted in 1867, King William was named *Bundesfeldherr* and given complete power of command over the armies of the member states.[1] Four years later, when the empire was established, this command was widened to include the troops of all German states except Bavaria, whose army in time of peace remained subordinate to the king of that state and was administered by the Bavarian Minister of War, although, in time of war, it too passed under Prussian command.

It was the contention of most German conservatives, and virtually all military officers, that—apart from the special arrangements made to satisfy Bavarian *amour propre*[2]—the king-emperor's authority over the national military establishment was subject to no limitation: that his right, for instance, to effect far-reaching changes in the organization of the army, which had been so hotly contested in the constitutional struggle, was now beyond question. They pointed out that the fourth paragraph of article 63 of the imperial constitution stipulated that 'The emperor determines the peace-time strength, the structure and the distribution [*Einteilung*] of the imperial army'. Jurists were apt to argue, however, that this provision was, at least in part, dependent on article 60 of the constitution, which provided for an imperial law governing the peace-time strength of the army. The scope of the emperor's powers under article

[1] See Schmidt-Bückeburg, *Militärkabinett*, pp. 96–108.

[2] The Württemberg army also occupied a special position. Although it was commanded by the Prussian ruler in war and peace, its officers were appointed by its own king and it had other privileges.

63, they contended, would necessarily be determined by the measures taken to implement article 60.[1]

The issue was not joined until 1874. Up to that time the size of the army was governed by the so-called 'iron law' of 1867 which provided for an army equivalent to 1 per cent. of the population, supported by an automatic annual grant of 225 thaler per man.[2] Originally scheduled to expire in December 1871, this law was extended for an additional three years. It was apparent, however, that implementation of article 60 could not be postponed beyond 1874 and that a fundamental decision would have to be made.

Given their belief in the unlimited nature of the royal power of command, it was clear that the army authorities would demand a perpetuation of the iron law or something very much like it. The emperor himself was convinced that his recent triumphs in the field had proved the validity of the position he had taken during the constitutional conflict, and he was determined that parliament must now be denied any effective influence over the army.[3] With his full approval, then, his military advisers drafted, for submission to the imperial Reichstag in 1874, a law setting the size of the army at 401,659 men, this figure to be considered permanent in time of peace until such time as there should be a 'declaration of a further legal modification'. Future modification, however, would depend upon government initiative. It was all too clear that the army was seeking to remove the strength of the army from the sphere of parliamentary debate and, since this would make the grant of funds an automatic matter, to emasculate the Reichstag's budgetary powers in so far as they applied to the army.[4]

The eagerness with which the army pushed this objective was well expressed by Albrecht von Roon, who had just retired as War Minister but was watching the progress of the bill anxiously.

> The King cannot give in [he wrote to a friend] without placing himself, his ministers, and his military principles as they apply to the past, in the pillory—to say nothing of the technical inadequacy and perversity [which such surrender would involve]. Bismarck too will appreciate that and, if he harnesses himself to the task with deter-

[1] See Huber, *Heer und Staat*, pp. 260–1 and the authorities cited.

[2] See above, Chapter IV, p. 178.

[3] Lucius von Ballhausen, *Bismarck-Erinnerungen* (Stuttgart and Berlin, 1921), p. 46.

[4] Huber, *Heer und Staat*, p. 265.

mination, he will succeed—despite all the thistles and thorns which the opposition sows, and all the holes and ruts which they try to dig—in pulling the wagon forward to its goal. An efficient army . . . is the only conceivable protection against the red, as against the black, spectre. If they ruin the army, then the end has come. Then *adieu* Prussian military renown and German glory![1]

Neither Bismarck's parliamentary skill,[2] however, nor the prestige of Helmuth von Moltke was sufficient to carry the bill in its original form through the Reichstag. The Chief of the General Staff sought to convince the deputies that the unsettled state of Europe, and, especially, the remarkable recovery of France, made it necessary for Germany to have a large army and one whose strength was not subject to sudden change. 'Through fluctuations in this figure', he warned the Reichstag, 'you bring uncertainty into all the many comprehensive preparations which must be made long in advance and worked out to the last detail. . . . Consider, that any reduction of this figure will have repercussions for twelve years.'[3]

Such technical arguments did not succeed in diverting the attention of the Reichstag from the real point at issue. Eugen Richter, who, over the next twenty years, was to prove himself the most formidable parliamentary critic of military affairs,[4] directed a blistering attack against the basic implications of the army plan. No civilized nation, he argued, could be expected to fix the size of its army for all time. This was a matter which must be determined by annual budgetary decisions of parliament; and the army would be well advised to avoid flouting this basic principle of constitutional law lest they drive a wedge between army and parliament.[5] Richter's views were supported

[1] Roon, *Denkwürdigkeiten*, iii. 390.

[2] Bismarck played a relatively small part in the controversy over the bill of 1874. He was ill and preoccupied with foreign affairs and his feelings about the bill seem also to have been mixed. He appears to have felt that the military were seeking to dispense with him as well as with parliament, and he took malicious pleasure in their confusion when opposition developed to their plans. See Eyck, *Bismarck*, iii. 70.

[3] L. Rüdt von Collenberg, *Die deutsche Armee von 1871–1914* (*Forschungen und Darstellungen aus dem Reichsarchiv*, Heft 4) (Berlin, 1922), p. 12.

[4] On Richter see M. Bonn, *Wandering Scholar* (New York, 1948), pp. 47–48. The soldiers came to fear, but also to respect, his views. During the hearings on the army bill of 1893 Waldersee wrote: 'The only man whose views deserve respect is Eugen Richter; he has already hit the nail on the head many times. He must really be a man of sharp intelligence.' Waldersee, *Denkwürdigkeiten*, ii. 286.

[5] Adalbert Wahl, *Deutsche Geschichte* (Stuttgart, 1926–36), i. 109.

by his own party—the Progressives—by the Catholic Centre party, led by Mallinckrodt, and by the left wing of the National Liberals under Eduard Lasker—a combination which doubtless confirmed Roon's fears concerning 'the red and the black spectre' but which was also sufficiently strong to block passage of the bill in its original form.

The government was, indeed, saved from complete defeat only by the timely intervention of Bismarck who, from his sick bed, arranged a compromise with the majority leaders of the National Liberals which was ultimately accepted by the greater part of the other opposition groups. In accordance with this the strength of the army was set at the figure requested by the government, but only for a period of seven years, at the end of which it had to be renewed by the Reichstag. This so-called *Septennat* was finally approved late in April, but not without some bitter opposition speeches which showed that the old wounds had been reopened. Both Richter and Mallinckrodt spoke against the bill in its final form, the Centre leader charging that 'the concept of militarism is more and more taking form and flesh and blood',[1] while Richter described the *Septennat* as 'a restriction placed by absolutism on the parliamentary system', and prophesied that 'this bit of absolutism will eat its way forward like cancer'.[2]

The emperor had assented to the amended version of the bill with disappointment and, apparently, with some resentment against Bismarck for his willingness to make concessions. But, as he wrote to Roon in May, 'really in our time seven years are almost half a century when one thinks of the seven years from 1863 to 1870! In this way we have the army organization intact for seven years and, after seven years, we will perhaps find ourselves *before*, or even *after*, another war; if not, then the population will have grown and we will have to increase the recruits by one per cent. . . .'[3] Even so, the emperor was alarmed by the tone of some of the parliamentary speeches and by the evident desire of certain deputies to pry into the internal affairs of the army, and his alarm was shared by members of his military entourage. It was probably the fear that, in future budget debates, the Reichstag might insist on discussing such matters as personnel problems and promotions that led to the adoption,

[1] Wahl, *Deutsche Geschichte*, i. 114.
[2] Eyck, *Bismarck*, iii. 76.
[3] Roon, *Denkwürdigkeiten*, iii. 409.

in the years after the defeat of 1874, of a very complicated defensive technique against such parliamentary pretensions. In brief, this involved the systematic removal of all matters of command and personnel policy from the jurisdiction of the one officer who regularly appeared before the Reichstag and who could be considered accountable to it for military affairs: namely, the War Minister.

Ever since the beginning of the constitutional system in Prussia the lot of the War Minister had been a hard one. As an officer he was bound by his personal oath of loyalty to his king and was expected to defend the royal power of command; as a minister of state he was bound by his oath to the constitution and was expected to countersign royal orders which affected the army and to bear responsibility for them before the *Landtag*. Conflicts of loyalty were frequent and the possibility of resolving them to the mutual satisfaction of king and *Landtag* remote.[1] But, if the position of the War Minister in the Prussian system was difficult, it became, in the words of one critic, 'monstrous and against all reason' under the empire.[2] In the first place, there was no imperial War Minister, partly because, in a strictly legal sense, there was no imperial army but only an army made up of contingents from the separate states,[3] and partly because, with the exception of Bismarck, there were no imperial ministers, the heads of the different departments of the government being secretaries of state under the Chancellor's supervision. In effect, Bismarck himself was the imperial War Minister, for he bore the ultimate responsibility for military affairs before the Reichstag.[4] But the Chancellor had no real control over the internal workings of the army, whereas the Prussian War Minister had authority over all the armed forces of the empire (with the exception of the Bavarian army) and supervised such common military institutions as the General Staff, the Division of Personnel (which was part of the Prussian War Ministry, al-

[1] See above, Chapter III, pp. 124–5, and Chapter IV, pp. 142–3.

[2] Schmitt, *Staatsgefüge und Zusammenbruch*, p. 34.

[3] This was the opinion of Laband. See his *Staatsrecht des deutschen Reiches* (5. Aufl., Berlin, 1914), iv. 5.

[4] Before his retirement in 1873, Roon made strenuous efforts to have himself recognized as imperial War Minister. Bismarck opposed this on the grounds that it would offend the rulers of the member states. His real reason was probably to avoid the creation of a minister whose rank would be virtually equal to his own. See Meisner, *Kriegsminister*, pp. 58–59; Roon, *Denkwürdigkeiten*, iii. 22–23, 34; Stosch, *Denkwürdigkeiten*, p. 137.

though administered by the Chief of the Military Cabinet), the schools and the *Kriegsakademie*, and the logistics and supply departments. In reality, if not in law, he was now more an imperial than a Prussian official; and, in the discussion of military affairs before the Reichstag, he, rather than Bismarck, generally represented the government. Because he did so and because he continued to countersign orders affecting the contingent army, the Reichstag regarded him as being responsible to them and directed questions at him which bore upon every aspect of the army's affairs. In a strictly legal sense he was not bound to answer such questions; in practice it was always difficult, and sometimes inexpedient, to refuse.[1] Even a man of such determination as Roon had not always succeeded in distinguishing between questions bearing upon the forces of the empire (which he could answer) and questions dealing with the Prussian army (which he could not) or between administrative matters (which he could discuss) and command questions (which the emperor considered none of the Reichstag's business). Roon's successor, General von Kameke, affected liberal political views and, in the parliamentary halls, he was inclined to be more compliant than Roon.[2]

To certain of the highest officers in the army the very existence of a constitutional War Minister had always seemed to represent a threat to the military prerogatives of the king. Edwin von Manteuffel, for instance, had always felt this way and, between 1857 and 1865, he had used all the powers of his curiously dual position—as Chief of the Military Cabinet, he was simultaneously head of the Division of Personnel in the War Ministry and chief of the bureau which handled the sovereign's military correspondence—to withhold from the War Minister information which might find its way to parliament. Thus he had generally refrained from transmitting to the minister royal communications to the commanding generals or orders on matters of military command which he had drafted, unless specifically instructed to do so by the king;[3] and he had

[1] On the difficulties of the War Minister's position, see especially Meisner, *Kriegsminister*, pp. 57–64; the same author in *Forschungen zur brandenburgischen und preußischen Geschichte*, l (1938), 95–98; Rüdt von Collenberg in *Wissen und Wehr* (1927), pp. 293–9; Huber, *Heer und Staat*, pp. 324–8.

[2] On Kameke, who was War Minister from 1873 to 1883, see Schmidt-Bückeburg, *Militärkabinett*, pp. 126 ff., and Meisner, *Kriegsminister*, p. 31.

[3] This had led to sharp clashes between Manteuffel and Roon, especially during

striven also, although with incomplete success, to remove all personnel matters—selection, promotion, decorations, punishments, and the like—from the War Minister's jurisdiction.[1]

The Chief of the Military Cabinet after 1871 was General E. L. von Albedyll.[2] In 1862, after twenty years of field service, Albedyll had been transferred to the Division of Personnel in the War Ministry, and there he had worked under Manteuffel until that officer was made Governor of Schleswig in 1865. For Manteuffel Albedyll had affection and veneration; he absorbed Manteuffel's principles as his own, and he frequently consulted him after he himself had become Chief of the Military Cabinet.[3] The eighteen years during which he stood at the elbow of the king-emperor may, indeed, be considered a kind of continuation of the Manteuffel régime; and, during them, Albedyll achieved his predecessor's ambition of removing the most vital matters of military administration from the effective control of the War Minister.

Even before the debate over the army bill of 1874, Albedyll had been working to weaken Kameke's authority,[4] and he was strengthened in his determination by the criticism of the army made by Richter and other deputies. Had such parliamentary attacks been continued, there is little doubt that he would have pushed his attack on the War Minister more vigorously. But in the last half of the 1870's both parliament and the army were preoccupied with other matters—the threat of war with France in 1875, the near-eastern crisis of the following year and the Russo-Turkish war precipitated by it, the Berlin congress of 1878, and the political revolution that was caused by Bismarck's break with the National Liberal party in 1879. During these events the problem of civil-military relations receded into the background. In 1880, for instance, when the first *Septennat*

the Danish war. See Roon Papers: Manteuffel to Roon, 8 July 1864.

[1] For a fuller treatment, see Craig, in *Political Science Quarterly*, lxvi (1951), 30-36.

[2] Between 1865 and 1871 the office was held by Hermann von Tresckow.

[3] See Schwedler in *Militärwissenschaftliche Rundschau*, ii (1937), 271.

[4] Albedyll's first victory was a royal decision of November 1873, confirmed in May 1874, that regulations concerning officers' courts of honour, a subject of some interest to the Reichstag, were to be considered matters of command and to fall in the jurisdiction of the Military Cabinet rather than the War Ministry. Schmidt-Bückeburg, *Militärkabinett*, p. 128. The idea of weakening Kameke was also implicit in the bill of 1874. Lucius von Ballhausen, *Bismarck-Erinnerungen*, p. 46.

expired, the Reichstag raised no serious difficulties over the government's request for an increase in the size of the army to 427,274 non-commissioned officers and men, and the debate on the estimates was neither so protracted nor so stormy as it had been in 1874.[1] It was not, indeed, until the foreign dangers had subsided and some semblance of order had been restored in the party system that the Reichstag turned a critical eye on the army again; and it was only then that the Chief of the Military Cabinet bent seriously to the task of emasculating the War Ministry.

In doing so he was supported by powerful allies, for both the Chancellor and the General Staff now approved of his designs. Bismarck's motives were both political and personal. His break with his National Liberal allies had created a chaotic situation in the Reichstag and had, in the end, made it much more difficult for him to control that body than it had been in the first years after the unification. Worried by the growth of the opposition parties and by the emergence of a militant socialism, the Chancellor seems now to have begun to regret the grant of universal suffrage and to view its future evolution with foreboding, and he was consequently determined that the Reichstag should not be given an opportunity to win any real measure of control over the last bulwark against revolution, the army. If reduction of the War Minister's powers would help avert this threat, he was willing to support it.[2] He regarded Kameke as a man who was too inclined to make damaging concessions to parliament and grumbled on one occasion that 'a parliamentary general on active service is always a disagreeable phenomenon, but one as War Minister is dangerous'.[3] Finally, Kameke was supposed to be in the confidence of the crown prince and Bismarck regarded all of the heir apparent's friends as conspirators against his own authority.

As for the General Staff, the bitterness which had sprung up between it and the War Ministry during the war against France

[1] Huber, *Heer und Staat*, p. 265.

[2] Schmidt-Bückeburg (*Militärkabinett*, pp. 129–30, 153–5) feels that Bismarck was motivated primarily by his desire to reduce the War Minister to the position of a secretary of state, like other imperial departmental heads. Meisner (*Kriegsminister*, pp. 68–70) feels that this is not sufficiently proved and places his emphasis on Bismarck's desire to strengthen the *Kommandogewalt* against parliamentary pretensions. See also Meisner in *Forschungen zur brandenburgischen und preußischen Geschichte*, l (1938), 94.

[3] Meisner in *Forschungen*, l. 95.

had not disappeared. General Staff officers resented the fact that, once the fighting was over, their chief was forced to revert to the role of subordinate to the War Minister. Moreover, throughout the 1870's, there was growing friction between the higher officers of the General Staff and the War Ministry, the former believing that they were advanced more slowly in rank than their contemporaries in the ministry.[1] Moltke himself, in his last years, paid little attention to this bureaucratic rivalry, for he was utterly absorbed in questions of war plans and mobilization schedules. But in 1882 there was appointed to the post of quartermaster-general a man of consuming ambition and overwhelming *Ressortpatriotismus*, Alfred von Waldersee. From the moment he stepped into the '*rote Bude*' on the Königsplatz, Waldersee was eager to free the General Staff from its dependence on the War Ministry. Unless this were done, he said blandly, 'we shall doubtless end up with the French state of affairs, where the minister commands the army'.[2] Waldersee cultivated Albedyll—indeed, he had been doing so ever since 1878[3]—and became his staunchest supporter; and as early as May 1882 he was confiding to his diary that 'the fight with the War Ministry is assuming ever greater dimensions, but I think we will carry it to a successful conclusion'.[4]

The reference to the widening scope of this complicated business was probably occasioned by a realization, on the part of both Albedyll and Waldersee, that their plans could not be effected unless they got rid of Kameke himself. The War Minister could not be expected to stand idly by while his prerogatives were diminished. A follower of the Scharnhorst–Boyen tradition, he believed not only that the army administration should remain united under the War Minister but also that it was to the interest of the army to remain on good terms with parliament, which necessarily involved allowing the deputies to have some share in military affairs. The idea of presiding over the dissolution of his own office and of spending the rest of his career laboriously explaining to parliament that neither he nor they had any authority over matters of command (which were in any case impossible to define logically) was utterly repugnant to him, and he made this abundantly clear to his colleagues.

[1] Schmidt-Bückeburg, *Militärkabinett*, p. 137.

[2] Waldersee, *Denkwürdigkeiten*, i. 220.

[3] Ibid., pp. 172, 174.

[4] Ibid., p. 220; Kessel, *Moltke*, pp. 693 ff.

It was apparent to Albedyll then that Kameke would have to go.

Events at the beginning of 1883 played directly into the hands of the Chief of the Military Cabinet. In January the opposition parties in the Reichstag launched an unexpected attack upon military expenditures. Windthorst, Vollmar, Schott, and Richter criticized such things as the excessive outlay for cavalry regiments, the pensioning off of officers at the so-called 'majors' corner', the amount of money spent on military bands, and the number of men who spent their term of service performing manual labour. Richter distinguished himself further by demanding the reduction of the term of service from three years to two and by describing the Guard regiments as 'parade troops' which possessed no military utility, and which consequently should be abolished. Against this last argument Kameke protested, and he was supported by other deputies, who pointed out that the decision as to whether there were Guard regiments or not was a command matter reserved to the emperor alone. Unabashed, Richter answered that the existence of the Guards was a matter of public knowledge on which the Reichstag had every right to comment and that he was fully justified in expressing his opinion that they were worthless and cost too much.[1]

This debate infuriated the emperor, who always resented reflections on the efficiency of his regiments,[2] and it gave Albedyll the opportunity for which he had been waiting. At the beginning of February the Chief of the Military Cabinet consulted Bismarck and found the Chancellor fully prepared to see Kameke forced out of office; and, in the following weeks, he discussed the question of a successor with both Bismarck and Waldersee.[3] Simultaneously, as the attacks in the Reichstag continued and were extended to include protests against the tax immunity of garrison towns, he found it easy to intimate to the emperor that Kameke was not showing enough vigour in his defence of the army. Under his influence, the emperor instructed the War Minister to inform the Reichstag that it had no authority in matters of command and, further, that the government did not intend to alter its tax arrangements. Kameke

[1] Reichstag, *Stenographische Berichte* (1882–3), ii. 990 ff., 1016 ff.

[2] See, for instance, Lucius von Ballhausen, *Bismarck-Erinnerungen*, p. 257.

[3] Schmidt-Bückeburg, *Militärkabinett*, pp. 140–1; Waldersee, *Denkwürdigkeiten*, i. 224.

made an effort to follow these orders, but, as a reward, he received only another long communication from the sovereign, insisting that a more strenuous effort would have to be made to show the Reichstag in its next session who really ruled the army. Kameke interpreted this as a sign that the emperor had lost confidence in him and immediately submitted his resignation.[1]

Albedyll had meanwhile decided that Kameke's successor should be Paul Bronsart von Schellendorf, who had been one of Moltke's 'demi-gods' during the French war. He required, however, that Bronsart agree to two important administrative reforms before being confirmed and—at the same moment that the emperor was consulting Bismarck and was being advised to accept Kameke's resignation[2]—Albedyll was laying his conditions before the candidate. Bronsart was asked to agree, first, that the Chief of the General Staff should be given the privilege, which he had possessed in the wars of 1866 and 1870, of direct access to the emperor without the War Minister being present when he availed himself of it; and, second, that the Division of Personnel in the War Ministry should be abolished and all personnel matters administered in the future by the Chief of the Military Cabinet independently.[3]

Bronsart was anxious for office and raised no objection to these terms. Moreover, when he was informed that the emperor had not been satisfied with Kameke's attitude in the Reichstag, he declared voluntarily: 'In the political realm I will oppose with severity and determination any attempt to endanger the rights of the Crown, as well as any pretension on the part of the political parties to win any influence whatsoever over the power of command.'[4] This reassured Albedyll and the other principal actors in this administrative drama; Kameke's resignation was accepted; the order transferring personnel matters to the Chief of the Military Cabinet was issued on 8 March; and, two months later, it was followed by the order granting immediate

[1] Lucius von Ballhausen, *Bismarck-Erinnerungen*, pp. 252, 259. Cf. Meisner, *Kriegsminister*, pp. 33–34.

[2] Schmidt-Bückeburg, *Militärkabinett*, p. 143. Albrecht von Stosch, Chief of the Admiralty, submitted his resignation at this time also, for he sympathized with Kameke's views. This was also accepted, doubtless to Bismarck's satisfaction, for he had had a long series of disputes with Stosch, and the Chief of the Admiralty was also close to the crown prince. On Kameke's fall, see also Bismarck, *G.W.*, vi c, 274.

[3] Schmidt-Bückeburg, *Militärkabinett*, p. 144.

[4] Meisner, *Kriegsminister*, p. 37.

access to the emperor to the Chief of the General Staff or his deputy, Waldersee.[1]

Writing in his diary at the end of March, Waldersee paid tribute to the adroitness of the Chief of the Military Cabinet. 'The wholly satisfactory solution', he wrote, 'and the dismissal of both Kameke and Stosch[2] is entirely to the credit of Albedyll who—with the approval, but at the same time the very careful abstention, of the Chancellor—handled the difficult matter very skilfully and has thereby earned great merit in the army and the fatherland.'[3] From his old mentor Manteuffel Albedyll also received praise for having destroyed the pernicious French theory that 'the War Minister is *quasi* chief of the army'.[4] But it is doubtful whether congratulations were really in order. What Albedyll had really done was to destroy the administrative unity which the army had enjoyed since the days of Scharnhorst and Boyen, and, in doing so, he had introduced a degree of interdepartmental rivalry that had been unknown before 1883. The War Ministry, the Military Cabinet, and the General Staff had become mutually independent agencies, but it was virtually impossible to define the limits of their spheres of competence and, between 1883 and 1914, disputes were frequent, acrimonious, and damaging to the efficiency of the army.[5]

Moreover, once they had won their freedom, neither the General Staff nor the Military Cabinet was content to leave matters there. The former became increasingly critical of the difficulties involved in co-ordinating its war plans with the supply services, which were still controlled by the War Ministry, and was apt to try to by-pass the ministry in the placing of ordnance and munitions orders.[6] Albedyll's ambitious successors, and especially General von Hahnke, who was Chief of the

[1] The order of 24 May affecting the General Staff is printed in Wohlers, *Generalstab*, p. 32.

[2] See p. 229, n. 2, above.

[3] Waldersee, *Denkwürdigkeiten*, i. 225.

[4] Meisner in *Forschungen*, l. 102–3.

[5] As early as February 1889 Franz von Roggenbach was fearful that the disorganization he detected in other branches of the state administration was communicating itself to the army. 'How could it be otherwise', he wrote to Stosch, 'with a War Minister who will no longer co-operate and a Chief of the General Staff who is one of the most suspicious people in the world.' This was a reference to a current struggle between Bronsart von Schellendorf and Waldersee. J. Heyderhoff, ed., *Im Ring der Gegner Bismarcks* (2. Aufl., Leipzig, 1943), p. 318.

[6] The Military Cabinet meddled in this sphere also, approving a request from Krupp's in 1891 without informing the War Ministry. Schmidt-Bückeburg, *Militärkabinett*, p. 192.

Military Cabinet from 1888 to 1901,[1] seemed bent on raising their office to the position enjoyed by the *Generaladjutantur* in the eighteenth century and subordinating the other departments of the army to it.[2] In his turn, the War Minister was not always content to be—as Kameke had prophesied he would be[3]—a 'Minister of the second class'. There were War Ministers who were resigned to the steady diminution of their functions—like Verdy (1889–90), who planned a transfer of some of his remaining functions to the Military Cabinet and the General Staff with the cheerful words, 'The new War Minister must make his debut in his office as a kind of suicide';[4] and Gossler (1896–1903), who seemed bent on nullifying the office completely.[5] But there were others who tried to win back the powers lost in 1883, and their efforts increased the internecine warfare that raged in the army in the years before the war.

The primary purpose of the changes of 1883 had been to render ineffective parliamentary attacks on the army. But the method employed had been so clumsy that it tended to defeat its own purpose. The War Minister had now been given the thankless task of turning away all questions on any but purely administrative and financial matters with the argument that he neither possessed knowledge of, nor had the authority to discuss, these matters. It was hardly to be expected that the Reichstag would be satisfied with this. Even Paul Bronsart von Schellendorf, who had been glad to accept Albedyll's conditions in 1883, came to regret his compliance when he began to understand the realities of the parliamentary situation. In two memoranda sent to the kaiser in 1889, he argued that the War Minister's function was not to avoid questions but to defend the army in parliament, that his voice would have no weight in the Reichstag unless it were recognized there that he possessed the confidence of the emperor, and that continued diminution of his prerogatives could only indicate that such confidence was non-existent.[6]

This was a warning that deserved more attention than it

[1] On Hahnke, see A. Graf von Monts, *Erinnerungen und Gedanken* (Berlin, 1932), p. 24.

[2] Schmidt-Bückeburg, *Militärkabinett*, pp. 197, 201, 220; Meisner, *Kriegsminister*, pp. 42, 44.

[3] Lucius von Ballhausen, *Bismarck-Erinnerungen*, p. 254.

[4] *Aus dem Briefwechsel des General-Feldmarschalls Alfred Grafen von Waldersee 1886–1891* (Berlin, 1928), p. 225. See also Schmidt-Bückeburg, *Militärkabinett*, pp. 175–6.

[5] See Gossler's personal notes of 1897 in Meisner, *Kriegsminister*, p. 44 and note.

[6] Schmidt-Bückeburg, *Militärkabinett*, pp. 167 ff., 177.

received. The Reichstag was quick to see that the War Minister had been rendered impotent, and the realization goaded the opposition parties on to new attacks on the army and, especially, on the agency which they rightly considered to be responsible for the minister's loss of power. In all of the military debates after 1883, the Military Cabinet was made a special target for parliamentary abuse, being described as another of those camarillas which had exercised such baleful influence in Prussian history and as a symbol of encroaching absolutism. Moreover, to a much greater extent than ever before, the deputies began to turn their serious attention to the actual policies of the Military Cabinet with regard to such things as selection and promotion, and the results of their investigations convinced them that the army was engaged in a deliberate plot to thwart social and political progress in Germany.

II

In the Prussian army there had been, over the years, a marked deviation from the principles of officer selection which had been laid down by Scharnhorst, Grolman, and Boyen.[1] The events of 1848 and the stress of the constitutional struggle had strengthened the idea that the officer corps was the only reliable bulwark against social upheaval; and the determination that it should remain so soon had its effect on selection policy.

When Edwin von Manteuffel was Chief of the Military Cabinet in the 1860's, for instance, his policy of 'rejuvenating the army in the higher commands and in general'[2] was guided by more than a mere desire for improved efficiency. Manteuffel did eliminate obviously unfit officers from the service, and was justly proud of the results of his efforts;[3] but his activities partook also of the nature of a political purge. Officers who entertained liberal opinions found promotion slow and were soon complaining about the spirit of espionage and thought control that was spreading in the regiments;[4] and, as early as December

[1] See above, Chapter II, pp. 42 ff., 79.

[2] Roon Papers: Manteuffel to Roon, 2 May 1860. See also the letters of 25 February and 11 June 1860.

[3] Later in his life Manteuffel said: 'That was my greatest political achievement; without this cleansing, the victories of 1864, 1866, and 1870 would not have been won. The officer corps at the beginning of the 50's was far worse than in 1806.' Demeter, *Deutsche Heer*, p. 20. On the fear induced in the officer corps by Manteuffel's rejuvenation measures, see Schweinitz, *Denkwürdigkeiten*, i. 88.

[4] Lenz, *Geschichte Bismarcks*, pp. 179–80.

1862, Theodor von Bernhardi was worried about the deleterious effects that these tendencies were having on army morale.[1] Manteuffel's vigilance could be carried to extraordinary lengths. When, for instance, he learned that the commandant of the garrison at Cologne was on friendly terms with several of the local merchants, he called in one of that officer's friends and interrogated him. The friend vouched for the commandant's reliability. 'But he goes around with civilians!' said Manteuffel. The friend repeated his assurances. 'Very well', said the Chief of the Military Cabinet, 'then we can count on him if the shooting begins?'[2]

If officers with progressive political ideas found the officer corps uncomfortable during the Manteuffel era, those with middle-class origins found it even more so. To Manteuffel such officers were objectionable not only because of the likelihood that they were contaminated by liberal opinions but also because he felt that their social class lacked the military spirit.[3] As early as March 1860 the military commission of the Prussian Chamber was objecting to the systematic elimination of *bourgeois* officers from the army,[4] and these complaints were repeated year after year.[5] The Chamber had an understandable fear that an officer corps predominantly anti-*bourgeois* in its opinions would be a standing threat to constitutional liberties; and this fear was heightened when, in 1865, an army representative admitted that, of 8,169 officers, 4,172 were nobles.[6] These figures assume added significance when it is remembered that, in the highest ranks of the army at this time—the generals and the colonels—well over 80 per cent. of the officers were of noble origin.[7]

Manteuffel's prejudice against middle-class officers was so deep that it permitted him to flout the principle laid down in the reform period that admission to the officer corps should be

[1] Bernhardi complained to the crown prince, who told him: 'If the affair stems from Manteuffel, there is nothing that can be done.' *Aus dem Leben Bernhardis*, iv. 339.

[2] Ibid. v. 30–31.

[3] This was a belief shared by Moltke, who said in 1861: 'We have to turn away a lot of the *bourgeoisie*, partly because they are useless young people who turn to military service because they can't get on in other careers, partly because they don't have the *Gesinnung* which must be preserved in the army.' Ibid. iv. 166.

[4] Ibid. iii. 284.

[5] See, for instance, Twesten, *Was uns noch retten kann*, p. 8.

[6] Löwenthal, *Verfassungsstreit*, pp. 247 ff.

[7] Demeter, *Deutsche Heer*, pp. 34–35; Vagts, *Militarism*, pp. 200–1.

conditional upon demonstration of educational qualification. He tried to justify his evasion of existing rules by arguing that it was unwise 'to require erudition from all officers', since 'the great majority . . . will consist always of qualified front officers and, for them, scholarly training is not necessary in such a high degree'.[1] In reality his objection stemmed from the fact that the tightening of educational requirements represented a threat to the social cohesiveness, and hence the political reliability, of the officer corps. In October 1861 a royal order stipulated that henceforth candidates for commissions would be required to present a certificate showing that they had reached the *Prima* in a *Gymnasium* or *Realschule* and could pass examinations in subjects required in the upper grades of such institutions. The order caused a storm of fury in the old officer class, who protested hotly that it marked the beginning of the thorough *bourgeoisification* of the army. In an anonymous letter to Manteuffel a group of officers asked plaintively: 'Instead of Dönhoffs, Dohnas, &c., will not the sons of rich bankers capture the places in the *Gardekorps*? Would an officer corps thus altered show the same attitude as it did in 1848? . . . Would it not be dangerous to offend the nobility so seriously?'[2]

Manteuffel thought that it would be. Without consulting the War Minister[3] he waged a determined battle against the order of October, persuading the king, first, to remind regimental commanders that character requirements were to be weighed equally with education and, later, to delay application of the order for four years.[4] Even after that time, the order was never applied in the spirit in which it was written.[5]

Manteuffel had operated according to the principle once defined by Lothar von Schweinitz in the words: 'Our power finds its limit at that point where our Junker material proves inadequate to fill the officers' billets.'[6] But that limit was passed when Germany was unified, and in the years that followed Manteuffel's policies became completely unrealistic. The army's

[1] Manteuffel to his son Hans Karl, 16 September 1864. *Deutsche Revue*, xxxviii (3) (1913), 198.

[2] Demeter, *Deutsche Heer*, pp. 88–89, 260–1.

[3] That is clearly the conclusion to be drawn from his letter of 19 February 1862 to Roon (Roon Papers).

[4] Demeter, *Deutsche Heer*, pp. 90–92.

[5] On these paragraphs on Manteuffel, see above, Chapter IV, p. 150, n. 1.

[6] Schweinitz, *Denkwürdigkeiten*, i. 259.

need for officers far outstripped the nobility's ability to supply them, partly because of the tremendous growth of the peace-time army—from 401,659 non-commissioned officers and men in 1874 to 760,908 non-commissioned officers and men in 1914[1] —and partly because of the economic decline or actual disappearance of the old noble families.[2] Despite the prejudices of officers like Manteuffel it was necessary to rely upon the middle classes to meet the army's demand, and the percentage of non-noble officers steadily increased. In contrast to the figures cited above for 1865, 70 per cent. of the officer corps as a whole, and 75 per cent. of the lieutenants alone, were *bourgeois* in the year 1913, while the percentage of noble generals and colonels had sunk from 80 per cent. to 52 per cent.[3] In addition the reserve officers' corps—the so-called *Einjährig-Freiwillige*, who, because of special educational requirements were permitted to secure reserve commissions after serving one year with the colours and meeting certain other requirements[4]—was almost exclusively drawn from the middle classes.[5]

The steady increase in the number of middle-class officers was well under way long before it was officially recognized or encouraged. It was not until March 1890 that Emperor William II, in a famous order, announced that 'the improved level of education of our people offers the possibility of widening the circles which will be considered for the expansion of the officer corps. Today the nobility of birth alone cannot, as formerly, claim the privilege of supplying the army with its officers.' The 'nobility of temperament' [*Adel der Gesinnung*] must, he added, now do its share, and he appealed to the sons of 'honourable *bourgeois* families in whom the love for King and Fatherland, a warm heart for the soldier's calling, and Christian morality are planted and nurtured'.[6]

The emperor's order is interesting not only as a belated acceptance of the facts of life but also as an indication of the

[1] Rüdt von Collenberg, *Die deutsche Armee*, p. 112.

[2] Demeter, *Deutsche Heer*, pp. 32–34, 69. By the end of the century only one-third of the *Rittergutsbesitzer* in the six eastern Prussian provinces were noble.

[3] Ibid., pp. 34–35.

[4] See above, Chapter II, p. 70.

[5] On the reserve officers, see Meinecke, *Preußisch-deutsche Gestalten und Probleme*, p. 177, and Elze, *Tannenberg*, p. 14.

[6] Demeter, *Deutsche Heer*, pp. 28–29. The order aroused some amusement among the irreverent, and a Berlin newsboy was heard shouting: 'Neustes Osterjeschenk des Kaisers! Janzer Adel abjeschafft! Allens nur noch Seelenadel!' C. Wedel, *Zwischen Kaiser und Kanzler* (Leipzig, 1943), pp. 90 ff.

way in which the army intended to guard itself against the danger that Manteuffel had fought against—the possibility, namely, that middle-class intrusion would break down the social and political cohesiveness of the officer corps. The officer corps and the reserve officers' corps were not to be opened to every intelligent candidate for a commission who might apply. The reference to Christian morality, for instance, was an intimation that Jews would not receive the entrée, while the emphasis on an *Adel der Gesinnung* clearly implied that there would be no place for social misfits or young men with unorthodox political views.

This last prohibition had, indeed, been made explicit in the military literature of the last decade. Writers in army periodicals were constantly pointing out that the forces of upheaval in society were becoming stronger; that 'whole masses had declared war on God and the King'; that in these circumstances the army was 'the only fixed point in the whirlpool, the rock in the sea of revolution that threatens on all sides, the talisman of loyalty and the palladium of the prince'.[1] The officer, whether on active service or in the reserve, was bound, they explained, by his personal oath of allegiance to the monarch. No one could be an officer who was not willing to subordinate his political convictions to those of his *Kriegsherr* and to give unflinching support to his policies. Officers on active service were not, of course, permitted to participate in politics, but reserve officers were, and they were told plainly what was expected of them. An instruction book prepared for their use made it clear that

> the officer in reserve status must never, while an officer, belong to a party which places itself in opposition to the government of our Emperor or of the *Landesherr*. If he feels conscientiously restricted by this, then he must request his dismissal. As an officer, he is his imperial master's 'man' in the old German sense of the word. Under no circumstances must he place himself in opposition to him. On the other hand, however, he is fully justified in making use of his political rights and intervening in the political struggle in behalf of the objectives which the government of the *Landesherr* and the Emperor pursue.[2]

Reserve officers who flouted these instructions suffered for it.

[1] 'Offizier als Erzieher des Volkes', *Militärwochenblatt* (Beihefte, 1882, Heft 2), p. 73.

[2] Quoted by the deputy Josef Wirth in a Reichstag debate in 1926. See *Stenographische Berichte* (1926–7), p. 8591.

Thus, for adhering to the *Freisinnige* party, the Reichstag deputy von Hintze lost his commission as major in the reserve;[1] and, in 1885, Prince Schönaich-Carolath, *Rittmeister à la suite* and parliamentary deputy, was stricken from the army rolls for having voted with the left in a matter touching on the royal prerogative.[2]

To fill its needs the army relied on the wealthier sections of the middle class and it demanded of them that they accept the feudal philosophy which had always reigned in the officer corps.[3] The experiment was successful, partly because growing affluence and the threat of socialism combined to make large numbers of the upper middle class conservative, if not reactionary, in their views, and partly because social aspiration made them anxious to be accepted by the older nobility. In imperial Germany the possession of a commission was an important sign of social acceptability, and it was eagerly sought after. In this respect, the character in Ompteda's novel,[4] who proudly prints his reserve rank and regiment on his calling cards, is typical of the social strata from which the new officers were now recruited, as is the reserve officer in Zuckmayer's *Der Hauptmann von Koepenick*, who dilates on the importance of the uniform and listens approvingly when his tailor says: '*Na*, so you have managed to become a reserve lieutenant—that is the chief thing—that is the thing you must be these days—socially, professionally, in every connexion! The doctorate is the visiting card, but the reserve commission is the open door—that's the essential thing these days!'

The new selection policy brought to the expanding army the officers it required and it had the incidental advantage of destroying the effectiveness of one of the stock criticisms made of the army in the Reichstag. It was no longer possible for parties like the National Liberal party to complain about restrictions placed on non-noble officers, since even the most exclusive regiments were breached by young men with middle-class

[1] Eyck, *Bismarck*, iii. 312.

[2] On this affair and the resultant uproar, see especially Waldersee, *Denkwürdigkeiten*, i. 257 ff.

[3] For fuller discussion, see Demeter, *Deutsche Heer*, p. 216, and, especially, Eckart Kehr, 'Zur Genesis des Königlich-Preußischen Reserveoffiziers', *Die Gesellschaft* (1928), ii. 495 ff., and 'Das soziale System der Reaktion in Preußen unter dem Ministerium Puttkamer', *Die Gesellschaft* (1929), ii. 254 ff.

[4] The character Gideon in the volume entitled *Eisen* in Ompteda's *Deutscher Adel*.

origins.[1] The development of this policy was, on the other hand, admirably calculated to increase the anti-militarism of the Social Democrats and their liberal allies. It could not be disguised that the standards set by the army for its officers were designed to prop up the system of absolutism. Moreover, as the feudal philosophy of the old officer corps was communicated to the new recruits it was apt to assume grotesque and objectionable forms. The wealthy sons of *bourgeois* families who flocked now to the colours aped and exaggerated the modes of thought, the manners, and even the vices of their aristocratic brothers in arms. They vied for distinction in the less pleasing aspects of garrison and Kasino life—the gambling,[2] the brawling, the drinking—and many an older officer was revolted by the changes effected by wealth in the traditional austerity and simplicity of the military career.[3] Nor could these signs of change be hidden from the Reichstag and the general public. In addition to his other failings, the new officer tended to cultivate, in all his public dealings, what he considered to be a proper aristocratic arrogance. The result—frequently caricatured in satirical journals like *Simplicissimus*—helped widen the gulf between the army and large sections of society. All in all the social policies of the army in the period after the unification had the result of converting 'the Prussian lieutenant, who up to this time had been on the average relatively modest, into the unbearable prig of the Wilhelmine era'.[4]

III

Many of the exaggerated traits of this product of social fusion were shared by the ruler who came to the imperial throne at the end of 1888, after the brief reign of Frederick III. William II was not without good qualities; it was generally agreed that he was intelligent, warm-hearted, and ambitious to win the respect and love of his subjects. But his intelligence was accompanied

[1] See Demeter, *Deutsche Heer*, pp. 35 ff., 38 ff.

[2] In an instructive passage in Spielhagen's *In Reih und Glied*, a wealthy banker boasts that his son has lost more money at the gaming tables than any of his aristocratic friends. For a defence of Kasino life against the charges frequently made against it, see Freytag von Loringhoven, *Menschen und Dinge*, pp. 40 ff.

[3] See, for instance, Lily Braun, *Memoiren einer Sozialistin* (Munich, 1909), i. 110 ff.

[4] Kehr in *Die Gesellschaft* (1928), ii. 500–1. See also Ritter, *Staatskunst und Kriegshandwerk*, i. 205.

by scorn for the opinions of others;[1] his warm-heartedness too often took the form of favouritism; and his ambition was qualified neither by patience nor prudence.[2] He venerated his grandfather, William I,[3] and sought to emulate him; but the monarch he most resembled was Frederick William IV.[4] Like that unfortunate ruler he had a flair for florid, but misleading, oratory, a jealous and demanding conception of the prerogatives of the Crown, and a habit of indecision in moments of crisis. Of that sense of political reality which was his great-uncle's redeeming quality he had inherited, however, no trace,[5] and his deficiencies in this respect had not been corrected by careful education in his youth. His tutors had discovered that William's interest in subjects requiring thought and study waned as rapidly as it was aroused, and one of them had said sadly: 'Prince William thinks he knows everything without having learned anything.'[6] The part of his youthful training which had made the greatest impression on him had been the military; but, rather than developing in him a true understanding of military problems, the chief effect of this had been to turn him into a kind of perennial Potsdam lieutenant, whose love for uniforms was so intense that he is reported to have insisted on wearing full admiral's regalia to performances of *The Flying Dutchman*,[7] who dined to *Ulanenmusik*,[8] and who preferred military companions, military manners, and military advice to any other.

[1] 'You old asses', he told a group of general officers on one occasion, 'think that you all know better than I because you are older; but that is absolutely not the case. What I wanted to order [with respect to colonial troubles in South-West Africa] would have been the only correct thing, but you old asses naturally knew better, and now your stupidity is avenging itself.' Zedlitz-Trützschler, *Zehn Jahre am deutschen Kaiserhof* (Berlin, 1924), p. 68. A similar scene led Prince Dohna to make the suggestive remark: 'He is and remains a parvenu.' Edgar Viscount d'Abernon, *An Ambassador of Peace* (3 vols. London, 1929–30), ii. 211.

[2] Bismarck said of him that he 'wanted to celebrate his birthday every day'. Gustav Stresemann, *Vermächtnis*, ed. by H. Bernhard (Berlin, 1932–3), iii. 374.

[3] In 1897 he wanted a commemorative medal struck to William I and presented to all soldiers and civil servants as a talisman against unpatriotic seductions. Fürst Chlodwig zu Hohenlohe-Schillingsfürst, *Denkwürdigkeiten der Reichskanzlerzeit* (Stuttgart, 1931), pp. 285–6.

[4] The similarity sometimes struck Waldersee. See *Denkwürdigkeiten*, ii. 287, 340.

[5] Nor did he compare favourably in this respect with contemporary rulers. In 1906 Holstein wrote: 'The cleverest diplomat in our time is King Edward. The least clever is our Emperor who is, above all, no politician.' Holstein, *Lebensbekenntnis*, p. 258.

[6] Rudolf Gneist, quoted in Eyck, *Bismarck*, iii. 557.

[7] Zedlitz-Trützschler, *Zehn Jahre*, pp. 89–90.

[8] See Hohenlohe's description of dinner with the emperor in *Reichskanzlerzeit*, p. 473.

This preference was shown not only in the company which William II selected for his moments of social ease,[1] but also in the ordering of his official business. The emperor organized his working week in such a way that he ordinarily gave audience to only one of the Prussian ministers, the War Minister—all others having to lay projects or petitions before him through the agency of the Civil Cabinet and its powerful chief, who had regular audiences every Monday and Wednesday morning. The Chancellor of the Reich, when he wished to discuss foreign affairs or matters affecting the federal states, saw the emperor on Saturday afternoon, but this was not invariable. In contrast, the Chief of the General Staff and the Chief of the Admiralty (later replaced by the Chief of the Marine Cabinet) each had one regular audience a week, while the Chief of the Military Cabinet discussed military matters with the emperor every Tuesday, Thursday, and Saturday morning.[2]

Nor does this official schedule tell the whole story. One of William's first acts after ascending the throne was to expand and reorganize the royal *maison militaire* and to give it the name royal headquarters—a title hitherto used only in time of war. This group now included all the general officers who were assigned to the emperor as adjutants and generals *à la suite*, the so-called *Flügeladjutanten* or aides-de-camp (generally younger Guard officers who had come to William's attention), and the chiefs of the Military and Marine Cabinets. The whole body was, after 1889, unified under a commandant of headquarters, who accompanied the emperor on his many journeys and, on such occasions, recorded royal orders on military matters and communicated them to the appropriate agencies, and who, when the emperor desired, was present at the audiences of other officials.[3]

Apart from the fact that this was a further step in the disintegration of the unity of army organization—(it was now extremely difficult to define the boundary between the sphere of competence of the Military Cabinet and that of the *Hauptquartier*)—the elaboration of the *maison militaire* had fateful political results. The emperor was always more intimate with members of his suite than he was with responsible ministers of state. He invariably had a high opinion of their talents—so high,

[1] See Zedlitz-Trützschler, *Zehn Jahre*, pp. 9, 216.

[2] Schmidt-Bückeburg, *Militärkabinett*, p. 178.

[3] Ibid., pp. 177–8.

indeed, that Philipp Eulenburg, who also possessed the kaiser's confidence in the first years of his reign, was moved to write:[1]

> Emperor William II (who, unlike his highly educated progenitors, 'finished' his education as an officer in the First Regiment of the Guards) sucked in like an infant at the breast the tradition that every Prussian officer is not only the quintessence of honour, but of all good breeding, all culture, and all intellectual endowment. How a man so clear sighted as William II could have attributed the last two qualities to *everyone* in Guards uniform has always been a puzzle to me. We will call it a combination of military Hohenzollernism and self-hypnotism. From this essence of all excellence the Emperor further distils a concentrated extract—denominated the A.D.C.

The emperor was not, perhaps, as clear sighted as Eulenburg believed. Once he had selected his A.D.C.s he had boundless confidence in them; he employed them on diplomatic missions which would have been better entrusted to professional diplomats;[2] and he solicited their advice on matters which, legally and logically, were beyond their competence.

There can be little doubt that William's desire to act according to the principle *sic volo, sic jubeo*, his inflated conception of the royal power of command, his contempt for the constitution,[3] and the violence of his reaction to any sign of independence on the part of the Reichstag were strengthened by the fact that he rarely moved outside this narrow military circle. It may be true, as Eulenburg wrote,[4] that there were more donkeys than foxes in royal headquarters. But among the emperor's confidants were men like Chief of the Military Cabinet Hahnke (1888–1901) and Chief of the General Staff Waldersee (1888–91)—men ambitious for personal power and impatient with the restrictions placed upon them by the constitutional system. If William's thoughts frequently turned, after political and social problems began to crowd in upon him, to the thought of a radical solution of all of Germany's ills by a military *coup d'état*, this was due in large part to the influence of his military entourage.[5] The members of William's private *Tabakskollegium* had no

[1] Fritz Haller, *Philipp Eulenburg, the Kaiser's Friend* (London, 1930), ii. 44.

[2] See below, Chapter VII.

[3] William once told his *Hofmarschall*, 'Die Verfassung habe ich nie gelesen und kenne sie nicht'. Zedlitz-Trützschler, *Zehn Jahre*, p. 201.

[4] Haller, *Eulenburg*, ii. 45.

[5] Ibid., 40–41. It is not intended to suggest here that the military alone thought in these terms. In the mid-90's politicians and industrialists like Stoecker, Miquel,

doubt that forcible dissolution of the Reichstag and the crushing of socialism would be a feasible military operation—General von Gossler referred to it as a *Kinderspiel*[1]—and Waldersee was generally considered to be the man who would direct it.[2] And if, despite the violence of William's private and public utterances, these plans came to nothing—thanks to the fundamental indecisiveness of William's character and, also, to the stubborn resistance of Bismarck's successors Caprivi and Hohenlohe[3]—the emperor's military advisers were nevertheless influential in creating and perpetuating a state of such tension between the government and the Reichstag that a complete breakdown of the constitutional system seemed always imminent. This they did by sniping from behind the *coulisses* at responsible ministers who sought a *modus vivendi* with the Reichstag and by denigrating them before the emperor in such a way as to weaken his confidence in them.

This was particularly irresponsible conduct in view of the fact that a good working relationship with parliament was more important for the army now than it had been even in the 70's and 80's. The days in which it had seemed desirable to permit the Reichstag to discuss the peace-time strength of the army as rarely as possible were now dead and beyond recall. In the spring of 1887 Bismarck had fought a long and bitter battle with the Reichstag for a new *Septennat* setting army strength at 468,409 non-commissioned officers and men, and he had forced new elections rather than consider a proposal which would have allowed the deputies to debate the size of the army every three years rather than every seven.[4] It had been a hollow victory. No sooner had the new law been pushed through than it was generally considered to be inadequate. A new bill, reorganizing the reserves, had to be brought before the Reichstag in December 1887 and, in 1890, another one, raising army

and Stumm-Halberg were working for strong action against the social democrats, and Hammerstein, the chief editor of the *Kreuzzeitung*, admitted that his own policy was 'to provoke the workers and have them shot'. Egmont Zechlin, *Staatsstreichpläne Bismarcks und Wilhelms II* (Stuttgart, 1929), pp. 125–6.

[1] Ibid., p. 92.

[2] 'People are thinking of a kind of *coup d'état* and of me as the man best qualified to execute it', Waldersee wrote in February 1895. *Denkwürdigkeiten*, ii. 338.

[3] See Fritz Hartung, 'Verantwortliche Regierung, Kabinette und Nebenregierungen', *Forschungen zur brandenburgischen und preußischen Geschichte*, xliv (1932), 335.

[4] See Eyck, *Bismarck*, iii. 448–68; Huber, *Heer und Staat*, pp. 267–8.

strength to 486,983. After the lapsing of the Reinsurance Treaty with Russia in 1890, the subsequent *rapprochement* of France and Russia and the rapid arming of the new partners, further increases became essential. In 1892 Waldersee's successor as Chief of the General Staff, Count Schlieffen, wrote to his sister: 'Our special enemies (Denmark not included) have almost double our strength. The relationship is something like 5: 3. . . . For me there is no doubt that this question cannot be put aside if Germany is not to collapse utterly. All men capable of service must be trained.'[1] But all men could not be trained without new increases and reforms and this meant new appeals to the Reichstag for authorization and for funds.

Such appeals were made with increasing frequency between 1890 and 1914, and even the parties which were normally friendly to the army were unhappy about the mounting debt made necessary by constantly heightened military expenditure—especially since the army's demands were soon supplemented by requests from the navy as well. The ministers who were primarily responsible for winning the assent of the Reichstag—the Chancellor and the War Minister—would have had a difficult time in any circumstances. But their task was made doubly difficult by constant criticism, on the part of the emperor and his military suite, of the tactics they employed to gain their objectives, and by bitter opposition by the *Hauptquartier* to anything that seemed to be a concession to the parliamentarians.

An illustration of this may be seen in the troubles experienced by Caprivi when he introduced his army bill in the fall of 1892. A soldier by profession, the Chancellor was as worried as Schlieffen by the apparent numerical superiority of the combined French and Russian armies, and he was anxious to secure a large increase in the strength of Germany's forces. He was convinced, however, that the Reichstag would consent to this only at a price. As he said in a memorandum of April 1892:

> There is no doubt that, unless at least a partial concession is made to the desire for annual establishment of the peace-time strength and the legal introduction of two-year service, a strengthening of the army is not to be attained. To conflict, dissolution, or even *coup d'état* we dare not allow it to come. The question is not whether the

[1] Schlieffen Papers (National Archives): Schlieffen to his sister Marie, 13 November 1892. During his term as War Minister Verdy had unsuccessfully championed the training of all eligibles.

three-year service in itself is preferable to two-year service, but whether we will give up the three-year service for infantry troops in order to strengthen our peace-time strength by 77,500 men. . . . Any attempt to carry the increase through without introducing two-year service can lead only to a defeat which must weaken the emperor's government within the Reich and abroad.[1]

Caprivi proposed not only to shorten the term of service but also to make other concessions, including the grant to the Reichstag of the right to debate army strength every five, rather than every seven, years, and he was supported in his views by the Chief of the General Staff and by the War Minister Kaltenborn.[2]

The emperor was persuaded to accept these terms with the greatest of difficulty. His desire was to demand the increase without any concessions whatsoever, and he seems to have believed that, if the Reichstag balked, it would be possible to have the bill passed by the Prussian *Landtag* and then forced on the rest of the Reich.[3] The three-year service was sacred in his eyes because it had been a basic feature of the army reforms of his grandfather, and this sentimental attachment was skilfully exploited by people like Waldersee, who told the emperor that he could find no better issue to fight on than this, and that parties which opposed it would succeed only in digging their own graves.[4] In August William solemnly told the assembled officers of the Guard Corps that he was firmly resolved to hold to the longer service and that 'if the parliament is so unpatriotic as to refuse an increase of the peace-time strength . . . he would rather settle for a smaller and better army than make that concession'.[5]

This was an embarrassing commitment, and it says much for the persuasive talents of Caprivi and his military supporters that they were able to talk the emperor out of it. By the end of the year William had agreed to their plan, although, characteristically, he weakened the possible good effects of his surrender by announcing in ringing tones that he would 'chase the half-mad Reichstag to the devil' if it now refused to accept the government bill.[6] It is impossible to say how much this state-

[1] Rüdt von Collenberg, *Die deutsche Armee*, p. 45.
[2] Huber, *Heer und Staat*, p. 270.
[3] Holstein, *Lebensbekenntnis*, pp. 157–60.
[4] Waldersee, *Denkwürdigkeiten*, ii. 214–15.
[5] Wedel, *Zwischen Kaiser und Kanzler*, pp. 189–90.
[6] Waldersee, *Denkwürdigkeiten*, ii. 276 ff.

ment contributed to Caprivi's subsequent difficulties in parliament. He did carry his bill through, roughly in the form in which he had devised it, but only after a dissolution and new elections and, even then, only after making further concessions to the opposition.[1]

From a personal point of view, Caprivi's victory was a costly one. To Hahnke and the emperor's military suite, having a general in the Chancellor's post had always been considered more dangerous than having a War Minister who took his parliamentary duties seriously.[2] After the passage of the bill they sedulously spread the opinion, expressed earlier by Waldersee, that Caprivi regarded the army 'as an object to be used in concluding deals between political parties'.[3] They also argued that the two-year service was generally unpopular in the army and that another feature of the law of 1893—a provision adding, to the three battalions in each regiment, an additional battalion at half strength—was militarily unsound.[4] To all of these arguments the emperor was susceptible; he was soon believing that, in giving way to Caprivi on the service issue, he 'had nearly done for himself with the army';[5] and, on at least one occasion, he reproached the Chancellor in the presence of other generals for not securing full-strength battalions.[6] Caprivi was too stiff-necked a man to seek protection by currying favour in the *Hauptquartier* and, as evidences of the kaiser's displeasure multiplied, he submitted his resignation and retired from office at the end of 1894.[7]

This startling example of the effectiveness of backstairs influence was followed by others during the chancellorship of Prince Hohenlohe-Schillingsfürst. Before the aged Bavarian statesman's term was over, the Military Cabinet, the *Hauptquartier*, and the perennial intriguer Waldersee had forced the

[1] Among other things, he reduced the demanded increase by 12,770 men. As a result there were still eligibles who could not be called to the colours. Rüdt von Collenberg, *Die deutsche Armee*, pp. 45–49. [2] See Hohenlohe-Schillingsfürst, *Memoirs*, ii. 461. [3] Waldersee, *Denkwürdigkeiten*, ii. 209–10.

[4] In October 1894 Holstein wrote: 'Waldersee and his gang have succeeded in persuading His Majesty that the half battalions of the Fourth Division should be made up to full strength.' Haller, *Eulenberg*, i. 257. [5] Ibid., p. 351.

[6] Zechlin, *Staatsstreichpläne*, pp. 129–30.

[7] Caprivi's popularity in the army was doubtless affected by the fact that his commercial treaties seemed to hurt the Junker landholding interest. Ibid., p. 117. For his resignation, see J. Alden Nichols, *Germany After Bismarck: The Caprivi Era, 1890–1894* (Cambridge, Mass., 1958) especially pp. 340 ff.

dismissal of one War Minister, one Foreign Minister, and one Minister of the Interior, and if Hohenlohe himself hung on until 1900 it was chiefly because he was less stubborn than his predecessor and less willing to take a stand on principle.

Hohenlohe's troubles began almost immediately after his assumption of office, when the War Ministry, under the energetic leadership of its new minister, Walther Bronsart von Schellendorf, undertook the reformation of the Prussian code of military justice. This was no idle whim on the part of the War Minister. The Prussian code of 1845, which now bound most of the German army, was hopelessly antiquated in comparison with the English, French, Italian, and Russian codes, all of which had more modern procedures and all of which provided for public hearings in at least certain types of trials. Since 1869, moreover, the Bavarian army had permitted public hearings, which seemed to argue the advisability of extending this principle to other components of the German army. This had been the feeling of an army commission which met in 1881 and recommended such extension; and it was certainly the opinion of the Reichstag, which had passed resolutions in favour of public trials in 1870, 1889, and 1892.[1] When new interpellations were raised in 1894, both Bronsart and Hohenlohe saw the wisdom of granting the Reichstag's demands, the former because he felt that this was the best way of persuading the Reichstag to fill out the half-strength battalions of 1893, the latter because he too desired amicable relations with parliament and because, in addition, as a sponsor of the Bavarian law of 1869, he was bound by his own past.[2] It seemed to the Chancellor, moreover, that continuation of secret trials hurt the army's reputation for impartial justice and put a weapon into the hands of the Social Democrats and other avowed anti-militarists.[3]

Even before Bronsart's draft was brought before the Prussian *Staatsministerium*, it was apparent that the emperor was hostile to the project. Bronsart sought to allay William's suspicion by writing into his bill provisions which would permit the emperor to quash guilty verdicts and to deny publicity in cases which involved military security or public morals.[4] The emperor, however, opposed publicity in any form and was encouraged in

[1] Bogdan Graf Hutten-Czapski, *Sechzig Jahre Politik und Geschichte* (Berlin, 1936), i. 280–1.
[2] Hohenlohe, *Reichskanzlerzeit*, pp. 44–45, 114–15.
[3] Hutten-Czapski, *Sechzig Jahre*, i. 281.
[4] Ibid., p. 283.

this intransigent position by the Chief of the Military Cabinet Hahnke, who adopted the view that 'the army must remain an insulated [*abgesonderter*] body into which no one dare peer with critical eyes'.[1]

The Prussian ministry, nevertheless, took up the Bronsart draft and approved it in November 1895. It subsequently appeared, however, that one of its members, the minister Köller, had communicated full details of the ministry's deliberations to Hahnke and to the chief of the *Hauptquartier*, General von Plessen, either in a desire to protect his own position with the emperor or with the wish of blocking implementation of the ministry's plans;[2] and this incident led to the first crisis in this long and tangled affair. For the ministry, describing Köller's conduct as a breach of confidence, decided that they could no longer serve with him and authorized Hohenlohe to request the kaiser to dismiss him.

The emperor, already angry at Bronsart,[3] was infuriated by this action, the responsibility for which he placed variously at the doors of Hohenlohe, the Foreign Minister Marschall von Bieberstein, and the Minister for Interior Boetticher.[4] It was, he said, an attack on the rights of the Crown, unparalleled in Prussian history;[5] and, although he finally gave in, he accompanied his surrender with a public reprimand to the ministry for seeking to dictate to him, pointing out that this might not 'be unusual in parliamentary states' but would not be tolerated in Prussia.[6] After this outburst of spleen, he administered a dressing down to Bronsart which the War Minister described as so insulting that he 'would have drawn his sword against any other man',[7] and gave a New Year's speech to the commanding generals in which he announced his inflexible opposition to public trials.[8]

[1] Hohenlohe, *Reichskanzlerzeit*, p. 116.

[2] Otto Hammann, *Der neue Kurs* (Berlin, 1918), pp. 80–81; Hartung in *Forschungen*, xliv. 336.

[3] In October the emperor was talking of taking Bronsart's order of the Black Eagle away from him and dismissing him from the army. Hohenlohe, *Reichskanzlerzeit*, pp. 114–15.

[4] Ibid., pp. 134–5, 199, 220. There is some reason to suppose that Marschall, who was having difficulties with the emperor in foreign affairs, and his aide Holstein were not disinclined to forcing the issue with the emperor in the hope that his personal government could be brought under control.

[5] Ibid., pp. 132–3.

[6] Ibid., pp. 138–9.

[7] Ibid., p. 151; Haller, *Eulenburg*, i. 344.

[8] Waldersee, *Denkwürdigkeiten*, ii. 363–4.

By this time the dispute had become a matter of public knowledge. It was discussed widely in the press, the *Kölnische Zeitung* in particular pointing out that Hahnke was the leader of the opposition to Bronsart's project.[1] Charges that a military camarilla was at work were freely made, and there was indignation over the fact that, at this time, the Military Cabinet transferred to inactive service five generals who were supposed to favour the Bronsart bill, one of whom, General Spitz, had helped to draft it.[2] In the circumstances, Hohenlohe felt compelled to point out to the emperor that the Reichstag would certainly refuse to strengthen the half-battalions of 1893 unless the government promised to bring a bill reforming military justice before them in the near future.

It is indicative of William's lack of understanding of the parliamentary situation that he should have instructed Hohenlohe, on 16 May, to brush aside any attempt on the part of the deputies to tie the battalion and the military justice issue together. The Chancellor should inform the Reichstag, he said, that these were separate issues, and that the military justice bill could not in any case be discussed at this time since it was still being considered by the federal princes.[3] Hohenlohe—apparently encouraged by Marschall[4]—decided that he could not be bound by the strict letter of these instructions. When the Reichstag session opened on 18 May, with a ringing denunciation of the political influence of adjutants delivered by deputy Haussmann,[5] the Chancellor did exert his principal efforts toward persuading the Reichstag to grant the kaiser the battalions he desired. But at the same time, when questioned about the justice issue, he announced that a bill would be laid before parliament in the autumn and that it would be in accord 'with the principles of modern legal theory'.[6] This was, in effect, a promise that the principle of publicity would be granted.[7]

Hohenlohe's declaration was enough to secure passage of the battalion bill, but the emperor and his military entourage were no more grateful for benefits received than they had been when Caprivi had passed his army bill. During the kaiser's northern

[1] Schmidt-Bückeburg, *Militärkabinett*, p. 207.
[2] Hohenlohe, *Reichskanzlerzeit*, p. 218.
[3] Ibid., pp. 225–6.
[4] Marschall drafted the declaration which Hohenlohe made in the Reichstag.
[5] Schmidt-Bückeburg, *Militärkabinett*, p. 207.
[6] Hohenlohe, *Reichskanzlerzeit*, pp. 228–9.
[7] Hartung in *Forschungen*, xliv. 340.

cruise in the summer of 1896, his military confidants persuaded him that both Bronsart and Marschall must now be dismissed, and Hohenlohe retained in office only if he would promise not to insist on the implementation of his declaration.[1] When this design came to the Chancellor's ears his first impulse was to submit his own resignation, but he was persuaded by Philipp Eulenburg that this would merely leave the emperor completely in the hands of those who were working for a *coup d'état*. Rather weakly, Hohenlohe agreed to a compromise. Bronsart would be replaced by General Gossler, the self-styled 'emperor's general', and the justice bill would be postponed, but Marschall would be retained at the Foreign Office.[2]

To save appearances Bronsart was appointed to the position of *Generaladjutant*, although he loudly protested that he had not been trained 'to sit in an ante-room and practise courtly arts'.[3] This preferment, however, deceived no one, and a rash of new attacks on the Military Cabinet broke out in the press. The prestige of the government was further shaken by a notice which appeared in the *Reichsanzeiger* on 20 August and which sought to portray the Military Cabinet as a harmless correspondence bureau with no political influence. The publication of this article at a time when the emperor was on an official trip to Russia led to speculation concerning its authorship and some not entirely derisive charges that the Military Cabinet was now directing the official organ of the government.[4] Hohenlohe sought to allay tension by announcing that a military justice bill would be laid before the Bundesrat in the autumn; but the emperor was still opposed to the principle of public trials, and autumn gave way to spring without any appreciable progress being made.

The continued baulking of the Reichstag's desires brought an end to any semblance of co-operation between that body and the government. In March the Budget Commission cut twelve million marks out of the government's naval estimates, which, in effect, made a workable bill impossible for another year. Two months later, after Prince Henry of Prussia had read to the crew of his ship a letter in which the kaiser referred to

[1] Ibid.

[2] Ibid., p. 341; Hohenlohe, *Reichskanzlerzeit*, pp. 242 ff.; Hutten-Czapski, *Sechzig Jahre*, i. 293–4.

[3] Hohenlohe, *Reichskanzlerzeit*, p. 253 and note; Hutten-Czapski, *Sechzig Jahre*, i. 295–8.

[4] Hartung in *Forschungen*, xliv. 342.

members of the Reichstag as 'vaterlandslosen Gesellen' and 'Schurken',[1] the Social Democrats, the Centre, and the Freisinnige party launched a full-scale attack upon William's personal government and the alarming growth in power of irresponsible agencies.[2] This last demonstration, which was marked by the careful silence of the Rightist benches during Richter's denunciations of malfeasance in high places, might have shaken more perceptive observers than the emperor and his military clique. Instead, it merely encouraged the camarilla to persuade William that he was ill served by his ministers and to urge him not only to complete his long nurtured design to get rid of Marschall, but to dismiss the Minister of Interior Boetticher as well, on grounds that he had not adequately defended the emperor against Richter's attacks.[3]

By the middle of 1897 a complete breakdown of the constitutional system seemed at hand, and rumours of an imminent *coup d'état* were more widespread than at any time since the beginning of the reign. Yet it is to be doubted whether the emperor ever seriously considered such a possibility. It gratified his dramatic sense to tell Waldersee—as he did in January 1897—that grim times were coming and that 'if it came to shooting' he knew he could rely on the former chief of staff;[4] but he always, in the end, flinched away from giving the order which Waldersee, for one, so ardently desired. And since he had no real intention of abolishing the system by force of arms, his conduct in relation to the Reichstag made very little sense. Both Caprivi and Hohenlohe had argued that, as long as there was a parliament with budgetary powers, it was better to seek an accommodation with it than to attempt to defy it in matters which were not, after all, of first importance. William preferred to regard all questions touching the army as of equal importance, to take his stand on the ill-defined concept of the royal power of command, to indulge in vain boasts and menaces, and then, in the end, to give way with the worst possible grace.

So it was with the military justice issue. After the fall of Marschall and Boetticher, William filled another whole year

[1] Hohenlohe, *Reichskanzlerzeit*, pp. 332 ff.

[2] Hartung in *Forschungen*, xliv. 345.

[3] Schmidt-Bückeburg, *Militärkabinett*, p. 211; Otto Hammann, *Bilder aus der letzten Kaiserzeit* (Berlin, 1922), p. 17; Erich Eyck, *Das persönliche Regiment Wilhelms II* (Zürich, 1948), pp. 163 ff.

[4] Waldersee, *Denkwürdigkeiten*, ii. 389 ff.

with noisy professions of his inflexible opposition to the proposed reform; but finally, in December 1898—thanks to Hohenlohe's patient insistence and, in part also, to the fact that his attention was now turning to the more exciting issues of foreign policy and imperialism—he signed the new code.[1] It was a curiously undramatic ending to a controversy which had aroused political passions for three years; and this ultimate concession could not repair the damage which William's tactics and his deference to irresponsible military advice had done to his own prestige and that of the army which he was so determined to defend.

IV

Two aspects of the battles of the Caprivi and Hohenlohe periods deserve special, if brief, attention, since they throw some light on the army's problems in the last years before the war. In the first case, it was clear that the disruption of the organizational unity of the army, which had been inaugurated in 1883, had now been carried to ridiculous and dangerous extremes. In the disputes of this period there had been nothing that even remotely resembled an informed army opinion, and the upper echelons of the service were frequently at hopeless odds. Not only the reasoned calculations of the army's political representative but even the technical plans of the Chief of the General Staff could be hopelessly jeopardized by the intervention of cabinet chiefs, adjutants, court generals, or self-appointed mentors like Waldersee. Once this habit of internal disharmony and rivalry had taken hold, it proved impossible to correct it. The emperor was temperamentally incapable of restoring unity to the army, and no Chancellor after Caprivi made a serious attempt to impose his own views upon it.[2] In the years before the war even the important question of expanding the army so as to keep abreast of foreign forces was affected by this situation. The General Staff, true to the principles of Schlieffen, continued to work for a truly universal military service which would train all eligibles. The War Ministry, under Einem (1903–9) and Heeringen (1909–13) resisted such expansion, placing its faith in a smaller quality army rather than a *Millionenheer*,[3] while the

[1] The code as finally accepted is described in Hutten-Czapski, *Sechzig Jahre*, i. 348–9.

[2] See Schmidt-Bückeburg, *Militärkabinett*, p. 227.

[3] Rüdt von Collenberg in Friedrich Thimme, ed., *Front wider Bülow* (Munich,

Military Cabinet was apt to take the view that too rapid expansion would make it necessary to take officers from sections of the population hitherto excluded from the officer corps and would thus lead to democratization.[1] The deficiencies of the German army at the beginning of the war were, no doubt, due to many factors,[2] but the war of opinions in the army itself certainly contributed in large part to them.

In the second place, the experience of the Caprivi and Hohenlohe period seemed, to important segments of the population, to be a striking confirmation of the prophecies of Mallinckrodt and Richter in 1874 concerning the growth of military absolutism. The fact that responsible ministers who enjoyed the confidence of parliament could be hounded from their posts by the emperor's military advisers seemed to be a plain indication that the army had become a state within the state, claiming the right to define what was, or was not, to the national interest and to dispense with those who did not agree with the definition. The very violence of the resistance to the principle of publicity in the military justice dispute appeared to confirm this and to show that the army, in effect, claimed immunity to the law that governed the rest of the nation and was resolved to remain, in Hahnke's phrase, an 'isolated body'. Finally, there was more than enough evidence, in the declarations of high-ranking officers and the public behaviour of very junior ones, to indicate that a significant part of the officer corps looked upon civilian society with a mixture of contempt and hostility and regarded themselves as forming a castle guard to watch over their master's unruly subjects and see to it that they did their duty.[3] The classic illustration of this attitude in pre-war Germany was, of course, the Zabern incident of 1913, when a young lieutenant touched off public disorders by making insulting references to

1931), pp. 159 ff. Einem himself blames the failures to expand the army on Bülow. Ibid., pp. 153 ff., and Karl von Einem, *Erinnerungen eines Soldaten, 1853–1933* (Leipzig, 1933), p. 109.

[1] Ziekursch, *Politische Geschichte*, iii. 256–7. The views are here expressed as Heeringen's, but they certainly stemmed from the Military Cabinet.

[2] Including the effect of high naval expenditure upon the budget and the debt.

[3] Eulenburg wrote in 1903: 'The army has become a castle guard and has to do sentry-go because we have not even yet contrived to win the hearts of the people. . . . The army will never look with anything but growing distaste on the "civilian", who was already sufficiently despised and now is called on to do great deeds for the social and economic state which the army called into existence by its achievements.' Haller, *Eulenburg*, ii. 163–4.

the people of Alsace and was backed up by his commanding officer, who regarded the matter as one affecting the prestige of the army, superseded the civilian authorities, declared a state of siege, and instituted wholesale arrests of people who mocked at his troops.[1] But there had been other incidents before Zabern which showed the same kind of military arrogance.

Even good patriots, who wanted Germany to have a big army and were willing to pay for it, were worried by these tendencies. It is significant that, in almost every session of the Reichstag from the end of the military justice dispute to the outbreak of the war, the army and its administration were subjected to searching criticism. The customary attack by the parties of the left upon the unwholesome influence of cabinet chiefs and adjutants continued; but these were supplemented now by a more systematic attempt to force the government to define the mystical concept of the power of command, which had been used so often in the past to withdraw vital aspects of army activity from parliamentary discussion.[2] Simultaneously, deputies turned their attention to the reduction of the War Minister's powers and the dominance of the Military Cabinet in matters of officer selection. With increasing frequency in the last decade of peace, demands were made that the War Minister—described by one deputy as 'a parliamentary whipping boy for the Military Cabinet'[3]—should be given back the powers lost in 1883 and authorized, as a responsible minister, to countersign all orders commissioning or dismissing officers.[4]

The army, while often irritated by these attacks,[5] remained unmoved. The last War Ministers of the pre-war period stoutly resisted their own rehabilitation, defended the changes of 1883, and either admitted that they could not define the power of command or defended it with arguments grown traditional by use. Thus, in 1914, Falkenhayn was speaking in terms which might have been employed by Edwin von Manteuffel, when he told the Reichstag that 'Only through the fact that the Prussian army is removed by the constitution from the party struggle and the influence of ambitious party leaders has it become what

[1] For a fuller treatment, see Erwin Schenk, *Der Fall Zabern* (Stuttgart, 1927); and, for the effect within the government see Hans-Günter Zmarzlik, *Bethmann Hollweg als Reichskanzler 1909–1914* (Düsseldorf, 1957), pp. 114–30.

[2] See Richter's attack on the *Kommandogewalt* in *Stenographische Berichte* (7 Dec. 1897), p. 78.

[3] Schmidt-Bückeburg, *Militärkabinett*, p. 235.

[4] Ibid., pp. 228–9, 234–8.

[5] See, for instance, Einem, *Erinnerungen*, pp. 70 ff.

it is: the secure defence of peace at home and abroad.'[1] Short of persuading the Reichstag to withhold all funds from the army —and, thus, to institute another struggle like that of the 1860's —there was no way in which the advocates of stricter control over the military establishment could force the acceptance of their views. Given the tension which prevailed in Europe after 1900, any such act of persuasion was politically impractical.[2] The army was privileged to remain a state within the state until the débâcle of 1918 gave the champions of constitutional government their long awaited opportunity.

[1] Schmidt-Bückeburg, *Militärkabinett*, p. 237.

[2] Not even the socialists were prepared to take any steps that could be interpreted as weakening the national defence; and some of them, like Bernstein, were so concerned over the uncertainty and danger of the international situation that they virtually repudiated the anti-militarist sections of their own Erfurt programme and became defenders of the standing army. The patriotism of the bulk of the Social Democratic party and the compromises it led to are discussed in Milorad M. Drachkovitch, *Les Socialismes français et allemands et le problème de la guerre 1870–1914* (Geneva, 1953), especially pp. 247–75.

VII

THE ARMY AND FOREIGN POLICY 1871–1914

'I would . . . never advise Your Majesty to declare war forthwith, simply because it appeared that our opponent would begin hostilities in the near future. One can never anticipate the ways of divine providence securely enough for that. BISMARCK *in 1875*.

Wär's möglich? Könnt' ich nicht mehr, wie ich wollte?
Nicht mehr zurück, wie mir's beliebt? Ich müßte
Die Tat vollbringen, weil ich sie gedacht,
Nicht die Versuchung von mir wies? *Wallensteins Tod.*

MORE dangerous than any of its activities on the home front during the period 1871–1914 was the influence which the German military establishment came to exert over the foreign policy of the empire. That the military chiefs had a legitimate role to play in the determination of Germany's foreign policy goes without saying, for the years of the armed peace were marked by periodic crises, and the possibility of war was a matter of almost constant concern to German statesmen. In no previous period of German history had there been so obvious a need for careful co-ordination of planning and action between the political leadership, the diplomatic representatives, and the armed services of the nation. No such co-ordination was ever achieved, a fact which is not the least important of the reasons for the failures of German foreign policy in this period. The army cannot, of course, be held entirely responsible for this, but its share in the responsibility is great.

The previous chapter has indicated the extent to which the leaders of the army regarded the military establishment as the true embodiment of the national interest. It was perhaps only natural that they should go farther and assume that soldiers were also better qualified than politicians or diplomats to determine the policies which would protect that interest. This assumption was sometimes openly and bluntly admitted; it is a recurring theme, for instance, in Waldersee's diaries and correspondence. But it underlay the activities also of soldiers like Schlieffen who were ostentatiously 'un-political' technicians but whose technical decisions had a disconcerting way of involving political commitments.

Even in the Bismarck period the army showed a desire to encroach upon civilian functions in the field of foreign policy. In the years after 1871 military representatives at German diplomatic missions abroad became impatient with their restricted technical functions and began to arrogate to themselves tasks of political reporting and negotiation which belonged properly to their civilian colleagues. In ordinary circumstances this development would have been easy to control. It soon became apparent, however, that the activities of the attachés were being encouraged by the General Staff. Indeed, when Waldersee became the leading luminary in that agency, it was clear that he aspired to the role of the emperor's chief adviser on matters of foreign policy. Distrusting both Bismarck's policy objectives and his agents abroad, Waldersee sought to transform the military attachés into an independent corps of observers, responsible to him and empowered with authority to send their reports directly to the emperor without reference to their chiefs of mission or to the Chancellor himself.

This ambitious project was—not without difficulty—defeated by Bismarck and Caprivi; and, after Waldersee's passing, the next chiefs of staff, Schlieffen and the younger Moltke, showed no inclination to revive it. Unlike their predecessor they had no desire to assume open responsibility for the direction of Germany's foreign policy and were content to restrict themselves to the task of formulating the plans which would guide the operations of the army in the event that the nation should once more find itself at war.

It can be argued, however, that this legitimate occupation, because it was pursued without proper consultation and coordination with the other policy-making agencies of the state, had a more disastrous effect upon Germany's foreign policy than any of Waldersee's designs. For Schlieffen and Moltke devised, and imposed upon the German army, the most rigid operational plan which had ever been accepted by any modern army, and one, moreover, which had dangerous political implications which were never fully understood by the political leaders of the country or, for that matter, by the soldiers themselves.

Once the master plan had been perfected by Schlieffen and accepted in its main outlines by Moltke, it had the inevitable result of depriving German diplomacy of the flexibility which it needed if it was to succeed in restraining Germany's ambitious allies in the interest of peace. At the same time it inspired in the minds of its adherents an urgent temptation to resort to war before the conditions upon which its chances of success depended had disappeared. During the crisis years from 1904 to 1914 that temptation grew steadily. At the height of the first Moroccan crisis Schlieffen was anxious for a war against France and Great Britain—a war which might prevent the greater war which he believed was otherwise inevitable. On that occasion the chief of staff was baulked by the emperor and his civilian advisers. But by 1914 even the civilians had gone so far in accepting the implications of the plan that their freedom of action had been destroyed; and, as a result, Germany entered a war which neither the technical virtuosity of her military planners nor the valour of her soldiers could win.

Before dealing with the fateful results of the military plans of the Wilhelmine period, it is important to recall Bismarck's conflict with the military in the sphere of foreign policy. This centred around the activities of the military attachés.[1]

I

The practice of attaching military representatives to the staffs of Prussian legations had its origins in the Napoleonic period. In 1800 Massenbach suggested that officers destined for high command in the Prussian army should be sent to the legations at St. Petersburg, Vienna, London, and Paris, to 'study the character of those who might be put in the future at the head of hostile or allied armies'.[2] This plan was not accepted at the time, but it was not forgotten. After the victory over Napoleon had been won, Grolman, Prussia's first post-war chief of staff, urged again that officers be sent to the chief diplomatic posts. In a memorandum of 12 February 1816 to War Minister

[1] The following section reproduces, with some alterations, the text of the first part of the author's article 'Military Diplomats in the Prussian and German Service: The Attachés, 1816–1914', *Political Science Quarterly*, lxiv (1949), 65–94. The note at the end of the chapter, dealing with the activities of the naval attachés, is also drawn from that article.

[2] Christian von Massenbach, *Memoiren zur Geschichte des preußischen Staates*, iii. 393. Quoted in Vagts, *Militarism*, p. 189.

von Boyen, he pointed out that other Powers had assigned officers to their legations, and he argued that it was high time Prussia followed suit.[1] Boyen took up the suggestion, and the first appointments were made in the same year.[2]

The motive for this innovation was originally technical rather than political. The military attachés were not meant to compete with the accredited diplomatic representatives in the collection of political information. Grolman made this clear in an instruction of 14 April 1816 which was approved by Hardenberg, the king's chief minister. 'The purpose of the assignment of these officers', wrote the chief of staff, 'is accurate knowledge of states from the purely military point of view. Their purpose is absolutely unpolitical, and they must avoid any meddling in politics and must, above all, observe the utmost caution and circumspection in their behaviour.'[3] They were specialists whose duty it was to keep their own government informed of the military strength of the country in which they served; and they were at the same time supposed, as Albrecht von Roon once said, to serve the chief of mission 'in the capacity of military *souffleur* and dictionary'.[4]

There can be little doubt that the technical services of the attachés were of a high order and that they adequately justified their creation in the period in which Prussia moved toward mastery in Germany. During the Crimean War, for instance, Prince Hohenlohe, the Prussian military attaché in Vienna, gave a convincing demonstration of the way in which technical military skill could supplement the legation's political reports. Since Prussia had concluded a defensive alliance with Austria at the outbreak of the war, it was important for the government to receive reliable information about the state of the Austrian army.[5] When Austrian military authorities evaded all of his requests for such information, Hohenlohe resorted to the standard processes of military intelligence. Thus, he worked out an accurate picture of the Austrian order of battle from study of

[1] Conrady, *Grolman*, iii. 29.

[2] Three majors and three captains were appointed to the most important legations. Considerations of economy, however, soon discouraged systematic appointments and it was not regular practice to have attachés at all posts until after the revolution of 1848. See Wohlers, *Die staatsrechtliche Stellung des Generalstabes*, pp. 46–47.

[3] Conrady, *Grolman*, iii. 30.

[4] Roon, *Denkwürdigkeiten*, ii. 248.

[5] Hohenlohe-Ingelfingen, *Aus meinem Leben*, i. 248.

the daily press supplemented by salon gossip and the reports of professional agents. With these aids also, he developed a remarkable skill in discovering and evaluating troop transfers within the empire, so that he was able to warn Berlin of Austrian moves which threatened to impair the treaty of neutrality.[1] As the first real staff officer to be assigned to the Vienna post,[2] Hohenlohe developed methods of analysis and appraisal which served as models for his successors; and, when the two German Powers fought their long duel for supremacy, the Berlin government benefited from the reliable intelligence estimates of the Vienna attachés.

The attachés in Paris also proved their worth in the period of the *Reichsgründung*. Throughout the 1860's they sent detailed and accurate reports on the French order of battle, the changes in recruiting policy, the deficiencies of military rail communication, and changes and experiments in ordnance. Two of the attachés participated actively in French campaigns—Stein von Kaminski in Mexico in 1863 and Walter von Loë in the Algerian rising of 1864—and these tours of duty supplied material for appraisals of French artillery effectiveness, fire discipline, and cavalry tactics.[3] As relations between Prussia and France deteriorated after 1867, the attachés in Paris maintained their reputation for accuracy and thoroughness. The frenzied attempts to reform the French army were calmly appraised; changes in army strength or mobilization schedules were noted and reported to Berlin.[4] Essentially, the reports of the Prussian attachés in Paris were in no way superior to those of their French counterpart in Berlin, Baron Stoffel. But while their dispatches were weighed carefully by the Prussian General Staff, Stoffel's description of the strength of Prussian arms merely aroused irritation in Paris and his warnings of Prussian

[1] Thus, Hohenlohe reported on 1 August 1854 that troop displacements indicated an imminent Austrian advance across the eastern frontier. The report was discounted in Berlin but was borne out by an Austrian agreement of 10 August with the Western Powers and the subsequent Austrian occupation of the Danubian Principalities. Ibid., pp. 250–1.

[2] His predecessors had not been drawn from the roster of the General Staff and, according to General Gerwien, had done little except go to dances. Ibid., p. 233.

[3] Loë, *Erinnerungen aus meinem Berufsleben*, pp. 59, 61 ff. See also L. von Schlözer, *Generalfeldmarschall Frhr. von Loë* (Stuttgart, 1914), pp. 62–63.

[4] J. M. von Radowitz, *Aufzeichnungen und Erinnerungen*, ed. by Hajo Holborn (Stuttgart, 1925), i. 140; E. Bircher and A. W. Bode, *Schlieffen: Mann und Idee* (Zürich, 1937), p. 47.

superiority were disregarded.[1] In this difference in the uses to which military reports were put lies part of the explanation for Prussia's victory in 1870–1.

In view of their services, no one in public life in Prussia could question the advantage of having military reporters attached to the legations abroad. Even Bismarck, who was on occasion contemptuous of the work of the attachés,[2] never attempted to abolish the institution. Nevertheless, as the attachés secured their position as an auxiliary arm of the diplomatic service, one difficulty arose which caused increasing concern. This was the problem of preventing the attachés from extending their sphere of activity beyond the limits laid down by Grolman in 1816 and duplicating, or even absorbing, the reportorial functions of the professional diplomatists.

This question arose because of the difficulty of drawing a sharp distinction between the work of the attaché and that of the regular diplomatic representative. Attempts to delineate their functions were, of course, made. At the beginning of the 1850's, for instance, an agreement between the Foreign Office and the Ministry of War specified that attachés, in their reports, would 'restrict themselves to military-technical subjects' and 'avoid whatever reached over into the political sphere'. Even at the time of this agreement, however, War Minister von Bonin insisted that military-technical subjects often involved political considerations and he stipulated that, in such event, the attaché should not be prevented from making his report.[3] Bonin's provision merely emphasized the impossibility of laying down hard and fast rules concerning the contents of dispatches. To overcome this difficulty, therefore, and to safeguard the diplomatic corps from the possibility that the attachés would establish themselves as independent political reporters, it was decided that all official correspondence between the attaché and his military superiors in Berlin must be conducted through the chief of mission, who would read his reports and transmit them

[1] Émile Ollivier, *L'Empire libéral* (Paris, 1895–1916), xi. 342.

[2] In 1879 Bismarck told Schweinitz that he knew the exact disposition of all Russian naval squadrons. Schweinitz murmured something about the services performed by military attachés, only to have Bismarck say bluntly: '*Ach was*, attachés! We get all that quite accurately through the Jews!' Schweinitz, *Denkwürdigkeiten*, ii. 80–81.

[3] H. O. Meisner, 'Aus Berichten des Pariser Militärattachés Freiherr von Hoiningen gt. Huene an den Grafen Waldersee, 1888–91', *Berliner Monatshefte*, 15. Jg. (1937), p. 959.

to the Foreign Office.[1] Even this rule, however, was relaxed after 1869, and the attaché, in so far as he was dealing with 'purely military-technical questions', was allowed to correspond directly with the War Ministry and the General Staff.[2] On the whole, it is clear that the regulations were so indefinite as to be susceptible of abuse.

Moreover, one diplomatic post was completely excluded from the operation of all existing regulations: namely, St. Petersburg, where the attaché, under the imposing title of 'military plenipotentiary', had special privileges. During the war of liberation against Napoleon, the close relationship between the Tsar and the Prussian King had been given formal expression in the exchange of personal adjutants (*Flügeladjutanten*) between the sovereigns; and this custom was perpetuated in the ensuing period. The *Pruski Fligeladjutant* in St. Petersburg was far more than a technical observer and he was in no sense subordinate to the Prussian minister, as were attachés at other capitals. His mission—as William I told Schweinitz in 1865—was to win the confidence of the Tsar and to serve as a means of direct communication between him and the Prussian King.[3] He was a member of the Tsar's personal suite and saw him daily, while his contact with the Prussian legation was apt to be infrequent and incidental. Schweinitz gives a clear picture of the unique position of the 'military plenipotentiary' in St. Petersburg. He wrote:

> My official position had the great advantage that I had nothing to do with any office or any superior but only with the two sovereigns; I wrote to no one except the King and was not obliged to accept, from either the War Ministry or the Foreign Office, commissions which I considered incompatible with the discretion imposed upon me by my wholly exceptional position.[4]

This military nexus between the Russian and Prussian courts had, as Alfred Vagts has pointed out, an essentially ideological

[1] When Hohenlohe was appointed military attaché in Vienna in 1854, General Reyher told him that the General Staff had strict orders to demand no direct reports from him; and the War Minister made it clear that his dispatches would have to be read and transmitted by the Prussian minister in Vienna. Hohenlohe customarily addressed his reports 'An die Königlichen Ministerien der Auswärtigen Angelegenheiten und des Krieges'. Hohenlohe, *Aus meinem Leben*, i. 242 ff., 254.

[2] Meisner in *Berliner Monatshefte*, 15. Jg. (1937), p. 959.

[3] Schweinitz, *Denkwürdigkeiten*, i. 174.

[4] Ibid., p. 181.

significance, and the exchange of military plenipotentiaries symbolized the union of conservative principles against the tide of revolution in Europe.[1] At the same time, however, since it constituted an independent channel of communication between Berlin and St. Petersburg, it gave rise to difficulties affecting the efficiency, the prestige, and the morale of the legation staff in the Russian capital. It is significant that Bismarck, who tolerated the existence of attachés at other capitals, was, from the beginning of his ministerial career, highly critical of the military plenipotentiary in St. Petersburg.[2]

Bismarck's attitude toward the St. Petersburg *Flügeladjutant* was partly the product of his general suspicion of military men in politics and his experience with a long series of special diplomatic missions carried out by political generals like Gustav von Alvensleben and Edwin von Manteuffel. He was always irritated by the soldier's penchant for giving undue weight in negotiations to such factors as honour, loyalty, and tradition; and he was aware that military bluntness and contempt for diplomatic niceties were apt to lead to a dangerous disregard of political realities.[3] But, quite apart from this general prejudice against the military, Bismarck had special reasons for disliking the military-diplomatic tie between St. Petersburg and Berlin.

In the first place, since the Prussian military plenipotentiary lived on terms of friendship with the Tsar, he received political information of the highest importance, information which was quite inaccessible to the legation staff. Aside from the deleterious effects of this arrangement upon the prestige of the professional diplomats, it was also inherently dangerous. The military plenipotentiary was obliged to inform neither the legation nor the Foreign Office of his findings. During the Crimean War, for instance, Lieutenant-Colonel Count Münster had transmitted vital information to the king and to members of the reactionary camarilla in Berlin; but the Minister President, Otto von Manteuffel, had remained ignorant of the

[1] Vagts, *Militarism*, p. 190.

[2] See his own criticism of the office in his memoirs (Bismarck, *G. W.*, xv. 389) and Lucius von Ballhausen, *Bismarck-Erinnerungen*, p. 381.

[3] See, for instance, Egmont Zechlin's account of the negotiations leading toward the so-called Alvensleben Convention of 1863 in which Alvensleben, in order to secure quick agreement, dangerously exceeded his instructions. *Bismarck und die Grundlegung der deutschen Großmacht*, pp. 436 ff.

content of the reports until he had employed a spy to steal them.[1] Under William I, this situation was corrected, and his cabinet always forwarded the reports of the military plenipotentiary to Bismarck. Nevertheless, they came secondhand and were often delayed, and this irritated the Minister President.

In the second place, since the military plenipotentiary was not bound by instructions from the Foreign Office, there was always a possibility that he would contradict or undermine official representations made by the legation. In the Crimean War, Münster had promoted a policy which was at such variance with that of the Foreign Office that his confidant, Leopold von Gerlach, wrote to him, 'Vous voulez être plus russe que les Russes eux-mêmes'.[2] Lack of co-ordination between the military and professional diplomats in St. Petersburg was a constant source of confusion. Schweinitz in the 1860's actually made a virtue out of wilful ignorance of the policy of the Foreign Office. In a passage in his memoirs he says that ignorance of the shifts and subterfuges of Prussian policy on the eve of the Austrian war was an advantage to him 'since, as an officer and a cavalier, I could not have defended them. . . . The military confidant of the two sovereigns had the task of representing the immutable laws of honour and almost sacred friendship even when *raison d'état* was in conflict with them.'[3] That there is some justice in Schweinitz's remarks as applied to the situation in 1866 cannot be denied, and his services in persuading the Tsar to maintain an attitude of neutrality during the war were important. Nevertheless, Bismarck could not be expected to approve this interjection of feudal standards into the realm of *Realpolitik*. Later, when he was Chancellor of the Reich and Schweinitz ambassador to Russia, Bismarck was reduced to fury by the general's refusal to make communications to the Tsar which he did not consider strictly truthful.[4]

Bismarck's dissatisfaction with the St. Petersburg arrangement came to a head in 1876, when the conduct of General von Werder, the Prussian military plenipotentiary, placed him in a

[1] On this famous scandal, see above p. 133, and the works cited there.

[2] Kurt Borries, *Preußen im Krimkrieg*, pp. 45–46. On Münster's policy in St. Petersburg, see 'Politische Briefe des Grafen Hugo zu Münster an Edwin von Manteuffel', *Deutsche Revue*, 38. Jg., especially pp. 183–97, 326–37.

[3] Schweinitz, *Denkwürdigkeiten*, i. 200–1.

[4] Ibid., p. ix.

decidedly awkward position.[1] Since the outbreak of the Bosnian revolt in the previous year, the Chancellor had striven to detach himself as much as possible from the ominous Austro-Russian rivalry which was developing in the Balkan area, and to pursue a policy of strict neutrality. His attempt to avoid any German commitment was, however, rudely challenged on 1 October 1876, when General von Werder informed him that the Tsar desired urgently to know what Germany's position would be if the present difficulties in the Near East should lead to a war between Russia and Austria.[2]

In any circumstances, this question would have been embarrassing to a man who was still attempting to preserve the fiction of the solidarity of the three Eastern courts. Bismarck knew that an unsatisfactory answer would give aid and comfort to that party in Russia which favoured *rapprochement* with France rather than Germany; he was equally certain that an answer which suggested German support of Russia would be used in Vienna by the Russians, with unfortunate results for Austro-German friendship.[3]

Bismarck's difficulties were increased, however, by the way in which the question had been presented. If it had been posed in accordance with accepted diplomatic procedure—in the form of a communication presented at the Foreign Office by the Russian ambassador—it could have been studied at some length and made the basis of negotiations which were recorded for future reference. The Russian use of Werder to address a question to the Foreign Office was unprecedented and hence, in Bismarck's eyes, suspicious. It was, he felt, a manœuvre of the Russian minister Gorchakov, designed to force a German commitment at no risk to the Russian government. 'We can never', the Chancellor wrote bitterly, 'hold the Russians to their word or make them responsible for what they say to us through Werder, because the commissions which Prince Gorchakov gives General von Werder for us reach the latter solely through the medium of verbal confidential conversation between a monarch and his "adjutant".'[4] Foreign Office replies to such

[1] Bismarck, *G.W.*, xv. 388 ff.

[2] *Die Große Politik der europäischen Kabinette, 1871–1914: Sammlung der diplomatischen Akten des Auswärtigen Amtes*, ii. 53. See also Eyck, *Bismarck*, iii. 246–7; Schweinitz, *Denkwürdigkeiten*, i. 348 ff.

[3] *Große Politik*, ii. 56.

[4] Ibid., p. 59.

questions, however, would be accepted by all Powers as formal expressions of German intentions.

The Chancellor, therefore, was infuriated with Werder's action and his instructions to the Foreign Office bristle with reprobation of the military plenipotentiary. 'It is really almost worse than *gauche* of Werder to offer himself as a Russian tool to help blackmail us for an embarrassing and untimely declaration.'[1] Werder's action was more than a *lapsus calami*;[2] it was a deplorable indication of political naïveté.

> When an officer completely unversed in politics, who has gradually become more intimately involved in Russian affairs than in our own, becomes . . . the sole representative and channel of German policy *vis-à-vis* Russian policy, then that is a diplomatic calamity; and it would be better for us not to be represented [in St. Petersburg] at all.[3]

Despite his attempts to delay the issue by forcing it back into regular diplomatic channels, Bismarck in the end had to answer the Tsar's question. He did so by expressing the hope that an Austro-Russian war would not take place, but he intimated clearly that, if such conflict should arise, Germany could not be expected to permit Austria's independence to be weakened or her position as a factor in the European balance to be jeopardized.[4] This rejoinder produced a perceptible coolness in St. Petersburg, an item which Bismarck undoubtedly added to the account of the unfortunate Werder. Certainly he did not forgive the military plenipotentiary. At the height of the incident, he had sought to have Werder recalled from the Tsar's entourage, and he had hoped that the attaché would at least be forbidden to send Russian communications to the Foreign Office in the future.[5] When William I refused to take any action against his personal representative in St. Petersburg, Bismarck retreated; but he marked Werder for future punishment and, although it took him ten years, finally succeeded in depriving him of his post.[6]

In all likelihood the Chancellor would have liked to do away with the post of military plenipotentiary as such and to supplant the *Flügeladjutant* with a simple attaché like those at other

[1] Ibid., p. 54. [2] Ibid., p. 55. [3] Ibid., p. 59.

[4] Ibid., pp. 72 ff., Schweinitz, *Denkwürdigkeiten*, i. 355 ff.

[5] Bismarck, *G.W.*, xv. 390; *Große Politik*, ii. 54.

[6] Waldersee, *Denkwürdigkeiten*, i. 296, 298; Schweinitz, *Denkwürdigkeiten*, ii. 82, 136–7.

missions. But, quite apart from the resistance which William I would have offered to any such suggestion, Bismarck had to reckon with the temperament of the Russian ruler as well. The fact was that Alexander II preferred diplomacy on horseback to the traditional methods of foreign offices. Indeed, in 1863 he had expressed his firm belief that, 'when soldiers deal with one another, all goes well; but, as soon as the diplomats step in, the result is unadulterated stupidity'.[1] Given this atmosphere at the Russian court, it was obviously inexpedient to restrict the privileges or abolish the position of the German military plenipotentiary.

Nevertheless, had Bismarck been able to foresee the future, he would have perhaps fought harder in 1876 to end the dual system of reporting at St. Petersburg or to impose more control over the military plenipotentiary, for the incident of 1876 was the first of a long series of difficulties which he and his successors had with the military diplomats. Nor were these restricted to the Russian post. Within the next decade, the military attachés at all capitals began to encroach upon the field of policy.

II

This new development was prefaced by two closely related events: the appointment, in 1882, of General Alfred von Waldersee to the post of quartermaster-general in the General Staff, and the General Staff's success, a year later, in winning both a position of complete administrative independence within the army structure and the privilege of direct access to the emperor. Waldersee, as has been indicated, was a political general. Bismarck, who came to detest him, said that his chief failing was that he never learned 'how to restrict himself to his military calling'.[2] Certainly Waldersee was not content with military honours. He aspired to the chancellorship at least and, throughout the 1880's, worked feverishly to ingratiate himself with both the crown prince and young Prince William so that his career would not be interrupted by the imminent change of reign.[3] Against the time of such elevation, he sought to make his position in the General Staff one of far-reaching influence. He had

[1] Zechlin, *Bismarck und die Grundlegung der deutschen Großmacht*, p. 494.

[2] H. Hofmann, *Fürst Bismarck, 1890–1898* (Berlin, 1913), i. 196. See also Maximilian Harden, *Köpfe* (33rd ed., Berlin, 1910), pp. 197–210.

[3] Waldersee, *Denkwürdigkeiten*, i. 222–3, 236 ff., 243, 249–250.

been one of the prime movers of the reorganization of 1883, and that change enabled him, as Moltke's deputy, not only to present his views at court but to deal independently with, and meddle in the affairs of, other governmental departments. Under his leadership, the General Staff now entered the sphere of foreign politics.

Waldersee had long considered himself to have a flair for foreign affairs. As chargé d'affaires in Paris in 1871, he had breathed the atmosphere of high policy and found it congenial. Now, as quartermaster-general, he felt that he could safely indulge the tastes developed ten years before. One of his first acts was to cultivate Holstein and Hatzfeldt in the Foreign Office on the principle that it is well to have friends in the centre of power.[1] Before another year was out he had managed to embarrass the German ambassador at Constantinople by advising the Sultan, through the agency of a German traveller, that it might be well for him to make plans for an eventual assault on French holdings in North Africa.[2] By the end of the 1880's he was frankly asserting the right of the General Staff to formulate Germany's foreign policy.

In Waldersee's schemes, the military attachés were to play an important part. As soon as he had become quartermaster-general, he had begun an active correspondence with them; and it became customary for them to send him not only copies of their official reports to the Foreign Office, but private letters containing information which they did not see fit to submit to the scrutiny of their chiefs of mission. A study of this private correspondence, which has been edited by H. O. Meisner,[3] makes it clear that the quartermaster-general encouraged the attachés to indulge in political reporting to an unprecedented degree; that he collaborated with them in devising means of escaping embassy control;[4] and that he considered it proper for

[1] Ibid., p. 223.

[2] Hajo Holborn, 'Deutschland und die Türkei', *Archiv für Politik und Geschichte*, v (1925), 140–1.

[3] See especially *Aus dem Briefwechsel des General-Feldmarschalls Alfred Grafen von Waldersee, 1886–1891* (Berlin, 1928). This is supplemented by selections from Waldersee's correspondence with York von Wartenburg in St. Petersburg, in *Historisch-Politisches Archiv*, i (1930), 133–92; and from his correspondence with Huene in Paris, in *Preußische Jahrbücher*, ccxxiv (1931), 125–48, and *Berliner Monatshefte* 15. Jg. (1937), pp. 958–1000.

[4] Engelbrecht, the attaché in Rome, used to send Waldersee long private reports and to consult him as to which portions of these he should communicate to his chief

them to represent the views of the General Staff in their dealings abroad, even when such views were at variance with those of the Foreign Office. The conclusion is also inescapable that Waldersee sought to transform the military attachés into a private diplomatic corps, at the service of the General Staff.

The first indication of the dangers involved in Waldersee's policy came during the Bulgarian crisis of 1887–8. The progressive worsening of Russo-German relations and the knowledge that diplomatic feelers were being put out between Paris and St. Petersburg had, by the end of 1887, produced the blackest pessimism in German military circles. With an alarming unanimity, army leaders believed in the inevitability of war. Having reached that conclusion, however, they adopted the further view that Germany and her Austrian ally must anticipate the action of their potential antagonists by launching a preventive war against Russia at a time of their own choosing. This was Waldersee's own conviction, and he was capable of expressing it with a sang-froid which, even today, is disconcerting. 'A good many men will be killed', he wrote in November 1887. 'However, as long as no one can prove to me that a man can die more than once, I am not inclined to regard death for the individual as a misfortune.'[1]

In Bismarck's opinion the military theory of prophylactic war bordered on the frivolous. It was, he said on one occasion, like committing suicide out of fear of death.[2] His own policy was guided by the desire to avoid war, or, if that was impossible, to delay its coming as long as possible.[3] In that spirit, in the last months of 1887, the Chancellor not only refrained from any threatening gestures against Russia but took measures to prevent foolhardy action on the part of Austria. Through the ambassador in Vienna he made it clear that the treaty concluded with Austria in 1879 was a purely defensive instrument and that Germany would not be obliged to support the Austrian empire if it precipitated a war with Russia.[4]

of mission. Schmettau in Brussels sent reports to Waldersee, on at least one occasion, by officer messenger rather than by diplomatic pouch. Deines in Vienna suggested the possibility of using a private code in letters to Waldersee which travelled by pouch, and Engelbrecht used one in 1891. See Waldersee, *Briefwechsel*, pp. 19–20, 22, 100–1, 132, 147–8, 159; *Denkwürdigkeiten*, ii. 217, n.

[1] Waldersee, *Briefwechsel*, p. 113.

[2] *The Memoirs of Prince Bülow* (Boston, 1931), iv. 609. [3] *Große Politik*, vi. 59.

[4] See the report of the ambassador in Vienna, December 1887, in *Große Politik*, vi. 13. See also Wertheimer in *Preußische Jahrbücher*, cci (1925), 267–8.

It was precisely here, however, that Bismarck found his policy crossed by the military. While Waldersee in Berlin sought to use Moltke's influence to convince the emperor of the necessity of immediate war against Russia[1] and irritated the Chancellor by some highly indiscreet remarks to the Austrian ambassador and the military attaché in Berlin,[2] the German attaché in Vienna, Major von Deines, had a series of confidential conversations with the Austrian chief of staff and with Emperor Francis Joseph. In these talks—as Moltke admitted later—Deines 'definitely allowed himself to be carried away by military passion'.[3] He made suggestions concerning advisable Austrian troop movements on the eastern frontiers; he discussed the possibility of removing the restrictions on the *casus foederis* in the treaty of 1879; and, in general, he gave the impression that an Austro-German assault on Russia was desired in Berlin.[4]

Confronted with an apparent attempt on the part of the General Staff to take over the direction of foreign policy, Bismarck reacted firmly and decisively. In a masterly instruction to Vienna at the end of December, he disabused the Austrians of false hope. He wrote:

> I cannot avoid the impression that it is the aim of certain military circles in Vienna to distort our *defensive* alliance. . . . We must both take care that the privilege of giving political advice to our monarchs does not in fact slip out of our hands and pass over to the General Staffs.

Germany had no intention of committing herself to support an Austrian attack on Russia.[5] At the same time, the Chancellor spoke some plain truths to the military chiefs in Berlin, pointing out that war would be foolhardy in view of the parliamentary situation and the impending change of ruler, and threatening to wash his hands of responsibility for policy if there was further

[1] *Von Scharnhorst zu Schlieffen*, pp. 218–19.

[2] As a result of these conversations Bismarck wrote a sharp letter to Waldersee on 7 December 1887 in which he said that he could not continue to take responsibility for German policy if he were 'exposed to interference of this kind from the military side and if, outside of the official channels, contradictory influences of an authoritative nature are exerted on foreign representatives and their cabinets'. Waldersee, *Denkwürdigkeiten*, i. 341.

[3] So Moltke to Herbert von Bismarck. *Große Politik*, vi. 61.

[4] Waldersee, *Briefwechsel*, pp. 127 ff., 131 ff., 137; *Große Politik*, vi. 61; Schweinitz, *Denkwürdigkeiten*, ii. 350–1; H. von Trützschler, 'Bismarcks Stellung zum Präventivkrieg', *Europäische Gespräche*, i (1923), 191.

[5] *Große Politik*, vi. 67, 69.

interference. By the end of December both Moltke and Albedyll, the Chief of the Military Cabinet and one of Waldersee's close associates, were assuring Bismarck that they had no intention of meddling in his sphere of activity,[1] and the military campaign to take over the direction of policy was in complete disarray.

While Bismarck was able now to solve the crisis short of war, he did not forget that his difficulties had been increased by the activities of the military attaché in Vienna. Aside from informing Deines that he had 'overstepped the boundary between political and military considerations',[2] he refrained from punitive action. But the incident increased his distrust of the attachés as such and made him more vigilant concerning the abuse of the institution.

There was good reason for vigilance. Despite the setback to his plans in 1887, Waldersee did not modify his ambitions. He was shrewd enough to bide his time until the domestic situation was clarified; but, as soon as William II was on the throne, he resumed the offensive. Not only did he continue to encourage the military attachés to circumvent the controls imposed upon them,[3] but he sought now to persuade the young emperor to free the attachés from subordination to their diplomatic chiefs. There was, he argued, no justification for the existing relationship. From the standpoint of ability, the attachés were superior to the diplomats with whom they served. As military technicians, they were better able to judge realities than their civilian colleagues; and, in reporting to Berlin, they had the courage of their convictions, whereas Bismarck's diplomats reported only what the Chancellor wanted to hear.[4]

Waldersee's argument was plausible, if not entirely honest. It was true that Bismarck was regarded in the diplomatic corps with a respect which bordered on awe—Eulenburg speaks of

[1] See Herbert von Bismarck's account of his talks with Albedyll and Moltke in *Große Politik*, vi. 59–62. Bismarck also showed Moltke the text of the secret Reinsurance Treaty with Russia. Ibid., vi. 63; Kessel, *Moltke*, p. 725; W. Kloster, *Der deutsche Generalstab und der Präventivkriegsgedanke* (Stuttgart, 1932), p. 24.

[2] He also advised the ambassador to request Deines's recall in the event of future misconduct. *Große Politik*, vi. 28–29, 57; Waldersee, *Briefwechsel*, pp. 137–8; Bülow, *Memoirs*, ii. 196–7.

[3] Thus, in a letter of 13 February 1889, he advised Engelbrecht, the attaché in Rome, to send political reports directly to him, 'since I am able at any time to bring them to His Majesty's attention'. Waldersee, *Briefwechsel*, pp. 217–18.

[4] Ibid., p. 262; Waldersee, *Denkwürdigkeiten*, ii. 31, 42.

the 'terrified fluttering at the thought of Jupiter's approach'[1]—and this probably made at least the junior members of the service over cautious in their reporting. Even senior diplomats had felt on occasion that too much control was exercised by Berlin over the embassies abroad.[2] But no one could honestly accuse the 'great ambassadors' of Bismarck's last period of truckling to the Chancellor. Reuss, Schweinitz, Hohenlohe, Münster, Hatzfeldt, and Radowitz were able diplomatists and men of independent judgement;[3] and nothing in their conduct supported the charges made by the Chief of the General Staff.

Waldersee's arguments, however, were not without effect upon William II, who shared the general's belief in the superiority of military to civilian intelligence. In a conversation with Waldersee in January 1889, the emperor agreed that something should be done for the attachés but said that he preferred to avoid a conflict with Bismarck at this time. As a temporary expedient, he suggested that the practice which had long applied to St. Petersburg could now be extended to other posts. Since certain attachés currently serving abroad were personal adjutants of the emperor, they could be privileged to send reports directly to him, without submitting them to the Foreign Office.[4] Waldersee accepted the suggestion eagerly; and subsequently the adjutants Engelbrecht in Rome and Deines in Vienna began direct correspondence with the emperor, while Huene in Paris sent reports to the sovereign by way of Waldersee's office.[5]

Bismarck was not slow in detecting these manœuvres and interpreting them as an attempt on the part of the chief of staff to establish 'an organized political bureau in which correspondence with all the military attachés plays a major role'.[6] In his

[1] Haller, *Eulenburg*, i. 182 ff.

[2] See, for instance, the correspondence between Robert von der Goltz and Bismarck in 1863. *Bismarck-Jahrbuch*, v. 238–9.

[3] Radowitz did, in referring to his service in the Foreign Office, write, 'To oppose the Bismarck of the 70's and 80's in any matter would have been impossible for me' (*Aufzeichnungen*, i. 264); but, as ambassador, he was not reluctant to contest the Chancellor's views on policy. For fuller discussion of the independence of Bismarck's diplomatic corps, see H. Rothfels, 'Die Erinnerungen des Botschafters Radowitz', *Archiv für Politik und Geschichte*, iv (1925), 389–90; Hajo Holborn, 'Bismarck und Werthern', ibid., v. 469 ff.; and Gordon A. Craig, *From Bismarck to Adenauer: Aspects of German Statecraft* (Baltimore, 1958), pp. 93–103.

[4] Waldersee, *Denkwürdigkeiten*, ii. 30.

[5] See Meisner's introduction to Waldersee's *Briefwechsel*, p. xviii.

[6] Waldersee, *Denkwürdigkeiten*, ii. 83–84.

last year he sought to tighten his control over the attachés;[1] and, when he fell from office, he appears to have passed on to his successor his concern over the increasing military encroachment upon the diplomatic sphere. Certainly Caprivi, although a soldier, proved to be as inflexible an opponent of Waldersee's plans as Bismarck himself. In the course of 1890 he issued two circular instructions stipulating that all reports of military attachés must be scrutinized in the future by the chiefs of mission and ordering the attachés once again to leave politics to the professional diplomats. He added insult to injury by declaring war on the most refractory of the military diplomats and proceeded systematically to recall Waldersee's correspondents from their posts. Between 1890 and 1895 the attachés in Paris, Vienna, St. Petersburg, and Rome were replaced; and, since their protector had himself fallen from grace in 1891,[2] the 'Waldersee system' was irretrievably ruined.

Caprivi's action did not—and could not hope to—end the historical conflict between the military observers on the one hand and the Foreign Office and the diplomatic service on the other. Chiefs of mission continued to experience difficulty in controlling their attachés' penchant for political speculation[3] and to be embarrassed by other activities of their military experts, as Count Münster in Paris was when his attaché, by disobeying the ambassador's specific prohibition against espionage, involved the embassy in the tangles of the Dreyfus affair.[4] Diplomats in general were made resentful by the knowledge that

[1] See Meisner in *Berliner Monatshefte*, xv. 959.

[2] On the circumstances leading to Waldersee's fall, see, *inter alia*, Wedel, *Zwischen Kaiser und Kanzler*, pp. 120–1, 123–4, 131–2, 134; Waldersee, *Denkwürdigkeiten*, ii. 172 ff., 176–9.

[3] See, for instance, the reports of the military attaché in Constantinople in 1898. *Große Politik*, xii. 571–5.

[4] The attaché, Colonel von Schwartzkoppen, entered relations with the French Major Esterhazy in 1893 and bought from him documents and other information. In 1894 Captain Dreyfus was charged with the sale of these papers and was arrested and imprisoned. Subsequently, when Münster questioned his staff about the affair, Schwartzkoppen, presumably on orders from Berlin, kept his relations with Esterhazy secret and persisted in this silence until the end of the affair. It was not until 1898 that Münster learned of his attaché's complicity. He quite rightly felt that, in his relations with the French government, he had been placed in a false position and said that 'the whole diplomatic service is greatly discredited by this wretched institution of military attachés'. See, *inter alia*, Friedrich Thimme, 'Botschafter und Militärattaché', *Europäische Gespräche*, viii (1930); O. von der Lancken, *Meine dreißig Dienstjahre* (Berlin, 1931), pp. 37 ff.; and Schwartzkoppen's own version of the affair in *Die Wahrheit über Dreyfus*, ed. by B. Schwertfeger (Berlin, 1930).

their reports were apt to make less impression on their emperor than the advice of former attachés who had been appointed, after their tours abroad, to William's *maison militaire*;[1] and this resentment was sometimes a source of bitter friction between the military and civilian members of German diplomatic missions.[2] Nevertheless, it must be admitted that, on the whole, the military attachés of the years immediately before the war obeyed the Caprivi instructions and that they observed the boundaries of their assigned task more faithfully than their counterparts in the naval service.[3] This is not difficult to explain. The General Staff had lost interest in Waldersee's grandiose schemes for emancipating the attachés, for its total energies were concentrated now on the technical problems of operational planning.

III

Ever since 1871 these problems had been difficult, thanks to Germany's geographical position. To the west lay France, a nation which still resented her defeat at Germany's hands and her loss of the provinces of Alsace and Lorraine. In the east stood Russia, always an uncertain quantity in international affairs. As early as April 1871 the elder Moltke had warned that the German-Russian friendship, which had been forged in the campaigns against Napoleon and strengthened by the close personal relations between the two ruling houses, could not be expected to last forever. 'Between the peoples themselves', he wrote, 'there is an unmistakable and mutual antipathy of faith

[1] In 1891, for instance, William, under the influence of Huene, the former Paris attaché, became convinced that France intended to attack Germany before the end of the year. When Münster dismissed this as inconsequential gossip, the emperor accused his ambassador of 'naïveté and childish trust' and said that he should be replaced by Generaladjutant Count Wedel, also—significantly enough—a former attaché. See *Große Politik*, vii. 295 ff. In general, the attachés, as Eulenburg said, were 'haloed in the Emperor's sight', and he frequently suggested that those recalled by Caprivi be employed on special diplomatic missions. See Haller, *Eulenburg*, ii. 44 ff., 50–51; Hohenlohe-Schillingsfürst, *Reichskanzlerzeit*, p. 195 and note.

[2] When Hintze, the military plenipotentiary in St. Petersburg, was recalled at the Tsar's request in 1911, it was whispered that his position had been systematically undermined by members of the embassy staff. See Gustav Graf von Lambsdorff, *Die Militärbevollmächtigten Kaiser Wilhelms II. am Zarenhof, 1904–1914* (Berlin, 1937), pp. 190 ff. In 1908 the military attaché in London, Major Ostertag, was dissuaded with difficulty from challenging Richard von Kühlmann to a duel because of remarks which the latter made to the ambassador about the policies of the military leaders in Berlin. See Wilhelm Widenmann, *Marine-Attaché an der kaiserlich-deutschen Botschaft in London, 1907–1912* (Göttingen, 1952), pp. 39–41.

[3] On the naval attachés, see note at end of this chapter.

and customs, and their material interests are in opposition.' The enhanced strength of the newly united Germany and the fact that the traditional enmity between Austria and Prussia was being replaced by a growing intimacy were now calculated to destroy the remnants of Russian friendship. This did not necessarily mean, of course, that Russia would resort to war. The Tsar's empire was still a backward country with a faulty administration, disorganized forces, and poor communications. It was likely that it would refrain from anything as hazardous as an assault upon Germany, 'unless it found an ally in western Europe'. But France was potentially just such an ally; and, if the Russians and the French came together and if war resulted, the military problem confronting Germany would be one of the nicest calculation.[1]

As is well known, the problem of keeping France and Russia apart was Bismarck's main preoccupation during his term as imperial Chancellor, and he handled it successfully for two decades. But, especially after 1878, there was an almost steady deterioration of Russo-German relations, and, long before the tie between Berlin and St. Petersburg was finally severed and the Franco-Russian *rapprochement* was effected in the 90's, the German General Staff had been making its plans for that unhappy eventuality.

The chief problem confronting the staff planners was whether, in the event of a two-front war, Germany's main forces should be directed against the eastern or the western enemy. With regard to this, the elder Moltke's views were flexible, changing as the political situation in Europe changed. In the 1870's, while France was still suffering from the political and military disorganization caused by the recent war, Moltke was inclined to believe that, at the outset of a major war, Germany's main strength should be mobilized in the west. In a memorandum of 3 February 1877 he argued that a decisive battle against the French armies might be expected within three weeks of the opening of hostilities, after which time German troops could be released to the Vistula front for the campaign against the Russians.[2] Within two years, however, Moltke had reversed himself completely and was writing: 'If we must fight two wars

[1] Graf Moltke, *Die deutschen Aufmarschpläne 1871–1890*, ed. by Ferdinand von Schmerfeld (*Forschungen und Darstellungen aus dem Reichsarchiv*, Heft 7) (Berlin, 1929), pp. 4–8.

[2] Ibid., p. 66.

150 miles apart, then, in my opinion, we should exploit in the west the great advantages which the Rhine and our powerful fortifications offer to the defensive and should employ all the fighting forces which are not absolutely indispensable [in the west] for an imposing offensive against the east.'[1]

This fundamental change in Moltke's strategical thinking was influenced primarily by France's rapid military revival in the late 1870's and by the strengthening of the fortifications around Paris and along the eastern frontiers. Since 1871 Moltke had become increasingly apprehensive concerning French recovery,[2] and he had no illusions concerning the effort and the length of time which it would take to impose a new defeat upon her once she was rearmed. 'We have already learned', he wrote in 1871, 'how difficult it is to end even the most victorious war against France.'[3] In 1877, while he thought it possible to count on an *Entscheidungsschlacht* against the main French force soon after the outbreak of war, he specifically warned against a subsequent attempt to beat France to her knees, arguing that 'it must be left to diplomacy to determine whether it can achieve peace for us on this one side, even if it can be done only on the basis of the *status quo ante*'.[4] By 1879 he seems to have lost faith even in this method of forcing a quick decision.

On the other hand, the chief of staff felt that the chances of knocking the Russians out of the war in a relatively short space of time were good, provided the German war against Russia was conceived as one of limited aims. Given the size of Russia, the strategy of annihilation (*Vernichtungsstrategie*] promised even less favourable results than in France, and any attempt to pursue it would probably degenerate into an offensive into the void.[5] But a series of hammer blows against the Russian armies in the western provinces, combined with a systematic attempt to encourage insurrection among such subject peoples as the Poles,[6] would hopelessly disorganize the Russian war effort. In

[1] Ibid., p. 77.

[2] Moltke's fear of French recovery led him in 1875 to favour, or at least to view with equanimity, the idea of a renewed assault on France. See Jähns, *Moltke*, pp. 572, 600; Heinrich von Treitschke, *Briefe*, ed. by M. Cornicelius (Leipzig, 1913–20), iii. 414; Winifred Taffs, *Lord Odo Russell* (London, 1938), p. 89; *Documents diplomatiques françaises*, 1st series, i. 441, 467. Cf. Kloster, *Präventivkrieg*, pp. 6–19.

[3] Moltke, *Aufmarschpläne*, p. 9.

[4] Ibid., p. 66.

[5] Ibid., p. 82; Gerhard Ritter in *Deutschland und Europa*, p. 90.

[6] 'Wir müßten dann alle Kräfte aufbieten und jedes Mittel ergreifen, namentlich Polen insurgieren, soweit Rücksicht auf Oesterreich dies gestattet.' Moltke,

the circumstances the Russian government would probably be amenable to negotiation, especially if the Germans offered reasonable terms. There was no reason why they should not do so, for, as Moltke said on one occasion, 'the Russians . . . have absolutely nothing which one could take from them after the most successful war; they have no gold, and we don't need land'.[1] Thus, in the chief of staff's view, 'we would have no interest in following up a victory in the kingdom of Poland with an advance into the interior of Russia, but it would enable us to send the greatest part of our armies to the Rhine by the railway routes best suited for that purpose'.[2]

The conclusion of the Dual Alliance of 1879, which assured Germany of active Austrian assistance in the event that she was attacked by Russia, led to no appreciable alteration in Moltke's plans for the two-front war. Austrian adhesion made the chances of success in the east greater, but not so much so that the allocation of troops to the two fronts could be changed. In the memoranda of January 1880, and in subsequent plans drawn up in his last years, Moltke continued to think in terms of a holding operation in the west until a decision had been reached in the east, and he was willing to contemplate initial reverses and even the loss of the left bank of the Rhine in order that the eastern campaign should achieve its objectives.[3]

How effective this strategy would have proved in the event of war we have no way of knowing. What can be said with some assurance, however, is that Moltke's plans reveal not only the most careful consideration of the technical aspects of Germany's military position but also an awareness of the political factors involved in war—the internal conditions of the countries opposed to Germany and the role of diplomacy in destroying the enemy coalition. Moltke possessed real political insight and in addition he had—despite his differences with Bismarck during the wars of the unification period—no hesitation in keeping the Chancellor informed concerning his operational plans.[4]

quoted in a telegram of Bülow to the Foreign Office, 16 September 1879. Moltke, *Aufmarschpläne*, p. 80.

[1] Lucius von Ballhausen, *Bismarck-Erinnerungen*, p. 139.

[2] Moltke, *Aufmarschpläne*, p. 80.

[3] Ibid., pp. 86, 89, 94–95, 145, 150–62.

[4] See, for instance, ibid., pp. 133–6, 137–45. For a fuller appreciation of Moltke's strategic thinking after 1871, see Ritter, *Staatskunst und Kriegshandwerk*, i. 288–95; Peter Rassow, 'Der Plan Moltkes für den Zweifrontenkrieg,' *Breslauer Historische Forschungen*, Heft 1 (1938); Kessel, *Moltke*, pp. 646 ff., 703 ff.

This appreciation of the political factors which must be considered in planning was notably lacking in the work of his greatest successor, Count Alfred von Schlieffen.

Schlieffen, who became Chief of the General Staff in 1891, after the brief tenure of Waldersee, had neither the philosophical breadth nor the diversity of interest which had characterized Moltke's thinking. He was the professional soldier pure and simple, completely absorbed in his calling and impervious to anything that lay outside it. It is perhaps indicative of the growing narrowness of view in the General Staff that this very attribute of Schlieffen should have made so deep an impression upon those who worked with him. General von Kuhl, who calls Schlieffen 'the most imposing personality with whom I came into contact in my long career of service', describes with admiration a staff ride during which an adjutant called the chief of staff's attention to the beauties of the Pregeltal. 'An insignificant obstacle', said Schlieffen, cutting off what doubtless struck him as a dangerously unprofessional line of thought.[1] The chief of staff was unfortunately capable of excluding a great many important factors from his thinking. Like many soldiers after him, he prided himself on being completely 'un-political', forgetting Clausewitz's wise dictum that 'war admittedly has its own grammar, but not its own logic', which must be supplied by politics. Few objective critics would deny that Schlieffen was a superb grammarian; but that unfortunately was not enough.

Thanks to the reversal of alliances which had taken place in the 1890's, Schlieffen was convinced that the two-front war which had absorbed so much of Moltke's attention was inevitable. When it came, he believed—as Moltke had believed—that 'Germany [would have] the advantage of lying between France and Russia and of separating these allies. . . . Germany must strive, therefore, first, to strike down one of the allies while the other is kept occupied; but then, when the one antagonist is conquered, it must, by exploiting its railroads, bring a superiority of numbers to the other theatre of war, which will also destroy the other enemy.'[2] Where Schlieffen came to differ with Moltke was on the question of where the initial thrust

[1] H. von Kuhl, *Der deutsche Generalstab in Vorbereitung und Durchführung des Weltkrieges* (Berlin, 1920), pp. 126–7.

[2] Generalfeldmarschall Graf von Schlieffen, *Dienstschriften*, hrsg. vom Generalstab des Heeres, ii (Berlin, 1938): *Die Großen Generalstabsreisen (Ost) aus den Jahren 1891–1905*, p. 222.

should be directed, for he believed that it must be delivered against France.

The materials thus far published do not make clear the stages by which Schlieffen reached this conclusion.[1] It seems likely that he was impressed by the construction at the end of the century of new Russian fortifications in the area of Ivangorod, Brest-Litovsk, Kovno, and Warsaw. This so-called Narew line barred the very area in which Moltke had planned his main attack.[2] Moreover, the great improvement which had been made simultaneously in the Russian railway net seemed to indicate that the Tsar's armies could be reinforced more speedily than was possible in Moltke's time. These facts argued against the possibility of a quick victory in the east, and Schlieffen had no stomach for a lengthy war of attrition.

At the same time, the chief of staff was more seriously concerned over the dangers of a French offensive than either of his immediate predecessors had been. He had none of Moltke's confidence in the possibility of remedying an initial withdrawal in the west by a counter-offensive on interior lines, since he felt that a simultaneous French attack in Lorraine and through Luxemburg in Belgium would deprive him of the necessary space for such a manœuvre.[3] To avoid this danger, Schlieffen, from 1892 on, began to think in terms of an initial offensive in the west.

Here, too, he was confronted with serious difficulties. If the French forces elected to remain behind their fortifications the German armies might exhaust themselves in costly frontal assaults and, even if they were successful in the end, they could hardly hope to be so in time to prevent the Russians from overrunning East Prussia. Therefore, 'an attack by the Germans upon the French fortresses does not seem advisable in a war on two fronts', for what was needed was 'a real *Entscheidungsschlacht*; a Solferino will bring us nothing; a Sedan, or at least a Königgrätz, must be fought'.[4]

The mention of the last two battles is significant. Königgrätz was an imperfect, Sedan a perfect, battle of encirclement; and, once Schlieffen had given priority to the western attack, he thought exclusively in terms of encirclement. He convinced

[1] On this point, see Peter Rassow, 'Schlieffen und Holstein', *Historische Zeitschrift*, clxxiii (1952), 302–4; G. Ritter, *Der Schlieffenplan: Kritik eines Mythos* (München, 1956), pp. 18 ff.

[2] Görlitz, *General Staff*, p. 131.

[3] See Rosinski, *The German Army*, p. 82.

[4] Schlieffen, *Dienstschriften*, ii. 222.

himself indeed, under the influence of Hans Delbrück's description of the battle of Cannae in his *History of the Art of War*, that the highest achievement of strategy was the crushing attack in the flank and rear of an enemy which had enabled Hannibal, in that battle, to destroy a numerically superior Roman army. To duplicate Cannae had, Schlieffen believed, always been the objective of the great commanders of the past;[1] and the Germans must strive to duplicate Cannae in their war against France.

The only way of doing this, however, was to strike across the neutral states which would separate the French left flank from the German forces; and Schlieffen was inexorably led to the acceptance of this expedient. Between 1897 and 1905 he evolved the plan which, in its most complete form, envisaged a massive manœuvre of envelopment in which the bulk of the German force in the west, pivoting upon Metz and Strassburg, would drive through Luxemburg and Belgium into the French rear, would cross the lower Seine, and then, wheeling to the east, would pin the shattered French forces back against their own fortresses and against the Swiss frontier.[2]

To assure this result Schlieffen was willing to assume great risks. In order that the German right wing should have the power necessary to enable it to smash its way through Belgium and northern France for a period of six weeks, he insisted that it must be roughly seven times as strong as the left wing, whose duty was to hold in Alsace. This offered the French the opportunity of crossing the upper Rhine and penetrating into southern Germany. Such an offensive, however, could hardly achieve decisive results, for it would remove troops from the critical area of northern France and would thus facilitate the main German advance. Schlieffen counted on his right wing's attaining a momentum which would carry it to Abbéville and the channel coast on the thirty-first day after mobilization. Once that had been achieved, the French, unable now to outflank their opponent, would be in a perilous position.[3]

The daring of this conception must arouse a reluctant ad-

[1] See Holborn in *Makers of Modern Strategy*, pp. 189–90. At Schlieffen's specific request the historical section of the General Staff elaborated this theme in a study entitled *Der Schlachterfolg, mit welchen Mitteln wurde er erstrebt?* See Freytag von Loringhoven, *Menschen und Dinge*, p. 99.

[2] Holborn in *Makers of Modern Strategy*, pp. 190–2; Rosinski, *The German Army*, pp. 82–83; Boetticher in *Von Scharnhorst zu Schlieffen*, pp. 259 ff.; Ritter, *Schlieffenplan*, pp. 38 ff.; Schlieffen, *Briefe*, p. 12.

[3] Holborn in *Makers of Modern Strategy*, pp. 193–4.

miration; and it is probably true that, if this plan had been carried out in 1914 in its original form and under the direction of an energetic and stubborn commander-in-chief, it would have achieved an overwhelming initial success.[1] But what then? Would that success have been so decisive that the French would have had to surrender? 'You cannot carry away the armed strength of a great Power like a cat in a bag', one senior general of the German army is reported to have said of Schlieffen's plan.[2] The war of 1870–1 had already demonstrated that the will to resistance and the ability to raise new armies can survive the most crushing initial defeats. There was no assurance that something of the sort might not happen again.

And even if France should surrender, what of France's allies? As early as 1905 it was likely that France would be supported not only by Russia but by Great Britain as well. Yet Schlieffen seems to have given little thought to the effect of Britain's participation in a future war.[3] He apparently shared the prevalent view that England was incapable of sending more than a token force to the Continent,[4] and his operational plans were based on the assumption that a complete defeat of France would persuade the British to make peace.[5] Only the profoundest disregard for the lessons of British history could have led to this conclusion. It is likely that, even if the British had been forced to leave the Continent, they would have continued to fight; and Schlieffen's future operations against Russia would have been gravely handicapped, not only by naval attacks on German commerce and industry,[6] but also by the constant threat of renewed invasion in the west.

Schlieffen's failure to consider these matters deeply stemmed perhaps from his conviction that, in modern conditions, no nation could tolerate a long war. Moltke had once prophesied gloomily that the next war would last for seven years and might

[1] Gerhard Ritter, however, feels that it was entirely too dependent on chance factors. *Deutschland und Europa*, p. 92 and *Schlieffenplan*, pp. 68 ff.

[2] Rosinski, *The German Army*, p. 85; Kessel in Schlieffen, *Briefe*, p. 14.

[3] Ritter in *Deutschland und Europa*, p. 93, and *Schlieffenplan*, p. 74.

[4] Even such a shrewd military observer as Hans Delbrück believed this. See his *Krieg und Politik* (Berlin, 1918–19), i. 243 ff., and Gordon A. Craig, 'Delbrück, the Military Historian', in *Makers of Modern Strategy*, pp. 275–6.

[5] Holborn in ibid., p. 203.

[6] Wilhelm Groener's chapter on England in his *Das Testament des Grafen Schlieffen* (Berlin, 1927), pp. 211–15, indicates that Schlieffen gave little thought to the possibilities of economic warfare.

last for thirty. Schlieffen, however, felt that such protracted conflicts were impossible 'in an age in which the existence of nations is based on the uninterrupted progress of trade and commerce. . . . A strategy of exhaustion [*Ermattungsstrategie*] is impossible when the maintenance of millions necessitates the expenditure of milliards'.[1] Believing this, it was easy for him to conclude that a battle that shattered the bulk of the organized forces of one of his antagonists in the first months of the war would destroy its will, and the will of its allies, to resist further. But this very conclusion betrayed the dangerous limitations of Schlieffen as a strategist. Mesmerized by visions of a greater Cannae, he disregarded not only the demographic, technological, and industrial factors which affect the war effort of Great Powers in the modern age, but also the political and psychological forces which are apt to make peoples fight even against hopeless odds.

Nor is it possible to argue that, despite these weaknesses, Schlieffen's plan was the only possible military solution for a Germany whose international position was hopeless and whose enemies possessed superior strength which they were determined to use against her. Schlieffen seems always to have believed that a war against France and Russia was inevitable and, by 1905, he was apparently resigned to the prospect of Britain adhering to the Franco-Russian cause. Yet when he became chief of staff in 1891 Russia was not yet hopelessly alienated from Germany and relations between Britain and Germany were far more cordial than relations between Britain and France. That the diplomatic alignments of Europe changed to Germany's disadvantage was due to the character of Wilhelmine foreign policy,[2] and particularly to such things as the new imperialism in Africa and the Far East, the exclusive tariffs against Russian grains, the naval programme,[3] the Baghdad railway

[1] Kuhl, *Der deutsche Generalstab*, p. 131.

[2] Even as late as 1901, Paul von Hatzfeldt, retiring as ambassador to the Court of St. James, could write: 'If people in Germany would only sit still, the time would soon come when broiled squabs would fly into our mouths. But these incessant hysterical vacillations of William II . . . will bring us all to destruction.' Baron von Eckardstein, *Lebenserinnerungen* (Leipzig, 1920–1), ii. 161.

[3] On the relationship between the tariff and naval policies and their results, see Eckart Kehr, 'Deutsch-englisches Bündnisproblem der Jahrhundertwende'. *Die Gesellschaft* (1928), ii. 24–31, and 'Die deutsche Flotte in den neunziger Jahren und der politisch-militärische Dualismus des Kaiserreiches', *Archiv für Politik und Geschichte*, viii (1927), 187–202.

scheme,[1] and the provocative encouragement of the Boers in South Africa.[2] All these policy innovations occurred during Schlieffen's term as chief of staff. He was presumably informed of them, since he was on intimate terms with Holstein in the Foreign Office and was privileged to read dispatches and other papers in that official's private study.[3] He could not but have been aware of their effect in alienating the sympathies of Germany's neighbours and thus endangering her security. Yet, despite his position as chief military adviser to the Crown, he remained as tolerant of the shortcomings of William's foreign policy[4] as he was of the egregious mistakes made by the emperor on those occasions when he assumed command in army manœuvres.[5] Not even the naval programme—which had no logical relation to Schlieffen's strategical plans for a future war and which therefore represented an unwise expenditure of man-power and money—aroused opposition on his part.[6] It is difficult to decide whether his blindness to political realities or his conviction that criticism would weaken the authority of the Crown was the stronger force in prompting this silence. But, if the completed

[1] On the role of the German military attaché at Constantinople in encouraging the emperor's interest in this, see Monts, *Erinnerungen*, pp. 393–4.

[2] See, *inter alia*, Eyck, *Wilhelm II*, pp. 253 ff.

[3] 'While I write here', Holstein wrote in 1897 to Ida von Stülpnagel, 'General Count Schlieffen sits beside me reading documents, which is usually the case once a week in troubled times.' Holstein, *Lebensbekenntnis*, p. 187. Holstein apparently hoped that Schlieffen would take a stand against at least some of the emperor's eccentricities and, in 1891, tried to effect a working arrangement between Schlieffen and Caprivi for that purpose. Ibid., pp. 155–6. Holstein and the chief of staff had been friendly since the 1870's. On their early relations, see Lancken, *Dienstjahre*, p. 58, and Hugo Rochs, *Schlieffen* (Berlin, 1921).

[4] In his memoirs, the later General and Reichswehrminister Wilhelm Groener, who was a member of the General Staff under Schlieffen, says that Schlieffen did object on one occasion to a scheme of William's for raising a special legion for service in East Asia. Wilhelm Groener, *Lebenserinnerung: Jugend, Generalstab, Weltkrieg*, herausgegeben von Friedrich Freiherr Hiller von Gärtringen (Deutsche Geschichtsquellen des 19. und 20. Jahrhunderts, Bd. 41, Göttingen, 1957), p. 77. Groener gives no date, but the protest was probably at the time of the Kiaou-Chau affair in 1897. See Hohenlohe, *Reichskanzlerzeit*, pp. 419–20. Against the broader implications of William's policies, however, Schlieffen did not protest.

[5] Criticism of the emperor's troop leadership was apt to be dangerous, and it had played its part in Waldersee's fall. See Wedel, *Zwischen Kaiser und Kanzler*, pp. 120–1; Waldersee, *Denkwürdigkeiten*, ii. 195. Schlieffen was accused in the army of encouraging the emperor's fantastic notions and even of rigging the manœuvres in which William participated in the emperor's favour. See Einem, *Erinnerungen*, pp. 144 ff. Friendly critics have said that his motive was to keep William's interest in the army alive and to prevent him from becoming completely naval minded. See Bircher and Bode, *Schlieffen*, pp. 118 ff.

[6] Holborn in *Makers of Modern Strategy*, p. 204. Cf. Kessel in Schlieffen, *Briefe*, p. 18.

Schlieffen plan is to be described as 'a project of desperation in a situation which had become hopeless',[1] then one must add that Schlieffen himself, by his failure to object to misguided strokes of policy, was partly responsible for the dangers of Germany's situation.

On the one notable occasion on which Schlieffen did intervene in an essentially political question he stood forth, not as a champion of a prudent and peaceful diplomacy, but—very much like his predecessor Waldersee—as an advocate of preventive war. This was in 1905, when he supported and encouraged Holstein's dangerous policy during the first Moroccan crisis.

In 1905 the French government undertook to extend their control over Morocco. To Holstein and Schlieffen this action provided an ideal opportunity to correct the setbacks of the last fifteen years and to remove future threats to German security. France, for the moment at least, could not expect strong support from her friends. The Russians were engaged in a disastrous war in the far east and were paralysed by revolution on the home front. The British army had been weakened and disorganized by the long war in South Africa, and the British government would probably be reluctant, despite the *entente* of 1904 with France, to engage in a continental conflict on behalf of their new partner. A diplomatic campaign against the French policy in Morocco, if it were energetic and uncompromising, might—Holstein and Schlieffen believed—succeed in creating a situation in which France would have to fight for reasons of prestige and public opinion; and such a war, even if Britain gave what aid she could, would soon end in German victory.

The German Chancellor in 1905, Bernhard von Bülow, later specifically denied that Schlieffen had 'recommended a preventive war on any occasion or ever sought to incite a war'.[2] This is probably true in the strictest sense of Bülow's words. But there is no doubt that Schlieffen was in a war-like mood in 1905. He was working on the December memorandum which was the most complete formulation of his plans for enveloping and crushing the French forces in the event of war, and it is natural that he should have been tempted to put those plans into effect while the Russians were powerless.[3]

[1] Ritter in *Deutschland und Europa*, p. 93.

[2] Letter to *Süddeutsche Monatshefte*, March 1921.

[3] The text of the Denkschrift of December 1905 will be found in Ritter, *Schlieffenplan*, pp. 145 ff.

Wilhelm Groener, one of his juniors in the General Staff in 1905, has written that Schlieffen felt it necessary to establish 'the security of the Empire's continental power, which he saw threatened by the Anglo-French combination which was supported by Russia'. Believing this, Schlieffen felt also that, in 1905, Germany was offered an opportunity to free herself and that, if this were missed, it might not recur.[1] That he would have welcomed war was no secret to the army, and his feelings were, for that matter, shared by other high-ranking officers, including the War Minister von Einem.[2]

If Schlieffen did not urge his policy upon Bülow it was simply because he felt that he did not need to. He could rely upon Holstein, with whom he was in closest contact throughout this period, to make war inevitable by skilful exploitation of the situation created by the French action.[3] And Holstein almost succeeded in doing just that. He was the driving force behind the emperor's visit to Tangier at the end of March,[4] the bullying campaign which forced the dismissal of the French Foreign Minister Delcassé in June,[5] the refusal to engage in direct negotiations with France over Moroccan affairs, and the insistence upon an international conference which was intended to create new opportunities for provocation.[6] He, too, stood behind the grim directive of December 1905 to the press chief of the German Foreign Office, which—apparently intended as a means of preparing public opinion for war—read:

I am afraid that at the conference at Algeciras there will be a tendency on the part of the French, perhaps encouraged by England but at any rate not prevented by her, to put Germany in a position in which she has only the choice between a heavy loss of prestige

[1] Groener, *Lebenserinnerungen*, pp. 84–85.

[2] See Einem, *Erinnerungen*, pp. 111–12. Gerhard Ritter, in *Schlieffenplan*, pp. 102–38, argues vigorously against this thesis but, while he demonstrates the weakness of some of the evidence, fails to explain away the testimony of Groener. It is interesting to note that, in two rather ambiguous passages in his introduction to Schlieffen's letters, Eberhard Kessel, while denying that Schlieffen's war plan of 1905 had 'a preventive war character', suggests that the Chief of Staff was in fact thinking personally in terms of preventive war during the Moroccan crisis and says plainly that he was as anxious to come to grips with France in 1905 as he had been in 1867. Schlieffen, *Briefe*, pp. 13 f., 52 ff., and, in addition, pp. 205, 207, 208.

[3] Lancken, *Dienstjahre*, p. 62. Groener makes the same point in his *Lebenserinnerungen* and emphasizes Schlieffen's close contact with Holstein.

[4] Holstein, *Lebensbekenntnis*, pp. xxxv, 238–9; Baron von Schön, *Memoirs of an Ambassador* (London, 1922), pp. 19 ff.; A. von Valentini, *Kaiser und Kabinettschef* (Oldenburg, 1931), p. 79.

[5] Eyck, *Wilhelm II*, pp. 398–401.

[6] Richard von Kühlmann, *Erinnerungen* (Heidelberg, 1948), pp. 246 ff.

in the world or an armed conflict. Such a conflict in the spring is expected by many here, and desired by many.[1]

Even if we did not have the testimony of men who discussed the Moroccan affair with Holstein in later years and who were confirmed in their belief that Holstein was working for war in 1905,[2] the very sequence of these events would be enough to prove that this was so.

The scheme, however, did not work. Bülow, in his usual airy way, followed Holstein's advice until the very end of 1905, when the crisis came to its head, but he did so apparently only because he regarded the dangerous German tactics as a way of bluffing the French into major concessions and of disrupting the Anglo-French *entente*. When the bluff did not work and Germany was confronted—as Holstein had expected she would be confronted—with a choice between war or diplomatic defeat, the Chancellor chose the latter alternative. He then proceeded to visit his wrath upon his adviser. Holstein's long career in the Foreign Office came to an end and, when he fell, Schlieffen fell with him.

In the case of the chief of staff, a riding accident was given as the reason for his retirement, but there was no doubt in the minds of the army hierarchy that this was only to save appearances. After announcing Schlieffen's resignation to his generals in January 1906, William II went out of his way to add: 'The Moroccan question has aroused the greatest tension in Germany and also in the army. I tell you here, however, that I will never fight a war for the sake of Morocco. In saying this, I am relying on your discretion, and it must not leave this room.'[3]

The principal effect of the policy followed by Germany in the first Moroccan crisis was to strengthen the Anglo-French *entente*, and it was no mere coincidence that the first Anglo-French staff talks were held in 1905. During his fourteen years

[1] Hammann, *Bilder aus der letzten Kaiserzeit*, p. 45.

[2] See Lancken, *Dienstjahre*, pp. 54–55, and Monts, *Erinnerungen*, pp. 191–2. Rassow in *Historische Zeitschrift*, clxxiii, gives a fuller discussion of this controversial question and an evaluation of the sources. Ritter, in *Schlieffenplan*, pp. 126–34, points out that there is no evidence in Holstein's dispatches or memoranda that he wanted war in 1905. This is not surprising; but it is hardly conclusive when one remembers that Holstein's desire for preventive war in 1887, which is not mentioned by Ritter, is not documented by papers from his own hand either. But see H. Krausnick, *Holsteins Geheimpolitik in der Aera Bismarck 1886–1890* (2. Aufl., Hamburg, 1942), pp. 117, 155 ff., 161.

[3] Einem, *Erinnerungen*, p. 114.

of reflection upon the problems of Germany's military security, Schlieffen had made no effort to ease those problems by urging a policy of caution and circumspection upon the emperor; and, at the end of that period, by his role in the Moroccan affair, he had helped make his country's military position more insecure than it had been at any time since his assumption of office.

For his advocacy of preventive war in 1905, Moltke's most gifted successor lost his post; but his influence continued, since his famous master plan was, with some later modification, accepted by his successor. It was not the happiest of legacies, as the history of the next nine years was to show.

IV

Much has been written about the technical modifications made in Schlieffen's plan between 1906 and 1914—the reallocation of forces and the redefinition of the mission of the left wing of the army invading France which had the effect of weakening the striking force of that right wing from which Schlieffen had expected so much.[1] These changes were doubtless important, but they need not concern us here. In a discussion of the role of the army in Germany's foreign policy before 1914, they are less significant than the fact that the basic concept of the plan was accepted without question by Germany's military leaders after Schlieffen had left the scene. For this retention of the plan encouraged the coming of war and made it inevitable that, when it came, Germany would have to fight it with tremendous political disadvantages.

Certainly the chances of war were greatly heightened by the effect which the Schlieffen plan had on Germany's relations with Austria, for in the long run it made Germany more dependent upon that Power than she had been earlier and weakened her ability to restrain the dangerous tendencies of Austrian policy.

The basic reason for this development was the fact that Schlieffen's rejection of the Moltke–Waldersee operational plans for an eastern war and the scant courtesy which he demonstrated toward Germany's ally alarmed and angered the Austrians. When he first came to office, the German chief of staff, in a letter to his Austrian counterpart, *Feldzeugmeister* Beck, had

[1] For a discussion of these changes, see Holborn in *Makers of Modern Strategy*, pp. 195–9; Kessel intimates that their importance has been exaggerated. Schlieffen, *Briefe*, pp. 15–16.

declared his intention of continuing in the line set by Moltke.[1] But from the start he showed none of Moltke's willingness to treat the Austrians like equals and, in his first conversations with Beck and in subsequent ones with the Austrian military attaché, he displayed an irritating taciturnity.[2] He allowed almost a year to elapse before making any overtures to the Austrians for an exchange of views on strategical questions, and it was not until the end of 1892 that he informed them, rather cursorily, that he was contemplating shifting Germany's main effort, in case of war, from the east to the west.[3] This change obviously made it necessary to overhaul all previous plans for the eastern campaign; and the Austrians, not unnaturally, expected that this would be done in collaboration with their ally. They had the greatest difficulty, however, in persuading Schlieffen to engage in anything that could be described as joint planning. The German chief of staff allowed long periods to pass without making any attempt to communicate with Vienna and, when he did make proposals, did so abruptly and with little consideration for the Austrian point of view.[4] It did not take much of this to arouse resentment in Vienna, and this increased and became more open as Schlieffen's preoccupation with the west deepened. Austrian officers were heard to grumble that if Germany intended to leave Austria in the lurch she would find that two could play that game.[5]

Schlieffen himself does not seem to have been concerned with the sentiment in Vienna, but, by the end of his term, it had begun to worry others in Berlin. Thanks to the mistakes of William's policy, Germany had few friends by 1906. With France and Britain reconciled, with the Russian tie to Paris closer than ever, and with the Italians showing a tendency to drift in the same direction, the partnership with Austria assumed new importance. For Austria alone, after all, stood between Germany and complete isolation.

This thought seems to have made a deep impression upon Germany's new chief of staff, Moltke the younger. This officer

[1] Glaise-Horstenau, *Franz Josephs Weggefährte*, p. 343.

[2] Ibid., p. 344; *Große Politik*, vii. 112; Ritter, *Schlieffenplan*, pp. 25, 27–29.

[3] Glaise-Horstenau, *Franz Josephs Weggefährte*, p. 346.

[4] Ibid., pp. 348–53, 377–8.

[5] The feeling that Germany was tending to dissociate herself from Austrian problems was strengthened by German warnings in 1896 that Germany would not consider a Russian occupation of Constantinople as a *casus belli*. Ibid., pp. 379–82.

possessed neither the strategical gifts nor the habitual sangfroid of his illustrious uncle.[1] An emotional man, given to strong doubts in his own ability,[2] he was a follower rather than an original thinker, and he accepted the basic premises of the war plans of his predecessor. At the same time, however, he recognized the indispensable role which Austria had to play in their execution, and he was frightened by the possibility that she might be unwilling to play it. He believed, therefore, that it was essential to repair the damage done by Schlieffen, even if this necessitated making new commitments to Austria in order to convince her of German loyalty.

In the circumstances this involved great risks. The most influential men in Austrian politics after 1906 were the Foreign Minister Aehrenthal, the man who was to follow him in that post, Count Berchtold, and Beck's successor as chief of staff, Conrad von Hötzendorf. All three were advocates of an expansionist policy in the Balkans and of the eventual elimination of Serbia as a threat to their designs there, and this policy was almost certain to invite Russian resistance.[3] They were eager to obtain a German promise of support in the event of war, and Moltke's desire to improve Austro-German military relations played into their hands.

In January 1909, taking as his excuse the agitation in Serbia which had continued since Austria's annexation of Bosnia in the previous year, Field Marshal Conrad wrote a long letter to Moltke. There was a strong possibility, he asserted, of an Austro-Serb war and an Austrian occupation of Serbia in the not distant future. If Russia should intervene when this contingency arose, he assumed that Germany, 'in conformity with the treaty of 1879', would join Austria. But since France might enter the war also, or since Germany might feel compelled to attack France as a means of preventing a subsequent attack on her own rear, it was necessary for Austria to know where Germany intended to direct her major effort, for this would influence her own plans.[4]

[1] On the circumstances of Moltke's appointment, which was opposed by both the War Minister and the Chief of the Military Cabinet, see Einem, *Erinnerungen*, pp. 148–9, and Hutten-Czapski, *Sechzig Jahre*, i. 410.

[2] See, for instance, Bülow, *Memoirs*, ii. 201–2.

[3] On Aehrenthal and Conrad, see, *inter alia*, G. P. Gooch, *Before the War*, i (London, 1936), 369 ff. On Berchtold, see ibid. ii (London, 1938), 373 ff.

[4] Feldmarschall Conrad, *Aus meiner Dienstzeit* (Vienna, Berlin, 1921 ff.), i. 631–4.

To this ambiguous epistle, Moltke answered on 21 January. He made no attempt to reject its underlying assumptions or to demand a clearer exposition of Austrian intentions. Instead, he completely accepted the notion that Austria might find it necessary to invade Serbia. Nor did he stop there. If she should do so, he said, and if Russia should intervene, 'that would constitute the *casus foederis* for Germany'. As soon as Russia began to mobilize, Germany would call up her whole fighting force.[1]

It is difficult to over-estimate the importance of this statement, for in the plainest terms it amounted to an admission that Austria had a right to expect German support even in a war caused by her own provocation. This was certainly an interpretation of the treaty of 1879 which would have been rejected flatly by the author of that instrument. Bismarck had always insisted that the dual alliance was a strictly defensive arrangement. In January 1887 he had denied that the treaty did or could require either signatory to subordinate its policies to, or place its forces completely at the disposal of, the other, since 'there are specifically Austrian interests for which we cannot pledge ourselves and there are specifically German interests for which Austria cannot pledge herself'. And in December 1887, at the height of the Bulgarian crisis, he had stated unequivocally in an instruction to Vienna that

> in order not to cancel the clear delimitation which now exists with regard to the *casus foederis*, we must not encourage the tendencies to which the Austrians are prone by pledging the armed force of Germany for the sake of Hungarian and Catholic ambitions in the Balkans. . . . For us Balkan questions can in no case constitute a motive for war.[2]

Moltke flatly disregarded this warning and, in effect, changed the treaty of 1879 from a defensive to an offensive instrument.[3] By doing so he placed his country at the mercy of the adventurers in Vienna. Conrad regarded Moltke's promises as 'binding written agreements',[4] and he and those who thought as he did were encouraged to pursue their fateful course in the Balkans.

[1] Ibid., pp. 380–1.

[2] *Große Politik*, vi. 27–28.

[3] For a fuller discussion, see Luigi Albertini, *Le origini della guerra del 1914*, i (Milan, 1942), 287–8; Heinrich Kanner, *Der Schlüssel zur Kriegsschuldfrage* (München, 1926), pp. 16–19; Helmut von Gerlach in *Die Weltbühne*, xxii (1926), 725; Bernadotte Schmitt, *The Coming of the War 1914* (N.Y., 1930), i. 13–18.

[4] Conrad, *Aus meiner Dienstzeit*, ii. 85.

In the same letter of 21 January, however, Moltke made other statements which deserve attention. In the case of a German mobilization which was inspired by Russian action, he said, it was doubtful whether France could refrain from taking similar measures. It must be assumed that France had some kind of an agreement covering the case of a Russo-German war and, in any event, 'two mobilized armies like the German and the French will not be able to stand side by side without resorting to war. . . . I believe, therefore, that Germany, when it mobilizes against Russia, must also reckon on a war with France.'[1] This being so, the bulk of German forces must be used at the outset against France. A quick decision could be expected here, however—Conrad seems to have assumed from subsequent exchanges that Moltke counted on a French war lasting only four weeks[2]—and when it had been reached German armies could be transported to the eastern front.[3]

At the very moment, then, that he was making commitments to Austria which increased the likelihood of war with Russia, Moltke insisted that the war must be fought in accordance with Schlieffen's prescription—that is, that it must start with a German attack on France. And this was to be true, apparently, regardless of France's attitude or of the general political situation in the west at the time the explosion came in the Balkans. Nothing could better illustrate the rigidity of thought in the German General Staff before 1914 or the dangerous pass to which its continued faith in the Schlieffen plan had brought it.[4]

Moltke had not, of course, dispatched his letter entirely on his own initiative. He informed Conrad that its contents had been communicated to the emperor and to Chancellor Bülow.[5] This fact cannot, however, lighten the tremendous responsibility which he must bear for this critical turn in German policy. He, after all, was the military expert. He had facts at his disposal which indicated that the German and Austrian armies might well be at a numerical disadvantage in a two-front war; and to a man who had his country's welfare at heart, these facts should have constituted an injunction to caution. Yet,

[1] Conrad, *Aus meiner Dienstzeit*, i. 381–2. [2] Ibid., p. 374.

[3] Ibid., pp. 383–4.

[4] After the war Bethmann Hollweg wrote: 'Our soldiers had only one war plan, based on the infallible and not disproved assumption that a war for Germany must be a two front war.' *Betrachtungen zum Weltkriege* (Berlin, 1919), i. 156.

[5] Conrad, *Aus meiner Dienstzeit*, i. 384.

despite his professed horror for war, he had no objection to taking a step which invited a conflict of European scope.

The chief of staff's attitude may be explained in part by his fatalism, to which on occasion he gave open expression.[1] Nor was he alone in this, for many of the highest officers in the German army were convinced that war was just a matter of time. It was natural for them to argue, therefore—as General von Eisenhart-Rothe argued during the manœuvres of 1913—that Bismarck's old advice against preventive war was out of date[2] and that it was more realistic to assume that France and Russia were implacable enemies of Germany and to seize the first favourable opportunity to deal with them before their rapid re-arming jeopardized the nice calculations of Schlieffen. After the second Moroccan crisis the soldiers expressed sharp condemnation of the policies which had prevented war from breaking out at that time;[3] and, in 1912, an American politician heard a group of general officers in Silesia accuse the emperor of having made Germany ridiculous in 1905 and in 1911, adding that they would not permit him to do so again.[4] Army sentiment was not without effect on William II. The French ambassador noted in 1913 that 'the impatience of the soldiers' was obtaining 'a greater hold over [the emperor's] mind',[5] and, in November of the same year, William told the King of the Belgians that war with France was unavoidable and was emphatically supported by his chief of staff, who said, 'This time we must finish with them!'[6]

This same tendency had been present in military thinking in 1887, but at that time Bismarck had firmly prevented it from affecting the course of policy. It was Germany's tragedy that the man who occupied the highest civilian position of authority during the last years of peace had none of Bismarck's determination to keep the soldiers within their proper sphere. As he admits in his memoirs, Bethmann Hollweg was a man who deferred to military advice whenever questions of German security were being considered;[7] and this meant in the end that the great decision of 1914 was made by the soldiers.

The story of the crisis of 1914 has been told so often that it

[1] See, for instance, his statement to Conrad in February 1913 that 'sooner or later a European war would come in which Germanism and Slavism would be the chief antagonists'. Ibid. ii. 144.

[2] Vagts, *Militarism*, p. 365.

[3] Ibid.

[4] Ibid., p. 419.

[5] G. P. Gooch, *Studies in Diplomacy* (London, 1942), pp. 55–56.

[6] Eyck, *Wilhelm II*, p. 692.

[7] Bethmann Hollweg, *Betrachtungen*, i. 156–7.

need be touched on only lightly here. The two points that must be emphasized are, first, that Moltke not only honoured the pledge of 1909 but encouraged the Austrians to take the steps that made this necessary, and, second, that he was so firmly committed to the Schlieffen plan that he violated all the laws of common sense in order to assure its being put into operation without interference.

In the first days after the assassination at Sarajevo, both civil and military authorities in Germany were united in believing that the Austrian government must take strong action against the Serbs. On 5 July the emperor met with the Chancellor, the Under Secretary of State for Foreign Affairs, War Minister von Falkenhayn, Chief of Military Cabinet von Lyncker, and *Generaladjutant* von Plessen. He read them a letter from the Emperor of Austria and a memorandum from the Ballplatz, both of which made it clear that the Austrians were contemplating a declaration of war and wished, before they took this step, to be assured of German support. All participants in the Kronrat agreed that they should be encouraged to go ahead and that Germany should come to Austria's aid in the event of Russian intervention.[1]

In agreeing with this decision, Bethmann Hollweg at least was probably won over by arguments advanced to prove that neither Russia nor France would in fact intervene in an Austro-Serb conflict. When in subsequent weeks—and especially after the Austrian ultimatum to Serbia—it became apparent that the Russian government would not disinterest itself in the plight of Serbia, Bethmann's position changed, and he sought desperately to find some way of reaching a peaceful solution in the Balkans.[2] For the soldiers, on the contrary, once the promise had been given to Austria there was no turning back; and the menacing news from St. Petersburg merely convinced them that nothing was now to be expected from negotiation and that it was more important to take the measures necessary to assure the success of their war plan.[3] In their eyes the crucial factor

[1] See Plessen's account, and the account of General Bertrab, Moltke's deputy, of a subsequent discussion with the emperor, in *Deutsche Gesandtschaftsberichte zum Kriegsausbruch 1914* (Berlin, 1937), p. 14. These are cited in Albertini, *Le origini*, ii (Milan, 1943), 146.

[2] For a contrary view, see Albertini, *Le origini*, ii. 441–54, where Bethmann is accused of playing a double game throughout.

[3] In his *Lebenserinnerungen*, p. 141, Groener says that when he heard of the

seemed to be that of timing. They were reasonably confident that, even if Russia started to mobilize her forces before Germany did, they would have little trouble in catching up, thanks to the excellence of their mobilization schedules. But could the same be said of the Austrians, who would have to hold the Galician front if war came? When, on 29 July, word reached Berlin of the measures of partial Russian mobilization, Moltke and Falkenhayn permitted themselves to be persuaded by Bethmann that similar measures were not yet necessary for Germany.[1] But, on the following day, the chief of staff's anxiety concerning Austria led him to take a step which cut directly across Bethmann's policy and made war virtually inevitable.

Without making any attempt to inform the emperor or the Chancellor, Moltke, on the evening of 30 July, sent a telegram to Field Marshal Conrad, urging him to mobilize his forces against Russia at once. According to a supplementary telegram from the military attaché in Berlin,[2]

> Moltke said that he judged the situation to be critical if the Austrian-Hungarian monarchy did not mobilize against Russia immediately. The excuse for counter-measures is provided by the Russian declaration . . . [Austria must] reject England's renewed proposal for the maintenance of peace. For the survival of Austria-Hungary, fighting through [*Durchhalten*] the European war is the only means. Germany will go along with her unconditionally.

The mention of England was a reference to an endeavour on the part of Grey to seek a basis for direct negotiation between Austria and Russia, an effort which was being supported by Bethmann. The Chancellor, indeed, was applying all the pressure he could in Vienna to make the Austrians consider this solution. When they received Moltke's advice to disregard Bethmann's efforts, the Austrians wondered, not unnaturally, who was in real authority in Berlin.[3] They did not, however, hesitate long and, at noon on 31 July, followed Moltke's counsel and ordered full mobilization against Russia.[4]

Simultaneously, the German government dispatched an ultimatum to St. Petersburg and, when no answer was received,

Austrian ultimatum he considered war unavoidable. This may be taken as a representative view in the General Staff.

[1] Albertini, *Le origini*, ii. 497–8.

[2] Conrad, *Aus meiner Dienstzeit*, iv. 152.

[3] Ibid., p. 153.

[4] See Ziekursch, *Politische Geschichte*, iii. 288; Eyck, *Wilhelm II*, pp. 748–50.

declared war on Russia on 1 August. This step, which even some of the soldiers regarded as unnecessary and ill-advised, was apparently due primarily to the urging of Moltke, who by this time had superseded the Chancellor in all but name.[1] It is likely that the chief of staff spent very little time in weighing the political advantages and disadvantages of the declaration against Russia. His thoughts were by now concentrated almost exclusively on the west, for the Schlieffen plan, as we have seen, demanded a German attack on France. The necessary dispositions for this had been made, and a note to the Belgian government, demanding free passage for German troops, had been drafted by the chief of staff as early as 26 July—two days before the outbreak of war in Serbia.

To Moltke's consternation, however, the emperor and the Chancellor were still uncertain about the advisability of attacking France, and their doubts were fortified by a wire from the ambassador in London on 1 August expressing the view that, if Germany refrained from an assault on France, Great Britain would remain neutral. The ambassador's opinion, which was based on a faulty interpretation of some remarks by Sir William Tyrrell, was not sound, but its effect on Moltke is instructive. The chief of staff explained to his royal master that it would be impossible at this late date to change Germany's war plans and arrange for an initial assault in the east for this would invite disaster.[2] Bethmann and the emperor had no answer for this and gave way, although William grumbled, 'Your uncle would have given me a different answer'.[3] An ultimatum had already been sent to Paris; the note to the Belgian government was now delivered. When both were rejected, Germany declared war on France and the invasion of Belgium began.

The student of German policy in the summer of 1914 cannot help but be struck by the fact that the crucial decisions were made by the soldiers and that, in making them, they displayed an almost complete disregard for political considerations. Historians are in general agreement that the responsibility for the First World War was not exclusively German. Yet, thanks to the soldiers, it seemed to be exclusively German to a large part

[1] See, however, Schmitt, *Coming of the War*, ii. 320–1.

[2] See Kühlmann, *Erinnerungen*, pp. 390–1. Moltke had terminated work on the großen Ostaufmarsch' in 1913 on the ground that it was superfluous. See Ritter, *Schlieffenplan*, p. 35. Cf. Groener, *Lebenserinnerungen*, pp. 145 f.

[3] Görlitz, *General Staff*, p. 155.

of the western world in 1914. In their insistence upon fighting their war *à la* Schlieffen, the military chiefs had seen to it that Germany took the initiative in declaring war on Russia and France and that she invaded Belgium; and these were actions which could not be hidden and which could not help but hurt the German cause in the eyes of the neutral Powers. Even if we accept the point of view of the soldiers that, for technical reasons, these steps were necessary—and this is not a position that is easy to defend—we must still ask why some attempt had not been made, by careful propaganda, to prepare the outside world at least for the advance through Belgium. The truth of the matter seems to be that the General Staff, far from asking the Foreign Office to devise a political justification for the invasion, did not see fit even to inform that organization of their plans except in the most general and misleading terms.[1]

In the fateful summer of 1914 there was, in short, none of that co-ordination of political and military strategy which is desirable when a nation goes to war. The technicians were too naïve to understand the necessity of such co-ordination. They had overborne the civilian authorities and brought war on in their own way, inspired by a faith in the Schlieffen plan that was so strong that it made political maladroitness seem unimportant.

But even when they are victorious in war, nations do not always escape the consequences of their political mistakes. In this case, Germany's soldiers could not win the conflict to which their fatalism and the inflexibility of their operational thinking had led them.

Note on the Activities of the Naval Attachés in the Pre-war Period

Perhaps the most striking example of the evils of political reporting on the part of military representatives at German embassies in the pre-war period is that afforded by the activities of the naval attachés in London. These men regarded themselves less as technical experts than as special envoys whose duty in London was to represent the interests of the imperial navy and to see that the Tirpitz expansion programme was not jeopardized by concessions made by the diplomats. As the diplo-

[1] There can be little doubt that Holstein and Bülow knew of the invasion plan. See Hutten-Czapski, *Sechzig Jahre*, i. 371–3. It is less easy to determine how much Bethmann knew. See Ritter in *Deutschland und Europa*, pp. 94–95.

mats sought a formula which would prevent the growing naval rivalry from causing an irrevocable breach between London and Berlin, the naval attachés made statements to British officials which could not be reconciled with the Foreign Office desire for a settlement; while in their reports to Berlin they represented British offers of agreement as attempts to dupe Germany. The unhappy effect of these tactics on the emperor, whose faith in his naval attachés equalled his confidence in his military informants, is evident in his marginal comments on their reports. If the failure to reach a naval accord was one of the causes of war in 1914, the naval attachés must share the responsibility for that conflict.

In February 1912 Bethmann Hollweg, struggling to find a basis for agreement with the British, complained to the emperor that his efforts were being crossed by the naval attaché, Captain Widenmann. In a recent conversation with Admiral Jellicoe, Widenmann had intimated that Germany's goal was a 2:3 capital ship ratio with Britain. This statement, wrote Bethmann, would give rise in England to

> incorrect notions concerning the goals which German policy is currently pursuing relative to the question of an accord over the naval armament of the two Powers. Above all, this incident is likely to confuse the issue there and to *impair seriously that confidence* which is the basis and necessary prerequisite for the favourable continuation of the exchange of views recently inaugurated. . . . Your Majesty will agree with me that the unity of direction in imperial foreign policy must be most seriously jeopardized, when it is interfered with by the military agents assigned to foreign missions, without instructions from the agencies responsible for this policy. . . . I therefore request most respectfully the authority to disapprove [Captain Widenmann's] . . . action and to issue to him a warning that he must in the future remain within the boundaries of his assigned functions.[1]

William's indignation at this request is made clear in the marginalia. With respect to the required disapproval of Widenmann's action, he wrote: 'No! He is an officer and can be disapproved only by the Supreme War Lord, not by his civilian superior.' Beneath this he added: 'I see in Widenmann's conversation absolutely no violation of his boundaries or his assigned functions.'[2]

[1] A. von Tirpitz, *Der Aufbau der deutschen Weltmacht* (Berlin, 1924), p. 294.
[2] Ibid.

Widenmann's nominal superior in London was the ambassador, Count Wolff-Metternich. Fully aware that the expansion of Germany's naval programme was poisoning Anglo-German relations, Metternich had repeatedly expressed his concern over the attaché's undisguised hatred of the English and his insistence upon portraying as insincere all English attempts to find a basis for naval agreement.

As early as December 1911 he urged Bethmann to recall Widenmann. When this advice was disregarded he adopted the practice of accompanying the attaché's reports with long refutations written for the emperor's eyes. This vain expedient was strongly supported by the Foreign Office, where Metternich's fears were shared; and, in March 1912, Kiderlen-Wächter informed the emperor that Widenmann's reports 'breathed a hatred and a distrust of England which, in my respectful opinion, are not justified and which . . . can only produce an unnecessary aggravation of the difficulties of our relations with England'.[1] This last stand of the professional diplomats, however, came to nothing. The emperor was now completely under the influence of his naval advisers, and he was in no mood to suffer criticism of his London informant. Instead, his long accumulated wrath descended on the head of Metternich. William had for some time regarded the ambassador as 'too flabby'[2] and as 'absolutely unteachable in naval questions'.[3] Now he concluded that 'Metternich is hopelessly incurable!'[4] and insisted that he be recalled.

The fall of Metternich was a kind of symbol for the complete victory of the Tirpitz fleet policy. In addition, it was proof that, in the sphere of policy determination, the naval staff and their foreign reporters had won the kind of position to which the army chiefs led by Waldersee had aspired in the 1880's. Certainly, as far as the vital London post was concerned, the naval attachés now completely disregarded the wishes of the chief of mission and the Foreign Office and followed the directions of the *Reichsmarineamt*. When Widenmann was transferred in September 1912 he was replaced by Captain E. von Müller, who shared all of his prejudices and pretensions. Müller nailed his colours to the mast in a letter to Tirpitz written shortly after his appointment:

[1] *Große Politik*, xxxi. 199.
[2] Ibid. xxiv. 116.
[3] Ibid., xxxi. 55.
[4] Ibid. xxxi. 194.

Experience teaches that when the inky diplomats want to accomplish anything, the making of concessions begins and, since England never gives anything for nothing—not even things which she doesn't own herself—one must be on guard that no conditions are proposed and championed by our diplomats that we—the Imperial Navy—cannot accept.[1]

Müller's fear of concessions was almost pathological. When, in June 1913, Winston Churchill, in private conversation with him, suggested the possibility of a naval holiday, Müller wrote to Tirpitz asking whether it would be wise to mention this conversation in his official report to Berlin, that is, in the report which would go to the Foreign Office and eventually to the emperor. Through a subordinate, Tirpitz answered that, in view of the 'universal desire for a permanent understanding with Britain', both the Reichstag and the Foreign Office might unfortunately be receptive to Churchill's idea. In the circumstances, then, it would be well for Müller to report the conversation as briefly as possible, and to state that the impression derived from it was that Churchill was seeking to delay or hinder the expansion of the German fleet because he feared that Britain could no longer maintain her superiority.[2] The naval attaché followed his instructions and twisted the report in a manner designed to prejudice the emperor against a possible arrangement.

In this plain distortion of the very purpose of diplomatic reporting, we can detect the bland assumption of the military and naval leaders that they alone had the right to determine the foreign policy of the empire. From this point until the outbreak of war, the attachés in London followed their own laws and determined, on the advice of their military superiors, what was fitting for the emperor's ears. In February 1914 Foreign Secretary von Jagow wrote in despair to his ambassador in London: 'Most disagreeable is the tendentious reporting of your naval attaché. Can you not keep him a bit more on leash? This everlasting baiting and calumniation of English policy is extraordinarily disturbing, especially since it is always used *en haut lieu* in argument against me.'[3]

[1] Tirpitz, *Aufbau*, pp. 355–6.

[2] Ibid., pp. 395–7.

[3] *Große Politik*, xxxvii. 105.

VIII

MILITARISM AND STATECRAFT
1914–1918

Laß es jetzt gut sein, Seni! Komm herab!
Der Tag bricht an, und Mars regiert die Stunde.
Wallensteins Tod

Die wahre Sicherheit unserer Zukunft, die wir anstreben müssen, kann niemals in der bloßen Machtvermehrung bestehen, sondern muss immer beruhen auf einer Verbindung von Macht und Politik.
HANS DELBRÜCK *in 1917.*

THE first two years of the World War were free from the clashes between civilian and military authority which had marked the wars of the unification period. Moltke and his successor Falkenhayn were too engrossed with the problems of military operations to think of political issues; and the Chancellor never attempted to interfere in the military conduct of the war. Yet this collaboration was purely adventitious, and it disappeared as soon as the civilian leaders began to face up to the problem which was posed by the campaigns of 1914 and 1915. For the tremendous, but inconclusive, battles of those years demonstrated that a definitive military victory for Germany was unlikely, if not impossible; and this brute fact forced the German government to consider the possibilities of ending the war, on terms not unfavourable to the nation, by negotiation.

The concessions to the enemy which would have been necessary to make any kind of negotiation feasible were, however, objectionable to the army High Command for strategical, political, and social reasons which will be discussed below; and, when Hindenburg and Ludendorff assumed leadership of the army in 1916, they did not hesitate to make their opposition felt. Because they were supported by powerful interest groups in the country and because public opinion in general, ignorant of the state of the war and uninformed concerning the issue at stake, had more confidence in the High Command than in the civilian leaders, they had their way. In the bitter political struggle that stretched from the end of 1916 until the middle of the following year, they created for themselves what has been called 'a silent dictatorship',[1] and in the subsequent period they were able to create and destroy chancellors at will, to force the dismissal of private servants of the emperor when their views did not coincide with their own, and to determine the objectives and the tactics of the Foreign Office.

In doing all this, however, they did not solve the dilemma in which Germany had been placed by the failure of the first campaigns and which was becoming increasingly difficult as the strength of the enemy grew. Stubbornly rejecting any suggestion that total victory might not be possible, the army chiefs sacrificed all other considerations to that of military expediency, generally discovering belatedly that their most inspired strokes of policy aided and comforted the enemy without bringing Germany any of the military advantages they had expected. Finally, having destroyed the last hopes of negotiation, they bolted into a desperate and ill-conceived campaign without making any attempt to co-ordinate their strategical thrust with a political offensive or to prepare public opinion in Germany for the possibility of failure. The result was not only defeat but revolution; and the world was provided with the classic illustration of the truth of Clemenceau's dictum that war is too serious a business to be entrusted to the direction of soldiers.

I

As the German armies drove across the borders of Belgium in 1914, a General Staff officer wrote in a letter: 'The spirit of the blessed Schlieffen accompanies us. The man who conceived all the ideas which we are executing will deserve the first monument when the campaign is over.'[2] The monuments that were erected after the first months of fighting, however, were humbler ones, and they did not celebrate a victory. The plan upon which so many hopes depended did, it is true, come perilously close to success. But from that moment when von Kluck's First Army—already worn out by six weeks of constant fighting—wheeled to the east rather than to the west of Paris and found itself attacked in the rear by Joffre's forces, things began to go wrong; and when Moltke conceived the unfortunate idea of committing his left wing to an offensive against Nancy, they went from bad to

[1] Görlitz, *General Staff*, p. 179.

[2] Groener, *Lebenserinnerungen*, p. 161.

worse. With the German armies caught in two violent and unco-ordinated battles, on the Marne and in Lorraine, the chief of staff, bewildered by the confused reports from the front, abandoned himself to that defeatism which had always been his dominant characteristic and permitted one of his subordinates to make the first critical decision of the war. Lieutenant-Colonel Hentsch, on 9 September, ordered Kluck's forces to break off hostilities and retreat behind the Aisne, and the German officer corps received a psychological blow from which it never fully recovered.[1]

Under energetic leadership, the situation in the west might still have been retrieved. Moltke, broken in spirit, retired from office on 14 September and was replaced by the War Minister, Erich von Falkenhayn. Momentarily at least, Falkenhayn seemed prepared to take up the fight with the vigour and determination that had characterized his parliamentary activity in peace-time; and he planned a resumption of the offensive in the Cambrai–Verdun sector. He was dissuaded by his chief of operations, Lieutenant-Colonel von Tappen, on the grounds that the planned attack would involve withdrawals in other sectors of the front, and decided instead to order his troops to assume the defensive along the line Noyon–Rheims–Verdun. With this decision, the whole theory of *Vernichtungsstrategie*, in which a generation of officers had been trained, was jettisoned, and the period of trench warfare was ushered in. In the words of one of the most thoughtful critics of modern strategy, 'if, on 9 September 1914, the German command suffered a signal setback through the breakdown of its famous plan of campaign, it is the 15th of that month, the morning on which Falkenhayn decided against a return to the mobile strategy of the first weeks, that must be considered to be the real turning point of the war'.[2]

This momentous change in strategy and the effect it was certain to have on the duration of the war, and—given the relative resources of the antagonists—its probable result, was not appreciated by the German public. The main reason for this, of course, was the fact that the principle of mobility continued to be applied, with apparently successful results, on the

[1] For a dramatic account of the Hentsch mission, see E. O. Volkmann, *Am Tor der neueren Zeit* (Oldenburg, 1933), pp. 47–83.

[2] Rosinski, *German Army*, p. 91.

eastern front. The tremendous victory which the combined talents of Hindenburg, Ludendorff, and Hoffmann won over the Russians at Tannenberg in August, the smashing of Rennenkampf's armies at the battle of the Masurian Lakes on 9 September, and the daring thrust at Lodz in November, which threw back the Russian advance into Silesia, had an exhilarating effect upon domestic opinion and kept the hope of imminent and total victory alive. But Falkenhayn was less impressed by the success of the Schlieffen strategy in the east and unconvinced that it could produce decisive results. His eyes were fixed on the west, which he considered to be the crucial theatre of the war, and he had committed himself to a strategy of holding on grimly to the positions won in the initial fighting and, periodically, of launching limited offensives which were designed to harass and wear down his antagonists. In November he struck an offensive blow of this nature at Ypres, simultaneously turning a deaf ear to the urgent pleas of Hindenburg and Ludendorff for reinforcements which would enable them, they argued, to expand the operation at Lodz into a massive encirclement of the main Russian armies in the bend of the Vistula. The plea of the eastern command that the war could be won in their theatre was, Falkenhayn wrote later, based on sophisms.

> This argument paid no heed either to the true character of the struggle for existence, in the most exact sense of the word, in which our enemies were engaged no less than we, nor to their strength of will. It was a grave mistake to believe that our western enemies would give way, if and because Russia was beaten. No decision in the East, even though it were as thorough as it was possible to imagine, could spare us from fighting to a conclusion in the West.[1]

Even the eventual failure at Ypres did not shake Falkenhayn's opinion. It is true that in 1915, because of the renewed Russian threat to Galicia, he allowed himself to be persuaded to turn his attention to the eastern front and to come to the aid of the hard-pressed Austrian armies. But the victory which Falkenhayn won at Gorlice in May 1915 and the successful assault on Warsaw, Kovno, and Novo-Georgievsk in August of the same year, were conceived as frontal attacks with limited objectives; Falkenhayn vigorously opposed all of Ludendorff's and Hoffmann's plans for more ambitious operations; and at the end of

[1] General von Falkenhayn, *The German General Staff and its Decisions, 1914–1916* (New York, 1920), p. 61.

1915 the Russian armies, though battered, were still in the field. Moreover, the chief of staff seems to have had no systematic plans for future operations in the east. His thoughts for 1916 centred on another limited offensive in the west to test the will of the allies—this time an assault on the great French fortress of Verdun.

If the chief of staff succeeded for the most part in imposing his strategical views on the army, he did so with difficulty, and the execution of his plans was accompanied by disputes which bade fair to split the army hierarchy into quarrelsome factions. Mention has been made above of the interdepartmental rivalry which existed in the army administration in the pre-war years, especially after the reorganization of 1883.[1] But the officer corps had never, in peace-time or in war, been torn by such violent dissension as in the years 1915 and 1916. Despite the fact that Falkenhayn combined in his own person the offices of chief of staff and War Minister,[2] and the further fact that he was strongly supported by the Chief of the Military Cabinet, General von Lyncker,[3] he was unable to maintain more than a semblance of unity in the upper reaches of the army.[4] The victories of Hindenburg and Ludendorff at Tannenberg and the Masurian Lakes had given those commanders a stature that was the equal of his own, and they had ardent champions, not only in their own headquarters, but in Berlin and Spa as well. Falkenhayn was accused by the 'easterners' of having, not only no recipe for victory, but no faith in ultimate success, and it was charged that he professed a hopeless policy of 'holding on' [*Durchhalten*] instead of attempting to smash the enemy. Hoffmann, the third and not the least gifted member of the eastern team, wrote in his diary in December 1914: 'The method of conducting the war in the west terrifies me. Falkenhayn is the

[1] See above, Chapter VI, pp. 230–1.

[2] Falkenhayn had insisted on this presumably to avoid the kind of differences which had arisen between the chief of staff and the War Minister during the war of 1870.

[3] When Moltke's nerves broke down, Falkenhayn had been the Military Cabinet's candidate for his position; and Lyncker remained loyal to the chief of staff until 1916. See Schmidt-Bückeburg, *Militärkabinett*, pp. 243–4.

[4] Under Falkenhayn there was at least no open friction between the three army administrative agencies. When Hindenburg and Ludendorff took over the Supreme Command, there were sharp differences between them and the Military Cabinet on matters of appointment, while the War Ministry was often disregarded completely, even in matters which concerned it. See Groener, *Lebenserinnerungen*, pp. 341–3, and Schmidt-Bückeburg, *Militärkabinett*, pp. 255–6.

evil angel of our Fatherland and, unfortunately, he has His Majesty in his pocket.'[1] Those who felt as Hoffmann did were resolved that Falkenhayn's influence over the emperor must be broken and that he must be replaced by the strong men of the east.

The conflict between Falkenhayn and the eastern command raged for eighteen months, and the antagonists seemed at times more bent on destroying each other than on fighting the common foe.[2] At the beginning of 1915 the chief of staff sought to strengthen his position by breaking up the eastern combination, and he ordered Ludendorff's transfer to a new army which was being formed under the command of General von Linsingen. This Hindenburg was able to prevent only by a frantic, and almost tearful, telegram to the emperor. The eastern command in its turn seems to have had some influence in the sovereign's decision at this time to reduce Falkenhayn's functions by appointing a separate War Minister.[3] By the summer of 1915 the rivals had descended to the level of name-calling and petty vindictiveness, and correspondence between them was abusive on both sides. There is evidence that each party attempted to influence the press in its favour;[4] and the easterners in addition complained that their exploits received inadequate recognition in the communiqués of the High Command. This sort of thing has not, of course, been unknown in other armies and in other wars, but it is doubtful whether there are many cases in which it was carried as far as it was here. In October 1915, when Falkenhayn—feeling it necessary to support Austria by an attack on Serbia and wishing to strengthen the Bulgarians, who were threatened from the direction of Salonika—began to withdraw troops from the eastern front for these purposes, Hindenburg and Ludendorff regarded this as a personal attack upon their position, and the field marshal actually composed a formal

[1] M. Hoffmann, *Die Aufzeichnungen des Generalmajors Max Hoffmann* (2 vols., Berlin, 1930), i. 62.

[2] For the most detailed and penetrating discussion of the conflict, see John W. Wheeler-Bennett, *Wooden Titan: Hindenburg in Twenty Years of German History* (New York, 1936), pp. 34–74.

[3] Schmidt-Bückeburg (*Militärkabinett*, p. 255) says that Falkenhayn gave up the War Ministry gladly because the dual strain was too much for him. But see Karl Heinz Janssen, 'Die Wechsel in der Obersten Heeresleitung 1916', *Vierteljahrshefte für Zeitgeschichte*, vii (1959), 341.

[4] See G. von dem Knesebeck, *Die Wahrheit über den Propagandafeldzug und Deutschlands Zusammenbruch* (Munich, 1927), pp. 63ff.

protest against Falkenhayn's strategy, embodying in it a flat refusal to release any more divisions.[1] The chief of staff, thanks to the support of the emperor, once more had his way, but it was his last victory.

Later in his life, Hindenburg was to admit that this controversy was unfortunate and that, if Ludendorff and he had known the whole military and political situation, they might have been more charitable toward the chief of staff's ideas.[2] Even if due weight is given to this belated apology, however, it is difficult to avoid the conclusion that, as a strategist, Falkenhayn had grave limitations. As the chief of his railway section wrote,[3] he never conceived a really great goal—that is, one which, if attained, would have had a perceptible effect on the future course of the war. There is a good deal to be said for Hoffmann's argument that the chief of staff let slip two great opportunities, in late 1914 and in mid-1915, to encircle and destroy the bulk of Russia's existing armies,[4] and that he was equally blind to the possibilities offered in the southern war theatre. The victory over Serbia was never exploited to the full; and, when Conrad von Hötzendorff urged an all-out assault upon Italy in the spring of 1916, Falkenhayn proved as inflexibly opposed to this as he had been to the projects of his eastern rivals.[5] Even in the western theatre, which he stubbornly insisted must be given priority over the others, the strategy which he followed throughout 1915 achieved no positive results but, on the contrary, gave the enemy an opportunity to build up his reserves of man-power and material and to exert increasing pressure upon the German lines.

The deficiencies of Falkenhayn's direction of the war were revealed with brutal clarity in 1916. In February the chief of staff hurled his full strength against Verdun. In his report recommending this objective to the emperor, he argued that, to retain this strongpoint, 'the French General Staff would be compelled to throw in every man they have. If they do so, the forces of France will bleed to death—as there can be no question of a voluntary withdrawal—whether we reach our goal or not. . . . For an operation limited to a narrow front Germany will

[1] Wheeler-Bennett, *Wooden Titan*, pp. 62–65.

[2] Hindenburg, *Aus meinem Leben* (Leipzig, 1920), p. 130.

[3] Groener, *Lebenserinnerungen*, p. 315.

[4] Hoffmann, *Aufzeichnungen*, ii. 84, 105, 131, 231–2.

[5] Ibid., pp. 131–2. Oskar Regele, *Feldmarschall Conrad, Auftrag und Erfüllung, 1906–1918* (Vienna, 1958), pp. 386 ff.

not be compelled to spend herself so completely that all other fronts are practically drained.'[1] These assumptions proved sadly in error. If the French had frightful losses before Verdun, the German losses were almost equal in number. Aside from this, Falkenhayn's commitment at Verdun tied up German forces so completely that he was powerless to come to the aid of Austria when, in June, Brusilov's offensive crashed through the Austrian lines at Lutzk and threatened the security of the whole eastern front. The allied offensive on the Somme, in the same month, demonstrated further how inadequate his estimate of enemy capabilities had been.

By the summer of 1916 German armies were on the defensive on every front, and the decision of the Romanian government, in August 1916, to throw their lot in with the allies merely underlined the bankruptcy of Falkenhayn's strategy. The strain of the last campaigns had visibly aged the vigorous and confident commander of 1914;[2] and his own staff officers were now sending deputations to Generaladjutant von Plessen in the hope that he would convince the emperor that the chief of staff must be replaced.[3] When the Chancellor added his influence, pointing out that Falkenhayn had quite clearly lost what popular support he had had, William II reluctantly gave way.[4] At the end of August, Hindenburg was called to the west from Brest-Litovsk and elevated to Falkenhayn's position, while Ludendorff was appointed first quartermaster-general of the army and assigned equal responsibility with the aged field marshal for future operational decisions.

The new supreme commanders inherited a strategical position which was perilously grave. The numbers and strength of

[1] Wheeler-Bennett, *Wooden Titan*, p. 66.

[2] Groener, *Lebenserinnerungen*, p. 315.

[3] The chief of the operations section of the General Staff, Colonel von Tappen, was a staunch Falkenhayn man. The discontented officers deputized Colonel Bauer, the next ranking officer in the Staff, to go to Plessen. See M. Bauer, *Der große Krieg in Feld und Heimat* (Tübingen, 1921), pp. 103–4.

[4] Since early summer, Bethmann had been convinced that Hindenburg must replace Falkenhayn but had been reluctant to press the case for fear of being accused of meddling in military matters. See Valentini, *Kaiser und Kabinettschef*, pp. 137 ff., 231–3. Satisfaction with the change was not universal. On 28 August, in a diary entry which is reproduced in his memoirs, Groener mentions a conversation with Colonel von Marschall (called Greiff) of the Military Cabinet. This officer viewed the impending change with terror and said that Ludendorff, 'in his boundless vanity and pride', would bleed the German people white and then make the monarchy assume responsibility for this. Groener, ibid., p. 316.

Germany's antagonists had grown impressively during the Falkenhayn period. Her own resources in man-power and material were already showing alarming signs of depletion, and there was reason to fear that her chief ally, Austria-Hungary, might be on the verge of general collapse. An objective appraisal of the situation might have been expected to throw serious doubt on the possibility of Germany's now winning a definitive military victory over the coalition arrayed against her. The Chancellor had already concluded that this was not to be hoped for. General Hoffmann had reached the same conclusion as early as October 1915, and he, like Bethmann, had begun to think that Germany's best chance of survival lay in the possibility of arranging a negotiated peace with one or all of Germany's enemies.[1]

Hoffmann, however, was in this respect, as in others, a *rara avis* in the army hierarchy, who were, in general, cold to the idea of seeking peace by diplomacy. Certainly the new supreme commanders, as they began their fateful term of office, were unresponsive to any suggestions of this nature, and the policies which they adopted in support of their military plans showed a complete disregard of the factors upon which successful negotiation would depend.

II

The obstacles to the use of negotiation to end the war were not, of course, all created by the military. If there was any possibility of a negotiated peace during the First World War, it could certainly be realized only if the German government were prepared to accept what amounted to a return to the *status quo ante bellum*. To make the average German understand the necessity of such a settlement would have been difficult, although probably not impossible. The man in the street had regarded the coming of war in 1914 as the result of a deliberate attack upon Germany by Russia, supported by France and Great Britain. In his eyes, therefore, it was a justifiable struggle in defence of the Fatherland. He was sure, moreover, that Germany would triumph over her enemies; and this faith, although somewhat diminished by the disappointments of the Moltke–Falkenhayn period, had been strengthened by the appointment of Hindenburg and Ludendorff to the Supreme

[1] Hoffmann, *Aufzeichnungen*, i. 93–94.

Command.[1] The idea that Germany should seek peace with the war criminals of 1914 and that she should do so, moreover, on terms that did not provide for added protection against future attacks on Germany would have bewildered and angered him, the more so because nothing that he read in his daily newspaper indicated that there was the slightest danger of German defeat. The first task of any government that intended to try to negotiate with the enemy was, therefore, to prepare public opinion for the step by indicating the reasons that compelled it.

Any such attempt, however, would have been opposed by the majority of the political parties and by powerful groups of vested economic interest, for they were firmly opposed to the thought of returning to the *status quo*. Of the parties, only the Social Democrats could claim to be preponderantly favourable to a peace of reconciliation, and even they had a wing which insisted that Germany must seek some territorial compensation for the suffering caused by the war.[2] The other parties without exception were annexationist to some degree; and the parliamentary bloc which controlled the Reichstag in the first two years of the war—the so-called *Kriegszielmehrheit*, composed of the National Liberals, the Centre party, and the Conservatives—were impassioned supporters of a programme of expansionist war aims which called for accretions of territory in both east and west. The groups outside the Reichstag were even more important. The president of the Pan-German League, Heinrich Class,[3] and Alfred Hugenberg, who was chief director of Krupp's, joint chairman of the chambers of commerce of Essen, Mühlheim and Oberhausen and president of the *Bergbaulicher Verein*, a union of the most important Ruhr concerns, had joined hands in August 1914 to promote what they called the *Kriegszielbewegung*. A memorandum on war aims drafted by them at the beginning of the following year formed the basis

[1] For an interesting appraisal of the popular reaction to the change in the High Command, see Albrecht Mendelssohn Bartholdy, *The War and German Society* (New Haven, 1937), pp. 25–26.

[2] In March 1915 the *Frankfurter Volksstimme*, a socialist paper, asserted that 'the renunciation of all demands of annexation is in itself not a serviceable programme. Social Democracy must put forward positive demands, and these demands can and must include modification in maps. All must not remain as it was.' Hans W. Gatzke, *Germany's Drive to the West* (Baltimore, 1950), pp. 18–19. This work is the most thorough study of the evolution of Germany's western war aims.

[3] On Class's philosophy and his important role in the annexationist movement, see his memoirs, *Wider den Strom* (Leipzig, 1932).

of the Petition of the Six Economic Organizations which was sent to the Chancellor in May 1915. This document, signed by representatives of the *Zentralverband Deutscher Industrieller*, the *Bund der Industriellen*, the *Bund der Landwirte*, the *Deutscher Bauernbund*, the *Reichsdeutscher Mittelstandsverband*, and the *Christliche Deutsche Bauernvereine*, demanded a truly impressive list of annexations when the war was won. Belgium was to be made militarily and economically dependent on Germany. France was to lose her coastal districts as far as the mouth of the Somme, as well as the district of Briey, the coal country of the north and the *Pas-de-Calais*, and the fortresses of Verdun, Longwy, and Belfort. 'A colonial empire adequate to satisfy Germany's manifold economic interests' was also demanded, in addition to the 'annexation of at least parts of the Baltic provinces and of those territories which lie to the south of them', since 'the great addition to our manufacturing resources which we anticipate in the west must be counterbalanced by an equivalent annexation of agricultural territory in the east'.[1]

The political power of the organizations represented in this petition and of the other groups, like the Pan-German League and the Army League,[2] which supported it, was a source of great concern to the moderates in the government, and in the first years of the war Bethmann-Hollweg, perhaps characteristically, had found it expedient to assume a highly equivocal position with regard to Germany's post-war objectives.[3] The Chancellor became aware, however, that the facts of Germany's military situation made the realization of the annexationist programme, or anything faintly resembling it, impossible; and, as he became himself more convinced that it was necessary to seek peace by negotiation, he may have hoped that the industrial and agrarian interests, the Pan-Germans, and the politicians would also face up to realities. If he did so, he was putting too high an estimate on the political intelligence of these groups, for they persisted in their demands until the very eve of the

[1] Gatzke, *Germany's Drive to the West*, pp. 38–47.

[2] The work of the Army League is described in the memoirs of its founder, General A. Keim, *Erlebtes und Erstrebtes* (Hannover, 1925). Its official magazine, *Die Wehr*, had a circulation of 108,000. It was annexationist from the beginning of the war. Gatzke, *Germany's Drive to the West*, p. 29. On the influence of the Pan-German League, see Alfred Kruck, *Geschichte des Alldeutschen Verbandes, 1890–1939* (Wiesbaden, 1954), especially pp. 66–80.

[3] 'For the sake of German unity no policy could be conducted during the war but a policy of the "diagonal".' Bethmann-Hollweg, *Betrachtungen*, ii. 35.

country's collapse. Moreover, their programme was supported by the army, and this support proved decisive, since the army became the controlling factor in German politics after the elevation of Hindenburg and Ludendorff to the High Command.

In explaining the army's support of the annexationist programme, it is not necessary to attempt to prove a community of economic interest between the officer corps and the members of the Six Economic Organizations. In view of the fact that the backbone of the officer corps had always been supplied by the old landholding families of the east and that the post-1870 corps had been expanded for the most part by recruits from the wealthiest middle-class families, it is doubtless true that economic considerations played no negligible part in determining the attitude of many officers towards the question of Germany's war aims. But other factors were fully as important, if not more so, in the thinking of the army hierarchy on this subject.

Certainly the question of future military security was a primary consideration among the highest officers of the army. The army command of 1870 had been dissatisfied even with the notable acquisitions which Germany had made as a result of her victory over Napoleon III, and the strength of Belfort and Verdun had been a perpetual reminder to General Staff officers of what they considered to have been excessive leniency on Bismarck's part. The very existence of an independent Belgium had come to represent to them a threat to German security; Schlieffen had lived in fear that the French would anticipate his plans by invading that country before German mobilization was complete. The future possession of Liège and the Flanders coast seemed indispensable to many staff officers of the war period, and some of them advocated the complete absorption of Belgium in an expanded Reich. The Belgian question was, indeed, one matter on which even Falkenhayn and Ludendorff possessed roughly similar views. In 1916 Falkenhayn had told the Chancellor that

> as far as the future of Belgium is concerned, there can be no doubt that the country must remain at our disposal as an area for the initial assembly of our troops, for the protection of the most important German industrial region, and as a hinterland for our position on the Flanders coast, which is indispensable for our maritime importance. From this demand automatically arises the necessity of

unconditional military domination of Belgium by Germany. . . . Without this . . . Germany would lose the war in the west.[1]

On 23 July of the same year Ludendorff was writing to a friend that 'Belgium's dependence [on us] must be an economic, military, and political one'.[2]

German security in the east also seemed to necessitate the annexation of new territories, for here the Germans had been poorly endowed by nature and there was no natural defensive barrier against the threat of Slavdom. Among the soldiers there was little agreement concerning what specific areas must be taken or in what form they should be attached to Germany. General von Seeckt, who was building in the east the reputation which was to make him the leader of Germany's post-war army, thought in terms of a system of German satellite states which would stretch from the Atlantic Ocean to Persia.[3] Hindenburg, who—as we gather from his attitude during the Brest-Litovsk negotiations of 1918—seemed to envisage a future of periodic wars with Russia, wanted to acquire land in the Baltic states and Poland which would enable him to manœuvre his left wing.[4] Ludendorff, more conscious than either of the others of the economic requirements of modern war, was as intent upon securing the grain lands of the Ukraine as he was on increasing Germany's war potential by industrial annexations in the west.[5] But, however they might differ in their specific ambitions, Germany's military leaders were united in opposing any return to the military position of 1914. The security of the nation, they insisted, forbade the re-establishment of the *status quo*.

And so, for that matter, did the maintenance of the social system of Germany, upon which the very position of the German army depended. Hans Gatzke has pointed out, with convincing documentation, that the basic aim of the *Kriegszielbewegung* was the maintenance and strengthening of the existing political, social, and economic order.[6] The intimation in the speech from the throne of 4 August 1914 that the end of the war would bring

[1] Gatzke, *Germany's Drive to the West*, p. 81.

[2] Knesebeck, *Propagandafeldzug*, p. 158.

[3] Seeckt Papers, Stück 90: Seeckt to General von Winterfeldt, 29 October 1915.

[4] See John W. Wheeler-Bennett, *The Forgotten Peace: Brest-Litovsk* (New York, 1939), p. 109.

[5] Arthur Rosenberg, *The Birth of the German Republic* (London, 1931), pp. 134–5.

[6] Gatzke, *Germany's Drive to the West*, pp. 130–1 and *passim*.

political and social reforms had led Heinrich Class to groan: 'Um Gotteswillen, damit ist der Krieg innenpolitisch verloren!'[1] The repetition of this hint in Bethmann's speech of December 1914 and in the speech from the throne in January 1916 led the ruling classes to fear that their existing privileges would be curtailed unless they did something about it. It became their hope that a strong peace might seduce the masses into a materialistic torpor and save Germany from being drawn into 'the democratic swamp';[2] it became their fixed belief that nothing would do more to promote social revolution than a peace which brought no tangible gains to Germany. As Baron von Gebsattel of the Pan-German League expressed it, renunciation of annexations would bring 'disappointment and embitterment . . . and the people, disappointed after all its achievements, will rise. The Monarchy will be endangered, even overthrown, and thereby the fate of our people will be sealed.'[3]

The fact that Gebsattel was a retired general is not without significance, for his views were shared by many in the officer corps. Of all the vested interests in Germany the armed services stood to lose most from political and social reform. Any extension of the principles of parliamentary government was bound to lead to the very kind of civilian control over the army that the military chiefs had been fighting since 1848. The reform of the Prussian electoral system, now being demanded by the parties of the left, would have the same effect. The rehabilitation of the War Ministry and the abolition of the Military Cabinet, the destruction of the feudal relationship between the king-emperor and his officers and the revolutionizing of selection and promotion procedures, the introduction of the militia system in place of the standing army—these and other dangerous changes could be expected if democracy or socialism resulted from the war. For the sake of its very existence, the army had to bring the German people territorial advantages which would drown the demands of its critics in shouts of enthusiasm and gratitude, and would leave the monarchical system stronger than it had been in 1914.

[1] Class, *Wider den Strom*, p. 307. Kruck, *Geschichte des Alldeutschen Verbandes*, p. 90.

[2] See the memorandum of Generallandschaftsdirektor Kapp to the Chancellor, May 1916, in R. H. Lutz, ed., *Fall of the German Empire* (2 vols., Stanford, 1932), i. 103.

[3] Ibid., p. 359. The same point was made in the so-called Petition of the Intellectuals, sent to the Chancellor in July 1916. See Class, *Wider den Strom*, pp. 395–8; Gatzke, *Germany's Drive to the West*, pp. 117–21.

Because a negotiated peace made the attainment of their territorial ambitions impracticable, the military leaders in the second half of the war did everything in their power to make it impossible. It was this that precipitated the struggle between Bethmann-Hollweg and the High Command which led in the end to the Chancellor's dismissal.

III

At the very moment when the German High Command was being reorganized in August 1916 there were indications that one at least of Germany's enemies was ready to discuss peace terms. The Russians were disillusioned and war-weary. As early as the autumn of 1915 the dismissal of Grand Duke Nikolas Nikolayevitch as commander-in-chief of the Russian armies had indicated a flagging of determination to fight on, for the grand duke had been an inveterate foe of the Germans. In July 1916 the Vice-President of the Duma, Protopopov, held conversations with Hugo Stinnes in Stockholm in which he expressed a personal desire for peace negotiations and intimated that there was a strong party in Russia of the same persuasion. The sudden dismissal in this same month of the pro-allied Foreign Minister Sazonov seemed to give additional weight to Protopopov's suggestions, for this event was the preface to the ascendancy of the President of the Council, Stürmer, a member of the empress's circle and a man with strong German sympathies. To some observers in Germany, these events seemed to indicate that peace with Russia could be had for the asking.[1]

The key to peace with Russia, however, was Russian Poland which had been in German hands since August 1915. Whatever other terms the Tsarist government might be prepared to accept, it could not agree to a settlement which did not return the greater part of Poland, with its capital Warsaw, to Russian possession. This possibility the German military leaders were unwilling to consider.

In July 1916, General von Beseler, the Governor-General of Warsaw, prepared a memorandum in which he advanced the notion that the German creation of a kingdom of Poland would permit the raising of at least three divisions of Polish volunteers, and that this would be the first step towards the establishment

[1] See Wheeler-Bennett, *The Forgotten Peace*, p. 9.

of a strong Polish army fighting for the German cause.[1] This paper was shown to Ludendorff, at this time still at eastern headquarters, and was then sent, with his enthusiastic support, to the Chancellor.

In his account of the Polish policy subsequently followed by Germany, Bethmann-Hollweg admits that his immediate reaction was to oppose any action along the line suggested by Beseler until he had a clearer picture of what was going on inside Russia.[2] This was a sensible attitude. But the soldiers had no desire to be hampered by caution or common sense; and, after the reorganization of the High Command in August, Ludendorff insisted on the implementation of the Beseler plan. He was to claim later on,[3] that he had been inadequately informed by the Chancellor concerning Russian affairs and had not even known of new conversations between Protopopov and the Hamburg banker Warburg which took place in October; and he implied that, but for this, he might not have been so precipitate. There is no reason, however, to doubt Bethmann's story that he forwarded all available information concerning the possibility of peace with Russia to Hindenburg, and that it had no effect. On 13 October the field marshal informed Bethmann that none of the reports reaching him gave him any assurance of an imminent settlement with Russia; therefore, military considerations demanded the raising of Polish troops as quickly as possible.[4] Without apparently making any new attempt to approach the Russians through private or diplomatic channels, Bethmann deferred to the military judgement;[5] and, on 5 November 1916, the German government proclaimed the establishment of an independent Poland, appealing at the same time for Polish volunteers.[6]

Prince Bülow described this decision as the greatest German

[1] Hutten-Czapski, *Sechzig Jahre*, ii. 290. The author was appointed in 1914 as an expert on eastern affairs in the Political Division of the General Staff and was later assigned to Beseler's office. On earlier suggestions that Polish troops might be raised, see ibid., pp. 281, 289, and Hoffmann, *Aufzeichnungen*, ii. 151–2.

[2] Bethmann-Hollweg, *Betrachtungen*, ii. 94.

[3] Erich Ludendorff, *Urkunden der Obersten Heeresleitung* (2. Aufl., Berlin, 1921), p. 300.

[4] Bethmann-Hollweg, *Betrachtungen*, ii. 95.

[5] Bethmann defends his yielding to the military by saying in effect that he never believed the Russians wanted peace and that, in any case, the Germans had to proclaim Polish freedom lest the Allies anticipate them in this. In general, his apologia is unconvincing and leaves the impression that he preferred not to fight on this issue. Ibid., ii. 95–106.

[6] Hutten-Czapski, *Sechzig Jahre*, ii. 304 ff.; Conze, *Polnische Nation*, pp. 209–20.

blunder of the war.[1] This, like a good many of the former Chancellor's opinions, is exaggerated; but the proclamation of the Polish kingdom, nevertheless, had far-reaching and unfortunate effects. If there had been a possibility of Russo-German negotiations before November, there was none after. The German declaration set off a series of violent attacks upon Stürmer in the Russian Duma, and the Tsar was compelled to dismiss him and to restore power to the nationalist, pro-allied parties.

At the same time, the military advantages which Beseler and Ludendorff had predicted would result from the declaration never materialized; nor could they do so in view of the territorial ambitions of the German military leaders. The Poles might have been willing to raise an army big enough to permit the transfer of German divisions to the western front[2] had they been given any assurance that their new kingdom would be territorially viable and politically independent. It was precisely this kind of assurance that the military leaders were unprepared to extend. Ludendorff, having blocked the return of Poland to Russia, was disinclined to allow it to escape from German control, either now or in the future. He had seen to it that no clear delineation of Polish frontiers was included in the text of the proclamation, thus leaving the door open for future German annexations.[3] In the months that followed, although he permitted the establishment of a provisional state council, he prevented its being given any real powers and he steadfastly resisted all suggestions of elections for a Polish diet, although this had been promised to the Poles in a supplementary declaration of 11 November. Moreover, while insisting on the raising of a Polish army, he refused to authorize the creation of an independent Polish command under Pilsudski, the man best qualified for the position, or to allow the inclusion in the new force of those Polish legions which had joined the Austrians earlier in the war. Finally, he became interested in the creation of a German puppet state in Lithuania and made promises of Wilna and adjoining Polish districts to pro-German elements there.[4]

[1] Monts, *Erinnerungen*, p. 171.

[2] Ludendorff expected four divisions to be raised within ten days of the declaration. Hoffmann, *Aufzeichnungen*, i. 148.

[3] On Beseler's position on self-government and the question of future German annexations, see Hutten-Czapski, *Sechzig Jahre*, ii. 275 ff.

[4] Ibid., pp. 339, 350, 355–6, 379, and, on the complicated question of the

Polish patriots, not unnaturally, came to believe that, even if they fought for Germany, they could expect few tangible signs of gratitude. This realization led to dissatisfaction which soon hardened into passive resistance to all German designs; and, by the spring of 1917, Poland, far from adding to German strength, was a centre of disaffection and a receptive target for allied propaganda.

The Polish affair was the first case in which the desires of the new Supreme Command were given precedence over broader considerations of politics. But it did not stand alone, and the unhappy fate of Bethmann-Hollweg's peace note of December 1916 supplied a new illustration of the extent to which the army was now, in fact, controlling German diplomacy.

In August 1916, at an imperial conference of military and civilian leaders, Bethmann had urged that Germany must seek peace and that the best method of doing so was through the good offices of President Wilson. The American president should be told, the Chancellor suggested, that Germany was prepared to negotiate and that she was willing, moreover, to give up Belgium, with the reservation that her relations with that country would be settled through direct negotiation after its restitution.[1]

In stressing the Belgian question, Bethmann had placed his finger on the crucial issue in any potential negotiations with the Western Powers,[2] and it is interesting to note what happened to his proposal concerning Belgium between August and December. The efforts to secure Wilson's services as a mediator were defeated by the President's absorption in the political campaign in the United States, and the German Chancellor hit upon the idea of issuing a declaration in behalf of peace on his own initiative, a declaration, moreover, which would make some reference to Germany's war aims. After securing the emperor's assent to this plan, he entered into negotiations with Count Burian, the Austrian Foreign Minister, in order that the interests of Germany's ally should be protected. The most significant aspect of these talks, however, was that Hindenburg was regularly consulted as they proceeded, and his views and those of Ludendorff inevitably coloured the end result.[3] Hindenburg,

legions, pp. 340–3, 366. Ludendorff says that Bethmann agreed that Wilna should go to Lithuania as early as August. *Urkunden*, pp. 298–9.

[1] Karl Helfferich, *Der Weltkrieg* (3 vols., Berlin, 1919), ii. 351.

[2] See the comments in J. V. Bredt, *Die belgische Neutralität* (Berlin, 1929), pp. 154–5, 168.

[3] See Erich Ludendorff, *Meine Kriegserinnerungen* (Berlin, 1920), pp. 243–5.

for instance, made it clear in November that he would insist upon guarantees for German security in Belgium and he indicated that these would include the possession of Liège and surrounding territory, German ownership or control of Belgian railways, a close economic relationship between the two countries, and recognition of Germany's right to occupy Belgium whenever it suited her purpose.[1] The Chancellor raised no specific objections to these demands but they must have aroused his strong misgivings. He knew at any rate that their disclosure would have the worst possible effect. He therefore strove to leave the question of Belgian guarantees conveniently vague in the programme of war aims agreed upon between the emperor, Burian, and the Supreme Command in late November, and in this he succeeded. But this meant that when the long discussed peace note was handed to the American chargé on 12 December, for communication to the Allied Powers, it gave no specific definition of war aims at all and did little beyond assert Germany's willingness to consider peace and her determination to fight on if this willingness were disregarded.[2]

The allies were not impressed by this ambiguous declaration and, in any event, they were being provided with a more accurate insight into Germany's post-war intentions in western Europe than that given by Bethmann's note. For, at the very moment when the Chancellor was seeking to create the impression that Germany favoured an equitable peace, the accelerated exploitation of Belgium for the benefit of German war industry and the forced transportation of Belgian labourers to Germany aroused new resentment at German brutality, while German encouragement of a separatist movement in the Flemish and Walloon districts indicated that a voluntary German restoration of Belgium was hardly to be expected. These new policies in Belgium were largely military in inspiration, dictated by the desire to make the 'Hindenburg programme' of increased production a success and, in part also, to solve the security question by winning the permanent sympathies of the Flemings and the Walloons. There can be no doubt that they greatly weakened the effect of the peace note of December.[3] Any inclination that the allies might have had to treat with the Germans vanished

[1] Gatzke, *Germany's Drive*, p. 142.

[2] Lutz, *Fall of the German Empire*, i. 398–9; Helfferich, *Der Weltkrieg*, ii. 364–5.

[3] Gatzke, *Germany's Drive*, pp. 151–61.

in the face of the Belgian policy and, when President Wilson issued his own peace note on 18 December, the allied answer was uncompromisingly negative. In his own answer to Wilson, Bethmann, now fully aware of the extent of the army's territorial ambitions, took refuge once more in ambiguities, and the possibility of negotiation faded away.[1]

The failure of the Chancellor's peace overtures weakened his prestige in governmental circles, a fact which was noted with satisfaction by the Supreme Command. For, although relations between Bethmann and the commanders had been excellent in August, they had deteriorated rapidly. In part this was the result of the influence exerted on the military chiefs by their departmental aides in the General Staff. These men, and their colleagues in the War Ministry, many of them relatively junior in rank, had been assigned tasks which were not always military in the traditional sense—tasks related to such matters as war production and transportation, allocation of man-power, press direction and censorship, and the like. Unprepared by their previous experience to deal with subjects which possessed any degree of political delicacy, they were apt to operate on the assumption that all problems could be solved by firmness.[2] When this was not the case, they had a natural tendency to attribute lack of determination to civilian officials, to the ministers, and ultimately to the Chancellor. The activities of Colonel Bauer, who was assigned responsibility for expanding the artillery resources of the army, provide an illustration of this tendency, for this undoubtedly able officer came to the conclusion that all the delays and inadequacies of the production programme were due to Bethmann's inability to 'lead' the nation and, having convinced himself of this, set about the task of convincing his chiefs of the same thing.[3]

This task of persuasion was not difficult, for Hindenburg was not a man who understood the delays and compromises of

[1] For the text of the German answer, which was delivered on 31 January 1917, see Ludendorff, *Urkunden*, pp. 342 ff.

[2] This is not intended as a blanket judgement. General Groener's direction of the *Kriegsernährungsamt*, and later of the *Kriegsamt*, was characterized by firmness but also by tact and considerable negotiating skill. See E. Kabisch, *Groener* (Berlin, 1932), pp. 35–36, 38, 40, 44, and Groener, *Lebenserinnerungen*, pp. 12, 328–73.

[3] See *Die Ursachen des deutschen Zusammenbruches im Jahre 1918*. (*Das Werk des Untersuchungsausschusses der deutschen Verfassunggebenden Nationalversammlung und des deutschen Reichstages*), 4. Reihe, ii. 26, 30. On Ludendorff's regard for Bauer, see *Kriegserinnerungen*, p. 13.

politics, and Ludendorff always put a higher valuation on strong words than on conciliatory gestures. The supreme commanders had been irritated by Bethmann's hesitations in the matter of the Polish declaration.[1] They were more so by the slowness with which the Chancellor had secured the passage in late 1916 of the universal war service bill (*Hilfsdienstgesetz*) which they believed fundamental to the success of the production programme.[2] Bethmann's peace-note they had viewed with scepticism, and Ludendorff at least seems to have concluded from it that the Chancellor's desire for a peace of reconciliation proved that he was not the man to inspire the German people with 'the true warrior impulse'.[3] The first quartermaster-general was, moreover, subject to the flattering attentions of heavy industry and pan-German circles and was probably not immune to the anti-Bethmann propaganda which they were spreading in their alarm over the Chancellor's peace plans.[4]

Hindenburg, for a time at least, seems to have taken the position that Bethmann was less at fault than some of his principal subordinates. In November the field marshal, in a startling revelation of the way in which military influence now extended into the civilian agencies, forced the resignation of Foreign Minister von Jagow, an official who, he said, was an intelligent man, but not one who could bang his fist on the table.[5] At about the same time Otto Hammann was forced out of his position as press chief in the *Idiotenhaus*, as General Staff officers were fond of describing the Foreign Office.[6] In December, Hindenburg trained his guns on the Vice-Chancellor, Karl Helfferich, who had displeased him by the way in which he had handled the war service bill in the Reichstag hearings, and he told one of Bethmann's aides that he had lost all confidence in Helfferich.[7] But by the end of the year the field marshal was beginning to share Ludendorff's feeling that the Chancellor was the real source of all

[1] Valentini, *Kaiser und Kabinettschef*, pp. 140–1.

[2] On the war service bill, see Mendelssohn Bartholdy, *War and German Society*, pp. 80–82, 84, and Helfferich, *Der Weltkrieg*, ii. 259–82. Also Kabisch, *Groener*, pp. 41–42.

[3] Ludendorff, *Kriegserinnerungen*, pp. 4, 243–4.

[4] Valentini, *Kaiser und Kabinettschef*, p. 141.

[5] Gatzke, *Germany's Drive*, p. 144.

[6] Hutten-Czapski, *Sechzig Jahre*, ii. 252–3.

[7] Valentini, *Kaiser und Kabinettschef*, pp. 141, 241 ff.; Helfferich, *Der Weltkrieg*, ii. 265–6, 272.

trouble, and he actually talked to the leader of the Conservative party about possible successors to Bethmann's post.[1]

Relations between Bethmann and the military leaders were decidedly worsened by the sharp conflict which took place between them in January over the question of the resumption of unrestricted submarine warfare. Since 1915, when the German government, in deference to American opinion, had forbidden submarine attacks upon neutral shipping, Bethmann had resisted any re-opening of the question. The pressure for war *à l'outrance* had increased sharply, however, through the latter months of 1916, inspired by annexationist groups and the Naval Command; and striking evidence was given of the effect of this in October, when the Centre party delegation in the Reichstag passed a resolution which said, in effect, that the Chancellor must be guided in this question by the views of the Supreme Command and that, if the latter decided that heightened submarine warfare was necessary, the delegation would support this judgement.[2] Even before this Bethmann had seen the handwriting on the wall and, in a note of 2 September to Germany's ambassador in Washington, had admitted that, if peace could not be secured by the President's mediation, the unrestricted U-boat war would have to be carried out in dead earnest.[3]

This was an accurate prognostication, for by the end of 1916 Hindenburg and Ludendorff had joined the ranks of the advocates of all-out war on the sea.[4] The supreme commanders were concerned over the volume of munitions shipments from the United States to the allies and were determined that this should be stopped at all cost.[5] The heightened interest of the army chiefs in the question was demonstrated at the end of December when Hindenburg bitterly criticized the Chancellor for seeking to exclude him from discussions dealing with it. Bethmann, nettled by the field marshal's tone, replied that the submarine issue could not, after all, be settled by the Supreme Command

[1] K. Westarp, *Konservative Politik im letzten Jahrzehnt des Kaiserreiches* (2 vols., Berlin, 1935), ii. 335. It proved difficult to find a successor for Bethmann, both now and later. See Hoffmann, *Aufzeichnungen*, i. 146.

[2] Lutz, *Fall of the German Empire*, i. 288. In his memoirs Bethmann says that this meant that he could no longer rely on a Reichstag majority in case of a dispute with the command on this issue. *Betrachtungen*, ii. 128. See also Rosenberg, *Birth of the German Republic*, p. 146.

[3] K. Forster, *The Failures of Peace* (Washington, 1941), p. 47.

[4] Helfferich dates their conversion from 31 August. *Der Weltkrieg*, ii. 382.

[5] Lutz, *Fall of the German Empire*, i. 297; Ludendorff, *Urkunden*, pp. 315 ff.

alone. Formal pledges made to the United States government in May 1916 were involved, and the decision as to whether they should be repudiated, the Chancellor said, 'is a political matter for which constitutionally I am alone responsible and which I cannot hand over to anyone else'. Repudiation would mean war with the United States, and Bethmann made no attempt to hide his revulsion to this idea. He would, he added, strive to reach agreement with the Supreme Command but, if this were not possible, the emperor would have to decide between them.[1]

For all of Bethmann's brave words the submarine issue was, in fact, settled by the Supreme Command alone. On 8 January the Chancellor received a telegram from Hindenburg requesting his presence at a conference at Pless. When he arrived there on the 9th, after having been carefully briefed by Helfferich concerning the logical fallacies in the naval case for resumption,[2] he was informed that the emperor had already been won over by the military. In the morning conference with the army and navy chiefs, Bethmann nevertheless argued vigorously against resumption. All of his arguments were countered by Hindenburg, who stated flatly that the army would receive material and psychological benefits from renewed submarine warfare; that a new allied offensive could be expected in the spring that would have the strength of the Somme offensive of 1916, and that every effort must be made to weaken it; that, if unlimited sea warfare were not begun before 1 February, he could not assume responsibility for the future course of operations; and that, conversely, he was prepared to accept full responsibility for all of the military consequences of renewal. He made it clear also that he did not take American intervention in the war seriously.[3]

When the Chancellor met with the emperor and the military chiefs in the evening, he was confronted, as he wrote later, with men 'who were no longer willing to allow themselves to be talked out of decisions which they had already made'.[4] The conference lasted only half an hour; and, after Bethmann had said that he

[1] Valentini, *Kaiser und Kabinettschef*, p. 243; Helfferich, *Der Weltkrieg*, ii. 397–8.

[2] Helfferich had worked over a memorandum of the Naval Command dated 22 December and had proved to his own satisfaction that, given an even greater percentage of sinkings than the navy predicted, the English would probably still receive more supplies than they were presently doing. *Der Weltkrieg*, ii. 404–7.

[3] Ibid., pp. 409–10; Valentini, *Kaiser und Kabinettschef*, pp. 144–5.

[4] Bethmann, *Betrachtungen*, ii. 137–8.

placed a higher evaluation on American aid to the allies than the Supreme Command but was unprepared to challenge their definition of the military necessities of the nation, the emperor cast his lot with the soldiers, and the entrance of the United States into the war was made inevitable.[1]

At the conclusion of the Pless conference, the Chief of the Civil Cabinet, Valentini, who shared Bethmann's dismay over the action taken, urged the Chancellor to submit his resignation. This idea had already occurred to Bethmann—he had, in fact, spent the afternoon wrestling with his conscience over this very point[2]—but he had concluded that it was not to the national interest to disclose the grave differences which existed between the civilian and the military leadership. He decided, in short, to assume before the German people a share in the responsibility for the decision made.[3] For this gesture he received no gratitude from the military chiefs. On 10 January Hindenburg urged the kaiser to dismiss his Chancellor and was dissuaded from pressing his demand only with difficulty. After 9 January Bethmann's days were numbered. He was protected only by the emperor's continued faith in him; and William was a slender reed on which to lean, subjected as he was from now on to daily criticism of the Chancellor, from the supreme commanders, and from the War Minister and the Chief of the Military Cabinet as well.[4]

It is possible that Bethmann might have strengthened his position if he had been willing to make peace with the soldiers and to become as wholeheartedly their man as his successor Michaelis was to be. But the Chancellor persisted in having beliefs of his own, even when he could not always translate them into policy, and one of the firmest of these was that, in order to maintain the war spirit of the nation, the government must remain loyal to its pledges of political reform. And now, at the very moment when the military campaign against him was coming to a head, he aided it by making renewed promises of such reform in his Reichstag speech of 27 February 1917.[5] This

[1] Typical of the army attitude was the comment of General von Mackensen when he learned of the decision, that 'only people without a sense of reality and convinced enemies of the existing state order' would be against it. Mackensen, *Aufzeichnungen*, ed. by W. Förster (Leipzig, 1938), p. 339.

[2] Helfferich, *Der Weltkrieg*, ii. 411.

[3] See L. Freiherr von Reischach, *Unter drei Kaisern* (Berlin, 1929), pp. 282–3.

[4] Valentini, *Kaiser und Kabinettschef*, pp. 149 ff.

[5] Reichstag, *Stenographische Berichte*, cccix (1917), 2375.

speech, which was approved by the middle parties and received with enthusiasm by the socialists, had far-reaching repercussions. It led, for one thing, to the creation in March of a special committee of the Reichstag 'for the examination of constitutional questions especially in regard to the structure of the representative body of the nation and its relationship to the government'.[1] It also reawakened interest in the question of the Prussian franchise; and this in turn persuaded the emperor, under Bethmann's urging, to issue the so-called Easter message of 7 April, in which he promised the abolition of the Prussian three-class electoral system and the reform of the upper chamber as soon as the war was over.[2]

It is not difficult to imagine the effect of these steps upon an officer corps which was generally conservative in its political views, which had long fought against the increase of parliamentary powers and which—as post-war revelations were to show[3]—was so fearful of democracy that it was already seeking to indoctrinate troops with the idea that the proponents of reform on the home front were as much Germany's enemies as were her foreign foes. Ludendorff's reaction to the Easter message was that it represented the kind of unwise concession to mob opinion that encouraged rather than prevented revolutionary agitation and that, moreover, it offered aid and comfort to the enemy by making it appear that the government feared that it was losing popular support.[4] The fact that the first major strikes of the war period—strikes caused, in Berlin at least, by food and fuel shortages[5]—broke out in this same month enabled Ludendorff to blame these alternately on the influence of the Russian revolution of March and on Bethmann's weakness. 'The government', he wrote later, 'increasingly let the direction of state business be taken out of its hands . . . by specific groups which, historically, were destructive rather than constructive [in their aims].'[6]

If anything more was needed to harden the Supreme Command's determination that Bethmann must go it was the revival

[1] Lutz, *Fall of the German Empire*, i. 261.

[2] *Ursachen des Zusammenbruches*, 4. Reihe, viii. 164–5.

[3] During the parliamentary investigations of the causes of Germany's collapse, a socialist deputy read at length from a pamphlet printed by the 10th Army for the troops which rang all the changes on this theme. Ibid., vii (1), 177, and R. H. Lutz, ed. *The Causes of the German Collapse in 1918* (Stanford, 1934), pp. 235–7.

[4] Ludendorff, *Kriegserinnerungen*, pp. 355–6, *Urkunden*, p. 292.

[5] Kabisch, *Groener*, pp. 47-48.

[6] Ludendorff, *Kriegserinnerungen*, p. 357.

of interest in negotiation for a peace of reconciliation. In April the Socialist party issued a manifesto in which, while repeating the arguments for political reform at home, it also called for 'a general peace without annexations and indemnities on the basis of the free international development of all peoples', and demanded that the government renounce 'the dreams of power of an ambitious chauvinism' and seek negotiations on this basis.[1] This document, which enraged all annexationist groups, infuriated the army command as well, for, in addition to their other reasons for supporting a policy of annexations, they now felt that the promise of booty was necessary to support the morale of weary front-line troops. This belief was reflected in a memorandum of June 1917 drawn up in the army's propaganda and intelligence section, which read:[2]

> Our propaganda [to troops] has the purpose of proving that a peace of renunciation or of understanding will not fulfil the needs of the German people but that only a victory and its consequences at the peace conference will bring about happy conditions for the German people and for each individual class.

The immediate reaction of the Supreme Command to the socialist manifesto was, therefore, to demand a more specific formulation of Germany's war aims than at present existed and one that would bind the civilian authorities to a programme that satisfied annexationist ambitions. In a series of conversations at Kreuznach in April and May they insisted that the nation be committed to a programme that went much further than anything contemplated in December 1916—which clearly envisaged the veiled annexation of Belgium, for instance, and which, in addition to extensive claims against France and Russia, included demands for new naval stations overseas and the creation of a large German *Mittelafrika*.[3]

The Kreuznach conversations served also to cause the first major differences between the emperor and his Chancellor. Bethmann fought strenuously against any specific formulation of war aims which could only lead, as he knew, to fantastic claims which would make future negotiation impossible; and, although he signed the minutes of the Kreuznach meetings, he

[1] *Ursachen des Zusammenbruches*, 4. Reihe, xii (1), 128–9.

[2] H. Thimme, *Weltkrieg ohne Waffen* (Stuttgart, 1932), pp. 250–1; quoted in Gatzke, *Germany's Drive*, p. 188.

[3] *Ursachen des Zusammenbruches*, 4. Reihe, xii (1), 200–4.

insisted, in private at least, that he was not bound by them and that he would pursue any possibilities of peace that might arise.[1] The emperor, however, frightened at the results of his Easter message, now clearly wished to atone for it in the eyes of the military by advocating the kind of peace they wanted, and he was highly critical of Bethmann's objections and reservations. Indeed, in a letter to the Chancellor in mid-May he reprimanded Bethmann sharply for having given him no positive guidance in the matter of war aims in three years of hostilities and for making it necessary for the emperor himself to formulate Germany's demands 'in accordance with his own wishes and those of his armed establishment'.[2]

The military leaders were quick to exploit this opportunity. Doubtless under Ludendorff's urging, Hindenburg now began a correspondence with the emperor which was calculated to increase William's doubts concerning Bethmann. On 19 June the field marshal sought to explain the disappointing results of the submarine warfare by arguing that the only reason that the allies went on fighting was that they were counting on an internal collapse in Germany, and he hinted broadly that this was due to Bethmann's encouragement of social unrest.[3] On 27 June he elaborated on the decline of the popular spirit for war and stated plainly that he doubted Bethmann's ability to revive it.[4] Even under this kind of pressure, however, the emperor remained doubtful of the advisability of change, and more forthright tactics were required before the soldiers secured their objective.

These they were now quite willing to employ. Accumulating war weariness and disillusionment concerning the possibility of attaining victory by use of the submarine had convinced the Centre party, under the leadership of Matthias Erzberger, that a new approach to peace must be made, in the form of a declaration by the Reichstag in favour of negotiation.[5] This idea was supported by the Socialists and the Progressives, and in July it was clear that a resolution would be introduced

[1] Westarp, *Konservative Politik*, ii. 85.

[2] *Ursachen des Zusammenbruches*, 4. Reihe, xii (1), 109–10.

[3] Ludendorff, *Kriegserinnerungen*, p. 358. [4] Ibid., p. 359.

[5] Erzberger's position in this matter is highly ambiguous. He was able to reconcile his support of a peace resolution with a continued desire for extensive annexations, and later said, 'This way I get Longwy-Briey by negotiation!' Prinz Max von Baden, *Erinnerungen und Dokumente* (Stuttgart, 1927), p. 114. For Erzberger's own account, see M. Erzberger, *Erlebnisse im Weltkrieg* (Stuttgart, 1920), chap. xix.

and would probably be passed. The Supreme Command fastened upon Bethmann's inability to head this off as the clinching proof of his inadequacy and launched their direct assault against him.

This took two forms. On the one hand, Colonel Bauer, long an inveterate foe of Bethmann's, entered negotiations with Reichstag deputies and intimated to them that Hindenburg and Ludendorff feared that Bethmann's retention of office was jeopardizing the hope of victory. With the ground thus prepared, Bauer persuaded the crown prince to come to Berlin and engage in discussions with the party leaders on the question of a change in the chancellorship. These talks revealed the fact that even those parliamentary leaders who favoured an increase of the Reichstag's powers and wanted new attempts made to negotiate peace with the enemy were ready and even eager to sacrifice Bethmann, who had promoted both those ideas, to the military, who were dead set against them.[1] A more striking illustration of the political incapacity of the Reichstag during the war could scarcely be provided.

Fortified by the knowledge that the Chancellor had lost the confidence of the parliament, Hindenburg and Ludendorff, on 12 July, telephoned their resignations to Berlin, saying that they could no longer co-operate with Bethmann. The emperor, although indignant at the nature of this forcing play, confessed to Bethmann that he was placed in an impossible position. The Chancellor was not willing to prolong his sovereign's embarrassment and, on 13 July, submitted his resignation and retired from office.[2]

IV

Bethmann's explanation that his resignation was caused by the loss of his Reichstag support could not disguise the fact that military pressure had been the real reason for his fall. And this,

[1] Bauer, *Der große Krieg*, pp. 141–2; Ludendorff, *Urkunden*, pp. 408 ff.; *Ursachen des Zusammenbruches*, 4. Reihe, ii. 30; Valentini, *Kaiser und Kabinettschef*, pp. 157 ff.; Bethmann-Hollweg, *Betrachtungen*, ii. 232–5. The parties interested in an early peace seem to have agreed with Erzberger that this would be facilitated by Bethmann's fall. The National Liberals, who supported Bethmann's ideas of political reform, criticized his failure to give strong leadership and to insist on territorial gains. See, for instance, R. von Rheinbaben, *Stresemann, the Man and Statesman* (New York, 1928), pp. 128 ff. The parties of the right had always opposed Bethmann.

[2] Bethmann-Hollweg, *Betrachtungen*, ii. 235–6; Ludendorff, *Kriegserinnerungen*, pp. 361–2.

of course, represented a significant turning point in the constitutional history of imperial Germany.

It will be remembered that during the war of 1870 the elder Moltke had sought to assert the principle that the Chancellor and the Chief of the General Staff were equally warranted and mutually independent agencies.[1] By this formula Moltke had hoped to draw a clear line between the spheres of politics and strategy and to protect himself from what he considered to be Bismarck's meddling in operational matters. Bismarck, however, had been able to defeat the chief of staff's claim and to maintain the principle of civilian responsibility for the overall direction of the war.

During the First World War Hindenburg and Ludendorff started their term at the Supreme Command by taking Moltke's principle for granted. Ludendorff was to write later that, with the outbreak of hostilities, 'the Supreme Command became an agency which shared responsibility with the Chancellor'.[2] Bethmann-Hollweg, unfortunately, never contested this claim, but himself drifted into an acceptance of the idea that, in political as well as military matters, the Supreme Command's views must be considered on the same level as his own and that, when there was a difference of opinion, the emperor must decide. Given the character of the emperor and his propensity for the military point of view, this meant, as the decisions concerning Poland and the submarine question showed, that arguments of military expediency were generally, in crucial matters, given more weight than political considerations.

This in itself represented a startling change in the relationship between the civilian and military leadership in time of war. But Hindenburg and Ludendorff were not content to stop there. In the July crisis of 1917 they claimed—and claimed successfully—the right of the High Command to demand the resignation of the Chancellor because of his pursuit of policies which, in Bismarck's time at least, were recognized as lying clearly within his sphere of competence; and they subsequently made good their right to nominate his successor.[3] This went far beyond anything that the elder Moltke had claimed and

[1] See above, Chapter V, pp. 213 ff.

[2] Ludendorff, *Kriegserinnerungen*, p. 5.

[3] William actually asked Hindenburg whom he wanted as Bethmann's successor and, in the end, appointed a man he had never met. See Kühlmann, *Erinnerungen*, pp. 501-2.

amounted to an assertion of the army's right of final decision in all matters of politics.

That this had a marked effect upon the whole theory of monarchical government in Germany goes without saying. It is true that the emperor's position had already been seriously weakened before July 1917. He had long since ceased to be supreme war lord in the sense that William I had been. To an increasing extent since 1914 William II had absented himself from the centre of military operations; and some of the weightiest military decisions of the war had been communicated to him only after they had been executed.[1] By the German people the emperor's military title was now regarded as a kind of fiction; they gave credit for Germany's victories to Hindenburg and Ludendorff rather than to their sovereign.[2] But no one, until July 1917, questioned the emperor's right to choose and dismiss his ministers as he saw fit; and the events of that month, taking place as they did in the hot glare of publicity, struck a blow at the very foundations of the monarchical system. It is ironical that that blow should have been delivered by the army, which had so steadfastly opposed political and social reform precisely because it might weaken the power of the Crown.

One man at least recognized the significance of the events of July. Arnold Wahnschaffe, Under Secretary of State in the *Reichskanzlei*, had written to Ludendorff on 10 July asking the general to give him authority to deny rumours, current in Reichstag circles, to the effect that the Supreme Command believed that the war would be lost if Bethmann remained in office. Ludendorff did not answer the letter until five days after the Chancellor's fall, and then in a rather offhand manner, saying in effect that a *démenti* would serve no useful purpose. Wahnschaffe returned to the charge in a letter of 21 July in which he pointed out that the prevailing opinion that the military had forced Bethmann out of office was more serious than the general seemed to think. 'The effect of those rumours continues and is growing, and it is a dangerous effect, seriously damaging the authority of the government and, indeed, threatening the stability of the state structure.' He again asked for a specific statement in which Ludendorff would repudiate the

[1] *Ursachen des Zusammenbruches*, 4. Reihe, ii. 33.

[2] Alfred Niemann, *Kaiser und Heer: Das Wesen der Kommandogewalt und ihre Ausübung durch Kaiser Wilhelm II* (Berlin, 1929), pp. 343, 367.

suggestion that the army was responsible for the change of chancellors.

The first quartermaster-general was sufficiently moved by this to have Colonel Bauer draft a letter to the new Chancellor Michaelis, in which he, rather evasively, disclaimed responsibility for Bethmann's fall and once more refused to issue a *démenti*, but in which he said that, if the Chancellor shared Wahnschaffe's concern, a meeting might be held to decide on a course of action. This letter, however, was never dispatched. Instead, Ludendorff wrote a curt note to Wahnschaffe in which he expressed resentment at the idea that he could have contributed through his behaviour to any weakening of the stability of the state and pointed out that he could claim, on the contrary, to have acted on repeated occasions as the saviour of the fatherland.

Wahnschaffe, rather doggedly, answered on 31 July that he would never question Ludendorff's services to the nation and that he had not, for that matter, made any accusations against the first quartermaster-general. He merely wanted to be able, with Ludendorff's help, to combat rumours which he did not believe to be true but which, unchecked, would have dangerous consequences. This last appeal had no effect and received no answer. Through a member of his staff, Ludendorff laid the whole correspondence before Michaelis, and the new Chancellor, who was heart and soul on the side of the military, informed Wahnschaffe that it would be unseemly for him to pursue the matter further.[1]

On the important and interrelated questions of negotiated peace and domestic reform, the army point of view now became binding upon both emperor and Chancellor. On 19 July the Reichstag passed the Peace Resolution which had contributed so powerfully to Bethmann's resignation, and announced that it was striving for 'a peace of understanding and the permanent reconciliation of all peoples'.[2] On the same day Michaelis made that famous and equivocal announcement in which he said that the objectives sought by the government were not incompatible with the resolution 'as I understand it'.[3] Subsequent

[1] This episode is discussed, and the correspondence is reproduced, in *Ursachen des Zusammenbruches*, 4. Reihe, ii. 34–38.

[2] Reichstag, *Stenographische Berichte*, cccx, 3573–6 (Verhandlungen, 19 July 1917).

[3] Ibid., p. 3572.

events were to show that the qualifying phrase robbed the endorsement of any meaning. Some indication of this was given, indeed, on 20 July when William II received delegates from the Reichstag parties for an exchange of views. The emperor harangued the group in a manner strongly reminiscent of his pre-war performances. He spoke of Germany's future treatment of her adversaries in a way which left no doubt of his support of annexationist programme and, in the course of remarks on recent operations in Galicia, said, 'When my Guards appear, there is no room for democracy'—a remark interpreted by many present as a repudiation of his Easter message.[1]

Meanwhile, the Supreme Command and the War Ministry gave covert support to the new *Vaterlandspartei*, an organization founded within two months of the passage of the Peace Resolution, and which, like the older *Kriegszielbewegung*, opposed domestic change and was insistent on a strong peace—or, as it described it, a 'Hindenburg peace'.[2] Both army and navy authorities permitted officers interested in joining this movement to evade regulations forbidding political activity by men in active service;[3] and Hindenburg and Ludendorff supported the movement's objectives by public assertions of Germany's ability to win complete military victory over her foes.[4] By means of the *Kriegspresseamt*, the army distributed writings of a patriotic and annexationist character which were calculated to spread the idea that any attempt to implement the Peace Resolution would baulk Germany of the total victory which she would otherwise win. Finally, through the *Vaterländischer Unterricht*, an information service for the troops, subtle propaganda against the resolution was spread and the necessity of territorial gains for Germany's future security was constantly emphasized. Here again attacks on the advocates of negotiated peace were accompanied by references to the dangers of democracy. An official army pamphlet of 1917 stated that

> In the spring of 1917 . . . the democratic parties of the German Reichstag began to attack our powerful monarchy, the Kaiser's power of command and the Prussian suffrage system. They wanted to compel the conclusion of a peace with renunciations by means of

[1] Helfferich, *Der Weltkrieg*, iii. 161; Gatzke, *Germany's Drive*, pp. 201–2.

[2] On the *Vaterlandspartei*, see Gatzke, *Germany's Drive*, pp. 206–14.

[3] Ibid., p. 215.

[4] See Ludendorff, *Kriegserinnerungen*, p. 369; Lutz, *Fall of the German Empire*, i. 370.

strikes and street demonstrations. . . . Those who do not stop the democratic and international efforts at the threshold are working for the enemy.[1]

It was in this frame of mind that the military approached every possibility of peace which arose from this time until the end of the war. Their intransigent opposition to anything but a peace of annexations was demonstrated on two occasions before the end of 1917: the first during the renewal of diplomatic activity in behalf of peace in August and the second during the deliberations which followed Russia's appeal for peace in November.

In a note to all belligerents, dated 1 August 1917, the Pope offered his mediation in the task of arranging a peace on the basis of mutual renunciation of conquests.[2] This principle did not, of course, cover the case of Alsace and Lorraine; and there was some question from the very beginning of the willingness of the French government to enter negotiations without a prior understanding that the provinces would be restored. It was consideration of this point that led Richard Kühlmann, who succeeded to the post of German Foreign Minister on 6 August, to conceive of an alternate idea, a direct approach to the British, in the hope that, if they could be assured that their own war aims—especially the restoration of Belgium—would be guaranteed, they would persuade the French to give up their demands with regard to Alsace and Lorraine. Kühlmann counted on his friendship with Sir William Tyrrell in the British Foreign Office to secure a hearing for his proposals.[3]

The Foreign Minister convinced Michaelis that his idea of talks with the British should be given priority over the papal proposals. This, in itself, spelled failure for the Pope's efforts, for he, from the outset, had made it clear to the Germans that he expected a clear statement on the future of Belgium from them. In principle Kühlmann favoured the restoration of Belgium, but he did not want to say so publicly, preferring to reserve this matter for bargaining purposes when negotiations with the British should begin. At the end of September, therefore, in a letter to Monsignore Pacelli, the German government

[1] Lutz, *Causes of German Collapse*, pp. 235–6; Gatzke, *Germany's Drive*, pp. 216–18.

[2] On the papal peace note, see especially M. Spahn, *Die päpstliche Friedensvermittlung* (Berlin, 1919); Gatzke, *Germany's Drive*, pp. 219–25; Helfferich, *Der Weltkrieg*, iii. 164–78; Epstein, *Erzberger*, pp. 216 ff.

[3] Kühlmann, *Erinnerungen*, pp. 471–3.

said that a statement on Belgium was impossible at this time, although it was hoped that it could be provided later on.[1]

Perhaps nothing would have been lost by this if Kühlmann had been empowered to make in secret the promises concerning Belgium which he did not want to make in public. But it was at this point that the Supreme Command entered the picture. On 11 September, at Schloß Bellevue, Michaelis and the Foreign Minister met with the emperor, Hindenburg, and Ludendorff and Admiral Holtzendorff of the naval staff to consider proposals which might be made to the British. When the Belgian question was raised the civilians argued the case for unconditional restoration so convincingly that the emperor overrode the objections of Holtzendorff, who wanted to retain the Flanders coast, and the supreme commanders, who insisted on the retention of Liège and its environs; and Kühlmann was apparently given a free hand to go ahead with his plans.[2]

This triumph was completely illusory. On 12 September, in a letter to Hindenburg and Holtzendorff summing up the results of the conference, Michaelis showed that he had been frightened by his own temerity on the previous day. In his plans for negotiation, he said, he was now counting on claiming Liège and the closest possible economic union between Belgium and Germany. This apologetic reversal of the Chancellor's position did not satisfy Ludendorff. On 14 September he composed a statement which embodied his considered views on Germany's requirements in any settlement.[3] In addition to the items mentioned by Michaelis, Germany must demand, he said, an extended occupation of Belgium, the annexation of the iron basin of Lorraine and of the Meuse valley as far as St. Vith, a number of new naval stations, and large African holdings. Two days later, in conversation with Count Westarp, Ludendorff was even more explicit with regard to his claims on Belgium. Economic union he interpreted now to include tariff arrangements, community of railways and ports, penetration of Belgian industry by German capital, and forced liquidation of French holdings.[4]

This memorandum, which was sent to Michaelis by Hinden-

[1] Kühlmann, *Erinnerungen*, pp. 484–5. Cf. Gatzke, *Germany's Drive*, pp. 225, 233.

[2] Georg Michaelis, *Für Staat und Volk* (Berlin, 1922), pp. 347–50; Kühlmann, *Erinnerungen*, pp. 481–2.

[3] Ludendorff, *Urkunden*, pp. 428–33; *Kriegserinnerungen*, pp. 413–19.

[4] Gatzke, *Germany's Drive*, p. 228; Westarp, *Konservative Politik*, ii. 552.

burg, with a note saying that it was in accordance with his own views,[1] was not communicated to Kühlmann, who proceeded with his attempts to make contact with the British in the spirit of the Bellevue conversations. The Foreign Minister's efforts came to nothing, in part perhaps because of the inefficient tactics of his Spanish intermediary, the Marquis de Villalobar.[2] The point is, however, that even if Kühlmann had succeeded in interesting the British in negotiation, he would have had nothing to offer them. The Supreme Command had once more asserted its dominance over emperor and Chancellor and had, in fact, formulated terms that were even more exaggerated than those which had ruined Bethmann's hopes for peace in 1916.[3]

Ludendorff had said, in his memorandum, that Germany had a right to make such demands, because her chances of victory were greater than those of the enemy. The general's confidence was undoubtedly inspired by the serious setbacks suffered by the allies in 1917—the failure of the Nivelle offensive and of the British push at Passchendaele—and it probably seemed to be confirmed by the Italian defeat at Caporetto in October and the outbreak of the Bolshevik revolution in Russia in November. But these blows to the allied cause were soon offset by new political blunders on the part of the Germans. The Russian revolution opened the way to new peace discussions, for the Bolshevik government sued for peace on 26 November. In the negotiations that followed, the Supreme Command gave another, and very public, demonstration of its conception of a peace settlement, and the treaty it imposed on the Russians brought more direct benefit to the allies than their own recent defeats had brought to Germany.

In the negotiations with the Bolsheviks, Kühlmann, who headed the German delegation, once more played an overly subtle game, trying to steer a course between the majority parties of the Reichstag, which still held to the spirit of the Peace Resolution, and the annexationists, who were, he knew, supported by the Supreme Command. In a discussion with the emperor and the military commanders on 19 December, he was

[1] *Ursachen des Zusammenbruches*, 4. Reihe, ii. 140.

[2] Kühlmann, *Erinnerungen*, pp. 485–7.

[3] In December, in a note to Chancellor Hertling, Hindenburg added to the already extensive bill of particulars a renewed demand for the Flanders coast, which he said he had been ready to sacrifice only as long as there was some hope of peace in 1917. *Ursachen des Zusammenbruches*, 4. Reihe, iii. 244, 265–6.

left no illusions about the thinking of the latter. Ludendorff made it clear that he desired the establishment of a personal union between Germany and Courland and Lithuania, the evacuation by Russia of Livonia and Esthonia and (with a sovereign disregard for earlier declarations concerning Poland) the annexation by Germany of a belt of Polish territory extending as far as Warsaw. Kühlmann argued against these claims with spirit[1] and the *Kronrat* adjourned without a firm decision.[2] The Foreign Minister then once more made the mistake of assuming that he had been given a free hand. He informed the party leaders in the Reichstag that he was prepared to negotiate on the basis of 'no annexations'.[3] Privately, he decided to follow a middle course: to take his stand on the principle of self-determination, which would, he believed, bring some accretions of territory to Germany without offending the majority parties or giving propaganda weapons to the allies.[4]

The weakness of these tactics was that they completely ignored the realities of Germany's political situation. The Supreme Command was willing to make concessions on unimportant points and even to permit the illusion of constitutional government, as it had in October, when Michaelis had retired from office under heavy attack from the Reichstag and when his successor Hertling had promised to follow the will of parliament in his foreign and domestic policy.[5] But the soldiers had no intention of relinquishing their control over things that mattered, like the question of peace conditions, or of permitting the Foreign Minister to defer to Reichstag opinion rather than to their own.

At Brest-Litovsk, where negotiations with the bolsheviks opened on 20 December, Kühlmann was able to win the support of Czernin, the Austrian Foreign Minister, and Hoffmann, the German military plenipotentiary, for his policy of negotiation on the basis of self-determination.[6] Announcement of this, how-

[1] It was during one of his exchanges with Hindenburg that he elicited the information that the field marshal wanted the eastern provinces for the manœuvreing of his left wing in the next war.

[2] Kühlmann, *Erinnerungen*, pp. 514–15; Wheeler-Bennett, *The Forgotten Peace*, pp. 108–9.

[3] Ibid., pp. 110–11.

[4] Kühlmann, *Erinnerungen*, p. 524.

[5] As Rosenberg says, the Reichstag leaders apparently forgot that Hertling was incapable of fulfilling any conditions; his government was 'no more than a constitutional cloak thrown over Ludendorff's dictatorship'. *Birth of the German Republic*, pp. 200, 203.

[6] Wheeler-Bennett, *The Forgotten Peace*, pp. 117 ff.

ever, led to an explosion at Kreuznach, where the Supreme Command accused Kühlmann of violating the 'agreement' of 18 December. The Foreign Minister rushed to Berlin in an attempt to persuade the emperor that the military demands were unreasonable; and he was joined in this effort by General Hoffmann, who was opposed particularly to Ludendorff's desire for extensive Polish annexations.[1] The supreme commanders were further enraged by these efforts. There was a highly uncomfortable meeting at Schloß Bellevue on 2 January, during which Hindenburg and Ludendorff showed scant courtesy for the imperial person, whispering together during his embarrassed explanations of his support of Kühlmann's policy and slamming the door behind them when they left the room.[2] There followed an awkward pause of five days. This was broken dramatically on 7 January when Hindenburg wrote a letter to the emperor in which he said that he and Ludendorff had been deeply wounded by the fact that the advice of a military subordinate had been preferred to their own. As for Kühlmann's policy, the field marshal wrote, 'Your Majesty will not demand that honest men, who have served Your Majesty and the fatherland loyally, should lend their authority and their names to negotiations [which they regard] with inner conviction as shameful for the Crown and the Reich. . . . I respectfully urge Your Majesty to make a fundamental decision.' In a letter to Hertling at about the same time Hindenburg made it clear that he was prepared to resign on this issue; and, in a conversation with the Chancellor on 12 January, Ludendorff intimated that he could no longer serve the emperor if Kühlmann and men who believed as he did—especially the Chief of the Civil Cabinet, Valentini—remained in office.[3]

Kühlmann tells us in his memoirs that Hertling and he advised the emperor to take a firm stand on the constitutional issue created by the field marshal's letter, and he would have us believe that they succeeded. Up to a point they did. William II sent a rather querulous letter to Hindenburg which suggested that he had violated the boundaries of constitutional propriety, and he enclosed a memorandum drawn up by Hertling and the

[1] On Hoffmann's intervention and Kühlmann's warning to the emperor to keep it secret from Hindenburg and Ludendorff, a warning that was disregarded, see Kühlmann, *Erinnerungen*, pp. 526–7.

[2] Ibid., pp. 528–9.

[3] Ibid., pp. 536–7.

Foreign Minister which discussed the relative responsibilities of the civil and military leaders in matters of foreign affairs, stressing the final responsibility of the Chancellor.[1] It is true also that the emperor refused to dismiss Kühlmann or to allow Hoffmann to suffer for his advice.[2] But, granted all this and the further fact that Hindenburg and Ludendorff did not resign, it can hardly be argued that the civilians won a victory in this crisis. At the very moment when the emperor was delivering constitutional lectures to his commanders, they were reaching into his household and forcing the dismissal of Valentini, who had supported Kühlmann's views on eastern annexations. The Chief of the Civil Cabinet was described around Berlin as 'a substitute for Kühlmann'[3] and, after he had been replaced by a creature of the Supreme Command, Hans Delbrück wrote: 'Have we come to a point in the monarchical system in Germany at which the Emperor dare not choose, not merely his ministers, but even the men of his personal entourage freely?'[4] The question could only be answered in the affirmative.

Moreover, even in the matter of eastern annexations, the military had their way. Before Kühlmann had returned to Brest-Litovsk it had been tacitly agreed that German acquisitions of Polish territory should more nearly approximate Ludendorff's desires than his own and Hoffmann's; and knowledge of this decision, which spread rapidly in Poland, caused strikes and other disorders in the 'kingdom' that had been founded in 1916. The subsequent German decision to detach the Ukraine from Russia and to hand over additional Polish territory to the new puppet state caused revolts in the volunteer army which General von Beseler had raised with such difficulty in Poland; several units broke through the Ukrainian front and joined the Bolsheviks, and the rest had to be transferred to the Isonzo front.[5] The refusal of the government to evacuate Courland and Lithuania and the islands of the Gulf of Riga showed that the ambitions of the Supreme Command in the Baltic area were also to be realized. When the peace of Brest-Litovsk was finally signed in March 1918, Kühlmann's idea of a moderate settle-

[1] Kühlmann, *Erinnerungen,*, pp. 538–42; Schmidt-Bückeburg, *Militärkabinett*, pp. 266 ff.
[2] Hoffmann, *Aufzeichnungen*, ii. 206.

[3] Valentini, *Kaiser und Kabinettschef*, pp. 183 ff., 187 ff.; Hutten-Czapski, *Sechzig Jahre*, ii. 451–2; Schmidt-Bückeburg, *Militärkabinett*, pp. 269–70.

[4] *Preußische Jahrbücher*, January 1918.

[5] Hutten-Czapski, *Sechzig Jahre*, ii. 458–62.

ment had long since been abandoned, and the terms imposed on the Bolsheviks were such as to delight allied propagandists, stir resentment and opposition among all the subject nationalities of eastern Europe, and cause dismay and disillusionment among those Germans who had persisted in believing that their country was fighting a defensive war rather than a war of conquest.

V

Since the beginning of the war, Hans Delbrück, Germany's most distinguished military historian, had written a monthly article on the course of the fighting and related topics in the pages of the *Preußische Jahrbücher*.[1] In these pieces the author of *The History of the Art of War* had stressed two ideas. The first was that the German army, even if the best in the world, did not possess so great a superiority over its antagonists as to be able to win victory by military means alone. It had staked everything on a strategy of destruction in 1914 and failed. It must now rely on political means to give added weight to its blows by causing differences among its enemies and convincing some or all of them that peace was preferable to a prolongation of hostilities. In the second place, Delbrück argued that the strongest bond holding the allied coalition together was the conviction that Germany would not accept a moderate result. 'We must look the facts in the face', he wrote in 1917, 'that we have in a sense the whole world leagued against us—and we must not conceal from ourselves that, if we try to penetrate to the basic reason for this world coalition, we will ever and again stumble over the motive of fear of German world hegemony.'[2] Until that fear was overcome by a political strategy based on a sincere disclaimer of territorial ambition, the war would go on, and Germany might be defeated.

Delbrück's hope that the government might disclaim a desire for annexations was disappointed by the events of 1917 and even more so by the negotiations at Brest-Litovsk, which he regarded as an almost disastrous blow to the German cause. Nevertheless, he had gone on urging that, before the Supreme

[1] These are conveniently collected under the title *Krieg und Politik* (3 vols., Berlin, 1918–19). On Delbrück's war writings see Gordon A. Craig, 'Delbrück, the Military Historian', in *Makers of Modern Strategy*, especially pp. 275–81.

[2] *Krieg und Politik*, ii. 187.

Command started the great offensive which everyone was expecting in the spring, it must first launch a political offensive by announcing Germany's willingness to negotiate on the basis of the restoration of Belgium and the evacuation of France. Even if the offer were turned down, the fact that it was made would strengthen the military drive when it began. Failure to make such an offer, on the other hand, would be to stake everything on the military card, with much less chance of success than in 1914.[1]

Delbrück was not alone in advancing this argument. In the early spring of 1918 Scheidemann, Erzberger, and Friedrich Naumann separately urged the idea of a political offensive and emphasized the necessity of a clear statement on Belgium; and the case was placed before Ludendorff in February in an extensive memorandum signed by Naumann, Alfred Weber, Robert Bosch, and others. The latter document not only talked of the potential effects of such a move upon the powers of resistance of the enemy but also pointed out that the German people must be convinced that every effort had been made to secure peace before they were asked to support a new military offensive.[2]

Ludendorff was unresponsive to these arguments and, in his answer to the February memorandum, completely ignored the suggestions concerning Belgium which were the heart of the document.[3] Similarly, when a member of the General Staff, Colonel von Haeften, prepared a proposal for a propaganda effort designed to take advantage of recent discussions in England of the possibilities of negotiation,[4] Ludendorff forwarded it to the Chancellor with indications of his interest, but only after carefully deleting Haeften's references to the critical nature of the Belgian question.[5] The first quartermaster-general had not, in fact, deviated in the least from his long-held conviction that Germany must win a strong peace which would include Belgium. The arguments he advanced in favour of this usually dwelt on Germany's security needs, but basically Ludendorff's motivation was political. In a letter to a friend in January

[1] *Krieg und Politik*, ii. 174 (Feb. 1918).

[2] Gatzke, *Germany's Drive*, pp. 252–3.

[3] *Ursachen des Zusammenbruches*, 4. Reihe, ii. 92–93.

[4] These had been touched off by publication in the press of a letter by the Earl of Lansdowne, urging the necessity of negotiated peace.

[5] Haeften's memorandum is in Ludendorff, *Urkunden*, pp. 473–8. See also Gatzke, *Germany's Drive*, p. 254.

concerning the pending proposals for political reform in Germany, he had written: 'I continually hope that the Prussian franchise falls through. If I didn't have that hope, I would favour the conclusion of any kind of peace. With this franchise, we cannot live.'[1] There could scarcely be a plainer admission of the general's belief that annexations were indispensable if the existing political system were to be maintained.

The great offensive of March 1918, upon which Germany's future depended, was, therefore, launched without the kind of political preparation which might have increased its chances of success. A month later, while the German armies were still advancing, Delbrück wrote, 'The great strategical offensive should have been accompanied and reinforced by a similar offensive which would have worked upon the home front of our enemies in the same way as Hindenburg and the men in field gray worked upon the front lines.' If only the German government had announced, fourteen days before the opening of the attack, that they firmly desired a negotiated peace and that they were willing to give up Belgium, what would the result have been? Lloyd George and Clemenceau might have regarded this as a sign of weakness. But now, as the offensive rolled forward, 'would Lloyd George and Clemenceau still be at the helm? I doubt it very much. We might even now be sitting at the conference table.'[2]

Without the aid of the political weapon, the spring offensive was doomed to failure. Despite Ludendorff's careful preparations, the German army was in no condition to strike a knockout blow against the enemy. Its numerical superiority was slight and, in reserves, it was definitely inferior to the allied armies. In certain important specialities, its equipment no longer matched that of the allies; its supply system was showing the effects of four years of war; and its fuel reserves were inadequate to supply its motorized vehicles. Ludendorff himself was sufficiently aware of these deficiencies to realize that he could not strike the enemy in accordance with the classic precepts of *Vernichtungsstrategie*. In his own words, 'tactics were to be valued more than pure strategy', which meant that he would attack at those points where it was easiest to break through rather than at those where the announced aim of the offensive could best be served. This policy of tactical improvisation was bound to be disastrous after

[1] Knesebeck, *Propagandafeldzug*, p. 164.

[2] *Krieg und Politik*, iii. 73.

the enemy had recovered from the shock of the first blows. In effect, the grand offensive of March had degenerated by June into a series of separate thrusts, unco-ordinated and unproductive.[1]

Neither the politicians nor the general public had any inkling of these facts, but doubts had begun to occur to some of the soldiers soon after the offensive got under way. At the beginning of June Colonel von Haeften composed another memorandum, again emphasizing the necessity of a political offensive.[2] When this document was forwarded by the Supreme Command to the Chancellor and the Foreign Minister, the passage that seems to have impressed Kühlmann most was one which read: 'Undoubtedly the successes of our arms, and especially the most recent ones, have already had a great effect upon our enemies. . . . But these successes alone will not bring us peace; for that we need a political victory behind the enemy front.'[3] This confirmed the Foreign Minister's worst fears; and, in the course of a rambling speech before the Reichstag on 24 June, he made some references to it, saying vaguely that 'an absolute end can hardly be expected from military decisions alone, without recourse to diplomatic negotiations'.[4]

The violence of the reaction to this utterance demonstrated once and for all the complete lack of realism of the annexationists and of the Supreme Command at this critical juncture of German affairs. Kühlmann was accused by the Conservatives, the National Liberals, and the *Vaterlandspartei* of undermining German morale. The Supreme Command demanded the Foreign Minister's dismissal and, by refusing flatly to have anything further to do with him, created a situation in which the emperor and the Chancellor felt they had to give way. And even before Kühlmann had handed over his office, the Supreme Command had written *finis* to any possibility of negotiation which might have remained. Haeften was ordered to discontinue his studies of a political offensive and, at a meeting with the Chancellor on 2–3 July, Hindenburg and Ludendorff made a final clarification of the Belgian issue. Belgium must be brought into the

[1] For an informed critique of Ludendoff's strategy in the spring offensive, see *Ursachen des Zusammenbruches*, 4. Reihe, iii. 239–73.

[2] Ludendorff, *Urkunden*, pp. 478–86.

[3] Ibid., p. 485.

[4] Reichstag, *Stenographische Berichte*, cccxii (1918), 5612; Kühlmann, *Erinnerungen*, pp. 572–3.

closest possible relationship with Germany by customs union, community of railways and the like. Flanders and Wallonia must be made into separate states. The country as a whole must be subject to long occupation, with the Flanders coast and Liège evacuated last; and any evacuation would depend upon the extent to which Belgium bound herself to Germany.[1]

This list of claims is interesting only as a final indication of the consistency with which the army command held to its territorial demands during the First World War, even after hard military facts had made their demands ridiculous. Exactly one month after Kühlmann's fall came 'the black day of the German army', when the British delivered their thrust east of Amiens and masses of allied tanks tore holes in the German lines. The initiative now passed to the Western Powers and, despite all of Ludendorff's frantic expedients, he was unable to stem the advance of their armies. On 3 October even his strong nerves had snapped, and he announced that an armistice must be concluded immediately. It was only then that the German people were able to see where the ambition and the political incapacity of the Supreme Command and its annexationist allies had led them. Their reaction to the disaster that was revealed to them was a violent one, and its principal victim was the monarchical system which the army had sought so long and so persistently to maintain.

[1] *Ursachen des Zusammenbruches*, 4. Reihe, ii. 346–7.

IX

THE ARMY AND THE REVOLUTION

1918–1920

Oh, how—*German* this German revolution is! How proper, how pedantic, how lacking in spirit, in verve and in grandeur!

ROSA LUXEMBURG.

Today, as yesterday, the army remains the basis of authority in the State. GENERAL VON LÜTTWITZ, *August 1919.*

NOT the least remarkable of the attributes of the Prussian army as a political organization was its ability to escape having to pay for its own mistakes. In 1848, for instance, it had been military abuses which had touched off the risings which took place in Berlin; yet, when the revolution was over, the army had experienced no real diminution of its powers and prerogatives; and, although Prussia was transformed from an absolute to a constitutional state, the military establishment was not forced to submit to any effective measure of civilian control.

Again in 1918 the army was faced with a revolution for which it was largely responsible, and this time the threat to its freedom was far greater than it had been seventy years before. The military collapse which the war-time policies of the Supreme Command had made inevitable released forces which, on 9 November, swept away the dynasty which the army had served since 1640 and transformed the Reich into a republic. Yet once more the army weathered the storm and once more it did so without any real loss of power.

It can scarcely be argued that this success was due to the collective political intelligence or the adaptability of the German officer corps. Had they been given a choice in November 1918, the majority of the officers would probably have preferred to fight to the end against any compromise with the new republican régime; and, even after an accommodation had been reached between the Supreme Command and Germany's new rulers, it was constantly jeopardized, and in March 1920 almost destroyed, by the counter-revolutionary aspirations of certain military groups. In the last analysis, the officer corps may be said to have been saved against its will; and this was possible because the majority of the German people in the years 1918–20—and this includes the leaders of the largest of the socialist parties—were far more fearful of communism than they were of an unreformed and unregenerate military establishment and, also, because a few of the army's leaders had the wisdom to realize this and to exploit it for all that it was worth. So deep, indeed, was the fear of communism and so skilful its exploitation by the military chiefs, that by the middle of 1920 the army was well on its way to becoming once more the state within the state that it had always been in the past.

I

One cannot help wondering whether the army would have been quite as successful in preserving its autonomous position in Germany's political life if the nation had managed to avoid a violent revolution in 1918. Had William II been wise enough, once the appeal for an armistice had been made to President Wilson, to realize that his own position and that of his son were insupportable, and had he surrendered the throne to one of his grandsons, it is possible that the dynasty would have survived and that Germany would have become a constitutional monarchy on the Western model.[1] The basis for such development was, indeed, provided by the series of important constitutional changes introduced by Prince Max von Baden's government and enacted by the Reichstag and the Bundesrat on 28 October 1918. Inspired by President Wilson's intimation that he could not negotiate with a government which was not in process of democratizing itself, these reforms satisfied political demands which had been made by the Centre, the Progressive, and the Social Democratic parties ever since the 1880's. They promised effective parliamentary government with a real measure of ministerial responsibility; and, most important in the present

[1] The reasons why the abdication issue was not faced up to in time are discussed in Andreas Dorpalen, 'Empress Auguste Victoria and the Fall of the German Monarchy', *American Historical Review*, lviii (1952), especially 33–38. Friedrich Meinecke wrote in his diary on 10 November that he had believed since August that the emperor should abdicate and that, if he had done so 'four or five weeks ago, he might perhaps—who will say so with any certainty?—have saved us from this catastrophe'. Meinecke, *Straßburg, Freiburg, Berlin, 1901–1919* (Stuttgart, 1949), p. 272.

context, they subordinated the military and naval commands to the civil government. The sacrosanct royal *Kommandogewalt* was virtually eliminated by a provision which made the Chancellor responsible for all actions taken by the emperor in his constitutional capacity; appointments of military commanders had to be countersigned by the Chancellor; and the once all-powerful Military Cabinet was brought once more under ministerial control.[1] In the October reforms the kind of restrictions which men like Manteuffel and Albedyll had feared in 1848, 1860, and 1883 seemed at last to have been imposed upon the army.

It is impossible to say how effective these reforms would have been in eliminating the abuses of the past, for they were never really put into effect. Within a week of their passage the naval mutiny at Kiel marked the beginning of serious revolutionary activity, and this was encouraged by the emperor's wilful refusal to lay down his office. When the Independent Socialist Kurt Eisner, convinced that only a radical break with the past would bring Germany peace, set up a soldiers and workers council in Munich and proclaimed the Bavarian republic on 7 November, the fate of the German monarchy was sealed. The Bavarian example was followed in Cologne, Frankfurt, Stuttgart, and Leipzig; and, by the morning of 9 November, Prussia was ringed round by revolution. Prince Max now yielded to the storm, handing the government over to the Majority Socialists; and, at two o'clock on the afternoon of 9 November, Philipp Scheidemann, in the name of that party, announced the establishment of a German republic.

To the army, the proclamation of the republic seemed to represent a much more serious threat than the reforms of October, the more so because it appeared likely that the republic would be socialist in character and would be guided, as far as military institutions were concerned, by the traditional socialist prejudice against the professional military tradition and the dominance of the General Staff. Yet this was only superficially true. In 1918 German socialism was hopelessly disunited; and the strongest of the socialist factions had long since ceased to be a revolutionary party. The Majority Socialists had declared the republic with the greatest of reluctance. 'We wanted to save the monarchy', the editor of *Vorwärts* said later, 'but, if some called,

[1] Reichsamt des Innern, *Reichs-Gesetzblatt*, 1918, pp. 1273–5.

"Long live the republic!", then there was nothing left for us to do but call with them.'[1] They had been forced ahead by the realization that, once the monarchy had been overthrown in the federal states, the unity of the Reich could not be preserved unless the central government were also transformed; and they were doubtless influenced also by the fear of leaving the initiative to the Independent Socialists and the spartacists, their rivals for the leadership of the proletariat. But even after the die had been cast, the Majority Socialist leaders showed no desire to press on with a genuinely socialist policy.[2] Their principal objective, indeed, was to restore internal order as quickly as possible lest the extremists drive Germany into the arms of bolshevism. The fact that this was so offered the army an opportunity to assume a commanding position in the counsels of the new régime at the very outset of its existence; and one man at supreme headquarters had the intelligence to realize this.

On 26 October Ludendorff had been dismissed from his post lest his growing megalomania jeopardize the negotiations with President Wilson which had been begun at his insistence three weeks before. His successor as first quartermaster-general was Wilhelm Groener, a Württemberger who had been chief of field-railway transport from 1914 to 1916, head of the agencies charged with promoting the economic mobilization programme in 1916 and 1917, and, most recently, chief of staff of the army of occupation in the east. In a supreme headquarters which was stunned by the disintegration of the military situation and which, after the arrival of the emperor and his suite on 29 October, was prey to all manner of fantastic plans, Groener soon revealed himself to be the most clear-headed and determined of the army's leaders. Although, in the first days after his arrival at Spa, he rejected any suggestion that the emperor should abdicate,[3] he quickly realized that this position was

[1] Quoted in John L. Snell, 'Republic by Default', a paper delivered before the American Historical Association at Chicago in December 1953.

[2] In 1919 Oswald Spengler wrote scornfully of the Majority Socialists: 'It is without parallel. They suddenly had what they had been working for for forty years, full power, and they regarded it as a misfortune.' *Preußentum und Sozialismus* (new ed., Munich, 1934), p. 9.

[3] In his *Lebenserinnerungen*, pp. 447 f., Groener explains his original position by saying: 'If my political instinct told me that the important question was the maintenance of the monarchy rather than that of the person of the monarch, nevertheless, as an officer and a representative of the officers, I had to strive to the

untenable and was soon urging that the only way in which William could restore confidence in the monarchy was to seek death in battle. When this advice was not accepted and when the emperor, under the influence of officers like *Generaladjutant* von Plessen, proposed to march into Germany at the head of his *Feldtruppen* and suppress the revolutionary agitations, it was Groener who prevented serious consideration of this project by bluntly telling his sovereign that the army would 'march home in peace and order under its leaders and commanding generals, but not under the command of Your Majesty, for it no longer stands behind Your Majesty'. Groener also opposed the equally unrealistic suggestion that William might abdicate as emperor but not as King of Prussia, although it was the onrush of events in Berlin rather than the first quartermaster-general's attitude which was decisive in blocking this experiment.[1]

Throughout his later career Groener's policy in 1918 was the subject of controversy and misunderstanding, and he was often accused of having shown a lack of devotion to the monarchy and of having been guided by secret republican convictions. In reality, dynastic loyalty and political partisanship had little influence on his actions. In the November crisis and subsequently, his policy was determined by considerations of *Staatsräson* beyond the comprehension of an officer corps which, in the shock of defeat and revolution, had given way to an impractical feudal romanticism. Perhaps his Swabian blood

utmost to see that the inner constitution of the army remained intact, and this depended on its personal relationship with the Emperor.'

[1] For a full discussion of the events at Spa, see the excellent account of Maurice Baumont, *The Fall of the Kaiser* (New York, 1931), which may be supplemented by Groener's description of his position there, which is reproduced in Beckmann, *Der Dolchstoßprozeß in München* (Munich 1925). In a laborious reconstruction, *Das Ende der Monarchie 9.11.18*, ed. by Werner Conze (Berlin, 1952), especially pp. 143–4, Graf von Westarp has challenged the validity of Groener's judgement concerning the loyalty of the troops to the emperor in a fight against the revolution. See the opposing evidence in Baumont, pp. 93, 224 ff. In any event, the question of loyalty was not paramount in Groener's thinking. As he says in his memoirs, he opposed the projected operation because, 'through the disintegration of the *Etappe* and the occupation of the sources of supply by the revolutionaries, the possibility of offering resistance to the enemy for more than a few days had disappeared, while at the same time the American break-through north of Verdun had brought the army into a catastrophic position'. These events could not help affect the course of a campaign against the home front unfavourably. Groener's statement to the emperor was made in sharper terms than it might have been because he was irritated by the *Wirklichkeitsfremdheit* of the emperor's advisers and because he wanted to prevent William from grasping at straws. *Lebenserinnerungen*, pp. 445, 460.

enabled him to be more realistic than the east Elbian paladins who stood at William's side at Spa. He was moved, in any case, by two clear and all-compelling convictions. Whatever else happened, the unity of the Reich must be maintained; and, at the same time, the army—that is, the officer corps—must be preserved as the protector of that unity, the guardian of national stability and development, and the source of 'moral-spiritual strength' for future generations.[1] Since William's frantic expedients promised to destroy both Reich and army, Groener opposed them uncompromisingly and effectively.

When the republic was proclaimed on the afternoon of 9 November, the first quartermaster-general reacted with none of that instinctive horror that affected his professional colleagues. He had had enough dealings with the Social Democrats during the war to realize that they were not very ardent revolutionaries and that their attitude toward the radicals and separatists was not much different from his own. He suspected that, in their present insecure position, they would welcome an offer of military support. At the same time, it was obviously to the interest of the officer corps to have the vacuum left by the fall of the monarchy filled by some governmental authority with a claim to legitimacy. Unless the officers could argue that they were serving such authority, they might lose control of the troops to the soldiers councils, which were already established in the *Etappe* and were now springing up among the front-line regiments.[2] Moreover, the Allied Powers had now transmitted the terms of armistice to the High Command; and Groener—concerned, as he wrote later, 'with keeping our weapons clean and the General Staff unburdened for the future'[3]—needed a civilian government which would assume the responsibility for accepting them.[4]

[1] *Lebenserinnerungen*, p. 467.

[2] On the councils, see Paul Gentizon, *L'Armée allemande depuis la défaite* (Paris, 1920), pp. 23–29.

[3] Groener, *Lebenserinnerungen*, p. 466.

[4] Groener's eagerness to avoid responsibility for terms which he knew would be harsh had already been shown on 6 November when he had agreed that the German armistice delegation should be headed by a civilian rather than a soldier. See General H. Mordacq, *L'Armistice du 11 Novembre 1918* (Paris, 1937), pp. 145–9. Harry Rudin's argument in *Armistice 1918* (New Haven, 1944), pp. 323–4 that the initiative for this change came from the civilian authorities, is true but loses its force in view of Groener's later statement that he 'could only approve [an arrangement whereby], in these unhappy negotiations, from which no good was to be expected, the army and the army command remained as free from blame as possible'. *Lebenserinnerungen*, p. 449.

These considerations led the first quartermaster-general on the night of 9 November to make his now famous telephone call to Friedrich Ebert, the leader of the Majority Socialists and the new Chancellor of the Reich. In the course of a brief conversation, he promised that the present High Command would continue its functions until the troops had been brought back to Germany in good order and perfect discipline. This was, at least implicitly, an admission that the army recognized the legitimacy of the new régime, but it was, nevertheless, a conditional recognition. Groener made it clear that the officer corps expected the government to aid it in maintaining discipline in the army, in securing the army's sources of supply, and in preventing the disruption of the railway system during the army's march home. And he stressed the fact that the officer corps looked to the government to combat bolshevism and was putting itself at the government's disposal primarily for that purpose.

Ebert accepted the offer and the conditions without hesitation, and thus the historic pact was concluded—a pact which, in the words of one authority, was 'destined to save both parties from the extreme elements of revolution but, as a result of which, the Weimar Republic was doomed at birth'.[1]

There is no reason to suppose that either partner contemplated this latter result; and, at the moment of the conclusion of their agreement, neither could have been very sanguine about its achieving even the former. Could Ebert control the situation in Berlin until army aid reached him? In the first days after the declaration of the republic, this seemed doubtful. Even at the time of the famous telephone call, his authority was extremely shaky, for he claimed the chancellorship on the basis of a constitution which no longer existed.[2] On the day following the telephone conversation he had to abandon this fiction. For when, on the afternoon of 10 November, he finally succeeded in forming a cabinet—the so-called Council of Peoples Repre-

[1] John W. Wheeler-Bennett, *The Nemesis of Power: The German Army in Politics, 1918–1945* (London, 1953), p. 21. For a measured judgement of Ebert's motives, see Arthur Rosenberg, *A History of the German Republic* (London, 1936), p. 50.

[2] Prince Max von Baden had handed his office over to Ebert and this in itself was unprecedented in German constitutional practice. Ebert, in accepting it, declared that he was doing so 'on the basis of the constitution of the Reich', despite the fact that that constitution had presumably been abrogated by the declaration of abdication and the proclamation of the republic. See Bredt, 'Der deutsche Reichstag im Weltkriege', *Ursachen des Zusammenbruches*, 4. Reihe, viii. 348–51.

sentatives, comprising three Majority Socialists (Ebert, Scheidemann, and Landsberg) and three Independents (Haase, Dittmann, and Barth)—the Independents refused to participate until he agreed that sovereign power resided in the soldiers and workers councils. On the same day, the soldiers and workers councils of Berlin met at Zirkus Busch and elected an executive committee, which henceforth claimed a right of control over the cabinet. Ebert's relations with the supervisory body were from the outset uncertain, the more so because it was under continual pressure from the left wing Independents and the spartacists who advocated a more revolutionary programme than he did himself. At the same time, the presence of large numbers of armed workers and the existence of irregular formations like the Peoples Naval Division made the situation in the capital highly inflammable.

The development of the situation in Berlin was watched with misgivings by Groener and his colleagues. Their immediate concern, of course, was to get the troops which were still stationed in France and Belgium back home. Once this was done, it might be possible to use the field army to strengthen Ebert's hand—indeed, to force the dissolution of the councils in Berlin, to disarm the civilian populace and the armed bands, and to force the speedy convocation of a National Assembly which would restore order to the Reich. Whether all this could be done would depend upon whether the *Feldtruppen* remained immune to the revolutionary contagion and permitted themselves to be used for these purposes. Groener was not optimistic on this score. The first quartermaster-general wrote later that from the outset he was inclined to believe 'that the revolutionary movement could no longer be put down by the troops of the purely peoples army that the old imperial army had long since become but only by specially raised and trained volunteer troops'. Such volunteers could not, however, be summoned up with 'a wave of the hand'; one must do what one could with the forces at his disposal, making every effort to maintain discipline and order.[1]

Discipline presented no very great problem while the troops were still west of the Rhine. On 12 November Ebert sent a

[1] Groener Papers: Memorandum of 1 June 1922. See also Reginald H. Phelps, 'Aus den Groener Dokumenten: I. Groener, Ebert und Hindenburg', *Deutsche Rundschau* (July 1950), p. 532.

telegram to Field Marshal von Hindenburg[1] requesting him to inform the army in the field that:

1. The relations between officer and rank and file are to be built up on mutual confidence. Prerequisites to this are willing submission of the ranks to the officer and comradely treatment by the officer of the ranks.
2. The officer's superiority in rank remains. Unqualified obedience in service is of prime importance for the success of the return home to Germany. Military discipline and army order must, therefore, be maintained under all circumstances.
3. The Soldiers' Councils have an advisory voice in maintaining confidence between officer and rank and file in questions of food, leave, the infliction of disciplinary punishments. *Their highest duty is to try to prevent disorder and mutiny.*

Groener was able to use this unequivocal confirmation of the traditional concept of command to stifle revolutionary agitation and to overawe the soldiers councils elected by the home-coming troops; and the evacuation was accomplished with perfect success and within the time limit set by the armistice terms of 11 November.

Once the German frontiers had been crossed, however, the situation deteriorated rapidly, for the most pressing desire of most soldiers was for demobilization. To prevent the army from melting away, Groener boldly tried to bend the regimental soldiers councils to his own purposes[2]—to turn them into propaganda units which would indoctrinate the troops with the necessity of remaining with the colours until the radicals in Berlin were put down.[3] His efforts—which culminated in an

[1] Text in 'The German Revolution', *International Conciliation*, no. 137 (Apr. 1919), p. 16; italics mine. According to this source the telegram was issued by the Wolff press bureau on 12 November, which probably means that it had been sent to Hindenburg on the same day or the day before. See Kurt Caro and Walter Oehme, *Schleichers Aufstieg: Ein Beitrag zur Geschichte der Gegenrevolution* (Berlin, 1933), pp. 11–12. Wheeler-Bennett, in *Nemesis of Power*, pp. 25–26, speaks of this telegram as having been read to delegates of the soldiers' councils at a meeting in Supreme Headquarters on the morning of 10 November. At that time, however, the Council of Peoples Representatives, which signed the telegram, had not yet come into existence. Wheeler-Bennett's account is apparently based on Jacques Benoist-Méchin, *History of the German Army since the Armistice*, i (Zürich, 1939), 56–57, which, in turn, seems to rest on a misreading of E. O. Volkmann, *Revolution über Deutschland* (Oldenburg, 1930), pp. 69–71.

[2] Groener Papers: Memorandum of 1 June 1922. Schüddekopf, *Heer und Republik*, pp. 20 ff.

[3] Groener worked especially through the council which had been established at Supreme Headquarters. This body was encouraged to issue manifestoes in favour of 'the Ebert government'. It was also informed, on 21 November, that it might

abortive Congress of Front Line Soldiers at Ems on 1 December[1] —did not counteract the prevailing desire for demobilization and succeeded only in awakening the suspicions of the executive committee of councils in Berlin and its left wing supporters. Already angered by reports of reactionary statements by divisional and regimental commanders and by a Supreme Command directive forbidding troops to wear red cockades or other symbols of revolutionary sympathy, the Independents began now to accuse the army leaders of seeking to promote counter-revolution and charged that Ebert was conspiring with the generals to this end. Moreover, on 8 December, when General Lequis, at the head of ten divisions of troops, reached the suburbs of the capital, the executive committee and the Independent members of the cabinet refused to authorize his entrance into Berlin.

This put Ebert in a very awkward position. He was strongly inclined at first to defer to the demands of his left wing colleagues, but he was prevented from doing so by a plain intimation from supreme headquarters that, unless the troops were admitted to the city at once, he could expect no further support from the army.[2] Before this threat Ebert bowed and, at the cost of alienating the Independents even farther, managed finally to persuade the cabinet to grant the authorization desired in Kassel. The army gained little, however, by its insistence. As soon as they were inside Berlin, Lequis's troops—most of whom belonged to local regiments and had families in the vicinity—simply evaporated; and, at the end of a week, the general had less than a thousand men under his effective control.[3] The chances that these would be able to disarm the citizenry or disband the councils was remote.

Moreover, the tactics employed by the army produced a reaction which threatened the very existence of the officer corps. On 12 December, the day after Lequis's forces entered the city, the cabinet, under the pressure of the executive committee,

become necessary to use force against the councils in Berlin. See Phelps in *Deutsche Rundschau* (July 1950), p. 533, and Volkmann, *Revolution*, pp. 79–80.

[1] The Ems congress was supposed to result in a ringing denunciation of the executive committee in Berlin, but it was stampeded by Emil Barth who advised the delegates that they were being misled by their officers. Volkmann, *Revolution*, pp. 80–81.

[2] Wheeler-Bennett, *Nemesis of Power*, pp. 29–30.

[3] Friedrich Wilhelm von Oertzen, *Die deutschen Freikorps, 1918–1923* (6th ed., Munich, 1939), p. 248.

issued a decree calling for the formation of a republican civil guard [*Freiwillige Volkswehr*], a force which was to be established on strictly democratic principles, outside the framework of the regular army, and which was presumably to reach a strength of 11,000 officers and men.[1] Four days later the first National Congress of Soldiers and Workers Councils was convoked in Berlin. This body immediately passed resolutions demanding the dismissal of Hindenburg and his staff and the dissolution of those favourite targets of German anti-militarists, the *Kadettenhäuser*. Then, warming to its task, the congress proceeded, by overwhelming vote, to pass a seven-point programme introduced by Walter Lampl of Hamburg. The so-called 'Hamburg points' called for the transference of command over the whole military establishment to the cabinet and the executive committee, the abolition of all insignia of rank, and the suppression of *Kadavergehorsam*, the election of officers by the troops, the suppression of the standing army, and the speedy creation of the *Volkswehr* provided for in the decree of 12 December.[2] Here were the elements of a truly revolutionary military policy and one which, if carried out, spelled an end to all of Groener's and Ebert's plans.

The reaction of the Supreme Command was immediate and violent. Hindenburg was furious at the effrontery of the delegates who dared suggest that he might be deprived of his epaulettes, and he instructed Groener to inform Ebert that he would fight the decisions of the congress 'to the last ditch'.[3] Groener himself seems momentarily to have lost confidence in his telephone partner. On 20 December, accompanied by Major Kurt von Schleicher, an officer who was destined to play a fateful role in the political history of the republic, the first quartermaster-general descended on Berlin in full regimentals[4] and icily informed the Majority Socialist leader that unless the demands of the congress were rejected out of hand the pact of December would lapse and Ebert would be thrown upon his own resources.

[1] See General Ludwig Maercker, *Vom Kaiserheer zur Reichswehr: Geschichte der freiwilligen Landesjägerkorps* (3rd ed., Leipzig, 1922), App. I. This reversed an earlier decision of the executive committee to refrain from attempts to raise a 'red guard' or anything of the sort. See Caro and Oehme, *Schleichers Aufstieg*, p. 11.

[2] See *Allgemeiner Kongreß der Arbeiter- und Soldatenräte Deutschlands, Stenographische Berichte*, pp. 61–65.

[3] Volkmann, *Revolution*, pp. 143–4.

[4] See the spirited description of their arrival in Berlin, in Caro and Oehme, *Schleichers Aufstieg*, p. 8.

This forcing play is understandable, but it is doubtful whether it was either necessary or wise. Was there, after all, the slightest possibility that the demands of the congress of councils would be put into effect? One who reads the debates of that congress cannot help but be reminded of the deliberations of the Prussian National Assembly of 1848—a body which, it will be remembered, also talked of the necessity of establishing a peoples army but which, once its rhetorical exercises were completed, did nothing to execute or to facilitate the execution of its demands.[1] The same thing happened in December 1918. The delegates who voted for Lampl's resolutions never seem to have realized that their implementation would depend upon the continued existence of a revolutionary political system—in fact, upon the continued existence of the system of councils. On 19 December most of those who had voted for the Hamburg points rejected a proposal for the continued exercise of legislative and executive power by the councils and demanded instead that elections for a National Assembly be held as soon as possible.[2] Moreover, in the elections for a new executive committee of the councils, all seats were won by Majority Socialists.[3] This meant that, within the framework of the existing government, Ebert's position was now stronger than it had been before the congress convened; and, that being so, the chances of any tangible results coming from the decree of 12 December or the Hamburg points were very slim, provided matters were allowed to take their course.

In view of this an immediate repudiation of the Hamburg points was hardly 'a question of life and death' for the officer corps, as Groener described it at the time;[4] and Ebert was justified in urging the first quartermaster-general not to force matters to a head.[5] But the army had its way and, at a joint meeting of the cabinet and the executive committee, attended by Groener and Schleicher, Ebert was forced to promise—although he did so in rather equivocal language—that the Hamburg points would not be applied in the field army.[6] The

[1] See above, Chapter III, pp. 110 ff.

[2] See *Ursachen des Zusammenbruches*, 4. Reihe, viii. 359, where these decisions of 19 December are described as marking 'die Schicksalsstunde des deutschen Volkes und seines Reiches'.

[3] This result was facilitated by the fact that the Independent Socialists boycotted the elections.

[4] Wheeler-Bennett, *Nemesis of Power*, p. 33.

[5] Volkmann, *Revolution*, p. 146.

[6] Ibid., p. 151.

immediate effect of this was to precipitate a crisis which, for the Supreme Command, was a near débâcle.

Infuriated by Ebert's action, the Independent Socialists began to stir up the soldiers and sailors councils in Berlin. Their activities, especially those of Emil Barth, had a direct influence on the decision of the most violent and undisciplined of these, the Peoples Naval Division, led by Emil Dorrenbach, to surround the Chancellory on 23 December and to take the Ebert government prisoner.[1] Ebert, using his secret telephone connexion with the Supreme Command at Kassel, appealed for help; but then, having managed to reach a compromise with Dorrenbach, sought to revoke his request. The Supreme Command had now, however, lost all patience. They insisted that the troops of General Lequis at Potsdam be ordered to attack the rebellious sailors in their headquarters in the imperial stables, and Ebert was forced once more to give way.[2]

In the fight at the *Marstall* on Christmas eve 1918 the imperial army suffered a greater humiliation than that suffered by royal troops in the same place on 19 March 1848.[3] Lequis by this time had only about 800 effectives. These forces, thanks to their possession of some light artillery pieces, managed, at the end of about two hours' fighting, to bring the beleaguered sailors to the point of surrender. But at that moment a hostile crowd of men and women, raised by Independent and spartacist leaders, debouched into the square and surrounded the regiments; and, after a few moments of indecision, the troops simply dropped their weapons and ran away. In a matter of minutes, and for the second time in their long history, the Prussian guards had been routed by a civilian mob.

II

What might not have happened now if this had been Paris or even Valparaiso? But it was Berlin, and Christmastide; the events at the *Marstall* had no immediate consequences; and the army was once more privileged to avoid paying for its mistakes. While the victorious crowds melted away to their homes, the warring socialist sects celebrated the season by exchanging recriminations. The Independent Socialists, after appealing in

[1] The sailors had been squabbling with Ebert concerning their pay for some time, and this incident was at least partly an attempt to blackmail the government.

[2] Volkmann, *Revolution*, p. 158.

[3] See above, Chapter III, pp. 100–5.

vain to the executive committee for immediate implementation of the Hamburg programme, resigned from the cabinet—a gesture whose only effect was to give Ebert complete control of the governmental machinery. A few days later the spartacists, in their first national congress, declared an end to the policy of co-operation with the Independents, transformed themselves into the German Communist party and plunged into a welter of fantastic plans for a *Putsch* which—in view of their previous actions—could not expect any mass support. And, while all this went on, the Supreme Command was given time to recover from the panic into which the defeat of 24 December had thrown them.

That panic had been real. In the first days after Lequis's discomfiture, in a meeting of the division chiefs at Kassel, the same officers who had been most active in urging the use of force to smash the revolution, now argued that it was useless to fight against fate, that the Supreme Command should dissolve, and that the officers should return to their homes to protect their families as best they could. Against these counsels of despair, Groener objected strenuously. Resignation would simply mean the destruction of the Reich. The maintenance of the authority of the government must remain the objective of the army. Since they had failed to maintain it by means of the war-weary troops brought back from France, they must find new troops; and the logical solution was to revert to a plan discussed in the past—to concentrate on raising volunteers, or free corps.[1]

Groener's views prevailed, although it is to be presumed that many who listened to them doubted their feasibility. Yet they were not impracticable. Even as they were being debated, the first of the free corps was conducting training exercises in Westphalia.

On 12 December—the same day on which the Peoples Representatives had issued their bootless decree concerning the formation of a *Volkswehr*—General Ludwig Maercker, the former commander of the 214th Infantry Division, had submitted a memorandum to his superior officers, setting forth his ideas for the creation of a volunteer rifle corps which could be used to defend Germany from anarchy. His plans had been approved by the Supreme Command, which also provided him with the necessary financial support; and he had set about raising his

[1] Volkmann, *Revolution*, p. 164.

force. He had no difficulty in finding recruits. Young officers whose units had disbanded, soldiers who had no desire to lose the comradeship and security of army life, demobilized men who discovered, after returning to their homes, that they had lost the ability to adjust themselves to the requirements of civilian society, and others who were disgusted or frightened by the political excesses of the revolutionary era, poured into the Franciscan convent at Salzkotten where Maercker had established his headquarters. Within a fortnight he had the rudiments of a fighting force and was worried only by the difficulty of obtaining necessary supplies.

The decision of the Supreme Command, after the fight at the *Marstall*, to pin its hopes on the kind of force he was raising solved this problem and at the same time encouraged other officers to follow Maercker's example. On 26 December Colonel Wilhelm Reinhard, formerly of the 4th Guard Regiment, met with some old comrades and set about organizing a free corps; and he was soon joined by Sergeant-Major Suppe, who had raised the force which protected the *Reichskanzlei* on 24 December. Meanwhile, at Potsdam, Major Stephani reorganized what was left of the old 1st Regiment of foot guards and the Imperial Potsdam Regiment and built up their strength by accepting former officers, professional men, cadets, and university students as volunteers. By Supreme Command directive, these units and others in the vicinity of Berlin, were placed under the command of General Walther von Lüttwitz, who took over Lequis's position as chief of *Generalkommando Berlin*.[1]

Ebert, who was sitting in the centre of the city, hourly expecting new risings on the part of the extreme left, was kept informed of these preparations and was simultaneously encouraged to do what he could in his own way to raise forces for the defence of the government. As a step in this direction, on 27 December, he summoned Gustav Noske to Berlin, appointed

[1] There is a tremendous literature on the free corps, and all of the officers mentioned above have written memoirs of one kind or another. Their tendency to exaggerate the importance of their own part in the events that followed, and their cavalier disregard for chronology and statistical accuracy, makes it impossible to say with assurance exactly when the various forces came into existence and how strong they were at any given moment. The above paragraphs, and much that follows, are based on the brilliant study of Robert G. L. Waite, *Vanguard of Nazism: The Free Corps Movement in Post-War Germany, 1918–1923* (Cambridge, Mass., 1952). See also Oberst a. D. Wilhelm Reinhard, *1918–1919: Die Wehen der Republik* (Berlin, 1933), pp. 59–62; and Oertzen, *Freikorps*, pp. 251–8.

him to one of the cabinet seats vacated by the Independent Socialists, and asked him to act, in effect, as Minister of Defence.[1] Noske had long been known in the party for his energy and determination, his contempt for the radical fringe, and also, it should be added, for his freedom from doctrinaire anti-militarism.[2] The first of these qualities he had demonstrated in restoring order to Kiel after the November mutinies; the others he was to display in Berlin in the weeks that followed. Immediately after accepting his post, he entered into close relations with Lüttwitz and with Majors von Stockhausen and Hammerstein, who had been appointed to Lüttwitz's staff. Simultaneously, he set about the task of raising troops.

This was not an easy task and, in view of the criticisms later levelled at Noske for having relied so heavily upon the free corps, it is well to remember the difficulties that confronted him. The truth was that few of the so-called 'republican' units which existed at this time were either politically sound or militarily effective. The watch regiments [*Wachregimenter*] and security forces [*Sicherheitswehren*] which had sprung up in the larger cities since November were generally recruited from revolution-minded soldiers of the *Etappe* army or from the unemployed; they had had no combat training and were badly disciplined; and the Berlin *Sicherheitswehr*, for instance, was to prove completely useless during the disorders of 5–6 January. The decree of 12 December, calling for the creation of a *Volkswehr*, had resulted in the formation of only a very few units; and, here again, the most active *Volkswehr* leaders were apt to be opposed to the government. The republican defence corps

[1] Gustav Noske, *Von Kiel bis Kapp: Zur Geschichte der deutschen Revolution* (Berlin, 1920), p. 63; and his *Aufstieg und Niedergang der deutschen Sozialdemokratie* (Zürich, 1947), p. 82.

[2] Noske's speech in the debate on the military budget of 1907 was so patriotic in tone that he was lampooned in *Lustige Blätter* in a poem which pointed out that, in time of war, when other reservists hesitated to join the colours, the nation would always be able to count on Noske.

> 'Noske schnallt den Säbel um,
> Noske geht aufs Ganze,
> Noske feuert, bum, bum, bum,
> Noske stürmt die Schanze,
> Noske schreit Hurra, Hurra!
> Noske hält die Wachen,
> Noske schießt Viktoria,
> Noske wird's schon machen.'

Noske, *Aufstieg und Niedergang*, pp. 29–30.

[*Republikanische Soldatenwehr*], raised in mid-November by the city commandant Otto Wels, had by January become almost as unreliable as the Peoples Naval Division. All in all, Noske was to discover that the only republican forces he could count on were the Regiment Reichstag, which was part of a new Republican Guard formed by the Majority Socialists in early January, and a unit called the *Maikäfer* raised by *Feldwebelleutnant* Schulze from the Replacement Battalion of the Guards Fusiliers.[1]

Despite this unpromising situation, Noske strove energetically to co-ordinate existing forces and to raise new ones. Simultaneously, he turned his attention to the security police, a force which numbered some 4,500 men but which had, thanks to its commander, the left Independent Emil Eichhorn, become a revolutionary rabble. As the first step toward reorganizing this body, Noske urged Eichhorn's dismissal; and government orders to that effect were issued on 4 January.

It was this action that precipitated the new disorders that Ebert feared. On 5 January the Independents and the communists resolved their differences for the moment and issued a joint manifesto, calling upon the proletariat to stage a mass demonstration of their resistance to Eichhorn's dismissal. On the following day 200,000 workers, carrying weapons and flags, poured into the streets of Berlin. In the *Reichskanzlei* Ebert and his colleagues sat throughout the morning receiving bulletins which reported the massing of columns in the Tiergarten, the occupation of the *Vorwärts* building and the Wolff Telegraphic Bureau by the spartacists, the refusal of the police to abandon Eichhorn, and other frightening news. It seemed that all would be lost unless determined counter-action was taken. Ebert turned to Noske and asked him to assume supreme command over an operation to end the disorders; and Noske answered: 'I don't mind. Someone must be the bloodhound. I will not shirk the responsibility.'[2]

When, however, Noske made his way, with some difficulty, through the crowded streets to the General Staff building on the *Platz der Republik* (formerly the *Königsplatz*), he was informed by Stockhausen and Hammerstein that matters were more

[1] On all this, see Harold J. Gordon, Jr., *The Reichswehr and the German Republic, 1919–1926* (Princeton, 1957), pp. 17–21.

[2] Noske, *Von Kiel bis Kapp*, p. 68.

desperate than Ebert seemed to think. There was little hope of successful military action at the moment. The free corps outside the city would not be fully equipped for another five or six days. Colonel Reinhard probably had enough men to hold on to the garrison area at Moabit. For the rest, the officers said—in words that unconsciously echoed the advice given by Prittwitz to his king in March 1848—the only advisable course was to evacuate the city in the hope that an effective attack might be launched from outside in a few days. Noske had perforce to accept this advice. He returned to Ebert and repeated it to his flabbergasted chief and then left the city.[1] In the days that followed, he sat in the girls' convent school at Dahlem, broadcasting scores of appeals for volunteers, authorizing officers to raise new forces, and listening to Lüttwitz's staff plan the operation against Berlin.

In bidding Ebert goodbye, Noske had said, 'Perhaps we'll have luck'. It seemed an apt remark in view of the turmoil in the streets of Berlin on 6 January and the defenceless state of the government. Yet once more, as in the first days after 24 December, the Ebert government was saved by the indecision and disunity of their antagonists. While 200,000 men stood in the streets, ready to 'save the revolution', the spartacist and Independent leaders could not agree on a specific course of action; and this failure of leadership broke the revolutionary mood of 6 January and turned the tide in Ebert's favour. Within two days the Independent Socialists were trying to call the whole business off and to devise a formula which would bring Ebert and the spartacists together.

Even if Ebert had wanted to consider this, it is unlikely that the soldiers would have permitted him to do so. The free corps were now ready; and, at long last, the destruction of bolshevism, so ardently desired by the soldiers, was to be carried out. On 10 January the operation against Berlin began with a successful attack by the Reinhard Brigade against spartacist headquarters in the munitions works at Spandau. On the same night, Stephani's Potsdam Free Corps attacked the Belle-Alliance Platz and, using flame-throwers, machine guns, mortars, and artillery, forced the spartacists in the *Vorwärts* building to capitulate. On the morning of the 11th, a cold rainy day, Noske, at the head

[1] Volkmann, *Revolution*, pp. 179–80.

of some 3,000 men, formed from Maercker's Volunteer Rifles and his own Iron Division from Kiel, entered the city from the south and west, marching through the Potsdamer Straße, the Leipzigerstraße, the Wilhelmstraße, and the Tiergarten to the further suburbs. There was no opposition. In the next four days Berlin was systematically occupied and the main boulevards and *Plätze* put under military guard. By 15 January the capital was completely in the government's hands.[1]

If there ever had been a chance of a bolshevist revolution in Germany it died during spartacist week in January 1919.[2] The government was never again so completely bereft of military power as it was in the first days after the fight at the *Marstall.* Volunteers now poured into free corps recruiting centres.[3] At the end of January Lüttwitz announced that he had enough troops to permit operations against provincial centres of disorder without jeopardizing the security of Berlin;[4] and the government began the great *Säuberungsaktion* which was to be completed successfully by June. In February and March spartacist insurrections in Bremen, Cuxhaven, and Wilhelmshaven in the north, Mühlheim and Düsseldorf in the west, and Halle in central Germany, were subdued by the free corps of Maercker and Lichtschlag. In the week of 5–13 March Reinhard crushed the second spartacist rising in Berlin, killing some 1,500 in the course of his operations. In April Maercker's Rifles restored order to Magdeburg and Braunschweig, while the Freikorps Goerlitz and Oberstleutnant Faupel took Dresden. In early May Maercker and Hülsen pacified Leipzig; and, finally, in the same month, an army composed of various of the volunteer formations and commanded by General von Oven, liquidated the communist government which had seized power

[1] Noske, *Von Kiel bis Kapp*, pp. 74–75; Waite, *Vanguard of Nazism*, pp. 60–62; Oertzen, *Freikorps*, pp. 262–9; Reinhard, *1918–1919*, pp. 69–79.

[2] Rosenberg calls the January fighting 'the battle of the Marne of the German revolution'. *German Republic*, p. 84. One of the Russians who were in Berlin in 1919 —perhaps Karl Radek—said, however, that one couldn't expect to make a revolution with the spartacists and Independents and that when you told a spartacist that the time for action had come, he said: 'Excuse me for a little while. I'd like to go home and put the table cloth that I inherited from my grandmother in a safe place.' Wipert von Bülow, *Deutschlands Weg nach Rapallo* (Wiesbaden, 1951), p. 40.

[3] By the summer of 1919 the total number enrolled in free corps was somewhere between 200,000 and 400,000. Waite, *Vanguard*, p. 40.

[4] Volkmann, *Revolution*, p. 201.

in Bavaria during the disorders following the murder of Kurt Eisner in February. Quiet now descended over the long troubled Reich.[1]

With this parade of victories in Germany's cities, the partners of 9 November had every reason to be satisfied. Ebert had defeated his leftist rivals; and although, in the elections of 19 January, his party had not won an absolute majority of the seats in the National Assembly, it had won more than any other party and, in union with the Centre and Democratic parties, was strong enough to draft a democratic constitution for Germany.[2] For his part, Groener had seen the unity of the Reich preserved and, quite as important, had witnessed the reorganization of Germany's armed forces, not on revolutionary lines, but in accordance with principles which he regarded as sound. For when the National Assembly at Weimar took up the question of military organization it made no attempt to return to the philosophy of the December decree or the Hamburg points. The majority of the delegates were concerned primarily with giving Germany an army strong enough to complete the restoration of internal order and to protect the frontiers; and, while they sought to provide constitutional provisions for democratic control of the military establishment,[3] they were entirely willing to

[1] For accounts of these operations, see Waite, *Vanguard of Nazism*, chap. iv, and the sources cited there. See also Volkmann, *Revolution*, pp. 215–36.

[2] The Majority Socialists won 163 of the 421 seats; the Centre 89; the Democratic party 74; the German Nationalists 42; the German Peoples party 22; and the Independent Socialists 22. On 11 February the Assembly elected Ebert President of the Reich. He requested Scheidemann to form a cabinet which, when organized, was composed of representatives of the three largest parties, with one non-party member, Count Brockdorff-Rantzau, who accepted the portfolio for foreign affairs.

[3] In accordance with the constitution of 1919, which was finally adopted in August, the President of the Reich was made supreme head of the army (article 47) and was to nominate and dismiss all general officers (article 46). He was authorized by article 48 to restore order in the event that public security in the Reich was endangered, acting 'if necessary with the aid of the armed forces', and was further empowered temporarily to suspend basic rights guaranteed by the constitution at such times. He was compelled, however, to inform the Reichstag of all measures taken under authority of this article; and such measures could be revoked on demand of the Reichstag. In general, the President's decrees had to be countersigned by the Chancellor or by the competent minister (article 50) which—since the Chancellor was dependent on the confidence of the Reichstag—implied a degree of parliamentary control. All members of the Reichswehr had to take an oath of allegiance to the constitution (article 176), and were subject, except in time of war, to civil, rather than military courts, the latter—including courts of honour—being abolished (articles 105, 106). The exclusive right of legislation with respect to the army was transferred from the provinces to the Reich; the separate contingents and

leave the internal administration and the command of the army in the hands of the old officer corps.

Thus, although the law for the creation of a Provisional Reichswehr, which was passed on 6 March 1919,[1] called for an army 'built on a democratic basis', it provided that the officers should be chosen, in the first instance, from among those who had proven themselves at the front or in the free corps, and, further, that, while the career of officer should be open to non-commissioned officers and men who proved themselves worthy of it, the decision as to their qualifications should be left to their battalion commanders. Groener's desire to preserve the imperial officer corps was quite clearly satisfied by these provisions; and the transition to a republican form of government did not, until 1935 at least, change the social composition of the officer class.[2] Moreover, the authority of the officer over his troops remained undiminished. The soldiers councils which had been instituted during the revolution were now replaced by elected confidential councils (*Vertrauensräte*), but these were restricted to the task of transmitting complaints to higher authorities and supervising the mess, the canteens and the quarters, and were specifically forbidden to concern themselves with exercise, field service, nomination of officers, or the right of command.[3]

The law of 6 March dissolved the old imperial army, yet a line of continuity between that force and the new Reichswehr is easy to discern. In its last stages, the imperial army had produced the nuclei of free corps; by the new law, the army was authorized to reabsorb the larger of those volunteer formations.[4] In the months that followed, Maercker's Rifles were to become the XVIth Brigade of the Provisional Reichswehr; Reinhard's

war ministers of Prussia, Saxony, Württemberg, and Bavaria were to disappear; and the administration of the army was henceforth to be handled by a single Reichswehr Ministry whose chief was a member of the Reich cabinet and could be questioned by the Reichstag (articles 6 and 79).

[1] *Reichsgesetzblatt*, 1919, no. 6755, pp. 295 ff.

[2] Benoist-Méchin (*German Army*, i. 165, n. 2) points out that, in 1913, 22 per cent. of the officer corps were of aristocratic birth. In 1921 the proportion was 23 per cent.

[3] This provision completed the destruction of the authority of the soldiers councils which had already been seriously weakened by a government decree of 19 January, for which see Noske, *Von Kiel bis Kapp*, pp. 94–95.

[4] Waite, in *Vanguard of Nazism*, pp. 78–79, makes the important point that the law of 6 March did not end the free corps movement, for not all the volunteer formations were re-integrated and some refused to enter the Reichswehr, continuing on their own with private support.

Free Corps of the Guard, the XVth Brigade; Hülsen's *Freikorps*, the IIIrd Brigade; and so forth. In their period of independent existence, moreover, some of the free corps had preserved the flags, badges, and archives of the imperial units from which they had been formed; in returning to the army, they transmitted these to their new regiments, which thus inherited the traditions of the past.[1] As the years passed, this cultivation of tradition was systematically pursued. After the Provisional Reichswehr had been transformed, by the law of March 1921, into the 100,000-man treaty Reichswehr, its commander, General von Seeckt, instituted a system of tradition companies under which each infantry company, cavalry troop, and artillery battery was regarded as representing a regiment or battalion of the imperial army and as being the custodian of its traditions.[2]

Once the new constitution was approved, both officers and men of the Provisional Reichswehr were required to take an oath of allegiance to that document. Yet, in view of what has been said above, it is clear that, from the outset, little enthusiasm was to be found in the army for the republic. The majority of the officers still remained loyal to the imperial régime whose military traditions they were seeking to perpetuate. As for the rank and file, it should be remembered that the bulk of the Provisional Reichswehr came from the free corps[3] and, further, that Noske—despite all his appeals for volunteers during the crisis of January—had never succeeded in raising any free corps which could be described as either democratic or republican.[4] For the most part the republic's first soldiers were either contemptuous of their political leaders or indifferent to politics, while, at the same time, they were completely in the hands of their officers—who also had the right to decide whether new volunteers were 'suitable' or not.[5]

On 9 November Groener had offered the support of the army to the new régime. That support had been forthcoming as long

[1] Benoist-Méchin, *German Army*, i. 172–4.

[2] Gordon, *Reichswehr and Republic*, p. 174.

[3] The new law envisaged the creation of a national army 'through the articulation of already existing volunteer formations . . . and the recruitment of similar formations'.

[4] Noske complains, indeed, that socialist newspapers would not even print his appeals for volunteers and that the working classes boycotted the volunteer movement instead of forming free corps of their own. *Von Kiel bis Kapp*, pp. 117–22.

[5] Benoist-Méchin, *German Army*, i. 166.

as the fight against bolshevism had continued. Could the government rely on the army when the threat from the left had disappeared? The very composition of the army raised doubts on this score; and the doubts were strengthened during the crisis precipitated by the arrival of the allied peace terms.

III

Ever since the conclusion of the armistice, the problem of the peace treaty had been the subject of intensive study at Supreme Headquarters; and it was one which particularly occupied the attention of the first quartermaster-general who realized that his hopes of maintaining the unity of the Reich and preserving the army might well depend on the nature of the allied terms. Groener possessed surprisingly optimistic views on the subject, however. He does not seem to have expected a dictated peace at all; and, later in his life, he wrote that he was counting, first, on German participation in the negotiations, which would permit German delegates to take advantage of the differences between the allies, and, second, on the common fear of bolshevism, which would make the allies eager to secure German aid for a crusade in the east.[1] Provided the government played its cards correctly, it should, he felt, be able to avoid a punitive peace settlement and, above all, it should be able to secure lenient military terms.

The first quartermaster-general was not, however, content to leave these matters entirely in government hands, but sought to play a role in foreign politics himself. As early as December 1918 he had managed, through an intermediary, to get in touch with Colonel A. L. Conger, chief of the Political Intelligence Section of U.S. Army H.Q. at Trier;[2] and he seems to have believed that, by opening his mind to this officer, he could influence General Pershing to work on Germany's behalf at the peace conference. Between December and March, at any rate, Groener carried on a series of long distance negotiations with Conger, transmitting his views in memoranda which were pre-

[1] Groener, *Lebenserinnerungen*, p. 484.

[2] On Conger, see especially Fritz T. Epstein, 'Zwischen Compiègne und Versailles: Geheime amerikanische Militärdiplomatie in der Periode des Waffenstillstandes 1918/1919: Die Rolle des Obersten Arthur L. Conger', *Vierteljahrshefte für Zeitgeschichte*, iii (1955), 412 ff. See also Karl Friedrich Nowak, *Versailles* (New York, 1929), p. 179 and Edgar Stern-Rubarth, *Graf Brockdorff-Rantzau: Wanderer zwischen zwei Welten* (Berlin, 1929), p. 98.

pared at Kassel (and after February, at Kolberg)[1] and which were then discussed with Conger by a certain Freiherr von Eltz. In general, Groener sought to convince Conger of three things: first, that if the peace were to be based on Wilson's fourteen points, the allies would not be justified in making any claims on the Rhineland or even in demanding the return of all of Alsace-Lorraine to France; second, that a joint campaign against bolshevism was necessary and feasible; and, third, that a strong army, based on the principle of universal service, was indispensable for Germany. In March 1919 Groener finally persuaded Conger to come to Kolberg to talk with him personally; and, in a discussion on the 19th in which Eltz and Schleicher participated, and in an elaborate dinner in the evening, attended by Hindenburg and other officers, the first quartermaster-general developed his case.[2]

Conger doubtless had official reasons for participating in these curious negotiations; and it is clear, from Groener's own account, that the American officer was circumspect in his statements and, indeed, tried his best to dampen Groener's enthusiasm—casting doubts especially on the possibility of the allies being willing either to support an eastern campaign or to allow Germany the kind of army Groener desired. Groener does not seem to have been discouraged by this in the slightest. On the contrary, it was at about this time that he informed Erzberger that there was a good chance that the allies would request German aid against the Soviet armies and that, if such a proposal were received, the members of the German peace delegation must immediately counter with demands for an end to the blockade, the evacuation of German territory presently occupied by allied troops, and a free hand in building up the army.[3] And, on 4 April, the first quartermaster-general undertook to instruct the Foreign Minister, Brockdorff-Rantzau, concerning the tactics which he should pursue during the peace negotiations, seeking to convince him that the allies would be badly split and the Americans sympathetic to Germany, and that a determined demeanour on the part of the German delegation would accomplish much.[4]

[1] The Supreme Command moved its headquarters from Kassel to Kolberg in mid-February.

[2] Groener, *Lebenserinnerungen*, pp. 489–91.

[3] R. H. Phelps, 'Aus den Groener-Dokumenten: II. Die Außenpolitik der O. H. L. bis zum Friedensvertrag', *Deutsche Rundschau* (Aug. 1950), p. 621.

[4] Groener's statement to Brockdorff-Rantzau was based on a memorandum

Brockdorff-Rantzau was somewhat flabbergasted by some of Groener's ideas—his suggestion, for instance, that the Foreign Minister must explain to the allies that the invasion of Belgium in 1914 had been absolutely necessary—and he was more than a little annoyed by Groener's intrusion into his own sphere of competence. He rather frostily pointed out that he would see that the requisite determination was shown at Versailles but that he regarded Groener's views in any case as over optimistic.[1] He remarked also that, if the German delegation found itself confronted with a difficult task, this was, after all, the fault of the army which had lost the war. On this cool note the conversation was terminated.[2] It left Groener apprehensive of government 'weakness' in the ensuing negotiations, and he therefore took the first opportunity offered him to ginger up the politicians.

On 24 April, therefore, in the course of a full cabinet meeting to which he had been invited in order to give an account of the military situation on the eastern frontiers, he pointed out that German forces in the Baltic lands and on the Polish border were now strong enough to protect German soil or, in union with the allies, to go on the offensive against the Soviet armies. This in itself gave the government great bargaining power which should be exploited to the full at Versailles. Above all, the German delegates must insist on the maintenance of an army based on universal service, and they must not be tempted by the thought that, by giving way on the army issue, they might win other concessions. In a spirited appeal to the members of the cabinet, Groener admitted that the army was not very popular in some quarters and that many Germans felt that it represented militarism and reaction. But, he added,

> only that government can govern which has military power—that is, a *Staatsgewalt*—behind it. I don't deny that there were a lot of things wrong with the old military establishment, but without power you can't rule. The Supreme Command takes the position

prepared by Major von Boetticher of the General Staff. A précis of this is given in Phelps, *Deutsche Rundschau* (Aug. 1950), pp. 616–17.

[1] Groener Papers: 'Besprechung mit Reichsminister Rantzau, 4. April 1919'; *Lebenserinnerungen*, p. 495. A rather exaggerated version of this conversation is to be found in Nowak, *Versailles*, pp. 195–7.

[2] Brockdorff-Rantzau's biographer points out that the Foreign Minister believed that, if Germany tried to manœuvre between the allies, she would lose the sound ground of principle and invite retaliation from all parties. Stern-Rubarth, *Brockdorff-Rantzau*, p. 87.

that this is not a question of counter-revolution or reaction but only of sound state power. Our only wish is for the government to trust us. If anyone thinks we can survive without this military power, he is wrong and would be even if there were a hundred Leagues of Nations.[1]

Groener's exhortations were as useless as his hopes were ill-founded. The Germans were never given an opportunity to exploit the differences among the allies or to offer their aid in a common fight against the Soviets. They went to Versailles not to negotiate but to receive peace terms; and the terms handed to them on 7 May were far worse than they had feared in their gloomiest moments. The military conditions alone were shattering. The German army was to be reduced to a volunteer force of 100,000 officers and men—the former, limited to 4,000, serving for twenty-five years, the latter for twelve. It was to be deprived of aircraft, tanks, and offensive weapons, and its General Staff, war academy, and cadet schools were to be dissolved. The Rhineland was to remain under occupation until the disarmament provisions were carried out and was to be permanently demilitarized, together with a strip 50 kilometres wide to the east of it. The battle fleet was to be replaced by a token force with no vessels exceeding 10,000 tons and no submarines. In addition, the emperor and the war leaders were to be surrendered for trial on charges of violation of the laws of war; and Germany was to acknowledge responsibility for the war.

When these terms reached him at Kolberg, Groener wrote in his diary: 'The proposals will be contested all the easier because they are so laughable.'[2] This, however, proved to be a vain hope. Even if the German people and their leaders had shown a united and inflexible opposition to the Versailles terms, it is doubtful whether they would have been able to win important modifications; and in reality, after the first explosion of indignation, neither the people nor the government showed any unity of view even on the tactics to be followed in seeking modifications. At Versailles bad feeling developed between the

[1] Groener Papers: 'Niederschrift über die Verhandlungen in der Sitzung des Reichsministeriums von 24. April 1919.' The discussion which followed Groener's statement is interesting chiefly because of Brockdorff-Rantzau's reiterated doubts concerning the possibility of winning the allies to a campaign against the Soviets and for the suggestion by the later ambassador Nadolny that the possibility of an arrangement with the Soviet Union should always be kept in mind.

[2] Groener, *Lebenserinnerungen*, p. 492.

civilian and the military members of the German delegation, and General von Seeckt in particular suspected Brockdorff-Rantzau of wishing to sacrifice the army in order to secure the amelioration of other parts of the treaty.[1] In Berlin the cabinet was split between the Chancellor, Scheidemann, who was unalterably opposed to the treaty in its present form, and Matthias Erzberger, who argued that it was useless to seek amendment of the terms and that it would be better to sign and hope for changes later.[2] It was Erzberger, for instance, who in mid-May persuaded the cabinet to drop its original intention of protesting against the reduction of the army to 100,000 men, a decision which was made without consulting the military experts at Versailles or the staff at Kolberg.[3] Erzberger's compliant attitude was well known to the allies, who were thus less inclined to concession than they might otherwise have been. As a result, when Brockdorff-Rantzau's counter-proposals were sent to them on 28 May, it was clear that there was little hope of substantial modification of the terms.

The realization that this was so, and that the military terms especially would probably remain unchanged, gave rise now to a movement in the officer corps in favour of outright rejection of the treaty regardless of the consequences. As early as mid-

[1] Officially Seeckt was not a delegate, but representative of the War Ministry serving in a consultative capacity. On his differences with Brockdorff-Rantzau, see especially Friedrich von Rabenau, *Seeckt: Aus seinem Leben, 1918–1936* (Leipzig, 1940), pp. 165–6, 175–6 (hereafter cited as Rabenau, *Seeckt*, ii); Alma Luckau, *The German Delegation at the Paris Peace Conference* (New York, 1941), p. 126; Victor Schiff, ed., *The Germans at Versailles* (London, 1930), p. 108. Hajo Holborn points out, in an analysis of the priorities given by Brockdorff-Rantzau's staff to the interests they wished to protect at Versailles, that Seeckt's suspicions were not entirely unfounded. Holborn, 'Diplomats and Diplomacy in the Early Weimar Republic', in *The Diplomats, 1919–1939*, ed. by Gordon A. Craig and Felix Gilbert (Princeton, 1953), p. 136. See also Gustav Hilger and Alfred G. Meyer, *The Incompatible Allies: A Memoir History of German-Soviet Relations, 1918–1941* (New York, 1953), pp. 90–91.

[2] For Erzberger's attitude, see Erzberger, *Erlebnisse*, pp. 371–3; Rabenau, *Seeckt*, ii. 175–6; Luckau, *German Delegation*, pp. 103–4; Nowak, *Versailles*, pp. 190 ff., 240–1. Epstein, *Erzberger*, pp. 301–27.

[3] The government had originally decided that every effort must be made to convince the allies that Germany needed an army of 300,000 and that 200,000 must be considered as an irreducible minimum. The later decision to accept the 100,000 figure was not discovered by the soldiers until 25 May. Seeckt immediately wrote a bitter letter to Brockdorff-Rantzau, accusing him of 'sacrificing Germany's honour'; and Groener protested to Scheidemann. Seeckt Papers, Stück 110: Besprechung im Hotel des Réservoirs in Versailles am 25. Mai 1919; Seeckt to Brockdorff-Rantzau, 26 May; Brockdorff-Rantzau to Seeckt, 27 May; Groener to Harbou, 27 May; Groener to Seeckt, 27 May. The incident caused a lasting coolness between Seeckt and Brockdorff-Rantzau.

May Groener learned that General Walther Reinhardt, who was *Chef der Heeresleitung* of the Provisional Reichswehr, favoured such a course and was quite willing, in the event of a renewed allied attack, to sacrifice western Germany and to fight a last-ditch battle in the east.[1] And Reinhardt was not alone. His views were shared by other high-ranking officers, notably by General von Below of the XVII Corps and General von Loßberg of the army of the south.[2]

To Groener this was dismaying intelligence. The aim of the army, he told some of his colleagues, should be 'to hold the sixty million Germans firmly together in one single state',[3] not to indulge in fantastic adventures which would lead to the atomization of the Reich. The trouble with the Prussians was that they were always dreaming of the glorious days of 1813;[4] they would not face realities. The grimmest of these realities was that the allies were prepared to fight for their terms; Colonel Conger was sure of that and had told one of Groener's agents so.[5] On the other hand, the German people were not prepared at all[6] and, if they were forced into war again, the results, for Reich and army, would be disastrous. When Hindenburg asked Groener whether honour might not require taking up weapons once more, the first quartermaster-general said drily:

> The significance of such a gesture would escape the German people. There would be a general outcry against counter-revolution and militarism. The Allies, baulked of their hopes of peace, would show themselves pitiless. The Officer Corps would be destroyed, and the name of Germany would disappear from the map.[7]

[1] Groener Papers: 'Stellungnahme des IGQM den militärischen Bedingungen im Friedensvertrage bei der Besprechung im KM am 15. Mai 1919'; Groener, *Lebenserinnerungen*, p. 493; Groener-Geyer, *General Groener*, pp. 142 f.; Fritz Ernst, *Aus dem Nachlaß Generals Walther Reinhardt* (Stuttgart, 1958), pp. 27–32.

[2] Despite the passage of the law of 6 March, the old war-time formations were still in existence.

[3] Groener, *Lebenserinnerungen*, p. 495; Nowak, *Versailles*, pp. 280–1.

[4] Groener, *Lebenserinnerungen*, p. 493.

[5] Ibid., pp. 497 ff. The allies were at this time discussing concrete plans for the occupation of northern Germany as far east as the Weser and for co-operation with the Czechs to cut off southern Germany. See *Foreign Relations of the United States: Paris Peace Conference*, vi. 501–50.

[6] So Groener concluded from the answers received to a questionnaire which he had had circulated to army corps headquarters at the end of May. See *Lebenserinnerungen*, p. 496.

[7] Volkmann, *Revolution*, pp. 280 f.

By 17 June, when the revised peace terms were received from the allies—with so few modifications that they were merely added in red ink to the original document[1]—Groener had managed to win a rather equivocal written admission from Hindenburg that military resistance would be hopeless.[2] Had the government simultaneously presented a united front in favour of accepting the terms, this indication of agreement on the part of the Supreme Command might have ended all talk of defying the allies. But the cabinet itself was badly split; in view of its inability to decide whether the treaty should be signed or not, Ebert had declared that the decision must be taken by the National Assembly; and this situation encouraged Reinhardt and his friends to try a forcing play. The chief of the army command summoned all of the commanding generals in the Reich to a meeting at Weimar to consider what attitude should be adopted with regard to the peace terms; and he invited Groener to attend as representative of the Supreme Command.

Groener went to Weimar fearing the worst;[3] and his fears were confirmed in a conversation *à deux* with Reinhardt on the afternoon of the 18th. Reinhardt asked him whether the Supreme Command would be willing, in the event that the cabinet should decide to accept the terms, to repudiate this action, break with the régime, and lead an insurrectionary movement in the east. Groener indignantly rejected this naked invitation to rebellion;[4] and, when the council of war opened on the morning of 19 June, he used all his gifts of eloquence and persuasion to show Reinhardt and his supporters how dangerous their plans were. If the legally constituted government of the country decided to sign the terms, he pointed out, and if the soldiers then refused to accept that decision, they would be regarded as rebels by the great majority of the German people; and it was highly unlikely that they would find support even in the eastern provinces. How true this last statement was was shown on the same evening, when Loßberg and some of the other generals met with a group of civilian notables and parlia-

[1] Luckau, *German Delegation*, p. 107.

[2] Hindenburg had nevertheless added to this admission the words 'but as a soldier I cannot help feeling that it were better to perish honourably than accept a disgraceful peace'.

[3] Groener, *Lebenserinnerungen*, p. 502.

[4] Volkmann, *Revolution*, pp. 282–3.

mentarians from eastern Germany. After listening to the soldiers outline their plans for a *Volkserhebung à la* 1813, the civilians almost unanimously declared that they would not be supported by the people and, thus, had no chance of success.[1] Under this cold douche some of the would-be Yorks became more thoughtful;[2] but they still insisted that they could not accept the treaty in its present form and, above all, that they would revolt rather than accept the war-guilt clauses.

This was an ominous conclusion to the Weimar talks for, as the events of the next few days proved, there was no hope of persuading the allies to drop the so-called *Schmachparagraphen.* When, on 22 June, the National Assembly authorized the new Bauer cabinet to sign the treaty if the war-guilt clauses were removed and when this was communicated to the Council of Four at Versailles, the allies answered curtly that the treaty must be signed unconditionally and, moreover, before the dead-line originally set on 17 June—namely, 6 p.m. of 23 June.

Once this answer was received, the sentiment for defiance received new impetus. Without waiting to see what the government would decide to do, Below and Loßberg plunged into frantic preparations in the east; General von Lüttwitz called his officers together to discuss whether or not they should take matters into their own hands; and even so level-headed an officer as Maercker, who was completely aware that there was no hope of effective military resistance to the allies,[3] went to Noske and appealed to him to set up a military dictatorship under his leadership.[4] Noske, whose attitude, even during the Weimar talks of 19 June, had been highly ambiguous, was sufficiently tempted by this to announce his intention of resigning from the cabinet and, in an impassioned harangue before a caucus of the Centre party delegates to the Assembly, to declare that the treaty must be rejected. Thus, as the dead-line neared, it appeared that anything might happen.

At this critical juncture, however, the two men who had

[1] Ibid., pp. 288 ff.; Rabenau, *Seeckt*, ii. 182, n.

[2] It was at this point that General von Stülpnagel, chief of the operations section of the Supreme Command, who had been attracted by Reinhardt's arguments, decided that resistance was impossible; and Seeckt seems to have done the same. Rabenau, *Seeckt*, ii. 182, n.

[3] Maercker admitted this in a newspaper article in July 1920. See Noske, *Aufstieg und Niedergang*, pp. 105–6.

[4] Maercker, *Vom Kaiserheer zur Reichswehr*, pp. 288 ff.

entered into partnership on 9 November once more demonstrated their courage and determination. Refusing to be stampeded by Noske's apparent defection, Ebert decided to ask the Supreme Command for a clear decision on the matter of acceptance, calculating that the National Assembly and the cabinet would be all too willing to follow whatever advice came from Kolberg. At about noon on 23 June, therefore, the President telephoned once more to Groener. He was prepared, he said, to throw his weight on the side of rejection if Hindenburg and Groener thought there was the slightest chance of successful resistance. But he needed a considered opinion by 4 o'clock in the afternoon, at which time the cabinet was meeting to take a final vote on the treaty.

Neither Hindenburg nor Groener had any reason to change the opinion which they had reached a week earlier. The only difference between them was that the field marshal lacked the moral courage to assume the responsibility for the decision, and found an excuse for not being present when Ebert telephoned again at four o'clock.[1] Groener, however, did not flinch from his unpleasant task. If the treaty were rejected and fighting broke out, he told the President, Germany's military situation was hopeless. As for the possibility of a military revolt against acceptance, he was sure that this would not materialize provided Noske made a public appeal to the army explaining the action taken and demanding the loyalty of every officer and man. Ebert followed this advice to the letter. He convinced Noske to abandon his vacillating course and to play the role demanded of him; the cabinet and the National Assembly followed along; and the peace terms were accepted, nineteen minutes before the ultimatum expired.

During this long crisis the decisive influence had been exercised by Wilhelm Groener. As on 9 November he had been animated by a desire to save the unity of the Reich and to preserve the officer corps for the future. Originally he had himself been too optimistic about what could be attained at Versailles; once the allies had made their position clear, however, he had

[1] Hindenburg's attitude is analysed at length in Wheeler-Bennett, *Wooden Titan*, pp. 220–1. In his memorandum of 1 June 1922 Groener defended Hindenburg's actions, saying that he had himself decided it was better to dissociate the field marshal from any responsibility for the advice to Ebert and that Hindenburg, realizing this, left the room until the call was completed, returning later to say: 'You are right but now you have to be the *bête noire* again.'

refused to allow his judgement to be clouded by private disappointment or by the high-flown rhetoric of the Reinhardts and the Loßbergs. As early as 19 May he told his staff officers at Kolberg that there was nothing that Germany could do which would induce the allies to give up their insistence upon the terms they had drafted unless it was to conclude an alliance with the Soviet Union, and this was something for which he would not accept the responsibility.[1] During the Weimar talks he had warned his fellow officers that wilful resistance to a government decision to accept the terms would destroy the officer corps and hand Germany over to revolution.[2] In the end his cold realism prevailed, for no attempt was in fact made to revolt against the government's decision. On the morning of 24 June General von Below told his command that resistance would be pointless; and the next day General von der Borne, Loßberg's commanding officer, informed the government that he would submit.[3]

In a speech to the officers of the Supreme Command on the evening of the same day on which he had given his counsel to Ebert, Groener said proudly: 'I have undertaken great responsibility by my action, but I will know how to bear it.'[4] He was fully conscious of the fact that he had now lost whatever popularity he had in the officer corps, and he would not have been surprised by the remark made later by a member of the Ehrhardt Brigade, that 'none of us could stand Groener after June 1919'.[5] But, as he retired from office, the first quartermaster-general could take comfort in the fact that he had prevented the officer corps from throwing away the position he had helped win for it during the revolutionary disorders and the days of Spartacus. The question now was whether the officer corps would be wise enough to refrain from tampering with his work.

IV

It was perhaps too much to expect wisdom from all of Germany's professional soldiers, considering the situation that confronted them after June 1919. It was bad enough in their eyes that the government should have signed a shameful peace; it was infinitely worse to discover that it intended to carry out the

[1] Groener, *Lebenserinnerungen*, p. 494. [2] Ibid., pp. 503 ff.

[3] Volkmann, *Revolution*, pp. 304–5.

[4] Seeckt Papers, Stück 111: 'Besprechung am 23. Juni 1919 abds. 6:30 im Gr. H. Qu.: Vortrag des Ersten Generalquartiermeisters.'

[5] Benoist-Méchin, *Histoire de l'armée allemande*, ii (Paris, 1936), 65.

military provisions that it had signed. The first steps to reduce the army to the 100,000 figure set at Versailles were taken almost immediately;[1] and the prospects of imminent unemployment not unnaturally aroused new thoughts of resistance in the minds of army and free corps commanders.

Simultaneously, the government was forced to make what appeared to be another shameful capitulation to the allies. In June the Western Powers decided to liquidate the curious situation in the Baltic lands where, since the beginning of the year, an army of free corps under the command of General von der Goltz had been waging war against the bolshevists and, simultaneously, against the local authorities who had originally solicited their help.[2] On 13 June the Council of Principal Allied Powers at Versailles demanded the evacuation by the Germans of all territory which had belonged to Russia before 1914,[3] and in August they repeated this demand with menacing overtones.[4] The German government sought to temporize but was forced to give in, thus infuriating local patriots who had taken pride in such German victories as the storm of Riga in May 1919.

More serious consequences were, however, to flow from the government's compliance. The Iron Division of Major Bischoff, for instance, greeted the order to return to Germany with open defiance, and its commander sought to make its obedience conditional upon—among other things—a government order reserving 30 per cent. of the places in the East Prussian Reichswehr for its members.[5] This attempt at blackmail failed and the

[1] In August, for instance, Seeckt, who was now head of the preparatory commission for the peace army, was complaining to the *Reichswehrministerium* about preference being given to front-line rather than staff officers in decisions as to which officers should be retained in the army. Seeckt Papers, Stück 111: Seeckt to R.W.M., 30 August 1919 (draft).

[2] The story of the Baltic adventure cannot be told in detail here. Brief accounts are to be found in Waite, *Vanguard of Nazism*, chap. v, and Volkmann, *Revolution*, pp. 237–45, 306–11. Goltz has told his story in General Graf Rüdiger von der Goltz, *Meine Sendung in Finnland und im Baltikum* (Leipzig, 1920), and *Als politischer General im Osten* (*Finnland und Baltikum*) *1918–1919* (Leipzig, 1936). See also August Winnig, *Am Ausgang der deutschen Ostpolitik: Persönliche Erlebnisse und Erinnerungen* (Berlin, 1921).

[3] *Documents on British Foreign Policy, 1919–1939*, edited by E. L. Woodward and Rohan Butler, 1st series, iii. 1 and note. This volume contains much new material on the last phases of the Baltic adventure. See also Phelps, 'Aus den Groener-Dokumenten: IV. Das Baltikum 1919', *Deutsche Rundschau* (Oct. 1950), pp. 830–40.

[4] *Documents on British Policy*, 1st series, iii. 47, 57; Goltz, *Meine Sendung*, pp. 240–1.

[5] See Goltz, *Meine Sendung*, pp. 245–50; Phelps in *Deutsche Rundschau* (Oct. 1950), p. 838; *Documents on British Policy*, 1st series, iii. 74–75.

Baltic freebooters were forced to come home. But they did so with a burning hatred for a government which had, in their opinion, robbed them of their conquests. Moreover, although some of the units dissolved upon reaching Germany, others either joined existing free corps or—as was the case with the Iron Division—maintained a separate existence under commanders who made no attempt to hide the fact that their ambition was to overthrow the existing régime. In December a British military observer wrote to his government concerning the imminence of a *coup d'état*:

the object of which is to overthrow the existing Berlin Government, establish a Military Dictatorship and refuse to accept the Peace Treaty. In general the plan is as follows: Spartacist riots will be arranged in Berlin and will be the excuse for the Iron Division in East Prussia and similar formations in Hanover and South Germany to march on Berlin. Ludendorff is quoted as one of the prime movers of the affair . . . Von der Goltz . . . Hindenburg and Mackensen are also concerned in the movement.[1]

As this report indicated, it was not only among the *Landsknechte* from the Baltic lands that the idea of a *coup d'état* was receiving attention. As early as July 1919 Captain Waldemar Pabst, a former staff officer who had organized the free corps of the Division of Horse Guards, went to Gustav Noske and urged him to join a group of officers who were prepared to overthrow the government. Noske declined and, two days later, ordered the dissolution of Pabst's division and the dismissal of the captain from the service. This did not discourage Pabst. He immediately became the leading spirit in a political organization called the *Nationale Vereinigung*, which included such notables as Ludendorff, Lüttwitz, Major von Stephani, and two old intriguers who had helped bring about Bethmann-Hollweg's fall in 1917, Colonel Bauer and Wolfgang Kapp.[2] This group's sole reason for existence was to plan the overthrow of the republican régime; and, although it did not succeed in this, it did precipitate the so-called Kapp *Putsch* of March 1920 which might easily have had grave consequences for the German officer corps.

There is little point in telling the story of the *Putsch* in any

[1] Ibid., p. 245. See also a second report by the same officer, ibid., pp. 249–53.

[2] See Noske, *Von Kiel bis Kapp*, p. 200; Volkmann, *Revolution*, p. 325; Waite, *Vanguard of Nazism*, p. 145 and note.

detail.[1] In brief, the National Union spent the latter part of 1919 in an elaborate propaganda campaign designed to discredit the government, while its leaders sought support in the officer corps and in rightist political circles. Even in these preliminary stages, the conspirators showed little regard for co-ordination of effort and a quite amazing ability to work at cross purposes. Kapp, who was designated as the civilian leader of the government-to-be, seems to have wanted to wait until the ground was fully prepared and to have expected no action until April or even July of 1920. Lüttwitz, an arrogant and very stupid man with the most rudimentary ideas of politics, had accepted Kapp's invitation to be the military leader of the rising, but subsequently showed no willingness to consider any of his co-conspirator's ideas. Lüttwitz seems to have believed for a time that he could simply browbeat Ebert and his associates into yielding voluntarily to a dictatorship. When these tactics failed to impress the government, he became increasingly impatient and finally launched the revolt without informing Kapp at all.

The incident which prompted Lüttwitz's action was the government's decision, in pursuance of its policy of reducing army strength, to dissolve the *élite* 2nd Marine Brigade of Captain Hermann Ehrhardt and the Baltikum Brigade of Bischoff's Iron Division, both of which forces were stationed at Döberitz, outside of Berlin. On 1 March 1920, responding to an appeal by Ehrhardt, Lüttwitz reviewed these troops and announced publicly that he would refuse to allow their demobilization. This should have been enough to warn the government that the danger of a rising was real. It was not until 9 March, however, that Noske, as Minister of Defence, saw fit to remove the troops at Döberitz from Lüttwitz's command and to entrust Admiral von Trotha with the task of completing their demobilization. This action infuriated Lüttwitz. Without consulting Kapp he went to Berlin and laid before Ebert and Noske a series of demands, including the return of the Ehrhardt Brigade to his command, the cessation of the whole policy of troop disbandment, and the replacement of General

[1] See, *inter alia*, Schüddekopf, *Heer und Republik*, pp. 82–85; Waite, *Vanguard of Nazism*, chap. vi; Wheeler-Bennett, *Nemesis of Power*, pp. 60–82.

Reinhardt, the present chief of the army command, by one of his own associates. When Noske refused these demands categorically, Lüttwitz turned to Ebert and demanded new elections, a presidential plebiscite, and the immediate appointment of a non-party government of experts. Ebert demurred, and Noske closed the interview by telling the general that the time had come for him either to obey orders or to resign.

Lüttwitz, however, did not resign; and Noske's belated decision on 11 March to remove him from his command and the government's order that Kapp, Pabst, and Bauer should be arrested came too late to be effective. On 12 March Lüttwitz told Ehrhardt that the time for action had come; and, at eleven o'clock in the evening, the brigade began its march to the capital.

Noske was informed of Ehrhardt's departure from Döberitz by a newspaper reporter's telephone call, and he hastily convoked a council of war to decide what should be done. In what has been called 'one of the most decisive conferences in the history of the Weimar Republic',[1] it was made clear to the dumbfounded Minister of Defence that, however happy the generals might be to defend the republic against attacks from the left, they were not prepared to adopt the same position when the rebels claimed to be patriots and nationalists. The chief of the army command, General Reinhardt, said stoutly: 'There can be no neutrality for the Reichswehr. The quicker we act, the quicker the spark will be put out!'; but he was supported only by Noske himself and Noske's chief of staff, Major von Gilsa.[2] The others present deferred to Seeckt, chief of the *Truppenamt* and, in effect, chief of staff of the army. Seeckt's attitude was summed up in the words:

> Troops do not fire on troops. Do you perhaps intend, Herr Minister, that a battle be fought before the Brandenburg Gate between troops who have fought side by side against the common enemy? . . . When Reichswehr fires on Reichswehr, then all comradeship within the officer corps has vanished.

To this there was no answer. Noske had finally been betrayed by the very generals who had lavished such praise on him in earlier days, and there was nothing left for him to do but join

[1] Waite, *Vanguard of Nazism*, p. 154. [2] Rabenau, *Seeckt*, ii. 222; Volkmann, *Revolution*, pp. 356–9; Ernst, *Reinhardt*, pp. 61 ff.

the convoy of cars in which the cabinet left Berlin at 5 a.m. on the road to Dresden. An hour later, Ehrhardt's men arrived at the Brandenburg Gate, where they were met by Lüttwitz, Ludendorff, and a very flustered Wolfgang Kapp, who did not know that his hour had struck until he saw Ehrhardt's battalions.[1]

As for Seeckt, he carefully retired to his home and remained there for the next four days. He had no intention of becoming involved personally in Lüttwitz's hazardous adventure, or at least not until he knew that it was going to succeed. This attitude was doubtless shrewd, but there is nothing admirable about it. Seeckt left his subordinates in the Ministry of Defence in the lurch and, in order to protect himself against all contingencies, even refrained from informing the commanders of the various army districts about the situation in Berlin. The result was an incredible amount of confusion. Lieutenant-Colonel Heye, Seeckt's chief assistant, who remained at his post in the Ministry of Defence, wrote later:

> All that day [13 March] telephone calls from officers in the army districts outside of Berlin had given me the impression that everywhere in the Reichswehr garrisons utter confusion reigned. They did not know who was entitled to give orders or what was going on. An added difficulty after a few days was that Lüttwitz gave orders to the Reichswehr in Berlin, whereas in the West and the South of the Reich, now the seat of the government, orders issued by Lüttwitz were not valid.[2]

Seeckt's policy of 'wait and see' threatened the officer corps with an even graver danger. While Kapp and Lüttwitz revealed to the country that, although they had been able to take Berlin, they had no constructive programme whatsoever, the government appealed to the workers to defend the republic. The general strike that followed was the decisive factor in defeating the *Putsch*. The enthusiasm with which it was carried out, moreover, was communicated to some elements in the Reichswehr. Dangerous signs of mutiny began to appear in certain garrisons; and, on 17 March, troops in Berlin actually put their officers under arrest.[3] This was enough to convince the officers in the

[1] Waite, *Vanguard of Nazism*, pp. 156–7 and note 48.

[2] Alma Luckau, 'Kapp Putsch—Success or Failure?' *Journal of Central European Affairs*, vii, no. 4 (Jan. 1948), p. 399.

[3] Ibid.

Bendlerstraße that they must get rid of Lüttwitz before it was too late. On the afternoon of the 17th, Heye—as spokesman for the officers of the Ministry of Defence—went to the general and told him that the insupportable situation in Berlin must not be prolonged and that he must declare the *Putsch* at an end and hand over the command of his troops to Seeckt. A stormy scene ensued in which Lüttwitz threatened Heye with his sword and Bauer showered him with epithets.[1] But, after Heye had left the room, even the stubborn general saw that the game was up. Kapp had already fled from Berlin; Lüttwitz and his staff now did the same.

It can be fairly argued that, in this miserable fiasco, the German officer corps had broken the bargain made for it by Wilhelm Groener on 9 November 1918. There were officers in March 1920 who were fully prepared to fight for the republic against the conspirators; General von Bergmann at Stuttgart, for instance, declared to his troops that he would not hesitate to support the legally constituted government. But in the upper reaches of the army hierarchy, only Reinhardt had been unambiguous in his willingness to defend the existing régime. The others had followed the line laid down by Seeckt; and there is no disguising the fact that Seeckt had been as insubordinate as Lüttwitz, even if in a somewhat different way.[2]

The Ebert government, then, would have been fully justified if it had taken reprisals against the officer corps and if it had sought, even at this late date, to start all over again and to create a truly republican army. Moreover, an energetic effort in this direction would probably have won wide support in Germany in March 1920, for the failure of the Kapp adventure was followed by a wave of anti-militarist feeling in all parts of the country.[3] Yet nothing of the sort happened, and the officer

[1] Luckau in *Journal of Central European Affairs*, vii. 400.

[2] On the basis of correspondence with Dr. Eugen Schiffer, the Ebert government's representative in Berlin during the *Putsch*, Harold Gordon reveals that on 13 March Seeckt went in mufti to the Ministry of Justice where Schiffer was being held in protective custody and assured him of his loyalty to the government. *Reichswehr and Republic*, p. 181. He also points out that, before the outbreak of the *Putsch*, Seeckt tried to head it off and even attempted to ease Lüttwitz out of the army. Ibid., pp. 102–4. All this is doubtless true but does not alter the fact that, when the *Putsch* came, Seeckt placed his loyalty to the army above his allegiance to the republic. The impression is inescapable that he was waiting to see what would happen before committing himself; and it is not weakened by his subsequent stern measures against the Kappists.

[3] Waite, *Vanguard of Nazism*, p. 168. It should always be remembered, of course,

corps was privileged once more to escape punishment for its sins.[1]

The principal reason for this was the fact that, in invoking the general strike, the government had given a new lease of life to the communist movement. In the first weeks after the collapse of the *Putsch* there were disorders in Berlin and Münster, and more serious troubles in the Ruhr, where a 'Red army', reputedly some 50,000 strong, captured all the important industrial towns and, by 20 March, dominated the entire area east of Düsseldorf and Mühlheim.[2] Confronted with this renewed threat from the left, Ebert and his colleagues felt that they could not permit themselves the luxury of chastising an indispensable ally for past unreliability. Therefore Ebert confirmed the final action taken by Lüttwitz during his short rule in Berlin and appointed Seeckt as commander-in-chief of all of the military forces of the Reich. Seeckt's first action was to call upon the same free corps who had tried to overthrow the government ten days before to defend it from the communist menace.[3]

that the Versailles Treaty prescribed what kind of army Germany would have and thus imposed restrictions on any government's ability to change it.

[1] As soon as the Kapp movement got into difficulties, there were negotiations between the nationalists and the *Deutsche Volkspartei*, in which Helfferich and others urged that an honourable way be found of dealing with the Kappists lest the Reichswehr suffer. Stresemann Nachlaß, vol. 217, container 3090, frames 139532 ff. The parties concerned agreed to seek an amnesty for the soldiers involved. A complete amnesty, however, was not immediately forthcoming. Lüttwitz, for instance, was still in exile in Innsbruck in 1922, whence he bombarded Stresemann with reproaches for not having secured an amnesty and with threats to return to Germany and start his movement all over again. Stresemann's correspondence with Lüttwitz, and with Ludendorff about Lüttwitz, is among the Stresemann Papers. See 245, cont. 3110, frames 143487, 143513, 143514 ff., 143580 ff., 143587 ff.; 246, cont. 3110, frames 143648–9, 143716 ff.; 247, cont. 3110, frame 143907.

[2] There can be little doubt that the original reports of these Red victories were greatly exaggerated. The 'capture' of the Ruhr towns was effected without bloodshed, the local Reichswehr detachments simply withdrawing without firing a shot. Two allied officers, sent to investigate conditions in the Ruhr in March, reported that, while there were communist bands at large, there was nothing that could be described as an 'army' and that the disorders had been deliberately played up by General von Kabisch's press bureau—acting presumably on orders from his superiors—in order to delay evacuation of the area as long as possible and to provide an excuse for keeping an army above treaty size. See J. H. Morgan, *Assize of Arms: The Disarmament of Germany and her Rearmament, 1919–1939* (New York, 1946), pp. 183–200. The hope of diverting the government's attention from the Kapp affair doubtless supplied another motive for such exaggeration.

[3] On this and the subsequent campaign in the Ruhr, see Waite, *Vanguard of Nazism*, chap. vii. See also Carl Severing, *Mein Lebensweg* (Köln, 1950), i. 256–75; Werner T. Angress, 'Weimar Coalition and Ruhr Insurrection', *Journal of Modern History*, xxix (1957).

While Ehrhardt's troops and Bischoff's *Baltikumer* restored order in central Germany, and the free corps of Rossbach, Faupel, Pfeffer, and Epp fought a bloody campaign in the Ruhr, thoughts of reprisals against the officer corps died away in official circles. Thus in his first appeal to his professional colleagues—which will be discussed more fully in another context[1]—Seeckt was able to intimate to them that the past was being conveniently forgotten and that 'there is no intention on the part of the responsible authorities of changing the principles upon which the organization of the Reichswehr rests'.[2]

This was true. There had been times since 9 November 1918 when the government had contemplated building a new kind of defensive force, and there had been times when—thanks to the political ineptitude of ranking officers—they had been given splendid opportunities to do so; but always in the end Ebert had remained true to his part of the original bargain with Groener. He did so now, and the old officer corps was permitted to survive and to play its part in the tragic story of post-war Germany.

[1] See below, Chapter X, pp. 385–6.

[2] Luckau in *Journal of Central European History*, vii. 403. In the original draft of this appeal of 18 April, Seeckt had written: 'All rumours concerning a complete dissolution or a basic reorganization of the Reichswehr are to be refuted most vigorously. No credence is to be given to newspaper accounts of that kind.'

X

THE 'NON-POLITICAL' ARMY: SEECKT AND GESSLER

1920–8

The mistake of all those who organize armies is to mistake the momentary for the permanent State. HANS VON SEECKT.

Geßler beherrscht die Innenpolitik, Seeckt ringt um die Außenpolitik. Etwas viel Präponderanz für ein so kleines Heer.
CARL VON OSSIETZKY, *July 1926*.

In the years that followed the Kapp *Putsch*, the German army was transformed from an aggregation of disparate and ill co-ordinated units with a resentful and demoralized officer corps into a homogeneous and perfectly disciplined force which, in quality at least, had no equal in Europe. By an adroit combination of passive resistance to, and skilful evasion of, the restrictive clauses of the Versailles Treaty, it advanced much farther along the road of military recovery than had been thought remotely possible by the men who had drafted those clauses in 1919; and, before the end of the decade, it had laid the foundations for its later expansion under Hitler.

In the same years, while ostentatiously abstaining from politics, the army steadily increased its influence in every aspect of state affairs and did not hesitate, on occasion, to arrogate to itself the initiative in matters of policy formulation, especially in the foreign sphere. This development, not unnaturally, caused concern in parliamentary circles, notably among the parties of the left, who were, nevertheless, powerless to control it.

The development of the Reichswehr into an efficient instrument of war and the growth of its prestige and influence in the state may be attributed primarily to the efforts of Hans von Seeckt and, to a lesser degree, to those of Noske's successor at the Reichswehr Ministry, Otto Geßler.

I

When Hans von Seeckt became chief of the army command in March 1920 he entered upon the last and most brilliant phase of an illustrious career. He had already won the highest honours which his profession could award and, although still unknown to the general public, was recognized by his colleagues as one of the most outstanding soldiers of his generation. In 1899, while still a mere lieutenant, he had been seconded to the Great General Staff in Berlin and had so distinguished himself in that *élite* body that, when war broke out in 1914, he was already chief of staff to the Third Army Corps. His planning of the operations around Soissons in 1914 had marked him for further preferment, and in 1915 Falkenhayn had appointed him as chief of staff to Mackensen's Eleventh Army on the eastern front. Here he had directed the successful break-through at Gorlice—a victory which established his reputation beyond any doubt. In the last years of the war he had been entrusted with the difficult task of co-ordinating the efforts of the central Powers in the east, serving as chief of staff to Archduke Karl of Austria and, later, as chief of the Turkish General Staff. When the war was finally lost, he was sent by Hindenburg and Groener to organize the retreat of the German armies from White Russia and the Ukraine and to establish a frontier defence force against the Poles and the bolsheviks. After successfully completing this mission, he had returned to Germany to be appointed as the War Ministry's representative on the delegation to Versailles.[1] Seeckt had been Groener's candidate for the post of chief of the army command when the war-time commanders retired from office in September 1919. The appointment had gone to Reinhardt but, even before the events of March 1920, there are indications that Seeckt's authority in army administration was greater than his nominal chief's; and, after the *Putsch* was over, he had supplanted him.[2]

The chief of the army command was, constitutionally at least, subordinate to the Reichswehr Minister who, in turn, was responsible to the Reichstag. Before he had assumed office, however, Seeckt had taken steps to avoid having his authority

[1] Seeckt's early career is treated at length in Hans von Seeckt, *Aus meinem Leben*, ed. Friedrich von Rabenau (Leipzig, 1938).

[2] Rabenau, *Seeckt: Aus seinem Leben, 1918–1936*, p. 197 (hereafter cited as Rabenau, *Seeckt*, ii); Moriz von Faber du Faur, *Macht und Ohnmacht* (Stuttgart, 1953), p. 77. Seeckt's resentment over Reinhardt's appointment, his failure to consult him regularly on matters affecting the *Truppenamt*, and Reinhardt's inability to control his subordinate, are discussed in Gordon, *Reichswehr and Republic*, p. 221.

curtailed by this provision. In January 1920 he had written to Noske that any direct contact, in matters of training, selection, administration, or command, between the minister and the army would be inadvisable, since the army would have no confidence in a political appointee. The Reichswehr should be placed under the direct control of a '*kommandoführende Persönlichkeit*' who would combine in himself all of the functions of the now defunct offices of Chief of the General Staff and Chief of the Military Cabinet, although he would presumably be responsible to the minister for his execution of those tasks.[1]

The confused events of February and March 1920 prevented any action being taken on this remarkable document; and neither then nor later was any effort made to clarify the relationship between the chief of the army command and the Reichswehr Minister. It is conceivable that another socialist minister might have contested Seeckt's claims;[2] the minister who succeeded Noske, and who remained in office until 1928, had no immediate inclination to do so. Otto Geßler, a member of the Democratic party and a former *Oberbürgermeister* of Nuremberg, agreed with Seeckt concerning the necessity of raising a strong and disciplined army and saw no point in raising difficulties over questions of administrative competence. This ceased to be true in 1925 and 1926;[3] but, until then, Seeckt was in effect given the power he had demanded. At the same time, Geßler proved himself to be an ideal collaborator in the general's designs. An adroit politician with an ingratiating manner, he was always at his best when the army was under

[1] Seeckt Papers, Stück 130: Seeckt to Reichswehrminister, 16 January 1920. See also Rabenau, *Seeckt*, ii. 466 ff., 471–2; Rosinski, *German Army*, pp. 158–9.

[2] There was some feeling in socialist circles that a general of liberal views should succeed Noske, but Ebert did not follow this advice. Caro and Oehme, *Schleichers Aufstieg*, p. 110.

[3] Gordon (*Reichswehr and Republic*, p. 333) believes that the beginnings of the breach between Geßler and Seeckt go back to 1923, when Geßler disapproved of Seeckt's policies as dictator and that their relations worsened in the last two years of Seeckt's term because the Minister resented his attempt to dominate him and to keep him away from the troops. Stresemann has written that, in 1925, Geßler supported the Locarno Pact 'in full opposition' to Seeckt—(Stresemann Papers, 272, cont. 3113, frame 147917)—but in his memoirs Geßler has denied that he knew Seeckt's views on this. Abroad, Geßler was generally regarded as Seeckt's tool, and this was not without importance in determining allied hesitation to relax military controls in Germany. See Gustav Stresemann, *Vermächtnis*, ed. by H. Bernhard (Berlin, 1932–3), ii. 44, 152; iii. 56.

fire in the Reichstag, showing a remarkable ability to drown leftist criticisms in floods of patriotic rhetoric and Bavarian humour.[1] To say that Geßler 'confined himself to signing the decisions of General von Seeckt'[2] is rather unfair to the minister; but he did secure Seeckt against attacks in press and parliament, and it was under the cover of his name and authority that Seeckt was able to carry out his work of reorganization.

The first step in that work was the task of overcoming the effects of the Kapp *Putsch*, and Seeckt addressed himself to this immediately. The ambiguity which had characterized his own behaviour during that affair disappeared as soon as the conspirators fled from Berlin. More clearly than most of his fellows, Seeckt realized how vulnerable the officer corps had become as a result of Lüttwitz's failure and—although he was able to avert retaliatory action by the government by taking advantage of the disorders in the Ruhr—he knew that another mistake like Lüttwitz's would certainly be disastrous. There must, he saw, be no more *Putsche* by members of the Reichswehr, and this must be made clear to every officer and man in that force.

This task of clarification Seeckt undertook on 18 April 1920, in his first order of the day to the officer corps, an order which opened with the ominous words:

> This is a crucial hour for the officer corps of the Reichswehr. Its behaviour in the immediate future will determine whether the officer corps will retain the leadership in the new army.

There was, the new commander went on to say, no sentiment in the government at the moment to change the organizational principles of the Reichswehr or even to visit pains and penalties upon those who had been misled by the 'political short-sightedness' of certain leaders in March. But henceforth, if the officer corps was to be preserved, 'irresponsible actions' could not be permitted. Therefore, in the future,

> any kind of political activity in the army will be prohibited. Political quarrels within the Reichswehr are incompatible with both the

[1] 'When Geßler smiles, we can laugh . . . Otto Geßler has the confidence of the homeland. Period.' *Die Weltbühne*, 21. Jg. (1925), i. 860. Geßler's technique is seen at its most effective in the debate on the Reichswehr law of 23 March 1921. See Reichstag, *Stenographische Berichte*, cccxlvii (1920–1), 2339–41; cccxlviii (1921), 3194–6, 3216–18. For a soldier's tribute to Geßler, see Dietrich von Choltitz, *Soldat unter Soldaten* (Zürich, 1951), p. 15.

[2] Général Nollet, *Une Expérience de désarmement* (Paris, 1932), p. 110; quoted in Wheeler-Bennett, *Nemesis of Power*, p. 89, n. 2.

spirit of comradeship and with discipline and can only be harmful to military training. We do not ask the individual for his political creed, but we must assume that everyone who serves in the Reichswehr from now on will take his oath seriously.

Those who do not condemn the unfortunate attempt made during the month of March at overthrowing the government, and those who still believe that a repetition would end in anything but new misfortune for our people and for the Reichswehr, should decide on their own that the Reichswehr is not for them.

The order ended with a reminder that the true source of Germany's present troubles was the Versailles Treaty and with a plain hint that officers could rely upon their top leadership to do everything possible to evade the provisions of that treaty.[1]

Although this declaration—which was echoed in public speeches made by Geßler at this time[2]—was received with some indignation by the most inveterate reactionaries in the army, who regarded Seeckt's rather unenthusiastic references to the oath to the constitution as a capitulation to democracy,[3] Seeckt demonstrated in the period that followed that he meant exactly what he said. The most outspoken of the kappists were quietly dropped from the army rolls,[4] and those officers who retained their positions after the army had been reduced to its treaty strength discovered that their tenure depended upon their ability to keep their political opinions to themselves, to devote themselves exclusively to their military tasks, and to obey their superiors without question. There were no exceptions to these rules, and Seeckt had no hesitation in reprimanding even general officers whose seniority was greater than his own when they seemed to question the wisdom of the course he had adopted.

In implementing the declaration of April 1920, moreover,

[1] Rabenau, *Seeckt*, ii. 239–40.

[2] Seeckt's order was sent to all army commands but not, apparently, to the press. On 16 April, however, in an important speech to the *Reichsverband deutscher Berufssoldaten*, Geßler had stressed the principal themes of Seeckt's declaration, emphasizing that 'terrible danger' would arise if 'the feeling of true comradeship' was destroyed by differences caused by political activity and saying: 'Like Germany, so also the Reichswehr is fighting for its life. The task of the professional soldier is to recognize discipline.' See *Frankfurter Zeitung*, 18 April 1920, p. 2.

[3] Generaladjutant von Plessen wrote at about this time: 'At the head of the General Staff an officer of the Alexander regiment pays allegiance to democracy.' Rosinski, *German Army*, p. 106.

[4] On the procedure used, see Caro and Oehme, *Schleichers Aufstieg*, pp. 111–12.

Seeckt showed no compunction about abandoning those useful allies, the free corps. The largest and most orderly of those formations had already been absorbed in the Reichswehr; those which had remained independent had neither the type of organization nor the respect for discipline that Seeckt required of his troops,[1] and they were, moreover, dedicated to the very type of political activity that he was now seeking to prevent. 'In the new Reichswehr', Seeckt wrote after his retirement, 'an absolutely strict discipline . . . had to be maintained. To surrender themselves unconditionally to that kind of discipline, the free corps were either unprepared or incapable.'[2] 'They were simply not suited for the work of peace.'[3]

If the great majority of the free corps could not be absorbed within the Reichswehr, neither could they be permitted to exist outside it. As will be seen below,[4] Seeckt felt compelled on occasion to rely on irregular formations for special purposes; but, when he did so, he subordinated them, however secretly, to Reichswehr control. He was not prepared to tolerate the existence of independent armed organizations, for he believed that the Reichswehr must possess a monopoly of armed strength within the Reich and, in addition to this, was determined that the Reichswehr must not again be confronted with the kind of situation which had embarrassed its leaders in March 1920. For this reason, he supported the government when, in August 1920, it enacted a law calling for the relinquishment by individuals and organizations of arms illegally possessed;[5] and, in other ways, he encouraged the dissolution of the forces which had fought in the Ruhr after the Kapp *Putsch*.[6]

These measures were intended to make the army once more a reliable instrument in the hands of its leaders. Whether it would also be a reliable instrument in the service of the Weimar Republic was another, and more doubtful, question. Seeckt's own allegiance was paid not to the republican régime—which,

[1] Gustav Stresemann once said to Briand that 'Seeckt never made any bones of the fact that he wanted to deal with real soldiers and scorned *Soldatenspielerei*'. Stresemann, *Vermächtnis*, iii. 15–16.

[2] Generaloberst von Seeckt, *Gedanken eines Soldaten* (Erweiterte Ausgabe, Leipzig, 1935), p. 96.

[3] Generaloberst Hans von Seeckt, *Die Reichswehr* (Leipzig, 1933), pp. 14–15.

[4] See below, pp. 401 ff.

[5] Wheeler-Bennett, *Nemesis of Power*, p. 91.

[6] Needless to say, the free corps did not disappear with the finality that was expected of them. Geßler was constantly explaining to the Reichstag, and Strese-

for all he knew, might be a transitory phenomenon—but to that permanent and imperishable entity, the German Reich.[1] In his view the army, too, owed its loyalty to the permanent state rather than to the régime of the moment, and its principal duty was to protect the interests of that permanent state. In one of his best-known essays, Seeckt rather vaguely admitted that the 'supreme leadership of the state' (*oberste Staatsleitung*)—which he did not otherwise define—must control the army. On the other hand, he added, 'the army has the right to demand that its share in the life and being of the state be given full consideration. It is subordinated to the state as a whole, which is incorporated in its leadership, not . . . to separate parts of the state organization'. Moreover, it must be granted 'full freedom in its development and in its way of life (*Eigenleben*)'. Yet again, 'in domestic and foreign policy the military interests represented by the army must be given full consideration along with the other necessities of state'. Finally, 'the army and its leaders must be assured of their rightful position in public life and must be protected against attacks'.[2]

It is difficult to tell from these cloudy phrases how far Seeckt was prepared to go in recognizing the existing régime, and the difficulty is increased by his added statement that 'the army serves the state, only the state; for it is the state'.[3] What Seeckt seems to be saying is that the army will co-operate with the government of the day as long as its rather exaggerated conditions are met.

What is perfectly clear, however, is that, although Seeckt

mann to the French, either that they did not exist or that they were harmless. This led *Die Weltbühne* (22. Jg. [1926], i. 210] to publish a parody of Körner's famous poem, 'Lützow's wilde Jagd', which read:

> Was glänzt dort vom Walde im Sonnenschein?
> Hör's näher und näher brausen . . .
> Es ist
> eine Formation, die nicht existiert, deren
> Angehörige lediglich die Ertüchtigung der
> Jugend betreiben, Waffen nicht besitzen
> und mit denselben äußerst vorsichtig
> umgehen, sodaß von einer unmittelbaren
> Gefahr für die Republik nicht gesprochen werden kann,
> Lützows wilde verwegene Jagd.

For the activities of the free corps after 1920, see Waite, *Vanguard of Nazism*, chap. viii, and Schüddekopf, *Heer und Republik*, pp. 130–46.

[1] Generaloberst von Seeckt, *Die Zukunft des Reiches* (Berlin, 1929), p. 11.

[2] 'Heer im Staat' (1928) in *Gedanken eines Soldaten*, especially pp. 92–93.

[3] Ibid., p. 93.

might insist that individual officers abstain from political activity,[1] he never doubted for a moment that the army as a whole had a right to intervene in both domestic and foreign politics whenever its interests—or the interests of the state of which it was 'the purest representative'[2]—seemed to be inadequately protected by the government of the day. And, long before he had written the essay cited above, Seeckt had demonstrated how far he was capable of extending that right.

II

In the first months after his assumption of office, however, Seeckt's energies were completely absorbed in the difficult task of making the Reichswehr an efficient military force. In the spring of 1920 the precise limitations within which he would have to work were not yet clear. Despite the apparent finality of the decisions made at Versailles, the German government still hoped for some amelioration of the peace terms; and Seeckt himself resolved to make a last attempt to win permission for a larger army than was provided for in the treaty.

In April, therefore, a note was dispatched to the allied governments urging that the unsettled state of Germany, the possibility of new revolutionary disturbances, and the constant Polish threat to German frontiers in the east made the reduction of the Reichswehr to the 100,000 figure dangerous. The government requested the Allied Powers to authorize the permanent retention by Germany of a force of 200,000 officers and men and to permit this force to equip itself with heavy artillery and, at least temporarily, with some military aircraft.[3]

To this request the allied governments replied on 22 June in the so-called Boulogne note in which they announced their unanimous insistence that the military clauses of the treaty be maintained in their entirety. They expected, they added, that 'no further requests for derogation from the military clauses'

[1] This abstention was also enjoined by law, for the Reichswehr law of March 1921, which was the basis of the permanent as opposed to the Provisional Reichswehr, forbade political activity by officers and men, including membership in political organizations and attendance at political rallies.

[2] Seeckt, *Gedanken eines Soldaten*, p. 92.

[3] House of Commons: Sessional Papers, 1921, xliii: 'Protocols and Correspondence . . . respecting the execution of the Treaty of Versailles of 28th June' [Cmd. 1325], 89–93. For a discussion of what the organization of the German army might have been like if this request had been granted, see J. H. Morgan, 'The Disarmament of Germany and After', *The Quarterly Review*, ccxlii (1924), 432–43.

would be submitted to them, 'as such requests can only receive a negative reply and consequently lead uselessly to further delay'.[1] To make their point abundantly clear, on 5 July Mr. Lloyd George and M. Millerand took the opportunity afforded by the opening of the Spa conference—to which the Germans had been invited in order to discuss reparations payments—to ask the German delegates a series of searching questions about the progress of disarmament.[2] These questions were highly embarrassing to the new Chancellor, Constantin Fehrenbach, and his Foreign Minister, Dr. Walther Simons. They were forced to admit that they were uninformed on the subject and to request a postponement until their military experts could be summoned to Spa.[3]

On 6 July Seeckt and Geßler arrived in Spa. Any possibility that the general might win permission to retain a 200,000-man army was already, in view of the attitude of the allies, remote, and it disappeared completely as a result of the maladroit tactics adopted by the Minister of Defence. Geßler had hardly descended from the train before he was telling newspaper reporters that he would 'resign' from the conference 'unless terms more favourable than those proposed were agreed upon'.[4] He then proceeded to the Villa La Fraineuse, where he edified the conference delegates with a very confused justification of the delay in disarming the civil population of Germany, adding that it would be impossible, 'in view of the existing unemployment and of the industrial stagnation, to reduce the effectives to 100,000 men. It would simply swell the number of unemployed.'[5] At this point Lloyd George—who had been eying the

[1] André Honnorat, *Un des problèmes de la paix: Le désarmement de l'Allemagne. Textes et documents* (Paris, 1924), pp. 22–24.

[2] On the Spa conference, see, *inter alia*, W. M. Jordan, *Great Britain, France and the German Problem, 1918–1939* (London, 1943), pp. 71, 85–88, 115, 136; Viscount d'Abernon, *An Ambassador of Peace* (London, 1929) i. 56–75; Harold Nicolson, *Curzon: The Last Phase, 1919–1925* (new ed., New York, 1939), pp. 203, 226–30; and the dispatches of *The Times*' special correspondent in *The Times* (London), 5–17 July 1920.

[3] Fehrenbach and Simons had some reason to be ill informed, since they had just assumed office as a result of the elections of 6 June 1920.

[4] *The Times*, 7 July 1920. Geßler's threats were recorded with some amusement by the British press. On 8 July *The Times* reported that the Reichswehr Minister was reproaching his colleagues for having misled him into believing that the allies would be conciliatory. On 10 July it noted that Geßler 'is reported to have resigned—for the 12th or 13th time during the last few weeks. His Ministerial career seems to have been marked by intermittent agitation.'

[5] Geßler's arguments were based on memoranda which had been worked out in

bemedalled uniforms of Seeckt and his aides with every evidence of displeasure[1]—rapped sharply on the table and remarked that the allies wanted, not disquisitions on the internal state of Germany, but facts and figures about disarmament, and that, unless these were produced, the conference might as well adjourn.[2]

To Seeckt fell the awkward task, on 7 July, of admitting not only that the German army was still far above treaty strength, but that no fewer than two million rifles were still unaccounted for in the hands of the civilian population. Seeckt's figures caused a sensible stir among the delegates, and he was sufficiently conscious of this to refrain from repeating Geßler's demands. Instead, he promised that every step would be taken to disarm the civilian population and to disband illegal formations, but requested that—since these tasks would require the use of regular troops—the reduction of the Reichswehr to treaty strength be stretched over a period of 15 months, not being complete before October 1921. He also asked that the Reichswehr be permitted to retain on its rolls 300 more surgeons and several hundred more administrators than the treaty stipulated, and that the number of small arms authorized for the force be increased also.[3]

Seeckt's forthright and unimpassioned exposition was more impressive than the ebullitions of his civilian colleague, but it won few concessions. Mr. Lloyd George told the Germans on 8 July that the requests for surgeons, bureaucrats, and small arms would be granted, but that the Reichswehr must be reduced to 150,000 men by 1 October 1920 and to 100,000 by 1 January 1921. Failure to achieve this on time, or delay in pushing on with the collection and surrender of illegal weapons, would be answered by allied occupation of further territory, in the Ruhr or elsewhere.[4] There was nothing that the Germans

his ministry during the last two months. See, for instance, Seeckt Papers, Stück 118: 'Nachrichtenstelle des R.W.M.: Behandlung der Frage des 200,000 Mann Heeres', 17 May 1920. Groener had used similar arguments in a letter to a British officer which, he hoped, would be read by Lloyd George. Groener Papers: Groener to Colonel Roddie, 10 June 1920.

[1] Lord d'Abernon, who was present at Spa, says that the British Prime Minister 'thought the appearance in uniform a signal instance of military arrogance and tactlessness', but adds that this feeling was not shared by allied soldiers. *An Ambassador of Peace*, i. 61–62.

[2] *The Times*, 7 July 1920.

[3] Ibid., 8 July 1920.

[4] Ibid., 9 July 1920.

could do but yield to these uncompromising terms, and they did so on 9 July.[1]

For Seeckt the Spa conference was, as his biographer admits, a 'political Kunersdorf'.[2] He had gone there with the intention of fighting for an army of 200,000 men; he had been confronted with an ultimatum.[3] On 10 July, after his return to Berlin, he gave a complete report to the assembled officers of the Reichswehr Ministry, accepting full responsibility for the decision to yield to the allied demands. 'There was no doubt', he said in his clipped tones, 'that those on the side of the Entente were in earnest in their willingness to break off the negotiations and impose their demands by force. The situation confronting us was like that of Versailles—accept or refuse. We could not say No.' What alternative was there, after all? There are people, Seeckt said, who talk of uniting with the Russians and defying the Western Powers, even at the cost of war. But this is an idea of 'unclear heads'; 'it is neither *Politik* nor *Kriegführung*, but a game'—and one which would destroy Germany.

> I do not underestimate the consequences of the delegation's decision for the internal state of Germany, nor for the Reichswehr. But I am convinced that this is our only road. . . . The fact that we must reduce the army to 100,000 men by 1 January 1921 will not be modified in any respect. . . . You must view the situation with clear eyes. There can be no one who feels it more painfully than I; but it must be. We must bear it.[4]

This address is interesting, partly because it is so reminiscent of the painful explanations which Groener had had to make to the officer corps in the course of 1919, and more perhaps because of the reference to co-operation with the Soviet Union. In point of fact, Seeckt was well aware of the possible advantages of an arrangement with the Soviets;[5] he was soon, as will be seen

[1] The protocol of 9 July, which embodied the allied terms, is printed in Honnorat, *Désarmement de l'Allemagne*, pp. 24–28. On the threat to occupy the Ruhr in case of default, see also *Foreign Relations of the United States*, 1920, ii. 394.

[2] Rabenau, *Seeckt*, ii. 284.

[3] Both Seeckt and Geßler, according to a later statement by the Reichswehr Minister, were honestly surprised by allied insistence on the Versailles terms. Stresemann Papers, 215, cont. 3090, frame 139316.

[4] Seeckt Papers, Stück 118: 'Ansprache des C.H.L. . . . an die Offiziere des R.W.M., gehalten am 10. 7. 20.' In his long citation from this speech, Rabenau has deleted all reference to the idea of uniting with the Russians. See Rabenau, *Seeckt*, ii. 284–6.

[5] The possibility of such arrangement was apparently much discussed in official circles immediately after Spa. The Stresemann Papers include an interesting

below, to work out a system of peaceful collaboration with the Red army. But he had no desire to be the junior partner in a joint Russo-German campaign against the West, for this would inevitably lead to the bolshevization of Germany. He was forced, therefore, to tell his officers that plans for the reorganization of Germany's armed forces must, for the immediate future, be based on the Spa stipulations.

If this was so, however, the chief of the army command was determined that the Reichswehr must make up in overall efficiency for what it must lose because of its limited size. He demonstrated this by the attention which he paid to matters of selection and training, the eagerness with which he grasped at the latest technical innovations, and the emphasis which he placed upon tactical and strategical improvements as he proceeded with his work.

The very necessity of reducing the army so sharply enabled Seeckt to start with an *élite* force. With respect to the officer corps, for instance, he was forced to dismiss three out of every four active officers; and, quite logically, he saw to it that it was the most intelligent officers and those who had proved themselves to be the most courageous and most reliable leaders of troops who were retained. In subsequent years, as new openings appeared in the officer corps, the most stringent requirements were laid down for aspirants to commissions. Educational attainments now became more important than they had ever been in the days of the empire or even in the days of Scharnhorst.[1] Without a certificate from a *Hochschule*, a youth could not hope to be considered as a candidate; and, even with that document, he had to complete a four-and-a-half-year training course, which included two years at a military school, before he received his commission. Nor did his training end there. There were always new courses to be taken and new tests to be met; and failure to meet them—failure on the part of an officer, for instance, to qualify for the grade higher than his own—meant dismissal.[2] Seeckt's personal preference was always for candi-

unsigned memorandum of about this date, arguing the necessity of closer relations with the Soviet Union. Stresemann Papers, 223, cont. 3091, frames 140431 ff.

[1] For the educational requirements of earlier periods, see above, Chapters II and IV. Some details on the educational requirements for officers are to be found in a speech by Groener in May 1928. Reichstag, *Stenographische Berichte*, ccxcv (1928), 13429.

[2] Rosinski, *German Army*, pp. 124–5; Rabenau, *Seeckt*, ii. 499–502.

dates who were of aristocratic birth and descended from the old military families,[1] for he believed in carrying the tradition of the old army over into the new; but he never permitted this bias to protect officers from the rigorous educational and training requirements which he had laid down, and, if his officer corps was predominantly upper class in composition, the intellectual *niveau* was high.

Seeckt was also in a position to be highly selective with regard to the rank and file, and he was so much so that he was frequently attacked by democratic and socialist journals. In 1926, for instance, an unsigned article in Carl von Ossietzky's magazine *Die Weltbühne* declared that

> the new army is recruited overwhelmingly from the agricultural districts [*platten Lande*]. Peasant boys, who are not eldest sons, go to the *Kommiß* just as gladly today as they did in the imperial period. That this material cannot appreciably raise the intellectual level of the army and especially of the non-commissioned officer corps, is beyond doubt. The insufficient urban part of the recruit-contingent shows an extremely small percentage of factory workers. Moreover, practically the whole of the recruit material comes from the national *Verbände*, &c.[2]

In these charges there was a good deal of truth. In accordance with regulations for the expansion of the army (*Heeresergänzungsbestimmungen*) of June 1921, the responsibility for recruiting lay in the first instance with the company commanders, who were supposed to use their personal contacts in a manner calculated to promote the best interests of the army—in other words, to keep their eyes open for promising material. Any citizen of the Reich who had passed the age of 17 could, of course, volunteer on his own initiative, but he was forced to submit to a *Prüfung* by an officer. These provisions were applied in such a way as to give preference to rural rather than urban volunteers and to exclude Jews, socialists, communists, and even outspoken democrats from the army.[3] On the other hand, it would be a mistake

[1] Wheeler-Bennett, *Wooden Titan*, p. 289; *Nemesis of Power*, pp. 98–99. With respect to the social composition of the officer corps during the Seeckt period the percentage of aristocrats is less important than the fact that less than 5 per cent. of the officers came from social groups which had been considered ineligible before 1914. So much for the 'democratization' of the army, which Geßler was so fond of hailing.

[2] *Die Weltbühne*, 22 Jg. (1926), ii. 49.

[3] Udo Hansen in *Die Weltbühne*, 22 Jg. (1926), i. 849 ff. It should be remembered that the predominantly rural and conservative complexion of the army was

to conclude that the officers charged with recruiting were indifferent to the educational qualifications of volunteers. In an army in which every enlisted man was expected to be capable of serving as a non-commissioned officer if the occasion arose, there was no place for illiterates; and it is worth noting that, in 1930, 9 per cent. of the total force had had secondary school education and 1 per cent. had graduated from secondary schools.[1] One of the best-informed writers on the German army of this period has concluded that 'the physical and intellectual standards of the rank and file were raised to levels hitherto unknown and unachievable in any force based upon conscription'.[2]

Throughout the Weimar period there were repeated references, in budget debates in the Reichstag, to cases of suicide or attempted suicide among the enlisted men of the Reichswehr. Whatever the reason for the high rate of suicide—and it was doubtless not unconnected with the twelve-year term of service[3] —it is unlikely that it can be attributed, as the army's critics often charged, to harsh discipline or the brutality of barrack life. During the Seeckt period considerable progress was made in improving the living conditions of the men, pay was increased and food improved, heightened emphasis was placed on sport and other recreational facilities,[4] and the disciplinary code was thoroughly reformed. The old barrier between officer and man was lowered, if not removed, and officers were encouraged to gain the friendship and the confidence of their troops. In general, this contributed to efficiency and—the suicides notwithstanding —to overall morale.

In the rigorous training programme which he enforced upon all ranks, Seeckt placed special emphasis upon technical and weapons training, co-ordination of arms, an effective system of

influenced also by the system of local selection employed, the high physical standards set, and the disinclination of working and middle-class youths of liberal and socialist views to enter the army. See Gordon, *Reichswehr and Republic*, p. 291.

[1] Wheeler-Bennett, *Nemesis of Power*, p. 99.

[2] Rosinski, *German Army*, p. 125. See, however, Choltitz, *Soldat unter Soldaten*, p. 24.

[3] In 1928, when a Centre deputy asked why there had been 135 attempts at suicide, with 87 deaths, in the last year, the Reichswehr Minister blamed this on the length of service, 'das menschenunwürdige System', forced on Germany by the Treaty of Versailles. Reichstag, *Stenographische Berichte*, cccxcv (1928), 13394, 13431.

[4] On the importance of the sports programme, see Choltitz, *Soldat unter Soldaten*, pp. 26–30.

communications, and a continued devotion to the Prussian tradition of mobility. The Versailles Treaty had, of course, placed difficult obstacles in his way by denying Germany the use of offensive weapons—including military aircraft, armour, and heavy artillery. But much could be accomplished within treaty limits. Every officer and man was trained in the expert use of small arms and machine guns and in methods of communication in the field; and officers were sent to the Berlin *Technische Hochschule* in order that the latest technical advances might be studied for possible military application. Studies of co-ordination and communication were encouraged and tested in elaborate exercises. Manœuvres with motorized units were held in the Harz mountains as early as 1921;[1] and in the winter of 1923–4 Lieutenant-Colonel von Brauchitsch, who was later to be commander-in-chief of the army, organized manœuvres to test the possibilities of employing motorized troops in co-operation with aircraft.[2] It was soon discovered also that much could be learned about tanks by exercises which employed motor-cycles, armoured cars borrowed from the police, and the clumsy 'armoured troop carriers' which the treaty allowed the Germans to keep. In 1924 a young captain named Heinz Guderian was responsible for a series of such exercises, on the ground and on paper, designed to explore the possibilities of the employment of tanks for reconnaissance purposes; and the same officer was soon working out theories of offensive employment of armour which were to be put into practice in the Low Countries and France in 1940.[3]

It seems remarkable, in retrospect, that the Reichswehr, in view of its restricted size and inadequate equipment, did not succumb to a purely defensive psychology. Had Reinhardt continued at the head of the army it is quite likely that this would have happened, for that officer believed that the recent war

[1] Rabenau, *Seeckt*, ii. 509.

[2] General Heinz Guderian, *Panzer Leader* (London, 1952), p. 21. On the Reichswehr's efforts to build up a secret air force, with fields in Germany and Russia, see Helm Speidel, 'Reichswehr und Rote Armee', *Vierteljahrshefte für Zeitgeschichte*, i (1953), 20–34.

[3] Guderian, *Panzer Leader*, pp. 21–28. Throughout the decade, steady progress was made in mechanizing the army. In December 1931 the British military attaché reported that the *Inspektion der Verkehrstruppen* had been transformed into an *Inspektion der Kraftfahrtruppen* and that a new mechanized transport centre had been established in Berlin. *Documents on British Pclicy*, 2nd series, ii. 519.

had demonstrated the limitations of mobile strategy, and that tactical and strategical doctrine must be revised in light of the experience gained in trench warfare. Under Reinhardt's influence the Reichswehr might have fallen prey to the *couverture* mentality and the 'fire kills' theory, which did so much to stifle imagination and initiative in the French army in these same years.[1] Seeckt, however, from the very beginning of his term in the *Heeresleitung*, emphasized the superiority of offensive to defensive strategy and based his whole training programme on the assumption that it was strategical mobility that won wars. Despite the fact that the Reichswehr would, in his opinion, probably be inferior in numbers and material to the armies of neighbouring powers for a long time to come, Seeckt held to the traditional Prussian view that 'destruction of the opposing army . . . is still the highest law of war, although at times it may assume a different appearance';[2] and he impressed upon his officers the idea that 'the goal of a modern strategy will be to force a decision with forces which are mobile and highly developed in operational capability . . . before the masses have begun to move'.[3] Here, in germ at least, was the idea of the *attaque brusquée* or lightning war which was to become dogma in the German army.

Even within the limitations of the treaty, then, Seeckt was able to accomplish a good deal for the new Reichswehr.[4] But he was not content to stop there. From the beginning, his public programme of reconstruction was supplemented with important secret practices and policies which were designed to evade and circumvent the stipulations of Versailles.

III

The Reichswehr under Seeckt was designed as a dual-purpose force capable of serving alternately as a highly efficient professional army or as the framework for a greatly expanded army in which its officers would take the highest commands, the best

[1] Irving M. Gibson, 'Maginot and Liddell Hart', in *Makers of Modern Strategy*, pp. 371–5. [2] Seeckt, *Gedanken eines Soldaten*, p. 56. [3] Ibid., p. 77; Rabenau, *Seeckt*, pp. 503–5. See also B. H. Liddell Hart, *The Other Side of the Hill* (rev. ed., London, 1951), p. 27. See also Manstein on his work in the Truppenamt in 1929–32. *Soldatenleben*, pp. 105 ff.

[4] Some of the measures mentioned above were, of course, technical breaches of the treaty—e.g. the armoured exercises would probably be considered such a breach even though no tanks were employed.

of its non-commissioned officers would become lieutenants, and the whole of the rank and file would serve as the N.C.O.s.[1] This cadre idea posed some very difficult problems, for the difference between a small army and a large one is not merely a matter of man-power but also of administration and of long-range supply and mobilization planning. If the transition were ever to be made effectively, an institutional network capable of serving a mass army had to be established and maintained from the beginning, and thousands of officers had to receive specialized training in duties which were, by treaty definition, illegal.

For one thing, the brain of the army, the general staff system, had to be preserved. The efficiency of this system in the old army had arisen from the intimate relationship between the Great General Staff in Berlin and the staffs of the various field units, and from the uniform training given to all members of the general staff corps regardless of assignment. The Versailles Treaty, while permitting the attachment of staff officers to the ten divisions of the Reichswehr,[2] had demanded the abolition of the Great General Staff and also of the *Kriegsakademie* which had been the source of supply for that body and the field units in the past. It would be extremely difficult to maintain any homogeneity of outlook between the divisional staffs if these stipulations were observed.

Seeckt had no intention of observing them. Some of the functions of the old Great General Staff he assigned to that section of the Reichswehr Ministry which was known as the *Truppenamt*;[3] others were handed over to other government departments. The historical and archival functions, which had, ever since the time of the elder Moltke, been considered of essential importance, were now performed in the new *Reichsarchiv*.[4] The topographical section was transferred to the Ministry of the

[1] Rosinski, *German Army*, p. 129. Seeckt mentioned the idea of the *Führerheer* for the first time in a memorandum entitled 'Basic Ideas for the Reconstruction of our Armed Forces' in 1921. See Rabenau, *Seeckt*, ii. 475. There were times when practically the whole rank and file *were* N.C.O.s. In 1922 the army estimates provided for 35,644 N.C.O.s and 40,000 lance corporals (*Gefreite*), leaving only some 20,000 men as privates. See Morgan in *Political Quarterly*, ccxlii (1924), 445.

[2] The Reichswehr was divided into seven infantry and three cavalry divisions, which were subordinate to two *Gruppenkommandos*. The districts of the infantry divisions were called *Wehrkreise*.

[3] In 1936, in an obituary of General Wever, Ludwig Beck spoke of his services in the *Generalstab des Reichsheeres* and made it clear that he was referring to the *Truppenamt*. See *Militärwochenblatt*, 11 June 1936.

[4] Rabenau, *Seeckt*, ii. 198.

Interior; the military railway section found a home in the Ministry of Transport, whose chief, from 1919 to 1922, was Wilhelm Groener;[1] some of the intelligence work was taken over by the Foreign Office; and, according to a British member of the Inter-Allied Commission of Control, a large number of staff officers carried on their work under the roof of the new Ministry of Pensions.[2] Since the officers performing these functions were often, nominally at least, civilians, it was difficult for the allies to interfere;[3] nor could they prevent retired staff officers from joining the *Vereinigung Graf Schlieffen*, which was also suspected of performing staff services.[4]

These measures of evasion did not solve the problems created by the abolition of the *Kriegsakademie*. But Seeckt handled these, too, with ingenuity. All officers were compelled to take the equivalent of the old entrance examination for the academy, and those who received the highest grades were selected as staff candidates and were given two years of training in schools established at the seven *Wehrkreis* centres. To secure uniformity of instruction, Seeckt prescribed the training directions for all seven commands and, in October 1923, added a third year of training for which the most promising students—the equivalent of Scharnhorst's *Selekta*—were transferred from the *Wehrkreise* to the Reichswehr Ministry in Berlin.[5] This system was followed, and was successful in supplying the staff needs of the army until 1932, when the need for disguise seemed less urgent and all officers in training did their work in Berlin in the so-called *Offizier-Lehrgänge*.[6]

[1] Groener, it will be remembered, had been chief of field transport in the first years of the war.

[2] Morgan, *Assize of Arms*, pp. 43–44.

[3] After Locarno the British especially seem to have lost any inclination to interfere; and by 1931 Sir Horace Rumbold, in a dispatch from Berlin concerning possible concessions to the Germans at the forthcoming Disarmament Conference, suggested that 'to concede the general staff means little in effect, as it already exists in everything but name'. *Documents on British Policy*, 2nd series, iii. 466. See also Major-General A. C. Temperley, *The Whispering Gallery of Europe* (London, 1938), pp. 221–2.

[4] On this society, see Rüdt von Collenberg, *Mackensen* (Berlin, 1940), p. 140.

[5] This may account for the fact that, according to a British report of January 1930, the telephone directory of the Reichswehr Ministry actually listed a branch called *Generalstab* which consisted of four sections under a Chief of General Staff, although the official Army List made no mention of this. The report noted also that a number of officers shown in the Army List to be serving with their regiments were actually at work in the ministry. 'Report of C.I.G.S. on the Military Situation in Germany', *Documents on British Policy*, 2nd series, i. 598–9.

[6] Rabenau, *Seeckt*, ii. 515–17.

If the preservation of the General Staff was considered an essential part of building for the army of the future, so was the maintenance of a mobilization and reserve system. From the moment when the Versailles Treaty was signed, the German military chiefs were preoccupied with the mobilization problem. Why, for instance, did it take repeated allied protests and, finally, a virtual ultimatum to force the German government to repeal the imperial conscription system and to have new laws passed validating voluntary enlistment?[1] The answer seems to be that the army leaders wanted the old conscription laws to remain on the statute books. For, if they did remain, then—even if only 100,000 men could serve in the army—every youth who was of age and physically fit would be legally liable to serve and could be ordered to register at district headquarters and, thereafter, to consider himself as being in a kind of reserve status.[2] This would have supplied the army administration with complete lists which would serve as the basis for mobilization planning. In 1919, as a matter of fact, the bureaucratic machine designed to handle these tasks of registration and list-maintenance was actually established, although it was called a 'demobilization' organization and existed ostensibly to administer the reduction of the army to treaty limits. This scheme was too elaborate to succeed. The very size of the demobilization organization,[3] and the frequent German requests that its term of life be extended, indicated that it was intended for purposes other than those that met the eye; and, after some very skilful detective work, the Inter-Allied Control Commission demanded, and in 1921 secured, its dissolution.[4]

This set-back, however, did not discourage Seeckt and his colleagues, and masked mobilization planning went on through

[1] See Honnorat, *Désarmement de l'Allemagne*, pp. 41, 46. The law ending military conscription was finally passed in July 1920, after a debate marked by lamentations over the passing of the system and a statement by Geßler to the effect that the change would not be permanent. See Reichstag, *Stenographische Berichte*, cccxliv (1920), 433-46.

[2] In May 1920 officers of the Inter-Allied Control Commission discovered that, at the time of demobilization, men fit for general service received papers similar to those given before the war to men entering reserve status—papers reminding them of their *legal* duty to report for annual musters, to obey their call-up in case of general mobilization, and to notify authorities of changes in address. Morgan in *Quarterly Review*, ccxlii (1924), 429.

[3] In the spring of 1920 it comprised 3,579 ex-officers, 16,392 N.C.O.s, and 8,517 men, none of whom was carried on army rolls. Ibid., p. 426.

[4] Ibid., p. 431.

this whole period. The accumulation of the necessary data on man-power resources seems to have been part of the duties of the so-called pensions centres (*Versorgungsstelle*) which apparently took over some of the functions of the *Landwehr Bezirkskommandos* of earlier days.[1] This work probably also fell within the province of those mysterious officials who were called district commissioners (*Kreiskommissare*)—former officers who had been appointed, at Seeckt's insistence, with the rather vague duty of encouraging military virtues among the inhabitants of their districts. Seeckt's biographer is very discreet in discussing the functions of these officials, but he insists that 'from this organization of District Commissioners there arose later a network which spread over a great part of Germany and which, while keeping military ideas alive, also frequently organized effective resistance. Here was the first beginning of a corps of reserve officers, of a frontier guard and even of a later reserve army.'[2]

Of more immediate importance than this long-range mobilization planning were the steps which Seeckt took to provide the army with an active reserve which would be prepared to take to the field immediately in the event of a national emergency. This aspect of Seeckt's work is illustrated by his activities in connexion with the so-called *Arbeits Kommandos* and with the security police.

As has been indicated above, Seeckt was disinclined to place any reliance in the free corps and, after the troubles in the Ruhr, agreed with the steps taken by the government to force their dissolution. Yet, in moments of national crisis, he was not averse to using auxiliary troops, provided they were placed under Reichswehr control;[3] and, in 1923, immediately after the French occupation of the Ruhr, when Lithuania seized Memel and the Poles began to demand frontier rectifications, he worked

[1] Ibid., p. 427; Manstein, *Soldatenleben*, pp. 105 ff., especially 111 ff.

[2] Rabenau, *Seeckt*, ii. 200. What the *Kreiskommissare* had to do with organizing reserve officers is not clear. In any event, this was the least of Seeckt's worries, since the regimental associations constituted an effective reserve. See Morgan in *Quarterly Review*, ccxlii (1924), 451.

[3] It may be mentioned that in May 1921, when Korfanty led a force of Polish irregulars into Upper Silesia and when the allies refused to permit the German government to send Reichswehr units into the province, free corps were raised with the tacit approval of the government and of Seeckt and helped to save the part of the province that Germany was permitted later to retain. Once the situation was saved, the government again demanded dissolution of the forces. On Seeckt's relations with the free corps in Silesia in 1921, see Rabenau, *Seeckt*, ii. 299 ff.

out an elaborate plan for raising a supplementary force to guard against an eastern attack. On 7 February 1923, after a series of conferences, an agreement was concluded between the Defence Minister and Carl Severing, the Prussian Minister of Police, with the approval of Ebert, the Chancellor Cuno, and the Prussian Minister President Otto Braun.[1] This provided for the creation of a reserve army composed of 'labour troops' or *Arbeits Kommandos*, which would be financed, garrisoned, and trained by the army and placed under the immediate authority of Lieutenant-Colonel Fedor von Bock, chief of staff of the Third Reichswehr Division, which was stationed in Berlin.[2] By September 1923 between 50,000 and 80,000 men had enrolled in what was to be known popularly as the 'Black Reichswehr', thanks to the energetic efforts of two former free corps commanders, Major Buchrucker and Leutnant Paul Schulz,[3] who were charged with the actual work of organizing the force. Buchrucker and his colleagues found their recruits in the various illegal *Verbände* which still existed and in the universities of Berlin, Jena, Leipzig, and Halle, whose students flocked to the colours with the full approval of the university authorities.[4]

In 1926 Geßler was interrogated concerning the Black Reichswehr by special investigating committees of the Prussian *Landtag* and the Reichstag and explained to both bodies, with characteristic effrontery, that the *Arbeits Kommandos* were not military formations at all. They were organized, he said in a memorandum to the Reichstag, to collect, sort, and destroy stocks of illegal weapons and other war materials in Berlin, the Ostmark, and Silesia, the existence of which represented a danger to the state. It was true, he added, that they were trained in the working of the various weapons, but only so that they would know whether those that they collected were

[1] Rabenau, *Seeckt*, ii. 328; Caro and Oehme, *Schleichers Aufstieg*, pp. 156–59; E. J. Gumbel, '*Verräter verfallen der Feme*': *Opfer, Mörder, Richter, 1919–1920* (Berlin, 1929), pp. 254–6; Oertzen, *Freikorps*, pp. 465–6.

[2] Bock was aided by Kurt von Schleicher, Kurt von Hammerstein, and Eugen Ott, all officers who were to rise to high positions in the army. See Wheeler-Bennett, *Nemesis of Power*, p. 92.

[3] Oberleutnant a. D. Schulz had founded the Bund Fridericus Rex at Fort Gorgas near Küstrin at the end of 1922. This whole group entered the *Arbeits Kommandos* after the Seeckt–Severing agreement. See *Die Weltbühne*, 21. Jg. (1925), ii. 239–58.

[4] E. J. Gumbel, *Verschwörer: Beiträge zur Geschichte und Soziologie der deutschen nationalistischen Geheimbünde seit 1918* (Vienna, 1924), p. 109; Waite, *Vanguard of Nazism*, p. 242.

usable or not. As for the fact that their existence was kept secret, this was to avoid arousing 'unjustified suspicion' on the part of the *entente* and providing the Western Powers with an excuse for conducting espionage in Germany.[1]

This declaration possesses a certain amusement value but bears no relation to fact. That the A.K. had been established as a volunteer frontier guard was openly admitted in 1926 by a member of Cuno's cabinet.[2] According to other reliable testimony, the labour troops had little, if anything, to do with the collecting of arms in Geßler's sense of the term. They were given extensive drills by Reichswehr officers and participated in army manœuvres. They attended the regular non-commissioned officers school in the Küstrin barracks and were used interchangeably with regular troops for guard and other duties in Berlin.[3] They were in every sense an active reserve force existing in defiance of the treaty and working in the closest co-ordination with the legally constituted army.

In the end, however, this experiment was a failure. The free corps elements in the A.K. were less interested in the possibility of a defensive war against the Poles than they were in an offensive action against the republican régime; and Buchrucker himself planned to use the four battalions which were under his command at Küstrin to capture Berlin. This plan was ruined by Ebert's declaration of a state of siege on 27 September, which gave full power to the military authorities.[4] Buchrucker had apparently been given to understand that Seeckt was sympathetic to his plans;[5] but Ebert's order inspired doubts in

[1] Caro and Oehme, *Schleichers Aufstieg*, pp. 147–8. For a discussion of Geßler's testimony before the *Landtag* committee, see *Die Weltbühne*, 22. Jg. (1926), i. 293 ff. In January 1926, Geßler described the A.K.s to Stresemann in the same manner as above and asked him to use his influence to keep any investigation of them secret lest German foreign policy be jeopardized. Stresemann wrote that he had 'the feeling that, aside from this consideration of the matter, other matters came into play, the discussion of which would be very unpleasant to the Reichswehr'. Stresemann Papers, 279, cont. 3100, frames 149449–50.

[2] Joseph Wirth. See Reichstag, *Stenographische Berichte*, cccxci (1926), 8589–90.

[3] See Waite, *Vanguard of Nazism*, pp. 245–6, and the authorities cited. For further details on the organization of the A.K.'s in 1923, with charts showing the main garrisons, strength figures, and the chain of command, see *Die Weltbühne*, 21. Jg. (1925), ii. 677 ff.

[4] See below, p. 416.

[5] According to an unsigned memorandum in the Stresemann papers, dated 'Anfang Dezember 1926' and apparently based on information deriving from Buchrucker, Seeckt had known of the projected *Putsch*. The memorandum states that Graf Westarp and two other Nationalist deputies had gone to him some time

his mind. He decided, therefore, to disband his troops but found, to his dismay, that they were determined to go ahead with the planned rising. As the only way out, then, he warned the local army command of what was pending; and steps were taken to nip the *Putsch* in the bud.[1]

The collapse of this curious affair made necessary the dissolution of the A.K. system as a whole. From this point on, although Seeckt extended Reichswehr facilities to a few favoured organizations,[2] he never again tried anything as elaborate as the labour battalion plan of 1923.

The chief of the army command did, however, throughout this whole period, possess another reserve force which could be employed in time of war to supplement the strength of the Reichswehr, namely, the police. Here Seeckt fought a protracted and successful battle against the Western Powers, who were conscious of the military capabilities of a police force and had, in the Versailles Treaty, stipulated that the members of the German police should have the same proportion to the total population as in the year 1913. In 1919 the German government established, in addition to the old *Ordnungspolizei*, which was under local control, a *Sicherheitspolizei*, under state control. In view of the heavy armament and large numbers of this body, the allies quite rightly regarded it as a military formation and, at the Spa conference, demanded its dissolution. In doing so, however, they authorized an increase in the *Ordnungspolizei* from 92,000 to 150,000 men, permitting it, moreover, to possess heavy machine guns and machine pistols.

in mid-1923 and asked him how he stood with regard to 'the movement in Küstrin'. Seeckt answered that he was 'informed concerning the matter' and that those 'who took measures in Küstrin could rely on him to be a man of action at the right moment. He knew what his patriotic duty was.' Westarp and the others were apparently satisfied that this ambiguous statement meant that Seeckt was prepared to unseat the Stresemann cabinet, by force if necessary. Stresemann Papers, 47, cont. 3167, frames 163234 ff. The weight of this evidence is somewhat offset by a letter which Westarp wrote to Friedrich von Rabenau in 1938, in which he said that as far as he could remember Seeckt refused to pledge Reichswehr aid for counter-revolutionary measures. Seeckt Papers, Stück 291: Westarp to Rabenau, 8 June 1938.

[1] On the Küstrin *Putsch* see Waite, *Vanguard of Nazism*, pp. 247–54, and Schüddekopf, *Heer und Republik*, pp. 167 ff., 177 ff.

[2] In his speech of 16 December 1926 Scheidemann claimed that the *Kleinkaliberschützenvereine* had been given the use of Reichswehr training facilities in Giessen, and he charged that the Reichswehr had ties with other organizations. Reichstag, *Stenographische Berichte*, cccxci (1926–7), 8579 ff. See also footnote 2, p. 405, below. In Silesia, moreover, Seeckt always maintained local defence units. See Gordon, *Reichswehr and Republic*, p. 260.

While these concessions were cheerfully accepted, every effort was made to evade the demanded dissolution of the *Sicherheitspolizei*. In the end, it was simply transformed into a new force, called the *Schutzpolizei*—a force which, under Seeckt's direction, rapidly assumed a military character, was grouped in units commanded by former army officers, was quartered in barracks, and participated in Reichswehr exercises and manœuvres. The close identity between this force and the Reichswehr was, of course, realized by members of the Inter-Allied Control Commission,[1] but the Western governments never acted effectively to check the evasions which their agents reported.[2] Indeed, after June 1925, the Western Powers abandoned their efforts to force the dissolution of the *Schutzpolizei* and concentrated on an attempt to limit the number of police quartered in barracks. In the end it was agreed that only 32,000 men must be so quartered and that they must have enlisted for twelve years. This was a rather backhanded authorization of an increase in the number of Reichswehr effectives; but there is no reason to believe that the Germans were content with the authorized figure. Seeckt's police reserve was generally believed to be closer to 70,000 in number than to 32,000.[3]

Even a brief account of the ways in which Seeckt and his aides evaded the terms of the treaty in order to build the army of the future would be incomplete without some reference to their work in providing that army with adequate sources of supply of munitions and the other sinews of war. In this connexion, the dogged efforts made by German soldiers to hide stocks of weapons from the Inter-Allied Control Commission need not concern us, for Seeckt himself did not regard them as very important. 'The accumulation of great reserve stocks', he was to write later, 'is the most uneconomical process imaginable, and also, in view of the natural obsolescence of material, of

[1] See Morgan in *Quarterly Review*, ccxlii (1924), 444.

[2] This is true of evasion in general, not only of those connected with the police. In January 1930 a British report stated that men who enlisted for twelve years in the Reichswehr were being released on various grounds after shorter periods, that a special category of men was apparently being enlisted for three years only, and that members of patriotic organizations were still being attached to regular units for short periods of training. The British military attaché estimated that in 1929 there was an excess of 7,000 men training in the depots. *Documents on British Policy*, 2nd series, i. 599. No action seems to have been taken on this or similar reports.

[3] The above discussion on the police question is based on Jordan, *Great Britain, France and the German Problem*, pp. 143–4.

doubtful military value.' It was more important, in his view, for the army to engage in joint planning with industry so that mass production of approved weapons and material could be begun at the strategically proper moment.[1]

Perhaps the best illustration of Seeckt's encouragement of this kind of planning, and the only one that need be given here, is that afforded by the relations between the army and the famous Krupp munitions firm. In accordance with the terms of the treaty, the greatest of German armaments establishments was restricted to the production of a single type of gun, and thousands of its machines and tools for munitions production were destroyed. In the subsequent period, the great plants at Essen, then, were turned to the manufacture of civilian goods. Behind this respectable screen, however, the traditional interests of Krupp were kept alive. A very active 'Research Department for Arms Production' worked on new designs for heavy guns, gun carriages, armour plating, and the like.[2] Nor did these plans remain on paper, for Krupp had subsidiaries abroad—the Bofors gun plants in Sweden, in which Krupp owned a controlling block of stock by 1925; a holding company named Siderius A. G., which controlled ship-building yards at Rotterdam, and machine and torpedo works at Utrecht and The Hague; and other holding companies at Barcelona, Bilbao, and Cadiz, where submarine construction and experimentation went forward.[3]

In all these enterprises the German army and navy were active partners. Representatives of the *Marineleitung* were privy to the developmental submarine work conducted in Holland, and Reichswehr officers had access to the Bofors proving grounds. A Krupp memorandum discovered after the Second World War mentions a formal agreement of 25 January 1922 between the *Reichswehrministerium* and Krupp, 'jointly to circumvent . . . the provisions of the Treaty of Versailles which strangled Germany's military freedom'. When the French entered the Ruhr in 1923 the 'Research Department' was hastily moved to Berlin, and the *Heeresleitung* collaborated in setting up a dummy corporation called Koch and Kienzle to camouflage its work. In 1925 Gustav Krupp arranged a four-day tour of the

[1] Seeckt, *Gedanken eines Soldaten*, pp. 60–61.

[2] Bernhard Menne, *Blood and Steel: The Rise of the House of Krupp* (New York, 1938), p. 378.

[3] Ibid., pp. 379–85.

leading Ruhr establishments for Seeckt and discussed with him the possibility of producing tanks in Sweden and the advisability of transferring part of the munitions industry from the Ruhr to central Germany.[1] It would be difficult to find a more perfect collaboration than that which existed between Krupp and the military establishment in these years.[2]

Seeckt did not, of course, restrict his activities to the task of maintaining good relations with Krupp and other private firms. He insisted that the army itself must assume responsibility for long-range economic planning, and, in November 1924, established a new branch in the Reichswehr Ministry which was intended to be a kind of economic general staff. Under the command of General Wurzbacher, this *Rüstamt* was assigned the task of ascertaining the total requirements in munitions, weapons, equipment, and clothing of an army of sixty-three divisions and a navy and air force to support it, of estimating the raw materials necessary for these requirements, of studying transport and other needs, and of maintaining liaison with industry at home and abroad.[3] The tradition established during the war by Walther Rathenau's economic staff was thus continued by Seeckt's *Rüstamt*; and his experiments in *Wehrwirtschaft* laid the basis for Hitler's later accomplishments in this field.[4]

Whether Germany's civilian leaders approved of all of the illicit preparations which have been discussed above is a question which would be difficult to answer. That they knew of them seems beyond doubt, for hints concerning all of them appeared, at one time or another, in the left-wing press.[5] But no one of Seeckt's civilian colleagues ever sought to divert him from his course or to convince him that his policy of evasions was

[1] Telford Taylor, *Sword and Swastika: Generals and Nazis in the Third Reich* (New York, 1952), pp. 44-45.

[2] Sums were drawn from the military budget to subsidize Krupp and other firms; and, by 1931, if not before, a separate budgetary grant of 2 million reichsmarks, ostensibly for 'war burdens' [*Kriegslasten*], was paid out directly to various munition firms. See *Documents on British Policy*, 2nd series, ii. 516.

[3] Wheeler-Bennett, *Nemesis of Power*, pp. 143-4.

[4] For further details of the experiments in *Wehrwirtschaft* in this period, see Godfrey Scheele, *The Weimar Republic* (London, 1946), pp. 110-19.

[5] Of Stresemann's awareness of rearmament activity there is now no doubt, and Hans Gatzke has described his attitude toward it as ranging from 'passive acceptance to active assistance'. *Stresemann and the Rearmament of Germany* (Baltimore, 1954), p. 107; also pp. 7-9, 37, 51, 80-84. Cf. Henry L. Bretton, *Stresemann and the Revision of Versailles* (Stanford, 1953), pp. 138 ff.

inconsistent with solemn German pledges made to other Powers; and it is hardly likely that he would have been impressed if they had done so.

IV

Of special interest in the history of Germany's evasion of the clauses of the Versailles Treaty is the story of Soviet–German military relations in this period. Seeckt's activities in this matter, moreover, are instructive in illustrating his fixed belief that the army was fully justified in taking the initiative in determining foreign policy when the interests of state and army required it.

Thoughts of a possible arrangement with the Soviet Union were certainly never far from Seeckt's mind in the first years after the defeat of 1918. For one thing he could not be blind to the possibility of promoting German military training and even German rearmament on Russian soil; for another, he was —as early as December 1918—determined that Germany must not remain isolated in international politics[1] and—despite ideological differences between Germany and the Soviet Union—the chance of an alliance between them was more likely than that of an alliance between Germany and any other Power. We have no way of telling what effect the subtle suggestions of Karl Radek had upon him during the days when that clever Soviet agent was holding *levées* for German staff officers and industrialists in his prison cell in the Lehrterstraße;[2] nor is it clear how receptive he was to the arguments of Enver Pasha, who apparently urged him to consider a *rapprochement* with the Soviets in 1919.[3] As we have seen, Seeckt was still sufficiently

[1] See Rabenau's account of the meeting in the General Staff building in December 1918 in which Seeckt argued that Germany's political future depended on her making herself *bündnisfähig*. Rabenau, *Seeckt*, ii. 118. E. H. Carr says, in *German-Soviet Relations between the Two World Wars* (Baltimore, 1951), p. 11, that in this context the word alliance could mean only Russia.

[2] Radek had been sent to Germany in 1918. He participated in the spartacist convention of December, and—after the disorders of January—was arrested and lodged in Moabit prison. He was given privileged treatment and was later moved to more comfortable quarters. He was visited by scores of officers, industrialists, and politicians, including Colonel Bauer, Felix Deutsch, Walther Rathenau, General von Reibnitz, and Admiral Hintze, and seems to have expounded to them his views on the natural affinity of the Soviet Union and a nationalist Germany. See Ruth Fischer, *Stalin and German Communism* (Cambridge, Mass., 1948), pp. 204–8.

[3] Enver also visited Radek, who later claimed that the Turkish leader 'was the first to explain to German military men that Soviet Russia is a new and growing world Power with which they must count if they really want to fight the Entente'. Carr. *German-Soviet Relations*, p. 22. See also Rabenau, *Seeckt*, ii. 306–7.

conscious of the threat of bolshevism in July 1920 to argue, after returning from Spa, that an accommodation with the Soviets was not practical politics.[1] At the same time, the rude rebuff given at Spa to his plans for a 200,000 man army must have led him to think more seriously of eastern possibilities; and we know for sure that, by the end of the year, he had established a special unit in the Reichswehr Ministry called *Sondergruppe R*, which was charged with studying possibilities of co-operation with the Red army.[2]

In May 1921 the first step towards the re-establishment of correct diplomatic relations between Germany and the Soviet Union was taken with the conclusion of a provisional economic agreement.[3] Shortly thereafter—the dating is still obscure—the Soviet government seems to have made formal application to the German government for aid in building up its armament industry.[4] Seeckt immediately dispatched a special military mission to Russia, headed by Colonel Oskar von Niedermayer, who claimed the title 'The German Lawrence' by virtue of his war-time activities in Persia and Afghanistan. Together with Gustav Hilger, a member of the German prisoners-of-war mission in Russia, Karakhan, Soviet Vice-Commissar for Foreign Affairs, and Victor Kopp, Niedermayer carried out a thorough examination of the armament factories and shipyards at Petrograd which the Soviet government had suggested might be restored with German financial and technical assistance. The Germans were appalled at the disorganized state of these works, and Niedermayer, upon returning to Berlin, recommended that their restoration would be beyond Germany's financial capacity and should not be attempted. This recommendation was followed.[5]

This did not end matters, however. In September 1921

[1] See above, p. 392. Seeckt's attitude on this occasion casts doubt on the evidence given by N. N. Krestinsky in the 1938 Moscow trials that in July 1920 Seeckt made approaches through Victor Kopp for Soviet–German collaboration against the *entente*. See Fischer, *Stalin and German Communism*, p. 264, and E. Wollenberg, *The Red Army* (London, 1938), p. 236.

[2] Carr, *German-Soviet Relations*, p. 57.

[3] This agreement was the result of protracted negotiations between Ago von Maltzan, head of the eastern division of the Foreign Office, and Victor Kopp, Soviet emissary charged with the discussion of matters dealing with prisoners of war. See Wipert von Bülow, *Deutschlands Weg nach Rapallo*, pp. 100, 147; Hilger, *Incompatible Allies*, pp. 65–68.

[4] C. F. Melville, *The Russian Face of Germany* (London, 1932), p. 199.

[5] Hilger, *Incompatible Allies*, pp. 194–6.

secret conversations were begun in the Berlin apartment of Colonel Kurt von Schleicher, in which the Soviet Commissar for Foreign Trade, Leonid Krassin, and General von Hasse, the head of the *Truppenamt*, participated; and in these talks the original scheme of rebuilding the Soviet armaments industry was broadened to include provisions for the supply of illegal weapons to Germany and the beginning of real collaboration between the Soviet and German General Staffs. To encourage German co-operation, the Soviet negotiators seem to have intimated that, with German aid, they would be prepared to attack Poland in the spring. As E. H. Carr has written,[1] they could hardly have meant this seriously; but there can be little doubt, in view of the exaggerated importance which Seeckt soon came to place on the Soviet tie, that this suggestion appealed to him. Hasse himself was sent to Moscow at the end of 1921 to consult with the Soviet chief of staff, and it was reported that his purpose was to talk of joint action in the event of a Polish war.[2]

Although the war did not materialize, an effective plan of collaboration did. The Reichswehr Ministry launched a private holding corporation under the name *Gesellschaft zur Förderung gewerblicher Unternehmungen* (G.E.F.U.) with offices in Berlin and Moscow and with a working capital (in 1923) of 75,000,000 reichsmarks.[3] Under the supervision of General von Borries and Major Fritz Tschunke, this organization financed the establishment of a Junkers aircraft factory at Fili near Moscow, a poison gas factory at Samara, and shell factories—under Krupp administration—at Tula, Leningrad, and Schlüsselberg. Plans for the building of submarines were also made, but nothing came of them.[4] For the money which it invested, the German army was to receive a share in the production of all plants.

Simultaneously, Niedermayer was sent back to Russia where

[1] *German-Soviet Relations*, p. 60.

[2] Ibid., p. 59.

[3] Hilger says that G.E.F.U. 'had speculated itself out of existence' by the mid-1920's and was replaced by a similar organization called *Wirtschaftskontor* (W.I.K.O.). *Incompatible Allies*, p. 194.

[4] Krupp's Dutch subsidiaries took over this work. The poison gas factory was never a success either, perhaps because of Russian incompetence or the mistakes of the German firm, Stolzenberg. Carr, *German-Soviet Relations*, p. 61. The Junkers plant at Fili was forced to close down in 1925 because of inadequate financing. See Wheeler-Bennett, *Nemesis of Power*, p. 129. For further details on the work of G.E.F.U., see George W. F. Hallgarten, 'General Hans von Seeckt and Russia, 1920–1922', *Journal of Modern History*, xxi (1949), 28–34.

he established a kind of branch office of *Sondergruppe R*, which was called *Zentrale Moskau*, which had administrative control over the purely military aspects of the secret accord. These included the training of German pilots and specialists in a Red army flying school near Lipetsk in Tambov province and in a tank school near Kazan. The *Zentrale* became the administrative centre for all German personnel connected with these projects, and Niedermayer in addition acted as an unofficial military attaché, sending his reports directly to the *Heeresleitung*.[1]

Seeckt's negotiations with the Russians were carried on with the knowledge and the approval of the civilian authorities.[2] Indeed, they were facilitated by a policy decision made by the civilians on their own initiative, for, in April 1922, at the Genoa conference, the Foreign Minister, Walther Rathenau, and Ago von Maltzan met with the heads of the Russian delegation and concluded a treaty of friendship with the Soviet Union in accordance with which both Powers agreed to a mutual renunciation of reparations claims, a renewed effort to facilitate Russo-German trade, and the immediate re-establishment of normal diplomatic and consular relations. The circumstances surrounding the conclusion of this treaty—which surprised and alarmed all Europe and which marked the first step toward the regaining of Germany's Great Power status—are so well known that they need not be described here. Seeckt's attitude towards Rapallo, however, in 1922 and in subsequent years, requires some comment.

Although the conclusion of the pact took place without his knowledge,[3] the chief of the army command was delighted by it, until he learned, with indignation, that it was the intention of the government to appoint Count Brockdorff-Rantzau as Germany's first ambassador to the Soviet Union. Seeckt still believed that Brockdorff-Rantzau had needlessly sacrificed the interests of the army at the Paris peace conference; and to the suggestion that he be sent to Moscow he reacted with the utmost violence.

In seeking to block the appointment, Seeckt seized upon a letter which Brockdorff had sent to the Chancellor in which

[1] Hilger, *Incompatible Allies*, pp. 196–7; Speidel in *Vierteljahrshefte*, i (1953), 20, 24–31, 43.

[2] Joseph Wirth was apprised of the negotiations at an early stage. See Carr, *Soviet-German Relations*, p. 59.

[3] See Rabenau, *Seeckt*, ii. 312.

the diplomat had warned against pushing the Rapallo policy too far.[1] In particular, Brockdorff had written:

> Any appearance of a military alliance on our part with the East would have the most detrimental effect on our relations with the West. The weighty disadvantage of the Rapallo Agreement lies in the military fears attached to it.
>
> A German policy oriented exclusively towards the East would at the present moment be not only precipitate and dangerous, but without prospect and, therefore, a mistake.

In a memorandum to the Chancellor, Seeckt interpreted these words as proof that Brockdorff-Rantzau regarded the Rapallo Treaty as a 'political blunder' and said that this in itself rendered him 'unfit for the post of German representative in Moscow'. This was, in fact, completely unfair to the former Foreign Minister. Brockdorff—as his close associate Hilger tells us—readily admitted that Rapallo had been a brilliant stroke.[2] He was convinced, however, that for Germany to pin all her hopes on the Russian card would be a mistake, for it would make Germany completely dependent on her essentially unreliable eastern neighbour while simultaneously frightening Britain and France into a solid front against Germany. Even in the military sphere he was not persuaded that Germany could gain as much from secret agreements with the Soviet Union as she could by exploiting the already apparent differences between the *entente* Powers. Essentially, although this is not explicitly stated in his letter, Brockdorff was arguing for the kind of policy of *finesse* practised successfully later by Stresemann—a policy of balancing between east and west and gaining advantages from both.

This kind of policy, however, Seeckt repudiated contemptuously. Germany, he said, must follow a policy of action, for if she stands still she will lose the very essence of her statehood. A policy of action necessarily means an anti-French policy and, since Poland is France's outpost in eastern Europe, an anti-Polish policy. 'Germany today is certainly not in a position to resist France. Our policy should be to prepare the means of doing so in the future.' Military collaboration with Russia is the

[1] Brockdorff-Rantzau's letter of 15 July 1922 and Seeckt's answering *pro memoria* to the Chancellor of 11 September have been printed in an article by Julius Epstein in *Der Monat* (Nov. 1948) and are reprinted in Schüddekopf, *Heer und Republik*, pp. 155–65.

[2] Hilger, *Incompatible Allies*, p. 92.

best way of advancing that preparation; and such collaboration is made possible by Germany's ability to provide Russia's technical needs and also by the mutual antipathy of the two Powers to Poland—a state which 'must disappear and will do so through her own inner weakness and through Russia—with our help'. Granted that the destruction of Poland may not come immediately, the very existence of Russo-German friendship, and the suspicion that a Russo-German military agreement also exists, will be enough to dissuade the Poles from joining in a French war of sanctions against Germany. Aside from this, it is needless to be concerned about the Western Powers, for they are so badly split that they will not interfere with German dealings with the Soviet Union. Therefore, full speed ahead with the eastern orientation!

Having made these points in defence of an exclusively eastern approach in policy, and having cheerfully admitted that the end objective was war,[1] Seeckt concluded by demanding that the direction of that policy should be in the hands of the soldiers, rather than of the Moscow embassy and the Foreign Office. Rather disingenuously he argued that this would spare the government embarrassment in case such things as details of secret rearmament came to light. But the real reason came at the very end of the memorandum. Seeckt wrote:

> The German nation, with its Socialist majority, would be averse from a policy of action, which has to reckon with the possibility of war. It must be admitted that the spirit surrounding the Peace Delegation at Versailles has not yet disappeared, and that the stupid cry of 'No more war!' is widely echoed. . . . It is true that there is a widespread and understandable need for peace among the German people. The clearest heads, when considering the pros and cons of war, will be those of the military, but to pursue a policy means to take the lead. In spite of everything, the German people will follow the leader in the struggle for their existence. Our task is to prepare for this struggle, for we shall not be spared it.[2]

Considering that this was written to Germany's leading civilian official, this is surprisingly frank. If it means anything, it is a firm request that the direction of Russian policy and the

[1] In one of his less guarded moments, Seeckt said in 1925: 'We must become powerful and, as soon as we have power, we will naturally take back everything we have lost.' Stresemann Papers, 272, cont. 3113, frame 147890.

[2] Schüddekopf, *Heer und Republik*, p. 165.

ultimate decision on the war that policy is to bring should be placed in army hands. This was too much even for the Wirth government to tolerate. Despite the categorical tone of Seeckt's *pro memoria* and despite his additional attempts to discredit Brockdorff-Rantzau,[1] the former Foreign Minister was sent to Moscow as ambassador and was vested with powers far exceeding those of the ordinary ambassador, for he was empowered to report directly to the President and was freed from any subordination to the Foreign Office or other agencies.

This represented a defeat for Seeckt and he resented it.[2] Despite the fact that Brockdorff himself, once he was installed in Moscow, abandoned his former reservations and became an impassioned advocate of the eastern orientation, the chief of army command never abandoned the belief that Russian policy should be strictly an army preserve. He continued, moreover, to act in that sense, with the result that there was no effective liaison between military missions to the Soviet Union and other branches of the executive, and the government often had only the sketchiest knowledge of the activities of, and the commitments made by, the soldiers. This became a source of concern even to those members of the government who were friendly to the Russians. Brockdorff, for instance, believed that Seeckt's enthusiasm for the Russian connexion led him to pay exorbitant prices for the military goods which Germany received from the Soviet Union; and—especially after a visit of General Hasse to Moscow in 1923, in which the chief of the *Truppenamt* talked openly of a great war of liberation to be launched in three to five years—he suspected that the soldiers might be making pledges to the Russians of which the government was not informed.[3]

This last suspicion may have been ill-founded. It must nevertheless be said that, despite the fact that Seeckt's work in

[1] The Seeckt Papers include a letter dated 14 October 1922 from Dr. Walther Simons to Seeckt, in which the former Foreign Minister and member of the Versailles delegation says that he has heard that the *Heeresleitung* is raising objections to Brockdorff's appointment and that he hopes that Seeckt is not being influenced by a belief that Brockdorff-Rantzau sacrificed army interests at Versailles, since such belief would be ill-founded.

[2] It is difficult to see how Wheeler-Bennett reaches the conclusion that Seeckt had 'won all along the line'. *Nemesis of Power*, p. 139.

[3] Hilger, *Incompatible Allies*, p. 200. This may explain why Hindenburg believed, at the time he assumed the presidency, that Germany had a military alliance with the Soviet Union. Stresemann Papers, 272, cont. 3113, frame 147822.

establishing the Russian connexion brought tangible military and political advantages to Germany in 1922–3, the chief of the army command tended increasingly to over-value the Soviet tie and, because of this, failed to see the possibilities of an active German policy on other fronts. It would be difficult to deny, for instance, that Gustav Stresemann's Locarno policy brought quite as many military and political advantages to Germany as Seeckt's policy in the east and did so, moreover, without abandoning the connexion made at Rapallo. Yet Seeckt conducted an embittered campaign against Stresemann's policy—a campaign which greatly increased the difficulties which the Foreign Minister had to overcome and which might even have been decisive in defeating Stresemann's efforts, if, at the crucial moment, both Hindenburg and Geßler had not thrown the weight of their influence on the Foreign Minister's side.[1] Seeckt's attitude during the fight over the Rhineland Pact and the question of Germany's membership in the League awakened fears in the hearts of many who admired his work in building up the army but who, nevertheless, recalled the results of army dictation in matters of foreign policy during the war.[2]

V

Meanwhile, Seeckt's influence in the field of domestic politics had also become a source of disquietude to supporters of the republican régime. To explain this it is necessary to refer briefly to his role in the series of crises which began with the French invasion of the Ruhr in January 1923.

In the twelve months that followed that event Germany experienced the most ruinous inflation in modern times, a revival of communist agitation on a dangerous scale, serious separatist movements in the Rhineland and Bavaria, and the first attempt of Adolf Hitler's National Socialist party to seize control of the state. As its troubles multiplied, the government—bereft of other forces with which to maintain internal order—was forced

[1] See Stresemann, *Vermächtnis*, ii. 152, 166; d'Abernon, *Ambassador of Peace*, iii. 169. Frau von Roon told Stresemann in July 1925 that Seeckt's wife was saying openly that 'efforts for reconciliation with France were senseless and her husband would take care that nothing came of them'. Stresemann Papers, 272, cont. 3113, frame 147935.

[2] As early as October 1922, in an article entitled 'Militärische Nebenregierungen und Seeckts Einmischung in die Politik', *Vorwärts* accused the general of seeking to use the methods of the war-time Supreme Command. See Rabenau, *Seeckt*, ii. 319.

to turn to the army; and, in September, a state of emergency was declared and full powers were given to Otto Geßler to restore order in the Reich. On the whole it must be admitted that the army did its duty, but there were moments when it was by no means certain that this would be the case. The attempted *Putsch* of the Reichswehr's auxiliaries at Küstrin has already been mentioned;[1] and it should be remembered also that the true danger of the Bavarian situation between September and November arose from the fact that the commander of the Bavarian Reichswehr, General von Lossow, was working with the separatist movement of State Commissioner Ritter von Kahr.[2] It was only when Adolf Hitler tried to stampede Kahr and his associates into a crusade against Berlin that Lossow changed sides and mobilized the forces that shot down Hitler's followers at the Feldherrn Halle on 9 November 1923.[3]

Moreover, throughout the troubles of 1923, Seeckt's own attitude was sufficiently ambiguous to arouse suspicions concerning his ambitions and ultimate intentions. During the emergency period, he showed not the slightest hesitation when it came to putting down disorders caused by leftist agitation; the suppression of the Zeigner government in Saxony—a government which was in danger of falling under communist domination—is a case in point.[4] On the other hand, he showed much more hesitation in dealing energetically with the situation in Bavaria. It is true that the Bavarian situation was a very delicate one and that Seeckt still wished to avoid a situation in which Reichswehr might have to fire upon Reichswehr.[5] But certain of his actions were of such nature as to give weight to the suspicions of those

[1] See above, pp. 403–4.

[2] For a good brief account of the development of the situation in Bavaria in 1923, see Halperin, *Germany Tried Democracy*, pp. 267–72.

[3] The story of the beer hall *Putsch* is now well enough known to make a detailed description unnecessary. For a recent account, see Wheeler-Bennett, *Nemesis of Power*, pp. 164–76.

[4] In the first week of October a coalition government of Social Democrats and communists was formed in Saxony, with the Social Democrat Zeigner as premier. Communist attempts to seize control of the police were blocked by Zeigner; but continuous disorders and an ill-planned communist rising in Saxony gave the Berlin government an excuse to move the Reichswehr in and depose the government. See Cuno Horkenbach, *Das deutsche Reich von 1918 bis heute* (Berlin, 1930), pp. 177–8, 180 ff.; Fischer, *Stalin and German Communism*, pp. 329 ff.

[5] This was also Geßler's position. In cabinet meetings on the Bavarian situation he urged compromise on the grounds that it was clear that the Reichswehr would not fight with enthusiasm. Stresemann Papers, 263, cont. 3009, frames 146165 ff.

who criticized him later for having protected himself against all possible contingencies. He had gone out of his way to seek a personal interview with Adolf Hitler in March 1923—a step which was surely more extraordinary than his biographer seems to believe.[1] Some time later, he established his wife in Munich, where she ran a kind of political salon which was frequented by politicians of pronouncedly anti-republican views.[2] After Ritter von Kahr had virtually broken off relations with the Berlin government and had ordered the Bavarian Reichswehr to take a special oath of allegiance to the government in Munich, Seeckt issued an order of the day of 4 November calling on all officers and men to obey their superior commanders; but the order made no mention of loyalty to the Weimar constitution.[3] Moreover, in a private letter to Kahr on the following day, Seeckt—while pleading with the Bavarian leader to refrain from meddling in military affairs—emphasized his own efforts to make the Reichswehr 'a pillar of the authority of the Reich, not of any particular government' and freely expressed his belief in the efficacy of 'national thinking', his antagonism to social democracy, his antipathy to the constitution, and his confident expectation that it would be changed soon—although, he hoped, without civil war.[4]

The fact of the matter is that, throughout the crisis months, Seeckt was seriously considering the possibility of taking power into his own hands, either by way of military dictatorship or in the form of a Seeckt chancellorship or, alternately, a three-man directorate in which he would be the chief figure. In connexion with the third of these possibilities he seems to have considered Lossow as a colleague,[5] although he apparently preferred Wiedfeldt, the ambassador in Washington, and the industrialist Minoux, and was actually negotiating with both of them at the beginning of November.[6] There exists, among his papers, a sixteen-page draft programme, which was presumably to be

[1] See Rabenau, *Seeckt*, ii. 347–8.

[2] Ibid., p. 344. Fritz Thyssen, in *I Paid Hitler* (New York, 1941), p. 84, hints broadly that Frau Seeckt's mission to Munich was intended to protect her husband's interests in case the nationalist groups there succeeded in taking full power in Germany.

[3] Rabenau, *Seeckt*, ii. 371.

[4] Seeckt Papers, Stück 154: Seeckt to Kahr, 5 November 1923.

[5] Rabenau, *Seeckt*, ii. 346.

[6] Ibid., pp. 346, 370–1; Reginald H. Phelps, 'Aus den Seeckt-Dokumenten: II. Seeckt und die Innenpolitik', *Deutsche Rundschau* (Oct. 1952), p. 1013.

put into effect by whatever government he formed—a programme which provided, among other things, for a strengthening of executive authority, a limitation of the Reichstag's powers by the creation of a new chamber of estates to balance it,[1] the substitution of *Berufskammern* for trades unions, and other features which were hardly calculated to arouse enthusiasm among democrats.[2]

It is possible that Seeckt was preparing to make his bid for power at precisely the moment when Adolf Hitler decided to make his own. On 3 November, at an audience with Ebert which took place in the presence of Geßler and Otto Meißner, Seeckt told the President that the time had come for a 'reconciliation with the Right' lest the troops be caught between two fires; and, when Ebert curtly rejected this suggestion, said that, in any event, it was impossible to go on with Stresemann as Chancellor. Ebert coolly advised him to tell this to Stresemann and telephoned the Chancellor to inform him that Seeckt and Geßler had something to say to him. Later, in Stresemann's office, Seeckt said: 'Herr Reichskanzler, it is impossible to carry on the fight under you. You don't have the confidence of the troops.' Stresemann asked whether Seeckt was claiming to speak for the Reichswehr; and Geßler hastily interjected to say that only he could do that. Seeckt remained silent; and the conversation was broken off.[3]

The Chancellor did not yield to the pressure of the military, and this fact and the events of 8–9 November in Munich took the initiative out of Seeckt's hands. Once Hitler's *coup de main* had failed, the prospects for any dictatorial régime became much

[1] This chamber, the idea for which may have been borrowed from the Italian fascists, was to represent the trades and professions.

[2] Rabenau, *Seeckt*, ii. 359–62. In the course of 1923, there were also some curious conversations between Seeckt and Heinrich Class of the Pan-German League, which in the end left Class feeling that Seeckt wished to become dictator of Germany but wanted someone else to accept the risks involved in trying to overthrow the government. See Kruck, *Geschichte des Alldeutschen Verbandes*, pp. 139–48.

[3] This account, which differs in marked respects from that given by Rabenau (*Seeckt*, ii. 367–8), is based on Geßler, *Reichswehrpolitik*, p. 299. It is interesting to note that Seeckt informed Commissioner Kahr that he had told Stresemann that the Reichswehr had no confidence in him. Seeckt Papers, Stück 154: Seeckt to Kahr, 5 November 1923. On 6 November, at a meeting of *Deutsche Volkspartei* deputies, rumours of Seeckt's statement to Stresemann led some of the deputies to urge that the Chancellor resign. Stresemann, called on the telephone, denied the truth of the story. Stresemann, *Vermächtnis*, i. 198–9.

less favourable. Thus, although Seeckt had been vested with full powers in a hurried cabinet meeting at midnight on 8 November, by the evening of the next day that grant was already beginning to lose its meaning. Ten days later Seeckt was writing to his sister that power had come to him too late; that 'envious people', 'rivals for power', the whole cabinet and all the parties in the Reichstag were now watering down the emergency powers they had given him, and that, in any case, the Western Powers would not permit him to retain them. 'And yet', he wrote bitterly, 'I see no other way to freedom [*ins Freie*] except some kind of dictatorship.'[1] But even the belated fall of the Stresemann cabinet on 23 November aroused no support now for a Seeckt directorate or anything of the sort,[2] and, in February, Seeckt reluctantly handed the executive power back to the civilian authorities.

The passing of the crisis year 1923 marked the beginning of the decline of Seeckt's personal authority in the Reich. By his actions in the latter part of that year he had alienated some of his former friends and supporters. The revelation of his personal ambitions had alarmed Gustav Stresemann and other party leaders, while, on the other hand, his failure to act decisively at a time when he might have been able to make himself dictator, exasperated anti-republicans like Heinrich Class and persuaded them to pin their hopes on more determined leaders like Hitler. The Küstrin *Putsch* and the other activities of the Black Reichswehr deepened the conviction of the leftist parties that Seeckt was, essentially, a threat to the Weimar régime. Finally, an ill-considered gesture of the chief of the army command during his period of emergency power probably caused misgivings among many men of moderate opinions as well. In January 1924, when Professor Ludwig Quidde, a veteran leader of German pacifism, wrote to Seeckt expressing concern about rumours of clandestine rearming, the general answered in an insulting and high-handed letter which, shortly thereafter, appeared in the press. Accusing Quidde of being a spokesman of 'international pacifism' and of favouring the execution of the Versailles Treaty 'in the interest of the French', Seeckt wrote:

Incidentally, I want to draw your attention to the fact that, in

[1] Rabenau, *Seeckt*, ii. 384.

[2] The British ambassador feared that this would bring at least a veiled military dictatorship. d'Abernon, *Ambassador of Peace*, ii. 272 ff.

case the questions touched upon in your letter should be discussed publicly, I should immediately act against you, on the basis of emergency powers; and this regardless of whether or not a proceeding of high treason would be instituted.[1]

Addressed as it was to a man of known probity and international reputation, this letter afforded a depressing glimpse of what a 'Seeckt régime' might mean for Germany.

It is safe to say that the doubts and suspicions aroused in 1923 played a part in defeating Seeckt's desire to succeed Ebert as *Reichspräsident*. For his elevation to the presidency, Seeckt made careful plans. His candidacy was to be managed by Kurt von Schleicher and was to be timed in such a way as to prevent involving Seeckt in the intrigues of the parties at too early a date. Not until the winter of 1925–6 were negotiations with the middle parties to begin, and, once their backing was assured, a campaign for popular support was to be instituted.[2] These schemes were thrown into hopeless disarray, however, by Ebert's sudden death in February 1925, and, to Seeckt's disillusionment, his name hardly figured in the subsequent presidential campaign. After the first inconclusive election, it was not to the chief of the army command but to the supreme commander of 1917–18 that the rightist and middle parties turned, and on the second ballot Hindenburg was elected.

Inevitably this event marked a diminution of Seeckt's personal authority, for the Reichswehr naturally accorded a degree of loyalty to their former commander that they had never given to Ebert, while, at the same time, the field marshal asserted the powers which his office gave him in the military sphere more vigorously than his predecessor had done.[3] And, if Seeckt's authority in the army was thus curtailed, so too was his political influence; and some indication of this was given in his failure to block Stresemann's Locarno policy later in the year.

The weakening of Seeckt's formerly impregnable position

[1] *Die Weltbühne*, xx. Jg. (1927), i. 160.

[2] Rabenau, *Seeckt*, ii. 412.

[3] On 12 May 1925 Stresemann noted in his diary: 'Somewhat dissatisfied apparently is General von Seeckt, who up to this time has had a unique position *vis-à-vis* the government and who naturally occupied a quite different position in relation to a civilian *Reichspräsident*, even though the latter was formally supreme commander of the Reichswehr, than he will now that a soldier like Hindenburg steps into that post with all the weight of his authority.' Stresemann Papers, 272, cont. 3113, frame 147816.

was not immediately appreciated. In December 1925 his inveterate critic Berthold Jacob could still write: 'The only real power in Germany is Seeckt. State of siege or not!';[1] and in the following month an article in *Die Weltbühne* by 'An Old Soldier' predicted that: 'Whatever happens, the Chief of the Army Command will not go into retirement silently and with resignation. The Geßler–Seeckt era can only find its conclusion amid thunder and lightning.'[2]

There were, it is true, some pyrotechnics before Seeckt left the centre of the stage, but they only illuminated the change in his fortunes. In October 1926 it was revealed in the press that the eldest son of the former crown prince had been permitted to participate in the autumn manœuvres of the Ninth Infantry Regiment; and it was subsequently made clear that this had been authorized by Seeckt without any attempt having been made to consult the Reichswehr Minister.[3] Within five days of the original disclosure, Geßler, with the backing of the cabinet, had asked Seeckt to resign; and—despite some frantic grasping at straws by Seeckt's adjutants and aides,[4] and an appeal to the *Reichspräsident* for support—Seeckt found it impossible to do anything but obey.

Seeckt's fall in 1926 has been interpreted variously as the result of a plot on the part of Schleicher, whom one writer calls 'the real Father Joseph of the Reichswehr Ministry',[5] of a belated gesture of independence on the part of Geßler, and of

[1] *Die Weltbühne*, 22. Jg. (1926), i. 34.

[2] Ibid., p. 588.

[3] Many new details on the background of this affair will be found in Reginald H. Phelps, 'Aus den Seeckt-Dokumenten: I. Die Verabschiedung Seeckts 1926', *Deutsche Rundschau* (Sept. 1952); and in Gordon, *Reichswehr and Republic*, pp. 261 ff.

[4] Oberstleutnant Werner von Fritsch, who was later to suffer an equally dramatic dismissal from the post of chief of the army command, urged Seeckt to defy Geßler's request, and Seeckt's adjutant Köstring told him: 'Ein Wink von Ihnen und wir tun doch alle, was Sie befehlen.' Phelps in *Deutsche Rundschau* (Sept. 1952), pp. 886, 888. See also Graf Kielmansegg, *Der Fritsch-Prozess, 1938* (Hamburg, 1949), pp. 24, 119.

[5] Benoist-Méchin, *Armée allemande*, ii. 329. See also Wheeler-Bennett, *Wooden Titan*, p. 298. Relations between Seeckt and Schleicher had deteriorated rapidly after the failure of Seeckt's presidential hopes. Seeckt seemed to blame this on Schleicher and henceforth opposed his ideas and, according to some witnesses, blocked his promotion. The theory that Schleicher used his influence to encourage Seeckt's dismissal in 1926 is strengthened by a remark of his to one of Seeckt's adjutants in 1927: '. . . when anyone treats me as Seeckt did, then I show my teeth and protect my own hide.' Phelps in *Deutsche Rundschau* (Sept. 1952), pp. 889–90.

accumulated resentment on the part of Stresemann,[1] while Seeckt himself seems to have felt that jealousy on the part of Hindenburg was largely responsible for the punishment meted out to him.[2]

It is clear, however, that the chief of the army command was the author of his own fall. It would be difficult to conceive of a more irresponsible action than his authorizing the prince's attendance at manœuvres, or one that promised to do more harm. It came on the heels of the Thoiry conversations between Stresemann and Briand, during which the German Foreign Minister had sought an acceleration of the evacuation of the Rhineland by the Western Powers, and had urged the withdrawal of the Inter-Allied Commission of Control. At Thoiry, Briand had been critical of continued evidence of illegal rearming in Germany and sceptical concerning the German government's ability to keep the military under control. 'Take care of your Reichswehr', he had said to Stresemann. 'I have the feeling that the Reichswehr does all sorts of things of which you have no knowledge. I don't take that too tragically. Soldiers are the same everywhere. But our policy ought not to suffer because of this.'[3] Seeckt's behaviour could only strengthen French doubts; and, unless the general were forced to pay for his indiscretion with his job, it was clear that Stresemann's policy would be hopelessly compromised. In view of what was at stake, there was no alternative to a demand for Seeckt's

[1] Stresemann was apparently growing increasingly suspicious of Seeckt and the army in general in 1926. In January he learned that the army was monitoring his telephone conversations. In February and again in June he was concerned about new rumours of rightist *Putsches* in which army elements were presumably involved. Stresemann Papers, 279, cont. 3100, frames 149451, 149466 ff.; 38, cont. 3145, frames 161753–4. Yet Stresemann repeatedly stated that 'in the whole question of Herr von Seeckt's dismissal, no kind of influence at all was exerted from the side of the Foreign Office or of the Foreign Minister'. Ibid., 45, cont. 3147, frames 162735, 162737, 162746; 278a, cont. 3100, frames 149367–8.

[2] When told on 22 October that Hindenburg was quite broken up over his resignation, Seeckt said: 'Yes, what good is that now? Had he said No then, we would both now be standing there and no one could do a thing to us!' Seeckt also suspected that Generals Joachim von Stülpnagel and von dem Bussche were part of a *Fronde* conspiring against him. Phelps in *Deutsche Rundschau* (Sept. 1952), pp. 888–9. For later personal reflections on his dismissal, see Rabenau, *Seeckt*, ii. 551–2, 558 ff., 564–5.

[3] Stresemann answered: 'Herr von Seeckt is not a man who suffers from illusions, but is fully aware of the situation in which Germany finds herself; and the matters which are brought forward from your side are matters of minor importance. . . .' Stresemann Papers, 43, cont. 3146, frames 162515 ff.

resignation; and this was appreciated by all members of the government, including Geßler.

Seeckt's fall was greeted with enthusiasm in republican circles. At the height of the crisis, *Vorwärts* had written that important principles were at stake, and that 'this is not simply a question of whether parliament or the military shall be the predominant factor in Germany; it is a question of democracy or militarism!'[1] When Seeckt had departed, it was believed that the first significant victory over militarism had been won, and that it must now be pushed home with a systematic attack upon the military system itself, upon the army's secret policies and dangerous connexions, upon its undemocratic selection and promotion system, and upon the man who had permitted the army to indulge in these abuses, Otto Geßler. Attacks upon these objectives were, in fact, made; but, despite the vigour with which they were conducted, they fell far short of complete success.

How far short they fell can be indicated by a brief mention of two incidents. The first came in December 1926 as a result of the revelation, in the *Manchester Guardian*, of the secret collaboration which had been going on between the German and Red armies since 1922. This had immediate repercussions in the German Reichstag where, on 16 December, Philipp Scheidemann, for the Social Democratic party, charged that the Reichswehr, far from being a reliable instrument of state policy, had become an independent political factor which 'follows its own laws and executes its own policy'. In an impassioned speech, which was frequently interrupted by cries of '*Landesverrat!*' from the Right benches and hoots and cat-calls from the communists, Scheidemann went beyond the disclosures of the *Guardian*, laying bare embarrassing details concerning the clandestine arrangements in Russia and, in addition, attacking the army for engaging in suspicious financial manipulation in the international market and for continued contact with illegal armed bands in Germany. He concluded by laying down a whole series of demands: the immediate dismissal of Otto Geßler; the definite severance of all ties between the Reichswehr and illegal formations; the strict accounting of all funds at the army's disposal, their itemization in the next budget, and civilian control of army expenditures in the future; a complete listing of all former officers working in any capacity for the Reichswehr Ministry; an end to

[1] Rabenau, *Seeckt*, ii. 573-4.

the policy of illegal rearming—which he described as militarily useless and politically disastrous; and the abrogation of all military arrangements with the Soviet Union.[1]

This speech touched off a debate in which, in addition to these demands, the Social Democrats also urged that action be taken on a proposal which had been collecting dust in committee rooms for some time. This was the so-called Loebe resolution, which called for the abolition of the present method of officer selection and the establishment of a political commission which would henceforth select officer candidates.[2] Thus, momentarily, it appeared as if virtually every aspect of the Seeckt army—its foreign ties, its financial freedom, its administration, and its selection policy—might be reformed by an aroused Reichstag.

Yet, as one journal remarked, even the Social Democrats seemed to be embarrassed by Scheidemann's speech, and sensitive to the charge that they had been unpatriotic in raising the army issue at all.[3] The debate of 16 December did lead on the following day to the fall of the second Marx government; but, in the protracted cabinet crisis that followed, the parties—including the Centre (which had shown some disposition to support Loebe's resolution) and the socialists themselves—appeared to be curiously reluctant to press the matters raised by Scheidemann and plunged with relief into the elaborate manœuvres which always accompanied the formation of a new government. A curtain of silence was once more dropped over the Reichswehr's Russian connexions, and—as if to indicate that this unfortunate episode was closed—in January 1927,

[1] Reichstag, *Stenographische Berichte*, cccxci (1926–7), 8577–83. In private conversations with Geßler and Stresemann in October, the socialist leaders had demanded that the army's ties with the armed bands be broken off; and, in similar talks in December, they asked for an explanation of the Russian arms shipments. Geßler said that the Foreign Office had been fully aware of them. Stresemann denied this, admitting that he had paid 30 million reichsmarks to the Soviet Union in 1923 for shipments made prior to his chancellorship but arguing that he and Ebert had decided then that the traffic should be broken off and that the Foreign Office had had no connexion with arms shipments since then. Apparently unsatisfied with these explanations, the socialists decided to take the matter to the Reichstag. Stresemann Papers, 45, cont. 3147, frames 162845 ff., 48, cont. 3167, frames 163462 ff.

[2] Rabenau, *Seeckt*, ii. 497. Frequent references to the Loebe *Vorschlag* were made in the debate of 16 December. See Reichstag, *Stenographische Berichte*, cccxci (1926–7), 8588, 8602 ff., 8609.

[3] *Die Weltbühne*, 22. Jg. (1926), ii. 943 ff.

when the *Münchener Post* published the names of Reichswehr officers on temporary duty in the Soviet Union, its editor was indicted for treason.[1]

Only one of the objectives sought by Scheidemann and Loebe was attained and even that not until another full year had passed. In February 1928 Otto Geßler was finally forced to resign when it was revealed that army administrators, in an attempt to increase the funds of the Reichswehr and thus gain a measure of freedom from budgetary limitations, had speculated heavily in the shares of a film company called 'Phoebus' which had then failed in a spectacular manner.

The disclosure of this sordid business revived the agitation for thorough-going reform of the army. On 20 January 1928 Carl Severing reminded the Reichstag that, during the First World War, the army had dictated the foreign and domestic policy of Germany, and that the German people was still paying for the disastrous results of military domination. Now, Severing charged, the army seemed bent on recapturing its war-time powers. It had 'a foreign policy of its own, a domestic policy of its own and, it seems to me, is beginning to have a financial and economic policy of its own as well'. Surely, he argued, the time had come to institute thorough-going reforms to correct these tendencies.[2]

Once more, however, the demands for basic reform were forgotten almost as soon as they were formulated. It is true that, in the debate on the military budget in March 1928, the Reichswehr's selection system was once more subjected to heavy criticism, and the necessity of establishing a 'democratic' army under civilian control was emphasized by several socialist deputies.[3] But even the socialists did not seem to find anything objectionable about the fact that Geßler had been succeeded at the Reichswehr Ministry by a former general, Wilhelm Groener—although this hardly squared with the principle of civilian dominance. Apart from this, it was all too clear that, for all parties, there were by this time more interesting things to think about than army reform. The third Marx government was falling to pieces and new elections were planned for May. Those elections were to be followed by the formation of the so-called

[1] Hilger, *Incompatible Allies*, p. 203, n. See also Gatzke, *Stresemann*, pp. 85–88.

[2] Reichstag, *Stenographische Berichte*, cccxciv (1927–8), 12255–6.

[3] Ibid. cccxcv (1928), 13382.

government of the Great Coalition, in which the socialists, the *Deutsche Volkspartei*, the *Bayrische Volkspartei*, the Democrats, and the Centre were to participate—a combination which, for the sake of unity on other issues, was tacitly to agree to leave the army alone.

And this meant, of course, that, despite the personal defeats suffered by Seeckt and Geßler, the army remained what they had made it—a remarkably efficient military instrument which had made good its claim to run its internal affairs without civilian interference and which continued to pay its allegiance not to the government of the day, or even to the republic,[1] but to that permanent state of which, in the view of its leaders, it was the purest representative.

[1] A socialist deputy, listening to one of the army's defenders make a long speech about the army's loyalty without making a single reference to the republican form of government, shouted: 'The word "republican" must be terribly hard to pronounce!' Reichstag, *Stenographische Berichte*, cccxcv (1928), 13414.

XI

THE ARMY IN POLITICS: GROENER AND SCHLEICHER

1928–33

> After the events of the last days, I am still quite happy that in the shape of the Nazis—who are, it is true, uncomfortable friends and who must be treated with the utmost caution—there exists a counter-weight. If they didn't exist, it would be necessary to invent them.
>
> KURT VON SCHLEICHER *in March 1932.*

> So hab' ich
> Mit eignem Netz verderblich mich umstrickt,
> Und nur Gewalttat kann es reißend lösen.
>
> *Wallensteins Tod.*

THE five years that followed the introduction of the Dawes Plan in 1924 were good years for Germany and were marked by economic prosperity and growing political stability. Hopes that the gains of this brief period might lead to the consolidation of the Weimar Republic were dispelled, however, by the repercussions of the stock market crash in the United States at the end of 1929. In the months that followed that event, all of the ills that had plagued Germany in 1923 were revived, and in more virulent forms. Political extremism grew in direct proportion to economic misery, and the republic was menaced now by a reinvigorated Communist party on the one hand and, on the other, by a National Socialist movement which commanded mass support on a national scale. In the face of this threat from left and right, the moderate parties showed no ability to co-operate. The so-called Great Coalition of 1928 was in full disintegration by the end of 1929; and the subsequent period was marked by a deplorable spectacle of intramural feuding and parliamentary bankruptcy. Under the double stress of its economic and its political troubles, the Reich in the early 1930's seemed to be on the point of disintegration or total collapse.

To this danger the German army could not be expected to remain indifferent in view of the fact that its leaders had grown accustomed to regarding themselves as the protectors of the Reich and the best-qualified interpreters of its essential interests. In the long series of crises which filled the years 1930–2, the military establishment, therefore, played an important role. Indeed, there is no period in German history in which representatives of the army intervened more frequently and more directly in the internal politics of the country; but, it must be added, there is no period in which the results of this intervention were more unfortunate. In their desire to end a political situation which threatened to degenerate into complete anarchy, the military chiefs rashly took upon themselves tasks of political negotiation and party manipulation for which they were not qualified. At the start they justified this activity by claiming that it was necessary to prevent the victory of the extremist parties; but, when their experiments proved unsuccessful, they looked with increasing approval to one of those parties and, in the end, concurred in its accession to power. There were doubtless many reasons for Adolf Hitler's elevation to the chancellorship in January 1933; but, in the last analysis, that event proved the validity of the maxim *exercitus facit imperatorem.*[1]

It is not the intention here to recount in detail the complicated political history of Germany in these years. In order to make clear the army's responsibility for Hitler's rise to power it will be enough, perhaps, to focus attention on two things: first, the spirited fight which Wilhelm Groener, Reichswehr Minister from 1928 to 1932, made against National Socialism, and the way in which he was repudiated by the army at the very moment when his policies promised to be successful; and, second, the cabinet-making activities of Kurt von Schleicher in the fateful year 1932.

I

Wilhelm Groener[2] had retired from active military service at the end of 1919 and, in the years when Hans von Seeckt was reorganizing the Reichswehr, he had had no direct connexion with army affairs. Between 1920 and 1923, he served the nation

[1] Meinecke, *Deutsche Katastrophe*, p. 76.

[2] The following account of Groener's term as Reichswehr Minister follows in the main the author's article, 'Reichswehr and National Socialism: The Policy of Wilhelm Groener, 1928–1932', *Political Science Quarterly*, lxiii (1948), 194–229. Some textual changes and additions have been made, and the documentation has been expanded.

as *Reichsverkehrsminister*, a post for which he was eminently qualified by his war-time service as director of field railways; and in this position he actively promoted the unification of the German rail system.[1] After the fall of the Cuno government in the fall of 1923, he returned to private life and spent his time composing a number of critical works on the Marne campaign of 1914. From this retirement he was recalled abruptly in 1928 when the Phoebus scandal forced the retirement of Otto Geßler.

The appointment of Groener to the *Reichswehrministerium* was determined by two factors: the desire of the *Reichspräsident* for a professional soldier as Geßler's successor and the pronounced change in the political climate in Germany in 1928. President Hindenburg regarded the Reichswehr as his special preserve; he exercised much more direct authority over it than his predecessor;[2] and he had no love for civilians meddling in military affairs. That he would insist upon a soldier taking over Geßler's post was certain. His military advisers realized, however, that the selection of a new minister would have to be guided also by considerations of general politics. In the first months of 1928, it was apparent that a major shift in political power in Germany was imminent and that the long exclusion of the Social Democratic party from office was coming to an end. Debates in the Reichstag in January showed that the existing government coalition was in course of dissolution;[3] national elections were expected in the near future; and it was generally conceded that the Social Democrats would make sweeping gains and dominate the next government.

In the circumstances, it was necessary to appoint a Reichswehr Minister who would be acceptable to the Social Democrats. This was all the more important in view of current Reichswehr armament plans. The military chiefs were intent upon winning Reichstag assent for the construction of a number of new heavy armoured cruisers, which would give Germany mastery of the Baltic and thus enormously strengthen her defences against

[1] H. Brauweiler, *Generäle in der deutschen Republik* (Berlin, 1932), p. 29. See also Scheele, *Weimar Republic*, pp. 203, 315.

[2] The extension of the President's authority over the army was forecast by Hindenburg's general order of 28 January 1926, entitled 'Befehlsbefugnisse im Reichsheer'. See Frhr. Marschall von Bieberstein, *Verfassungsrechtliche Reichsgesetze* (2nd ed., Mannheim, 1929), pp. 736 ff.

[3] See, for instance, the note on the debate of 20–21 January in Horkenbach, *Das deutsche Reich von 1918 bis heute*, p. 248.

Poland.[1] Violent opposition to such a programme could be expected from the Social Democratic party, and a Reichswehr Minister who did not inspire some respect in socialist circles could hope for little success in promoting the necessary construction.

The Reichswehr officials who discussed the appointment with Hindenburg therefore urged the selection of Groener as a man whose war record qualified him for the post and who—by virtue of his reputation as a 'democratic general'—would be least objectionable to the socialists.[2] The calculation was a sound one. Groener was appointed at the end of January. Six months later, as a result of socialist gains in national elections, the Marx government fell from office and a new coalition was formed by Hermann Mueller. No attempt was made, however, to challenge Groener's appointment and he was retained in the new ministry.[3]

In view of the circumstances governing his appointment, it is probably true that the new Reichswehr Minister made the mistake of assuming that he had more personal authority in the Reichswehr than was actually the case. He knew, of course, that there were members of the officer caste who still resented the policy he had followed in 1918 and 1919 and that, in some circles, he was considered a 'November criminal'. But he tended to minimize this factor because of his confidence in his ability to work with the army chiefs. They were, he announced happily, 'his friends, his old comrades, his colleagues';[4] they were, moreover, all men who had followed his leadership without hesitation in 1918 and 1919. Hindenburg, his former chief at Spa, was now President of the republic and commander-in-chief of the Reichswehr, and Groener confidently expected that the old marshal would follow his advice, in political affairs which affected the military, as he had done in the earlier period. The very fact that, in 1918 and 1919, Groener had assumed

[1] Horkenbach, *Deutsche Reich*, pp. 251, 262.

[2] According to Wheeler-Bennett, Groener's appointment was pushed most energetically by Kurt von Schleicher, who canvassed the general officers and, with the aid of Hindenburg's son, overcame the President's initial objections. *Wooden Titan*, pp. 300–1; *Nemesis of Power*, pp. 195–7.

[3] The Mueller cabinet was an attempt to revive the so-called Great Coalition of 1923. Groener was perhaps the only Reichswehr Minister acceptable to all of the partners in this combination. On the formation of the Mueller cabinet, see Horkenbach, *Deutsche Reich*, pp. 255–6.

[4] Groener Correspondence: To Richard Bahr, 22 May 1932.

the responsibility for decisions which Hindenburg himself should have made seems to have strengthened the new Reichswehr Minister in this rather unwise conclusion. As he told Heinrich Bruening on one occasion, he was convinced that 'Hindenburg would always in the last instance follow his counsel, since he, in order to protect Hindenburg's renown, had sacrificed his own irreproachable reputation in the interest of the nation'.[1] As for the other Reichswehr leaders, there seemed to be no question that they would defer to his political judgement. Heye, Seeckt's successor as *Chef der Heeresleitung*, had been on Groener's staff at Spa;[2] Hammerstein, who succeeded Heye in 1930, had also been junior to him in the service; and neither of these officers had pronounced political convictions of his own.[3] Finally, the strongest political influence among the general officers, General Kurt von Schleicher, had been one of Groener's closest personal friends since before the World War and was, indeed, considered by the new Reichswehr Minister as his 'adopted son'. Groener had a high opinion of Schleicher's political intelligence and, once he had taken over his post, he placed Schleicher at the head of the newly created *Ministeramt* of the Reichswehr Ministry, a political liaison body between the armed services on the one hand and the Reich ministries and the political parties on the other.[4] In this position, as Groener's 'Cardinal *in politicis*',[5] Schleicher soon became indispensable to the new Reichswehr Minister, but it seems clear that the latter always believed that Schleicher, in the last analysis, would recognize his superior authority in political matters.[6]

[1] Heinrich Bruening, 'Ein Brief', *Deutsche Rundschau* (July 1947), p. 3. Hindenburg greeted his new Reichswehr Minister with cordiality and soon granted him the privilege of giving critiques at manœuvres, a right which previous ministers had not possessed. See Brauweiler, *Generäle*, p. 31.

[2] Volkmann, *Revolution*, p. 58; Wheeler-Bennett, *Wooden Titan*, pp. 195, 199–200.

[3] Until April 1932 Groener generally spoke of Hammerstein with enthusiasm, although he often added that the *Chef der Heeresleitung* was incurably lazy. For other judgements, see Ulrich von Hassell, *Vom anderen Deutschland* (2nd ed., Zürich, 1946), p. 314; Bruening in *Deutsche Rundschau* (July 1947); and Wheeler-Bennett, *Nemesis of Power*, pp. 199 and *passim*.

[4] Scheele (*Weimar Republic*, pp. 97–98) regards the *Ministeramt* as the first attempt in Germany to create an inter-service directive body and holds that it was the precursor of Hitler's O.K.W.

[5] The term is Groener's own. Groener Correspondence: To General von Gleich, 4 January 1930.

[6] For Groener's view of the partnership, see Groener Correspondence: Walter Oehme to Groener, 12 January 1933, and the enclosed questionnaire which Groener had completed for Oehme.

This confidence that the Reichswehr and its chiefs would follow his political leadership was not immediately challenged. It was only after he addressed himself to the problem of National Socialism that Groener had reason to doubt his earlier optimism.

During his first two years of office Groener does not seem to have concerned himself with the Hitler movement. The functions of the Reichswehr Ministry, embracing as it did both military and naval affairs, left him little time to think about a party which still seemed to be of minor importance. Moreover, his major task in this period was the securing of funds for the completion of *Panzerkreuzer A*, the first of the so-called 'pocket battleships'. On this issue, socialist opposition to expenditure for armaments caused two major cabinet crises and led Groener, in November 1928, to threaten to resign his post if construction were delayed; and it was not until mid-1929 that the completion of the vessel—the future *Deutschland*—was finally assured.[1]

By that time, however, more serious issues confronted Germany. In the course of 1929, the solidarity of the Mueller cabinet, never very strong, declined progressively; and the death of Stresemann in October loosened still further the ties that had bound the government partners together. With the Social Democrats and the *Volkspartei* indulging in mutual recriminations, the cabinet was incapable of giving leadership to a nation now suffering from extreme economic depression. As unemployment figures began to mount, anti-republican movements received thousands of new adherents. The communists became increasingly active on a national scale, while, in elections in Baden and Saxony, the National Socialists demonstrated that they were fast becoming a force of political consequence. Meanwhile the bitterness with which the rightist parties conducted their campaign against the Young Plan revealed a new and ugly note in German politics.

To the Reichswehr Minister, Germany at the end of 1929 seemed to be reverting to the chaos of 1918. In the circumstances, he felt compelled to warn the Reichswehr that it must be prepared to prevent a complete disintegration of the national unity.

[1] Horkenbach, *Deutsche Reich*, pp. 255–8, 260, 262, 273, 278; Friedrich Stampfer, *Die vierzehn Jahre der ersten deutschen Republik* (Karlsbad, 1936), pp. 480–2; Otto Braun, *Von Weimar zu Hitler* (New York, 1940), pp. 250–3; Wheeler-Bennett, *Nemesis of Power*, pp. 189–94. *Panzerkreuzer A* (the *Deutschland*, later the *Lützow*) was launched at Kiel on 19 May 1931.

In January 1930 he issued a general order to the army, an order which is interesting, not only as a recapitulation of Groener's conception of the role of the army in the state, but also as his first open attack upon National Socialism.

Referring to the rapid growth and the apparent revolutionary intentions of both the communists and the nazis, the order stated flatly: '[The nazis] are to be distinguished from the communists only by the national base on which they take their footing.' Greedy for power, 'they therefore woo the *Wehrmacht*. In order to use it for the political aims of their party, they attempt to dazzle us . . . [with the idea that] the National Socialists alone represent the truly national idea.' But, the order continued, the destruction of the present political system by either the communists or the nazis would be a disaster, for it would bring civil war in its train, 'a catastrophe for state and economy'. It is the responsibility of the Reichswehr to prevent such an eventuality.

> It is the sacred task of the *Wehrmacht* to prevent the cleavage between classes and parties from ever widening into suicidal civil war. In all times of need in the history of a people, there is one unshakable rock in the stormy sea: the idea of the state. The *Wehrmacht* is its necessary and most characteristic expression. It has no other interest and no other task than service to the state. Therein lies the pride of the soldier and the best tradition of the past. . . . [The *Wehrmacht*] would falsify its essence and destroy itself if it descended into the party conflict and itself took party. To serve the state—far from all party politics to save and maintain it against the terrible pressure from without and the insane strife at home—is our only goal.[1]

The association of National Socialism with communism in this order is an interesting illustration of the way in which Groener identified the present situation with the crisis of 1918, when the army had been employed to fight bolshevism. In this connexion his views were summed up in a conversation between one of his aides and the British military attaché in May 1930. 'The trouble about the "Brown Shirts"', this officer said, 'is that their principles and theories are entirely *destructive*. They wish to destroy the present fabric of the State, but have no constructive programme with which to replace it, except a

[1] Groener Papers: 'Reichswehrministerium, Erlaß, 22. Januar 1930.' Reprinted in Groener-Geyer, *General Groener*, pp. 266–8.

form of mad-dog dictatorship. The movement is therefore, in the long run, far more akin to Bolshevism than to Fascism.'[1]

At the same time, Groener realized clearly that, in the present state of Germany, National Socialism was a much more dangerous force than communism. The army would always defend the state against the communists; of that, there was no doubt. But there had been moments in the past, in 1920 and 1923, in which the army had shown itself to be reluctant to oppose the aspirations of groups which claimed to represent the 'national idea'. And in 1930 Groener feared that, unless the Reichswehr leaders took a decided stand against National Socialism, the bulk of the officers' corps might be seduced from its allegiance to what he called the 'idea of the state'. Adolf Hitler had already announced, in a speech of March 1929, that the army's responsibility was not to 'this lazy and decayed State' but to the German people, who yearned for release from parliamentarism and 'democratic Marxism';[2] and, since then, such National Socialist organs as the *Völkischer Beobachter* and the *Deutscher Wehrgeist* had been openly inviting the Reichswehr to repudiate its oath to the republic and to make common cause with the movement that was destined to bring order, stability, and, incidentally, an enlarged military establishment to Germany. On the younger officers of the army especially these arguments were not without effect.

This was demonstrated clearly enough by the so-called Leipzig trial which stirred up so much excitement in Germany in 1930. In February three junior officers of the Reichswehr were arrested and charged with spreading National Socialist propaganda within the ranks of the army. Although he tried originally to treat this matter as a simple breach of discipline, the attitude of the culprits compelled Groener in the end to have them tried before the *Reichsgericht* in Leipzig for high treason. The trial ended with the officers in question being sentenced to eighteen months fortress detention. Before that result had been reached, however, an alarming amount of evidence had been put into the record concerning political discontent in the garrisons; and, more important, Adolf Hitler,

[1] *Documents on British Policy*, 2nd series, i. 478.

[2] See Schüddekopf, *Heer und Republik*, pp. 281–7; Krausnick in *Vollmacht des Gewissens*, pp. 186 ff.

in a dramatic appearance as a witness, had been given an excellent opportunity to express his high regard for the army and his intention of advancing its interests once he had come to power.[1]

From Groener's standpoint, the sequel to the Leipzig trial was as important as its result, for he found himself roundly and publicly abused by a number of former officers of distinction for having brought the matter into court. Hindenburg's friend Oldenburg-Januschau, the former Major-General Graf von der Goltz and Seeckt himself were particularly outspoken, the last-named—who might have been expected to approve of the punishment of political agitation in the army—accusing Groener of weakening the spirit of comradeship and solidarity within the officer corps.[2] Groener defended himself energetically, pointing out that the essence of the officer corps was its discipline and its *Überparteilichkeit*, its neutral position above the strife of parties, and in a public letter to Goltz he made it clear that he was determined to insist on these qualities. 'It must not', he wrote, 'be party programmes or resounding slogans drawn from them that determine the manner in which the Reichswehr serves the fatherland, but the will of the *Reichspräsident* and those higher leaders appointed by him.'[3]

It was, however, precisely the attitude of those higher officers that concerned Groener after the Leipzig case. He began to discern that the much-praised political neutrality which Seeckt had imposed upon the Reichswehr had been dangerous in its consequences.[4] When junior officers began, like the defendants

[1] For fuller treatment of the case, see Reginald H. Phelps, 'Aus den Groener-Dokumenten: V. Der Fall Scheringer-Ludin-Wendt', *Deutsche Rundschau* (Nov. 1950), pp. 915–22.

[2] For Seeckt's attitude, see Rabenau, *Seeckt*, ii. 657, 663. In this period Groener grew increasingly critical of Seeckt and said that he expected him at any moment to be found 'walking arm in arm with Herr Goebbels'. Groener Correspondence: To General von Gleich, 28 December 1930. For Schleicher's concern over the rightist attacks, see 'Neue Dokumente zur Geschichte der Reichswehr, 1930–1933', *Vierteljahrshefte für Zeitgeschichte*, ii (1954), 401–3.

[3] Groener Correspondence: To General v. d. Goltz, 6 October 1930. See also Groener to Kammerherr von Oldenburg-Januschau, 21 October 1930; and *Documents on British Policy*, 2nd series, ii. 515–20.

[4] Speaking of Seeckt's attitude in political matters, Groener said: 'He offered his subordinates riddles concerning his own convictions, and many of them must have concluded that a somewhat Right radical point of view was the one best calculated to win favour with the Supreme Commander despite all the stern orders which he in fact issued but which no one took seriously.' Nor, he added, had things improved under Heye, 'weil der gute Onkel kein Kerl war und sich von den

at Leipzig, to criticize the Reichswehr leadership for its lack of patriotism, it was the duty of the commanding officers to correct those views, by giving them some idea of political and economic realities, by explaining the effort it had taken to build up the *Wehrmacht* to its present state and by revealing the logical weaknesses in National Socialist propaganda. Too many of the commanding officers, however, shunned all political discussion with their juniors, either because of lack of political knowledge or because they were afraid that, if they should defend the Weimar system, they would be considered 'not national'. 'We must conclude from these events', Groener wrote, 'that in the future we should appoint as leaders of the officers' corps only such persons as possess the courage of their convictions and sufficient spiritual authority to educate the youth of the present. . . .'[1]

This intimation that the officers' corps must at long last give an unequivocal sign of allegiance to the Weimar system was, in a sense, a reflection of Groener's own relationship to the civilian government which had taken office in March 1930—the government of Heinrich Bruening.

Despite Groener's earlier insistence that the army must never 'descend into the party conflict', it is clear that Bruening's appointment to the chancellorship had in large part been the result of army influence subtly exerted in the *Reichskanzlei*. In the winter of 1929–30, as the Mueller government tottered to its fall, Groener himself became convinced that further attempts to form a coalition between the Social Democrats and the middle-class parties would be fruitless. He was inclined, therefore, to consider a proposal put forward by his most intimate adviser, Kurt von Schleicher, and he ended by accepting it, authorizing Schleicher to use his political gifts to secure the President's approval, and undertaking to bring his own influence and that of the *Chef der Heeresleitung* to bear for the same end.

The Schleicher plan envisaged the formation of a radically new political combination, a cabinet composed of men unhampered by a narrow conception of party loyalty, governing from the standpoint of the national interest alone and relying for its authority upon the support of the *Reichspräsident*.[2] Such a

Leutnants auf der Nase herumtanzen ließ'. Groener Correspondence: To Gleich, 26 April 1931.

[1] Groener Papers: 'Reichswehrministerium, Erlaß (Geheim), 6. Oktober 1930 (Nr. 486. 30 g. WIa).'

[2] Groener Correspondence: To Gleich, 4 January 1930. In January Groener

government, resorting whenever necessary to the use of emergency decrees, would be welcomed by a people bewildered by the bickering of the old parties. Groener and Schleicher were aware, of course, that the Reichstag could not be entirely ignored. For that very reason they seem from the start to have favoured the appointment of Bruening as Chancellor; for Bruening would assure the co-operation of his own party, the Centre, while his military record would commend him to the President and his sound fiscal views to the industrialists who controlled the *Volkspartei*. Aside from that, they seem to have calculated that a strong presidential government would appeal to important elements in the Nationalist party and might indeed free that party completely from the radical leadership of Hugenberg.[1] In the last analysis, they do not seem to have worried about difficulties in the Reichstag; if such developed, the new government could appeal to the nation.

The government projected by Groener and Schleicher during the winter months took actual form when Bruening assumed office in March 1930. From the start, Groener was enthusiastic about the new Chancellor and was convinced that the solution to the national emergency had been found. In Bruening, he felt, the parties, whose quarrels had done so much to weaken national unity, had met their master. 'He operates cleverly with the parties while keeping his real views hidden. His attitude in parliament toward the babblers [*Quatschköpfe*] is nothing short of an aesthetic pleasure. I have concluded a firm alliance with him and, as long as the *Reichspräsident* goes along with us, we shall be through with the *Parlament* one way or another.'[2] Germany at last had a civilian government which

was thinking of a government which might include such men as the Nationalist rebels Treviranus and Lindeiner, Moldenhauer and Curtius of the *Volkspartei*, Bruening, and even the current Chancellor Mueller, if he could be detached from his party. 'I advised M. not long ago', he wrote to Gleich, 'that he ought to bid his party farewell [*valet sagen*] in order to rise to the position of a real statesman.' That Schleicher was engaged in negotiations for the formation of the new cabinet is indicated by Groener's note that, during the Christmas vacation, 'my Cardinal *in politicis* . . . accomplished excellent work behind the *coulisses* and prepared the ground for future development'.

[1] In this connexion, Groener and Schleicher strongly supported the policy of Treviranus, which aimed at breaking the power of 'Hugendabel, the keyhole politician' in order to make the Nationalists *bündnisfähig*. Groener Correspondence: To Gleich, 4 January, 21 July 1930.

[2] Groener Correspondence: To Gleich, 28 December 1930.

embodied those qualities of discipline and *Überparteilichkeit* which Groener felt so important in the army, and he became convinced that Germany's salvation depended on the new Chancellor's retention of office. 'Most of all,' he wrote in April 1931, 'I count on Bruening.... I have never known a statesman, chancellor, minister (or) general who combined in his head as much positive knowledge and political clarity and adaptability as Bruening.'[1] To his old faith in the army as the true element of stability in the state, Groener now added a complete allegiance to Bruening, and he expected the Reichswehr to stand behind him in his support of the new government.

There seems to be no doubt that the Reichswehr would have supported the Bruening government if Hitler had been foolish enough, at any time in these years, to risk a *Putsch* on the order of his attempt in 1923. Bruening discussed the possibility of such a rising with the Reichswehr chiefs on several occasions and found that they had complete plans for such an eventuality.[2] Groener himself was in no doubt concerning the willingness and the ability of the Reichswehr to smash a Hitler *Putsch.* 'The Reichswehr', he said to Friedrich Meinecke, 'will do what it is ordered to do, and *damit Basta!*',[3] and to his friend Gleich he predicted that, if Hitler should resort to force, he would encounter 'the unqualified employment of the power resources [*Machtmittel*] of the state. The Reichswehr is so completely in our hands that it will never hesitate in this eventuality. Hammerstein is the man to strike with *brutality*, quite differently than Seeckt in 1923–24.'[4]

It soon became evident, however, that the decisive question would be not what attitude the Reichswehr would take if the nazis grasped the initiative, but whether it would support an attempt on the part of the Bruening government to strike out at the nazis. In the last months of 1930 and throughout the whole of 1931, it became increasingly apparent that the Bruening government would have to take some decision with regard to the National Socialist movement. The government had not developed the great resources of strength expected by its founders. When difficulties had appeared in the Reichstag it

[1] Groener Correspondence: To Gleich, 26 April 1931.
[2] Bruening in *Deutsche Rundschau* (July 1947).
[3] Meinecke, *Deutsche Katastrophe,* pp. 68–69.
[4] Groener Correspondence: To Gleich, 26 January 1932.

had appealed to the nation; but that appeal, in September 1930, had been a tragic miscalculation. The September elections made the National Socialist party the second strongest party in Germany, while leaving the government in a position of uncomfortable dependence upon the Social Democrats.[1] Now, while Bruening's policy of fulfilment became increasingly unpopular, the National Socialist party continued to grow in strength. As it did so, the excesses of its members increased, despite the professions of legality made by its leader; and the resort to violence was especially marked in the case of the *Sturm Abteilungen*, the party's private army and the backbone of its power.

II

It was the question of the S.A. which, by widening the breach between the Reichswehr and the civilian authorities, was to precipitate not only Groener's fall as Reichswehr Minister but the collapse of the Bruening government as a whole. Yet on the surface there seemed to be no reason for differences between the army and the civilian leaders on this issue; for the S.A. was a source of danger to both. It was, for one thing, responsible for a good part of the disorders which characterized German life in the early 1930's. Quite apart from that, this irregular nazi soldiery not only represented a menace to the state but threatened to be a military competitor of the Reichswehr itself, a development which could be expected to arouse suspicion on the part of army leaders.

Groener himself dated the danger of the S.A. to state and Reichswehr from the appointment of Roehm as its commander at the beginning of 1931. Before that, the S.A. was a 'relatively harmless affair'; after Roehm had begun to centralize the S.A. and improve its discipline and its co-ordination it became 'increasingly unbearable'. The S.A. became

> an absolute private army with all the signs of such an organization, which in all its parts was planned, articulated and organized in a fabulous manner and through a great propaganda was placed increasingly firmly into the hands of the Fuehrer. Thus the danger

[1] The attempts to win over the Nationalists had failed miserably. After September 1930 the Bruening government could muster a majority in the Reichstag only so long as the Social Democrats supported them. See the election figures in Horkenbach, *Deutsche Reich*, p. 319.

for the state became extraordinarily great, for despite all the declarations of legality . . . such an organization has its dynamic in itself and cannot simply be declared now legal and now illegal.[1]

There seems no reason to doubt that Groener, both as a soldier and as a member of the Bruening government, was firmly convinced from the beginning of 1931 of the necessity of removing this potential threat to the state, and that he regarded the dissolution of the S.A. by Reich decree as the best means of accomplishing this purpose. Yet throughout 1931, as the danger increased in intensity, he made no attempt to implement his conviction and, even after he had become Reich Minister of the Interior, he still postponed the decisive step.

For this delay there were two main reasons. The first was the legal question posed by any such project of dissolution. It would be extremely difficult to justify the dissolution of the S.A. by presidential decree, unless the decree equally proscribed organizations like the *Reichsbanner* and the *Stahlhelm*, which were in some respects similar to the S.A. Yet action against the *Reichsbanner*, the uniformed but unarmed organization of the Social Democrats, would almost certainly be followed by the withdrawal of that party's support from Bruening; while, at the same time, Hindenburg's active interest in the *Stahlhelm* made it unlikely that he would agree to any restriction of its activities.[2]

[1] Reichstag, *Stenographische Berichte*, cmxlvi (1931–2), 2547 ff. Major Ernst Roehm had actually joined the German Workers' party before Hitler. He was active in the formation of the party's 'gymnastic and sports division', which was founded in 1921 and which later changed its name to *Sturm Abteilung* (S.A.). Roehm was always more interested than Hitler was in developing the S.A. as a military force; and friction on this point led to a break between the two men in 1924–5, as a result of which Roehm resigned his party offices. See Alan Bullock, *Hitler: A Study in Tyranny* (New York, 1953), pp. 56, 65–66, 112–13, 115–16. Between 1925 and 1930 the S.A. was led by the former free corps commander, Hauptmann a. D. Franz Pfeffer von Salamon, who emphasized the S.A.'s political and propaganda tasks at the expense of military training. Friction between the party's Political Organization (P.O.) and Pfeffer led to the latter's retirement in 1930. Hitler then for the first time took over command of the S.A., offering the post of chief of staff to Roehm. Roehm accepted and reverted to his earlier ideas. Starting in January 1931 he completely reorganized the force, increased its size from 250,000 to 400,000 and inaugurated a heightened programme of military training. See Walter Görlitz and Herbert A. Quint, *Adolf Hitler: eine Biographie* (Stuttgart, 1952), pp. 261–5, 289–90, 310–11.

[2] In October 1929, the Prussian government issued a decree of dissolution against the *Stahlhelm* because of its activities in the Rhineland. Hindenburg intervened personally and engaged in a lengthy and acrimonious dispute with Prussian authorities. See Braun, *Von Weimar zu Hitler*, pp. 299 ff.; Horkenbach, *Deutsche Reich*, p. 289. Groener wrote on one occasion: 'The old man of the mountain . . .

The second reason for the delay was Groener's realization that a simple dissolution of the S.A. would not strike at the roots of the problem. Since the Leipzig affair the Reichswehr Minister was aware that the S.A. was gradually winning support within the Reichswehr itself.[1] To some officers it was the living embodiment of Hitler's promise to give them a large army in which advancement would be more rapid. Others were impressed by the influence it was winning over German youth[2] and defended it on pedagogical grounds.[3] There were, moreover, many staff officers who regarded a war against Poland to regain the Corridor as inevitable and desirable,[4] and they naturally opposed the dissolution of a valuable auxiliary force. Groener was scornful of the ambitions of this last class. Writing in 1931, he described a Polish war as 'a utopia', but added: 'Unfortunately, strategy is a contagious disease which by preference affects heads which are not exactly filled with wisdom. . . . It has long been known that I make merry at the busy strategists. But *jedes Tierchen braucht sein Pläsierchen*.'[5] Groener knew that the planners would continue to plan and that all possible military resources, including the S.A., would figure in their calculations.

Determined as he was that the S.A. should be dissolved, the Reichswehr Minister realized, therefore, that such action would arouse criticism even inside the army, unless it were accompanied by measures which would disarm the critics. Specifically, he felt that the state would have to find the means of performing the most practical of the functions now performed by the S.A. At the outset, this would involve remedying the situation that had been created by the allies in 1919, increasing the size of the

is the protector of the *Stahlhelm*.' Groener Correspondence: To Gleich, 1 November 1931.

[1] Groener Correspondence: To Gleich, 21 September 1931.

[2] After the elections of 1930, the British military attaché reported that the officers of the Reichswehr were impressed by the growth of National Socialism. 'It is the *Jugendbewegung*', they said. 'It can't be stopped'. *Documents on British Foreign Policy*, 2nd series, i. 512 n.

[3] Meinecke, *Deutsche Katastrophe*, pp. 70–71.

[4] See the statements of Blomberg and Blaskowitz during the Nuremberg trials. *Nazi Conspiracy and Aggression* (Washington, 1947), vi. 414, 417.

[5] Groener Correspondence: To Gleich, 21 September 1931. Somewhat later Groener wrote: 'Completely stupid rumours are continually circulating as if we could spirit aircraft out of the silk hat; and even instructors in the ordnance schools whisper mysteriously that Russia is crammed full of German tanks and other machines. Among us *sancta simplicitas* is not to be extirpated.' To Gleich, 1 November 1931.

Reichswehr and basing it on the principle of universal service, so that the youth of Germany would turn to the army rather than to the nazi organization. Before any action should be taken against the S.A., then, Groener and Bruening hoped to persuade the Powers to concede to Germany the right of supplementing the existing Reichswehr with a militia of some 200,000 men, recruited in accordance with the principle of universal service.[1] Quite apart from the effect this would have on soldiers who thought in terms of numbers, the creation of such a militia would, Groener believed, ease the domestic situation, by enabling the government to provide for 'hundreds of thousands of young Germans whom the terrible unemployment leaves in the streets'.[2]

As an alternative, or perhaps supplementary, plan Groener thought of bringing all existing semi-military organizations directly under state control. This might be done, he thought, by forming a gigantic sport organization or *Wehrsportverband*. Primarily designed to advance the physical training of German youth, this organization too would have a political purpose. It would 'alleviate differences and accustom the hostile *Verbände* to working together for the fatherland'.[3] And it would, he hoped, offer more attractions to German youth than the Hitler organization.

Although the Bruening government in 1931 tentatively drew up a decree directed against the semi-military organizations,[4] nothing was done to put it into effect. Instead, the Chancellor proceeded with what Groener called his *Spiel mit fünf Kugeln à la Bismarck*,[5] designed to secure, among other things, some concessions to Germany in the question of armaments. Feelers were put out to the British;[6] Bruening, in the course of his tour of the European capitals to discuss the reparations question, had an encouraging talk with Mussolini;[7] and Groener himself discussed

[1] Meinecke, *Deutsche Katastrophe*, pp. 72–73.

[2] Interview in the *Augsburger Postzeitung*, 20 October 1932.

[3] Ibid. Meinecke, who was close to Groener, says that he thought for a time of placing this *Wehrsportverband* under the control of the *Stahlhelm*. *Deutsche Katastrophe*, p. 100. Cf. 'Neue Dokumente' *Vierteljahrshefte*, ii (1954), 416.

[4] Groener Correspondence: To Gleich, 1 November 1931.

[5] Ibid., 20 September 1931.

[6] See, for instance, *Documents on British Policy*, 2nd series, i. 556–7, 583 ff.

[7] Groener Correspondence: To Gleich, 20 September 1931. On Bruening's extensive tour of the capitals, see also André François-Poncet, *Souvenirs d'une Ambassade à Berlin* (Paris, 1946), pp. 20 ff.

Germany's legitimate military needs with the French ambassador.[1]

While these negotiations were proceeding, Groener was personally opposed to any action against the S.A. Officially, however, he soon found it difficult to maintain this attitude, for, in the reorganization of the cabinet in October 1931 he added the duties of Reich Minister of the Interior to those he already performed. Immediately, this duplication of function made Groener the object of criticism and pressure from the parties of the right and the left alike. Almost every step taken by him in his capacity of Minister of the Interior was described by opponents of the government—and by Groener's personal enemies within the Reichswehr—as a dangerous involvement of the army in party politics.[2] On the other hand, in his negotiations with the ministries of the *Länder*, Groener was subjected to increasing pressure from the Social Democratic government of Prussia, which demanded that action be taken against the S.A. on a national scale and which regarded Groener's hesitation as proof that the Reichswehr was bent on protecting the Hitler movement.

Groener realized that failure to satisfy the Social Democrats might endanger the cabinet. Nevertheless, he continued to oppose action that might compromise Bruening's international discussions. His chief duty in his new post, he wrote, was that of 'covering . . . [Bruening's] rear in internal affairs, so that he has freedom for negotiations abroad'.[3] On 18 November, in a long instruction to Zweigert, his state secretary in the Ministry of the Interior, Groener specifically disclaimed any intention of using new police measures against the S.A. Instead, he spoke of a new spiritual and moral offensive against disturbers of the peace. 'The *Reichsinnenminister* must no longer merely sit in a room, busied with documents and bureaucratic labours. He must go out before the people and speak to them without an intermediary.' To facilitate this approach, he ordered Zweigert to set up a new unit in the ministry, 'if I may use the customary

[1] Groener Correspondence: To Gleich, 1 November 1931.

[2] When Groener assumed the functions of Reich Minister of the Interior, the *Völkischer Beobachter* spoke of a disguised 'military dictatorship'. The new arrangement aroused some criticism in the Reichswehr also and after Groener's fall Hammerstein described the coupling of the offices as a mistake. 'Neue Dokumente,' *Vierteljahrshefte*, ii (1954), 424.

[3] Groener Correspondence: To Gleich, 1 November 1931.

military expression—a little Operations Section', which would map a radio and press propaganda programme, gather statistics on breaches of the peace, and prepare daily reports for the minister.[1]

Beyond this, however, Groener was not prepared to go. Thus, in December, when representatives of the Information Bureaux of the *Länder* met in conference at the Ministry of the Interior to discuss the nazi problem, they were actually forced to listen to a report which expressed confidence in Hitler's intentions of holding to the ways of legality and in his sincerity in attempting to keep his party hotheads under control and which insinuated that any action against the party or the S.A. might cause worse ills to descend on the country. The Prussian representative protested hotly against this report and complained about the ministry's curious reluctance to offend the National Socialists; and the conference ended with most representatives agreed that the Reich government was demonstrating an inadequate grasp of the situation.[2]

However disturbed he may have been by these protests, Groener persisted in his passive policy. He was encouraged in this by Schleicher who, already involved in negotiations with the nazis to an extent unsuspected by his chief, held that the time had not come for action and who dismissed the complaints of the *Länder* as a Social Democratic plot to compromise Groener politically.[3] Moreover, a new factor had by this time to be considered in formulating plans of action. It was clear by the end of the year that Bruening could hope for no striking foreign success, at least until the late spring. Yet Hindenburg's term of office would expire in March and the new elections would certainly involve the nation in widespread disorders and might very well bring Hitler to power. Bruening hoped to avoid both contingencies by eliminating the elections and securing the assent of the parties to a prolongation of the presidential term. Since this would necessitate negotiations with Hitler, it was

[1] Groener Correspondence: To Zweigert, 18 November 1931.

[2] Groener Papers: 'Vortrag, Konferenz der Nachrichtenstellen der Länder in dem Reichsinnenministerium, 14. Dezember 1931.'

[3] As late as March 1932 Schleicher was describing the nazis as a necessary counterweight to the socialists and was writing that if there were no nazis, 'it would be necessary to invent them'. Groener Correspondence: Schleicher to Groener, 25 March 1932. The letter is printed in full in Gordon A. Craig, 'Quellen zur neuesten Geschichte: II. Briefe Schleichers an Groener', *Die Welt als Geschichte*, xi (1951), Heft 2, p. 130.

plainly inadvisable to resort to any action which might persuade him to veto the projected plan. 'If our plan succeeds,' Groener wrote, 'it will be a great victory for the chancellor; but very delicate manipulation [*ein sehr feines Spiel*] is necessary in order, at home and abroad, to join the different pieces of weaving into the proper pattern and in order to prevent any disturbance.'[1]

Groener seems to have expected Hitler to agree without too much difficulty to the planned prolongation of Hindenburg's term. In his estimation of the Fuehrer he was no wiser than many other German leaders of this period. He was amused at Hitler's habit of becoming completely drunk with words;[2] but at the same time regarded him as a man seriously worried by the demands of the radicals in his party. A note in one of his papers describes Hitler as a 'modest, orderly man who wishes for the best'.[3] When, therefore, after a series of talks in which Bruening, Groener, Schleicher, and Hitler participated in early January, the Fuehrer refused to agree to the constitutional prolongation and took refuge in the argument that it would be a breach of the constitution,[4] the Reichswehr Minister was rudely surprised and considerably cast down. 'Our defeat in the question of the presidential elections', he wrote to his friend Gleich, 'is *very bad*, and we must now do everything possible in order to secure Bruening's position. For he *must* remain. I fight for that for official and personal reasons.'[5] And at the end of January, calculating that Hindenburg could hope at best for 35 per cent. of the total vote in new elections, he gloomily admitted that Hitler might very well win the presidential office.[6]

Even in his most pessimistic moments, however, Groener did not lose his determination to dissolve the S.A., and the possibility of an eventual Hitler victory in Germany strengthened his feel-

[1] Groener Correspondence: To Gleich, *Christfest*, 1931.

[2] 'Sachlichen Gesprächen weicht er aus und phantasiert gleich wieder durch alle Jahrhunderte der Geschichte. Er redet wie in einem Trance-Zustand mit weltverlorenem Blick, dann gehts los mit einem Sturzfall von Wörtern, Phrasen, und Bildern, ohne Komma und Punkt, bis er total erschöpft sich ausgegeben hat.' To Gleich, 24 January 1932.

[3] Groener Papers: 'Auszug aus Führerbesprechung im Reichswehrministerium, 11. Januar 1932'. See also Groener's later comments on Hitler to the British ambassador. *Documents on British Policy*, 2nd series, iii. 114.

[4] On the January conversations, see J. Goebbels, *My Part in Germany's Fight* (London, 1935), pp. 15 ff.; Wheeler-Bennett, *Wooden Titan*, pp. 352 ff.; R. T. Clark, *The Fall of the German Republic* (London, 1935), pp. 343 ff.

[5] Groener Correspondence: To Gleich, 24 January 1932.

[6] Ibid., 26 January 1932.

ing that the Reichswehr must be secured against this formidable military competitor before such victory was consummated. He made no attempt to hide his views from the nazis. Indeed, in January, while warning Hitler not to depart from the ways of legality, the Reichswehr Minister openly expressed his disapproval of the S.A. 'The *Wehrmacht* is the highest institution in the state,' he said; and it would not be replaced or even influenced by non-professional military organizations. The government intended at a later date to enlarge the army by a militia and absorb the best elements of the various semi-military organizations. But if Hitler dreamed of subordinating the army to his own militia, as had happened in Italy, he had better revise his views.[1] In March, when visited by Goering and Frank, Groener repeated this warning and said that he intended to absorb the S.A.,[2] and Hitler's strong showing in the elections of that month seems to have strengthened rather than weakened his determination.[3] Still he delayed action month after month, hoping for the elusive victory abroad which would rehabilitate the government and give added weight to his action. 'Really', he wrote at the beginning of April, '. . . [Bruening] should win some successes soon in the sphere of foreign and economic policy. *Darin liegt meines Erachtens des Pudels Kern.*'[4]

III

At this juncture of affairs, however, Groener was forced into action by a new turn of events. In the last days before the March elections, a series of raids by the Prussian police upon nazi headquarters had led to the capture of papers which seemed to be plans for a seizure of power by the S.A. in the event of a Hitler victory at the polls.[5] Groener himself doubted the genuineness of these discoveries, pointing out that, if the nazis had such plans, they would not be so stupid as to entrust copies to local

[1] Groener Papers: 'Auszug aus Führerbesprechung im Reichswehrministerium' 11. Januar 1932.' Also Schüddekopf, *Heer und Republik*, pp. 330 ff.

[2] *Augsburger Postzeitung*, 20 October 1932. See also the altercation between Groener and Goering in the Reichstag on 10 May. Reichstag, *Stenographische Berichte*, cmxlvi (1931–2), 2543 ff. Groener stated that he had warned Goering that 'there is no armed force, there is no party army, there is no organization of this nature which is not in the hand of the State'.

[3] Groener Correspondence: To Gleich, 2 April 1932.

[4] Ibid.

[5] Braun, *Von Weimar zu Hitler*, p. 381; Konrad Heiden, *Der Fuehrer* (New York, 1944), p. 447; François-Poncet, *Souvenirs*, pp. 39–40.

headquarters.[1] But the discoveries made by Severing's police were sufficiently alarming to increase the desire of the *Länderregierungen* for action, and in the first week of April the Bavarian government requested a meeting of representatives of the *Länder* to discuss the co-ordination of security measures in the forthcoming run-off elections.

This meeting was held at the *Reichsinnenministerium* on 5 April and was decisive in determining Groener's attitude toward the S.A. Led by the Prussian and Bavarian representatives, the majority of the meeting confronted Groener with what was in effect an ultimatum. Sharply criticizing the lack of leadership shown by the *Reichsinnenministerium*, they insisted that immediate action be taken to remove the threat of the Storm Troops; and they hinted strongly that, unless the Reich government took the initiative, they would proceed against the S.A. separately.[2]

This threat was effective for two reasons. In the first place, as Groener said later, if the states proceeded separately against the S.A., 'then, in this serious question, a heterogeneous legal situation would be produced within the area of the Reich, a situation clearly unbearable for the authority of the Reich and the cause of order'.[3] In the second place, it was clear to Groener that failure to act now would involve the loss of Social Democratic support, and that that would weaken the Bruening government fatally. Although he wrote to Bruening that party considerations need not influence the government, and that the decision with regard to the S.A. must be taken 'solely on the basis of *Staatsräson*',[4] Groener was aware that the party which had acquiesced in Bruening's tenure of power would no longer endure a passive policy on the part of the government. At the conclusion of the meeting on the 5th, therefore, he assured the *Länder* delegates that he was fully prepared to use the most extreme measures against the nazis and that he would urge the Chancellor and the President to agree to a dissolution of the S.A. and S.S. by emergency decree, to be issued immediately after the conclusion of the elections.

Once that promise was given, Groener went vigorously to his

[1] Groener Correspondence: To Gleich, 6 April 1932.

[2] Groener Correspondence: To Bruening (Draft), 10 April 1932. Also Groener-Geyer, *General Groener*, pp. 294 ff.

[3] *Augsburger Postzeitung*, 20 October 1932.

[4] Groener Correspondence: To Bruening (Draft), 10 April 1932.

task, as if relieved to have his previous reasons for delay overruled. And, at the outset, his own enthusiasm was equalled by that of the army chiefs. In a meeting in the Reichswehr Ministry on 8 April, at which the pending action was discussed, Hammerstein announced his eagerness to support the proposed dissolution in the most uncompromising terms and Groener was gratified by the 'complete agreement between me and the generals'.[1] On the same afternoon, in a telephone conversation with *Staatssekretär* Pünder, chief of the *Reichskanzlei*, Schleicher not only supported the projected S.A. prohibition but tended to assume complete responsibility for it, saying proudly that, while he had hitherto counselled Groener to delay action against the S.A., he was now convinced that the psychological moment had arrived.[2]

In view of the attitude of the army chiefs, Groener may be excused for not being seriously concerned when, on the morning of 9 April, Schleicher suddenly suggested a new procedure for dealing with the S.A. Direct dissolution of the S.A., without warning, might, he argued, enable Hitler to pose as a martyr before the country. Would it not be more effective for the Minister of the Interior publicly to outline the abuses of the S.A. and to insist that Hitler make his organization conform to a given set of conditions within a definite period of time? If Hitler complied, his position in the country and in his own party would be seriously weakened. If he refused to comply, the government could proceed to put a decree of dissolution into effect.

In this suggestion, Groener discerned no fundamental change in his aide's attitude. He assumed merely that, for direct action, Schleicher preferred to substitute 'a tactical feint, in keeping with his manner of thinking'.[3] Groener himself had little liking for the method advocated by Schleicher. It would merely, he thought, give Hitler a chance to write insulting replies to the Minister of the Interior, and it would lower the dignity of the government.[4] Nevertheless, he was willing to have the method

[1] Groener Papers: 'Chronologische Darstellung der Vorkommnisse, die zu meinem Rücktritt als Reichswehr- und Reichsinnenminister geführt haben', October 1932.

[2] Groener Papers: 'Memorandum vom Staatssekretär der Reichskanzlei, 30. Mai 1932.' Correspondence: To Gleich, 18 June.

[3] Groener Papers: 'Chronologische Darstellung.'

[4] Ibid.; Correspondence: To Bruening (Draft), 10 April.

discussed. Schleicher's plan was, indeed, given a full hearing after Bruening's return to Berlin on 10 April, the date of Hindenburg's definitive victory at the polls. In a meeting at the *Reichskanzlei*, in which the military chiefs, the Chancellor, the Minister of Justice, and state secretaries Meißner, Zweigert, and Pünder participated, Schleicher argued his case, but failed to convince the group. Bruening associated himself firmly with Groener's plan for immediate dissolution of the S.A., stating that his recent election tour had convinced him that such action was imperative. At the end of the meeting it was decided that the Chancellor would go to the President on the following morning and procure his assent for the necessary emergency decree.[1]

Here again Groener expected no difficulties. He had already discussed the S.A. question with President Hindenburg on 9 April and come away with the impression that the President was ready to sign a decree of dissolution. Meißner, of the President's entourage, had assured him on 10 April that the President would not hesitate to sign such a decree.[2] Nevertheless, as the government proceeded with its plans, Hindenburg's behaviour became alarmingly erratic. On the morning of 11 April he promised to sign the necessary emergency legislation. Later in the same day, however, he abruptly reversed this decision, apparently on the advice of his son; and it was necessary on 12 April for Bruening and Groener to go to him and recapitulate all of the arguments which made the prohibition necessary. After Groener had promised to assume full responsibility before the Reichstag and the public for the action to be taken, Hindenburg promised his assent.[3] After that had been procured, events moved swiftly. On the 13th the full cabinet approved the decree of prohibition and on the following day it was promulgated throughout the Reich.

Whatever doubts Groener might have had in the past about the political expediency of the prohibition of Hitler's military organization, he had never doubted that such prohibition would

[1] Groener Papers: 'Memorandum vom Staatssekretär der Reichskanzlei, 30. Mai 1932.' See also Reginald H. Phelps, 'Aus den Groener-Dokumenten: VII. Das S.A.-Verbot und der Sturz des Kabinetts Brüning', *Deutsche Rundschau* (Jan. 1951), pp. 24–25. Bruening wrote later, in *Deutsche Rundschau* (July 1947), that he privately considered the dissolution premature. In April 1932, however, he seems to have supported Groener without hesitation.

[2] Groener Papers: 'Chronologische Darstellung.'

[3] Groener Correspondence: To Gleich, 25 April 1932.

be in the best interests of the Reichswehr. Despite all of Hitler's assurances, the Hitler troops represented a threat to state security; and responsible Reichswehr leaders would, he thought, recognize that 'the spook of the S.A.' must be removed.[1] Yet, at the very moment when that removal was made possible, Groener discovered to his shocked surprise that the Reichswehr leaders no longer supported his policy, and, worse, that his most trusted colleague, Schleicher, had set out deliberately to sabotage it.

On the day following the promulgation of the decree of prohibition, Schleicher came to Groener with the alarming news that a storm of disapproval was sweeping through the Reichswehr Ministry and the army as a whole. Disaffection was so pronounced, Schleicher announced, that it was apparent that the Reichswehr was not prepared to accept the decree, and he had grave fears for Groener's continued tenure as Reichswehr Minister. Groener pointed out that it was not the right of the Reichswehr to oppose any act of state; it had merely to obey; but—as he wrote later—Schleicher 'would not admit that my objection was valid'.[2]

Groener was already the recipient of an angry letter from the crown prince, deploring the decree,[3] and he expected similar criticism from retired army officers who were attracted by Hitler's promises to increase Germany's military strength. But disaffection within the active ranks of the Reichswehr was something which could be prevented by the army chiefs themselves. As Groener wrote later, there was no agitation within the navy, for the simple reason that Admiral Raeder forbade any open criticism of the government's action.[4]

It soon became evident, however, that Schleicher and Hammerstein were not anxious to stamp out criticism. Ever since the defeat of his own plan for dealing with the S.A., Schleicher's conduct had been, to say the least, ambiguous. When Oskar Hindenburg had come to him on 11 April to express his concern over the pending prohibitory decree, Schleicher had said that

[1] Groener Correspondence: To Gleich, 25 April 1932.

[2] Groener Papers: 'Chronologische Darstellung.'

[3] Groener Correspondence: Crown Prince to Groener, 14 April. The crown prince expressed dismay that Groener should wish to destroy 'the wonderful human material that is gathered together in the S.A. and S.S. and which is getting valuable training there'.

[4] Groener Correspondence: To Gleich, 22 May. Raeder, *Mein Leben*, i. 270–1.

he himself was 'completely disinterested' in the S.A. question, a curious statement from one who had been so enthusiastic about dissolving the S.A. only three days earlier.[1] And now an even more questionable manœuvre of Schleicher's became apparent. On 16 April Groener received from Hindenburg an irritable letter, published simultaneously in the press, complaining about the suspicious and possibly treasonable activities of the *Reichsbanner*. Coming as it did so soon after the prohibition of the S.A., this could only be regarded as a criticism of the government's policy. Aside from this, the flimsy evidence that Hindenburg cited to justify his strictures of the *Reichsbanner* Groener recognized as emanating from the files of the *Wehrmachtabteilung* of the Reichswehr Ministry, a section immediately under Schleicher's supervision; and further investigation disclosed that, contrary to all ministerial procedure, they had been transmitted to the President by Hammerstein.[2]

Because of his long friendship with Schleicher, Groener was reluctant to accept even this evidence of Schleicher's double game; but he was seriously worried by what appeared to be a growing antagonism between the civilian government and the Reichswehr. On the 17th, therefore, he suggested to Schleicher that he, Schleicher, and Hammerstein, with their wives, should dine together in 'one of the big hotels', as a kind of public gesture of harmony and that at the same time Schleicher should send an order to all army commands putting an end to false rumours. Schleicher appeared to agree with this, but never referred to it again; and Groener was forced reluctantly to conclude that the army chiefs had no desire publicly to support the policies of their own minister.[3]

Indeed, in the next weeks, a malicious undercover campaign was waged against Groener in the Reichswehr Ministry itself. Charges that he had gone over to the Social Democrats, even to the extent of becoming a doctrinaire pacifist, were freely bandied about.[4] His second marriage was described as *unstandesgemäß* and much capital was made of the unfortunately premature birth of his child.[5] Feelers were put out to Admiral Raeder to secure his assent for a joint request on the part of the army and

[1] Groener Papers: 'Chronologische Darstellung.'
[2] Groener Correspondence: To Gleich, 25 April 1932.
[3] Groener Papers: 'Chronologische Darstellung.'
[4] Groener Correspondence: To Gleich, 21 December 1932.
[5] Braun, *Von Weimar zu Hitler*, p. 384.

navy commands for Groener's dismissal.[1] Attempts were made even to alienate his personal adjutants, although these, like the approach to Raeder, failed. Against this whispering campaign Groener had only one recourse, to go to the President and demand the dismissal of Schleicher and Hammerstein. This he refused to do for fear it would lead to a conflict which would precipitate the fall of Bruening at the very moment when his foreign negotiations showed promise of fruition.[2]

Groener's position became completely insupportable, however, at the beginning of May. On 10 May, in the Reichstag, his dissolution of the S.A. was subjected to a scathing criticism by Hermann Goering, in a speech in which the nazi leader openly appealed to the Reichswehr against its civilian chief. Groener's answer was delivered to the accompaniment of an almost uninterrupted howl of abuse from the nazi benches, a circumstance which deprived him of his customary aplomb and led him into an unwise attempt to answer his many hecklers.[3] The impression left by his speech was an unfortunate one; but, as one observer pointed out, the whole session of the Reichstag had the appearance of being staged. It seemed almost as if the nazis were ordered to provoke Groener into indiscretions and 'in this way to give the generals a suitable excuse' for urging his retirement.[4] Some validity is given to this conclusion by the fact that, immediately after the Reichstag session, a rumour that Groener was seriously ill was circulated in Berlin; and Schleicher blandly suggested to him that he ought to apply for sick leave.[5] The Reichswehr Minister refused, but it was clear to him that his continued tenure in office would be a source of embarrassment to Bruening. On 13 May, after consulting the Chancellor, he resigned his office.

By sacrificing himself, Groener hoped to prolong Bruening's term, but he was clear-sighted enough to recognize that there was now little chance of that. He remembered that Schleicher, once so enthusiastic about Bruening, had been suspiciously cool toward him since the previous winter.[6] He recalled that Hinden-

[1] Groener Papers: 'Chronologische Darstellung'; Correspondence: To Richard Bahr, 22 May; To Gleich, 22 May 1932.

[2] Groener Correspondence: To Gleich, 22 May 1932.

[3] Reichstag, *Stenographische Berichte*, cmxlvi (1931–2), 2546 ff.

[4] Georg Decker in *Die Gesellschaft* (June 1932), pp. 465–6.

[5] Groener Correspondence: To Gleich, 18 June 1932. Raeder, *Mein Leben*, i. 271.

[6] Groener Correspondence: To the editor of the *Münchener Neueste Nachrichten*, 5 August 1932.

burg had of late been given to grumbling about the Chancellor. 'The old man', Groener wrote angrily in the first days after his resignation, 'has become difficult, as became evident in the S.A. prohibition. He . . . has curtly and without any feeling of shame let me go and, as things stand, he will act no differently toward Bruening.'[1] It was a sound prophecy. At the end of May, after Schleicher had told the President that Bruening no longer enjoyed the confidence of the army, the Chancellor was dismissed as unceremoniously as his Reichswehr Minister.

IV

There was no doubt in Groener's mind that the *spiritus rector* of the plot which had overthrown the government was Schleicher, and he never completely forgave the general for the double game he had played since April. In November 1932, answering a letter in which Schleicher sought a reconciliation, Groener wrote: 'Scorn and rage boil in me because I have been deceived by you, my old friend, disciple, adopted son, my hope for people and fatherland.'[2]

At the same time, Groener found it difficult to discern the reasons for Schleicher's change of course and was bewildered concerning his objectives.[3] This is perhaps understandable. Even after more than twenty years, we can still only guess at the nature of Schleicher's long-range plans. There is, however, no very great mystery about his motives and his immediate aims. Schleicher was still intent, as he had been at the time of the formation of the Bruening government in 1930, upon freeing Germany from the anarchy of party politics and the dangers of parliamentary instability. He had hoped that Bruening would lead the way out of the political swamp. But, instead of giving the authoritarian leadership which was needed, Bruening, in the general's opinion, had gradually become a mere pawn in the hands of the Social Democrats. The Chancellor and Groener had actually allowed themselves to be forced by the socialists

[1] Groener Correspondence: To Gleich, 22 May 1932.

[2] Groener Correspondence: To Schleicher, 29 November 1932. A reconciliation was nevertheless effected in the latter part of 1932. See Craig in *Die Welt als Geschichte*, xi (1951), 132–3.

[3] Groener thought that he might be aiming at a monarchical restoration, for he maintained intimate relations with the crown prince. Groener Correspondence: To Gleich, 18 June 1932. For other views of his aims see 'Zum Sturz Brünings: Dokumentation', *Vierteljahrshefte für Zeitgeschichte*, i (1953), 267–75, and *Documents on British Policy*, 2nd series, iii. 169.

into an ill-considered action against the nazis—ill-considered because, even if successful, it could only benefit the Social Democrats in a manner which, in view of their attitude on military matters, would not be to the interest of the Reich or the army.[1]

It was necessary, then, Schleicher thought, to try the experiment of 1930 over again, with a new and more determined political combination which would derive its powers from the President and govern, if necessary, by decree. This new government's first order of business would be to reduce the Social Democrats to impotence so that when the time came to act against the nazis there would be no doubt in anyone's mind that such action was being taken in the national interest rather than for the benefit of the left. Schleicher fully intended to deal with the nazis in time, but in his own devious way. He was confident that he would be able to split Hitler's party and detach important elements to his side; and he had already, without Groener's knowledge, or that of Hitler, indulged in exploratory conversations with certain nazi dignitaries which were designed to subvert their loyalty to the Leader.[2] What Schleicher intended after the nazis had been disposed of is not clear; but he was probably thinking of a fundamental constitutional reform which would end parliamentary confusion—if not parliamentary government—and allow Germany to stand before the world as a united and disciplined nation—as those words were understood in army circles.[3]

It is surely unnecessary to comment on the risks involved in a programme which proposed to eliminate the Social Democrats before dealing with the more dangerous threat on the right and which rested on the dubious assumption that its author would prove to be more adroit politically than the leader of the nazis.[4]

[1] That Schleicher was not alone in thinking this is shown in a report from the British embassy in late May. Speaking of the S.A. *Verbot*, this said: 'The country garrisons complained that a serious and one-sided blow had been dealt to those classes which were prepared to volunteer for the defence of the country and the continued existence of the *Reichsbanner* was regarded as a sign that the Bruening government had opted for the Left parties and for a pacifist policy generally.' *Documents on British Policy*, 2nd series, iii. 140 ff.

[2] See 'Zur Politik Schleichers', *Vierteljahrshefte*, vi (1958), 88 f., 115; Krausnick n *Vollmacht des Gewissens*, pp. 194 f.; Braun, *Von Weimer zu Hitler*, p. 327.

[3] See Wheeler-Bennett, *Nemesis of Power*, p. 245.

[4] In a letter to Gleich on 22 May 1932, Groener wrote: 'Schleicher relies on his adroitness to lead the Nazis about by the nose . . . but perhaps [they] are even more adept than he in the uses of cunning and misrepresentation.' On 18 June he added to the same correspondent, the tag from *Faust*: 'Er glaubt zu schieben, doch er

But Schleicher was never one to doubt his own capacities, and he launched his plan with an assurance which bordered on nonchalance. Nor did he hesitate to stake the reputation and the prestige of the army upon the success of his design. In all of his manœuvres from this point until the end of January 1933, Schleicher claimed to speak in the name of the army, with some justification, it may be added, since the top echelon of the army command—Hammerstein, Adam, Bredow, and Ott—were his friends and disciples,[1] while his influence with the district commanders had been attested by their attitude in the May crisis.

The last unhappy phase in the history of the Weimar Republic was one, therefore, in which the army was more continuously and intimately involved in domestic politics than it had been under either Seeckt or Groener. This was made abundantly clear in the negotiations which led to the formation of the Papen government. It was Schleicher who urged Hindenburg to appoint Franz von Papen as Bruening's successor, who first broached the matter to Papen himself, who nominated most of his ministerial colleagues, and who conducted the negotiations which were designed to win Hitler's forbearance as the new cabinet began its work. And in all this, as Papen himself has written, 'Schleicher left . . . no doubt that he was acting as spokesman for the army, the only stable organization remaining in the State'.[2]

The first fruits of Schleicher's grand design were hardly impressive. Papen's appointment as Chancellor was received with considerable stupefaction by a country which, with reason, had never been able to take the gentleman jockey, and war-time military attaché in the United States, very seriously;[3] and wits

wird geschoben.' See also Meinecke's considered judgement of Schleicher in *Deutsche Katastrophe*, p. 75.

[1] Hammerstein was *Chef der Heeresleitung*; Adam, head of the *Truppenamt*; Ott, chief of the *Wehrmachtabteilung*; and Bredow, Schleicher's successor as head of the *Ministeramt* after Schleicher became Reichswehr Minister.

[2] Franz von Papen, *Memoirs*, translated by Brian Connell (London, 1952), p. 151. Papen is a highly unreliable witness on the events of this period, but there is no reason to doubt this statement. On Schleicher's role in the formation of this cabinet, see also Lutz Graf Schwerin von Krosigk, *Es geschah in Deutschland* (3rd ed., Tübingen, 1952), p. 117.

[3] On hearing of Papen's appointment, Seeckt wrote: 'Habemus Papen . . . Ein sympathischer Kerl. War unter mir in der Türkei Chef des Stabes. Seine amerikanische Tätigkeit im Kriege ist etwas unbequem.' Seeckt Papers: To his wife, 31 May 1932.

were quick to point out that the only qualifications for a ministerial portfolio in the new government seemed to be a background in the *Gardekürassier* Regiment or the title Freiherr.[1] The initial criticism deepened as the consequences of Schleicher's negotiations with Hitler became apparent. In return for an equivocal promise to support the new government, Hitler had been assured that new elections for the Reichstag would be held and that the decree abolishing the S.A. would be repealed.[2] The Reichstag was consequently dissolved on 4 June and the S.A. *Verbot* rescinded on the 15th. Hitler immediately turned his full attention to the task of scoring new gains in the forthcoming elections, and he loosed his liberated storm troopers against his opponents. A new wave of violence swept over the country, reaching its peak in riots at Altona on 17 July when fifteen persons were killed and fifty injured.

These events, which weakened whatever meagre popular support the new government possessed, did not disturb Schleicher or cause him to deviate from his course. He agreed with his fellow cabinet ministers—for he had undertaken to serve as Reichswehr Minister in Papen's government—that it would be expedient to reimpose the ban on political demonstrations and parades,[3] even if this was likely to strain Hitler's 'tolerance' to the breaking point. But at the same time, he insisted that the time had come to strike out at the Social Democrats, and in a way designed simultaneously to placate Hitler and to advance the government's plan of centralizing political authority in the country.[4] The main stronghold of Social Democratic power since 1929 had been the Prussian government; and Prussia was currently governed by a Socialist-Centre coalition government, the Braun–Severing government, although this no longer represented a majority in the *Landtag* and was ruling *ad interim*. Schleicher proposed the deposition of the Prussian ministers and their replacement by a Reich Commissioner; and, to justify such high-handed action, he secured from friendly sources within the Prussian Ministry of the Interior what purported to be evidence that the Prussian department of police was under

[1] Hans Schlange-Schöningen, *Am Tage danach* (Hamburg, 1947), p. 77.

[2] See Goebels, *Germany's Fight*, pp. 83–84, 88, 99–102.

[3] This was done on 18 July. Since the lifting of the S.A. *Verbot*, 99 persons had been killed and 1,125 wounded in political demonstrations, according to Carl Severing in *Mein Lebensweg*, ii. 346.

[4] Wheeler-Bennett, *Nemesis of Power*, p. 252.

communist influence, that it had been lax in dealing with communist demonstrations and that, consequently, it was responsible for the disorders at Altona and elsewhere.[1]

Papen was in full agreement with the proposed plan. After securing the approval of the President and ordering General Gerd von Rundstedt, commanding *Wehrkreis III*, to alert his troops for immediate action, the Chancellor and the Reichswehr Minister on 20 July informed the flabbergasted Prussian ministers[2] that they were to be replaced by a Reich Commissioner in the person of Papen. The angry officials protested loudly but in vain, and, on the same day, were physically ejected from their offices. Neither on the 20th nor on succeeding days did anything resembling active resistance materialize, for neither the *Reichsbanner* nor the trade unions were, in the opinion of their leaders, strong enough to oppose the government's stroke, and the police could not be counted on to test their strength against that of the local garrisons.[3]

For Papen and Schleicher, however, this well-executed coup was an empty victory. Neither it, nor Papen's success in freeing Germany from reparations at the Lausanne conference, nor even his carefully calculated withdrawal from the Disarmament conference on 23 July served to increase the reputation or the popularity of the government; and this was made unmistakably clear in the national elections of 31 July. When the votes were counted and the Reichstag seats apportioned, it was patent that the Cabinet of Barons had been rejected by an overwhelming majority of the people. The only two parties upon whom Papen could rely with any assurance—the Nationalists and the *Volkspartei*—won only forty-four seats between them. On the other hand, the nazis—whose thunder Schleicher and Papen had hoped to steal by their coup in Prussia—doubled their representation, winning 230 seats and becoming the largest party in the Reichstag.[4] There was now no hope that Hitler would

[1] Ibid., p. 253. Papen, *Memoirs*, p. 189.

[2] Braun did not attend the meeting because of illness, but Severing and two of his colleagues met with Papen and Schleicher. See Severing's account in *Mein Lebensweg*, ii. 348–51.

[3] Ibid., pp. 354–7. See also Braun, *Von Weimar zu Hitler*, pp. 405–6; and Albert Grzescinski, *Inside Germany* (New York, 1939), pp. 155, 158–9, 161. Grzescinski had been police president of Berlin since November 1930, and was now deposed.

[4] The Social Democrats received 133 seats, a loss of 10; the Centre and Bavarian Peoples party won 97 seats between them. The communists increased their representation from 77 to 89.

tolerate Papen further. The nazi chief burned for power and, when it was refused him in the now famous interview with Hindenburg on 13 August, he wasted no time in going on the offensive. When Papen met the Reichstag for the first time on 12 September, he was forced to dissolve it immediately, for the nazis and the communists combined to defeat him overwhelmingly in a vote of confidence.[1] This necessitated new elections and, when they were held, in the first week of November, Papen fared little better than he had in July. Ninety per cent. of the votes cast were still against the government.

In mid-October Josef Goebbels had written in his diary: 'The Reichswehr has already fallen away from the Cabinet. Upon what will it base itself now?'[2] The remark was perceptive, if premature. It was only after the November elections that army support was withdrawn from Papen, and this, of course, was Schleicher's doing. The general had, without doubt, become increasingly displeased with Papen in the weeks since the July coup, for the Chancellor had not only developed an irritating habit of making up his own mind on important issues, but was also in a fair way to supplanting Schleicher in the affections of the President. But it was the November election results which raised more basic differences. The most salient feature of the elections was the sharp setback suffered by the nazis—a loss of two million votes and thirty-four Reichstag seats. To Schleicher this proved that the time had come to put into effect the second part of his programme, the operation designed to split the National Socialist party. He was aware that Gregor Strasser, the leader of that party's powerful political organization, was deeply discouraged by the election returns, and believed that they foreshadowed a precipitous decline in party fortunes. Schleicher thought that Strasser would be willing to join a new government and that he would be supported by important elements of the party, including Roehm. To make this new combination possible, however, Papen would have to step down, for neither Strasser nor Roehm would be prepared to serve under him.

Papen, on the other hand, had developed a love for office which was—despite all the disclaimers which he makes in his

[1] See Papen's own account of this well-known incident in *Memoirs*, pp. 207–9, where he accuses the nazis of abandoning 'elementary rule[s] of democratic procedure'.

[2] Goebbels, *Germany's Fight*, p. 170.

memoirs—to persist until 1945. He had no intention of stepping down. He would, he insisted, make a last effort to secure, by negotiation with the parties, a workable parliamentary majority. If this failed, as it almost certainly would, he would summon Hitler and demand that he either demonstrate that he could obtain such a majority or that he enter the cabinet as Vice-Chancellor. If Hitler refused, then all attempts to observe constitutional propriety must be abandoned. The Reichstag—and if necessary the opposition parties, and the trade unions—should be dissolved and the cabinet should rule quite openly by presidential decree backed by the authority of the army.

With the President's backing, the first steps of the Papen programme were taken. The parties were canvassed and emphatically rejected the suggestion that they support the cabinet. For five days, between 19 and 24 November, Hindenburg, his secretary Meißner, and Papen conducted acrimonious negotiations with Hitler, only to receive in the end his flat refusal to accept anything but a grant of full power.[1] After that there was nothing left for Papen but the third alternative—the open violation of the constitution; and in an interview with Hindenburg and Schleicher on 1 December, he proposed this.

The fact that the President, despite his sincere desire to remain true to his constitutional oath,[2] gave his approval to Papen's plan, shows how completely he had fallen under the spell of the *Herrenreiter*. Hindenburg, indeed, proved wholly impervious to all of the rather disingenuous arguments which Schleicher now made in favour of legality, and he was frankly sceptical of the general's claim that he could destroy the nazis without departing from the letter of the constitution. He preferred, he said, to go on with Papen. In consequence, Schleicher was compelled to resort to the same kind of forcing play which had served to get rid of Groener and Bruening. He brought the influence of the army to bear against the Chancellor.

At a meeting of the full cabinet on 2 December Schleicher came out flatly against the Papen proposals. They would, he said, lead in all probability to a simultaneous insurrection on the part of the nazis and the communists; they would possibly

[1] On these negotiations, see Bernhard Schwertfeger, *Rätsel um Deutschland* (Heidelberg, 1948), pp. 156–78; and Otto Meißner, *Staatssekretär unter Ebert, Hindenburg und Hitler* (Hamburg, 1950). Meißner and Wilde, *Machtergreifung*, pp. 113 f.

[2] On Hindenburg's attitude to the oath, see Schwertfeger, *Rätsel um Deutschland*, p. 157.

precipitate a general strike by the trade unions; and they might even, by the domestic anarchy which they caused, tempt the Poles into launching an attack against East Prussia. The army simply did not have the strength to cope with a war fought simultaneously on the domestic and foreign fronts; and it was doubtful—in view of the political unreliability of some of its components—whether it was capable even of dealing firmly with the domestic risings. To support his argument, Schleicher summoned Colonel Eugen Ott of the *Wehrmachtabteilung* of the Reichswehr Ministry; and this officer reported in the gloomiest terms upon a study which his staff had made of army capabilities in the conditions foreseen. Ott fully corroborated the arguments of his chief.[1] As he wrote later:[2]

> I informed the Minister of Defence that, although administrative measures under a decree of emergency could be set in motion immediately, detailed study had shown that the defence of the frontiers and the maintenance of order against both Nazis and Communists was beyond the strength of the forces at the disposal of the Federal and State Governments. It was therefore recommended that the Reich Government should abstain from declaring a state of emergency.

John Wheeler-Bennett is surely justified in describing this testimony as an inglorious confession of weakness.[3] No responsible army leader since 1918 had ever admitted doubts concerning the Reichswehr's ability to control domestic dissidents; if anything, army commanders had tended at times to err on the side of over-confidence. If true, Schleicher's disclosure was a scathing indictment of the way in which he and his friend Hammerstein had administered the army since 1930.[4] So determined was Schleicher, however, to unseat Papen that he was quite willing to run the risk of being accused of responsibility for the weaknesses he delineated. And he was successful. Frightened by the sombre picture which he painted, the cabinet voted

[1] On this meeting see, *inter alia*, Papen, *Memoirs*, pp. 220–2; Meißner, *Staatssekretär*, pp. 245–6; and, for Ott's report, G. Castellan, 'Von Schleicher, von Papen et l'avènement de Hitler', *Cahiers d'histoire de la guerre* (Jan. 1949).

[2] Papen, *Memoirs*, p. 222.

[3] *Nemesis of Power*, p. 265.

[4] For evidence that Ott at least believed what he reported, see 'Neue Dokumente', *Vierteljahrshefte*, ii (1954), 427. Groener, apparently on the basis of what he heard of the meeting of 2 December, was highly critical of Hammerstein and wondered whether he should not have appointed Blomberg as *Chef der Heeresleitung* in 1930. Groener Correspondence: To Gleich, 21 December 1932.

solidly against the Papen solution. The Chancellor repaired to Hindenburg who listened in silence to the news. Then the President said: 'My dear Papen, you will not think much of me if I change my mind. But I am too old and have been through too much to accept the responsibility for a civil war. Our only hope is to let Schleicher try his luck.'[1]

Thus Schleicher himself—rather reluctantly, since he knew that his political talent was best exercised behind the scenes—became Chancellor in the first week of December. A few days later, Goebbels wrote cheerfully in his diary: 'A Jew has written a book called "The Rise of Schleicher", of which a huge edition is being published. A great pity, since when it appears in the shop windows von Schleicher will have disappeared from the political stage.'[2] Once again the little doctor's gift of prophecy was working well. Schleicher's chancellorship, which marked the highest point of army influence in the history of the republic, was brief and inglorious. It was notable, however, in one respect. Despite its brevity, it was long enough for Schleicher and the generals who supported him to execute a remarkable volte-face. In early December they were determined that Hitler must not come to power and confident that they could prevent this. By late January they were determined that he *must* come to power and frightened lest something should occur to postpone his doing so.

The failure of Schleicher's chancellorship was made inevitable within a week of his assumption of office. He had staked everything on his ability to detach Gregor Strasser from Hitler's side, and his confidence in his influence over Strasser was, in fact, justified. He erred, however, in assuming that Strasser's defection would break up the National Socialist party;[3] and, basically, his mistake arose from his over-estimation of Strasser's capacities and his under-estimation of Hitler's political genius in moments of crisis.

On 3 December Schleicher invited Strasser to join his cabinet as Vice-Chancellor and Minister-President of Prussia. For the

[1] Papen, *Memoirs*, p. 223.

[2] Goebbels, *Germany's Fight*, p. 213. The reference is probably to Kurt Caro's and Walter Oehme's *Schleichers Aufstieg* which was published in January 1933, although it may have been to Rudolf Fischer's *Schleicher, Mythos und Wirklichkeit*, which was published at about the same time.

[3] Otto Braun warned Schleicher that no appreciable part of the nazi party would follow Strasser. Braun, *Von Weimar zu Hitler*, p. 432.

next five days there were heated discussions in the inner circles of the nazi party, with Strasser urging that the offer must be accepted in order to avoid new elections which might be disastrous for the party, and Goering and Goebbels staunchly opposing this course as being the rankest kind of defeatism. After momentary hesitation, Hitler vetoed the Strasser policy and, on 7 December, accused the chief of the party's political organization of seeking to replace him as Leader. Strasser hotly denied the charge and, on the following day, resigned from the party. But there his resistance stopped. Far from seeking to carry all or part of the party with him, as Schleicher had expected, he washed his hands of the whole business and took his family off for a vacation in Italy.

Hitler, on the other hand, in an explosion of that demoniac rage which always cowed his party comrades when they were exposed to it, threatened to commit suicide if the party fell to pieces and then proceeded to smash the political organization which Strasser had ruled so long, to set up a new central party commission under Rudolf Hess, and to bully the deputies and gauleiters into new pledges of unconditional loyalty.[1] By mid-December the party was unquestionably united behind the Leader; and that fact spelled failure for the scheme which Schleicher had elaborated in the cabinet meeting of 2 December.

The Chancellor was forced then to do what Papen had done before him—to make the dismal round of the parties, seeking support which would give him a workable majority when the Reichstag re-convened. But here his past record for deviousness told against him in his negotiations with the middle and left parties, while the promises he made in order to allay their suspicions alienated the parties of the right. Remembering the *coup* in Prussia, the directorate of the Social Democratic party not only rejected Schleicher's initial overtures, and advised the trade union leadership to do the same,[2] but was openly scornful when the Chancellor promised fundamental reforms to relieve unemployment and a scheme of land settlement to alleviate the distress of the peasantry. The only tangible effect, indeed, of the last mentioned plan was to destroy what support Schleicher

[1] For this crisis in the Nazi party, see Bullock, *Hitler*, pp. 215–17, and Görlitz and Quint, *Hitler*, pp. 355–8; Bracher, *Auflösung*, pp. 681 f.; Meißner and Wilde, *Machtergreifung*, pp. 137 ff.

[2] For Schleicher's negotiations with the socialists and the trade unions, see Braun, *Von Weimar zu Hitler*, p. 437, and Noske, *Aufstieg und Niedergang*, pp. 310–11.

had in conservative circles, for, on 12 January, the *Landbund* delivered a broadside against the government, accusing it—as it had once accused Bruening—of desiring to impose agrarian bolshevism on the eastern districts of the Reich. The persistence with which Schleicher clung to his agrarian policy—and his threat to publish details of the *Osthilfe* scandals of 1927–8 if the resistance of the *Landbund* did not cease—not only influenced the decision of the Nationalist party to withdraw its support from the government—a step announced on 20 January—but sensibly weakened Schleicher's popularity in the army, whose officer corps, after all, was still recruited from the very families which would suffer most from the execution of his projects.[1]

Schleicher ended up then with even less party backing than his predecessor. And, this being so, he was forced to go to the President and make precisely the same request that his predecessor had made on 1 December. On 23 January he told the President that the Reichstag must be dissolved and that Germany must be ruled, under article 48 of the constitution, by what amounted to military dictatorship. Hindenburg was a very old and infirm man who suffered frequent lapses of memory, but he had no difficulty in remembering the arguments which Schleicher had used against this very solution only two months before.

> On December 2 [he said] you declared that such a measure would lead to civil war. The Army and the police, in your opinion, were not strong enough to deal with internal unrest on a large scale. Since then the situation has been worsening for seven weeks. The Nazis consider themselves in a stronger position, and the left wing is more radical in its intentions than ever. If civil war was likely then, it is even more so now, and the Army will be still less capable of coping with it. In these circumstances I cannot possibly accede to your request for dissolution of the Reichstag and *carte blanche* to deal with the situation.[2]

The President ordered Schleicher to go on with his search for a majority, and the Chancellor went through the motions of doing so. But Schleicher was well aware that his fall was only a matter of days away, and he felt that the time would be better

[1] H. W. Blood-Ryan, in his book *Franz von Papen: His Life and Times* (London, 1940), p. 180, says that Papen bombarded officers in the Reichswehr whose families had estates with circular letters protesting against Schleicher's agrarian policy. This seems unlikely, and in any case it would have been unnecessary.

[2] Papen, *Memoirs*, p. 236.

spent in influencing the choice of a successor. This was, after all, a matter which vitally concerned the army, and Schleicher still claimed to speak for that body.

Practically speaking, there were only two possible successors: Hitler and Papen. Hitler, whose fortunes had seemed to be on the downgrade in January, had been strengthened by the establishment of relations with a group of Rhenish-Westphalian industrialists and bankers who assumed responsibility for the debts of his party and were openly calling for his elevation to power.[1] The ebb-tide of party fortunes seemed to have turned, and in local elections the nazis had registered heavy successes within the past weeks. Hitler's appointment to the chancellorship would have seemed a certainty if it had not been for Hindenburg's past record of opposition to him and the President's deep affection for Papen. There was no doubt that Papen wanted office again; and, in view of Hindenburg's feelings, he had an excellent chance of getting it.

Of the two solutions Schleicher preferred the first. His reasons for this were not entirely rational and certainly by no means free of personal prejudice. But he seems to have calculated—as so many others did—that if Hitler assumed the responsibilities of office he would become more moderate in his views and would be susceptible to management by other agencies, notably by the army. This would be particularly true, if, as Schleicher hoped, he himself were made Reichswehrminister.[2] If, on the other hand, Papen became Chancellor, Hitler might well raise the standard of revolt, and the army would be placed in the awkward position of having to defend Papen. Schleicher did not believe that it would fight cheerfully for that discredited politician, or that it should be forced to do so.

In the last days of January 1933 Schleicher was desperately anxious lest a new Papen government be formed. On 27 January he asked Hammerstein to use the occasion of General von dem Bussche's customary report to the President on personnel affairs in the officer corps to sound Hindenburg out on his intentions. Hammerstein did so and was severely snubbed for his pains, being told that he would be better advised to spend his time

[1] Bracher, *Auflösung*, p. 687. See Bullock, *Hitler*, pp. 220–2, and Papen's disclaimer of any responsibility for arranging this alliance in *Memoirs*, pp. 227–32.

[2] Hammerstein in *Frankfurter Hefte*, xi (1956), 165, 'Neue Dokumente', *Vierteljahrshefte*, ii (1954), 431.

thinking of ways of improving manœuvres rather than in meddling in political matters. However, the President added, 'I have no intention whatever of making that Austrian corporal either Minister of Defence or Chancellor of the Reich'.[1] This alarmed Schleicher even farther. Two days later, when he went to the President to tell him that the cabinet was resolved to resign unless the powers requested on the 23rd were granted, he tried to argue that the formation of a new Papen government would be disastrous for Germany. The only response he received was a set speech accepting his resignation.[2]

Until the formation of a new government, of course, Schleicher was still Chancellor and Minister of Defence and, with his friend Hammerstein, had direct command over the army. But on 29 January Schleicher learned that General Werner von Blomberg, commanding *Wehrkreis I* and currently a member of the German delegation to the Disarmament conference,[3] had been ordered by the President to return to Berlin and to report to him personally rather than to the Bendlerstraße, as custom required. This seemed to denote an intention on Hindenburg's part of removing the army from the control of its present commanders by appointing Blomberg as Minister of Defence, after he had promised army support to Papen. In short, if Schleicher and Hammerstein were to block Papen, they were, they thought, going to have to move fast.

The true measure of their desperation in these last days is shown by the fact that the idea of arresting the President and his entourage was frankly discussed by Schleicher's intimates.[4] More important, at least two plain intimations of army support were made to Hitler. On the afternoon of 29 January Hammerstein—the man who Groener had believed would oppose a nazi seizure of power 'with brutality'—was dispatched by Schleicher to ask Hitler about the state of his current negotiations with Papen and to tell him that, if he thought that Papen was planning to form a government which would exclude him,

[1] Görlitz and Quint, *Hitler*, p. 362; Wheeler-Bennett, *Nemesis of Power*, p. 280.

[2] In March 1933, in an interview with an English journalist, Schleicher gave what would appear to be an exaggerated version of this scene, in which, among other things, he said that Hindenburg accused him of 'having made a mess of the Reichswehr'. 'Schleicher's Political Dream', *New Statesman and Nation*, 7 July 1934.

[3] After its brief withdrawal from the conference, the German delegation had returned in December 1932.

[4] See, for instance, Görlitz and Quint, *Hitler*, p. 364 and Hermann Foertsch, *Schuld und Verhängnis: Die Fritschkrise im Frühjahr 1938* (Stuttgart, 1951) pp. 28–29.

the generals would be willing 'to influence the position'.[1] That same night Werner von Alvensleben, one of Schleicher's close associates, went—again at the general's request—to Goebbels's house where a group of nazi chieftains was anxiously awaiting final confirmation of Hitler's appointment as Chancellor and of the President's willingness to dissolve the Reichstag. Alvensleben took the occasion to say to Hitler: 'If the Palace crowd are only playing with you, the Reichswehr Minister and the Chief of the *Heeresleitung* will have to turn out the Potsdam garrison and clean out the whole pig-sty from the Wilhelmstraße.'[2]

These were astonishing *démarches*, so astonishing, indeed, that Hitler does not seem to have known what construction to place upon them and secretly took precautions to guard against an army *Putsch*, which might be directed against himself. The Fuehrer's suspicion, while understandable, was unjustified. At this crucial moment in German history, the army command was on his side and contemplated no further action unless Hindenburg gave power to Papen.[3] Nothing of the sort was necessary; and Hitler became Chancellor on 30 January without any military intervention on his behalf. But surely the will was as important here as the deed would have been; and Hitler himself later admitted that 'if . . . the Army had not stood on our side, then we should not be standing here today'.[4]

V

It is appropriate at this point to ask whether the attitude of Schleicher and Hammerstein in January 1933 should properly be represented as a last-minute reversal of position. Was it not,

[1] Hammerstein in *Frankfurter Hefte*, xi (1956), pp. 165 f.; Hammerstein may also have been sent to obtain some assurance of Schleicher's inclusion in a Hitler cabinet. See Gerhard Ritter, *Carl Goerdeler und die deutsche Widerstandsbewegung*, (Stuttgart, 1954), p. 130.

[2] Wheeler-Bennett, *Nemesis of Power*, pp. 283–4; Hammerstein in *Frankfurter Hefte*, xi (1956), 169.

[3] In 1935 Hammerstein wrote that no military preparations for any kind of *Putsch* by the Potsdam garrison had been made. He added: 'Wohl aber wäre ich bereit gewesen, mich beim Herrn Reichspräsidenten noch einmal sehr energisch einzusetzen, wenn er die 7-prozentige Regierung ernannt hätte und nicht die nationalsozialistische Regierung. Das gleiche wollte Schleicher.' Hammerstein in *Frankfurter Hefte*, xi (1956), 169. During the Nuremberg trials, Hermann Goering said that Schleicher had offered Hitler the use of military force to block Papen, in return for the defence post in Hitler's cabinet. It is more likely that Alvensleben said this than that Schleicher did. See Ritter, *Goerdeler*, p. 468; and, for other aspects of this complicated question, Schüddekopf, *Heer und Republik*, pp. 356–7.

[4] Speech of 23 September 1933, quoted in Wheeler-Bennett, *Nemesis of Power*, p. 285.

after all, implicit in everything that they had done since May 1932, when they had forced Groener from office? However Groener's own policy may be judged—and he is certainly open to criticism for having allowed army representatives to play party politics in the first place—there can be no doubt of his determination to prevent Hitler from becoming Chancellor of the Reich or of his willingness to use force to prevent that. But the responsible leadership of the army—the district commanders and the staff chiefs in the Bendlerstraße, who supported Schleicher against Groener in May 1932—were, like most members of the officer corps ever since 1918, far less happy over the thought of attacking rightist dissidents than they would have been if asked to turn against the left. In face of National Socialism, moreover, they were always of two minds. They heartily disliked Hitler and rejected with contempt the thought of his leading the nation; but they also admired the disciplined forces which stood behind him, and had no desire to destroy them. Instead they set out to attempt to seduce those forces from their Leader. But the tactics which they employed to reach this goal merely increased the kind of political confusion in which Hitler thrived. The generals were far more successful in weakening those political parties which were genuinely opposed to National Socialism than they were in dividing Hitler's party; and, as intriguers, they were hopelessly outclassed by the Fuehrer and his paladins.

In the long run, then, the frantic expedients of the generals facilitated Hitler's rise to power; and, in January 1933, they recognized this and put the army seal of approval on his appointment as Chancellor. The only alternative, as they saw it, was an open fight against National Socialism under a discredited leader, Franz von Papen, and for this they had no stomach. Even at this late date, when all their elaborate schemes had proven to be bankrupt, they were still, however, able to persist in their old delusions. Hitler, they thought, would respect them for the opposition they *might* have offered to his accession. Hitler would recognize the army's paramount influence in political decisions. Hitler would allow himself to be managed and, if he did not, he could be disposed of.

Of all the mistakes made by political generals in the long history of the Prussian army, this was the greatest and, for the nation, the most tragic.

XII

HITLER AND THE ARMY

1933–45

We are often pure fools in political and legal affairs. But we are what we are as a result of our upbringing and education and we shall do well not to try to be any different. GENERAL GÜNTHER BLUMENTRITT.

Deveroux. Doch sieh, wir sind Soldaten, und den Feldherrn
Ermorden, das ist eine Sünd' und Frevel,
Davon kein Beichtmönch absolvieren kann.
Buttler. Ich bin dein Papst und absolviere dich.
Entschliesst euch schnell!
Deveroux. (*Steht bedenklich.*) Es geht nicht.

Wallensteins Tod.

THROUGHOUT the course of German history the Prussian army, and the German army which grew out of it and inherited its traditions, had been a law unto itself, acquiescing in directions issued by the political heads of the state for the most part only when it suited its purpose to do so. Even in the days of the monarchy, there were practical limitations to what the sovereign could command his army to do; and it is doubtful whether any monarch after Frederick II believed that he could expect blind obedience from his soldiers. If Frederick William III did so, he discovered at Tauroggen that he was wrong.[1] His successor, Frederick William IV, was under no illusions on this score, and his opposition to the inclusion of a military oath in the constitution of 1848 was prompted by the belief that the army would not stand for it.[2] During the constitutional conflict of the 1860's, William I showed himself extremely sensitive to army opinion, as it was expressed to him by Edwin von Manteuffel, and on more than one occasion rejected possible solutions to the dispute with the Chamber because he feared the reaction of the officer corps.[3] As for William II, one need only recall, in this connexion, the way in which he was forced by the Supreme Command to dismiss Bethmann-Hollweg, despite his

[1] See above, Chapter II, p. 59.

[2] See above, Chapter III, p. 118.

[3] See, for instance, Chapter IV, pp. 157–9.

personal confidence in that statesman.[1] Finally, when the monarchy gave way to the republic, the army became even less amenable to control, acting, as has been seen, with scant regard for—and sometimes in complete disobedience of—the wishes of the responsible political leadership of the nation.[2]

In view of this history it is understandable that publicists and German 'experts' in the outside world should have been so ready to believe that, despite the so-called *Machtübernahme* of Adolf Hitler in January 1933, the army was still the master of the political situation in Germany and that, if the new leader failed to respect its prerogatives and defer to its policy desires, it would unseat him.[3] It is easy to see also why ranking members of the officer corps—Schleicher's closest associates, for example —should have believed the same thing. But no calculation could have been more erroneous. In the course of his twelve years of office, Adolf Hitler was to impose upon the army a control more rigid than any in its long existence, and to compel the obedience of its officers even to commands which violated their historical traditions, their political and military judgement, and their code of honour.

Had Hitler sought to assert this kind of domination over the military establishment in the first months of his power, it is quite possible that he would have met violent resistance. But the Fuehrer was never one to act precipitately, and, in dealing with the army, he employed the arts of ingratiation and seduction before showing his hand. It was only at the beginning of 1938, after the integrity of the officer corps had been sapped and its will to resistance weakened, that he threw aside the façade and, in a series of swift and brutal manœuvres, arrogated to himself personal command over the armed forces. That action was not challenged by the army leadership. Nor was the long series of humiliations that followed, humiliations the like of which no previous ruler would have dared inflict upon those who wore the uniform.

Indeed, swallowing their pride, the officers as a class followed their master to the bitter end, and in doing so inevitably assumed a large share of the responsibility for the crimes of his

[1] See above, Chapter VIII, pp. 323 ff. [2] See above, Chapters IX–XI, *passim*.

[3] Many examples could be cited of this belief, which was further strengthened by the events of June 1934. A correspondent in *The New Statesman and Nation* of 21 July 1934, for instance, predicted that the Reichswehr would continue to be 'masters of the situation' even if it preserved 'the Hitler-Göring façade'.

régime. It is this that must not be forgotten, even when we pay tribute to those representatives of the officer corps who risked and lost their lives in the conspiracy of 1944. For the most significant aspect of the officers' revolt was that it failed, and it did so because the great majority of the army's leaders refused to participate in it.

Thus, the long political history of the Prussian army ended with the bulk of the officer corps desperately foreswearing politics and frantically seeking, like the central figure in Zuckmayer's powerful drama *Des Teufels General*, to escape the political guilt of their generation by complete absorption in their military tasks—technicians operating in the void to the point of unreason,[1] but nevertheless Hitler's collaborators in the destruction of their country.

I

Nothing could have been more deferential and circumspect than the new Chancellor's behaviour in his first dealings with the army. Hitler went out of his way to express his respect for the traditions of the officer corps and his determination that its honourable place in the state should be maintained. Within a few days of his elevation to power, he poured his heart out to a gathering of the heads of the armed services, emphasizing that it was his dearest wish that the services should be permitted to work, with greater resources and more freedom than ever before, on the development of Germany's military strength.[2] Shortly thereafter, in a grandiose ceremony at the Garrison Church in Potsdam, he spoke in almost fulsome terms of the army's role in German history, and, if his remarks were received with sceptical amusement by cynics like Schleicher,[3] they made a favourable impression on most of his uniformed auditors. Old Field Marshal Mackensen said after the meeting, 'We German officers used to be called representatives of reaction, whereas we were really bearers of tradition. It is in the sense of that tradition that Hitler spoke to us, so wonderfully and so directly from the heart, at Potsdam.'[4]

[1] Ignaz Pollmüller, 'Die Rolle der Reichswehr von 1918 bis 1933', *Frankfurter Hefte*, 1. Jg., Heft 9 (Dec. 1946), p. 838.

[2] Wheeler-Bennett, *Nemesis of Power*, p. 291.

[3] In December 1933 Schleicher sent a note from Potsdam to Wilhelm Groener which read: 'Hearty Christmas greetings from the old soldier city whose name has been much taken in vain during the past year while no trace of its spirit can be discovered.' See Craig in *Die Welt als Geschichte*, xi (1951), 133.

[4] Rüdt von Collenberg, *Mackensen*, p. 149. Foreign observers were also misled

There was to be very little left of the old tradition when Hitler got through with it, but in 1933 there were no intimations of the future. The Fuehrer seemed disposed even to restore some of the features of the imperial military system. To the gratification of the officers, a new army law of 20 July 1933 abolished the jurisdiction of the civil courts over the military and did away with the system of elected representatives of the rank and file—the *Vertrauensmänner* whose very existence recalled the soldiers councils of 1918.[1]

In the field of foreign policy also, the soldiers found that Hitler was most accommodating to military interests. Although he criticized communism in some of his speeches, he made no attempt to repudiate the Soviet-German treaty of 1926, and its term was prolonged when it came up for renewal in May.[2] Moreover, at Geneva, where the conference on disarmament was limping along, the new government not only followed the intransigent line first established by Bruening and Papen—insisting upon equality of status with the other Powers—but also, by skilful use of the arts of delay and obfuscation, avoided committing the nation to any plan which would involve future controls on German arming. And when these tactics had begun to lose their effectiveness, and when the other Powers actually agreed on a concrete plan for general reduction of armaments, Hitler, in October 1933, abruptly withdrew from the conference, a step which caused grave misgivings among some of his diplomats[3] but was generally approved by his soldiers, who saw in it the beginning of a new and promising era for the army. Indeed, the action at Geneva seemed to give substance to promises which Hitler had been making to them since January to the effect that the *Truppenamt* could begin to revise its peace-time and mobilization schedules in an upward direction and that it was only a question of months before the army could begin exercises with real tanks.[4]

It was probably not until the very end of 1933 that doubts

by the ceremony, and G. K. Chesterton wrote an article on it entitled 'The Return of Prussianism'. See S. D. Stirk, *The Prussian Spirit* (London, 1941), p. 20.

[1] Wheeler-Bennett, *Nemesis of Power*, p. 300.

[2] Erich Kordt, *Wahn und Wirklichkeit* (Stuttgart, 1947), p. 63.

[3] See Craig, 'The German Foreign Office from Neurath to Ribbentrop', in *The Diplomats*, p. 414.

[4] Görlitz, *General Staff*, p. 247. The first tank battalion was formed at Ohrdruf in 1934. Liddell Hart, *Other Side of the Hill*, p. 121.

began to occur to some of the soldiers. It was discovered, for instance, that Hitler was not after all going to maintain the hitherto cordial relations with the Soviet Union and that the treaty of 1926, while not repudiated,[1] was to become a dead letter. The negotiations with the Polish government and the subsequent German–Polish declaration of 26 January 1934 came as an unpleasant surprise to the disciples of Seeckt within the army and to all of those who had regarded a war against Poland as a certain eventuality. When the ambassador to Moscow, Rudolf Nadolny, returned to Germany to conduct a personal campaign against the new departure, he found ready listeners among officers in the East Prussian garrisons.[2] This opposition, however, never assumed the dimensions of Seeckt's spirited fight in defence of the Russian tie in 1925. This was partly because President Hindenburg, who was always less enthusiastic about the connexion with the Red army than Seeckt had been, gave it no support;[3] and it was due also to the fact that, throughout the first months of 1934, the attention of the army's leaders was engrossed by other matters of more immediate importance to them.

For one thing, in January some doubt was cast upon the genuineness of Hitler's many professions of devotion to the traditions of the army, for when Hammerstein retired as chief of the army command it became known that Hitler desired the appointment of Walter von Reichenau as his successor. The administrative appointments made since January 1933 had not all, it should be noted, been greeted with universal approbation by the senior officers, but they had on the whole been acceptable. If Werner von Blomberg, who had been appointed as War Minister when Hitler became Chancellor, was too enthusiastic about National Socialism for the taste of some of his colleagues, he was at least a soldier of known ability and, in addition, possessed the confidence of Hindenburg. If Blomberg, more-

[1] It was never in fact repudiated and, at the time of the negotiation of the Nazi-Soviet Pact in 1939, the German ambassador informed the Russians that his government regarded it as a valid instrument. See *Nazi-Soviet Relations, 1939–1941: Documents from the Archives of the German Foreign Office*, edited by R. J. Sontag and J. S. Beddie (Washington, D.C., 1948), pp. 29–30.

[2] Friedrich Hoßbach, *Zwischen Wehrmacht und Hitler, 1934–1938* (Wolfenbüttel und Hannover, 1949), pp. 37–38.

[3] Hindenburg also had little sympathy for Nadolny. See Picker, *Hitlers Tischgespräche*, p. 432. On Nadolny's campaign and his subsequent dismissal, see Rudolf Rahn, *Ruheloses Leben* (Düsseldorf, 1950), pp. 83–84.

over, had been excessively ruthless in clearing Schleicher's set out of the Bendlerstraße, his replacements had generally been above reproach. Ludwig Beck, for instance, who took General Adam's place at the *Truppenamt*, was regarded as one of the best strategists in the army. But the Reichenau appointment could not be justified in the same way. Reichenau had the reputation of being a *Streber* and of being outspokenly National Socialist because he believed it would bring him advancement; and he was known to possess completely unorthodox views on discipline and the relationship between officers and enlisted men, going so far as to engage in athletic competition with the troops of his command.[1] By officers in his age bracket he was little liked, and even his selection in the spring of 1933 as head of the *Ministeramt* had aroused criticism. Now, when his name was put forward as Hammerstein's successor, opposition was general in the higher ranks, and the army's two group commanders, Rundstedt and Leeb, made no secret of the fact that they would find it very difficult to work with him if he were appointed.[2]

The decisive role in this affair, however, was played by Hindenburg. When he learned of Hitler's desire to have Reichenau appointed, the President was deeply angered, principally, one gathers, because he regarded this as an attempt to meddle with his own prerogatives. Apart from this, he considered Reichenau unqualified for the post in question. 'He has never even held a divisional command', the field-marshal said to Papen, 'and now I am supposed to entrust the whole army to him. The idea is ridiculous!' When Blomberg had the temerity to notify the President that he would resign if Reichenau were not appointed, Hindenburg told him that, since the War Minister's position was a political one, he was at liberty to resign for political reasons. But, as a soldier, he had no right to challenge a Presidential decision in military matters. To do so, the President suggested, was tantamount to insubordination.[3]

Thanks to Hindenburg, then, the Reichenau candidacy was blocked, and Hammerstein's place was taken by Colonel-General Werner von Fritsch, a long-time member of the inner circle of

[1] On Reichenau, see Wheeler-Bennett, *Nemesis of Power*, p. 298 and Foertsch, *Schuld und Verhängnis*, pp. 31–32. [2] Görlitz, *General Staff*, p. 282.

[3] Papen, *Memoirs*, p. 288, and his testimony at Nuremberg in *Nazi Conspiracy and Aggression*, Supplement A, p. 484. See also Walter Görlitz, *Hindenburg: Ein Lebensbild* (Bonn, 1953), p. 417.

the General Staff, an officer who had fought with distinction in the First World War and had served as Goltz's chief of staff in the Baltikum, and who had later been one of Seeckt's most intimate aides. Fritsch had everything that Reichenau lacked: a long experience in command and the general respect of his colleagues. Hitler was wise enough not to try the impossible; he accepted Fritsch because he could do nothing else, doubtless taking comfort in the fact that the new chief of the army command had remained aloof from politics since Seeckt's fall[1] and had never expressed unfavourable views on the subject of National Socialism and its leader.

In retrospect, the Hammerstein 'crisis' seems trivial enough, but it was not unimportant. The army leaders had been given a glimpse of the real Hitler, who was determined that sooner or later he would assert his domination over them; but they do not seem to have reflected very deeply on the revelation afforded them. The fact that they had had their way gave them a false sense of confidence, confirming them in their belief that they would always have their way when they wanted to do so. And this belief, which was dangerous precisely because it made them disinclined to take any action against Hitler in these early years when action might have been effective, was now further strengthened by what seemed to be a victory for the army in a much more serious affair. This was precipitated by the ambitions of Ernst Roehm, the commander of the National Socialist party's *Sturm Abteilungen*.

Roehm had watched Hitler's delicate manœuvring with the army with growing disgust. Since he had taken command of the S.A. in 1931 he had expanded it into a force of some one and a half million men and, in the past year, he had begun to form within it special aviation, motor, engineer, intelligence, and medical units, and had established an S.A. *Ministeramt* and a press bureau. It was clear that he aspired to make of the S.A. the true army of the National Socialist era—the *Volksheer* which would be the school of the nation—and that he thought of himself as the Scharnhorst of the new age.[2] He was infuriated because Hitler seemed disinclined to take the same view; and in a remarkable interview with Hermann Rauschning in the

[1] In 1926 Fritsch advised Seeckt to oppose his dismissal order, if necessary by force. See above, Chapter X, p. 421, n. 4.

[2] Görlitz and Quint, *Hitler*, p. 423.

early months of 1934, he gave vent to his rage and disappointment.[1]

> Adolf is a swine, [he swore]. He will give us all away. He only associates with the reactionaries now. His old friends aren't good enough for him. Getting matey with the East Prussian generals. They're his cronies now. . . . Adolf knows exactly what I want. I've told him often enough. Not a second edition of the old imperial army. Are we revolutionaries or aren't we? *Allons, enfants de la patrie*! If we are, then something new must arise out of our *élan*, like the mass armies of the French Revolution. If we're not, then we'll go to the dogs. We've got to produce something new, don't you see? A new discipline. A new principle of organization. The generals are a lot of old fogeys. They never have a new idea. . . . I'm the nucleus of the new army, don't you see that? Don't you understand that what's coming must be new, fresh and unused? The basis must be revolutionary. You can't inflate it afterwards. You only get the opportunity once to make something new and big that'll help us lift the world off its hinges. But Hitler puts me off with fair words.

Hitler was all too conscious of Roehm's feelings, but he had no desire to follow the daring course plotted by the S.A. chief. Even if it were possible to effect the grandiose military reorganization of which Roehm dreamed, the net result would be to place Hitler at the mercy of his ambitious subordinate. Apart from this, any attempt to implement Roehm's schemes would certainly precipitate a conflict with the army leadership, which could not be expected to sit idly by as the Reichswehr was absorbed in a peoples army. Hitler did not want a breach with the army at this time. He knew that the death of Hindenburg could be expected within a matter of months, that that event would surely bring a crisis in his own fortunes, and that it would be well to have the army at his side at that dangerous moment. But he did not want a break with Roehm either. He tried to temporize; he appointed Roehm to the cabinet; and he used the 'fair words' of which the S.A. commander complained.

Admission to the cabinet, of which Blomberg was also a member, merely increased Roehm's importunity, and he used his preferment to force his views on the War Minister. In February 1934, for instance, he laid before his ministerial colleagues a plan for the co-ordination of all of the armed forces of

[1] Hermann Rauschning, *Hitler Speaks* (London, 1939), pp. 154–5.

the state and the party under one ministry, of which he himself would presumably be the head.[1] This angered Blomberg. For all of his inclination to National Socialism, the War Minister possessed orthodox views on the subject of army organization and the privileged position of the Reichswehr in the state. He took the Roehm plan to the *Heeresleitung*, where the reaction was one of indignation and alarm. The generals were able to dispose of Roehm's scheme by an appeal to Hindenburg, who majestically rejected it; but they realized that this did not end what had become a serious threat to their prerogatives and that more decisive action was needed.

This was Blomberg's view in particular and, in the spring months of 1934, he seems to have devoted himself to the double task of strengthening Hitler's preference for the army and convincing him to take firm steps against the S.A. Blomberg had once expressed the thought that, whereas it had been a point of honour for the Prussian officer to be correct, it was 'the duty of the German officer to be crafty';[2] and it cannot be denied that there was a lack of directness about his actions here. His decision in February to permit the National Socialist party emblem to become part of the uniform insignia of the armed forces, and his announcement in April that indoctrination in National Socialist principles would be included in the army training programme,[3] were far from popular in the officer corps, but they were doubtless introduced in spite of this, in order to show Hitler that he could rely on the army in a showdown with the S.A. This was probably true also of the eight-point statement issued to the armed forces on 25 May under the title 'The Duties of the German Soldier', which was written in the new *völkisch* style and which said proudly that the army's first duty was to protect 'the Reich, the people now united in National Socialism, and its living space [*Lebensraum*]'.[4] This was certainly a far cry from the *Überparteilichkeit* upon which

[1] Wheeler-Bennett, *Nemesis of Power*, p. 309.

[2] Hermann Rauschning, *The Revolution of Nihilism* (New York, 1939), p. 123.

[3] Krausnick in *Vollmacht des Gewissens*, p. 222; G. Castellan, *Le réarmament clandestin du Reich 1930–1935* (Paris, 1954), pp. 432 f.

[4] This document was signed by Blomberg and Hindenburg. See *Militärwochenblatt*, 118. Jg. (11 June 1934). The editors wrote that this statement marked 'the end of an epoch in which the Wehrmacht stood apart from the life of the *Volk* and nation as a "*Staatsheer*", an epoch in which the people's principles of life were not its principles, and in which its ideals were not, and could not be, shared by all'.

Seeckt and Groener used to insist, and Hitler could have asked for no more generous avowal of support.

At the same time, Blomberg and Reichenau seem to have done their best to encourage Hitler's opposition to Roehm's pretensions; and their efforts became more insistent as signs began to multiply by the middle of the year that the radical wing of the National Socialist party was becoming restive and was agitating for a new wave of revolution.[1] Hitler was passing through one of those strange fits of indecision that often preceded his most frightening outbursts of violence; and some of his lieutenants—notably Goering and Himmler, who had private reasons for wishing the liquidation of the S.A.—despaired at the Fuehrer's vacillation. These now found allies in the army chiefs. While Reichenau collaborated with Himmler in devising the kind of measures that would be needed to remove the S.A. threat,[2] Blomberg seems to have brought more direct pressure to bear upon the hesitant Chancellor. There is evidence to indicate that on or about 21 June he intimated to Hitler that, unless necessary measures were taken to ensure the maintenance of internal peace throughout the Reich—that is, unless steps were taken to bring the radicals under control—the President might declare martial law and call upon the army to restore order.[3] This warning ended Hitler's hesitations. He spent the next ten days planning the action against Roehm and, on 30 June, he struck with unparalleled ferocity.

The story of the Blood Purge of 30 June has been often told and need not be repeated here. In the present context the salient point is that, while it was going on, the leaders of the army did nothing. For forty-eight hours, while Himmler's S.S. committed wholesale murder from one end of the country to the other, they remained completely passive.[4] Even when it was clear that people who had no connexion with the S.A.—includ-

[1] See Foertsch, *Schuld und Verhängnis*, pp. 49–54; Manstein, *Soldatenleben*, pp. 187–89.

[2] Hermann Mau, 'Die zweite Revolution — Der 30. Juni 1934', *Vierteljahrshefte für Zeitgeschichte*, i (1953), 133.

[3] Wheeler-Bennett, *Nemesis of Power*, p. 320.

[4] Army units did give some technical assistance to the police and the S.S. and, in Bavaria, occupied some key positions. See Mau in *Vierteljahrshefte*, i (1953), 133 and Castellan, *Le réarmement clandestin*, p. 441.

ing Ritter von Kahr, two of Franz von Papen's aides and Generals von Schleicher and Bredow—had been shot out of hand, the army did not move. Papen, who narrowly missed death himself, found this behaviour incomprehensible and later asked General von Fritsch why he had not intervened to end the killing. The chief of the army command gave him the kind of answer which was to be given to similar queries on many occasions in the years that followed. The army wanted to intervene, he said, 'but they could not move without explicit orders from Blomberg or Hindenburg. However, Blomberg had rigidly opposed any intervention, and Hindenburg, the commander-in-chief, could not be reached and seemed to be wrongly informed'.[1] The ambiguous phrasing of this statement makes it impossible to tell whether Fritsch ever in fact urged Blomberg to give the necessary orders or how, for that matter, he knew Hindenburg's views if he could not reach him.[2] It is difficult to avoid the conclusion that the leaders of the army closed their eyes to the slaughter and their minds to everything but the thought of the advantages which the elimination of the S.A. would bring to them.[3]

This was doubtless in accordance with the dictates of 'realism', as that term was understood in the nazi era, but it was, to say the least, flagrantly irresponsible. And worse was to follow. How, for instance, was one to interpret the Order of the Day which Blomberg issued to the army on 1 July, in which he spoke of the Fuehrer's 'soldierly decision and exemplary courage' in wiping out 'mutineers and traitors'? Was the last phrase meant to include Blomberg's former comrades-in-arms, Schleicher and Bredow? Apparently so, for at the beginning of August General von Reichenau, interviewed by a reporter from the *Petit Journal*, said: 'The death of Schleicher, our former chief, caused us grief, but we are of the opinion that for some time he had ceased to be a soldier.'[4] There is no evidence that Reichenau was repri-

[1] Papen, *Memoirs*, pp. 318–19. See also his remarks at Nuremberg in *Nazi Conspiracy and Aggression*, Supplement A, pp. 443–4.

[2] Wheeler-Bennett suggests, indeed, that the army saw to it that no requests for intervention reached the President and that this was the reason why Field Marshal von Mackensen, who wanted the army to step in, could not get in touch with Hindenburg. *Nemesis of Power*, pp. 328–9.

[3] The S.A. was not completely eliminated, although it was said in Berlin that this was only because it was mentioned in the Horst Wessel song. It ceased, however to be a military force of any consequence or future.

[4] Quoted in *Deutsche Allgemeine Zeitung*, 7 August 1934.

manded for this statement, which was widely quoted. Indeed, the majority of the senior officers of the army seemed perfectly willing to accept the fantastic charges of conspiracy and treason which Hitler made against Schleicher and Bredow[1] for this made it unnecessary for them to protest against the murders.[2] Yet this, as Rauschning has written, could only be described as a moral capitulation, and its long run effect upon army morale was bound to be disastrous.[3]

Nevertheless, the prevailing attitude at the Bendlerstraße in the summer of 1934 was a compound of relief and satisfaction. Roehm had been disposed of; the army had once more demonstrated its ability to protect its own interests; and it remained now only to consolidate this victory by some formal manifestation of a public nature. There followed, then, the episode of the reciprocal pledges.

On 1 August Field Marshal von Hindenburg died and, on the same day, Hitler announced the amalgamation of the offices of President and Chancellor and his assumption of the dual post under the title Fuehrer and *Reichskanzler*. On 2 August the leaders of the armed services and every officer and man in the Reichswehr made the following declaration:[4]

> I swear by God this sacred oath, that I will yield unconditional obedience to the Fuehrer of the German Reich and *Volk*, Adolf Hitler, the Supreme Commander of the Wehrmacht, and, as a brave soldier, will be ready at any time to lay down my life for this oath.

This seems to have been a purely voluntary action by the

[1] Hitler outlined the plot which was supposed to have been concocted by Roehm and Schleicher, with the support of 'a foreign Power', in his speech of 13 July in the Reichstag. See Norman H. Baynes, *The Speeches of Adolf Hitler, 1922–1939* (London, 1942), i, especially 311 ff. How little he believed in it himself may be judged from his statement that Roehm and Schleicher deserved death for talking secretly with a foreign diplomat, even if it should transpire that 'they talked about nothing save the weather, old coins and like topics'. Ibid., pp. 323–4. Schleicher doubtless still had political ambitions—see 'Schleicher's Political Dream', *New Statesman and Nation*, 7 July 1934, and editorial comment in issue of 14 July—but the charges made by Hitler have been pretty conclusively disproved. See, *inter alia*, Bullock, *Hitler*, pp. 268–9.

[2] In the upper ranks of the army there was talk of an investigation of Schleicher's death and a protest to Hindenburg. In the end, the only defence of the dead officers was a statement by Field Marshal von Mackensen before the Vereinigung Graf Schlieffen to the effect that 'the personal honour' of Schleicher and Bredow had not been affected by their political activities. See Krausnick in *Vollmacht des Gewissens*, pp. 240 f.

[3] Rauschning, *Revolution of Nihilism*, p. 157. See also Rudolf Pechel, *Deutscher Widerstand* (Zürich, 1947), p. 138; Faber du Faur, *Macht und Ohnmacht*, p. 158.

[4] *Militärwochenblatt*, 119. Jg., Nr. 8 (25 Aug. 1934), 283–4; Ritter, *Goerdeler*, pp. 136 ff.

army. As far as we know, nothing had been said in the pre-Purge negotiations with Hitler about such a pledge; and, strictly speaking, there was no need for one. The army was already bound by a formula of 1 December 1933, in accordance with which its members swore 'as brave and obedient soldiers' to serve 'people and fatherland at all times'. The arguments of the *Militärwochenblatt*, that a new oath was necessary as a sign of the army's confidence in the Fuehrer and because the existing oath was a departure from the old Brandenburg-Prussian tradition of a personal tie between the ruler of the state and his soldiers,[1] do not provide a very plausible explanation for the change. It is more likely that Blomberg, who was the author of the new formula,[2] persuaded the *Heeresleitung* to offer it to Hitler in order to elicit a reciprocal declaration from him.

That declaration the Fuehrer gave. In a letter to Blomberg on 20 August—the day after a popular plebiscite had approved his amalgamation of the Presidency and the Chancellorship—he wrote:[3]

> Today . . . I want to thank you, and through you the Wehrmacht, for the oath of loyalty taken to me as its Fuehrer and Supreme Commander. Just as the officers and soldiers of the Wehrmacht have pledged themselves to the new State in my person, so will I at all times regard it as my highest duty to intercede in behalf of the stability and inviolability of the Wehrmacht, in fulfilment of the testament of the late *Generalfeldmarschall;* and, in accordance with my own desire, to fix [*verankern*] the army as the sole bearer of arms [*einzige Waffenträger*] in the nation.

In these last words—which, even as they were being written, were being contradicted by the favours Hitler was showering on Himmler's S.S.[4]—the army chiefs saw a binding promise of future security, and they doubtless believed that this justified

[1] *Militärwochenblatt*, 119. Jg., Nr. 8 (25 Aug. 1934), 283–4. 'Certainly', the editors wrote, 'loyalty to an idea or an institution is conceivable and possible, but it is the good old German tradition that [the military oath] is taken to the prince, the Fuehrer, as a person.' Thus, the oath of 1919, to the constitution, was 'an oath anyone could take' and the oath of December 1933 was not much better.

[2] See Bernhard Schwertfeger, 'Hindenburgs Tod und der Eid auf den Fuehrer', *Die Wandlung*, iii (1948), 563–77.

[3] Schwertfeger, *Rätsel um Deutschland*, p. 553.

[4] A few months after the oath was taken, a consignment of heavy arms was sent to the East Prussian S.S. The local Reichswehr commander protested but was ordered to give way by the Defence Ministry itself. See Rosinski, *German Army*, p. 118.

all their own acts of commission and omission during the past six months. They apparently did not see that they had already yielded ground to the tyrant which could never be recovered, that 'the inviolability of the Wehrmacht' had already been breached by the unpunished murder of Generals von Schleicher and Bredow, and that their old boast that the army stood above parties and represented the state alone had been fatally compromised by the new oath which they had taken so unhesitatingly. If they had pondered the passage in Hitler's letter in which he spoke of the Wehrmacht pledging itself 'to the new State *in my person*', they might have been less complacent as they looked to the future. Those few words expressed the totalitarian philosophy which was to destroy Germany. Yet, when Hitler's ambitions had brought the nation to the brink of disaster, the careless commitment of 2 August 1934 was to make effective preventive action by the army impossible.

II

In one of those rambling monologues to which he used to treat his dinner guests during the war years, Hitler made an interesting confession. He had, he admitted, sought in his first years of power to avoid any conflict with the Wehrmacht, but only until he was able to introduce conscription.

> Once that was accomplished, the influx into the Wehrmacht of the masses of the people, together with the spirit of National Socialism and with the ever-growing power of the National Socialist movement, would, I was sure, allow me to overcome all opposition among the armed forces, and in particular in the corps of officers.[1]

If this is an accurate description of Hitler's views in 1934 and 1935—and one can never be entirely sure of the reliability of Hitler's reminiscences—his estimate of the probable results of conscription was shrewd and was certainly borne out by the facts.

Any hope that the army could maintain its independence within the state and at the same time exercise a restraining influence on the policies of the nazi leader rested, in the last analysis, upon the ability of its leaders to maintain the unity and discipline of the officer corps. In Seeckt's time, there was

[1] *Hitler's Secret Conversations, 1941–1944.* With an introduction by H. R. Trevor Roper (New York, 1953), p. 403.

no doubt about this; but after his passing, and especially after 1930, there had been indications that sympathy for National Socialism was growing among the junior officers and that they were inclined to be increasingly critical of the more conservative views of their superiors. This tendency was probably checked to some extent by the S.A. crisis, which had the effect of closing army ranks against the party interlopers. In normal circumstances it might even have been checked definitively by the new chief of the army command, for Fritsch enjoyed greater respect and popularity among both junior officers and enlisted ranks than his easy-going predecessors, Heye and Hammerstein.[1] But, once the inflation of the army got under way, any hope of this disappeared.

Expansion began immediately after Germany's withdrawal from the Disarmament conference and the League of Nations in October 1933. In the course of the next year, the *Heeresleitung* formed cadres for twenty-four divisions, began the mechanization of part of the cavalry, and started to build up an air force. Before much progress had been made, however, Hitler had raised his sights. On 16 March 1935 he announced the unilateral repudiation of the military clauses of the Versailles Treaty, the re-introduction of universal conscription, and the prospective establishment of an army with a peace-time strength of thirty-six divisions. Within the next three years this figure was to be stepped up even further and, by the autumn of 1939, the army comprised fifty-two active divisions.

General Siegfried Westphal has given a graphic description of what this meant for the German officer corps. Of the 4,000 officers in the army in 1933, 450 were medical or veterinary officers. Of the remaining 3,550 active troop leaders and General Staff officers about 500 were transferred to the newly established *Luftwaffe* in 1934. That left only about 3,000 officers and, even when they had been supplemented by newly commissioned N.C.O.'s from the treaty army and about 1,000 police officers, who had been trained in army garrisons,[2] they were a totally inadequate basis for an army which was to be increased fourfold in four years. In that brief period 25,000 new officers had to be added to the rolls.[3]

[1] Kielmansegg, *Fritschprozeß*, p. 29; Siegfried Westphal, *Heer in Fesseln: Aus den Papieren des Stabschefs von Rommel, Kesselring und Rundstedt* (Bonn, 1950), p. 49.

[2] See above, Chapter X, pp. 404–5.

[3] Westphal, *Heer in Fesseln*, pp. 65–66.

In these circumstances it was impossible for the officer corps to exert the kind of unifying and formative influence upon the new arrivals that it had exerted during the rapid expansion of the 1880's and 1890's.[1] Inevitably the inner homogeneity of the officer corps dissolved, and its members came to possess widely different political views and social attitudes.[2] Moreover, after 1936, officer candidates, like the enlisted conscripts, were mostly youths who had been subjected to party indoctrination in school, and many of them were apt to be intolerant or contemptuous about everything in the past, including the traditions which Seeckt and his followers had cherished.[3] Nor was this the only thing that weakened the former unity of the officer corps. Even among the older officers professional standards and caste loyalties began to suffer. The breakneck rearmament, which opened a way to preferments to which junior officers in the early 1930's would never have dared aspire, let loose new and ugly passions. Ambition, jealousy, opportunism, willingness to seek outside aid in securing promotion—always present in military, and other, organizations—now permeated all ranks. In particular, there was a sharp increase in the number of those who were willing to seek a connexion with the nazis in the interest of self aggrandisement. In 1933 Reichenau had been one of very few officers regarded as pro-nazi; by 1936 there were hundreds like him. At the same time, many officers who were in their hearts opposed to Hitler and all he stood for now felt it expedient to keep their views to themselves, not knowing which of their fellows or superiors might be convinced nazis—or which, for that matter, might be S.S. agents, for it was known that Reinhard Heydrich, the Gestapo chief, was slipping his men into the regiments.[4]

Thus, the first effect of the rapid rearmament programme was

[1] See above, Chapter VI, pp. 236 ff.

[2] In an absorbing book, which reconstructs the events of these years in the form of a drama, General Adolf Heusinger has an officer say: 'The division of the officer corps becomes greater all the time. Against the few officers of the 100,000 man army stand the great number of newcomers. There are countless decent fellows among them but also many unknown quantities (*Nieten*). Party people, others who are only looking for personal advantage, and even people who have ruined their lives. Seeckt would be horrified. We need many, many years in order to integrate these alien elements.' Heusinger, *Befehl im Widerstreit: Schicksalsstunden der deutschen Armee, 1923–1945* (Tübingen and Stuttgart, 1950), pp. 43–44. See also p. 21.

[3] See Peter Bor, *Gespräche mit Halder* (Wiesbaden, 1950), pp. 106–7.

[4] See, *inter alia*, Rauschning, *Revolution of Nihilism*, pp. 152–6; Görlitz, *General Staff*, pp. 299–300.

to destroy the cohesiveness of the officer corps and to leave it a rather heterogeneous body whose members fell into three broad categories: a group, composed for the most part of the most senior officers, which remained true to the tradition of an autonomous army, standing aloof from the parties and devoting itself to the service of the state, and which was resolved to defend this tradition if it was possible to do so; a second group, constantly growing in size, of 'Party soldiers', who considered the complete nazification of the army as right and necessary and who were completely uncritical in their allegiance to the Fuehrer; and a large mass of neutralists, who did their jobs and, for the rest, rigorously abstained from expressing opinions on political or administrative problems, lest they jeopardize their careers.[1] With the officer corps thus split, Hitler was placed in an excellent position to assert his absolute dominance over the army and to purge it of unbelievers whenever he decided it was expedient to do so.

Hitler did not risk a real test of strength with the army until almost three years from the date of his repudiation of the Versailles military clauses, but during those years he became steadily more irritated with the army command and more contemptuous of the officers for whom he had once had such exaggerated respect.

There were a number of reasons for this. For one thing, there were profound differences of opinion between the Fuehrer and the *Heeresleitung* concerning the nature and extent of German rearmament. The army chiefs had not been consulted before Hitler's dramatic announcement of 16 March 1935, and they were quite as thunderstruck by it as the rest of the world. Their surprise passed more quickly than their misgivings concerning the possibility of attaining the goals set by Hitler. Fritsch believed that a threefold expansion was the most the army could undergo without a serious loss of efficiency and, although he finally concurred even in the re-introduction of two-year conscription in 1936, he did so with a lack of enthusiasm which

[1] Fabian von Schlabrendorff speaks of all Germany being divided into 'Nazis, *Nichtnazis* and anti-Nazis' and says bitterly, 'The *Nichtnazis* were almost worse than the Nazis. Their lack of character caused us more trouble than the despotism and brutality of the Nazis.' *Offiziere gegen Hitler* (Zürich, 1946), p. 16. See also General Hans Speidel, *Invasion 1944: ein Beitrag zu Rommels und des Reiches Schicksal* (Stuttgart, 1949), pp. 29–30, where the author differentiates between 'thinking soldiers', 'party soldiers', and '*Nur-Soldaten* (just soldiers)'.

puzzled and disgusted Hitler. Moreover, his direction of the rearmament programme was both too methodical and too economical for Hitler's taste. Fritsch believed in developing new units and supplying them systematically and was far more interested in building on old lines than in striking out on new. While Hitler's mind dwelt on the programme of mechanization and the rapid development of the tank and air arms, Fritsch tended to think of such things as heavy artillery, engineers, railroad troops, and communication services, which interested the Fuehrer far less.[1] Since most of Fritsch's experience had been in periods where the army budget was severely limited, he could not get used to Hitler's free and easy ways with money. Thus, Hitler was always protesting 'against the homeopathic-like quantities which the Wehrmacht demanded . . . today an order for ten howitzers, tomorrow for two mortars, and so on'.[2] All in all Hitler was led to the conclusion that the army chiefs were not sufficiently grateful for the opportunities he had given them and not imaginative enough to take advantage of them.

The *Heeresleitung*, on the other hand, was horrified by the pace set by Hitler—by the constant necessity of dividing established companies and batteries in two so that their parts could serve as the basis for new units, by Hitler's lack of interest in building up an army reserve, by the mechanization of units before tests had been made to establish its advisability, by the insistence upon the adoption of unproved weapons, and the tendency to rely upon what seemed to be unrealistic production estimates. As far as they could see, the army could not possibly solve the many problems raised by all this until the year 1943 and, in the immediate future, it would be in a dangerously disorganized condition. This belief led the army leaders to another conclusion which caused friction with Hitler: namely, that adventures in foreign policy must be avoided at all costs until army efficiency had been restored. This was Fritsch's own view, and it was also that of the Chief of the General Staff, Ludwig Beck, who was constantly warning his colleagues that the other Powers had come close to war with Germany during the abortive nazi *Putsch* in Vienna in July 1934 and that they

[1] Westphal, *Heer in Fesseln*, pp. 62–63; Liddell Hart, *Other Side of the Hill*, p. 38; Kielmansegg, *Fritschprozeß*, p. 28; Faber du Faur, *Macht und Ohnmacht*, p. 160.

[2] *Hitler's Secret Conversations*, pp. 514–15.

would certainly strike at the first evidence of German aggression.[1]

Hitler did not believe this, and he had no intention of allowing the soldiers to dictate Germany's foreign policy. His determination on this point was made abundantly clear in the spring of 1936 when he decided on his own initiative to repudiate the Locarno Treaty and to reoccupy the demilitarized Rhineland.

Perhaps nothing did more to destroy Hitler's respect for the generals than their behaviour on this occasion.[2] The orders to the army command were issued on 2 March and immediately elicited a flood of protests. Fritsch, Beck, and Blomberg tried to persuade the Fuehrer to alter the nature of the operation. Hitler rejected all of their suggestions, although he appears to have made a perhaps sarcastic promise to withdraw his troops in the event that the French sent an army into the area. When the German battalions moved into the Rhineland on 7 March, the agitation of the soldiers increased, as well it might, since they knew that there were no reserves available if fighting broke out. And for the moment it looked as if their fears might be justified. From London, ambassador Hoesch and his military attaché, Geyr von Schweppenburg, were cabling frantically that the chances of British intervention were at least 50:50—an intimation that so disconcerted Blomberg that he begged Hitler to withdraw the units which had crossed the Rhine and occupied Saarbrücken, Trier, and Aachen. The dire warnings of the soldiers momentarily impressed even Hitler. Far from demonstrating what he was later to describe as 'amazing aplomb',[3] he was decidedly nervous until the crisis was past. But he held firm and, in doing so, not only won his first great victory over the Western Powers, but also scored a decided moral victory over his military advisers. Never again did he place much stock in their predictions. They were, he believed, incurable pessimists, who need not be taken seriously.[4]

Aside from destroying his regard for the judgement and even

[1] See, for instance, his memorandum of 1934 in Wolfgang Foerster, *Ein General kämpft gegen den Krieg: Aus nachgelassenen Papieren des Generalstabschefs Ludwig Beck* (Munich, 1949), pp. 26–27.

[2] Bor, *Gespräche mit Halder*, p. 111.

[3] *Hitler's Secret Conversations*, p. 211.

[4] On the Rhineland affair, see the accounts in Hoßbach, *Zwischen Wehrmacht und Hitler*, and Geyr von Schweppenburg, *Erinnerungen eines Militärattachés, London 1933–1937* (Stuttgart, 1949). On the French side, see the interesting material in Assemblée nationale: Commission d'enquête parlementaire sur les événements survenus en France de 1933 à 1940: Rapport et Témoignages (Paris, 1951).

the courage of his soldiers,[1] the effect of the Rhineland affair was to increase Hitler's faith in what he described, in a speech of 15 March 1936, as his '*schlafwandlerische Sicherheit* (sleep-walker's assurance)' in foreign affairs.[2] Almost immediately, he plunged into a new venture which disturbed the military chiefs. In July 1936, immediately after the outbreak of the civil war in Spain, he began to send military assistance to the insurgent cause.

The aid to Franco was admittedly on a small scale, being confined for the most part to weapons shipments, a tank battalion led by General von Thoma—which was used primarily to train Spanish armoured units[3]—and the so-called Condor Legion, which comprised four fighter-bomber, four fighter, one reconnaissance, and two seaplane squadrons detached from the *Luftwaffe*.[4] But the army was not reassured by this. However small the shipments to Spain, they represented a dangerous drain on Germany's military resources during the most critical period of her own rearmament.[5] Moreover, it was no secret that some elements in the party were eager for greater involvement in Spain. Hitler's first ambassador to the Burgos government, the former free corps leader Faupel, not only wanted the army to send as many as four divisions of infantry troops to the Iberian peninsula but wished them to fight under his own command. To block schemes like this, the top officials of the War Ministry seem to have worked in secret collaboration with the Foreign Office, where the Spanish adventure was also unpopular, and, in the end, they managed to undermine Faupel's position and force his retirement.[6] Despite this success, however, the Spanish affair remained, at least until mid-1937, a source of constant disquiet to Fritsch and Beck, who never knew when it might not precipitate a major war for which they were not prepared.

The attitude of the army leadership is well expressed in a memorandum which Beck handed to his chief in January 1937.[7]

[1] Foertsch, *Schuld und Verhängnis*, p. 74.

[2] Bullock, *Hitler*, p. 343.

[3] See Liddell Hart, *Other Side of the Hill*, pp. 122–3. By dilution of German personnel, Thoma had four battalions of tanks under his command by 1938, plus thirty anti-tank companies.

[4] Görlitz, *General Staff*, p. 307.

[5] See *Jodl Diary*, entries of 14 January, 27 March, 30 March 1937.

[6] See *Documents on German Foreign Policy, 1918–1945* (Washington, D.C., 1949 ff.), series D, iii. 50, 149, 168.

[7] Foerster, *Ein General kämpft*, pp. 44–47.

The Chief of the General Staff took as his theme the proposition that 'the Wehrmacht today bears 100 per cent. the responsibility for all or any warlike developments' and, in lines which implied the strongest criticism of the foreign policy of the Reich, laid down the reasons why the army must oppose any move which might invite war. Despite the government's success in building up German industry and alleviating unemployment, the nation was in a situation in which reserves of raw materials and food supplies were being consumed as fast as they were accumulated.

> Experts have made the point that the situation of 1936 was like that of 1917. . . . We are entering the new year without food reserves; the harvest expectations have proved to be illusory; we will not be able to reach the new harvest without stretching things; and increased imports of fats—and, this time, of grains, too—are anticipated. If it should come to developments of a warlike nature in May or June of 1937, our position would be inconceivable.'

Moreover, Beck added, when one speaks of war, he should remember that the important thing is the morale of the people. 'Today an anxious disquietude affects the masses; they fear war; . . . they see no justifiable grounds for war.' If a conflict comes, the army will be blamed for it, for

> our people in their *pietas* towards the army (*unser militärfrommes Volk*) place a confidence in the Wehrmacht which hardly knows limits. . . .[1] Almost exclusively upon the army rests the responsibility for coming events. In face of this truth there can be no evasion.

No warlike developments did come in May or June, and the tension in Wehrmacht headquarters began to relax as the months passed without major international incident. Yet Beck's apprehensions were well founded. There was no stopping Hitler now. He had tested the Western Powers' will to resistance in the Rhineland and Spain; he saw no reason to believe that they would stand up to him any more firmly in the future than they had in the past; and he began to feel that the time had now come to implement the ideas of expansion in eastern Europe which he had first sketched in *Mein Kampf* in the 1920's. On 5 November 1937, in a now famous conference with his military and diplomatic aides, the Fuehrer announced that 'the aim of German policy was to make secure and to preserve the racial

[1] This sentence is cited in L. B. Namier, *In the Nazi Era* (London, 1952), p. 13, and I have used his translation.

community, and to enlarge it. It was, therefore, a matter of space', which must be acquired, by force if necessary, in Europe. Germany's first objective, he announced, was the absorption of Austria and Czechoslovakia. It was his 'unalterable resolve to solve Germany's problem of space at the latest by 1943–1945'; but such solution would come sooner if domestic events in the western countries or the development of differences between Britain, France, and Italy presented a suitable opportunity.[1]

In the long discussion that followed Hitler's initial statement, Blomberg, Fritsch, the Foreign Minister Neurath, and even Goering seem to have expressed doubts or raised questions concerning the advisability of proceeding with any such programme.[2] The soldiers especially pressed Hitler hard on certain points: the absolute necessity of avoiding a situation which would lead to joint Anglo-French intervention; the inadvisability of relying on Italy's power to prevent France from attacking Germany's western frontiers in superior strength even in the event of a simultaneous Franco-Italian war; the present weakness of Germany's western fortifications; the dangers of underestimating the strength of Czechoslovakia's 'little Maginot line'; and much else. These observations must have struck Hitler as the replaying of a record which he had heard in March 1936, and his reaction to it this time was one of deep resentment. For the moment he hid this, answering the points raised civilly enough and even reassuring Fritsch, who asked if he should postpone the leave which he was to begin on 10 November, by saying that he planned no action in the immediate future. But it is almost certain that it was the cool reception which the soldiers gave to his views that persuaded him that the time had come to show the army leadership that he was its master and that its duty was obedience rather than criticism.[3]

Other factors probably played a part in Hitler's decision. For one thing, he was perhaps influenced by the insinuations which Heinrich Himmler and his associate Heydrich had been making for some time against the army and especially against Fritsch. For this undercover campaign Heydrich had private

[1] *Documents on German Policy*, series D, i. 29 ff.

[2] Only Admiral Raeder seems to have been completely silent, although Goering only questioned the advisability of action before the German forces had returned from Spain.

[3] It is perhaps significant that the first rumours that Fritsch was on his way out began to circulate in November. See Kielmansegg, *Fritschprozeß*, p. 34.

reasons—he had been dismissed from the officer corps on a morals charge and was resolved to avenge this—while to Himmler it was part of a systematic effort to extend the control of the S.S. over the armed forces. Himmler had doggedly pursued this objective ever since the Blood Purge of 1934. His first success had come during the aftermath of that event, when he was given the right to form three regiments of S.S. General Service troops (S.S. *Verfügungstruppen*) which were to be reserved for police operations.[1] The army had agreed to this reluctantly and, ever since, had viewed Himmler's efforts to expand these forces with the gravest suspicion. On the one hand, Fritsch refused to permit the special regiments to assume military functions or even to practise military ceremonial, forbidding them, for instance, to perform the ancient and cherished army torchlight ceremony, the *Zapfenstreich*; on the other, he constantly pressed for an admission that, if and when war came, the S.S. troops would pass immediately under army command. To Himmler, whose ambitions now ran considerably farther than Roehm's had, and who hoped ultimately to subordinate all of the armed forces to his personal control, Fritsch became an object of special detestation, a man who must be removed at all costs.

The S.S. chief, then, took every opportunity to intimate to Hitler that the army was a hatching ground for plots against him and that Fritsch was the chief conspirator. There was, it must hastily be said, nothing to this. Far from being a conspirator, Fritsch might more accurately be described as a complete defeatist, believing that Hitler was 'Germany's destiny for good or evil'. He refrained from political speculation and timidly shunned relationships which might be believed to be political. He once wrote, with perhaps an unconscious reference to Schleicher's fate, 'I never go out. I decline all [invitations from] foreign ambassadors as a matter of principle, and I never invite them myself.' To an American correspondent who asked him about army influence in foreign policy, he answered curtly, 'The army does not mix in politics'.[2] This was no political general, and Hitler had nothing to fear from him.

On the other hand, so persistent was the belief abroad that

[1] Wheeler-Bennett, *Nemesis of Power*, p. 341. For army concern over the increased strength of the S.S., see Krausnick in *Vollmacht des Gewissens*, pp. 253 f.

[2] Kielmansegg, *Fritschprozeß*, p. 30. See, however, Pechel, *Deutscher Widerstand*, pp. 139–40.

the army would one day 'deal with' Hitler that Fritsch's name constantly figured in journalists' accounts of non-existent plots; while, even in Germany, critics of the régime often said hopefully that Fritsch 'werde es schon machen'.[1] The S.S. leaders did not hesitate to advance this as proof of their highly coloured charges against the chief of the army command, and, although Hitler probably did not fully believe their stories, he must certainly have been irritated by this evidence of the high regard in which Fritsch was held and angered by the knowledge that there were people who actually believed that a general would dare to rise against him.

Finally, Fritsch's essential decency played into the hands of his enemies. A profoundly religious man, he was revolted by the religious programme of the National Socialist party, and especially by the so-called 'German Christian' movement, which distorted and paganized Christianity, attacked the established churches, and propagated its doctrines in the schools. Characteristically, he did not give personal expression to his feelings, but he did not object when others in the army did. There were many officers who felt as strongly as he did on this subject and, in the latter half of 1937, a rage of church-going swept the army. In the garrisons, church parade became obligatory, and battalion commanders who had previously not been remarkable for their piety attended with notebooks in which to jot down the names of lieutenants in their command who were absent.

This protest was given sharper form at the end of the year when the Protestant army chaplains drew up a memorandum which they were permitted to send to the Fuehrer, in which they strongly attacked the party's anti-religious policy and said: 'The Party and State today combat not only the churches. They combat Christianity. . . . The situation has become wholly intolerable.' Since this document appeared in the foreign press,[2] it amounted to a public demonstration against the régime. The S.S. chiefs, who were actively promoting the crusade against religion, made the most of it; and there can be little doubt that, coming as it did on the heels of the meeting of 5 November, the

[1] Westphal, *Heer in Fesseln*, p. 49.

[2] It was printed in the *New York Times* of 29 November 1937. See also *The Times* (London), 6 December 1937 and 10 February 1938; and, in general, Micklem, *National Socialism and the Roman Catholic Church* (New York, 1939), especially pp. 47, 107 ff., 143, 201–2, and Westphal, *Heer in Fesseln*, p. 21.

incident further inflamed Hitler's anger at the army leadership and further inclined him to action against it.

Moreover, he was resolved to act quickly now, for—despite his assurance to Fritsch on 5 November—he was already revising his foreign policy time-table. Two weeks after the conference with the generals, Hitler received a visit from Lord Halifax, and what the British statesman had to say persuaded him that he could safely accelerate his pace. The Halifax mission was the opening gun in Neville Chamberlain's campaign to solve all European problems, in Halifax's words, 'on the basis of realism, even if the realities to be dealt with were unpleasant for one party or another'. It rapidly appeared that there was no reason for the Germans to fear any of this unpleasantness, for, when he turned to concrete European problems,

> Halifax admitted of his own accord that certain changes . . . could probably not be avoided in the long run. The British did not believe that the *status quo* had to be maintained in all circumstances. Among the questions in which changes would probably be made sooner or later were Danzig, Austria and Czechoslovakia.[1]

On top of this comforting disclosure came equally heartening news from France. The German ambassador in Paris reported that the French Foreign Minister, Delbos, had admitted that, while France was not disinterested in central Europe, 'she had no essential objection to a further assimilation of certain of Austria's domestic relations with Germany's'.[2] This was almost too good to be true;[3] and there seemed to be no excuse for further delaying the drive to the east. Still, before it could be launched, it would be prudent to put the military house in order. The time had come when it was necessary to have an army which knew the meaning of 'positive loyalty'. Reasonably certain that he could rely on the rank and file and on the junior officers, Hitler decided to purge the upper echelon of his military establishment.

An occasion for this was provided in January 1938 when it became widely known that Field Marshal von Blomberg's second marriage, contracted the previous month, was a *mésalliance* of the most embarrassing kind. The fact that the Minister of War

[1] *Documents on German Policy*, series D, i. 69–70. [2] Ibid., p. 83.

[3] For other reports that may have encouraged Hitler, see Gordon A. Craig, 'High Tide of Appeasement: The Road to Munich, 1937–1938', *Political Science Quarterly*, lxv (1950), 23–24.

had married a woman with a police record compromised the honour and tradition of the whole officer corps; and, at Beck's insistence, Fritsch went to Hitler and convinced him that Blomberg must go.[1] This raised the question of succession to his post, and Fritsch himself was the obvious choice. But Himmler was determined to prevent his appointment and laid before Hitler a *dossier* purporting to show that Fritsch was guilty of homosexual practices. There is reason to believe that these charges had been known to Hitler for at least two years,[2] and his failure to act upon them previously indicates that he knew they were false, as they were subsequently proven to be. But they served his purpose now. In a dramatic scene at the *Reichskanzlei*, Fritsch was identified by an accuser provided by Himmler and Heydrich, and, as he choked with fury, Hitler demanded that he resign.

Here again was one of those moments in the history of the Third Reich when decisive action might have radically changed the course of future events. The atmosphere in Berlin in the last days of January 1938 was not unlike that on the eve of the purge of 1934;[3] and the air was filled with rumours to the effect that the army at long last was prepared to make its stand against the tyrant. Yet once again the moment was allowed to pass. Fritsch himself, shaken by the confrontation in the *Reichskanzlei*, now showed how illusory were all the hopes placed in him. It is possible that he might have brought most of the officer corps to his side if he had raised the standard of revolt. Whether the army as a whole would have followed him is more difficult to say, and he made no attempt to find out. In 1926 he had had no hesitation about urging Seeckt to employ force to prevent his dismissal; in June 1938 he was to admit that he himself should have done the same thing;[4] but at the moment of decision, in January, he could not convince himself that action was either feasible or advisable. The German people, he told himself, was too much under Hitler's spell to understand or support a

[1] *Jodl Diary*, entry for 26 January. He found that Goering had been ahead of him.

[2] Ibid., entry for 28 January; Kielmansegg, *Fritschprozeß*, pp. 44–45, 105; H. Rosenberger in *Deutsche Rundschau*, November 1946.

[3] Karl Heinz Abshagen, *Canaris* (Stuttgart, 1949), p. 177.

[4] Kielmansegg, *Fritschprozeß*, p. 122. Thus, Fritsch joined the distinguished company of Groener, who admitted that he should have acted in 1932 (Meinecke, *Deutsche Katastrophe*, p. 74), and Hammerstein, who regretted not having acted in January 1933.

military *Putsch*, least of all one led by an officer with criminal charges hanging over him. The charges, of course, were false, but—. And in any case there was the oath of August 1934, and no Fritsch could in honour break his oath. Overwhelmed by the enormity of Hitler's conduct toward him, Germany's first soldier meekly submitted his resignation.[1]

And, if Fritsch would not act, none of the commanding generals was prepared to do so.[2] They were imperfectly informed about what was going on and in a state of high confusion. Some of those who did know of the charges against Fritsch were indignant but cautious. One of the lessons that Hitler has taught our generation is that, if a falsehood is fantastic enough, it is apt to make people suspect that there may be a kernel of truth in it. In 1938 this suspicion doubtless occurred to some of the generals and lamed their will to action.[3] Meanwhile, those who were in Berlin, at least, allowed themselves to be drawn into discussions about successors for Blomberg and Fritsch and, when Hitler slyly suggested that Reichenau might be the man for one or the other post,[4] they were so alarmed that they drifted away from the main point at issue—which was, after all, the slanderous attack upon the reputation of their commander and, by implication at least, upon their collective honour. In their anxiety to block Reichenau, and even more dangerous candidates,[5] they were manœuvred into agreeing to the appointment of Walter von Brauchitsch as Fritsch's successor; and they failed to see, until it was too late, that Brauchitsch had been nominated by Hitler because he, like Paul Bronsart von Schellendorf in 1883,[6] was perfectly willing to emasculate his office before he assumed it. Indeed, when Brauchitsch was first approached on 28 January[7]

[1] Kielmansegg, *Fritschprozeß*, pp. 120–1; Krausnick in *Vollmacht des Gewissens*, pp. 286–9.

[2] Görlitz, *General Staff*, p. 319; Ritter, *Goerdeler*, pp. 144–7.

[3] Wheeler-Bennett (*Nemesis of Power*, p. 369) says that Beck wished to strike against Hitler on 27 January. This is supported neither by Kielmansegg nor by Foerster. One gathers from Foerster's account that Beck was completely confused, that he had at least two interviews with Hitler on the matter and that it was not until later that he was freed from the belief that Hitler had acted in good faith. *Ein General kämpft*, pp. 70–71.

[4] Hitler told Keitel on 27 January that Reichenau was 'too superficial—too jumpy', yet on the following day professed to want him as Fritsch's successor. *Jodl Diary*, 27 and 28 January. See also Foertsch, *Schuld und Verhängnis*, pp. 103 ff.

[5] Goering's name, and even Himmler's, seem to have appeared in the discussions. Blomberg, indeed, nominated Goering as his own successor.

[6] See above, Chapter VI, pp. 229–30.

[7] It is perhaps significant that Hitler did not admit the possibility of Brauchitsch's

by General Keitel, the head of the *Wehrmachtamt*, who had been authorized by Hitler to conduct negotiations with candidates for Fritsch's position, he promised that, if he were appointed, he would make every effort to bring the army closer to the State and the State's ideology and, in the next few days, he agreed without hesitation to far-reaching administrative and personnel changes in the army. As Keitel's confidant Jodl wrote in his diary, Brauchitsch was ready to agree to everything.[1] This was, indeed, to be his outstanding trait throughout his three years' tenure of office.

It was not until 4 February 1938—long after the tactical moment for action had passed—that the generals learned the full and humiliating details of what was in store for them. On that day, the Fuehrer announced the resignations of Blomberg and Fritsch, the appointment of Brauchitsch as commander-in-chief of the army, and the promotion of Hermann Goering to the rank of field marshal. Blomberg was to have no successor. Instead, Hitler decreed,

> Henceforth I will personally exercise immediate command over the whole armed forces. The former *Wehrmachtamt* in the War Ministry becomes the High Command of the Armed Forces (*Oberkommando der Wehrmacht*), and comes immediately under my command as my military staff.

This intimation that the General Staff of the army was to be superseded, or at least reduced in importance, by a new creation was made doubly galling by the appointment of Keitel, a man of no character and a thorough-going admirer of Hitler, as the head of the O.K.W. Keitel was given rank equivalent to that of Reich Minister and was authorized, as Hitler's deputy, to exercise the former functions of the War Minister. Finally, the retirement of thirteen high ranking generals—including such friends and supporters of Fritsch as Leeb, Kleist, Lutz, Kress von Kressenstein, Pogrell, Liese and Niebelschütz—and the transfer of forty-four others to new duties was announced. These were the personnel changes agreed to by Brauchitsch, and they represented a purging of the potentially dissident elements in the higher ranks of the officer corps.[2]

appointment until 31 January in a discussion with Beck and General von Rundstedt. Wheeler-Bennett, *Nemesis of Power*, pp. 370–1; Foertsch, *Schuld und Verhängnis*, pp. 102–3.

[1] *Jodl Diary*, entries of 28 and 29 January.

[2] For the public announcement, see the *Berliner Tageblatt*, 5 February 1938. The

There was no disguising the crushing nature of this defeat at Hitler's hands. The Austrian corporal, whom the generals had permitted to come to power in 1933 because they were sure they could control him and whom they had, they believed, forced to do their bidding in June 1934, had now dropped the mask and revealed what had been his intentions with respect to the army ever since he had come to power. The time had come at last when the army, like every other institution in the country, had to submit to the process of *Gleichschaltung*. And that meant an end to the old conception of the army as a state within the state. It was now painfully clear that in the National Socialist state the army was expected to be a body not only of efficient technicians but also of true believers; and those who were unwilling to accept these conditions could expect to be dealt with as were Fritsch and the sixteen generals who followed him into retirement.

That was the essential meaning of the decrees of 4 February. The Fuehrer, as has been well said, 'had outmanœuvred, defeated, humiliated and dragooned the German army'.[1] And these indignities, in which the army acquiesced, were the forerunners of worse indignities to come.

III

In one of the many books written by German soldiers since the end of the war, General Friedrich Hoßbach has sought to place the blame for everything that happened up to 1938 upon the shoulders of Werner von Blomberg and for everything that happened thereafter on the heads of Brauchitsch and his chief of staff Franz Halder. Of Blomberg he has written:[2]

> The fund of trust which the German people, since earliest times and since and despite the loss of the war in 1918, placed in the soldier involved for Blomberg the moral obligation of being the attorney of reason and of forming a barrier against totalitarian claims on the part of the State. It is the tragedy of modern German

New Statesman and Nation in its issue of 12 February said, 'Hitler's second purge shows an immense advance in poise and technique over his previous performance. . . . The June massacre made an impression of panic; it was the act of a young and insecure despotism.' Now, 'the Totalitarian State has achieved something approaching final perfection'. To leave the purged generals alive, for instance, was a sign not of weakness but of self-confidence.

[1] Wheeler-Bennett, *Nemesis of Power*, p. 373.

[2] Hoßbach, *Zwischen Wehrmacht und Hitler*, p. 76.

history that Blomberg was, neither as a soldier nor as a statesman, a strong personality, forceful and creative, guiding and leading. His intelligence lacked the foundation of a firm character.

As to Brauchitsch and Halder, Hoßbach charges that they 'placed the reputation of the High Command at the disposal of an immoral political leadership and weakly gambled it away. . . . In respect to the security of the nation, they failed to exert their political, military and moral responsibility.'[1]

No one who reflects upon the history of the nazi era will feel disposed to quarrel with these strictures at least as far as they apply to Blomberg and Brauchitsch.[2] Yet there is, of course, little justification for making them bear the full weight of responsibility. Everything that Hoßbach says of them applies with equal force to many others—indeed, to the great majority of the commanding officers of the German army. Individually and collectively, they shirked their obligations to the German people.

So grave a charge should not be made idly, least of all by an historian. Yet is it not the historical record that validates the accusation? For three hundred years the army had claimed that it was the truest embodiment of the state and the ordained protector of the national interest, and, in return for its services in this capacity, it had demanded and obtained special rights and privileges. It had fought implacably, and on the whole successfully, to maintain this preferred position and, in the course of doing so, had vitiated all attempts to create a viable democracy in Germany. Thus, it was largely due to its efforts that the German people were deprived of the most effective defence that any people can have against the excesses of absolutism and the whims of dictatorship; and, because this was true, the army necessarily incurred the obligation to protect the German people from such things. The very fact that the army had sponsored the rise of Hitler to power in 1933 made that obligation a heavier one. At the very least, the *militärfrommes Volk* had a right to expect its army to remain true to its own political traditions and

[1] Ibid., p. 202.

[2] With respect to Halder, these views would appear to call for modification. See Martin Horn, *Halder, Schuld oder Tragik* (München, 1948) and, especially, Kurt Sendtner, 'Die deutsche Militäropposition im ersten Kriegsjahr', in *Vollmacht des Gewissens*, pp. 480 ff.

to prevent Hitler from acting in a way calculated to destroy the national interest.

Perhaps one should say 'try to prevent Hitler', for it is possible that, in view of the strength of the nazi régime by 1938 and the growth of National Socialist convictions even in the army, no conceivable action by the generals could have succeeded in preventing him from doing precisely what he did do to Germany. But the important point here is that the great majority of those who were in a position to take action neither did so nor recognized that they had any obligation to do so; and it is in this failure that the responsibility of the officer corps lies.

Whatever excuses existed for inactivity before 1938 were invalidated by the decrees of 4 February and by the events that followed immediately thereafter. The reorganization of the High Command had been influenced to a large degree by Hitler's rage at the lack of enthusiasm which his soldiers showed when he revealed his foreign policy plans to them on 5 November. It was a brutal warning that henceforth the army was to have no opinions on foreign policy but was merely to execute the plans laid before it; and it was driven home by the peremptory orders, handed to the generals on 9 March, for the occupation of Austria and, after that *coup* succeeded, the directive a month later for the preparation of a campaign against Czechoslovakia.

To one man at least the role in which Hitler had cast the army, that of passive executor of his grandiose designs, was insupportable. The Chief of the General Staff, Ludwig Beck—whom Meinecke includes among 'those unfortunately not very numerous ranking officers who could count as the true heirs of Scharnhorst'[1]—had felt that even the Austrian operation was an unjustified gamble for the army in its current state of preparedness (an opinion corroborated by the tangle into which the German armoured column managed to get itself on the Linz road)[2] and he believed that a drive against Czechoslovakia would precipitate a war which would destroy his country. It was, he felt, inconceivable that German soldiers, who knew the limitations of the nation's military resources, should close their

[1] Meinecke, *Deutsche Katastrophe*, p. 146.

[2] Although this has been hotly denied by German tank commanders, it has been supported by Hitler himself, who said in 1942: 'On the stretch from Linz to Vienna we saw over eighty tanks immobilized by the side of the road—and yet what an easy road it was!' *Hitler's Secret Conversations*, p. 164.

minds to the inevitable consequences of Hitler's orders and simply obey them.

Beck's own position is made clear in a statement to Brauchitsch, which deserves to be quoted at length, if only because it was not accepted by the majority of his fellows.[1]

> What are at stake here [he said in July 1938] are decisions which in the last analysis affect the existence of the nation. History will burden [the highest commanders of the army] with blood guilt if they do not act in accordance with their professional and political knowledge and conscience. Their soldier's duty of obedience has its limit at that point where their knowledge, their conscience and their responsibility forbids the execution of a command.
>
> If, in such a case, their advice and warnings are not listened to, then they have the right and the duty before their people and before history to resign their commands. If they all act with a determined will, the execution of an act of war becomes impossible. In this way they save the fatherland from the worst possible fate, from destruction.
>
> Any soldier who holds a leading position and at the same time limits his duty and task to his military charge, without being conscious of his supreme responsibility to the nation, shows lack of greatness and of understanding of his task.

Beck strove with all his might to make his chief Brauchitsch and other of the commanding generals see his point, and he succeeded at least in persuading a group of them to meet with Hitler and to express their misgivings concerning his course. At this meeting, which took place at Jüterborg on 15 August, Hitler dismissed all his generals' doubts, while at the same time making no secret of his irritation at the necessity of doing so. His attitude left Brauchitsch disinclined to any further efforts along the lines suggested by Beck; and, on 18 August, the Chief of Staff handed in his resignation in disgust.[2]

He was succeeded by Franz Halder, an able soldier and a confirmed foe of Hitler ever since the blood purge of 1934. Halder felt as strongly as Beck had done that the Fuehrer must be prevented from precipitating a war that could lead only to national disaster; and, at least in the period before the Munich conference, he was willing to use more direct measures to prevent it than those advocated by his predecessor. In the tense autumn weeks of 1938 Halder co-operated with resistance

[1] Förster, *Ein General kämpft*, p. 103.

[2] See Krausnick in *Vollmacht des Gewissens*, pp. 326, 330.

forces within the Foreign Ministry who were trying to warn government circles in London that Hitler could be stopped now only by unflinching opposition, and simultaneously made feverish preparations for a *coup de main* against Hitler in case war actually came. Tentative plans were laid for a military seizure of power to be directed by General von Witzleben, commander of Wehrkreis III Berlin, and executed by the Potsdam (23.) Division of Generalmajor Graf Brockdorff-Ahlefeldt; the co-operation of Graf Helldorf, the Berlin Polizeipräsident, was confidently expected; General Adam, the commander of the western armies, had promised his support; and a special force was being organized to carry out the arrest of Hitler himself.[1] How reliable these arrangements would have been if they had been tried, it is impossible to tell. The important thing about them is that they would have come into effect only if Hitler tried to go to war; and, when the western cave-in at Munich averted that possibility, they were abandoned.

The most fateful effect of Munich was that it became an excuse for inactivity on the part of the soldiers.[2] From now on Brauchitsch and his associates took the position that resistance to Hitler was impossible, at least until he had suffered a crushing defeat in the diplomatic or military field which would destroy his prestige with the people and the troops.

It must, of course, be admitted that it was much more difficult to plan resistance after Munich than before.[3] Even so, the post-Munich attitude is hard to defend. Its essential irresponsibility is evident as soon as we remember that there was now little likelihood of any diplomatic alignment arising which would defeat, or even impress, Hitler, while there was a certainty of war unless the soldiers acted to prevent it. And the kind of war that Hitler had in mind would be no limited conflict which would produce a minor setback and enable the soldiers to disembarrass themselves of the Fuehrer. By May 1939, at least, the soldiers must have known that Hitler was thinking in the most grandiose terms. For, in that month, he told them of his plans 'to attack Poland at the first opportunity', spoke

[1] On Halder's 1938 plans, see Krausnick in *Vollmacht des Gewissens*, pp. 332–64; and Ritter, *Goerdeler*, pp. 183–96.

[2] On 29 September 1938 Jodl expressed the hope in his diary that doubters and unbelievers would now be converted to faith in Hitler; and he was not to be disappointed.

[3] Ritter, *Goerdeler*, pp. 224–9.

blithely of the possibility of Britain and France entering the war, and talked of the necessity of occupying Dutch and Belgian bases as a protective measure as soon as the fighting began. And three months later, the vaulting ambitions of the Fuehrer were even more starkly revealed. On 22 August, in a statement to the leading commanders of his three services, he informed them of the pact about to be concluded with the Soviet Union, stated that this now made possible a war of extermination against the Poles but added that, in due course, 'we will crush the Soviet Union' as well. Here was a vision of unlimited, ever expanding war, war against all the Powers, war which could only end in total disaster. But no voices were raised in protest on 22 August, although the shape of that ultimate catastrophe must have loomed before the faces of many of the soldiers present.

And, having failed to act to prevent the war, the majority of Germany's commanders failed also to act to stop it, even after the first exhilarating victories had passed away and the period of attrition and defeat had set in. While Beck and his devoted followers kept the flame of resistance alive, their fellows for the most part abandoned themselves to competition for the professional spoils of war, answering appeals from opposition leaders evasively, if they answered them at all.[1] Not even the growing contempt that Hitler evinced toward them[2] and the insults and abuse he heaped on them—like his assumption of personal command over the army in 1941 with the words 'This little affair of operational command is something anyone can do!'[3] or his cashiering of General Heim before Stalingrad for failure to execute commands impossible of execution[4]—stayed them in their course. Their attitude was felt as a betrayal by many who had long put their trust in the army and who now began to blame Germany's sufferings on the generals as much as on Hitler. Of such critics, Goerdeler wrote in 1943, 'Es sind nicht törichte Männer, die das sagen; es sind Männer, die ein warmes Herz für Deutschland und für den deutschen Soldaten haben, die aber darüber verzweifeln, daß man sehenden Augens, denkenden Verstandes und fühlenden Herzens von Verbrechern

[1] On this attitude of Paulus and Manstein in 1942, see Ritter, *Goerdeler*, pp. 342 ff.

[2] 'I distrust officers who have exaggeratedly theoretical minds', Hitler said in 1942. *Hitler's Secret Conversations*, p. 187. He implemented this distrust by a deliberate reduction of the functions of the General Staff. See Westphal, *Heer in Fesseln*, p. 97.

[3] Wheeler-Bennett, *Nemesis of Power*, p. 255.

[4] Bor, *Gespräche mit Halder*, pp. 222–4.

und Narren das Vaterland in den Abgrund führen und die deutsche Jugend und die deutschen Männer willenlos in Tod und Verstümmelung treiben läßt'.[1]

It was, indeed, only when the allied landings in North Africa and the defeat at Stalingrad showed what lay at the end of the road that the generals began to talk of active resistance. In his brilliant study of the events leading up to the officers' revolt of July 1944, John Wheeler-Bennett says that, in 1943, 'the number of converts to Opposition became positively embarrassing';[2] but he makes it clear also that there were many more who talked about it than who were willing to act. When it came to the sticking point, the courage of many failed, while to others the oath of 2 August 1934 presented an insuperable obstacle. These last were willing to act, provided someone disposed of Hitler first, but they would not violate their solemn obligation to their supreme commander while he was living. One can appreciate the moral dilemma in which they found themselves,[3] even if one happens to believe that, in contrast to Beck's essentially Christian attitude, those who held to their fealty to a man who himself recognized no moral obligations were imprisoned by an outworn feudal philosophy. Yet surely there is much justification for the comment of a German writer who says:[4]

> It is astonishing that the generals always speak only of their military duty toward their superiors but not of their duty to the soldiers entrusted to them, most of whom were the flower of the people. One can certainly not require anyone to kill the tyrant, if his conscience forbids him to do so. But must not one require of these men that they expend the same care and scrupulousness on the life of every single man among their subordinates? The reproach of not having prevented the slaughter of many hundreds of thousands of German soldiers must weigh heavily on the conscience of every single German general.

This statement assumes added weight when one recalls that, even when they became nominal members of the opposition, the generals continued to fight for Hitler, despite the fact that they had lost confidence in his conduct of the war, despite the

[1] Ritter, *Goerdeler*, p. 354.

[2] Wheeler-Bennett, *Nemesis of Power*, p. 695.

[3] It is well described in Heusinger, *Befehl im Widerstreit*, pp. 386–8.

[4] Helmut Lindemann, 'Die Schuld der Generäle', *Deutsche Rundschau*, January, 1949.

fact that his intervention in tactical matters violated their professional standards, despite the fact that his explicit order that there must be 'No operations!' and that every inch of ground must be held to the bitter end meant the needless loss of German lives. They fought on while they considered whether they should join the conspiracy; they fought on when the attempt on Hitler's life was made and failed; they fought on while the new wave of proscriptions passed over the officer corps; and they were still fighting hopelessly amid the ruins of their country when Hitler put a bullet through the roof of his own mouth in the bunker in Berlin.

To the very end the commanders of Germany's armies showed the technical virtuosity and the physical courage which had always, since the recovery from Jena and Auerstädt, been characteristic of the Prussian officer corps. But what most of them failed to demonstrate in these last desperate years was what they had failed to demonstrate when Hitler stood on the threshold of the chancellorship in 1933, what they had failed to demonstrate when he loosed his murderers on the land in June 1934, what they had failed to demonstrate when Schleicher was killed and Fritsch disgraced: namely, any trace of the moral courage, the spiritual independence, and the deep patriotism which had marked the careers of such great soldiers of the past as Scharnhorst, Boyen, and Gneisenau. Without these things, their other gifts were without value; and they themselves were powerless to avert the disaster which had been so largely the result of their political irresponsibility.

ALPHABETICAL LIST OF BOOKS AND ARTICLES CITED

ABSHAGEN, KARL HEINZ, *Canaris* (Stuttgart, 1949).

ALBERTINI, LUIGI, *Le origini della guerra del 1914* (3 vols., Milan, 1942 ff.).

ALTROCK, CONSTANTIN VON, 'Jena und Auerstädt. Ein Rückblick und Ausblick', *Militärwochenblatt* (Beihefte, 1907).

—— *Vom Sterben des deutschen Offizierkorps* (Berlin, 1922).

ANDERSON, EUGENE N., *Nationalism and the Cultural Crisis in Prussia, 1806–1815* (New York, 1939).

—— *The Social and Political Conflict in Prussia, 1858–1864* (Lincoln, Nebraska, 1954).

ANGRESS, WERNER T., 'Weimar Coalition and Ruhr Insurrection', *Journal of Modern History*, xxix (1957).

ANSCHÜTZ, G., *Die Verfassungsurkunde des preußischen Staates* (Leipzig, 1912).

Assemblée nationale: Commission d'enquête parlémentaire sur les événements survenus en France de 1933 à 1940: Rapport et Témoignages (Paris, 1951).

Die auswärtige Politik Preußens, 1858–71: Diplomatische Aktenstücke, herausgegeben von der Historischen Reichskommission (Oldenburg, 1931 ff.).

BAUER, M., *Der große Krieg in Feld und Heimat* (Tübingen, 1921).

BAUMONT, MAURICE, *The Fall of the Kaiser* (New York, 1931).

BECKMANN, *Der Dolchstoßprozeß München* (München, 1925).

BENOIST-MÉCHIN, JACQUES, *Histoire de l'armée allemande depuis l'armistice* (2 vols., Paris, 1936 ff.).

—— *History of the German Army since the Armistice*, i (Zürich, 1939).

BERGENGRÜN, ALEXANDER, *Staatsminister August Freiherr von der Heydt* (Leipzig, 1908).

BERNHARDI, THEODOR VON, *Aus dem Leben Theodor von Bernhardis* (8 vols., Leipzig, 1893–1906).

BETHMANN HOLLWEG, THEOBALD VON, *Betrachtungen zum Weltkrieg* (2 vols., Berlin, 1919, 1922).

BIGGE, W., *Feldmarschall Graf Moltke: ein militärisches Lebensbild* (2 vols., München, 1901).

BIRCHER, E., and BODE, A. W., *Schlieffen: Mann und Idee* (Zürich, 1937).

BISMARCK, OTTO VON, *Briefe an seine Braut und Gattin*, ed. by Fürst Herbert Bismarck (Stuttgart, 1900).

—— *Briefe an seine Gattin aus dem Kriege 1870/71* (Stuttgart, 1903).

—— *Die gesammelten Werke* (1. Aufl., 15 vols., Berlin, 1924 ff.).

Bismarcks Großes Spiel. Die geheime Tagebücher Ludwig Bambergers, ed. by Ernst Feder (Frankfurt a. M., 1932).

BLOOD-RYAN, H. W., *Franz von Papen: His Life and Times* (London, 1940).

BLUME, W. VON, 'Politik und Strategie. Bismarck und Moltke, 1866 und 1870/71', *Preußische Jahrbücher*, cxi (1903).

BLUMENTHAL, ALBERT COUNT, *War Journals 1866 and 1870–71* (London, 1903).

BOEHN, MAX VON, *Biedermeier. Deutschland von 1815–1847* (Berlin, n.d.).

BONN, MORITZ J., *Wandering Scholar* (New York, 1948).

BOR, PETER, *Gespräche mit Halder* (Wiesbaden, 1950).

BORN, STEPHAN, *Erinnerungen eines Achtundvierzigers* (Leipzig, 1898).

BORRIES, KURT, *Preußen im Krimkieg* (Stuttgart, 1930).

BOYEN, HERMANN VON, *Erinnerungen aus dem Leben des Generalfeldmarschalls Hermann von Boyen*, ed. by Friedrich Nippold (3 vols., Stuttgart, 1889–90).

BOYEN, H. VON, *Erinnerungen aus dem Leben des Generaladjutanten Kaisers Wilhelm I. Hermann von Boyen*, ed. by W. von Tümpling (Berlin, 1898).

BRACHER, KARL DIETRICH, *Die Auflösung der Weimarer Republik* (2. Aufl., Stuttgart, 1957).

BRANDENBURG, ERICH, *Die Reichsgründung* (2 vols., Leipzig, 1914).

—— ed., *König Friedrich Wilhelms IV. Briefwechsel mit Ludolf Camphausen* (Berlin, 1906).

BRAUN, LILY, *Memoiren einer Sozialistin* (2 vols., München, 1909).

BRAUN, OTTO, *Von Weimar zu Hitler* (New York, 1940).

BRAUWEILER, H., *Generäle in der deutschen Republik* (Berlin, 1932).

BREDT, J. V., *Die belgische Neutralität und der Schlieffensche Feldzugplan* (Berlin, 1929).

BRETTON, HENRY L., *Stresemann and the Revision of Versailles* (Stanford, 1953).

BRONSART VON SCHELLENDORF, PAUL, *Geheimes Kriegstagebuch, 1870–71* (Deutsche Geschichtsquellen des 19. und 20. Jahrhunderts), ed. by Peter Rassow (Bonn, 1954).

—— *The Duties of the General Staff* (3rd rev. Eng. ed., London, 1908).

BRUENING, HEINRICH, 'Ein Brief', *Deutsche Rundschau* (July, 1947).

BÜLOW, B. V., *Memoirs of Prince von Bülow* (Eng. trans., 4 vols., Boston, 1931).

BÜLOW, WIPERT VON, *Deutschlands Weg nach Rapallo* (Wiesbaden, 1951).

BULLOCK, ALAN, *Hitler: a Study in Tyranny* (New York, 1953).

BUSCH, MORITZ, *Tagebuchblätter* (Leipzig, 1899).

CARO, K., and OEHME, W., *Schleichers Aufsteig: ein Beitrag zur Geschichte der Gegenrevolution* (Berlin, 1933).

CARR, E. H., *German-Soviet Relations between the Two World Wars* (Baltimore, 1951).

CARSTEN, F. L., *The Origins of Prussia* (Oxford, 1954).

CASTELLAN, G., 'Von Schleicher, von Papen et l'avènement de Hitler', *Cahiers d'histoire de la guerre* (Jan. 1949).

—— *Le réarmement clandestin du Reich, 1930–35* (Paris, 1954).

CHOLTITZ, DIETRICH VON, *Soldat unter Soldaten* (Zürich, 1951).

CLARK, CHESTER W., *Franz Joseph and Bismarck: The Diplomacy of Austria before the War of 1866.* (Cambridge [Mass.], 1934).

CLARK, R. T., *The Fall of the German Republic* (London, 1935).

CLASS, HEINRICH, *Wider den Strom. Vom Werden und Wachsen der nationalen Opposition im alten Reich* (Leipzig, 1932).

CLAUSEWITZ, GENERAL CARL VON, *Hinterlassene Werke über Krieg und Kriegführung* (3 vols., Berlin, 1857).

COCHENHAUSEN, F. VON, ed., *Von Scharnhorst zu Schlieffen* (Berlin, 1933).

COCHENHAUSEN, F. VON, 'Vor 125 Jahren. Politische und militärische Führung im Feldzug 1814', *Wissen und Wehr*, xx (1939).

CONRAD VON HÖTZENDORF, FELDMARSCHALL, *Aus meiner Dienstzeit* (5 vols., Vienna, Berlin, 1921).

CONRADY, E. VON, *Leben und Wirken des Generals Carl von Grolman* (3 vols., Berlin, 1894–6).

CONZE, WERNER, *Polnische Nation und deutsche Politik im ersten Weltkrieg* (Köln, 1958).

CRAIG, GORDON A., 'Army and National Socialism, 1933–1945: The Responsibility of the Generals', *World Politics*, ii (1950).

—— *From Bismarck to Adenauer: Aspects of German Statecraft* (Baltimore, 1958).

—— 'High Tide of Appeasement: The Road to Munich, 1937–1938', *Political Science Quarterly*, lxv (1950).

—— 'Military Diplomats in the Prussian and German Service: The Attachés, 1816–1914', ibid. lxiv (1949).

—— 'Portrait of a Political General: Edwin von Manteuffel and the Constitutional Conflict in Prussia', ibid. lxvi (1951).

—— 'Quellen zur neuesten Geschichte: ii. Briefe Schleichers an Groener', *Die Welt als Geschichte*, xi (1951).

—— 'Reichswehr and National Socialism: The Policy of Wilhelm Groener, 1928–1932', *Political Science Quarterly*, lxiii (1948).

D'ABERNON, VISCOUNT, *An Ambassador of Peace* (3 vols., London, 1929–30).

DAWSON, WILLIAM HARBUTT, *The German Empire* (2 vols., New York, 1919).

DEHIO, LUDWIG, 'Bismarck und die Heeresvorlagen der Konfliktszeit', *Historische Zeitschrift*, cxliv (1931).

—— 'Edwin von Manteuffels politische Ideen', ibid. cxxxi (1925).

—— 'Die Pläne der Militärpartei und der Konflikt', *Deutsche Rundschau*, ccxiii (1927).

DELBRÜCK, HANS, *Geschichte der Kriegskunst im Rahmen der politischen Geschichte* (7 vols., Berlin, 1900–36).

—— *Krieg und Politik* (3 vols., Berlin, 1918–19).

DEMETER, KARL, *Das deutsche Heer und seine Offiziere* (Berlin, 1930).

DETTE, ERWIN, *Friedrich der Große und sein Heer* (Göttingen, 1914).

Deutschland und Europa: Festschrift für Hans Rothfels, ed. by W. Conze (Düsseldorf, 1951).

The Diplomats, 1919–1939, ed. by Gordon A. Craig and Felix Gilbert (Princeton, 1953).

Documents on British Foreign Policy, 1919–1939, ed. by E. L. Woodward and Rohan Butler (London, 1949 ff.).

Documents on German Foreign Policy, 1918–1945: From the Archives of the German Foreign Ministry (Washington, D.C., 1949 ff.).

Dokumente der deutschen Politik, herausgegeben von Hans Volz, Bd. III. Teil I (Berlin, 1942).

DORN, W. L., 'The Prussian Bureaucracy in the Eighteenth Century', *Political Science Quarterly*, xlvi (1931), xlvii (1932).

DORPALEN, ANDREAS, 'Empress Auguste Victoria and the Fall of the German Monarchy', *American Historical Review*, lviii (1952).

DRACHKOVITCH, MILORAD M., *Les Socialismes français et allemands et le problème de la guerre, 1870–1914* (Geneva, 1954).

DROYSEN, J. G., *Briefwechsel*, ed. by R. Hübner (2 vols., Stuttgart, 1929).

—— *Das Leben des Feldmarschalls Grafen Yorck von Wartenburg* (Neue Ausgabe, 2 vols., Berlin, 1954).

—— *Geschichte der preußischen Politik* (5 vols., Berlin, 1865 ff.).

DROZ, JACQUES, *L'Allemagne et la Révolution Française* (Paris, 1949).

DUNCKER, MAX, *Politische Briefwechsel aus seinem Nachlaß*, ed. by J. Schultze (Deutsche Geschichtsquellen des 19. Jahrhunderts, xii) (Stuttgart, 1923).

ECKARDSTEIN, BARON VON, *Lebenserinnerungen* (3 vols., Leipzig, 1920–1).

EINEM, GENERALOBERST VON, *Erinnerungen eines Soldaten, 1853–1933* (Leipzig, 1933).

EISENMANN, LOUIS, *Le Compromis austro-hongrois de 1867* (Paris, 1904).

ELZE, WALTHER VON, *Der Streit um Tauroggen* (Breslau, 1926).

EPSTEIN, FRITZ T., 'Zwischen Compiègne und Versailles: Geheime amerikanische Militärdiplomatie in der Periode des Waffenstillstandes 1918/1919: Die Rolle des Obersten Arthur L. Conger', *Vierteljahrshefte für Zeitgeschichte*, iii (1955), 412 ff.

EPSTEIN, KLAUS, 'The Development of German-Austrian War Aims in the Spring of 1917', *Journal of Central European Affairs*, xvii (April 1957).

—— *Matthias Erzberger and the Dilemma of German Democracy* (Princeton, 1959).

ERGANG, ROBERT, *The Potsdam Führer: Frederick William I, Father of Prussian Militarism* (New York, 1941).

ERNST, FRITZ, *Aus dem Nachlaß Generals Walther Reinhardt* (Stuttgart, 1958).

ERZBERGER, M., *Erlebnisse im Weltkrieg* (Stuttgart, Berlin, 1920).

EYCK, ERICH, *Bismarck: Leben und Werk* (3 vols., Zürich, 1941–4).

—— *Das persönliche Regiment Wilhelms II* (Zürich, 1948).

FABER DU FAUR, MORIZ, *Macht und Ohnmacht: Erinnerungen eines alten Offiziers* (Stuttgart, 1953).

FALKENHAYN, GENERAL VON, *The German General Staff and its Decisions, 1914–1916* (New York, 1920).

FESTGABE FÜR H. RITTER VON SRBIK, *Gesamtdeutsche Vergangenheit* (München, 1938).

FISCHER, FRITZ, 'Deutsche Kriegsziele, Revolutionierung, und Separatfrieden im Osten 1914–1918', *Historische Zeitschrift*, clxxxviii (1959).

FISCHER, RUTH, *Stalin and German Communism* (Cambridge [Mass.], 1948).

FÖRSTER, WOLFGANG, *Ein General kämpft gegen den Krieg: Aus nachgelassenen Papieren des Generalstabschefs Ludwig Beck* (München, 1949).

FOERTSCH, HERMANN, *Schuld und Verhängnis: Die Fritschkrise im Frühjahr 1938 als Wendepunkt in der Geschichte der nationalsozialistischen Zeit* (Stuttgart, 1951).

Foreign Relations of the United States.

FORSTER, K., *The Failures of Peace* (Washington, D.C., 1941).

FRANÇOIS-PONCET, ANDRÉ, *Souvenirs d'une ambassade à Berlin* (Paris, 1946).

FREYTAG-LORINGHOVEN, FREIHERR VON, *Menschen und Dinge wie ich sie in meinem Leben sah* (Berlin, 1923).

—— *Politik und Kriegführung* (Berlin, 1918).

FRIEDJUNG, H., *Der Kampf um die Vorherrschaft in Deutschland, 1959 bis 1866* (10. Aufl., 2 vols., Stuttgart, 1916–17).

—— *Öesterreich von 1848 bis 1860* (2. Aufl., 2 vols., Stuttgart, 1912).

FRIEDRICH II, *Œuvres de Frédéric le Grand* (31 vols., Berlin, 1946–57).

—— *Die Werke Friedrichs der Großen in deutscher Übersetzung*, ed. by G. V. Volz (10 vols., Berlin, 1913–14).

—— *Die politischen Testamente*, übersetzt von Friedrich von Oppeln-Bronikowski (Berlin, 1922).

FRIEDRICH III, KAISER, *Tagebücher von 1848–1866*, ed. by H. O. Meisner (Leipzig, 1929).

—— *Das Kriegstagebuch von 1870/71*, ed. by H. O. Meisner (Berlin, 1926).

FRIEDRICH KARL, PRINZ VON PREUSSEN, *Denkwürdigkeiten aus seinem Leben*, ed. by Wolfgang Förster (2 vols., Stuttgart, 1910).

FRIESE, CHRISTIAN, *Rußland und Preußen vom Krimkrieg bis zum polnischen Aufstand* (Berlin, 1931).

GACKENHOLZ, H., 'Der Kriegsrat von Czernahora vom 12. Juli 1866', *Historische Vierteljahrschrift*, xxvi (1931).

GATZKE, HANS W., *Germany's Drive to the West: A Study of Germany's Western War Aims during the First World War* (Baltimore, 1950).

—— 'Russo-German Military Collaboration during the Weimar Republic', *American Historical Review*, lxiii (1958).

—— *Stresemann and the Rearmament of Germany* (Baltimore, 1954).

GAXOTTE, PIERRE, *Frederick the Great* (New Haven, 1942).

GEBHARDT, BRUNO, *Wilhelm von Humboldt als Staatsmann* (2 vols., Stuttgart, 1899).

GENERALKOMMANDO DES GARDEKORPS, 'Zum 18. März 1848', *Preußische Jahrbücher*, cxii (1903).

GENTIZON, PAUL, *L'Armée allemande depuis la défaite* (Paris, 1920).

GERLACH, ERNST LUDWIG VON, *Aufzeichnungen aus seinem Leben und Wirken, 1795–1877* (2 vols., Schwerin, 1903).

GERLACH, HELMUT VON, 'Wenn Generäle entscheiden', *Die Weltbühne*, xxii (1926).

GERLACH, LEOPOLD VON, *Denkwürdigkeiten aus dem Leben Leopolds von Gerlach* (2 vols., Berlin, 1892).

GESSLER, OTTO, *Reichswehrpolitik in der Weimarer Zeit*, herausgegeben von Kurt Sendtner (Stuttgart, 1958).

GEYR VON SCHWEPPENBURG, LEO FREIHERR, *Erinnerungen eines Militärattachés: London, 1933–37* (Stuttgart, 1949).

GLAISE-HORSTENAU, EDMUND VON, *Franz Josephs Weggefährte* (Zürich, Leipzig, and Vienna, 1930).

GOEBBELS, JOSEF, *My Part in Germany's Fight* (London, 1935).

GÖRLITZ, WALTER, *Hindenburg: Ein Lebensbild* (Bonn, 1953).

—— *History of the German General Staff* (New York, 1953).

—— and QUINT, H. A., *Adolf Hitler: eine Biographie* (Stuttgart, 1952).

GOLLWITZER, H., 'Bayern 1918–1933', *Vierteljahrshefte für Zeitgeschichte*, iii (1955), 381 ff.

GOLTZ, COLMAR VON DER, 'Roßbach und Jena: eine kriegsgeschichtliche Studie', *Militärwochenblatt* (Beihefte, 1882, 1883).

GOLTZ, RÜDIGER GRAF VON DER, *Meine Sendung in Finnland und im Baltikum* (Leipzig, 1920).

—— *Als politischer General im Osten (Finnland und Baltikum) 1918 und 1919* (Leipzig, 1936).

GOOCH, G. P., *Before the War* (2 vols., London, 1936, 1938).

—— *Frederick the Great: The Ruler, the Writer, the Man* (New York, 1947).

—— *Studies in Diplomacy* (London, 1942).

GORDON, HAROLD J., *The Reichswehr and the German Republic, 1919–1926* (Princeton, 1957).

GROENER, WILHELM, *Das Testament des Grafen Schlieffen* (Berlin, 1927).

—— *Lebenserinnerungen: Jugend, Generalstab, Weltkrieg*, herausgegeben von Friedrich Freiherr Hiller von Gärtringen (Deutsche Geschichtsquellen des 19. und 20. Jahrhunderts. Bd. 41, Göttingen, 1957).

GROENER-GEYER, DOROTHEA, *General Groener* (Frankfurt a. M., 1955).

Die Große Politik der Europäischen Kabinette 1871–1914: Sammlung der diplomatschen Akten des Auswärtigen Amtes (Berlin, 1912 ff.).

GRZESCINSKI, ALBERT, *Inside Germany* (New York, 1939).

GUDERIAN, GENERAL HEINZ, *Panzer Leader* (London, 1952).

GUMBEL, E. J., '*Verräter verfallen der Feme': Opfer, Mörder, Richter, 1919–1920* (Berlin, 1929).

—— *Verschwörer: Beiträge zur Geschichte und Soziologie der deutschen nationalistischen Geheimbünde seit 1918* (Vienna, 1924).

HAAKE, PAUL, 'König Friedrich Wilhelm III., Hardenberg und die preußische Verfassungsfrage', *Forschungen zur brandenburgischen und preußischen Geschichte*, xxvi (1913)–xxxii (1919).

HAEFTEN, HANS VON, 'Bismarck und Moltke', *Preußische Jahrbücher*, clxxvii (1919).

HAENCHEN, KARL, 'Aus dem Nachlaß des Generals v. Prittwitz', *Forschungen zur brandenburgischen und preußischen Geschichte*, xlv (1933).

—— 'Neue Briefe und Berichte aus den Berliner Märztagen des Jahres 1848', ibid. xlix (1937).

—— *Revolutionsbriefe 1848: Ungedrucktes aus dem Nachlaß König Friedrich Wilhelms IV. von Preußen* (Leipzig, 1930).

HALDER, FRANZ, *Hitlers als Feldherr* (München, 1949).

HALLER, FRITZ, *Philipp Eulenberg, the Kaiser's Friend* (2 vols., London, 1930).

HALLGARTEN, GEORGE W. F., 'General Hans von Seeckt and Russia, 1920–22', *Journal of Modern History*, xxi (1949).

HAMMANN, O., *Bilder aus der letzten Kaiserzeit* (Berlin, 1920).

—— *Der neue Kurs* (Berlin, 1918).

HAMMERSTEIN, KUNRAT FREIHERR VON, 'Schleicher, Hammerstein und die Machtübernahme 1933', *Frankfurter Hefte*, xi (1956).

HARBOU, ANDREA VON, *Dienst und Glaube in der Staatsanschauung Albrecht von Roons* (Berlin, 1936).

HARDEN, MAXIMILIAN, *Köpfe* (33. Aufl., Berlin, 1910).

HARTUNG, FRITZ, *Deutsche Verfassungsgeschichte vom 15. Jahrhundert bis zur Gegenwart* (2. Aufl., Leipzig, 1922).

HARTUNG, FRITZ, 'Verantwortliche Regierung, Kabinette und Nebenregierungen im konstitutionellen Preußen 1848–1918', *Forschungen zur brandenburgischen und preußischen Geschichte*, xliv (1932).

—— *Volk und Staat in der deutschen Geschichte: Gesammelte Abhandlungen* (Leipzig, 1940).

HASSELL, ULRICH VON, *Vom anderen Deutschland* (2. Aufl., Zürich, 1946).

HEIDEN, KONRAD, *Der Fuehrer* (New York, 1944).

HELFFERICH, KARL, *Der Weltkrieg* (3 vols., Berlin, 1919).

HENDERSON, E. F., *Blücher and the Uprising of Prussia against Napoleon, 1806–1815* (London, 1911).

HEUSINGER, A., *Befehl im Widerstreit: Schickalsstunden der deutschen Armee, 1923–45* (Tübingen and Stuttgart, 1950).

HEYDERHOFF, JULIUS, ed., *Im Ring der Gegner Bismarcks. Denkschriften und Politischer Briefwechsel Franz von Roggenbachs mit Kaiserin Augusta und Albrecht von Stosch, 1865–1896* (2. Aufl., Leipzig, 1943).

HILGER, GUSTAV, and MEYER, ALFRED G., *The Incompatible Allies: A Memoir History of German–Soviet Relations, 1918–1941* (New York, 1953).

HINDENBURG, GENERALFELDMARSCHALL O. VON, *Aus meinem Leben* (Leipzig, 1920).

HINTZE, OTTO, *Die Hohenzollern und ihr Werk* (7. Aufl., Berlin, 1916).

—— *Historische und politische Aufsätze* (2. Aufl., Berlin, 1908).

—— *Staat und Verfassung: Gesammelte Abhandlungen zur allgemeinen Verfassungsgeschichte*, ed. F. Hartung (Leipzig, 1941).

—— *Zur Theorie der Geschichte*, ed. by F. Hartung (Leipzig, 1942).

'Hitlers Brief an Reichenau vom 4. Dezember 1932', *Vierteljahrshefte für Zeitgeschichte*, vii (1959), 429–37.

Hitler's Secret Conversations, 1941–1944, with an introduction by H. R. Trevor-Roper (New York, 1953).

HÖHN, REINHARD, *Verfassungskampf und Heereseid: Der Kampf des Bürgertums um das Heer, 1815–1850* (Leipzig, 1938).

HÖPFNER, OBERST VON, 'Grolman', *Militärwochenblatt* (Beihefte, 1843).

HOFFMANN, MAX, *Die Aufzeichnungen des Generalmajors Max Hoffmann*, ed. K. Nowak (2 vols., Berlin, 1930).

HOFMANN, H., *Fürst Bismarck 1890–98* (3 vols., Berlin, 1914).

HOHENLOHE-INGELFINGEN, PRINZ KRAFT ZU, *Aus meinem Leben, 1848–1871* (4 vols., Berlin, 1897–1906).

HOHENLOHE-SCHILLINGSFÜRST, CHLODWIG FÜRST ZU, *Denkwürdigkeiten der Reichskanzlerzeit*, ed. K. A. v. Müller (Stuttgart, 1931).

—— *Memoirs of Prince Chlodwig zu Hohenlohe-Schillingsfürst* (2 vols., London, 1906).

HOLBORN, HAJO, 'Bismarck und Werthern', *Archiv für Politik und Geschichte*, v (1925–6).

—— 'Deutschland und die Türkei', ibid., v (1925–6).

HOLSTEIN, FRIEDRICH VON, *Lebensbekenntnis*, ed. by W. Rogge (Berlin, 1932).

HONNORAT, ANDRÉ, *Un des problèmes de la paix: Le désarmement de l'Allemagne. Textes et documents* (Paris, 1924).

HORKENBACH, CUNO, ed., *Das Deutsche Reich von 1918 bis heute* (Berlin, 1930).

HORN, MARTIN, *Halder: Schuld oder Tragik?* (München, 1948).

HOSSBACH, FRIEDRICH, *Zwischen Wehrmacht und Hitler, 1934–1938* (Wolfenbüttel and Hanover, 1949).

House of Commons: Sessional Papers, 1921, xliii: 'Protocols and Correspondence . . . respecting the Execution of the Treaty of Versailles of 28th June' (Cmd. 1325).

HUBER, ERNST R., *Heer und Staat in der deutschen Geschichte* (1. Aufl., Hamburg, 1938).

HÜBNER, R., *Albrecht v. Roon: Preußens Heer im Kampf um das Reich* (Hamburg, 1933).

HUMBOLDT, WILHELM, *Wilhelm und Caroline von Humboldt in ihren Briefen*, ed. by Anna von Sydow (5 vols., Berlin, 1906–16).

HUTTEN-CZAPSKI, BOGDAN GRAF, *Sechzig Jahre Politik und Gesellschaft* (2 vols., Berlin, 1935–6).

IRVINE, DALLAS D., 'The French and Prussian Staff Systems before 1870', *Journal of the American History Foundation*, ii (1938).

—— 'The Origin of Capital Staffs', *Journal of Modern History*, x (1938).

ISAACSOHN, SIEGFRIED, *Geschichte des preußischen Beamtenthums vom Anfang des 15. Jahrhunderts bis auf die Gegenwart* (3 vols., Berlin, 1873–84).

JÄHNS, MAX, *Feldmarschall Moltke* (new ed., Berlin, 1894).

—— *Geschichte der Kriegswissenschaften vornehmlich in Deutschland* (3 parts, München, 1889–91).

JANSSEN, KARL HEINZ, 'Die Wechsel in der Obersten Heeresleitung 1916', *Vierteljahrshefte für Zeitgeschichte*, vii (1959).

JANY, CURT, *Geschichte der königlich-preußischen Armee bis zum Jahre 1807* (3 vols., Berlin, 1928–9).

—— *Geschichte der königlich-preußischen Armee: IV. Die königlich-preußische Armee und das deutsche Reichsheer 1807 bis 1914* (Berlin, 1933).

JEISMANN, KARL-ERNST, *Das Problem des Präventiv-krieges im europäischen Staatensystem mit besonderem Blick auf die Bismarckzeit* (München, 1957).

JORDAN, W. M., *Great Britain, France and the German Problem, 1918–1939* (London, 1943).

KABISCH, ERNST, *Groener* (Berlin, 1932).

KAEBER, ERNST, *Berlin 1848: Zur Jahrhundertfeier der März-revolution im Auftrage des Magistrats von Groß-Berlin* (Berlin, 1948).

KAEHLER, S. A., *Wilhelm von Humboldt und der Staat* (München, 1927).

KAMINSKI, KURT, *Verfassung und Verfassungskonflikt im Preußen 1862–66* (Königsberg and Berlin, 1938).

KANNER, HEINRICH, *Der Schlüssel zur Kriegsschuldfrage* (München, 1926).

KAYSER, WALTHER, *Marwitz* (Hamburg, 1936).

KEHR, ECKART, 'Das soziale System der Reaktion unter dem Ministerium Puttkammer', *Die Gesellschaft* (1929), ii. 253 ff.

—— 'Deutsch-englisches Bündnisproblem der Jahrhundertwende', ibid. (1928), ii. 24 ff.

—— 'Die deutsche Flotte in den neunziger Jahren und der politisch-militärische Dualismus des Kaiserreiches', *Archiv für Politik und Geschichte*, viii (1927).

KEHR, ECKART, 'Soziale und finanzielle Grundlagen der Tirpitzschen Flottenpropaganda', *Die Gesellschaft* (1928), ii. 211 ff.

—— 'Zur Genesis des kgl. preußischen Reserveoffiziers', ibid. 492 ff.

KEIM, A., *Erlebtes und Erstrebtes* (Hannover, 1925).

KESSEL, E., 'Die Wandlung der Kriegkunst im Zeitalter der französischen Revolution', *Historische Zeitschrift*, cxlviii (1933).

—— 'Zu Boyens Entlassung', ibid. clxxv (1953).

—— *Moltke* (Stuttgart, 1957).

KEUDELL, R. VON, *Fürst und Fürstin Bismarck: Erinnerungen aus den Jahren 1864–72* (Berlin, 1901).

KIELMANSEGG, GRAF, *Der Fritsch-Prozeß 1938* (Hamburg, 1949).

KLEIN-WUTTIG, ANNELIESE, *Politik und Kriegführung in den deutschen Einigungskriegen* (Abhandlungen zur mittleren und neueren Geschichte, lxxv) (Berlin, 1934).

KLOSTER, W., *Der deutsche Generalstab und der Präventivkriegsgedanke* (Stuttgart, 1932).

KNESEBECK, G. VON DEM, *Die Wahrheit über den Propagandafeldzug und Deutschlands Zusammenbruch* (München, 1927).

KOHN, HANS, 'Arndt and the Character of German Nationalism', *American Historical Review*, liv (1949).

—— 'The Paradox of Fichte's Nationalism', *Journal of the History of Ideas*, x (1949).

KOHN-BRAMSTEDT, ERNST, *Aristocracy and the Middle Classes in Germany: Social Types in German Literature, 1830–1900* (London, 1937).

KORDT, ERICH, *Wahn und Wirklichkeit* (Stuttgart, 1947).

KOSER, R., 'Zur Geschichte der preußischen Politik während des Krimkrieges', *Forschungen zur brandenburgischen und preußischen Geschichte*, ii (1889).

KRAUSNICK, H., *Holsteins Geheimpolitik in der Aera Bismarck 1886–1890* (2. Aufl., Hamburg, 1942).

—— 'Vorgeschichte und Beginn des militärischen Widerstandes gegen Hitler', *Die Vollmacht des Gewissens*, herausgegeben von der Europäischen Publikation e. V. (Bonn, 1956).

KRIEG, THILO, *Constantin v. Alvensleben* (Berlin, 1903).

Kriegsministerium, *Das Königliche Preußische Kriegministerium 1809—1 März. 1909* (Berlin, 1909).

KRUCK, ALFRED, *Geschichte des Alldeutschen Verbandes, 1890–1939* (Wiesbaden 1954).

KÜHLMANN, RICHARD VON, *Erinnerungen* (Heidelberg, 1948).

KÜNTZEL, G., and HASS, M., *Die politischen Testamente der Hohenzollern* (Leipzig, 1919).

KUHL, H. V., *Der deutsche Generalstab in Vorbereitung und Durchführung des Weltkrieges* (2. Aufl., Berlin, 1920).

LABAND, *Staatsrecht des deutschen Reiches* (5. Aufl., Berlin, 1914).

LAMBSDORFF, G., *Die Militärbevollmächtigten Kaiser Wilhelms II. am Zarenhofe, 1904–1914* (Berlin, 1937).

LANCKEN, V. D., *Meine dreißig Dienstjahre* (Berlin, 1931).

LAVISSE, E., *La jeunesse de Frédéric le Grand* (Paris, 1891).

LEBER, JULIUS, *Ein Mann geht seinen Weg: Schriften, Reden und Briefe*, herausgegeben von seinen Freunden (Berlin, 1952).

LEHMANN, MAX, *Freiherr vom Stein* (3 vols., Leipzig, 1902–5).

—— *Knesebeck und Schön* (Leipzig, 1875).

—— *Scharnhorst* (2 vols., Leipzig, 1886/1887).

—— 'Zur Geschichte der preußischen Heeresreform von 1808', *Historische Zeitschrift*, cxxvi (1922).

—— 'Werbung, Wehrpflicht und Beurlaubung unter Friedrich Wilhelm I.', ibid. lxvii (1891).

LEIDOLPH, E., *Die Schlacht bei Jena* (2. Aufl., Jena, 1901).

LENZ, MAX, *Geschichte Bismarcks* (4. Aufl., München, 1913).

—— '1848', *Preußische Jahrbücher*, xci (1898).

LETTOW-VORBECK, OSCAR VON, *Der Krieg von 1806 und 1807* (4 vols., Berlin, 1892–9).

—— *Geschichte des Krieges von 1866* (Berlin, 1896).

LIDDELL HART, B. H., *The Other Side of the Hill* (rev. ed., London, 1951).

LINDEMANN, HELMUT, 'Die Schuld der Generäle', *Deutsche Rundschau* (Jan. 1949).

LOË, FREIHERR VON, *Erinnerungen aus meinem Berufsleben* (2. Aufl., Stuttgart, 1906).

LÖWENTHAL, F., *Der preußische Verfassungsstreit, 1862–1866* (Altenburg, 1914).

LUCIUS VON BALLHAUSEN, R. S., *Bismarck-Erinnerungen* (Stuttgart and Berlin, 1921).

LUCKAU, ALMA, 'Kapp Putsch—Success or Failure?', *Journal of Central European Affairs*, vii (1948).

—— *The German Delegation at Versailles* (New York, 1941).

LUDENDORFF, E., *Meine Kriegserinnerungen* (Berlin, 1920).

—— *Urkunden der Obersten Heeresleitung über ihre Tätigkeit 1916–18* (2. Aufl., Berlin, 1921).

LUTZ, R. H., ed., *The Causes of the German Collapse in 1918* (Stanford, 1934).

—— ed., *Fall of the German Empire* (2 vols., Stanford, 1932).

MACKENSEN, AUGUST VON, *Briefe und Aufzeichnungen des Generalfeldmarschalls aus Krieg und Frieden*, ed. Wolfgang Förster (Leipzig, 1938).

MAERCKER, GENERAL LUDWIG, *Vom Kaiserheer zur Reichswehr: Geschichte der freiwilligen Landesjägerkorps* (3. Aufl., Leipzig, 1922).

Makers of Modern Strategy: Military Thought from Machiavelli to Hitler, ed. by Edward Mead Earle in collaboration with Gordon A. Craig and Felix Gilbert (Princeton, 1943).

MANSTEIN, ERICH VON, *Aus einem Soldatenleben 1887–1939* (Bonn, 1958).

MANTEUFFEL, EDWIN VON, 'Briefe des Generalfeldmarschalls Freiherr Edwin v. Manteuffel an seinen Sohn Hans Karl', *Deutsche Revue*, xxxviii (III), 1913.

MARCKS, ERICH, *Kaiser Wilhelm I.* (4. Aufl., Leipzig, 1900).

—— *Männer und Zeiten* (2 vols., Leipzig, 1912).

MARSCHALL VON BIEBERSTEIN, F. FREIHERR, *Verantwortlichkeit und Gegenzeichnung bei Anordnungen des Obersten Kriegsherrn. Studie zum deutschen Staatsrecht* (Berlin, 1911).

—— *Verfassungsrechtliche Reichsgesetze* (2. Aufl., Mannheim, 1929).

Marwitz, F. von der, *Aus dem Nachlasse Friedrich August Ludwigs von der Marwitz* (2 vols., Berlin, 1852).

Mau, Hermann, 'Die zweite Revolution—Der 30. Juni 1934', *Vierteljahrshefte für Zeitgeschichte*, i (1953).

Maude, F. N., *1806, the Jena Campaign* (London, 1909).

Max von Baden, Prinz, *Erinnerungen und Dokumente* (Stuttgart, 1927).

Meerheimb, F. v., 'Graf v. Wrangel, Kgl. Pr. Generalfeldmarschall', *Militärwochenblatt* (Beihefte, 1877).

Meier-Welcker, Hans, 'Die Stellung des Chefs der Heeresleitung in den Anfängen der Republik', *Vierteljahrshefte für Zeitgeschichte*, iv (1956).

Meinecke, Fr., 'Boyen und Roon, zwei preußische Kriegsminister', *Historische Zeitschrift*, lxxvii (1896).

—— *Das Leben des Generalfeldmarschalls Hermann v. Boyen* (2 vols., Stuttgart, 1895–9).

—— *Die deutsche Katastrophe: Betrachtungen und Erinnerungen* (3. Aufl., Wiesbaden, 1947).

—— *1848: Eine Säkularbetrachtung* (Bonn, 1948).

—— *Erlebtes, 1862–1901* (Leipzig, 1941).

—— *Preußisch-Deutsche Gestalten und Probleme* (Leipzig, 1940).

—— *Radowitz und die deutsche Revolution* (Berlin, 1913).

—— *Staat und Persönlichkeit* (Berlin, 1933).

—— *Straßburg, Freiburg, Berlin, 1901–1919* (Stuttgart, 1949).

Meisner, H. O., 'Aus Berichten des Pariser Militärattachés Freiherr von Hoiningen gt. Huene an den Grafen Waldersee (1888–91)', *Berliner Monatshefte*, 15. Jg. (1937).

—— 'Briefwechsel zwischen Waldersee und Yorck v. Wartenburg, 1885–94', *Historisch-Politisches Archiv*, i (1930).

—— 'Graf Waldersees Pariser Informationen 1887', *Preußische Jahrbücher*, ccxxiv (1931).

—— *Der Kriegminister, 1814–1914, ein Beitrag zur militärischen Verfassungsgeschichte* (Berlin, 1940).

—— 'Militärkabinett, Kriegsminister und Reichskanzler zur Zeit Wilhelms I.', *Forschungen zur brandenburgischen und preußischen Geschichte*, l (1938).

Meissner, Hans Otto and Wilde, Harry, *Die Machtergreifung: ein Bericht über die Technik des nationalsozialistischen Staatsstreiches* (Stuttgart, 1958).

Meissner, Otto, *Staatssekretär unter Ebert, Hindenburg und Hitler* (Hamburg, 1950).

Melville, C. F., *The Russian Face of Germany. An Account of the Secret Military Relations between the German and Soviet Russian Governments* (London, 1932).

Mendelssohn Bartholdy, Albrecht, *The War and German Society* (New Haven, 1937).

Menne, Bernhard, *Blood and Steel: The Rise of the House of Krupp* (New York, 1938).

Meusel, Friedrich, 'Marwitz' Schilderung der altpreußischen Armee', *Preußische Jahrbücher*, cxxxi (1908).

Meyer, A. O., *Bismarck: Der Mensch und der Staatsmann* (Stuttgart, 1949).

—— 'Kronrat vom 29. Mai 1865', *Festgabe für Srbik* (Berlin, 1938).

Meyer, Henry Cord, *Mitteleuropa in German Thought and Action, 1815–1945* (The Hague, 1955).

MEYERINCK, GENERALLT. VON, 'Die Tätigkeit der Truppen während der Berliner Märztage des Jahres 1848', *Militärwochenblatt* (Beihefte, 1891).

MICHAEL, HORST, *Bismarck, England und Europa, vorwiegend von 1866–1870* (München, 1930).

MICHAELIS, GEORG, *Für Staat und Volk* (Berlin, 1922).

MICKLEM, NATHANIEL, *National Socialism and the Roman Catholic Church* (New York, 1939).

Ministère des Affaires Étrangères, *Documents diplomatiques français (1871–1914)* (Paris, 1929 ff.).

MOLTKE, HELMUTH VON, *Die deutschen Aufmarschpläne 1871–1890* (*Forschungen und Darstellungen aus dem Reichsarchiv, VII*), ed. by F. v. Schmerfeld (Berlin, 1928).

—— *Gesammelte Schriften und Denkwürdigkeiten* (8 vols., Berlin, 1891–92).

—— *Militärische Werke* (13 vols., Berlin, 1892–1912).

—— *Moltke in der Vorbereitung und Durchführung der Operationen.* (Kriegsgeschichtliche Einzelschriften herausgegeben vom Großen Generalstab. Heft xxxvi) (Berlin, 1905).

MONTS, A. GRAF V., *Erinnerungen und Gedanken*, ed. by K. Nowak and F. Thimme (Berlin, 1932).

MORDACQ, GÉNÉRAL H., *L'Armistice du 11 Novembre 1918* (Paris, 1937).

MORGAN, J. H., *Assize of Arms: The Disarmament of Germany and her Rearmament, 1919–1939* (New York, 1946).

—— 'The Disarmament of Germany and After', *The Quarterly Review*, ccxlii (1924).

MUHLEN, NORBERT, *The Incredible Krupps* (New York, 1959).

MÜNSTER, H. ZU, 'Politische Briefe des Grafen Hugo zu Münster an Edwin von Manteuffel', *Deutsche Revue*, xxxviii (1913).

NADOLNY, RUDOLF, *Mein Beitrag* (Wiesbaden, 1955).

NAMIER, L. B., *In the Nazi Era* (London, 1952).

Nazi Conspiracy and Aggression (8 vols., and 2 supplements, Washington, D.C., 1946 ff.).

Nazi-Soviet Relations, 1939–1941: Documents from the Archives of the German Foreign Office, ed. by R. J. Sontag and J. S. Beddie (Washington, D.C., 1948).

'Neue Dokumente zur Geschichte der Reichswehr 1930-33', ed. by Thilo Vogelsang, *Vierteljahrshefte für Zeitgeschichte*, ii (1954).

NEUMANN, FRANZ, 'Germany and Western Union', *Proceedings of the Academy of Political Science*, xxiii (1949).

NEWTON, LORD, *Lord Lyons, a Record of British Diplomacy* (2 vols., London, 1913).

NICHOLS, J. ALDEN, *Germany after Bismarck: The Caprivi Era, 1890–1894* (Cambridge, Mass., 1958).

NICOLSON, HAROLD, *Curzon: The Last Phase, 1919–1925* (new ed., New York, 1939).

NIEMANN, ALFRED, *Kaiser und Heer: Das Wesen der Kommandogewalt und ihre Ausübung durch Kaiser Wilhelm II* (Berlin, 1929).

NIRRNHEIM, OTTO, *Das erste Jahr des Ministeriums Bismarck und die öffentliche Meinung* (Heidelberg, 1908).

NOLLET, GÉNÉRAL, *Une expérience de désarmement* (Paris, 1932).

NOSKE, GUSTAV, *Von Kiel bis Kapp: Zur Geschichte der deutschen Revolution* (Berlin, 1920).
—— *Aufstieg und Niedergang der deutschen Sozialdemokratie* (Zürich, 1947).
NOWAK, KARL FRIEDRICH, *Versailles* (New York, 1929).

OERTZEN, F. W. VON, *Die deutschen Freikorps 1918–23* (6. Aufl., München, 1939).
'Offizier als Erzieher des Volkes', *Militärwochenblatt* (Beihefte, 1882, Heft 2).
OLDEN, RUDOLF, *The History of Liberty in Germany* (London, 1946).
OLLECH, MAJOR VON, 'Carl Friedrich Wilhelm von Reyher', *Militärwochenblatt* (Beihefte, 1860, 1861, 1869, 1870, 1873–6, 1879).
OLLIVIER, ÉMILE, *L'Empire libéral* (18 vols., Paris, 1895–1916).
ONCKEN, HERMANN, *Großherzog Friedrich I. von Baden und die deutsche Politik von 1854–71. Briefwechsel, Denkschriften, Tagebücher* (2 vols., Stuttgart, 1927).
—— *Die Rheinpolitik Kaiser Napoleons III. von 1863 bis 1870 und der Ursprung des Krieges von 1870/71* (3 vols., Stuttgart, 1926).
Origines diplomatiques de la Guerre de 1870/71. Recueil de Documents publié par le Ministre des Affaires Étrangères (Paris, 1909 ff.).

PAPEN, FRANZ VON, *Memoirs*, trans. by Brian Connell (London, 1952).
PECHEL, RUDOLF, *Deutscher Widerstand* (Zürich, 1947).
PERTZ, G. H., and DELBRÜCK, H., *Das Leben des Feldmarschalls Grafen Neithardt von Gneisenau* (5 vols., Berlin, 1864–80).
PETERSDORFF, H. VON, *Friedrich Wilhelm IV.* (Stuttgart, 1900).
PHELPS, REGINALD H., 'Aus den Groener Dokumenten', *Deutsche Rundschau*, 76. Jg. (1950).
—— 'Aus den Seeckt Dokumenten', *Deutsche Rundschau*, 78. Jg. (1952).
PICKER, HENRY, *Hitlers Tischgespräche im Führerhauptquartier 1941–42* (Bonn, 1951).
POLLMÜLLER, IGNAZ, 'Die Rolle der Reichswehr von 1918 bis 1933', *Frankfurter Hefte*, 1. Jg., Heft 9 (Dec. 1946).
PONSONBY, SIR F., *Letters of the Empress Frederick* (London, 1929).
POSCHINGER, H. VON, ed., *Unter Friedrich Wilhelm IV.: Denkwürdigkeiten des Ministerpräsidenten Otto von Manteuffel* (3 vols., Berlin, 1901).
PRATT, E. A., *The Rise of Rail-Power in War and Conquest, 1833–1914* (New York, 1915).
PRIESDORFF, KURT VON, ed., *Soldatisches Führertum* (7 vols., Hamburg, 1936).

Quellen zur deutschen Politik Österreichs, 1859–66, ed. by H. Ritter von Srbik (Oldenburg, 1934–8).

RABENAU, F. V., *Seeckt: Aus seinem Leben 1918–36* (Leipzig, 1940).
—— 'Zur 90. Wiederkehr des Todestags des Generalfeldmarschalls v. Boyen', *Militärwissenschaftliche Rundschau*, iii (1938).
RACHFAHL, FELIX, 'König Friedrich Wilhelm IV. und die Berliner Märzrevolution im Lichte neuer Quellen', *Preußische Jahrbücher*, cx (1902).
RADOWITZ, JOSEF VON, *Ausgewählte Schriften und Reden*, ed. by Friedrich Meinecke (*Der deutsche Staatsgedanke*, erste Reihe, xvi) (Munich, 1921).
RADOWITZ, J. M. VON, *Aufzeichnungen und Erinnerungen aus dem Leben des Botschafters J. M. von Radowitz*, ed. by Hajo Holborn (2 vols., Stuttgart, 1925).

RAEDER, ERICH, *Mein Leben* (2 vols., Tübingen, 1956).

RAHN, RUDOLF, *Ruheloses Leben: Aufzeichnungen und Erinnerungen* (Düsseldorf, 1950).

RASSOW, PETER, 'Der Plan Moltkes für den Zweifrontenkrieg, 1871–1890', *Breslauer Historische Forschungen*, Heft 1 (1938).

—— 'Schlieffen und Holstein', *Historische Zeitschrift*, clxxiii (1952).

RAUSCHNING, HERMANN, *Germany's Revolution of Destruction* (New York, 1939).

—— *Hitler Speaks* (London, 1939).

REDLICH, JOSEPH, *Emperor Francis Joseph of Austria: a Biography* (New York, 1929).

REGELE, OSKAR, *Feldmarschall Conrad, Auftrag und Erfüllung, 1906–1918* (Wien, 1958).

'Die Reichswehr in Bayern und der Münchener Putsch 1923', herausgegeben von Thilo Vogelsang, *Vierteljahrshefte für Zeitgeschichte*, v (1957), 91 ff.

Reichstag: Verhandlungen: *Stenographische Berichte*.

REINHARD, OBERST, A. D., *1918–19: Die Wehen der Republik* (Berlin, 1933).

REISCHACH, L. FREIHERR VON, *Unter drei Kaisern* (Berlin, 1929).

REVERTERA, FRIEDRICH GRAF, 'Rechberg und Bismarck 1863 bis 1864', *Deutsche Revue*, xxviii (4) (1903).

RHEINBABEN, ROCHUS BARON VON, *Stresemann, the Man and the Statesman* (New York, 1929).

RHEINDORF, KURT, *Die Schwarze Meer- (Pontus-)Frage vom Pariser Frieden von 1856 bis zum Abschluß der Londoner Konferenz von 1871* (Berlin, 1925).

RITTER, GERHARD, *Friedrich der Große: ein historisches Profil* (Leipzig, 1936).

—— *Die preußischen Konservativen und Bismarcks deutsche Politik* (Heidelberg, 1913).

—— *Carl Goerdeler und die deutsche Widerstandsbewegung* (Stuttgart, 1955).

—— *Der Schlieffenplan: Kritik eines Mythos* (München, 1956).

—— *Staatskunst und Kriegshandwerk: Das Problem des 'Militarismus' in Deutschland*, i (München, 1954).

—— *Stein: eine politische Biographie* (2 vols., Stuttgart, 1931).

ROCHS, HUGO, *Schlieffen* (Berlin, 1921).

ROHDEN, PETER RICHARD, 'Die klassische Diplomatie im Kampfe um das europäische Gleichgewicht', *Europäische Revue*, xv (1939).

ROON, A. GRAF VON, *Denkwürdigkeiten* (5. Aufl., 3 vols., Berlin, 1905).

ROSENBERG, ARTHUR, *The Birth of the German Republic* (New York, 1931).

—— *A History of the German Republic* (London, 1936).

ROSENBERG, H., 'The Rise of the Junkers', *American Historical Revue*, xlix (1944).

—— *Bureaucracy, Aristocracy and Autocracy: The Prussian Experience, 1660–1815* (Cambridge [Mass.], 1958).

ROSENBERGER, HEINRICH, 'Die Entlassung des Generalobersten Freiherrn von Fritsch', *Deutsche Rundschau*, 69. Jg., Heft 8 (Nov. 1946).

ROSINSKI, H., 'Die Entwicklung von Clausewitz' Werk "Vom Kriege" im Lichte seiner "Vorreden" und "Nachrichten" ', *Historische Zeitschrift*, cli (1935).

—— *The German Army* (rev. ed., Washington, D.C., 1944).

ROTHFELS, H., 'Die Erinnerungen des Botschafters Radowitz', *Archiv für Politik und Geschichte*, iv (1925).

ROTHFRITZ, HERBERT, *Die Politik des pr. Botschafters Grafen Robert v. d. Goltz in Paris, 1863–69* (Abhandlungen zur mittleren und neueren Geschichte, lxxiv) (Berlin, 1934).

RUDIN, H., *Armistice, 1918* (New Haven, 1944).

RÜDT V. COLLENBERG, L. K. G. W., *Die deutsche Armee von 1871 bis 1914* (Forschungen und Darstellungen aus dem Reichsarchiv, Heft 4) (Berlin, 1922).

—— 'Die staatsrechtliche Stellung des preußischen Kriegsministers von 1867 bis 1914', *Wissen und Wehr*, viii (1927).

—— *Mackensen* (Berlin, 1940).

'Rühle von Lilienstern', *Militärwochenblatt* (Beihefte, 1847).

SCHARFENORT, L. VON, *Die königlich-preußische Kriegsakademie, 1810–1910* (Berlin, 1910).

SCHEELE, GODFREY, *The Weimar Republic* (London, 1946).

SCHENK, ERWIN, *Der Fall Zabern* (Stuttgart, 1927).

SCHENK, H. G., *The Aftermath of the Napoleonic Wars: The Concert of Europe—an Experiment* (New York, 1947).

SCHEVILL, FERDINAND, *The Great Elector* (Chicago, 1947).

SCHIFF, VICTOR, ed., *The Germans at Versailles* (London, 1930).

SCHLABRENDORFF, FABIAN VON, *Offiziere gegen Hitler* (Zürich, 1946).

SCHLANGE-SCHÖNINGEN, HANS, *Am Tage danach* (Hamburg, 1947).

'Schleicher's Political Dream', *New Statesman and Nation* (7 July, 1934).

SCHLIEFFEN, GENERALFELDMARSCHALL GRAF VON, *Dienstschriften hrsg. vom Generalstab des Heeres*, ii (Berlin, 1938): *Die Großen Generalstabreisen (Ost) aus den Jahren 1891–1905.*

—— *Briefe*, herausgegeben von Eberhard Kessel (Göttingen, 1958).

SCHLÖZER, L. V., *Generalfeldmarschall Freiherr von Loë* (Stuttgart, 1914).

SCHMIDT-BÜCKEBURG, R., *Das Militärkabinett der preußischen Könige und deutschen Kaiser* (Berlin, 1933).

SCHMITT, BERNADOTTE, *The Coming of War 1914* (2 vols., New York, 1930).

SCHMITT, CARL, *Staatsgefüge und Zusammenbruch des zweiten Reiches: Der Sieg des Bürgers über den Soldaten* [*Der Deutsche Staat der Gegenwart*, Heft 6] (Hamburg, 1934).

SCHMITZ, ELISABETH, *Edwin von Manteuffel als Quelle zur Geschichte Friedrich Wilhelms IV.* (München and Berlin, 1921).

SCHMOLLER, G., 'Die Entstehung des preußischen Heeres von 1640–1740', *Deutsche Rundschau*, xii (1877).

SCHNABEL, FRANZ, *Deutsche Geschichte im 19. Jahrhundert* (4 vols., Freiburg i. B., 1925 ff.).

SCHÖN, W. E., *Memoirs of an Ambassador* (London, 1922).

SCHOLTZ, GERHARD, *Hermann von Boyen, ein Lebensbild* (Berlin, 1936).

SCHRÖTTER, ROBERT FREIHERR VON, 'Die Ergänzung des preußischen Heeres unter dem ersten Könige', *Forschungen zur brandenburgischen und preußischen Geschichte*, xxiii (1910).

SCHÜDDEKOPF, OTTO-ERNST, *Das Heer und die Republik: Quellen zur Politik der Reichswehrführung 1918 bis 1933* (Hannover und Frankfurt a. M., 1955).

SCHULTZ, W. VON, *Die preußischen Werbungen unter Friedrich Wilhelm I. und Friedrich dem Großen* (Schwerin, 1887).

SCHWARTZKOPPEN, *Die Wahrheit über Dreyfus*, ed. by B. Schwertfeger (Berlin, 1930).

SCHWARTZENBERG, ADOLF, *Prince Felix zu Schwarzenberg* (New York, 1946).

SCHWEDLER, GENERALLEUTNANT VON, 'Gen. d. Kav. Emil v. Albedyll zum 40. Todestag (13. Juni 1937), *Militärwissenschaftliche Rundschau*, ii (1937), 269 ff.

SCHWEINITZ, H. L. VON, *Denkwürdigkeiten des Botschafters H. L. von Schweinitz*, ed. by W. von Schweinitz (2 vols., Berlin, 1927).

SCHWEND, K., *Bayern zwischen Monarchie und Diktatur* (München, 1954).

SCHWERIN VON KROSIGK, LUTZ GRAF, *Es geschah in Deutschland* (3. Aufl., Tübingen, 1952).

SCHWERTFEGER, BERNHARD, *Die großen Erzieher des deutschen Heeres: Aus der Geschichte der Kriegsakademie* (Potsdam, 1936).

—— 'Hindenburgs Tod und der Eid auf den Fuehrer', *Die Wandlung*, iii (1948).

—— *Rätsel um Deutschland* (Heidelberg, 1948).

SEECKT, HANS VON, *Aus meinem Leben*, ed. by F. von Rabenau (Leipzig, 1938).

—— *Die Reichswehr* (Leipzig, 1933).

—— *Die Zukunft des Reiches* (Berlin, 1929).

—— *Gedanken eines Soldaten* (Erweiterte Ausgabe, Leipzig, 1935).

SENDTNER, KURT, 'Die deutsche Militäropposition im erstern Kriegsjahr', *Vollmacht des Gewissens* (Bonn, 1956).

SETON-WATSON, R. W., *Britain in Europe, 1789–1914* (Cambridge, 1937).

SEVERING, CARL, *Mein Lebensweg* (2 vols., Koln, 1950).

SHANAHAN, WILLIAM O., *Prussian Military Reforms, 1786–1813* (New York, 1945).

SOSSIDI, ELEFTHERIOS, *Die staatsrechtliche Stellung des Offiziers im absoluten Staat und ihre Abhandlungen im 19. Jahrhundert* (Berlin, 1939).

SPAHN, M., *Die päpstliche Friedensvermittlung* (Berlin, 1919).

SPEIDEL, HANS, *Invasion 1944: ein Beitrag zu Rommels und des Reiches Schicksal* (Stuttgart, 1949).

SPEIDEL, HELM, 'Reichswehr und Rote Armee', *Vierteljahrshefte für Zeitgeschichte*, i (1953).

SPENGLER, OSWALD, *Preußentum und Sozialismus* (new ed., München, 1934).

SRBIK, H. RITTER VON, *Deutsche Einheit* (4 vols., München, 1935–42).

STADELMANN, RUDOLF, 'Das Duell zwischen Scharnhorst und Borstell im Dezember 1807', *Historische Zeitschrift*, clxi (1940).

—— *Das Jahr 1865 und das Problem von Bismarcks deutscher Politik* (München, 1933).

—— *Scharnhorst, Schicksal und geistige Welt* (Wiesbaden, 1952).

—— *Moltke und der Staat* (Krefeld, 1950).

—— *Soziale und politische Geschichte der Revolution von 1848* (Munich, 1948).

STAMPFER, FRIEDRICH, *Die vierzehn Jahre der ersten deutschen Republik* (Karlsbad, 1936).

STEEFEL, LAWRENCE, *The Schleswig-Holstein Question* (Cambridge [Mass.], 1932).

STEGLICH, WOLFGANG, *Bündnissicherung oder Verständigungsfriede: Untersuchung zu dem Friedensangebot der Mittelmächte vom 12. Dezember 1916* (Göttingen, 1958).

STEIN, FREIHERR VOM, *Briefwechsel, Denkschriften und Aufzeichnungen*, ed. by E. Botzenhart (7 vols., Berlin, 1931 ff.).

—— *Staatsschriften und politische Briefe*, ed. by Friedrich Thimme (Leipzig, 1921).

STERN-RUBARTH, EDGAR, *Graf Brockdorff-Rantzau: Wanderer zwischen zwei Welten* (Berlin, 1929).

STOLBERG-WERNIGERODE, OTTO GRAF ZU, *Anton Graf zu Stolberg-Wernigerode: ein Freund und Ratgeber König Friedrich Wilhelms IV.* (München, 1926).

STOSCH, *Denkwürdigkeiten des Generals und Admirals Albrecht von Stosch*, ed. by Ulrich von Stosch (Stuttgart, 1904).

STRESEMANN, GUSTAV, *Vermächtnis*, ed. by H. Bernhardt (3 vols., Berlin, 1932–3).

Stufen und Wandlungen der deutschen Einheit, ed. by Kurt von Raumer and Theodor Schieder (Stuttgart, 1943).

TAFFS, WINIFRED, *Lord Odo Russell* (London, 1938).

TAYLOR, TELFORD, *Sword and Swastika: Generals and Nazis in the Third Reich* (New York, 1952).

TEMPERLEY, MAJOR-GENERAL A. C., *The Whispering Gallery of Europe* (London, 1938).

THIMME, FRIEDRICH, 'Botschafter und Militärattaché. Ein document humain zur Dreyfus-Affäre', *Europäische Gespräche*, vii (1930).

—— *Front wider Bülow. Staatsmänner, Diplomaten und Forscher zu seinen Denkwürdigkeiten* (Munich, 1931).

—— 'König Friedrich Wilhelm IV., General von Prittwitz und die Berliner Märzrevolution', *Forschungen zur brandenburgischen und preußischen Geschichte*, xvi (1903).

THIMME, H., *Weltkrieg ohne Waffen* (Stuttgart, 1932).

THYSSEN, FRITZ, *I Paid Hitler* (New York, 1941).

TIRPITZ, ALFRED VON, *Der Aufbau der deutschen Weltmacht* (Berlin, 1924).

TREITSCHKE, HEINRICH VON, *Briefe*, ed. by M. Cornicelius (3 vols., Leipzig, 1913–20).

—— *German History in the Nineteenth Century* (7 vols., New York, 1915–19).

TRUTZSCHLER, H. VON, 'Bismarcks Stellung zum Präventivkrieg', *Europäische Gespräche*, i (1923).

TSCHIRSCH, OTTO, *Geschichte der öffentlichen Meinung in Preußen vom Baseler Frieden bis zum Zusammenbruch des Staates* (2 vols., Weimar, 1934).

TÜMPEL, LUDWIG, *Die Entstehung des brandenburgisch-preußischen Einheitsstaates im Zeitalter des Absolutismus, 1609–1806* (Untersuchungen zur deutschen Staats- und Rechtsgeschichte, ed. by Otto von Gierke, 124. Heft) (Breslau, 1915).

TWESTEN, CARL, *Was uns noch retten kann* (Berlin, 1860).

UNGER, W. VON, *Blücher* (2 vols., Berlin, 1907–9).

Die Ursachen des deutschen Zusammenbruches im Jahre 1918 (Das Werk des Untersuchungsausschusses der deutschen verfassunggebenden Nationalversammlung und des deutschen Reichstages 1919 bis 1928) (Berlin, 1920–9).

VAGTS, ALFRED, *A History of Militarism* (New York, 1937).

VALENTIN, VEIT, *Geschichte der deutschen Revolution, 1848–49* (2 vols., Berlin, 1930–1).

VALENTINI, A. VON, *Kaiser und Kabinettschef* (Oldenburg, 1931).

VARNHAGEN VON ENSE, K. A., *Blücher* (new ed., Berlin, 1933).

VAUPEL, R., *Stimmen aus der Zeit der Erniedrigung* (Berlin, 1923).

—— *Die Reorganisation des Preußischen Staates unter Stein und Hardenberg. Das Preußische Heer vom Tilsiter Frieden bis zur Befreiung, 1807–1814* (Publikationen aus den Preußischen Archiven, xciv, Leipzig, 1938).

VERDY DU VERNOIS, J. VON, *With Royal Headquarters, 1870–71* (London, 1897).

Verhandlungen der constituierenden Versammlung für Preußen 1848 (Berlin, 1848).

VOLKMANN, E. O., *Am Tor der neuen Zeit* (Oldenburg, 1933).

—— *Revolution über Deutschland* (Oldenburg, 1930).

Von Scharnhorst zu Schlieffen, ed. by F. von Cochenhausen (Berlin, 1933).

WAHL, ADALBERT, *Beiträge zur Geschichte der Konfliktszeit* (Tübingen, 1914).

—— *Deutsche Geschichte von der Reichsgründung bis zum Ausbruch des Weltkrieges* (4 vols., Stuttgart, 1926–36).

WAITE, ROBERT G. L., *Vanguard of Nazism: The Free Corps Movement in Post-War Germany, 1918–1923* (Cambridge [Mass.], 1952).

WALDERSEE, *Aus dem Briefwechsel des Generalfeldmarschalls Alfred Grafen von Waldersee, 1886–91*, ed. by H. O. Meisner (Berlin, 1928).

—— *Denkwürdigkeiten des Generalfeldmarschalls Alfred Grafen von Waldersee*, ed. by H. O. Meisner (3 vols., Stuttgart, 1923–5).

WEBER, ALFRED, *Farewell to European History or the Conquest of Nihilism* (Eng. trans., London, 1947).

WEBSTER, C. K., *The Foreign Policy of Castlereagh, 1812–15* (London, 1931).

WEDEL, C., *Zwischen Kaiser und Kanzler* (Leipzig, 1943).

WERTHEIMER, EDUARD VON, 'Ein k. und k. Militärattaché über das politische Leben in Berlin, 1880–1895', *Preußische Jahrbücher*, cci (1925).

WESTARP, GRAF VON, *Das Ende der Monarchie 9.11.18*, ed. by W. Conze (Berlin, 1952).

—— *Konservative Politik im letzten Jahrzehnt des Kaiserreiches* (2 vols., Berlin, 1935).

WESTPHAL, SIEGFRIED, *Heer in Fesseln: Aus den Papieren des Stabschefs von Rommel, Kesselring und Rundstedt* (Bonn, 1950).

WHEELER-BENNETT, JOHN W., *The Forgotten Peace: Brest Litovsk* (London, 1938).

—— *The Nemesis of Power: The German Army in Politics, 1918–1945* (London, 1953).

—— *Wooden Titan: Hindenberg in Twenty Years of German History* (New York, 1936).

WIDENMANN, WILHELM, *Marine-Attaché an der kaiserlich-deutschen Botschaft in London, 1907–1912* (Göttingen, 1952).

WINNIG, AUGUST, *Am Ausgang der deutschen Ostpolitik: Persönliche Erlebnisse und Erinnerungen* (Berlin, 1921).

WOHLERS, GÜNTHER, *Die staatsrechtliche Stellung des Generalstabes in Preußen und dem deutschen Reich* (Bonn, 1921).

WOLFF, A., *Berliner Revolutions-Chronik* (Berlin, 1852).

WOLLENBERG, E., *The Red Army* (London, 1938).

ZECHLIN, EGMONT, *Bismarck und die Grundlegung der deutschen Großmacht* (Stuttgart, 1930).

— *Staatsstreichpläne Bismarcks und Wilhelms II 1890–94* (Stuttgart, 1929).

ZEDLITZ-TRÜTZSCHLER, GRAF, *Zwölf Jahre am deutschen Kaiserhof* (Berlin, 1924).

ZIEKURSCH, JOHANNES, *Politische Geschichte des neuen deutschen Kaiserreiches* (3 vols., Frankfurt a. M., 1925 ff.).

ZMARZLIK, HANS-GÜNTER, *Bethmann Hollweg als Reichskanzler 1909–1914* (Düsseldorf, 1957).

'Zum Sturz Brünings: Dokumentation', *Vierteljahrshefte für Zeitgeschichte*, i (1953).

'Zur Erinnerung an General von Griesheim', *Militärwochenblatt* (Beihefte, 1854).

'Zur Politik Schleichers gegenüber der NSDAP 1932', herausgegeben von Thilo Vogelsang, *Vierteljahrshefte für Zeitgeschichte*, vi (1958), 86 ff.

INDEX